MW01539234

Interpreting Tocqueville's *Democracy in America*

Interpreting Tocqueville's *Democracy in America*

Edited by Ken Masugi

Rowman & Littlefield Publishers, Inc.

ROWMAN & LITTLEFIELD PUBLISHERS, INC.

Published in the United States of America
by Rowman & Littlefield Publishers, Inc.
8705 Bollman Place, Savage, Maryland 20763

British Cataloging in Publication Information Available

Library of Congress Cataloging-in-Publication Data

Interpreting Tocqueville's Democracy in America
/ edited by Ken Masugi.
p. cm.
Includes bibliographical references.
1. Tocqueville, Alexis de, 1805-1859.
De la démocratie en Amérique.
2. United States—Politics and government.
3. United States—Social conditions—To 1865.
4. Democracy. I. Masugi, Ken.
JK216.T7193I58 1991
321.8—dc20 91-25538 CIP

ISBN 0-8476-7711-7 (hardcover : alk. paper)
ISBN 0-8476-7712-5 (pbk : alk. paper)

Printed in the United States of America

™ The paper used in this publication meets the minimum requirements of American National Standard for Information Sciences—Permanence of Paper for Printed Library Materials, ANSI Z39.48–1984.

Dedicated to the memory of
John Adams Wettergreen,
defender of liberty.

Contents

Introduction

Alexis de Tocqueville (1805-59) is so frequently quoted that his readers may not probe beneath the enticing surface *Democracy in America* presents. Many would remain content with picking and choosing from his text, reading him as others do Montaigne or Nietzsche, for aphoristic insights into modern life. Thus Tocqueville remains an inexhaustible resource for journalists and other popularizers, who use his marvelous insights to add the weight of authority to their opinions. Such a familiarity with Tocqueville led *New York Times'* columnist Russell Baker to satirize college students quoting Tocqueville to their advantage—fawned on by intimidated professors who had not read the primary source![1] The essays in this book prepare their readers to approach Tocqueville's text more deeply by seeking to destroy any illusion of that "excessive familiarity which breeds contempt and of misuse which breeds disgust."[2] Today, in light of Gorbachev, the most frequently quoted example of Tocqueville's insight—his prediction that Russia and America would divide the world between them—serves our intention well, by raising enduring questions about the scope of statesmanship and human choice.

At the very end of Volume I, first published in January 1835, Tocqueville reiterates that he and his contemporaries "live at a time when there is a general tendency toward equality in human affairs."[3] Continuing his prediction of the future course of the world and the influence of the Anglo-Americans, he describes the "great nations," Russia and America, having "grown in obscurity," now seeming to advance "toward the same goal."[4] While other nations have "nearly

---

[1]Russell Baker, "Off the Top of De Tocq," *New York Times*, Nov. 23, 1976, p. 33.
[2]Leo Strauss, *Natural Right and History* (Chicago: University of Chicago Press, 1953), p. 1. Strauss refers here to the Declaration of Independence.
[3]Alexis de Tocqueville, *Democracy in America*, ed. J.-P. Mayer, trans. George Lawrence (Garden City, N.Y.: Doubleday, Anchor Books, 1969), vol. I, "Conclusion." Hereinafter cited as *Democracy*. We will occasionally correct this translation. Some of our contributors will use the older edition of Phillips Bradley, trans. Henry Reeve, rev. Francis Bowen, 2 vols. (New York: Alfred J. Knopf, Vintage Books, 1945). They have in many instances used this translation as a basis for their own.
[4]Ibid., p. 412.

reached their natural limits," the Russians and the Americans "alone march easily and quickly forward along a path whose end no eye can yet see."[5] Tocqueville portrays a Russian "at grips with men." Moreover,

> America's conquests are made with the plowshare, Russia's with the sword.
>
> To attain their aims, the former relies on personal interest and gives free scope to the unguided strength and common sense of individuals.
>
> The latter in a sense concentrates the whole power of society in one man.
>
> One has freedom as the principal means of action; the other has servitude.
>
> Their point of departure is different and their paths diverse; nevertheless each seems called by some secret design of Providence to hold in its hands the destinies of half the world.

Now one curious thing about this prediction is that it occurred well before Russia became Communist. It suggests a warning to us immediately: Even a non-Marxist Soviet Union—such as the one possibly emerging now—might still want to divide the world between itself and the United States. An end to twentieth-century wars of ideology does not preclude a return to the nineteenth-century wars of balance of power or national interest.

There remains, however, something even more noteworthy about Tocqueville's Russia. If this is the age of equality, as Tocqueville stressed from the book's first words, then how can Russia remain a throwback to previous, nondemocratic ages? Though but one exception to the rule, it threatens to dominate half the world. (There is no evidence to suggest that Russia represents the soft despotism Tocqueville discusses later in Volume II, Part IV, as opposed to the plain old hard despotism in Russia.[6]) So we are faced with a

---

[5]Ibid., pp. 412-13.

[6]Incidentally, the exception of Russia also makes us reconsider the exception of the South in Tocqueville's account. (See chaps. 2 and 10 in vol. I.) The South is somewhat un-American, because it would rather fight than trade.

paradox: Does not this observation about Russia—which is not elaborated on anywhere else in Tocqueville's work, so far as we know—contradict what is said throughout *Democracy in America* and indeed in just a few paragraphs before—that the age of equality is inevitable?[7]

Thus Tocqueville forces us to raise other questions about his intent. How free are statesmen to shape events? How does the age of equality constrain them? How does the "irresistible" 700-year democratic revolution epitomized in America confine nations and private individuals? Moreover, how should Americans rule themselves, given the "irresistible" democratic revolution? These questions in turn raise a more fundamental one: What is man's capacity for political life, for the life of ruling and being ruled?

In concluding the Introduction, he maintains that "I did not intend to serve or to combat any party; I have tried to see not differently but further than any party; while they are busy with tomorrow, I have wished to consider the whole future."[8] That is, Tocqueville may appear to be partisan, but his intent extends further, as a teacher of a "new science of politics" for a "world itself completely new."[9] He would educate democracy by taming its excesses and educating it to its flaws. Perhaps the best summary of the scope of Tocqueville's project and how it relates to his view of history is to be found in the concluding paragraphs of the book:

> I am aware that many of my contemporaries think that nations on earth are never their own masters and that they are bound to obey some insuperable and unthinking power,

---

[7]Cf. our reflections on the last sentence of Francis Fukuyama's "The End of History?" *The National Interest,* Number 16 (Summer 1989), p. 3, in "Tocqueville and 'The End of History?' Soft or Hard Historicism?" *The Proposition,* Nov.-Dec. 1989, pp. 5-9. Fukuyama's application of Alexandré Kojève's interpretation of Hegel to international relations is anticipated by John Adams Wettergreen, "Is Snobbery a Formal Value?" *Western Political Quarterly* (March 1973), vol. 26, pp. 109-29. How does the end of ideology or the triumph of one ideology over all others affect political debate and the ultimate political conflict, international relations? Can the end of politics mean anything other than the end of philosophy, and hence the end of human life?

[8]According to Robert Eden, "Tocqueville and the Problem of Natural Right," forthcoming in *Interpretation,* this is the only instance in Strauss's publications of a reference to Tocqueville.

[9]*Democracy,* p. 12.

> the product of preexisting facts, of race, or soil, or climate.
>
> These are false and cowardly doctrines which can only produce feeble men and pusillanimous nations. Providence did not make mankind entirely free or completely enslaved. Providence has, in truth, drawn a predestined circle around each man beyond which he cannot pass; but within those vast limits man is strong and free, and so are peoples.
>
> *The nations of our day cannot prevent conditions of equality from spreading in their midst.* But it depends upon themselves whether equality is to lead to servitude or freedom, knowledge or barbarism, prosperity or wretchedness. [Emphasis added.]

It is far from the case that the great political questions are over, that "history has ended." In fact they remain alive, in that liberty, knowledge, and prosperity are still very much at risk. Equality is inevitable, but civilization is not.

Thus Tocqueville attempts to make issues other than equality the focus of men's political interest. He emphasizes instead the means of accommodating die-hard aristocrats to the new democratic order. So Tocqueville warns of the tyranny of the majority, the soft despotism of a schoolmaster, ever-centralizing administration that threatens to stifle individual freedom, a philosophic and a commercial materialism; a dull people, indifferent to and unformed by the beautiful and the good, a trading nation. Thus in Tocqueville's view, we democrats are everything that Rousseau, and other insightful men, despise about modern man. Yet we Americans also have our associations, our extraordinary ability to work together for the common good; our charities, our religion, and our often outrageous local and national pride. We are able to make self-interest operate in the most ingenious, self-effacing, and humane ways. If we are a trading people, we are also, or at least were, a religious people. We have our democratic envy but also our democratic love of equality of opportunity. While arguing that his "chief aim in writing" *Democracy in America* is to combat indifference to public life, he later refers to the need to allow the individual "to keep the little freedom, strength, and originality left to him."[10] At times Tocqueville's democratic individual resembles Nietzsche's last man. Yet Tocqueville's historicism, if it be such, does not lead to the fanaticism of a neo-Darwinian, Marx, or Nietzsche, or the enervation of Mill or other nineteenth-century historicists—those who believe that the human condition is ineluctably determined by its historical circumstances.[11]

But consider, in this light, Tocqueville's own implicit self-categorization as a kind of democratic historian. Note how he would appear to limit the scope of statesmanship in the modern, democratic age.

> In reading historians of aristocratic ages, those of antiquity in particular, it would seem that in order to be master of his fate and to govern his fellows a man need only be master of himself. Perusing the histories written nowadays, one would suppose that man had no power, neither over himself nor over his surroundings. Classical historians taught how to command; those of our own time teach next to nothing but how to obey. In their writings the author often figures large, but humanity is always tiny.
>
> If this doctrine of fatality, so attractive to those who write history in democratic periods, passes from authors to

---

[10]Ibid., pp. 670-71.

[11]Consider the warning against superficially imposed historical patterns from the statesman of the twentieth century, Sir Winston Churchill.

> It was the custom in the palmy days of Queen Victoria for statesmen to expiate upon the glories of the British Empire, and to rejoice in that protecting Providence which had preserved us through so many dangers and brought us at length into a secure and prosperous age. Little did they know that the worst perils had still to be encountered and that the greatest triumphs were yet to be won.

And going on to describe the growth of British power, Churchill observes:

> Surely that was the end of the tale as it was so often the end of the book. History showed the rise, culmination, splendour, transition and decline of States and Empires. It seemed inconceivable that the same series of tremendous events through which since the days of Queen Elizabeth we had three times made our way successfully, should be repeated a fourth time and on an immeasurably larger scale. (Winston S. Churchill, *The World Crisis*, 6 vols. [New York: Charles Scribner's Sons, 1923, 1951], vol. I, pp. 1-2.)

Of course Churchill would live to see disaster emerge on a fifth and even larger scale, with the British Empire left barely even a shadow of its former self. But Churchill was not deceived by doctrines of historical necessity because of his prudence—derived from his knowledge of history and his activity of statesmanship.

> readers, infects the whole mass of the community, and takes possession of the public mind, it will soon paralyze the activities of modern society and bring Christians down to the level of Turks.[12]

Plainly, Tocqueville wishes to preserve freedom, not to clear the path for despotism. But what can be the political effect of saying we are in the grips of a tide that moves us inevitably? He does not point to the possibility of statesmanship which can modify that tide. Yet, as he later insists, his very purpose in writing is to combat the apolitical inclinations of the modern world.[13] Men today are interested in commerce and the activities of the private sphere; public life means little to them. This in turn points us to Tocqueville's explanation of the duties of the statesman and the philosopher or "moralist":

> In such a country where unhappily skepticism and democracy exist together, philosophers and men in power should always strive to set a distant aim as the object of human efforts; that is their most important business.

"The moralist," Tocqueville explains, will try to encourage men to think in terms of long-term projects and resist the "thousand daily petty urges" that distract them from true happiness and prosperity. Contemporary equivalents of the building of the pyramids or the cathedrals cross the mind. (Or one thinks of the canal on which Faust works himself to death.) Rulers, Tocqueville avers, would attempt to "banish chance, as much as possible, from the world of politics"; they would attempt to "give men back that taste for the future which neither religion nor social conditions any longer inspire. . . ."[14] A moral-political substitute must be found for the immortality of the soul. But how does one "banish chance, as much as possible," without destroying human freedom? This

---

[12]*Democracy*, p. 496. Note Allan Bloom's praise of Tocqueville: "Tocqueville taught me the importance of the university to democratic society. His noble book, *Democracy in America*, gave voice to my inchoate sentiments." *The Closing of the American Mind* (New York: Simon & Schuster, 1987), p. 246.

[13]*Democracy*, p. 671.

[14]Ibid., pp. 548-49. Incidentally, this chapter, chap. 17 of pt. II, is located in the very middle of vol. II.

proposed goal for contemporary statecraft is a long way from the best regime of classical political philosophy, as reflected in Lincoln's speeches on the principle of equality.

We see that Tocqueville's argument about inevitability may be intended for moral-political purposes.[15] The necessity of equality provides the basis for the freedom to choose different versions of the good life. Here, in chapter 17 of Part II, Volume II, Tocqueville proposes questionable political solutions for vast, seemingly extra-political questions.[16] Elsewhere, he focuses on associations, town meetings, and juries, emphasizing the role of ordinary individuals who unite and work together for common purposes. Perhaps one can hardly blame Tocqueville for slighting the possibility of great statesmen, when modern Europeans on the continent have had so few leaders to take pride in. The Napoleons were a source of further miseries, after all. And Abraham Lincoln saw a problematic side to his own rise, as he anticipates in the Lyceum Address.[17] Hence Tocqueville did not anticipate—but who else did?—the statesmanship of Lincoln. But to his discredit, it appears he did not take into account the possibility of such a man, who would perform his work by refining the *principles* on which the nation was founded. Indeed for Tocqueville there is no principled American founding in the Declaration of Independence. Rather, he saw the improvement of democracy—or the slowing of its atomizing tendencies—arising from the people's mores.

> The social state is commonly the result of circumstances, sometimes of laws, but most often of a combination of the two. But once it has come into being, it may itself be considered as the prime cause of most of the laws, customs, and ideas which control the nation's behavior; it modifies

---

[15]Tocqueville scholars owe an immeasurable debt to Marvin Zetterbaum's reflections on the political rhetoric of the inevitability thesis in *Tocqueville and the Problem of Democracy* (Stanford: Stanford University Press, 1967).

[16]But Machiavelli and the early moderns who followed him politicized metaphysics and science. This chapter of *Democracy* is a prime example of the power of the modern project.

[17]"Address Before the Young Men's Lyceum of Springfield, Illinois: The Perpetuation of Our Political Institutions," *Collected Works of Abraham Lincoln*, ed. Roy P. Basler (New Brunswick, N.J.: Rutgers University Press, 1953), vol. II, pp. 108-15.

even those things which it does not cause.[18]

Here the political appears to be largely a response to the social, which in turn reflects greater historical trends. But as we see later in Volume II, the decent mores taming American democracy are crumbling as the skepticism of the democratic age makes religious faith more difficult or more fanatical.[19] We can see political life dissolving into the bureaucratized mass society Tocqueville describes in Part IV of Volume II. Will there be a Russia—that is, some non-democratic alternative—to exempt democratic life from such a fate? The concluding words of the book do not lead us to believe so. The only alternative to despotism of either the democratic or non-democratic sort appears to be moderate liberal democracy, which appears in turn to contain its own self-destructive tendencies.

In defense of a contrary, fundamentally political understanding of man, John Adams Wettergreen maintained that Tocqueville "mis-evaluated the human desire to rule." He adduced as evidence Tocqueville's belief that modern tyrants would resemble school-masters—a clear error on Tocqueville's part. Wettergreen went on to observe that "[t]his is an error characteristic of modern political philosophy from Machiavelli on: the assumption that human nature (or a part of humanity) is nonpolitical."[20] Tocqueville came to believe that the new despotism would not be of the sort that befell the peoples of antiquity. "More detailed study of the subject and the new ideas which came into my mind during five years of meditation [following the completion of Volume I] have not lessened my fears but have changed their object." Democratic nations would have a kinder, gentler tyranny, so to speak, one which would "degrade men rather than torment them."[21] (Note that he speaks here of Christian and of democratic nations; he does not deny the possibility of savage tyrannies ruling in Asia—recall his comments on the despotism of Turkey.) So, according to Tocqueville, the political task for modern, western democracies is rather different. The question at

---

[18]*Democracy*, p. 50.

[19]Ibid., see, e.g., vol. II, pt. I, chaps. 1-7, and pt. II, chaps. 11-12.

[20]"Our Problems, and Tocqueville's," Correspondence, *The Claremont Review of Books*, Spring 1988, p. 14.

[21]*Democracy*, p. 690.

issue between him and Wettergreen—whether as long as men remain men, that is, as long as human nature exists, the political questions remain the same—is of immense practical significance. How confident can we be that history will be so kind as to mellow future despotism; that is, make the age of equality irrevocable, putting an end to history, as it were? Will human life ever be free of the dangers of the political condition? Does not the statesman, at the height of his powers, claim suzerainty not only over his space but over time as well?

We are faced again with, not relieved of, the need to choose our fate—whichever reading of Tocqueville we accept. In other words, our reading of Tocqueville brings us back to the crucial role of the statesman, the man who must choose wisely on behalf of his community. Here Tocqueville, who concedes too much to history, does not provide sufficient guidance on the first principles of such a statesman. The overarching principle of the American regime is equality, as Lincoln and the Founders understood it. But Tocqueville portrays equality to be a force, not a moral-political principle which reflects teachings of natural right. Equality as a matter of historical necessity cannot provide moral-political guidance. Moreover, after Tocqueville completes *Democracy in America,* he never returns to America's themes; it is not even a topic of his letters. America served a temporary, purely instrumental purpose for him.

The conception of equality as a force partly explains why Tocqueville never mentions the Declaration of Independence. Equality cannot be *the* American principle because it is the modern principle simply, an inevitable historical tendency. Thus statesmen cannot take guidance from equality but must rather acknowledge it as a necessity. In America this low understanding of equality as a force separates one from the best teachers of politics: the Founders and Abraham Lincoln.[22]

---

[22]On this and other points, we must acknowledge the influence of Harry V. Jaffa's work on the American regime for our understanding of political things. See especially *Crisis of the House Divided* (Chicago: University of Chicago Press, 1982, repr. Seattle: University of Washington Press, 1973, originally published 1959, Garden City, N.Y. Doubleday Press); *How to Think About the American Revolution: A Bicentennial Cerebration* (Durham, N.C.: Carolina Academic Press, 1978); and *American Conservatism and the American Founding* (Durham, N.C.: Carolina Academic Press, 1984).

* * *

The essays in this book consider Tocqueville's ambiguous legacy in three areas: his place in the history of political philosophy, his understanding of American political institutions, and his study of American character.

In the first section, on Tocqueville's place in Western political thought, two eminent European scholars, Jean-Claude Lamberti and Wilhelm Hennis, consider the status and dignity of democratic life in Tocqueville's thought and reflect on his relationship to Jean-Jacques Rousseau. Bruce James Smith explores the extent to which Tocqueville can be regarded as a classical liberal—that is, one who regards individual well-being as primary. Taking the preservation of human decency in the modern world as his theme, Peter Augustine Lawler contrasts Tocqueville and Marx through an interpretation of Tocqueville's chapter on pantheism. Finally, Catherine Zuckert reflects on whether Tocqueville can be considered a sociologist (one who understands man in terms of subpolitical categories) or a political theorist, thus summarizing the primary question of this section: To what extent is Tocqueville's endeavor philosophic? To take up later contributor John Marini's suggestion, does Tocqueville stand to Rousseau, as the respectable Locke stood to the heretical Hobbes?

The second section features Tocqueville's study of American political and economic institutions, with implications for both American principles and contemporary politics. Following Thomas West's essay on Tocqueville's misunderstanding of the Founders' principles, James Schleifer contrasts his and Jefferson's understandings of fundamental political concepts. John Adams Wettergreen recounts the blessings of capitalism, which Tocqueville praised. Wettergreen is supported by Edward Banfield's critique of what he takes to be Tocqueville's French aristocratic understanding of America and his critique of capitalism. John Marini explores the roots of the modern bureaucratic state. James Ceaser reflects on the institutions that Tocqueville thought would improve democracy—the law, intellectuals, and the jury—and indicates why their roles and effects have changed.

The final section of the book considers American mores as observed by Tocqueville and how they fare today. Robert Bellah's essay indicates the role Tocqueville's analysis can play in devising a more satisfying way of life. Ralph Hancock's study of the key theme of religion makes clear the extent to which its political role has changed and abided since Tocqueville wrote. Two extended analyses of the place of self-interest, by Delba Winthrop and George Anastaplo, indicate its broad significance, as well as its limitations, for understanding American mores. William Richardson's essay on Tocqueville's grim view of blacks and Indians also reminds us that his French horizon is not necessarily the same as Lincoln's American horizon. America's abolition of slavery, if ultimately a case of self-interest, is the crucial issue in the understanding of American politics and mores. Closely studying a part of *Democracy* often read with bemusement today, William Kristol reminds us that Tocqueville's notion of democratic excellence requires women of a certain character. Concluding the volume, prominent Thai scholar Sombat Chantornvong gives a Tocquevillean analysis of contemporary political life in various Asian countries, illuminating Tocqueville's worldwide significance in this age of democratic revolution.

* * *

This volume would have been impossible without the initiative and dedication of The Claremont Institute for the Study of Statesmanship and Political Philosophy—especially Christopher Flannery and Douglas Jeffrey, co-directors of the Institute's Bicentennial of the Constitution Project, and Larry Arnn, its President. The book originated from a Bicentennial of the Constitution conference on *Democracy in America,* held on the book's sesquicentennial, in January 1985. In the intervening years, essays have been added. Peter W. Schramm, then-President of the Institute, encouraged the conference and the book.

This project was generously supported by grants from the National Endowment for the Humanities. In typesetting, Richie Scurry took her usual painstaking care. Assisting with proofreading were Lucas Morel, Jeffrey Schultz, Steven Lenzner, and David Green. Finally, the contributors themselves deserve extra thanks for the patience they displayed while the project slowly crept toward completion.

— Ken Masugi

July 4, 1990

Contributors

Ken Masugi, former Director of the Bicentennial Project of The Claremont Institute for the Study of Statesmanship and Political Philosophy, has been Special Assistant to Chairmen Clarence Thomas and Evan J. Kemp, Jr., of the Equal Employment Opportunity Commission. With J. Jackson Barlow and Leonard W. Levy, he is co-editor of *The American Founding* (1988).

George Anastaplo is Professor at Loyola University School of Law. He is author of books on the American Constitution and American political thought and politics, including *The Constitutionalist, Human Being and Citizen, The Artist as Thinker,* and *The Constitution of 1787: A Commentary.*

Edward C. Banfield is George D. Markham Professor of Government Emeritus at Harvard University. His latest book is *Here the People Rule.*

Robert N. Bellah is Elliott Professor of Sociology at the University of California at Berkeley. In addition to his recent co-authored *Habits of the Heart,* he has written *Tokugawa Religion, Beyond Belief, The Broken Covenant, The New Religious Consciousness,* and *Varieties of Civil Religion.*

James W. Ceaser is Professor of Government at the University of Virginia and author of *Presidential Selection* and *Reforming the Reforms.*

Sombat Chantornvong is Professor of Political Science at Thammasat University, Bangkok, Thailand. In addition to having translated Western classics such as *The Federalist* into Thai, he writes on Asian and Thai politics and political thought and has served at high levels in the Thai government.

Ralph C. Hancock is Associate Professor of Political Science at Brigham Young University. He has published on American political thought and is author of *Calvin and the Foundations of Modern Politics.*

Wilhelm Hennis is Professor of Political Science at Freiburg University in West Germany. He writes on political theory and problems of contemporary German politics.

William Kristol is Chief of Staff to the Vice President of the United States. He has written numerous articles on political theory and American politics.

Jean-Claude Lamberti was Professor at the University of Paris and author of *Tocqueville and the Two Democracies.*

Peter Augustine Lawler is Associate Professor of Political Science at Berry College. He has published on Tocqueville and other subjects concerning American politics.

John Marini is Associate Professor of Political Science at the University of Nevada, Reno. He is co-editor of *The Imperial Congress* and author of a forthcoming work on Congress and the bureaucracy.

William D. Richardson is Associate Professor of Political Science at Georgia State University. He is the author of a book on Melville's *Benito Cereno* and several articles on American political thought.

James T. Schleifer is Professor of History and Director of the Gill Library at the College of New Rochelle. He is author of *The Making of Tocqueville's "Democracy in America"* and editor and translator of a forthcoming edition of Tocqueville's *Democracy.*

Bruce James Smith is Assistant Professor of Political Science at Allegheny College. He is author of *Politics and Remembrance.*

Thomas G. West is Professor of Politics at the University of Dallas. He is author of *Plato's "Apology of Socrates"* and co-translator (with Grace Starry West) of *Four Texts on Socrates.* He is now completing a book on the American Founding.

John Adams Wettergreen was Professor of Political Science at San Jose State University. At the time of his death in 1989 he had nearly completed a manuscript on bureaucracy, which will be published by Harper & Row.

Delba Winthrop is Lecturer in Extension Studies at Harvard University. She has published numerous articles on Aristotle, Tocqueville, and Solzhenitsyn, and is completing a book on Tocqueville.

Catherine H. Zuckert is Professor of Government at Carleton College. She is editor of *Understanding the Political Spirit* and author of *Natural Right and the American Imagination.*

Political Thought

"I have tried to see not differently but further than any party. . . ."

1

Two Ways of Conceiving the Republic

Jean-Claude Lamberti

When Alexis de Tocqueville observes the new order born in America, he does so through the eyes of a French aristocrat whose family, let us not forget, had suffered greatly through the French Revolution. His father and mother, his aunt and uncle, his maternal grandparents and his great-grandfather, the old Malesherbes, were arbitrarily arrested and thrown into prison under the Convention. No plotting, no crime could be held against them. But Malesherbes had bravely assumed his role as a lawyer during the King's trial, and he was guillotined, as were almost all the other members of his family. However, Alexis's mother and father escaped a similar fate and no more—they were saved at the last moment by Robespierre's fall from power on the 9th of Thermidor, year II (28 July 1794), which led to their liberation as well as to that of many other prisoners. But Alexis de Tocqueville's mother was henceforth to be afflicted by a sort of depression and never recovered her health. When her husband, Count Hervé, who was twenty when he was incarcerated, came out of jail a few months later, his hair had turned completely white. It would take too long to talk of all his relatives, close and distant, who perished. It is enough for us to realize that the author of *Democracy in America* was brought up in a very old noble family, a victim of the French Revolution, whereas, in fact, it was open to the new ideas and sensitive to the ideals of 1789. But 1789 was not 1793, and Tocqueville was constantly to question himself as to the reasons why the fine élan of liberty and equality of 1789 could, in the space of a few years, end up in the bloody Terror.

When Alexis de Tocqueville discusses in America an orderly and peaceful democracy, he cannot but compare it bitterly with the first French Republic. For him, the first image of democracy outside America is that of the republic which foundered in bloodshed, and when he writes his first masterpiece, the horror of revolutionary memories is as much in his mind as the felicitous success of the American republic. But he does not say so and, in general, the comparison remains implicit in *Democracy in America,* which gives it a great penetrating force in people's minds. But it is easier for the French reader than for the American reader to accept the suggestions made in the text. Still, if the American reader is prepared to recall that *Democracy in America* is a book written by a French aristocrat, meant first and foremost to be read by his compatriots, he will easily realize that the work is not only a painting of the happiest of republics but also a complex picture whose background contrasts strongly with its foreground.

In order to dispel any doubt that there might be concerning this interpretation, it would be enough to consult the rough drafts of *Democracy in America* at Yale University, where they have been admirably classified and conserved by Professor Paul Lambert White and then by his former student, Professor George W. Pierson. For instance, it is possible to read therein a text entitled, "On the different ways of conceiving of a republic." The text in question begins thus:

> What is understood by "Republic" in the United States, is a regular state really founded on the enlightened will of the people. It is a government in which resolutions mature over a long period, are not discussed in haste and are executed when the time is ripe. What is called the Republic in the United States is the tranquil rule of the majority . . . but the majority itself is, however, not omnipotent; above it in the moral world are to be found humanity and reason, and in the physical world, acquired rights.

And in the margin he had added:

> In all countries in which this republic would be practicable, I would be a republican.

Perhaps for an unpublished text, so central to our topic, the reader will not hold it against us if we give a rather long quotation, setting it beside the passage quoted above, which Tocqueville writes about another republic he prefers not to mention.

> According to certain people in Europe, the Republic is not the rule of the majority, it is the rule of those who speak in their name. It is not the people who get in these sorts of governments, it is those who desire the greater well-being of the people. The republican government is, moreover, the only one with the recognized right to do all it wishes and which must not force itself to follow any divine or human law in order to attain the goal it has fixed for itself. . . . When I see one of those so-called republicans, I always seem to see the Executioner in ceremonial dress . . . standing on the scaffold. . . .[1]

The opposition, as strong as it is simple, between the American republic and the first French republic is at the starting point of Tocqueville's reflection, but he does not stop there, and he cannot content himself with the confrontation of the two historical entities. On the contrary, as his reflection progresses, he tends to define ideal models which borrow certain significant features from historical entities but do not claim to describe them entirely and make it possible to answer the questions which appear to him to have the greatest pertinence to political theory. In other words, *Democracy in America* is not one of those American travelogues, so common in the nineteenth century, nor yet a simple study of American institutions, as is sometimes believed. It is a work of political theory which starts from the reasoned observation of the American republic and its successes to build up, thanks to the comparative method, a model of liberal democracy. Tocqueville uses the comparative method in the same way as Montesquieu, and he builds models of the same nature as the ideal-types of Max Weber.

---

[1]*Inédits de Yale*, Cahier CV, h, 2, pp. 68-71.

In this short study, we propose to highlight the stages in this theoretical elaboration. First of all, the author reasons on the opposition of the two democracies: on the one hand, liberal democracy, American style; and, on the other, the democracy inherited from the French Revolution and the errors of Rousseau, the Jacobin myths and the corruption of the public mind, whose distant origins go back to the administrative monarchy. A further step in the analysis is taken when, in the second part of *Democracy in America*, the author shows the ambivalent tendencies of democracies, and then it can be understood how democracy bears in itself the seeds of its own ruin. Finally, we should like to ask ourselves whether Tocqueville's reflections make it possible to distinguish a democratic model of general scope from the American model in the nineteenth century which constitutes the first example of liberal democracy. If this distinction proves to be possible, then there will open up a way to understanding what democracy outside America can be.

The Two Democracies

The first half of *Democracy in America*, published in 1835, opposes the ideas and political practices of the Americans to Rousseau's conceptions and the passions of the French Revolution. As early as in the Introduction, Tocqueville deplores the fact that in France "the religionists are the enemies of liberty and the friends of liberty attack religion,"[2] and as soon as he tackles the study of American civilization, he shows that it is "the result of two distinct elements which in other places have been in frequent disagreement, but which the Americans have succeeded in incorporating to some extent one with the other and combining admirably. I allude to the spirit of religion and the spirit of liberty."[3]

---

[2]Alexis de Tocqueville, *Democracy in America*, ed. Phillips Bradley, trans. Henry Reeve, rev. Francis G. Bowen, 2 vols. (New York: Alfred J. Knopf, Vintage Books, 1945), Introduction, p. 13. Hereinafter cited as *Democracy*. To facilitate comparison with the original text published by Gallimard of Paris in *Oeuvres Complètes, d'Alexis de Tocqueville*, tome 1, vols. I and II, all references to *Democracy in America* will indicate the volume (I or II), then the section (A, B, C, or D, for volume II), chapter number, as well as page. *Oeuvres Complètes*, hereinafter cited as O.C.

[3]*Democracy*, vol. I, chap. 2, p. 45.

To a great extent, this first opposition explains the difference in conceptions relative to the fundamental concept of sovereignty. On this matter, the text quoted earlier in this study is patently clear, but the texts in *Democracy in America* are no less clear:

> I hold it to be an impious and detestable maxim that, politically speaking, the people have a right to do anything; and yet I have asserted that all authority originates in the will of the majority. Am I, then, in contradiction with myself? A general law, which bears the name of justice, has been made and sanctioned, not only by a majority of this or that people, but by a majority of mankind. The rights of every people are therefore confined within the limits of what is just.[4]

In the America of 1835, religious or Puritan convictions and the morality of their descendants hold such a sway over justice that the majority finds itself limited thereby. In France, on the contrary, the opposition of the revolutionaries and the Church, as well as the bad habits born of royal absolutism, have contributed to spreading a conception of the absolute sovereignty of the people, the theoretical expression of which is to be found in Jean-Jacques Rousseau's *Contrat Social*.[5] And assuredly, it is a severe denunciation of Rousseau's thesis that is seen in this passage:

> Some have not feared to assert that a people can never outstep the boundaries of justice and reason in those affairs which are peculiarly its own; and that consequently full power may be given to the majority by which it is represented. But this is the language of a slave.[6]

Such different conceptions of sovereignty result very logically from completely opposite ideas on the notion of "Constitution." From the idea of limited sovereignty, shared by the Americans and the Liberals in France, stems the idea, already dear to Montesquieu, of a balance and separation of public powers as well as the search

---

[4]Ibid., chap. 15, p. 269.
[5]*Du Contrat Social*, bk. 2.
[6]*Democracy*, vol. I, chap. 15, p. 269.

for guarantees of rights and, in the first instance, individual liberties. Conversely, Rousseau's disciples challenge all separation of powers and go as far as to assert that general will is always capable of shifting the bounds of individual rights.[7] It is striking indeed to note that the Constitution of 1793, which in Tocqueville's time served as a real reference for the French Republicans, is the exact opposite of the Constitution of the United States of America: a collegiate executive of twenty-four members rather than presidential powers invested in one man; one single chamber instead of two; and a rigid conception of the relationship between different powers, unlike the balance in the separation of powers which American tradition interprets simply and modestly, faithful therein to the true teachings of Montesquieu.[8] The comparison cannot be completed without noting that in America the Federal Constitution created a stable political order and enjoyed the quasi-religious respect of all citizens, whereas, from the time of its great revolution, France had known quite an exceptional constitutional instability. Even more than by these contrasts in matters constitutional, Tocqueville was struck by the opposition of the administrative structures in the two countries, and he was the first to feel all the importance of this. According to him, it was principally the absence of administrative centralization which, in the United States, tempered the risk of tyranny by the majority,[9] while in France, the centralized administration served revolutionary tyranny, after having been the instrument of the absolute power of kings. But Tocqueville's analysis goes even further: Over and above the institutions, it embraces those values which direct the public spirit. And there again, the differences are very real, although on both sides of the Atlantic, reference is made to the values of liberty and equality.

Since the Revolution, equality of rights had reigned in France—equality before the law, before justice, before taxation—as well as equal rights to access to state services. But this equality is not to be

---

[7]*Du Contrat Social.* See especially bk. 1, chap. 7. "There can be no sort of fundamental law obligatory for the body of the people, not even a social contract."

[8]Cf. *The Federalist,* especially No. 47 by James Madison.

[9]*Democracy,* vol. I, chap. 16, p. 281.

confused with what Tocqueville calls "equality of condition"; otherwise, why would he have begun his book by writing, "Among the novel objects that attracted my attention during my stay in the United States, nothing struck me more forcibly than the general equality of condition among the people."[10] If, in his eyes, equality of condition is a new object, it is because it is different from the equality of rights existing in France, and in order to grasp this difference, nothing is more enlightening than this page from his travel journals, in which he describes the most original aspects of American equality:

> I am speaking of equality in the context of social life; that equality that results in certain individuals gathering in the same places, sharing their ideas and their pleasures, uniting their families. . . . In America, as in France, men are ranked according to certain categories. In the course of social life, common habits, education and especially wealth establish these classifications; but these rules are neither absolute, nor inflexible, nor permanent. They create passing distinctions yet do not form classes as such.[11]

Thus, equality of condition presupposes equality of rights but does not just amount to that; it also comprises social mobility and what the ancients used to call equality of esteem. Now, the latter components were not yet greatly developed in France in 1835. For Tocqueville, equality of condition is the mainspring that affects all aspects of American life and transforms all human relationships.[12] Tocqueville understood that the feeling of similitude in men is the most powerful imaginary product of the social democratic state. Given certain conditions, in America, men who live unequally from unequal situations nevertheless feel themselves to be equals. Thus egalitarian claims never degenerate into demands for absolute equality, applied to all aspects of life. However, Tocqueville notes that the social democratic society leads to two forms of equality:

---

[10] Ibid., Introduction, p. 3.

[11] *O.C.*, tome V, vol. I, p. 279.

[12] *Democracy*, vol. II, C, p. 5; in particular, p. 190: "Equality of conditions turns servants and masters into new beings and places them in new relative positions."

> There is, in fact, a manly and lawful passion for equality that incites men to wish all to be powerful and honored. This passion tends to elevate the humble to the rank of the great; but there exists also in the human heart a depraved taste for equality, which impels the weak to attempt to lower the powerful to their own level and reduces men to prefer equality in slavery to inequality with freedom.[13]

But, in the United States, laws and manners orientate the need for equality toward its noble form and, as Tocqueville noted, the Americans knew how to oppose the idea of rights and feelings of envy.[14]

The passion for equality was less well controlled in France, for the revolutionary struggle had exacerbated it. "Democratic nations," wrote Tocqueville, "are at all times fond of equality, but there are certain epochs at which the passion they entertain for it swells to the height of fury. This occurs at the moment when the old social system, long menaced, is overthrown after a severe internal struggle, and the barriers of rank are at length thrown down."[15] It may be that here the author is remembering Montesquieu who had already demonstrated that democracy can be corrupted by an "extreme spirit of equality"[16] and had outlined certain circumstances conducive to this spirit. "The great successes to which the people contribute substantially give them such pride that it is no longer possible to lead them."[17] And the great victories of the Revolution and the Empire had, in fact, exacerbated egalitarian demands.

In the United States, the generating force behind democratic society is the peaceful equalization of conditions, but in France it was the Revolution that played this role. And Tocqueville perceived only too well the difference between the demands for equality, characteristic of democracies, and the extreme form adopted by egalitarian passion both during and after democratic revolutions. Thus it is that he was able to write that the great

---

[13]Ibid., vol. I, chap. 3, p. 56.
[14]Ibid., p. 17.
[15]Ibid., vol. II, B, chap. 1, p. 102.
[16]Montesquieu, *L'esprit des Lois*, bk. VIII, chap. 3.
[17]Ibid., chap. 4.

advantage of the Americans is that "they are born equal instead of becoming so."[18]

* * *

In revolutionary terms, liberty sometimes seems to be merely a means of attaining equality and, in any case, is a secondary value. On the contrary, in liberal philosophy, liberty is situated at the apex of the hierarchy of values and has a certain value both as an end and as a means. But although he was born into an aristocratic family, Tocqueville did not share the prejudices of his class; he realized that in the future, liberty could survive only when allied to equality. "Liberty," he wrote in the preparatory notes to his *Democracy*, "for democratic peoples will never be founded except on the basis of respect for equality. All those who in the centuries to come will try to establish and found liberty on the basis of aristocracy will fail."[19] His conception of liberty is in contradiction with the idea of aristocratic liberty—that is to say, limited to a few—and on this point he differs from those of his own station, his own kinsman, Chateaubriand for instance. He professes a doctrine of liberty that is very clearly democratic, as is shown by this text written in 1836:

> According to the modern notion, the democratic notion and, I dare say, the just notion of liberty, each man being presumed to have received from Nature the necessary lights for his conduct, is endowed at birth with an equal and imprescriptible right to live independent of his fellow men, in all that concerns himself, and to control his own destiny as he sees fit.[20]

But if, henceforth, it is indispensable to ally liberty and equality, it is difficult to strike a balance between the two demands.

Lack of balance is highly probable and risks being fatal for liberty. It is this point which preoccupies Tocqueville most of all, as can be seen when one reads the famous chapter entitled "Why Democratic Nations Show a More Ardent and Enduring Love of

---

[18]*Democracy*, vol. II, pt. II, chap. 3, p. 108.
[19]Tocqueville, Cahier CV, p. 9.
[20]*O.C.*, tome II, vol. I, p. 62.

Equality Than of Liberty."[21] The Americans' major success has consisted in maintaining a certain balance between the fundamental values of democracy. This was also the ideal of the Constituent Assembly in France in 1789. But the French Revolution failed to achieve it, and it was liberty that was sacrificed to revolutionary passions. Tocqueville's contemporaries were acquainted with *Considérations sur la Révolution francaise* by Mme. de Stael, first published in 1818 and frequently reprinted. In general, from this book they retained the notion of an opposition between the Constituent Assembly and the Convention, the one inspired by Montesquieu, the other by Rousseau, and with Mme. de Stael, they opposed the spirit of 1789 and that of 1793. The most common conclusion reached was marked by great skepticism about the possibility of balancing the demands for liberty and those for equality. Tocqueville also perceived the difficulty and, as much as any other, reflected upon the failure of the Constituent Assembly. He did realize, however, that solidarity between the two values was indispensable, and he searched for the reasons for the balance achieved in America so as to draw the political consequences from this on his return to France.

The Ambivalent Tendencies of Democracies

Between the publication of the first half of *Democracy in America* in 1835 and that of the second volume, five years elapsed, devoted to fresh reflections. It is here that is situated what Professor George W. Pierson has wittingly called "the second journey to America," a totally imaginary voyage, composed solely of readings, studies, and a sort of intense intellectual rumination, interrupted only by observation and, moreover, by political action since, after an abortive attempt in 1837, Tocqueville succeeded in being elected to the Chamber of Deputies in 1839. As it became more profound, his reflection went beyond the oversimple opposition between American democracy and the first French Republic, and he succeeded in highlighting the ambivalent tendencies of the two democracies.

---

[21] *Democracy*, vol. II, pt. II, chap. 1, pp. 99-103.

The contradiction is situated not only between two historical experiments but right inside the motor forces behind any democracy. The examples considered until then retain their value and their opposition remains meaningful, but only insofar as they are extreme situations. In order to construct a theoretical model of democracy, it is necessary to pick out the most pertinent features of each of the societies observed and to link them in such a way that the intellectual instrument thus formed may assist us in answering the basic question posed by the future of democracies; namely, on what conditions can liberty be safeguarded in democratic societies, taking into account the threats that weigh heavy on it and which are born of democratic society itself? As has often been underlined, Tocqueville always asks himself what must be done so that the social democratic state may lead to a liberal democracy and not to a democratic despotism. But he does not content himself with posing this question purely from the political point of view and, indeed, his interrogation is threefold—political, cultural, and economic—as the last sentence of *Democracy in America* reminds us:

> The nations of our time cannot prevent the conditions of men from becoming equal, but it depends on themselves whether the principle of equality is to lead them to servitude or freedom, to knowledge or barbarism, to prosperity or wretchedness.

For intellectual life, equalization of social conditions entails contradictory consequences that Tocqueville analyzes with a rigor that prefigures the more recent efforts of the sociology of knowledge. At first glance, it favors the independence of minds and the flight of the intellect but, on reflection, it seems that progress is never sure and that the excesses of conformity or those of individualism may lead to a regression. The breaking of those hierarchical links forming the framework of society in the centuries of aristocracy ends up ruining the authority of tradition. "Everyone shuts himself up tightly within himself and insists upon judging the world from here."[22] The Reformation, the philosophy of Descartes,

---

[22]Ibid., A, chap. 1, p. 4.

the philosophical method of the eighteenth century express in different ways the intellectual individualism which accompanied the equalization of condition. However, according to Tocqueville, man cannot bear complete intellectual independence; he must place somewhere an authority in the intellectual and moral worlds, but in the democratic centuries this eternal truth receives a particular application: Men then tend to place authority in the opinion of the mass.[23] And in democratic societies, Tocqueville asserts, "faith in public opinion will become a species of religion, and the majority its ministering prophet."[24] Then a serious risk is discovered that Tocqueville evokes in disquieting terms—"a sort of enormous pressure of the mind of all upon the individual intelligence."[25]

Threatened on the one hand by the conformity of the mass, intelligence runs the risk, on the other, of remaining sterile if men do not know how to temper their individualism by associating with one another. And in this hypothesis, Tocqueville is not afraid to conclude that society would revert to barbarism.[26] Indeed, the equalization of condition isolates individuals and tends to create a splintered society in which interactions become dangerously impoverished. Now, Tocqueville notes:

> Feelings and opinions are recruited, the heart is enlarged, and the human mind is developed only by reciprocal influence of men upon one another.[27]

The author of *Democracy in America* adopts a position midway between those who believe that democratic individualism will automatically entail the regression of civilization and those who see therein the source of sure progress. According to him, everything depends on men's skill in voluntarily compensating for the most pernicious tendencies of democratic societies, by all possible means and especially by creating associations, which the Americans were so good at doing. However, the citizens of

---

[23]Ibid., chap. 2.
[24]Ibid., p. 12.
[25]Ibid., p. 11.
[26]Ibid., vol. II, C, chap. 21, pp. 277-78.
[27]Ibid., chap. 5, p. 117.

democracies must be aware of the very risks of their societies, and as for Tocqueville, he strives to dissipate the illusion of automatic progress:

> It is believed by some that modern society will be always changing its aspect; for myself, I fear that it will ultimately be too invariably fixed in the same institutions, the same prejudices, the same manners, so that mankind will be stopped and circumscribed; that the mind will swing backwards and forwards forever without begetting fresh ideas; that man will waste his strength in bootless and solitary trifling, and, though in continual motion, that humanity will cease to advance.[28]

At the heart of democratic ambivalence lie individualistic tendencies. Tocqueville does not combat these, for he knows that they are inscribed in the nature of democratic societies,[29] and for him, as for all liberal philosophers, the goal of political societies is nothing more than the well-being of individuals. Tocqueville distinguishes individualism and egoism and, if he has faith in the individual, he constantly draws attention to the dangers of excessive individualism. In the intellectual sphere, as has been seen, individualism can bring liberty and the advance of intelligence or, just as well, can lead very isolated minds to submit themselves to a conformity which bears the seeds of all regression. In economic life, the same ambivalence of democratic tendencies can be traced: Economic individualism can be a source of prosperity, but its excesses can lead to new misery.

In its Tocquevillian definition, individualism is essentially a fault of public-spiritedness, and the orientation of societies toward individual and commercial activities can only accentuate this tendency.

> Individualism is a mature and calm feeling, which disposes each member of the community to sever himself from the mass of his fellows and to draw apart with

---

[28]Ibid., C, chap. 21, pp. 277-78.
[29]Ibid., B, chap. 2.

> his families and his friends, so that after he has thus formed a little circle of his own, he willingly leaves society at large to itself.[30]

Now, it is obvious that the interest shown in business strongly develops individualistic tendencies and risks sapping the virtues of public life. Politically, Tocqueville is a liberal, but with regard to economic liberalism, he keeps his distance, to a certain extent. His economic thought owes a great deal to the major representatives of the liberal school, Jean-Baptiste Say and N. Senior, but also to Alban de Villeneuve-Bargemont, author in 1834 of *A Treatise on Christian Political Economy.* On occasion, he deems it necessary to correct the abuses of the economy for social reasons, and he defends a wide and noble conception of utilitarianism, which anticipates the one to be championed a few years later by his friend John Stuart Mill. Moreover, in his eyes, one of the reasons for the American success stems indeed from a conception of self-interest rightly understood, capable of going beyond narrow egoism, of allying itself to moral and religious ideals and of combating excessive individualism.[31] The love of material well-being, which prompts activity in democratic societies, can become dangerous once it goes beyond a certain point, and Tocqueville shows in a famous chapter "How Excessive Care for Worldly Welfare May Impair That Welfare."[32]

Democratic societies spontaneously grant greater attention to economic interests than to long-term political interests, and *Democracy in America* shows the main political dangers resulting from this. On the one hand, the democratic principle may find itself thwarted by the birth of a new aristocracy, born of industry.[33] On the other hand, Tocqueville especially wishes to draw his French readers' attention to the danger of an excessive interest in business in certain circumstances, particularly when the habits of liberty are not yet consolidated, as was the case in France in 1840; the taste for physical gratifications among them has grown more

---

[30]Ibid., p. 104.
[31]Ibid., pp. 8-9.
[32]Ibid., p. 16.
[33]Ibid., p. 20.

rapidly than their education, and their men are carried away and lose all self-restraint at the sight of the new possessions they are about to obtain.

The risk, then, is that they would be the victims of too narrow a conception of their interest and that "the better to look after what they call their own business, they neglect their chief business, which is to remain their own masters."[34] In the end, the triumph of economic individualism and the excessive passion for material gain can lead to the ruin of welfare, or to a new aristocracy, or even facilitate the establishment of a new despotism.

An idea often expressed by Tocqueville is that individualism, while granting more liberty to each and every one, introduces the risk of a new despotism. There is in that an aspect of the ambivalence of egalitarian societies which does not always appear at first glance. "The principle of equality," writes Tocqueville, "begets two tendencies: The one leads men straight to independence and may suddenly drive them into anarchy; the other conducts them by a longer, more secret, but more certain road to servitude."[35] Tocqueville is not afraid of fleeing anarchy; he knows full well that in an industrial and commercial society, order, in the eyes of all, is essential; in the centuries of democracy, it is civil society that demands order and does not need it to be imposed on it from the outside by political power. The real risk lies elsewhere; it has its roots in the ambivalent tendencies of democratic societies, and Tocqueville devotes the fourth part of the *Democracy* of 1840 to demonstrate how the ideas of men as well as their feelings threaten to conduct them along "the secret road to servitude." But the despotism that could establish itself in democratic societies would differ from the one that had been experienced by societies in Antiquity, and would not resemble revolutionary tyranny. "It would be more extensive and more mild; it would degrade men without tormenting them."[36] As far as leaders are concerned, Tocqueville does not fear that in democratic societies they would resemble tyrants, but rather "guardians." At the end of the *Democracy* of

---

[34]Ibid., pp. 14, 149.
[35]Ibid., D, chap. 1, p. 304.
[36]Ibid., chap. 6, p. 335.

1835, Tocqueville had depicted the tyranny of the majority by borrowing its traits both from the conformity of majority opinion in America and the tyranny of the French revolutionary assemblies, but in the famous chapter which he devotes to this new despotism which threatens democracies, he presents a more personal construction and one which has greater prophetic value. He had noted this himself in the margin of the manuscript: "New despotism. It is in the portrayal of this that resides all the originality and depth of my idea. What I wrote in my first work was hackneyed and superficial."[37] At the heart of this famous text in which Tocqueville announces the appearance of the welfare state, we are going to find these men, similar, equal, isolated, and strangers to one another as it were; in short, we are going to find individualism again:

> I seek to trace the novel features under which despotism may appear in the world. The first thing that strikes the observation is an innumerable multitude of men, all equal and alike, incessantly endeavoring to produce the petty and paltry pleasures with which they glut their lives. Each of them, living apart, is as a stranger to the fate of all the rest; his children and his private friends constitute to him the whole of mankind. As for the rest of his fellow citizens, he is close to them, but does not see them; he touches them, but he does not feel them; he exists only in himself and for himself alone; and if his kindred still remain to him, he may be said at any rate to have lost his country. Above this race of men stands an immense and tutelary power, which takes upon itself alone to secure their gratifications and to watch over their fate. That power is absolute, minute, regular, provident, and mild. It would be like the authority of a parent if, like that authority, its object was to prepare men for manhood; but it seeks, on the contrary, to keep them in perpetual childhood.[38]

What a terrible punishment of individualism is that "servitude of the regular, quiet, and gentle kind" which "does not tyrannize,

---

[37]*Inédits de Yale*, Cahier CV, g.

[38]*Democracy*, vol. II, D, chap. 6, p. 336.

but it compresses, enervates, extinguishes, and stupefies a people, till each nation is reduced to nothing better than a flock of timid and industrious animals, of which the government is the shepherd."[39] As can be seen, this new despotism does not have to impose itself through violence; it is born of democratic society itself and answers certain of its demands. Nothing can better illustrate than this example the ambivalence of democratic societies which may lead to servitude as to liberty.

Democracy Outside America

What remains to be done now is to examine the observations on which Tocqueville's analysis rests and the democratic societies to which it can be applied. The ambivalence of democratic tendencies is examined especially on the basis of a comparison between France and the United States, but *Democracy in America* also contains other comparisons, with Latin America and with England in particular. We likewise have at our disposal the report presented by Tocqueville on January 15, 1848, to the Academy of Moral and Political Sciences on M. Cherbuliez's work entitled *On Democracy in Switzerland.*

This study, therefore, antedates the Constitution of September 12, 1848, endowing Switzerland with a stable Federal Council and two chambers elected by universal suffrage. Such a reorganization of the country's institutions rendered obsolete the criticisms which Tocqueville had not failed to formulate with regard to the former confederal structure, and in particular concerning the weakness of the real powers of the confederal government. Yet, the author of *Democracy in America* had clearly announced that in the long run, the federal government would take more and more power, a prediction which was confirmed not only by the Constitution of September 12, 1848, but also by its revision in May 1874 and by all the subsequent changes. In its central section, Tocqueville's report compares the institutions of the Swiss cantons and the constitution of the State of New York. The author certainly does not praise the

---

[39]Ibid., p. 337.

ways in which the Swiss make use of pure democracy; ways which, in his estimation, are minor and tend to become exceptional. "The pure democracies of Switzerland," he declares, "belong moreover to another age; they can teach us nothing of the present, nor of the future."[40] And even in what Tocqueville calls the representative democracies of Switzerland, "the people," he writes, "have kept for itself the direct exercise of a part of its power,"[41] so that, in certain cases, representative democracy may degenerate into pure democracy. Moreover, the comparison with the representative democracy of the state of New York brings out a double inferiority: In the cantons, there is but one legislative assembly, and the separation of powers has no meaning as such there, for judicial power and executive power are overdependent on the legislative assembly.

As the Swiss had already been living for a long time in a Republic when the French Revolution broke out, it was often imagined that they were closer to modern liberty than the other peoples of Europe, but Tocqueville notes that this is not the case; indeed, most of their cantonal governments have remained oligarchies. With his customary realism, he was careful not to believe in the myth, born of the theories of Jean-Jacques Rousseau, concerning the democratic virtues and spirit of the mountain race. According to Tocqueville, M. Cherbuliez ought to have entitled his book *On the Democratic Revolution in Switzerland* because, for over fifteen years, the country had been in a state of revolution. As he notes:

> Democracy there is less a regular form of government than a weapon customarily used to destroy, and sometimes to protect, the old type of society. One can very well study the particular phenomena which accompany the revolutionary state in the democratic era in which we are living, but not depict democracy in its permanent, tranquil place.[42]

That is perhaps the crucial point: In Europe, it is possible to observe the seeds of democratic revolution but not democracy in its pure state.

---

[40]Ibid., app. 1, p. 356.
[41]Ibid., p. 357.
[42]Ibid., p. 353.

Even in England, Tocqueville was able to observe a mixed social state, characteristic of an age of transition between pure aristocratic reform and pure democracy. And even if it is gradually accomplished, this transition has the same results as a revolution. After his first journey to England in September 1833, Tocqueville wrote:

> If by "revolution" one understands every fundamental change in the laws, every social change, every substitution of one regulating principle for another, England is assuredly in a state of revolution, for the aristocratic principle which was the vital principle of its constitution loses a little of its strength every day; and it is likely that, within a certain lapse of time, the democratic principle will have replaced it. But if by "revolution" one understands violent, abrupt change, England does not appear to me to be ripe for such an event; and I can even see many reasons for thinking that it never will be.[43]

He was able to measure on the spot the skill of the English in defusing revolutionary tendencies; he saw the effects of the Reform Bill of 1832; and during his second journey in 1835, he was to study the new Poor Law of August 14, 1834, whose principal mover was the economist N. Senior with whom he was to remain on friendly terms until the end of his life. In his eyes, the basic difference between France and England stems from the nature of, and the alliance formed by, the ruling classes in the two countries. The aristocracy of England remains open, while the nobility of France "separates itself from the rest of the nation." "'Gentleman' and 'gentilhome,'" Tocqueville notes, "have obviously the same origin, but in England, 'gentleman' is applied to any well-bred man, whatever his birth, whereas in France, 'gentilhome' is applied only to someone of noble birth."[44] In such conditions, one understands why the nobility of France whipped up more violent hatred than the aristocracy of England. For Tocqueville, it is the difference between the elites of the two countries which, to a large extent, explains the way in which they evolve toward democracy. In France, the movement

---

[43]*O.C.*, tome V, vol. 2, p. 36.
[44]Ibid., p. 37.

imposes itself through revolutionary outbursts, while the English evolve gradually by proceeding through reform.

All the comparisons lead to one and the same conclusion: In Europe observers come across only mixed situations in which the aristocratic principle is still more or less violently opposed to the democratic principle. It is only in America that one can look on democracy in its pure state, in its perfect simplicity. Tocqueville wrote to the Comte Molé in 1835:

> In America, all the laws are to some degree the result of the same thoughts. The whole of society, so to speak, is founded on one single fact; everything springs from one single principle. America could be compared to a great forest criss-crossed by a multitude of straight paths which reach the same point. It is merely a question of finding the intersection, and all will become clear in the twinkling of an eye.

And the author of *Democracy in America* showed how equality of condition could explain all aspects of American life, its vitality as well as its laws and its manners.

When, at the end of the first volume, he examines the "Principal Causes which Tend to Maintain the Democratic Republic in the United States,"[45] Tocqueville demonstrates that the laws contribute more to the maintaining of such a republic than "the physical circumstances of the country, and the customs more than the laws."[46] And in order to establish his demonstration, he has recourse to a comparison between the United States and those states founded in America by the Spanish. In no single one of these states has aristocracy been able to survive, yet democratic institutions have really been successful only in the United States. Nevertheless, the states of South America have also benefited from vast territories and immense natural resources, but they have often suffered from bad legislation. And Mexico, whose laws are inspired by those of the United States, has been unable to accustom itself to the peaceful government of democracy, notes Tocqueville, for its manners were out of harmony with its laws.

---

[45] *Democracy*, vol. I, p. 17.
[46] Ibid., chap. 17, pp. 330-34.

But if the principal cause of the success of the Republic is to be looked for in the agreement between manners and democratic laws, it must be admitted that the United States of America enjoys a three-fold privilege, part and parcel of what Tocqueville calls their starting point. First, the religion of the earliest immigrants was perfectly attuned to their republican convictions; secondly, the absence of administrative centralization and the custom of local self-government, which has greatly contributed to the prosperity of America and spurred its citizens to a high degree of political education; last but not least, the absence of violent social revolution at the origin of democracy in America. Tocqueville declares this fact to be "of considerable importance," and right from the start of the *Democracy* of 1840, he notes: "The social condition and the Constitution of the Americans are democratic, but they have not had a democratic revolution."[47]

Tocqueville noted with great perspicacity the particular circumstances which favored democracy in America, but he did not admit for all that the latter could develop only in America. To put it in present-day terms, let us say that his work cannot serve as an argument for the thesis of American exceptionalism. Moreover, were this thesis admitted in an absolute way, with all that it implies, it would have an antidemocratic significance, for it would imply that democracy is an illusory ideal, which cannot be translated into hard facts, unless by exception. In our opinion, it is being truer to Tocqueville's thought to consider that a regime of liberty is difficult to maintain in centuries of democracy and that the success of the United States was facilitated to a large extent by particularly favorable circumstances, in the vanguard of which must be placed the absence of revolution.

Indeed, as we have already had the occasion to underline, a great revolution exacerbates egalitarian and individualistic tendencies. That is why Tocqueville is able to write: "The great advantage of the Americans is that they had arrived at a state of democracy without having to endure a democratic revolution."[48] The genesis and the structure of the second half of *Democracy in*

[47]Ibid., vol. II, pt. I, chap. 1, p. 7.
[48]Ibid., pt. II, chap. 3, p. 108.

America can be explained by the author's desire to distinguish what is characteristic of democracy and what results from the mixture of democratic demands and revolutionary passions. Fresh light is cast on the work through the comparison of the situation in France and that in the United States, and the distinction of democratic characteristics and revolutionary traits is worked out via the methodical confrontation of the two democracies.[49]

The first *Democracy* describes the American institutions, the second is more general, more philosophical; it offers a theoretical model of democracy, stripped of revolutionary features but, very often, stripped also of American characteristics. In the work published in 1840, the author also strives to show what democracy outside America is. In order to understand this, it would seem necessary to be able to draw a line between what is American and what is democratic in at least three spheres: the state, society, and the standard of economic development. The United States forms a federation which does not know administrative centralization. It is not vital for a democratic state to have a federal structure unless it be a large state.[50] But in the end, it seems to Tocqueville that democracy must lead to centralization. On the latter point, his thoughts varied, and Professor Seymour Drescher has produced a remarkable analysis of the various stages.[51] Following his journey to America, Tocqueville declared above all that the prosperity of a country was related to the absence of heavy administrative structures. In 1835, his reflections on the installation of an administration charged with applying the new Poor Laws in England led him to think that centralization was characteristic of the period of transition between aristocracy and democracy. But from 1838 on, he deemed that democracy itself was generally directed toward centralization and that the American state appeared then as an

---

[49]For fuller developments on these points, see Jean-Claude Lamberti, *Tocqueville et les deux démocracies* (Paris: Presses Universitaries de France, 1983), published in the U.S. as *Tocqueville and the Two Democracies* (Cambridge, Mass.: Harvard University Press, 1988). Hereinafter cited as Lamberti, *les deux démocracies*.

[50]See *The Federalist* No. 9 (Alexander Hamilton), and Montesquieu, *L'esprit des Lois*, bk. IX, chap. 1.

[51]Seymour Drescher, *Dilemmas of Democracy: Tocqueville and Modernization* (Pittsburgh, Pa.: University of Pittsburgh Press, 1968).

exception to this rule, a fact which could be explained by special circumstances.

A reading of the *Democracy* of 1840 also makes it possible to separate the ideal type of democratic society from the image of American society, but, in the main, commentators have scarcely been interested in this exercise. In the first part, and in certain chapters of the third part, Tocqueville is at pains to pick out the particularities of the American system and especially the links between America and England. This he does strongly at the beginning of the work when he underlines the exceptional nature of the American situation on the intellectual level, and then, more discreetly, but still clearly, half-way through the book. On the other hand, the last chapters of the third part (from chapter 18 to chapter 26) and all the chapters of the fourth part are very general and visibly concern the distant future of democratic societies. It is in the second part that the difficulty is greater, but, in general, American society is presented there as an instance of democratic society; the seemingly most "American" chapters of this section are strongly oriented toward France, and the readers of the July Monarchy had no trouble in recognizing therein a liberal political program for the years to come.[52]

What still remains to be done is to reply to a tricky question: Is an American-style democracy possible without the economic prosperity of the Americans? The problem is particularly acute today when one asks oneself about the changes of democracy outside America. Since the studies of Seymour M. Lipset, Robert Dahl, and Bruce M. Russett,[53] it has been admitted that there is a relationship between the level of economic development and forms of political development. Without doubt, the correct functioning of democracy presupposes a minimal level of prosperity, but that is not to say that democracies are valid only in those countries considered rich according to today's norms. The examples of Athens or America as

---

[52]For more details, see Lamberti, *les deux démocracies.*

[53]Seymour M. Lipset, "Some Social Requisites of Democracy: Economic Development and Political Legitimacy," *American Political Science Review* (vol. LIII, March 1959, pp. 69-105); Robert Dahl, *Modern Political Analysis* (Englewood Cliffs, N.J.: Prentice Hall, 1963); Bruce M. Russett, *Trends in World Politics* (New York: Macmillan, 1965).

described by Tocqueville are there to remind us that the economic standard required is relatively modest and that cultural factors are every bit as important for political development as economic factors. Without professing here to reply to the preoccupying question as to the most desirable political regime for under-developed countries, it is possible to underline two important points, while remaining faithful to Tocqueville's inspiration.

Democracy in America warns us against any unidimensional conception of development: The economy may well have the role of a permissive condition, but not that of a determining cause, and political and cultural factors, laws and manners, Tocqueville would have said, count just as much as economic factors. Tocqueville has shown us that to the social democratic state there may correspond two very different political regimes, and his thought can be prolonged today by the theories on development which show that to each stage of socio-economic development, there may correspond a plurality of political forms.[54]

Democracy in America is not a mere description of the institutions and manners of the Americans. In some way or another, the work always deals with democracy outside America as well: First of all, because Tocqueville's starting point is the comparison between American democracy and the first French Republic; secondly, because the author develops a reflection on the ambivalent tendencies of democracy, well controlled in America but much less controllable in those countries submitted to democratic revolution; and, finally, because the second half of the work deals much more with democracy than with America.

If Tocqueville's masterpiece has retained a lasting attraction, it is not because it provides us with a more or less faithful portrait of the America of yesteryear, but because it offers us an ideal type of democracy which allows us, even today, to ask the question which is the most important one for us: How can we defend liberty, which is under threat?

---

[54]See, for instance, A.F.K. Organski, *The Stages of Political Development* (New York: Alfred Knopf, 1965).

2

In Search of the "New Science of Politics"

Wilhelm Hennis

In a well-known passage, Hannah Arendt defended the thesis that the occidental tradition of political thought is marked by a clearly datable beginning and an equally clear-cut termination. "Our tradition of political thought had its definite beginning in the teachings of Plato and Aristotle. I believe it came to a no less definite end in the theories of Karl Marx."[1] This may well be true. But in Alexis de Tocqueville (1805-1859), Marx's contemporary and senior by thirteen years, we see once more a thinker who has that bold thought shared by all who can properly be called "political thinkers": Everything depends upon government and upon politics—or, in other words, the most important of the sciences (*Wissenschaften*) is political science.[2]

Was Tocqueville a political scientist? It seems to me that this question, which might appear rather superficial and pedantic, opens a path not only to a more precise understanding of Tocqueville, but also to the reactivation of questions basic to the field.[3]

---

[1]Hannah Arendt, *Between Past and Future* (New York: Viking Press, 1968), p. 17.

[2]Aristotle, *Nicomachean Ethics*, 1094a (politics as the most important and leading science); Hobbes, *De Cive*, Preface ("certainly the most valuable"); Rousseau, *Confessions*, bk. 9 (everything depends upon the art of government). What Friedrich H. Tenbruck has sketched as "*Die Glaubensgeschichte der Moderne*" (*Zeitschrift für Politik*, N.F. 23 [1956], pp. 1-15) is discernible in the succession of those sciences in which recent generations have placed their hopes, from political economy to ecology.

[3]With regard to the wealth of facets in recent Tocqueville research, see Robert Nisbet, "Many Tocquevilles," *The American Scholar*, 46 (1976-77), pp. 59-75.

That Tocqueville was not a scientist (*Wissenschaftler*); that even had he wished to be one he would not have been a good one; that his intentions were totally other than those of a political scientist; and that his work belongs to the history of political rhetoric—these are judgments to which authorities on Tocqueville, thorough admirers of the great Frenchman, feel themselves compelled. However, there is a significant line from Tocqueville himself which opposes this view. In the "Introduction" to Part I of *Democracy in America,* Tocqueville writes: "A new political science is needed for a world itself quite new." (*"Il faut une science politique nouvelle à un monde tout nouveau."*)[4] This sentence, placed at a dramatic point in this highly dramatic introduction,[5] can scarcely be understood as anything but an indication of the ambition of its highly ambitious author. Should we not read Tocqueville's *Democracy in America,* and his entire corpus for that matter, as an answer to this need? This is the question I wish to answer.

To be able to do this, we must first deal with three established notions concerning Tocqueville's writings which would distort the view of his "new political science," assuming that it exists. The first is the opinion that there is no scientific intent underlying Tocqueville's work; that he is a liberal thinker of the first order, but not a scientist. To so characterize him, however, is to fail to recognize the peculiarity of his scientific purpose and to thereby misunderstand his continuing, timeless significance. The second view is closely linked to the first. He who sees in Tocqueville the liberal thinker in an age of emerging democracy and understands his book on America only as a "tract for the times," will be inclined to regard him as the great successor of Montesquieu. This picture of Tocqueville as Montesquieu's successor appears to be one of the most firmly settled views in the research on Tocqueville. In contrast, I would like to demonstrate that Montesquieu does not supply the

---

[4]Alexis de Tocqueville, *Democracy in Ameria*, ed. J.-P. Mayer, trans. George Lawrence (Garden City, N.Y.: Harper & Row, 1966), p. 12. Hereinafter cited as *Democracy.* Citations will include volume and page numbers. The citations in parenthesis refer either to J.-P. Mayer's *"édition definitive," Oeuvres Complétes* (hereinafter cited as *O.C.*), or to the Beaumont edition (hereinafter cited as B).

[5]*Democracy*, vol. I, p. 6 (*O.C.*, I, p. 5).

key to an understanding of Tocqueville, and that to view him within this tradition leads to a failure to understand his modernity. Tocqueville's actual teacher, if one is to be ascribed to him, is Rousseau. The third obstacle standing in the way of an understanding of Tocqueville is the fixation on a problem that was not even his; i.e., the tension between freedom and equality allegedly central to his work. Tocqueville's actual problem was that of freedom and solidarity, of individuality and sociality; and it is here that his significance for our own age lies. I shall attempt to establish these three theses in order then to proceed with a systematic treatment of at least the basic ideas of Tocqueville's "new political science."

I

When an undisputedly great author remarks in the introduction to his principal work that an era which is quite new demands a new political science, it ought to be obvious that this suggestion is to be taken seriously and that the work itself may be readable as a response to this challenge. But such a reading seems to be anything but obvious.[6] Is there any scientific purpose at all behind Tocqueville's work? Even James Bryce, otherwise full of admiration for Tocqueville's book, could no longer recognize its scientific character. In Bryce's words, written in 1888, fifty-three years after the appearance of the first volume of *Democracy in America:* "Let it only be remembered that, in spite of its scientific form, it is really a work of art quite as much as a work of science. . . ." And even more pointedly: "The *Democracy in America* is not so much a political study as a work of edification."[7]

George W. Pierson, again no petty critic but a man who devoted his entire life to research on Tocqueville, comes to a similar

[6]The first to follow this suggestion were Jack Lively in *The Social and Political Thought of Alexis de Tocqueville* (Oxford: Clarendon, 1962) and Jürgen Feldhoff in *Die Politik der egalitären Gesellschaft. Zur soziologischen Demokratie—Analyse bei A. de Tocqueville* (Cologne: Westdeutscher Verlag, 1968), p. 117ff.

[7]James Bryce, "The Predictions of Hamilton and Tocqueville," in *Studies in History and Jurisprudence* (Oxford: Oxford University Press, 1901), vol. I, p. 325.

conclusion.[8] Tocqueville's book on America is allegedly full of defects, and Pierson can explain the book's rank and enduring acclaim only by the personality of its author and by the fact that Tocqueville was a sociologist, one of the first in France. This is a dubious honor, as it results from identifying nothing but defects and errors in the classic.

It is to Otto Vossler that we owe the most thorough and informative attempt to prove the unscientific character of Tocqueville's work. His 1973 book on Tocqueville is again a testimonial of love and admiration for its object.[9] Yet he contends that whoever looks for a scholarly purpose and intent in Tocqueville's literary work is on the wrong track. Tocqueville is

> . . . a Frenchman writing for France, for political education and therewith a better future for his countrymen. He aims for a political effect and is not seeking pure knowledge for knowledge's sake. He is not interested in science, but in practical political utility and success.
>
> He writes neither as historian nor as sociologist, but as concerned political educator and admonisher, as passionate Frenchman—and it is as such that both he and his work are to be judged.[10]

For Vossler, the determinative bar to Tocqueville's book on America being scientific lies in a sentence in the "Author's Introduction" to the first volume: "I admit that I saw in America more than America; it was the shape of democracy itself which I sought . . . so as at least to know what we have to fear or hope therefrom."[11] This sentence purportedly shows first, that Tocqueville did not seek knowledge for the sake of knowledge; second, that he sought knowledge for its practical utility; and third, that he pursued this knowledge for the sake of a particular object:

---

[8]George Wilson Pierson, *Tocqueville and Beaumont in America* (New York: Oxford University Press, 1938).

[9]Otto Vossler, *Alexis de Tocqueville: Freiheit und Gleichheit* (Frankfurt a. M.: V. Klostermann, 1973). Hereinafter cited as Vossler, *Freiheit.*

[10]Ibid., pp. 65, 83.

[11]*Democracy*, vol. I, p. 12 (O.C., I, p. 12).

France. As far as Vossler is concerned, each of these intentions separately, not to mention cumulatively, precludes Tocqueville's work from being scientific.[12]

Now it is certainly true that Tocqueville seeks scientific knowledge for its utility as an intellectual aid to France. But must this preclude it from being scientific in character? If I understand it correctly, no one strove for knowledge for the sake of knowledge until the middle of the nineteenth century. In no field of knowledge was knowledge for its own sake the central concern, but rather, it was always a matter of the meaning of knowledge, or, in Max Weber's terminology, its *Wertbeziehung.* The meaning could be theoretical, practical, or technical. The *science politique* of Tocqueville still stands squarely in the tradition of political science as a practical-philosophical discipline.[13] As with everyone before him, the knowledge he seeks in this field is sought not for its own sake but for the sake of correct action.[14] Nor can the fact that Tocqueville pursues his study of democracy in America for the sake of France keep it from being a scientific contribution to our understanding of the era.

Gerhard Krüger[15] has described the modern concept of science as being defined by the attempt to achieve the double emancipation from natural sensuous experience and from the bonds of the practical community surrounding the researcher. In the historical-political sciences, too, there has been no shortage of attempts to supplement the obviously fallible human power of judgment with more precise, universal instruments of measurement and observation. Outside the realm of quantifiable magnitudes (with which political science is only peripherally concerned), the results to date of these efforts have been minuscule. But the modern demand upon

---

[12]Vossler never tires of testifying that Tocqueville is "no scientific mind, not a philosopher at all" (Vossler, *Freiheit,* pp. 91, 151). The demand for a new political science is thus not to be taken seriously.

[13]Regarding this tradition, see Wilhelm Hennis, *Politik und praktische Philosophie* (2d ed.; Stuttgart, 1977).

[14]Aristotle, *Nicomachean Ethics,* 1095a, pp. 5-6; 1103b, p. 27. The purpose of political knowledge is not changed in Machiavelli or Hobbes, either. They only radicalize it.

[15]Gerhard Krüger, *Grundfragen der Philosophie* (Frankfurt a. M.: V. Klostermann, 1958).

the researcher that he radically abstract himself from the "prejudices" and value standards of his political community has triumphantly prevailed. Oriented to the standard of theoretical science, "[i]t must know," in Krüger's words, "in order to know, and not for the purpose of leading a social life."[16] Such an understanding of science is entirely foreign to Tocqueville. But can this justify denying him any scientific intention whatsoever, and thereafter, in the manner of Vossler, no longer looking for such an intention in Tocqueville's works? Tocqueville wanted to become acquainted with democracy in America, to subject it to scientific examination, even if only "so as to know what we [i.e., the French of his time] have to fear or hope therefrom." Hope and fear refer to a good, to the manner in which life is conducted in community—not just any sort of life in common, but that which is possible for the French. Only when such hope and fear legitimately enter into scholarly inquiry can the normative problems of politics or, if you will, the question of the ends toward which our lives are directed, be appropriately addressed.[17] For Tocqueville this was self-evident. To take this fact as an indication of the unscientific character of his findings reveals more about our contemporary understanding of science than about Tocqueville.

The addressee of Tocqueville's book on America (his *ouvrage politico-philosophique,* as he always called it)[18] was certainly not the scientific community. It was directed toward those who were responsible for France's destiny. In Tocqueville's terminology, which is identical with that of Plato and the entire tradition, it was directed toward the "legislators," the "leaders" of France. The point of view, the scholarly perspective in Tocqueville's work, is also that of an imaginary legislator, of a statesman in search of the knowledge he needs. This has been one of the classical scholarly approaches to political science since Plato's *Laws.* In the United States, Tocqueville seeks and finds lessons "from which

---

[16]Ibid., p. 183.

[17]Hans Jonas argues for a "heuristic of fear" in *Das Prinzip Verantwortung* (Frankfurt a. M.: Insel Verlag, 1979).

[18]Cf. James T. Schleifer, *The Making of Tocqueville's "Democracy in America"* (Chapel Hill, N.C.: University of North Carolina Press, 1980), pp. 83, 165. Hereinafter cited as Schleifer, *Making.*

we"—and that means especially the legislators—"can derive benefit." To ask questions in this manner was to take a scientific perspective and was not merely an attempt at popular education, which for the modern scholar is apparently the very epitome of an unscientific design.[19]

If one seeks to salvage to some extent the scientific character of Tocqueville's work by classifying it in the pre- and early history of sociology,[20] this, too, conflicts with Tocqueville's own understanding of his work. He spoke only very condescendingly of Saint-Simon and his school and of Comte. And what, if not his self-understanding as a political scientist, could have prompted him, in his capacity as president of the *Academie des Sciences Morales et Politique,* to deliver an important lecture on "Politics as Science"—which in any case provides us with a certain insight into his systematic understanding of the required "new" science? I will deal briefly with the contents of this lecture, Tocqueville's only extended statement concerning his idea of political science.[21] Confronted with the conventional objection that the field of politics is too polymorphous, too unstable to support the foundations of a science, Tocqueville distinguishes that which belongs to the art of statesmanship from politics as a science. Politics as a science is constant; the art of governing is elastic. Politics as a science "lies grounded in the very essence of man, in his interests, his capacities and his instincts, whose direction changes with the times but whose essence is unchanging, imperishable as his species itself." This science teaches "which laws best suit the general and enduring being of man." Tocqueville continues: The "greatness" (*grandeur*) of this science prevents many intellects from noticing it. However, if one were to observe "this significant science" attentively, the various elements of which it is composed would palpably emerge, and one

---

[19]This aspect of Tocqueville's scientific perspective is penetratingly analyzed by Seymour Drescher in *Dilemmas of Democracy: Tocqueville and Modernization* (Pittsburgh: University of Pittsburgh Press, 1968), pp. 23ff. ("He was always a politician or a potential politician addressing other politicians and citizens," p. 25.)
[20]Most forcefully, Jürgen Feldhoff, *Die Politik der egalitären Gesellschaft*, p.117ff.
[21]*O.C.*, B, IX, p. 111ff. The most important passages are in the collection edited by Albert Salomon, *Alexis de Tocqueville: Autorität und Freiheit* (Zürich: Rascher, 1935), pp. 138-52. Hereinafter cited as Salomon, *Autorität.*

would arrive at a precise conception of the whole.

For such an observer, the great writers would no longer present such a mass of confusion. Some, the very great, seek

> . . . the natural laws of the societal body and the rights which the individual exercises, i.e., the laws which best suit the societal structures depending upon which characteristics they possessed from their origins and which they acquired. They seek the governmental systems appropriate according to situation, place and time. These are the great authors: Plato, Aristotle, Machiavelli, Montesquieu and Rousseau, to mention only some of the most illustrious names.

But, he asks rhetorically, why must one demonstrate the existence of political science in a country where its power has made itself manifest on every hand?

> You deny the existence and deeds of political science! Look around yourselves! . . . Who has so altered the face of the modern world that were your grandfather to return to earth, he would recognize neither the laws, the morals, the clothing nor the customs which he once knew—scarcely even the language which he once spoke? In short, who brought about the French Revolution, this most momentous event in history?

Was it the politicians of the eighteenth century, the princes, the ministers, the great feudal lords? Nothing of the kind!

> The great creators of this colossal Revolution were precisely the men of that time who had never taken part, even in the slightest degree, in the affairs of state. Everyone knows that political writers, political science, and often even the most abstract science planted in the minds of all our fathers the new seeds from which suddenly grew so many political institutions and statutes unknown to their forefathers. . . .
>
> Among all civilized peoples, political science gives birth to the general ideas, or at least lends them their form. From

> these then later arise the events in whose midst the politicians move and the laws which they think they are inventing. . . . The barbarians are the only ones in whose politics one recognizes only practice. Our Academy, gentlemen, has the task of preparing a place for this useful and fruitful science and of determining its field of activity. This is its honor, but also a danger.

It is a danger for the very reason that this science could prosper only under the condition of freedom. Tocqueville's speech is a subtle treatment of the decline of freedom under the dictatorship of Louis Napoleon.

Now if one knows only (and I am getting ahead of myself) that a fundamental axiom of Tocqueville's political science was that "everything in politics is only derivative and symptomatic, except for the ideas and feelings of the people, which embody the causes of everything else,"[22] and if one does not know that Tocqueville was equally convinced that "political societies are not the products of their laws, but are from the very beginning determined by the feelings, beliefs, ideas, and habits of the hearts and minds of their members,"[23] then one will not be able to understand why he felt compelled to ascribe such greatness to this science. But if what he says in his speech to the Academy is true (i.e., that political science "forms something like an intellectual atmosphere around every society, which the spirits of the ruled and the rulers inhale and from which they alike, often unconsciously, draw the principles of their behavior"),[24] then it is understandable why he attributes such fundamental importance to this science and why he feels himself a part of it.

Nevertheless, one might question whether it is really to the point to ask whether Tocqueville should be read as a political scientist or a sociologist. Is not what Tocqueville has to say to us the same in either case? But this is not so. To read Tocqueville as a sociologist is to pose questions or ascribe questions to him which

---

[22]Letter, Oct. 26, 1853, in Salomon, *Autorität*, p. 215 (*O.C.*, B, VII, pp. 300-01).

[23]Letter, Sept. 17, 1853, ibid., p. 214 (*O.C.*, B, VI, pp. 226-27).

[24]The address to the *Academie des Sciences Morales et Politiques*, in Salomon, *Autorität*, p. 144.

were not his. We cannot really get a reply from an author who did not regard himself as a sociologist by posing him sociological questions. On the other hand, we cannot receive or understand what he may have had to say to us if we refuse to receive it in the language which he speaks. Everyone knows that in translating a poem from one language to another, much is lost. But how much more must be lost when we are deaf to the questions expressed in the idiom of a particular science because we believe it will yield the correct and, for us, "relevant" scientific sense only when we have (to use the modern term) "reconstructed" the texts to conform to our own questions.

To understand Tocqueville as a sociologist is to fundamentally misunderstand him. For all truly political thought, the relationship between man and citizen is the central political problem, but for sociological thought it is a problem which no longer exists.[25] As successor to Machiavelli and Rousseau, Tocqueville fights once again the specifically Western struggle against the disjunction between the private and the public. He does this in the tradition, and using the categories, of classical political science. In a letter dated October 26, 1853, Tocqueville complains:

> We belong to another era. We are to a certain extent antediluvian animals which might soon be displayed in natural history museums to show how beings once looked that loved freedom, equality and honesty. All are strange tastes, which presuppose totally different organs on the part of this world's present inhabitants.[26]

It is a "totally different" manner of thinking which distinguishes the political science of Tocqueville from the incipient sociology of his time and from that of ours. Not that Tocqueville would automatically be understood if he were to be read as a political scientist, but one bars every possibility of understanding Tocqueville when one is not prepared to understand him as he himself wanted to be

---

[25]This is the basic idea of Siegfried Landshut's *Kritik der Soziologie und andere Schriften zur Politik* (Neuwied: Luchterhand, 2d ed., 1969). Hereinafter cited as Landshut, *Kritik*. See also his introduction to *Alexis de Tocqueville: Das Zeitalter der Gleichheit* (Stuttgart: A. Kröner, 1954). Hereinafter cited as Landshut, *Zeitalter*.
[26]See n. 22.

understood. Nothing in his work evidences an affinity, everything evidences a decided enmity, toward the emerging sociological thought of his time. In his entire work, Tocqueville's concern was nothing but to attempt to prevent the separation of man from citizen. He was not concerned, as was his younger contemporary, Marx, with the elimination of this polarity in a definitive solution to this problem. More realistically than Marx, Tocqueville could conceive of this problem's solution only in the shape of egalitarian democratic tyranny. To prevent this form of solution to the problem was the driving force behind his passionate intellectual effort.

Just as access to an understanding of Tocqueville's thought is obstructed when we overlook the fact that he reflected on the problem of politics in the categories of classical political science, so also do we obstruct our access to him when we, as it were, give him the wrong genealogy in the history of political thought. Tocqueville himself precipitated this fate in a peculiar way.

II

Insofar as the effectiveness and *brisance* of a political thinker is concerned, his placement in a particular family tree is not a matter of indifference. A thinker in the tradition of Plato is more "exciting" than one in the tradition of Aristotle; and the relation of Hegel to Kant and of Marx to Ricardo is the same in this regard. In an often-quoted passage from one of Tocqueville's letters composed during the time he was working on his second volume on America, he wrote: "There are three men in whose company I find myself for a while each day: Pascal, Montesquieu and Rousseau."[27] Let us leave Pascal to one side. Diez del Corral has sympathetically investigated Tocqueville's connection to him.[28] That Tocqueville stands in the intellectual tradition of Montesquieu is a commonplace since Royer-Collard's comparison of the first volume of *Democracy in America* with *The Spirit of the Laws*. Tocqueville

---

[27]Letter to Kergolay on Nov. 10, 1836 (*O.C.*, XIII, 1, p. 418). In Salomon, *Autorität*, p. 193.

[28]Luis Diez del Corral, *La mentalidad politica de Tocqueville con especial referencia a Pascal* (Madrid: Real Academia de Ciencias Morales y Politicas, 1965).

is the "faithful pupil of Montesquieu" (Raymond Aron), the Montesquieu of the nineteenth century. And Rousseau? An influence is "not identifiable" writes Otto Vossler,[29] who within the space of a few years published a large monograph on Rousseau and one on Tocqueville which especially emphasizes Tocqueville's aristocratic family tradition. The same social origins, the same concern with freedom, the same open and unbiased spirit—what could be easier than to name Montesquieu and Tocqueville in the same breath? What could be more erroneous than to place Tocqueville, the great gentleman, in a closer relationship with the petty bourgeois from Geneva, the resentful outsider, the patriarch of the Revolution, Jean-Jacques? However, I know of no "epistemological-sociological" chain of reasoning that is more decisively misleading than this one.

Certainly, it is fruitful to compare Montesquieu and Tocqueville, especially with regard to Tocqueville's theory concerning the new forms of despotic domination. Certainly, the younger man stands in a sort of succession to the man born 116 years (and what years!) before him. Nor could he have anything against our seeing in him a new Montesquieu. Indeed, he wanted to accomplish something similar to what that great man of his own social station had achieved. But under what radically changed conditions! They are worlds apart with regard to their places in fundamentally different societies, and with regard to the experiences which each sought to master intellectually. "A new political science is needed for a world itself quite new." There can be no doubt that this sentence, which is our starting point and which contains a judgment of the old political science, is essentially directed toward Montesquieu. In *Democracy in America* there is a whole series of passages which begin roughly: "I am not speaking about . . ." and continue with familiar viewpoints of Montesquieu which Tocqueville classifies as indisputable, common-sense positions not meriting further elaboration.[30] Typical of this

---

[29]Vossler, *Freiheit*, pp. 51, 204. Although Vossler emphasizes with such love of detail Tocqueville's attachment to his great-grandfather, Malesherbes, he mentions not one word concerning the close friendship between Malesherbes and Rousseau. If one accepts Vossler's thesis concerning Tocqueville, the "family man," Rousseau must have been rather close to him.

[30]Cf., for example, *Democracy*, vol. I, p. 286 (*O.C.*, I, 1, p. 326); *Democracy*, vol. II, pp. 608-09 (*O.C.*, I, 2, p. 257).

sort of tacit dismissal of Montesquieu is Tocqueville's examination of honor in the United States, a classic example of a paradigm change. Montesquieu is not mentioned at all. At the beginning of chapter 29 of *The Spirit of the Laws* is the statement: "I assert, and it appears to me, that I have written this work only for the purpose of proving this contention: The spirit of moderation must govern the legislator." Tocqueville writes in order to prove a totally different contention; namely, that equality, absent fortunate countervailing forces such as exist in America, could lead to the degradation of man. He seeks to cultivate understanding for moderation, the unavoidable mediocrity of democracy. He reconciles himself to it but is not fond of it. The weak, dull souls which it can produce trouble him, and all his maxims of statecraft aim at nothing other than the repeated creation of incentives to stronger spiritual sensitivity within the framework of unavoidable moderation. What he fears is that the citizens of democracies "may in the end become practically out of reach of those great and powerful public emotions which do indeed perturb peoples but which also make them grow and refresh them."[31] For that which is distilled from Montesquieu, he has nothing but scorn. "I have always considered what is called a mixed government to be a chimera."[32] And what, if not Montesquieu's theory of despotism, is the target of the following proud passage?

> The chief and, in a sense, the only condition necessary in order to succeed in centralizing the supreme power in a democratic society is to love equality or to make believe that you do so. Thus the art of despotism, once so complicated, has been simplified. One may almost say that it has been reduced to a single principle.[33]

According to Montesquieu, the "principle," the pernicious motive, of despotic domination is, as we know, fear (*crainte*). Tocqueville's work on democracy closes with a full "General Survey" that reads like a tortured exercise in diligence. The actual

---

[31]Ibid., vol. II, p. 619 (*O.C.*, I, 2, p. 269).
[32]Ibid., vol. I, p. 232 (*O.C.*, I, p. 262).
[33]Ibid., vol. II, p. 654 (*O.C.*, p. 309).

conclusion can be found at the end of Part IV, Chapter 7, a continuation of Part IV, Chapter 6, which bears the title, "The Sort of Despotism That Democratic Nations Have to Fear." This, the actual conclusion of the entire work and, at the same time, of his analysis of despotism, reads (and I believe that one need not have learned to stalk the semantic nightingale from Leo Strauss to catch the allusion): "Let us then look forward to the future with that salutary fear (*crainte salutaire*) which makes men keep watch and ward for freedom, and not to that flabby and idle terror (*cette sorte de terreur molle et oisive*) which makes men's hearts sink and enervates them."[34] It is surely no coincidence that in the final sentence of a work dealing with modern despotism, fear is called "salutary."

In this penultimate chapter, Tocqueville compares the dangers of aristocratic times with those of democratic times. Naturally, he knew that *The Federalist* No. 47 states: "The oracle who is always consulted and cited on this subject [of the preservation of liberty and separation of powers] is the celebrated Montesquieu." But since Madison had written these words, the world had changed completely. The endangered good remained the same: freedom and human dignity. However, the dangers lurked elsewhere. They were harder to recognize in the age of equality than in the era of personal rule. Thus Tocqueville remarked: "Other dangers and other needs [than in aristocratic times] face the men of our own day. . . . The political world changes, and we must now seek new remedies for new ills."[35]

Montesquieu had little to tell Tocqueville concerning either the identification of the new evil (the degradation of mankind in individualistic egoism and *amour propre*) or the new remedy (democratic sharing of responsibility). Rousseau, on the other hand, could tell him much. In all of Tocqueville, I find not one sentence which would contradict Rousseau's teachings when these are correctly understood. On the contrary, there are countless of his lines which strike one as pasted-in excerpts from Jean-Jacques' work, for, all differences aside, the latter's writings bear a

---

[34]Ibid., p. 676 (*O.C.*, p. 335).
[35]Ibid., p. 675 (*O.C.*, p. 334).

fundamental affinity with Tocqueville's romantic soul.

In the fragments for *The Ancien Régime,* Tocqueville portrays the change in the ideas and feelings of the French between the king's relinquishment of absolute power and the beginning of the elections for the Estates-General.

> At first one thinks only of the formation of the Estates-General. Thick tomes are hastily filled with undigested erudition. One labors to reconcile the Middle Ages to the conceptions of the present. Finally, the question of the old Estates-General disappears completely. One discards the whole mess. In the beginning, one only speaks of how the powers might be better balanced, the relationships between classes better regulated. Soon, however, one follows, pursues, then frantically chases the idea of pure democracy. At first, Montesquieu is quoted and explained; in the end one speaks solely of Rousseau. He became the only teacher of the Revolution in its heyday and will remain such. . . .[36]

Thus, I believe that the key to understanding Tocqueville—his principles and his political maxims as they relate to the new despotism—is to be found in Rousseau insofar as it can be found in any "forerunner." Montesquieu may have been Tocqueville's mentor as far as the form or the analytic ordering of subjects is concerned.[37]

---

[36]Quoted in Landshut, *Zeitalter,* p. 240.

[37]George W. Pierson in *Tocqueville and Beaumont,* p. 769, reduces the influence of Montesquieu to the stylistic similarity of the chapter headings. A rebuttal of this aside of Pierson is undertaken by Melvin Richter, "The Uses of Theory: Tocqueville's Adaptation of Montesquieu," in Melvin Richter, ed., *Essays in Theory and History* (Cambridge, Mass.: Harvard University Press, 1970), pp. 74-102. Richter sees Tocqueville as Montesquieu's successor primarily in terms of method, in an adoption of Montesquieu's analytic categories. But the differentiation of circumstances, institutions and morals is not peculiar to Montesquieu. We find it from Plato and Aristotle to Rousseau, in every political thinker who approaches the ordering of a polity from the perspective of a legislator, i.e., with an eye to purpose and formative potential. It belongs to the unquestioned tools even of Rousseau; that is, the Rousseau of the "maxims of government," which Roger D. Masters worked out in *The Political Philosophy of Rousseau* (Princeton: Princeton University Press, 2nd ed., 1976 [1968]).

Richter places Tocqueville in the context of that style of thought which J.G.A. Pocock has named "civic humanism." Machiavelli, Harrington, Montesquieu, the Scots, *The Federalist,* among many others are assembled by Pocock within a great community: "civic humanism." This connection is too tenuous to make Tocqueville the

Rousseau is Tocqueville's real teacher when it comes to substance; indeed, the substance which is at issue: human freedom.[38]

In this essay I cannot deal more closely with the fundamental agreement between Rousseau's and Tocqueville's thinking—an agreement not extending to details, of course, but one consisting in the manner in which Tocqueville sees the problem of politics, the future of man under the conditions of equality. Examples must suffice. When one stumbles across a connection between Rousseau and Tocqueville, one is almost in danger of underestimating the differences which naturally exist between them: Rousseau, still under the conditions of the *ancien régime*, intellectually anticipated the society of equals, while Tocqueville encountered such a society in full development in America, self-confident and secure in its continued existence. Indeed, the belief that a large state could not exist as a republic (much less, a democracy) was one of the firmest convictions of political theory. Tocqueville saw before his eyes in America a huge empire, organized in a republican and democratic fashion, whose existence was less endangered than any of the great European monarchies. Further, it is without exception with Rousseau's categories that he explains this astonishing state of affairs and sees and understands what is happening in America. When he writes in summary that America's federal form allows it to enjoy "the power of a great republic and the security of a small one," it matches almost word for word a sentence from Rousseau's

---

"pupil" of Montesquieu.

38The thesis that Rousseau was Tocqueville's "teacher" naturally requires that one very clear distinction be made: Tocqueville writes in totally changed circumstances. Rousseau's revolutionary principles (popular sovereignty, freedom, and equality) are now prevailing law. One must live with them and make them fruitful. Tocqueville's political world also stood open for change. It was no longer a matter of a prudential, practical-philosophical *"science du legislateur,"* but rather of actual tasks and possibilities for the legislator, at whose disposition the constitutional and administrative order by and large stood.

How little Montesquieu and how much Rousseau signified for a theoretical mind of Tocqueville's time in understanding the contemporary world, is underscored by Lorenz von Stein. Von Stein (born in 1815 and thus ten years younger than Tocqueville) wrote in his *The History of the Social Movement in France, 1789-1850* (Totowa, N.J.: Bedminster Press, 1964): "Montesquieu merely showed what the old constitution might have been, not what the new one was to be" (p. 108). Allan Bloom refers to the "intimate relation" between Tocqueville and Rousseau—a surprising discovery for him, as well. See his "The Study of Texts," in Melvin Richter, ed., *Political Theory and Political Education* (Princeton: Princeton University Press, 1980), pp. 135-37.

work on Poland.[39]

But more basically, which traditional thinker could have supplied Tocqueville with the categories he needed in order to understand the fundamental destiny of the new world, i.e., democracy? Or who could have helped him understand a country in which the will of the people expressed itself through the laws, public opinion, and the prejudices of the masses—a will limited by morals grounded in a religiosity of seemingly modest demands, but for that reason all the more powerful? Tocqueville appropriated Rousseau's concept of freedom in describing the republic as defined by the "slow and quiet action of society upon itself," distinguishing it from constitutional monarchy, in which authority "in a sense outside the body social, influences it and forces it to progress." "In the United States the motherland's presence is felt everywhere."[40] All the maxims of Rousseau's political genius had aimed at producing this result. "It is a just observation," Tocqueville quotes Hamilton, "the people commonly intend the PUBLIC GOOD. This often applies to their very errors." Who could overlook the fact that Hamilton was quoting Rousseau?[41] According to Tocqueville, the society of equals stands before the alternative of the egalitarian, free republic and egalitarian despotism. For the individual, this alternative means being a citizen or a subject—*citoyen* or bourgeois. Tocqueville sees, as Rousseau had, the moral problem in a world in which equality has ruptured the ties of dependence and belonging. In every conceivable way, egoism must be broken, diverted, circumvented, by forcing men to concern themselves with the affairs of others as well as their own. To lay upon men the bonds of brotherhood, or to tie these bonds anew, as the case may be, and to make them legitimate—this is

---

[39]*Democracy*, vol. I, p. 264 (*O.C.*, I, 1, p. 300); Rousseau, *The Government of Poland*, XI, toward the end (*O.C.*, Bibl. de la Pleide III, p. 1010), translated with an introduction and notes by Willmoore Kendall (Indianapolis: Bobbs-Merrill, 1972). To be sure, Montesquieu, too, saw the possibility of a federated republic which would benefit from the intrinsic health of (small) numbers and, at the same time, thanks to the federation, command the advantages of a great republic (*The Spirit of the Laws*, IX, 1). Regarding this question of utmost importance to Tocqueville, cf. Schleifer, *Making*, pp. 112-18.

[40]*Democracy*, vol. I, pp. 362, 53, 85 (*O.C.*, I, 1, pp. 412, 56, 95) (*"la patrie se fait sentir partout*).

[41]Ibid., p. 139 (*O.C.*, p. 156).

Rousseau's central problem, formulated in the first lines of *The Social Contract*. And Tocqueville is concerned with the same thing. Perhaps the most frequently used word in Tocqueville's work is the word "bonds" (*liens*). No more than did Rousseau does Tocqueville wish to extinguish the individuality of the person. However, for the sake of morality and the nobility of the soul, man, who is threatened by "individualism" (Tocqueville's term for what Rousseau called *amour propre*[42]) and abandoned to his egoistic weakness in the egalitarian, anomic, "unfettered" society, must be surrounded in every conceivable way with the bonds of brotherhood. Only the political order which tears the individual out from behind the walls of his ego can secure these bonds and continually tighten them.

Tocqueville is no more a liberal than is Rousseau. To the extent that they are, they are liberals of a very special kind. Neither is interested in the governmental order from the perspective of bourgeois liberalism, i.e., out of the motive of securing freedom for the individual. Certainly the individual needs freedom and guarantees of this freedom, too. But this freedom is active, oriented to the social and political order, and its services are constantly laid claim to by the social and political order—the freedom of the *citoyen,* not of the bourgeois. What must be cultivated is the spiritual disposition to freedom, the "taste for freedom," the "satisfaction of being free . . . dependent not upon man but upon God and the law." This freedom unites men; it is not the freedom of the individual who withdraws into his own private space.

Tocqueville shares with Rousseau a thoroughly pedagogical, formative view of the political problem. If Rousseau could say that Plato's *Republic* was the most magnificent book written on education, Rousseau's philosophical endeavor itself centered on nothing so much as the elevation of man to his true nature, needful to him and perhaps possible. As is well known, *The Social Contract* is presented in summary form in the *Emile,* a book which Tocqueville must have known especially well; parallels to the *Emile* are particularly evident in the second volume of

---

[42]Jean-Claude Lamberti, *La Notion d'Individualisme chez Tocqueville* (Paris: Presses universitaires de France, 1970).

Democracy in America.[43]

The moral-educational probing is tied to something else which is important to an understanding of Tocqueville in the light of Rousseau. If we distinguish in politics or pedagogy between principles and maxims, the *Emile* is almost exclusively a compendium of instructions, of maxims of the pedagogical art. Indeed, the book presents itself thus in its first sentence: "This collection of reflections and observations, without order and almost without cohesion. . . ." *The Social Contract,* on the contrary, bears the subtitle, "or Principles of Political Right" (*ou principes du droit politique*). In the first sentence of *The Social Contract* one reads: "I wish to determine whether there can be in the bourgeois order of life, any kind of principle (*règle*) for a legitimate and incontestable form of government."

Generally then, one sees in the political Rousseau only the man of the "principles"—Freedom, Equality, Popular Sovereignty—the doctrinaire of the *Contrat Social.* In Germany this is a tradition extending back to Kant. But *The Social Contract* is only a fragment of a planned larger work on "Political Institutions." That never-completed work would in any case have dealt with much more than principles. Even at the conclusion of *The Social Contract* itself, Rousseau writes, "After the true axioms of constitutional law are established and an attempt has been made to provide the state with its foundation . . ." (IV, 9). That is, there is to be a consideration of this foundation with the help of the maxims of the art of governing. Three-quarters of *The Social Contract* deals with the art of governing—not with principles as general rules, but with how to "lend drive and will" to the body politic, with what "must be done for its preservation" (II, 6), and with how one "must alter general goals according to the circumstances in establishing a good state" (II, 11). The perspective (what is fashionably termed the "theoretical interest" [*Erkenntnisinteresse*], but is more properly called the "need to know" [*Wissensbedürftigkeit*]) from which the knowledge of political science in Rousseau's sense, beyond the question of universally applicable principles, is sought, is the

43This is true above all of the third section of vol. II, which treats of the "Influence of Democracy on Mores Properly So-Called."

perspective of the legislator and, in the course of time, of the statesman. His knowledge, viewed as a whole, is empirical, substantive, and saturated with experience. Like the Greek *phronesis,* it is prudential and practical in character, able to differentiate one situation from another. Precisely in these matters, Tocqueville could have learned at least as much from Rousseau as from Montesquieu.[44]

III

Guided by Tocqueville's relationship to Rousseau, we find the path into the deeper levels of his thought. What Rousseau says of himself in anti-Cartesian fashion (namely, that he feels and senses before he thinks) is also true of Tocqueville. He considers men's feelings as more important, more fundamental to their life together, than their thinking, i.e., than their rationally considered rights and interests. "I am convinced," he writes in a previously quoted letter dated September 17, 1853, "that political societies are not the products of their laws but are, from the very beginning, determined by the feelings, beliefs, ideas, and habits of the hearts and minds of their members, and that these latter days are in turn formed through nature and through education."[45] Tocqueville's concerns do not originate in his head; the head is an organ of the worrying and hoping soul. Like Rousseau, Tocqueville is convinced that "the true greatness of man consists exclusively in the accord between the feeling for freedom and religious sentiment" and that the question at issue is "the enlivening and taming of the soul."

If that is so, Tocqueville's true problem cannot be that of freedom and equality, as one reads everywhere. Just as our epistemological-sociological prejudices cause us to see Tocqueville in the tradition of Montesquieu instead of that of Rousseau, so do we

---

[44]Here I must let these suggestions and assertions suffice and hope at a later time to be able to portray in greater depth Tocqueville's "inspiration" (the term is perhaps more fitting than any other) by Rousseau. Only a completely rigidified picture of Rousseau (e.g., that of the theoreticians of *"identitaren Demokratie")* could make the reference to their relationship appear so questionable. (Cf. the convention report by Jutta Höffken in *Politische Vierteljahrschrift,* 21 [1980], p. 410.)
[45]*O.C.,* B, VI, pp. 226-27. Salomon, *Autorität,* p. 214.

ascribe to him a problem which is, in fact, the dominant real-historical problem of the nineteenth century and still, to some extent, of our century: the power struggle of the third and fourth estates, liberal bourgeoisie and proletariat or, if you will, of freedom and equality, liberalism and democracy. Real-historically, these were the stakes in the struggle over education, the franchise, power, and taxes. From the side of the bourgeoisie, this struggle was reflected in the thought of men from John Stuart Mill to Max Weber and Carl Schmitt. But Tocqueville is no bourgeois. His situation, his philosophical instinct, and his bias toward freedom and human dignity, permit him the same distance from the real-historical conflicts of the period after the Revolution as Rousseau enjoyed in the period preceding it.[46]

Tocqueville always saw but one alternative for the future: either an unfree, egalitarian society of disconnected and weak individuals under the domination of a new despotism, or the free egalitarian society of those who remain free through close association. Each of these possibilities is defined by equality. They differ in the association, the spiritual and political league, which makes it possible for equals to preserve their strength and therewith their freedom. Democracy, the equality of conditions, furthers the danger of men succumbing to the *amour propre* of individualism. There is no road leading back to aristocracy, to a society founded upon an inequality which binds all men tightly together. Even the old, pre-democratic idea of freedom is finished. "According to the modern, the democratic, and—I dare say—the correct conception of freedom, every man has from his birth onwards an equal and perpetual right in everything which touches on himself alone," from which it follows that "the sovereign will can only proceed from the coming together of the decisions of all wills." "From this point on, obedience"—Tocqueville here means personally owed obedience—"has also lost its moral foundation; and

---

[46]Naturally, this must be taken with numerous grains of salt. Tocqueville, the active politician, had his place in the political class conflicts of his day—he always remained a "defender of property" (Andre Jardin). Michael Hereth convincingly discusses the stale thesis that Tocqueville is the classical author for the opposition of freedom and equality. *"Die Gleichheit als Gegner der Freiheit?"* in *Aus Politik und Zeitgeschichte* B 31/80 (August 2, 1980), p. 34ff.

between the manly and proud virtues of the citizen and lowly compliance of the slave there is no middle ground."[47]

Thus men's mutual detachedness, the other side of equality, threatens freedom; and Tocqueville's "new political science" sees itself faced with the specific task of "showing men what they must do to escape tyranny and degeneration once they become democratic." This, Tocqueville wrote in 1836, after the appearance of the first volume of *Democracy in America*, was the most general idea with which one could summarize the meaning of his book.[48]

IV

With that we can finally turn our attention to the task of representing, at least in outline, Tocqueville's "new political science." Tocqueville, and still more the Tocqueville literature (to which we owe so much for the understanding of the man), make this difficult. Tocqueville, like every political philosopher, wrote with a purpose: He wished to reconcile democracy and Christianity, convinced that "only freedom (I mean, moderate and regular) and religion, in a joint effort, can pull men out of the swamp into which democracy casts them as soon as one of these supports is missing."[49] He also wants to reconcile the men of his own class to democracy, and he does nothing which could detract from this purpose. Why call Rousseau the forefather of the revolution, why talk of fraternity, when this third concept of the revolutionary trinity has been so besmirched? But the linkage of freedom, equality, and fraternity concerns Rousseau, and it is fraternity, the equivalent of the friendship which supports harmony in the *polis*, that points to

---

[47]From the essay of 1836 on "*L'etat social et politique de la France avant et depuis 1789*" (in Landshut, *Kritik*, pp. 141-42). The strict rejection of all personal domination and thus of the subordination of one person to another in the new state of affairs (the core of Rousseau's concept of freedom) appears to me to be Rousseau's most important legacy. And just as with Rousseau, it is all the more crucial that those consequently abandoned to individual isolation (*Vereinzelung*) be joined together through intensive "social contracting." That is the fundamental idea, common to Rousseau and Tocqueville, of the "*science politique nouvelle*." The new science of associations is only its most important subdiscipline.

[48]Letter to Kergolay, Dec. 26, 1836 (*O.C.*, XIII, 1, p. 431). Salomon, *Autorität*, p. 193.

[49]Letter of Dec. 1, 1859 (*O.C.*, B, VII, p. 295). Salomon, *Autorität*, p. 213.

those central ideas from which something like a "system" of his "new political science" can be inferred. In sentences which, once again, sound very "Rousseauian," the elderly Tocqueville wrote to a female friend in 1856:

> You can hardly imagine, honorable lady, how painful and terrible it is for me to live in this moral isolation, to feel as if I were living outside the intellectual community of my country and time. Solitude in the desert would be no more difficult for me than this isolation in the midst of humanity. For, I will confess to you this weakness, isolation has always frightened me; and to be happy and even serene, I always had to live in a certain concord with others and to be able to count upon the understanding of my own kind—perhaps more than one can reconcile with wisdom. To me especially the line applies: "It is not good to be alone."[50]

Since Aristotle's definition of man as a being characterized by speech (i.e., characterized in a special way by sociality and requiring the political community in order to develop fully as *zoon politikon*), there have been many linkages made between anthropology and politics. They occur in the central themes of classical political philosophy, of modern rational natural law, and even in the work of Marx—at the end of these efforts and purportedly superseding them. None of them seems to me to be more valid or more modern in its "hoping hopelessness" than that of Tocqueville.

The bitterness of loneliness is a primeval human experience. Tocqueville affirms this; but he radicalizes an experience suffered so much more prevalently in modern society by making this oldest pronouncement of our Judeo-Christian conception of human history the basis of his entire political thought: It is not only oppressive and sad, it is *not good*—it weakens and destroys spiritual strength and the soul of man if he is not torn from behind the walls of his ego into constant social and brotherly responsibility. The broadest association in which this can be accomplished is the state. In

---

[50]Letter of Jan. 1, 1856, to Madame Swetchine, (*O.C.*, B, VII, p. 295). Salomon, *Autorität*, p. 224.

aristocracy, this happened "naturally" on account of the historical abundance of social *"liens."* In the society of equals it must be pursued "artificially." However, this is possible only on a basis which is in each instance historically given and therefore fortuitous and contingent. America shows how it can be done, for there the circumstances, the laws and morals, held off an even greater danger of isolation stemming from equality of conditions. It is the task of the legislator, of the "leaders of society" (from whose ideal perspective and for the sake of whose enlightenment Tocqueville's political science is pursued) to utilize all the ties in a given social fabric, to strengthen or "artificially" reestablish them in order to promote the bonds of brotherhood. Even when he insists that that which was "natural" in aristocratic society must be pursued "artificially" in the society of equals, Tocqueville is not a rational constructionist. Entirely within the footsteps of Rousseau, he seeks social ties within the given. To establish these ties and protect them from harm is the task of the "leaders of society," just as it is the task of the educator to guide the pupil in accordance with his talents and the circumstances.

If the interpretation of Tocqueville's political science takes as its starting point the statement, "It is not good to be alone," we are past the relationship of freedom and equality and are dealing with human togetherness in mutual dependency and aid. Here lies Tocqueville's central thought, in the light of which everything else, even his doctrine of the new despotism, is explicable. I will clarify this by referring to the chapters on individualism in the second volume of *Democracy in America.*

In aristocratic societies, all men are linked to their fellow citizens above, below, and inside their order of rank. In a manner of speaking, they are adjacent to one another. They are therefore almost always "closely tied to something outside themselves," and thus often ready "to forget themselves." In democratic ages, on the other hand, devotion to another human being would be rarer. "The bond of human affection stretches and loosens." Under the conditions of equality, every class comes closer to the others and mixes with them. Men become indifferent and "at the same time, alien to one another. . . . Aristocracy formed of all citizens a long chain that reached from the peasant up to the king; democracy breaks the chain and segregates each link unto itself."

> Thus, not only does democracy make men forget their ancestors, but it also clouds their view of their descendants and isolates them from their contemporaries. Each man is forever thrown back on himself alone, and there is danger that he may be shut up in the solitude of his own heart.[51]

This is despotism's golden opportunity. Fearful by nature, it perceives in men's isolation the surest guarantee of its own duration. No vice of the human heart so suits it as does egotism. "A despot will lightly forgive his subjects for not loving him, provided they do not love one another. . . . Despotism, dangerous at all times, is therefore particularly to be feared in ages of democracy."[52]

How is one to combat this? "Citizens who are bound to take part in public affairs must turn from their private interests and occasionally take a look at something other than themselves." In the common management of the community's affairs, everyone notices that "he is not as independent of his fellows as he used to suppose and that to get their help he must often offer his aid to them." One must endeavor to attract the esteem and affection of those in whose midst one must live.

> Those frigid passions that keep hearts asunder must then retreat and hide at the back of consciousness. Pride must be disguised; contempt must not be seen. Egotism is afraid of itself.[53]

In America, the perfected democracy, Tocqueville sees that it is possible—was possible there at any rate—to combat the democratic isolation which leads morally to the numbing of hearts and politically to despotism. "The Americans have used liberty to combat the individualism born of equality; and they have won." By preventing the centralization of administration, America's lawgivers gave every region "its own political life so that there should be an infinite number of occasions for the citizens to act together

---

[51]*Democracy*, vol. II, p. 478 (*O.C.*, I, 2, p. 106).
[52]Ibid., p. 481 (*O.C.*, p. 109).
[53]Ibid., pp. 481-82 (*O.C.*, pp. 110-11).

and so that every day they should feel that they depended on one another. That was wise conduct."

Squarely on the path cut by Rousseau, Tocqueville virtually gushes: The free institutions which the Americans possess and the political rights of which they make such active use

> . . . provide a thousand continual reminders to every citizen that he lives in society. At every moment they bring his mind back to this idea, that it is the duty as well as the interest of men to be useful to their fellows. Having no particular reason to hate others, since he is neither their slave nor their master, the American's heart easily inclines toward benevolence. At first it is of necessity that men attend to the public interest, afterward by choice. What had been calculation becomes instinct. By dint of working for the good of his fellow citizens, he in the end acquires a habit and taste for serving them.[54]

The great means of spreading this inclination are the "associations," the unifying alliances, sometimes for political purposes but more importantly those "which arise in bourgeois life and have no political purpose." How important such alliances are for Tocqueville is generally known. It is precisely here that he seems to be continuing Montesquieu's teaching concerning the freedom-preserving function of the *pouvoirs intermédiares.* But that is entirely incorrect; at least the context is so totally different that the reference to Montesquieu rather clouds the meaning of "associations" in Tocqueville's writings. The intermediate powers of Montesquieu have their place only in monarchy; their presence "forms the essence of the monarchical form of government" (*Spirit of the Laws,* II, 4). Mechanically, they are necessary to prevent the degeneration of monarchy into despotism. Because Tocqueville's concept of freedom is entirely different from that of Montesquieu, the task of Tocqueville's "associations" in preserving freedom, in morally establishing both community and freedom, is totally different. I cannot demonstrate here how subtly Tocqueville

---

[54]Ibid., p. 484 (*O.C.*, p. 113).

distances himself from Montesquieu on this point. Tocqueville insinuates that even in relation to aristocratic society, to which alone Montesquieu's teaching applies, Montesquieu recognized only the cruder, more mechanical aspects of the limitation of power. These are "easy to comprehend."[55] There is in Montesquieu no discussion of the "less well-known but not less powerful barriers" of inclination, morals, religion, provincial prejudice, custom, and public opinion, which had formed themselves like an "invisible ring" around the old power of the state.[56] Montesquieu, child of the Enlightenment, had underestimated religion and thus failed to recognize the actual reason for the duration of despotic regimes, whose roots lay in religious feeling and not in fear. In the same way he misperceived the power of religious and moral restraints in constitutional monarchy, where they hindered despotic degeneration. Tocqueville's teaching concerning associations is also thoroughly imbued with the observational acuity and the moral spirit of Rousseau. This, as he emphasizes, "*science nouvelle*"[57] of the art of association becomes the "fundamental science"—*science mere*—in democracy.[58] The individual would sink into impotence and debility, and culture itself would be threatened by barbarism if men did not avail themselves constantly of associations. "Feelings and ideas are renewed, the heart enlarged, and the understanding developed only by the reciprocal action of men one upon another."[59] These lines contain the true essence of Tocqueville's "political science."

---

[55]Ibid., vol. I, p. 286 (*O.C.*, I, 1, pp. 326-27).
[56]Ibid., p. 287 (*O.C.*, p. 327).
[57]Ibid., vol. II, p. 486 (*O.C.*, I, 2, p. 114). The chapter entitled "Of the Use Which the Americans Make of Associations in Civil Life," begins with a clear distancing from the "*pouvoir intermédiaries*" of the old regime: "*Je ne veux pas parler. . . .*" The designation of "*science nouvelle*" also distinguishes his teaching on "*associations secondaires*" (his consistent choice of words) from that of Montesquieu.
[58]Ibid., pp. 488, 494 (*O.C.*, pp. 117, 174). Tocqueville's belief in the power of associations must be viewed in the context of the manifold associational movements of the time (Buchez, Lacordaire, Lamennais, St. Simon, and the early socialists). Tocqueville's position within the thought of his time has, in the absence of even a minimally satisfactory biography, virtually not been researched at all. An overview is provided by Maxime Leroy, *Histoire des ideés sociales en France*, vol. II: *De Babeuf à Tocqueville* (Paris, 1962).
[59]*Democracy*, vol. II, pp. 486-87 (*O.C.*, pp. 114-15).

This being so, it is clear that the true object of political science, its systematic center, must be the factors which promote or, as the case may be, oppose "human interaction." What brings men together? What drives them apart? The modern answer, already found in the Enlightenment and in Hobbes, is clear: interest. Tocqueville, no less than Rousseau, knew that to move men one must appeal to their interests.[60] But as on the one hand the "human mind" inclines to the banal, material, and useful, so on the other hand it is "naturally drawn toward the infinite, the spiritual, and the beautiful. Physical needs hold it to the earth, but when these are relaxed, it rises of its own accord."[61]

Lasting ties can be established only on the basis of ideas, passions, and feelings, which always bind men together, even if in hatred toward one another. When "[n]o longer do ideas, but interests only" bind men together (democracy's specific danger), "it would seem that human opinions were no more than a sort of mental dust open to the wind on every side and unable to come together and take shape."[62] When, as in France before the February Revolution, "restricted goals and points of view which are taken from private life and its interests" progressively take the place of "general views, sentiments and ideas,"[63] the commonweal goes downhill, and revolution is just around the corner. What these lines from the well-known address of January 27, 1848, to the Chamber of Deputies express of contemporary political concern, also forms the deepest foundation of Tocqueville's political theory. That men must be bound together in the state by ideas and views held in common, that not interests but feelings and opinions form the social cement, that only they prevent isolation and the dissolution of the chain—this is the persistent theme of Tocqueville's truly theoretical work, the second volume of *Democracy in America*.

It is easily seen that "no society could prosper without such beliefs." Without ideas in common, there can be no common action;

---

[60]Classically stated in Jean-Jacques Rousseau, *The Government of Poland*, chap. IX, p. 79.

[61]*Democracy*, vol. II, p. 424 (*O.C.*, I, 2, p. 44).

[62]Ibid., p. 396 (*O.C.*, p. 15).

[63]Address to the Chamber of Deputies on Jan. 27, 1848; Landshut, *Kritik*, p. 254.

without common action, there are of course men, but there is no societal body.

> So for society to exist and, even more for society to prosper, it is essential that all the minds of the citizens should always be rallied and held together by some leading ideas; but that could never happen unless each of them sometimes came to draw his opinions from the same source and was ready to accept some beliefs ready made [*croyances toutes faites*].[64]

Dogmatic convictions are no less indispensable for man's "living alone than for acting in common with his fellows." It is not conscious choice which causes men to adopt most of their views without examining them for themselves—"the inflexible laws of his existence compel him to behave like that."[65] *La loi inflexible de sa condition*—one must search long and hard to find any more decisive anthropological declaration in Tocqueville.

Tocqueville's *"cogito"* is diametrically opposed to that of Descartes. One might formulate it as follows: "I am able to be a man among men because I, like all the others, accept most things unexamined." In the name of freedom and human dignity, Tocqueville rehabilitated prejudice. "[A]ny man accepting any opinion on trust from another puts his mind in bondage." Tocqueville continues, "[I]t is a salutary bondage, which allows him to make good use of freedom."[66] Men cannot survive without dogmatic beliefs. Their possession is desirable; and of all dogmatic beliefs, regarded from a purely worldly and scientific perspective, religious beliefs are "the most desirable of all."[67] There is "hardly any human action . . . which does not result from some very general conception which men have of God, of His relations with the human race, of the nature of their soul, and of their duties to their fellows." These ideas are "the common spring from which all else originates." All religions which remain within this realm and do not strive to go

---

64*Democracy*, vol. II, p. 398 (*O.C.*, I, 2, p. 16).
65Ibid. (*O.C.*, p. 17).
66Ibid., p. 399 (*O.C.*, p. 17).
67Ibid., p. 408 (*O.C.*, p. 27).

beyond it "impose a salutary control on the intellect," and though they do not save men in the next world, they "greatly contribute to their happiness and dignity in this."[68]

I shall leave to one side the many advantages which religion confers on democratic peoples in particular—the central point of comparison between America and France—and only direct attention once more to that central political idea which is almost a warranty of salvation: the combating of egotism by means of socialization. From Machiavelli, via Hobbes, to Rousseau, the relation of the Christian belief in God to patriotism is the core problem of modern political theory. All three men tried, as Rousseau said of Hobbes in *The Social Contract*, "to reunite the two heads of the eagle." This is Tocqueville's problem, as well, and with Rousseau he can say: "Everything which destroys social unity is without value. All institutions which bring man into contradiction with himself are worthless." Tocqueville expresses it in a letter as follows:

> I should like it if the priests would tell men more often that they, even as Christians, belong to one of these great human associations which God has doubtless founded in order to make visible and palpable those ties by which individuals are bound to one another. These associations are called peoples, and their territory the motherland. I wish that we might stamp it deeply on each and every soul—everyone belongs first to this collective entity and only then to himself.[69]

Here is someone who actually believes he can look over God's shoulder—to see that God "doubtless" founded the great associations in order to make visible and tangible the ties, the *liens*, by which individuals are bound together. There must be no indifference regarding the motherland; nor dare one make of this indifference a spiritless virtue, "which weakens some of our noblest instincts." "When a people's religion is destroyed, doubt invades the highest faculties of the mind and half paralyzes all the rest." Such a skeptical state "inevitably enervates the soul, and relaxing

---

[68]Ibid., pp. 408-09, (*O.C.*, I, 2, pp. 27-28).
[69]Letter dated Oct. 20, 1856 (*O.C.* [B], VI, p. 347), in Salomon, *Autorität*, p. 226.

the springs of the will, prepares a people for bondage."[70] Again and again he states that skepticism always seemed to him to be "the worst evil in the world."[71]

> What one finds most scarce today are the passions, genuine and powerful passions which hold life together and guide it. We can no longer desire, no longer love and no longer hate. Skepticism and humanitarianism completely paralyze us; make us incapable of performing either good or evil in a grand style; force us to flutter clumsily around a myriad of petty things, of which not one attracts us, powerfully repels us or forcibly arrests us.[72]

V

Tocqueville has always been regarded as a great liberal thinker whose major concern was how freedom could be preserved in equality. That he, who was, if a liberal, then "a liberal of a new sort;" would be in this manner misunderstood, was one of Tocqueville's constant worries. On March 22, 1852, he wrote:

> They are absolutely set upon making me a party man, although I am not one. They ascribe passions to me and I only have opinions; or better, I have only one passion—the love of freedom and human dignity.[73]

It is hard to see where the typical liberal aims could ever have been Tocqueville's. He had but one aim, and for its sake he sought to harness politics and the political order: "to combat the weaknesses of the human heart." The weakness of man lies in egotism; spiritual

---

[70]*Democracy*, vol. II, p. 409 (*O.C.*, I, 2, p. 28).
[71]Letter dated August 1, 1850 (*O.C.*, B, VI, p. 154) in Salomon, *Autorität*, p. 207. Certainly Tocqueville, as a modern man, must have repeatedly had to wrestle with skepticism within himself. Nevertheless, it is a fundamental misunderstanding to think that Tocqueville's way of thinking can be reduced to the formula of "skeptical liberalism" (thus, R. Leicht in Höffken, *Politische Vierteljahrschrift*, p. 408, and *Süddeutsche Zeitung*, July 26/27, 1980).
[72]Letter dated August 10, 1841 (*O.C.*, [B], VI, p. 117) in Salomon, *Autorität*, ibid., pp. 197-98.
[73]Letter dated March 22, 1837 (*O.C.*, pp. 70-71) in ibid., p. 193.

self-degradation follows upon it. The ever-present weakness of men is intensified by their isolation, the dissolution of the *liens* of the old society in the society of equals. Therefore, "the world itself quite new" demands a new political science, for not the ruler, but political rule, political life together is what must render our weakness assistance. It is precisely for this reason that political science is the most important of all the sciences.

The diagnosis of the new form of despotism has been regarded as Tocqueville's greatest achievement in the field of political science. One can only agree with this. However, his accomplishment is obscured, his institutional reflections are given undue weight, when he is viewed from the scientific perspective of our time, and it is overlooked that Tocqueville is, precisely here, a political scientist in the tradition of Plato and Rousseau—a moral historian or, if you will, an analyst of the order and disorder of the human soul in the age of democracy.

In order to make Tocqueville's concerns more understandable to the modern mind, we might do well to elucidate Tocqueville's analysis of egalitarian despotism with the help of the categories of Max Weber.

The evil with which Montesquieu was still confronted was absolute monarchy which threatened to degenerate into unrestricted personal rule, the "despotism" of Louis XIV and his successor. Tocqueville wrote within the context of an entirely different world: a democratic world, in which even Caesaristic rule, such as that of both Bonapartes, legitimized itself in a plebiscitary-democratic way. This democratic Caesarism no longer bears the character of personal rule, i.e., of personal loyalty. The chain is broken, the new master is faceless. He is not interesting, and Tocqueville had nothing to say about him. Thus Tocqueville writes that "despotism corrupts the man who submits to it much more than the man who imposes it,"[74] and, "I am much less interested in the question who my master is than in the fact of obedience."[75] If we adopt Tocqueville's analytic tools for the recognition of despotic dangers, the "strong man" is of no interest.

---

[74]*Democracy*, vol. II, p. 668 (*O.C.*, I, 2, p. 325).
[75]Ibid.

He is, as Tocqueville said of Napoleon I, a mere accident.

Tocqueville's theme is no longer personal domination, but in Max Weber's sense, rationally legitimated domination and the specific motives to submission which are necessary for it in the age of equality. In aristocratic times, the motives for submission and obedience to a certain extent follow the master; in democratic times, things are reversed. Here the motives for submission are the controlling theme; domination follows submission: *oboedientia facit imperantem.* The character of domination is not defined by the ruler, but principally, as in classical politics, by those who obey: either free men or slaves. Thus, Tocqueville's indifference regarding the character of the ruler.

Nowhere, at least not overtly (but remember that he is addressing the "leaders of society"[76]), does Tocqueville revert to what he considers an antiquated theme—the analysis of contemporary rule from a personal perspective. He seeks in vain for a word for the new sort of oppression which threatens democratic peoples, a word that would

> . . . exactly express the whole of the conception I have formed. Such old words as "despotism" and "tyranny" do not fit. The thing is new, and as I cannot find a word for it, I must try to define it.[77]

What he describes are the small souls' motives for submission in a system of domination which legitimizes itself rationally, objectively, through increasing provision of security and social welfare. He never speaks of a personal "ruler," but rather of the "sovereign," the "tutelary power" or, most often, entirely matter-of-factly, the "central power." The image of "regulated, mild and peaceful servitude" which he draws is much more easily assimilable with some of the outward forms of freedom than one might think, so that "it would not even be impossible for it to build its nest in the very shadow of popular sovereignty."

---

[76]Concerning who these might actually be, Tocqueville is as unclear as Rousseau was. Here lies the objective-sociological and theoretical dilemma of every political theory in the age of equality.

[77]*Democracy*, vol. II, p. 666 (*O.C.*, I, 2, p. 324).

> [Men] console themselves for being under schoolmasters by thinking that they have chosen them themselves. Each individual lets them put the collar on, for he sees that it is not a person, or a class of persons, but society itself which holds the end of the chain.[78]

Tocqueville could not yet form a mental picture of the extent to which men in the democratic and technical-scientific civilization of our time would become slaves to the conditions of this civilization. The pampering of *amour propre,* the encouragement of every sort of emancipation from one's duties to others, has become the guiding maxim of democratic politics in all Western nations. We have difficulties conceiving what Tocqueville could have meant by freedom. Tocqueville's freedom (here, too, in conformity with Rousseau) has nothing to do with freedom from distress, burdens, or the circumstances in which man may find himself vis-à-vis nature or his own kind. But rather, it is a matter of independence, of man's self-reliance in little things. Rousseau prepared the path for him, but Tocqueville, among the theoreticians of politics, is nevertheless the first realistic analyst of that disenchantment of the modern world resulting from rationalism, industry, improved productivity, and bureaucracy. Certainly, and he clearly says so, the concepts of despotism and tyranny do not fit. But what he describes is the illegitimacy of relations which are illegitimate and inhuman even when (and perhaps are made even more illegitimate because) they find popular approval.

Here is the key to the significance which Tocqueville attaches to morals in democracy. Political analysis must turn from the structures of rule to the structures of obedience. Thus, he says again and again that he is concerned not with the ruler, but with obedience. Nowhere—in any case not explicitly, although certainly implicitly—is Tocqueville concerned with the illumination of rule, but rather with that illumination which might awaken the souls of citizens. That is his actual theme, his only theme: How can we prevent the degradation of souls in an age of equality which has

[78]Ibid., pp. 667-68 (*O.C.*, p. 325).

been willed by destiny? For Tocqueville as for Rousseau, man in his humanity is defined by his freedom. He can choose the high road or the low road. Keeping him from choosing the more comfortable path is what determines the many institutional suggestions and considerations to be found in Tocqueville. In themselves they are unimportant and dated.[79] What is important is that man's sense for the higher things be preserved and that his sensitivity to greatness be prevented from falling asleep. Therefore he writes at the end of his major work, and I quote it again:

> Let us then look forward to the future with that salutary fear which makes men keep watch and ward for freedom, and not with that flabby, idle terror which makes men's hearts sink and enervates them.[80]

The political world changes, "and we must now seek new remedies for new ills."[81]

This challenge toward the end of *Democracy in America* is a response to the demand for a new political science in the "Author's Introduction." Tocqueville formulates the theme of this science as an appeal to the "legislator":

> It would seem that sovereigns now only seek to do great things with men. I wish that they would try a little more to make men great, that they should attach less importance to the work and more to the workman, that they should constantly remember that a nation cannot long remain great if each man is individually weak, and that no one has yet devised a form of society or a political combination which can make a people energetic when it is composed of citizens who are flabby and feeble.[82]

---

[79]Naturally, the institutions and empirical characteristics of America furnished him with the material for his principal work. And certainly the descriptions and reflections which these occasioned are fascinating and "classic." But the "*science politique nouvelle*," his basic philosophic-political concern, lies beyond these empirical characteristics.

[80]*Democracy*, vol. II, p. 676 (*O.C.*, I, 2, p. 335).

[81]Ibid., p. 675 (*O.C.*, p. 334).

[82]Ibid., p. 676 (*O.C.*, pp. 334-35).

I believe that I have found what Tocqueville was really concerned with in some lines by Erhart Kästner (the Greek Kästner). They are in the volume of his literary remains, *Der Hund in der Sonne* ("The Dog in the Sun") and helped to give it its peculiar title. I would like to quote them:

> There is a wonderful line in Seneca: "*Calamitosus animus futuri anxius*"—deeply unhappy is the soul that anxiously thinks about the future. How true. He who thinks about the future is not happy. But to think anxiously about the future is human. It is a truth of the first order and one with which we must live: Only with the look toward the uncertain, the anxious care, the prospective view, the hope at worry's threshold, the fear for the future—only then does that which distinguishes man begin. Without thought for the future is the dog in the sun. There is no doubt that the dog in the sun has received unexpected honors in modern times. He has become the great promise. The leaders of peoples have promised the tormented and untormented the dog in the sun for so long that in some countries he has become the model. Gradually it is becoming clear what lies at the bottom of it—a colossal contempt for humanity.[83]

Tocqueville was not the first who saw through the new despotism, the degradation of man by modern civilization. This title belongs to Rousseau. But the service of having first elevated this little theme of the dog in the sun, modern servitude, through comprehensive analysis, to the central theme of political science—this accomplishment is most certainly Tocqueville's.

---

[83]Erhart Kästner, *Der Hund in der Sonne* (Frankfurt a. M.: Insel Verlag, Suhrkamp-Taschenbuch, 1975), p. 5.

3

A Liberal of a New Kind

Bruce James Smith

Prodded into self-description by the criticism of an old friend, Alexis de Tocqueville called himself "a liberal of a new kind." Tocqueville's claim to novelty, privately made, is the corollary of Tocqueville's public plea for "a new science of politics . . . needed for a new world."[1]

While many have acknowledged the originality of Tocqueville's ideas, the extent of Tocqueville's claim has not been fully appreciated. Liberals have generally viewed Tocqueville as providing a new vantage point on what John Stuart Mill called "the great problem in government," that of preventing "the strongest from becoming the only power." Sympathetic critics, like Mill, saw in Tocqueville a kindred spirit who knew that the chief end of political science was to "repress the natural tendency of the instincts and the passions of the ruling body to sweep away all barriers which are capable of resisting." The dangers posed by majoritarianism were only a new variety of the perennial political problem, the same, in Mill's phrase, "now as ever." The history of Tocqueville scholarship has helped to fix Mill's somewhat diminished view of Tocqueville's claim to novelty. In particular, the restoration of

---

[1]Letter to Stoffels, July 24, 1836, in *Memoir, Letters, and Remains of Alexis de Tocqueville*, ed. Gustave de Beaumont (London: Macmillan, 1861), vol. 1, p. 402. Unless otherwise cited, all letters come from these volumes and are hereinafter cited by correspondent, date, volume, and page number; other materials in these volumes will be cited as de Beaumont, *Memoir*. Alexis de Tocqueville, *Democracy in America*, ed. Phillips Bradley, trans. Henry Reeve, rev. Francis G. Bowen (New York: Alfred J. Knopf, Vintage Books, 1945), vol. I, p. 7. Hereinafter cited as *Democracy*.

Tocqueville to his deserved prominence has been the result, in part, of his having come to be seen as the prophet of democratic authoritarianism. When viewed through this retrospective prism, Tocquevillian liberalism *is* the old liberalism confronted by new circumstances. I propose to take Tocqueville's claim to novelty more seriously than Mill.[2]

Such a view of Tocqueville's claim raises some interesting questions, I think, but questions for which the answers are difficult to make out. If the new political science is a new kind of liberalism, is the old science the old kind of liberalism? Is Tocqueville's work, then, as much a critique of the old liberalism as a warning about the illiberal inclinations of egalitarian societies? Why did Tocqueville believe a new kind of liberalism was necessary? What are its characteristics? What does it mean to be "an old lover of liberty" in democratic times? It was Tocqueville's commitment to what he called "constitutional institutions" that established his liberal credentials.[3]

I

In theory and practice, Tocqueville said that he advocated "always the same course—regulated liberty." Mill understood Toqueville almost exclusively in institutional terms. If power is to be "render[ed] . . . safe, it must be fitted with correctives and counteractives." But Tocqueville's opinion of institutions was more complex.[4]

---

[2]John Stuart Mill, *Collected Works* (Toronto: University of Toronto Press, Routledge and Kegan Paul, 1977), vol. 18, p. 200. Hereinafter cited as Mill, *Works*. In drawing out the novel characteristics of Tocqueville's liberalism and its relation to what I call "the old liberalism," I have proceeded in two ways. First, I have made special use of J. S. Mill's two reviews of Tocqueville's *Democracy*. Second, in trying to talk about a coherent perspective that might properly be described as the old liberalism, I have found the work of Lionel Trilling and Robert Denoon Cumming particularly helpful. This assumption of coherence in liberal thought must remain controversial. This much can be said: Tocqueville attempted to differentiate himself from other liberals by emphasizing the novelty of his views, while Mill spoke of "the school of Locke and Bentham."

[3]Letter to A. Stoffels, Jan. 4, 1856, vol. 1, p. 429; Letter to de Beaumont, May 1, 1852, vol. 2, p. 203; Gustave de Beaumont, *Memoir*, vol. 1, p. 49.

[4]Letter to de Beaumont, May 1, 1852, vol. 2, p. 203; Mill, *Works*, vol. 18, pp. 64, 203.

In his review of the first part of the *Democracy*, Mill understands Tocqueville's constitutionalism as primarily concerned with the "restraint" of power. There is much to support this view. Tocqueville held that "unlimited power is itself a bad and dangerous thing." His praise of Madisonian political mechanics is generous. Tocqueville's reflections on the operation of the American constitutional "machine" (the phrase is Mill's) are profound and in keeping with the liberal tradition's concern with dividing power. In Mill's view, part one of the *Democracy* is essentially a description of the American "institutions" and their "practical working." Taking Tocqueville's claim to novelty seriously does not cause us to reject Mill's account, but rather to question its sufficiency. Two considerations suggest themselves.[5]

The first concerns Tocqueville's *Madisonianism*. Madisonian liberalism erects its state on the principle: "Extend the sphere." Madison grounds his conclusions on a consideration of the dangers and shortcomings of small republics. Tocqueville, on the other hand, is brought to endorse strong national government not because of the inherent difficulties of public life on a small scale, but because "the existence of great nations is unavoidable." Tocqueville is a Madisonian, not by preference, but by "the necessity of the case." Tocqueville does not doubt that, had modern conditions not made the large state necessary, the small state would afford mankind more happiness and freedom than all the sophisticated "precautions" (again, the phrase is Mill's) of liberal constitutionalism.[6]

Tocqueville's mania for literary precision is well known, and his order of presentation in the *Democracy* is a self-conscious one. Tocqueville's treatment of American constitutionalism comes after his treatment of the township, the first "focus of action." Tocqueville begins with the township, he says, because it is the only "natural" association. While other, more complex, political institutions are the products of human reason, the township seems to come from God. The difficulty is not the existence of the township (which is "coeval with . . . man"), but its freedom, which is "an

---

[5]*Democracy*, vol. I, p. 270; Mill, *Works*, vol. 18, pp. 65, 68.

[6]Alexander Hamilton, James Madison, John Jay, *The Federalist* No. 10 (New York: E. P. Dutton & Co., 1937), p. 47; *Democracy*, vol. I, p. 168; Mill, *Works*, vol. 18, p. 57.

infrequent and fragile thing." The *unreason* of the township has two aspects. Composed of "coarser materials" than other political institutions, the township resists the plastic arts of the legislator. It is the recalcitrance of municipal matter that makes the freedom of the township so "infrequent" and "fragile." As the people become more "intelligent" (that is, the more they place confidence in human reason), the more easily "disgusted" they become with the "numerous blunders" of municipal government.[7]

The liberal state, with its confidence in rational artifice and its propensity for mechanistic institutional solutions, was particularly ill-suited by both method and temperament to preserve "the immunities" of the township. There was no small irony in this, for the liberals were lovers of liberty and had fought the good fight against absolutism in its monarchial, republican, and imperial guises. The difficulty lay in the failure of the old liberalism to appreciate the place of the township in free government, that municipal institutions are the "strength" of free nations. Municipal institutions taught citizens not only how to "use" their liberty, but also how to "enjoy" it. The old liberalism, with its Lockean emphasis on the distinction between liberty and license, understood the first problem well enough, but was quite ignorant of the second. It thus risked confusing "the external forms of independence" with "the spirit of liberty."[8]

The problem, however, went beyond the liberal's method, which confused form and substance in these matters (and thereby ignoring Tocqueville's famous warning); it extended to the liberal temperament. Even among Tocqueville's friends such as Vivien, there was a marked preference for centralization. (As members of the Drafting Committee for the Constitution after the fall of the July Monarchy, Tocqueville and Lamennais could not even get the issue of "local liberties" discussed.) Among American liberals, antagonism to municipal immunities stretches from Madison to Grant McConnell. This antipathy has solid liberal credentials and is rooted in the accurate perception that it is especially in the

---

[7]*Democracy*, vol. I, p. 62.

[8]Lionel Trilling, *The Liberal Imagination* (New York: The Viking Press, 1951), p. 126. Hereinafter cited as Trilling, *Imagination*. *Democracy*, vol. I, pp. 62-63.

township, with its "coarser materials," that the tyranny of the majority is apt to weigh most heavily. Indeed, Tocqueville's own reflections on the power of local magistrates in America confirm this. These considerations suggest the complexity of the problem of liberty under egalitarian conditions. Tocqueville's sense of this complexity informs his liberalism at every turn.[9]

While Tocqueville's constitutionalism partakes of "the conservative principle" of the division of powers, such institutional mechanics cannot be understood apart from the manners and customs of a people. Any "system of counter-balance" must find its ground "in the memories and habits of the people." It is the particular sentiments of a people that attach "the relative strength[s]" to the several "wheels" of a constitutional machine and determine their interaction one with another. In Tocqueville's view, institutions "exercise[d] only a secondary influence over the destinies of man." How, then, should we understand Tocqueville's extended treatment of American institutions?[10]

To say that institutions are of secondary importance is not to say that institutions are unimportant. Tocqueville intends his discussion of the township to provide a context for his constitutional reflections. His treatment of institutional mechanisms is to be understood in relation to other "structures" which are more "instinctive." The new liberalism teaches the necessity, but also the necessary humility, of constitution-making. Tocqueville means to combat the pretensions to which the old liberalism is subject and the illusions to which such pretensions give rise, both of which threaten liberty.[11]

Tocqueville's view of the necessity of constitutional government is most succinctly stated in the notes for the projected second volume of his history of the French Revolution.

---

[9]Alexis de Tocqueville, *Recollections*, eds. J.-P. Mayer and A. P. Kerr, trans. George Lawrence (Garden City, N.Y.: Doubleday & Co., 1970), pp. 169-70. Hereinafter cited as *Recollections*. Grant McConnell, *Private Power and American Democracy* (New York: Vintage Books, 1966). Especially *Democracy*, vol. I, chap. 4, pp. 216-19, 272-73.

[10]*Democracy*, vol. I, p. 113. Alexis de Tocqueville, *Journey to America*, ed. J.-P. Mayer, trans. George Lawrence (New Haven, Conn.: Yale University Press, 1960), p. 55. Hereinafter cited as *Journey to America*. Letter to N. W. Senior, August 25, 1847, vol. I, p. 84; *Recollections*, pp. 172-73, 176-77; Letter to Corcelle, Sept. 17, 1853, vol. 2, p. 237.

[11]Letter to Corcelle, Sept. 17, 1853, vol. 2, pp. 237-38.

> Local liberties may exist for some time without general liberties when such local liberties are traditional, habitual, customary, rooted in memories; or, on the other hand, when despotism is relatively new. But it is senseless to believe that while general liberties are suppressed such local liberties can be voluntarily created. This is the dream of some among us, *pure* dream.[12]

The lover of liberty, under modern conditions, must also be a constitutionalist. Liberal constitutionalism, however, not only risks mistaking "the outward form of independence" for the "substance" of liberty but, ignorant of its own limitations, may unwittingly contribute to the decay of the "spirit" necessary for the maintenance of a free way of life. In particular, a constitution founded on the principle of "ambition . . . counteract[ing] ambition" must finally feed the democratic taste for centralization, if only because it ignores and obscures the need for "attachment" to a set of institutions.[13]

When Tocqueville comes to discuss "causes which mitigate the tyranny of the majority in the United States," there is no mention of constitutional limitations, but rather curious praise for such things as trial by jury. The discussion of this institution complements Tocqueville's earlier and equally curious treatment of municipal government. From the vantage point of liberalism, their curiosity consists of this: Tocqueville praises these institutions not so much for their ability to restrain the power of the magistrate as for their ability to instill love of the laws and forestall the erosion of public spirit.[14]

The institutional mechanics of the old liberalism had been a response to what it saw as the physics of civil society. But Tocqueville's exploration of the relations of forms to the substance of liberty under conditions of equality and his misgivings about the

---

[12]Alexis de Tocqueville, *"The European Revolution" and Correspondence with Gobineau*, ed. and trans. John Lukacs (Westport, Conn.: Greenwood Press, 1974), p. 170. Hereinafter cited as *European Revolution*.

[13]*Democracy*, vol. I, p. 342; vol. II, p. 337; Madison, *The Federalist* No. 51, p. 264; *Recollections*, p. 168.

[14]*Democracy*, vol. I, pp. 281-97.

adequacy of institutional solutions pointed to the need for a more thorough reconsideration of the liberal categories. For "I soon perceived that the influence of [the general equality of condition] extends far beyond the political character and the laws . . . and that it has no less effect on civil society than on the government."[15]

II

From one vantage point, liberalism originated in the discovery of *society* as a self-subsisting entity independent of political arrangements. Among the important consequences of this discovery were changes in the tasks of political theory. Locke's efforts at "clearing the ground a little" extended beyond epistemology to political speculation. The appropriate tasks of political theory became the clarification of the content of society and the investigation of the proper relations between civil society and the political order which rests upon it.[16]

In its investigation into the content of civil society, liberalism showed a preference for what Lionel Trilling has called "hard reality" and a distrust of certain aspects of the inner life. In this, liberals silently followed Hobbes for whom even the inward glance was beset with the anxieties of the outside and "full of others." The images of society which the old liberalism found most compelling were of "hard bodies . . . knock[ing] against each other."[17]

But Hobbes's deduction was not only an "inference made from the passions," it was also an attempt to bring certain passions into prominence at the expense of others. The anxieties of the psychology of collision gave rise to a desire for mastery of a recalcitrant Nature, but also to a sense of certain limits to the capacity of human reason in ordering the social world. Both liberal confidence in rational calculation and its sense of the limits of reason found their origin in the effort to clarify the content of civil society. The

---

[15]Ibid., p. 3.

[16]John Locke, *Essay Concerning Human Understanding*, ed. Alexander Campbell Fraser (New York: Dover, 1959), vol. 1, p. 14.

[17]Trilling, *Imagination*, p. 215. Robert Denoon Cumming, *Human Nature and History* (Chicago: University of Chicago Press, 1969), vol. 2, pp. 93, 337. Hereinafter cited as Cumming, *Human Nature*.

efficacy of reason required a means to simplify at once mind and society and provide a theoretical bridge between them. Liberalism found this in the idea of *interest*.[18]

But while the idea of interest opened a wider field of action to reason and enhanced its capacity for control, it was not without costs to what Tocqueville called "the soul." As Trilling put it,

> [L]iberalism [has] tend[ed] to select the emotions . . . that are most susceptible of organization. . . . [In establishing] its vision of a general enlargement and freedom and rational direction of human life—it drifts toward a denial of the emotions and the imagination. And in the very interest of affirming the confidence in the power of the mind, it inclines to constrict and make mechanical its conception of the nature of the mind.[19]

Trilling generously treated this tendency to "simplify" the emotions and the imagination as a result of "the unconscious life of liberalism." Bentham, at least, knew very well the implications of the idea of interest for the sentiments.

> But by the interest [man] is at the same time diverted from any close examination into the springs by which his own conduct is determined. From such knowledge he has not, in any ordinary shape, anything to gain—he finds not in it any source of *enjoyment*. [Emphasis added.][20]

The idea of interest presupposed certain understandings about the nature of human action. If the range of human action or liberty was to be enhanced, it was necessary to divest the inner life—the life of the sentiments—of its joy. If all liberals did not share Bentham's contempt for the sentiments, most saw them as impediments to enlarging the scope of liberty. At the least, the affections were seen as too weak and uncertain to be a dependable spur to

---

[18]Thomas Hobbes, *Leviathan*, ed. Michael Oakeshott (Oxford: Basil Blackwell, 1960), p. 82.

[19]*Democracy*, vol. I, p. 35. Trilling, *Imagination*, pp. xii-xiv. See also Sheldon S. Wolin, *Politics and Visions* (Boston: Little, Brown, 1960), pp. 298-300, 341.

[20]Jeremy Bentham, *Bentham's Handbook of Political Fallacies*, ed. H. A. Larrabee (Baltimore, Md.: The Johns Hopkins Press, 1952), p. 236.

human activity. And perhaps more important, the complexity of both their origins and their objects made them less amenable to the control of a calculating reason. Indeed, the primitive origins of the affections and their frequent attachment to a narrow and parochial experience made them likely targets of the hostility of an expansive and enterprising reason.[21]

By defining human action in terms of the interests, the old liberalism thought it had solved the problem of lethargy which had brought to a tragic end the attempts of the ancient republics to expand the scope of human action. The error of the ancient republic, it was thought, lay in the confidence it placed in the political affections, which were untrustworthy, often difficult to arouse, and liable to decay. The interests, on the other hand, seemed to be grounded in man as man and drew their force from the human creature's perennial sense of deprivation.[22]

Tocqueville was well aware of these difficulties, but suspected, however, that the old liberalism, despite its heroic effort at clarification, had made a serious analytical error, an error with grave consequences for human liberty.

> Those who think that, by turning aside men's attention from important subjects, you can enable them to act more vigorously in the small field which is left to them, apply to the human mind the laws of matter. Steam-power or water-power move small wheels all the better when the large wheels are out of gear; but our minds do not obey the laws of mechanics.

This was indeed the "paradox" of liberalism. For in the very effort to make the world accessible to reason and thereby expand the scope and efficacy of human action, liberal theory tended to develop a conception of the human mind that "justif[ied] the limitation" or the narrowing of the life of the emotions, denying them, in Trilling's

---

[21]L. T. Hobhouse, *Liberalism* (London: Oxford University Press, 1974), p. 9.

[22]Consider in this regard the discussion of the weakness of "moral (and) religious motives" (*The Federalist* No. 10, p. 45) and the positive danger of "interesting too strongly the public passions" (*The Federalist* No. 49, p. 258).

phrase, "their full possibility."[23]

This paradox centered on the account which the old liberalism gave of the emotions and their relation to reason. It was especially this relation which concerned Tocqueville in his effort to clarify the content of civil society and reformulate the nature of its relationship to the political order. (We have already anticipated the difficulties here in noting Tocqueville's view of the tension between the independence of the township and the increasing intelligence of the people.[24])

The old liberalism conceived of the content of civil society as the complex interactions of interested and rational individuals. Tocqueville acknowledged the power of this account, especially in democratic societies, but signaled his departure from what Mill called "the school of Locke and Bentham" by describing civil society as a matrix of "opinions," "sentiments," and "customs." In Tocqueville's account, the interests lose their special stature as "hard reality," and are seen to enjoy a portion of their power as a consequence of certain opinions and sentiments which are characteristic of the egalitarian psyche. Their power obtains less from their more intimate connection with man as man than from the vantage point of equality.[25]

Tocqueville's view of the place of interest in democratic societies is more complex than is commonly thought. Tocqueville's reflections on the status of interest originate in his consideration of the nature of the patriotism under conditions of equality. He offers the well-known distinction between instinctive patriotism and a patriotism of rational calculation. The first is that "disinterested and undefinable feeling which connects the affections of man with his birthplace." This variety of patriotic attachment "does not reason, but acts from the impulse of faith and sentiment." The second "species of attachment," thinks Tocqueville, "is perhaps less generous and less ardent, but . . . more fruitful and . . . lasting." Patriotism of rational calculation "grows by the exercise of civil

---

[23]Letter to the Comtesse de Circourt, Nov. 26, 1856, vol. 2, p. 248; Trilling, *Imagination*, pp. xii-xiii.

[24]*Democracy*, vol. I, p. 63.

[25]Cumming, *Human Nature*, vol. 2, p. 141.

rights and . . . is confounded with the personal interests of the citizen."

> A man comprehends the influence which the well-being of his country has upon his own; he is aware that the laws permit him to contribute to that prosperity, and he labors to promote it, first because it benefits him, and secondly because it is in part his own work.[26]

What is the relation of these two varieties of political attachment and their implications for democratic society? Here, Tocqueville appears to suggest that this relation is historical. Instinctive patriotism was appropriate for the youth of the race, but modernity has destroyed its power and only a patriotism of rational calculation is now accessible to us. Tocqueville would seem to agree with Mill that the older form of patriotism was "childlike," or with Hobhouse that the ties of kinship and neighborhood are effective only within narrow limits, and are therefore inappropriate for the new emerging democracies.[27]

In the American notebooks, however, Tocqueville reveals his doubts about the liberal project. "But to what extent can the two principles of individual well-being and the general good in fact be merged? How far can a conscience, which one might say was based on reflection and calculation, master those political passions which are not yet born, but which certainly will be born?" While self-interest is forever hovering before the eyes of democratic man, Tocqueville feared that interest alone would suffice neither as a basis for political vitality nor as a bond of political allegiance under egalitarian conditions. And while Tocqueville insisted upon the importance of the covenant of "reciprocal aid" in democracies, he also knew that France's political difficulties were, in part, the result of the disappearance of common sentiments and opinions and the effort of the middle class to found politics solely upon interest. The principle of interest, as a basis for political liberty, is subject to two difficulties. The doctrine of self-interest tends to confine the

---

[26]*Democracy*, vol. I, pp. 250-51.

[27]Ibid., p. 252; see also pp. 254-55; Mill, *Works*, vol. 18, p. 86; Hobhouse, *Liberalism*, p. 9.

application of human reason to a narrow field of human endeavor, truncating the development of political prudence and discouraging political activity. Moreover, political allegiance founded upon interest unaided is jeopardized by the mutability and inconstancy of interest. If political liberty was to survive under modern conditions, it would have to be more than an "interest," it would have to be a "cause."[28]

It was in the structure of civil society that Tocqueville looked for remedies to these difficulties. The preference of "the school of Locke and Bentham" for the hardness of man's relation with an external (and recalcitrant) reality had led the old liberalism to define the content of civil society primarily in terms of an alliance between the interests and a calculating reason. Early on, Tocqueville rejected the old liberalism's methodological vantage point.

> My head is cool, and my reason may even be called calculating; yet I am possessed by violent passions, which carry me away without persuading me, and conquer my will, though my judgment remains unconvinced.

Such reflections not only pointed up the limitations of the old liberalism's method, but suggested means through which the weaknesses of reason and the interests might be remedied. In its anxiety and its pride, the old liberalism had construed too narrowly the content of civil society. "But men," Tocqueville knew, "have sentiments and principles as well as material interests."[29]

This insight had great importance for Tocqueville's view of civil society and raises certain questions about the character of patriotism and the relation of "instinct" and "reason." First, even in his advocacy of a rational, calculating patriotism, Tocqueville's mood is one of "regret" over the weakening of public instincts and contrasts with the unmistakable pleasure Mill finds in "mankind hav[ing] outgrown the childlike, unreflecting, and almost instinctive love of country which distinguishes a rude age." More importantly, Tocqueville's further reflections go far toward

---

[28] *Journey to America*, p. 211; *Democracy*, vol. I, p. 408; vol. II, pp. 7, 149; Letter to Freslon, March 16, 1858, vol. 2, p. 429.

[29] Letter to Stoffels, Oct. 18, 1831, vol. 1, p. 393; *Democracy*, vol. I, p. 175.

rehabilitating the political instincts. Tocqueville never doubted "the superiority of a power that rests on the instinct of human patriotism, so natural to the human heart." Tocqueville's reformulation of the content of civil society begins with this question: What is the status of "a loving heart" in democratic societies?[30]

The practice of the Americans, who "talk much" of their attachment to country, is suggestive.

> The Americans . . . are fond of explaining almost all the actions of their lives by the principle of self-interest rightly understood. . . . In this respect I think they frequently fail to do themselves justice; for in the United States as well as elsewhere people are sometimes seen to give way to those disinterested and spontaneous impulses that are natural to men; but the Americans seldom admit that they yield to emotions of this kind; they are more anxious to do honor to their philosophy than to themselves.

The Americans, apparently, *say* one thing and *feel* another. Tocqueville cautions, however, against attaching too much importance to their "language."[31]

These self-interested explanations extend to liberty itself. While public liberty is, "so to speak, the only pleasure an American knows," the calculating reason of the democrat defends his liberty, for the most part, in instrumental terms only. The difficulty is more serious than it first appears. Curiously, the sentiments and joys upon which a free way of life rests, tend to lose their persuasive power under egalitarian conditions. This does not mean that democratic men do not love liberty, but it does mean that the affection for liberty is more difficult to preserve or pass on. It is in this context that the doctrine of self-interest rightly understood takes on significance. On the one hand, "by its admirable conformity to human weaknesses it easily obtains great dominion" over democratic men. On the other hand, "it gradually draws them [to

---

[30]Mill, *Works*, vol. 18, pp. 86-87; *Democracy*, vol. I, p. 175. See also Letter to Stoffels, April 22, 1832 (vol. 1, p. 34) where Tocqueville insists that "a loving heart" is the only foundation in this world; and Letter to Corcelle, July 6, 1836 (vol. 1, p. 25) where Tocqueville argues for the greater reliability of "instinct" over "reason."

[31]*Democracy*, vol. I, p. 408; vol. II, p. 130.

virtue] . . . by their habits," that is, by the public sentiments it silently cultivates. In other words, it is precisely because the principle of self-interest is subject to "crude" formulations that cause men to "neglect" their liberty, that self-interest must be "rightly understood."[32]

In one sense, to the extent that the old liberalism attempted to give a descriptive account of civil society, it sometimes paid more attention to what democratic men *said* than to what they *felt*; but in another sense, to the extent that liberalism emphasized the status of the interests and the life of rational calculation, it tended to further denigrate the "pleasure" of liberty. Tocqueville's reformulation of the content of civil society aimed, above all, at the restoration of the sentiments to their proper place in an account of human liberty.

We have already called attention to the old liberalism's preference for the simplicity and the primordial status of the interests. To the extent that liberalism accorded the sentiments a place in "hard reality," it followed Hobbes in attempting to break down sentiment into its component parts, which turned out to be a species of interest mediated (or distorted) by habituation and embedded in custom. The accretions of time, which gave the affections their distinctive hue, were, however, but a kind of coloring (in Hume's phrase, a sort of "gilding and staining"), lacking the substantiality of those interests which were their origin. As mediated interests, the sentiments were a kind of confusion, and the old liberalism took a certain pleasure in unmasking them. In short, the liberal account of the sentiments was part of the larger liberal project of demystifying the natural world.[33]

Tocqueville acknowledged the truth of this argument, that the affection of the aristocrat for his family or the democrat's exultant patriotism were forms of "self-love" or self-interest. But the liberal taste for anatomizing the sentiments obscured important political truths. The sentiments were more than simple accretions. They too could claim a primordial status, bound up, as they were, with the "first images which the external world casts upon the

---

[32]Ibid., vol. I, p. 260; vol. II, pp. 131, 149.
[33]Cumming, *Human Nature*, vol. 2, pp. 208-32.

dark mirror of the mind." These images are presented by the matrix of human relations within which a new *self* finds itself and are "the primal cause" of "the prejudices, habits, and passions which will rule his life." The nature and implications of "self-love" are more complex than the old liberalism imagined, and this is reflected in the complexity of human relations that characterize civil society.[34]

Civil society no longer appears as the collective result of the interactions of interested individuals, each armed with a calculating reason, but rather as a tableau of passions, sentiments, and opinions mediated by human reason through time. Taken together, such a tableau is properly described as the spirit of a people or national physiognomy, but Tocqueville takes this idea further than predecessors such as Montesquieu or Burke. Certain amalgams of passions, sentiment, and opinion are "tenacious" and inflexible, others are more "elastic." Still others, "like the flow of the Rhone," disappear only to reappear again later.[35]

The new science must give an account of the relations among these complex and diverse elements. The new liberalism is especially concerned with *les moeurs*, a term through which Tocqueville hopes to capture the richness of the relations of civil society.

> I apply it not only to manners properly speaking, what one could call habitual feelings, but also the different notions which men hold, to the various opinions current among them, and to the totality of ideas which make up their habits of thought. . . . [And] the more I study the cause of the movements of human affairs, whether in practice or from books, the more I remain convinced that all events are consequences except the notions and sentiments dominant in a people: these are the real causes of all the rest.

The complexity of human affairs derives from the discontinuities between the interests, the opinions, and the affections. And

---

[34]*Democracy*, vol. I, pp. 27-28, 52, 98. See also "Tour in Sicily" in de Beaumont, *Memoir*, vol. 1, pp. 120-21.

[35]Letter to Beaumont, Nov. 3, 1853, vol. 2, p. 245. J.-P. Mayer, *Alexis de Tocqueville: A Biographical Study* (Gloucester, Mass.: Peter Smith, 1966), p. 89; *European Revolution*, p. 152.

Tocqueville knew that the "cause" of liberty would depend upon how well democratic statesmen understood these dynamics.[36]

III

For Tocqueville no less than for "the school of Locke," the problem of human liberty was to be understood against the fabric of civil society. But with Tocqueville's reformulation of the content of civil society, the problem of human liberty had changed its form. Hobhouse said of liberalism that its first aspect was negative. Historically, as well as methodologically, the liberal critique aimed at removing obstacles, "a clearance of obstructions." As a political principle, this involved "an opening of channels for the flow of free spontaneous vital activity." While different circumstances have often put widely varying interpretations on what obstructions ought legitimately to be cleared, liberalism has not altered its view of the nature of human action so well synopsized by Hobhouse.[37]

This rather happy view of human activity was grounded on the status the old liberalism accorded to the interests. While government was necessary, Locke argued, to protect and advance "civil interests," in protecting these, a liberal politics left human beings free to "acquire what they farther want." Liberals may disagree over what exactly it is that human beings "farther want." Indeed, such disagreement is probably an essential ingredient of liberalism. But liberals have always shown great confidence in human beings "farther want[ing]." All human activity took its character and drew its strength from the ubiquity of the interests.[38]

Among those interests, liberty itself occupied a prominent place. For this reason, the cause of human liberty could be conceived as a ground-clearing operation. True, Lockean man's readiness to delegate authority and his calculating patience in the face of lesser or occasional tyrannies perhaps should have given the old liberalism

---

[36]Letter to Bonchitte, Sept. 23, 1853, quoted in Jack Lively, *The Social and Political Thought of Alexis de Tocqueville* (Oxford: Clarendon Press, 1962), p. 53.
[37]Hobhouse, *Liberalism*, pp. 14, 28.
[38]Wolin, *Politics and Vision*, p. 302.

pause. But in the struggle to remove obstacles to the development of human freedom, such concerns were historically peripheral.

Tocqueville's view of human liberty is less complacent. We have already glimpsed one aspect of this. While it is always in men's interest to remain free, the pursuit of interest often obscures the true value of human liberty, giving it the appearance of an instrumentality. Tocqueville's attention is, rather, focused on the *love* of liberty. He speaks of liberty most often in the language of affection—as a "taste." It is liberty's "intrinsic glamour"—the "noble pleasures" of speaking, acting, and breathing freely—that interests him. In such discussions, Tocqueville slips into almost mystical prose, confessing that the love of freedom is a "lofty aspiration that defies analysis" (and adding ominously that "the man who asks of freedom anything other than itself is born to be a slave").[39]

The theorist puzzles over this problem.

> I have often asked myself what was the source of that passion for political liberty which has inspired the greatest deeds of which mankind can boast. In what feelings does it take root? From where does it derive nourishment?

But despite the opacity of the most "exalted" of pleasures, Tocqueville does not leave us without at least provisional or partial answers to what must be considered the central questions of "the new science."[40]

The love of liberty is, to some extent, "instinctive" and "unconscious," but a free people must turn these "natural instincts" into "intelligent, deliberate, and lasting tastes." Such independence of "spirit" partakes of a certain "firmness," of "caprice," even of "irritability," but also of "generosity" and "self-devotion." Tocqueville places particular emphasis on this last quality. "All free nations are serious because their minds are habitually absorbed by

---

[39]*European Revolution*, p. 167. Alexis de Tocqueville, *The Old Regime and the French Revolution*, trans. Stuart Gilbert (Garden City, N.Y.: Doubleday, Anchor Books, 1955), pp. 168-69. Hereinafter cited as *Old Regime*.

[40]Edward T. Gargan, *De Tocqueville* (N.p.: Hillary House, 1965), p. 77; *Democracy*, vol. II, p. 101.

the contemplation of some dangerous or difficult purpose."[41]

Perhaps the first thing to note about Tocqueville's descriptions is that the "taste" for liberty seems to have its foundation in a certain kind of *character.* And while the last citation emphasizes an almost democratic purposiveness, there is also something in Tocqueville's account that is reminiscent of more aristocratic notions—liberty understood as immobile resistance, the tenacity and endurance of those possessed of greatness of spirit. Thus, while the love of liberty "has created the most energetic nations," the *notion* of liberty derives from a fixed and lofty self-possession.[42]

Tocqueville's fullest treatment of liberty is contained in his praise of those notorious illiberals who founded Massachusetts Bay. Nothing, thought Tocqueville, was "more curious" nor "more instructive" than those Puritan legislators who "constantly invaded the domain of conscience." Tocqueville is taken by the remarkable union of austerity and freedom that he finds in the Puritan polity. He quotes Winthrop: "Liberty is maintained and exercised in a way of subjection to authority."[43]

It was his fundamental agreement with Winthrop that underlies Tocqueville's "dream" of uniting the party of liberty and the party of religion, and his insistence that liberty and religion are so "bound up together" that each is weakened when separated from the other. "These two tendencies, apparently so discrepant, are far from conflicting; they advance together and support each other."[44]

> I believe that, as a general principle, political freedom rather increases than diminishes religious feeling. There is a greater family likeness than is supposed between the two passions. Both have in view universal and, on the whole, immaterial blessings; both aim at a certain ideal perfection of the human race, the contemplation of which lifts the

---

[41]*European Revolution*, p. 167; *Democracy*, vol. I, pp. 356-60; vol. II, pp. 173, 233, 285; "France Before the Revolution," in de Beaumont, *Memoir*, vol. 1, pp. 254-58.

[42]"France Before the Revolution," de Beaumont, *Memoir*, p. 256.

[43]*Democracy*, vol. I, pp. 38-41, 44-45.

[44]Letter to Corcelle, Nov. 15, 1843, vol. 2, p. 71; Letter to Stoffels, July 24, 1836, quoted in Mayer, *Alexis de Tocqueville*, p. 16; *Democracy*, vol. I, p. 46.

mind above the consideration of petty personal interests.[45]

The "family likeness" between "religious feeling" and political liberty has to do with the compatibility and interconnectedness of their *aims*. The love of liberty and the yearning after heaven are both, one might say, among the higher *tastes* of the soul. These tastes "support" one another. Each is likely to be weaker or to lose its way in the absence of the other. Conjoined, however, they bring forth "heroic passions" and "glorious deeds."[46]

We are now better able to describe the taste for liberty. While liberty is established "in the midst of storms" and "perfected by civil discord," it takes its bearings and acquires its seriousness from some authoritative ground which has "invaded" the "conscience" or the "soul" and established itself there. Like Winthrop's speech to the General Court, the conscience is the meeting ground of authority, sentiment, and reason. The conscience recollects, recovers, and persuades. It identifies objects of affection and reverence and *explains* their worthiness. It is from this Archimedean point in the character of individuals and peoples that the taste for liberty emanates. This taste "lifts the mind above the consideration of petty personal interests" to "the contemplation of . . . dangerous and difficult purpose[s]." While political liberty makes its appearance in the guise of agitation, disputation, and uncertainty, its stormy and discordant qualities are in the service of and strengthen "a voluntary obedience" to some fixed, enduring, and exalted purpose.[47]

The special difficulty and task of liberalism is at once the preservation of a free people's exalted purposefulness while creating and maintaining the "apparently so discrepant" forms of genuine political agitation and disputation which "habitually absorb" them in actions "dangerous and difficult." As I have tried to suggest, the failure of the old liberalism in this regard was at base doctrinal. In conceiving of both mind and society in terms of interest

---

[45]Letter to Kergorlay, Oct. 19, 1843, vol. 1, p. 360.

[46]Letter to Corcelle, Oct. 23, 1854, vol. 2, p. 284.

[47]*Democracy*, vol. I, pp. 44-45, 256. For an account of the relation of the soul and political liberty, consider Tocqueville's discussion of the significance of Plymouth Rock (p. 35).

and describing human action as "farther wanting," liberalism obscured the affective roots of the taste for liberty, and thereby risked mistaking the "form" for the "spirit" of liberty.

Under conditions of equality, the gravity of the liberal confusion over the origins of the love of liberty increases. Again, the difference between the old and the new liberalism is underlined by reference to Mill's commentary on the *Democracy*. It is significant that while he shares Tocqueville's concern with the immense power of the majority in democracies, Mill continues to discuss strength and weakness in the language of physics, as an external relation of the "individual" and the "mass." In democracies, Tocqueville argues that the relations between the "stronger" and the "weaker" must be understood in conjunction with the profound psychological changes wrought by the doctrine of equality. (This Mill explicitly rejects.) For Tocqueville, the power of the new sovereign went well beyond the problem of "the insecurity of right under the popular form of government," or even the moral force of majority opinion. The issue confronting liberalism was nothing less than the degradation of the human soul.[48]

The new liberalism took the "primary fact" of equality as its starting point. To fully appreciate the extent of Tocqueville's departure from the old liberalism, it is necessary to return to a portion of our earlier argument. Liberalism's predilection for the outer life and its account of human liberty in terms of external relations was accompanied by a certain complacency regarding the springs of human action. The old liberalism drew its confidence from the integrity of the self. The centrality of the interests in the liberal self was only the most prominent feature of a more general conception of the human mind as formed independent of others. Each self, thought Adam Smith, "has a principle of motion of its own." But the spiritual dynamics of equality that Tocqueville traced called into question the conclusions of the liberal theory of action and the integrity of the liberal self. The most important of these dynamics is the tendency of equality to undermine those opinions and dry up those sentiments from which the taste for

---

[48]Mill, *Works*, vol. 18, pp. 194-96; *Democracy*, vol. I, pp. 8, 280.

liberty derives its "nourishment." The error of the old liberalism was in considering the *independence* of human beings in a condition of equality apart from their *weakness*.[49]

Tocquevillian epistemology and psychology emphasize the dualism of the egalitarian psyche, that the democratic mind is subject to "very contrary propensities." On the one hand, the intellectual pretensions of equality cause individuals to fix "the standard of their judgment in themselves alone." Put somewhat differently, democracy tends to equalize the weights of the differing opinions of human beings. Finding his own opinion no less weighty than those of his fellows, the democrat is disposed "not to trust any man" and to place little stock in traditional authority or received opinions. Locke's account of human judging in nature—that it takes place in solitude—becomes for Tocqueville a description of the psychology of democratic judgment. "Everyone shuts himself up tightly within himself and insists upon judging the world from there." As each is interested, so each can (and should) judge. But independence, Tocqueville insists, is only one side of the egalitarian psyche. "In the principle of equality I very clearly discern two tendencies; one leading the mind of every man to untried thoughts, the other prohibiting him from thinking at all."[50]

Paradoxically, in assuring the *independence* of his judgment, equality denies to the democrat the *power* to judge.

> At periods of equality men have no faith in one another, by reason of their common resemblance; but this very resemblance gives them almost unbounded confidence in the judgment of the public; for it would seem probable that, as they are all endowed with equal means of judging, the greater truth should go with the greater number.

Behind the self-confidence of the democrat lurks self-doubt; behind the pride of independent judgment, the weakness of a solitary man. When the "private judgment" of the democrat is extended to questions of "God and human nature," that is, to those questions which concern the authoritative aims of religion and the political order,

---

[49]*Democracy*, vol. I, p. 3; vol. II, p. 311; Wolin, *Politics and Vision*, p. 292.
[50]*Democracy*, vol. II, pp. 4, 12, 311.

> . . . every man accustoms himself to having only confused and changing notions on the subjects most interesting to his fellow creatures and himself. His opinions are ill-defended and easily abandoned; and in despair of ever solving by himself the hard problems respecting the destiny of man, he ignobly submits to think no more about them.[51]

Without "a salutary restraint on the intellect," without the enduring and exalted objects of self-devotion that depend upon "a principle of authority" for their maintenance, the taste for political liberty atrophies.

> Such a condition cannot but enervate the soul, relax the springs of the will, and prepare a people for servitude. Not only does it happen in such a case that they allow their freedom to be taken from them; they frequently surrender it themselves. When there is no longer any principle of authority in religion any more than in politics, men are speedily frightened at the aspect of this unbounded independence. The constant agitation of all surrounding things alarms and exhausts them. As everything is at sea in the sphere of the mind, they determine at least that the mechanism of society shall be firm and fixed; and as they cannot resume their ancient belief, they assume a master.[52]

As with the "opinions," so with the "feelings"—equality tends "to isolate [men] from one another" and "to concentrate every man's attention upon himself." More exactly, egalitarian opinions have the effect of circumscribing the heart and narrowing the range of human attachment, disposing "each member of the community to sever himself from the mass of his fellows." This "mature and calm feeling" Tocqueville calls *individualism*. The isolation of the affections to which equality tends is both spatial and temporal. Ironically, Tocqueville finds the causes of such isolation to be two related phenomena generally praised by liberals (even perhaps the very aims of liberal social policy); namely, social mobility and the

---

[51] Ibid., pp. 11, 22-23.
[52] Ibid., pp. 22-23.

expansion of the middle class. As the uncertainty and inconstancy of social condition in democracies effaces "the trace of generations," the illusions of those of modest means give them "the habit of always considering themselves as standing alone."[53]

Both the intellectual and emotional lives of the middle class are characterized by a certain independence. Such independence has been an opinion and a feeling, but it has been more; it has been a badge of courage and a battle cry. Tocqueville's critique of liberalism is, in part, a political sociology that focuses on the character and propensities of this class. I have drawn a stark Tocquevillian portrait of the tendencies of the mind and heart in democratic times. These tendencies predominate especially among the middle class.

In order to give a more full account of this class, it is first necessary to add another aspect to this portrait—the love of physical well-being. This third component derives, to some extent, from the spiritual isolation just discussed, insofar as the taste for physical gratification flourishes where the affections have narrowed and the doctrine of interest has slighted the inner life of the emotions. This taste, Tocqueville tells us, is the "most natural" to men of "scanty fortune" (that is, those "neither rich nor powerful enough to exercise any great influence over their fellows," but who have "sufficient . . . fortune to satisfy their own wants"). In Tocqueville's description of the middle class, one can discern the outline of Lockean man.[54]

Liberals have always seen a close connection between private and public prosperity. True, Locke suspected that liberal man, careful of his properties, might be inclined to delegate his public responsibilities, but Locke also thought the interests, armed with reason, were far-seeing enough to save themselves. Although Tocqueville agreed that commerce and political liberty were, in some respects, natural allies, the politics of the French middle class convinced him that the "commercial spirit" might also stifle "public spirit." While the love of physical well-being is a "tenacious" taste, it is also a "gentle" one "that easily comes to terms with any type of government that allows it to find

---

[53]Ibid., pp. 23, 104-06.
[54]Ibid., pp. 105, 137.

satisfaction." The old liberalism had noted with pleasure the political patience of the commercial classes, seeing in their distaste for "extreme measures" a guarantee against the excesses of public life that had contributed to the decay of the ancient republics. But as Tocqueville knew, the same inclinations which preserved the middle classes from revolution jeopardized public life itself. If commerce sometimes gave rise to notions that "prepare men for freedom," the taste for physical well-being was also "exclusive" and tended to crowd out other tastes, including even the taste for liberty. Indeed, there is something quite immoderate about the moderation of the middle classes.[55]

The political difficulties posed by the tastes of the middle class went beyond their gentleness and patience. The middle classes were especially subject to certain illusions. Locke had known that the pursuit of physical well-being skewed human reason, but as Tocqueville saw it, this distortion of the rational capacity was much more extensive than "the school of Locke" had imagined. These illusions are especially costly to the preservation of political life. At the least, such men "think they have no time" for the "useless engagements" and "idle amusements" of public life. More ominously, "men who are possessed by the passion for physical gratification generally find out that the turmoil of freedom disturbs their welfare before they discover how freedom serves to promote it." Too careful of their "small fortunes," they mistake the tumultuousness and "civil discord" that attend political liberty for "anarchy," and they are "always ready to fling away their freedom at the first disturbance." Tocqueville's political sociology is a profound critique of the middling condition.[56]

I began this discussion with the suggestion that, while the old liberalism knew that liberty depended upon a certain relation between the strong and the weak, it was dangerously mistaken about the nature of strength and weakness under conditions of equality. In this regard, Tocqueville's relation to the old liberalism is dia-

---

[55]Ibid., pp. 149, 268; Letter to Buller, June 21, 1846, vol. 2, p. 76; *Recollections*, p. 78. By way of contrast, see Mill's praise of the commercial spirit (Mill, *Works*, vol. 18, p. 197).

[56]*Democracy*, vol. II, pp. 149-50.

lectical. The old liberalism had constructed a foundation for liberty and human action out of three related components: the independent judgment of the solitary man, liberation from the constraints of tradition and the sentiments, and a conception of human activity grounded in the rational calculation of self-interest. Tocqueville systematically confronted this liberal infrastructure, showing not only the inadequacy of the liberal account, but also its perils. The opinions and feelings of liberal man, far from assuring his liberty, threatened to take it from him. Curiously, while liberalism had come into the world as criticism, it had been reduced unwittingly to description and nurtured the worst tendencies of equality.

Uncertain as to other more exalted purposes, the democrat comes to believe that the interests are over-mighty and ubiquitous, and must always be, therefore, first consulted. As with the Americans, this opinion soon enjoys the authority of the majority. Such democratic opinions are complemented by democratic tastes, the "most natural" of which is the love of physical well-being. Bentham had been right. The interests "diverted" men from "any close examination" of "the springs" of their own conduct by depriving "such knowledge" of action of that pleasure which properly belongs to it. Thus the independence so cherished by the old liberalism not only narrowed the objects of human action and the range of human attachments, it threatened to dry up the very springs of human passion.

Tocqueville's new science is just such a "close examination" of the springs of human action made in an effort to recover certain joys. In discussing the passions, Tocqueville distinguishes two general types: "petty desires" and "great irregularities of passion." These two kinds of passion differ not only as to their objects, but also as to what might be called the quality of their pleasures. The "petty desires" aim at "small objects," the purpose of which is the making of life "more comfortable and convenient." The aims of the "great" and "irregular" passions are grander: "to build enormous places, to conquer or to mimic nature, to ransack the world." And while the satisfaction of the petty desires brings "small enjoyments," the great and irregular passions bestow "exalted pleasures" even in the pursuit of their objects. The lesser desires cry out for "daily and casual" satisfactions; the greater passions can be satisfied only "from time to time." They are "long desires" which elevate perseverance and endurance into virtues. The old liberals had discovered the tenacity and dependability of the interests, but overlooked the peculiar "restlessness" of interested motion. While men "bent upon" physical well-being "desire eagerly," their frame of mind is "at once ardent and relaxed . . . [and] death is often less dreaded by them than perseverance in continuous efforts to one end."[57]

While the passions may derive from a common source (Tocqueville hints at this, calling the primordial passion "self-love"), this self-love is sometimes mediated and enlarged, particularly by the claims of religion and the political order, and it is this transformation that accounts for the substantial differences between the greater and lesser passions. In any case, the taste for liberty, it would seem, is intimately connected with these higher passions. For the old liberals, the capacity for action came "from the womb." For Tocqueville, human activity was more problematic. The relations of the greater and lesser passions are more ambivalent than their common origin might suggest. In particular, "ardor . . . in small matters" dissipates "zeal for momentous undertakings." It is this concern with the problem of passion, or rather with its disappearance, that finally separates Tocqueville from the old liberals. While liberalism feared the energy of the state, it never doubted the energy of the individual. Tocqueville knew better.

> If men continue to shut themselves more closely within the narrow circle of domestic interests and to live on that kind of excitement, it is to be apprehended that they may ultimately become inaccessible to those great and powerful public emotions which perturb nations, but which develop them and recruit them.

Taking his bearings from Hobbes rather than Locke, Tocqueville suspected that the greatest danger to human liberty was not a state which prevented men from exercising their liberty, but one which encouraged them to refuse the burdens of action.[58]

---

[57]Ibid., pp. 101, 138, 140, 145-46, 159.

[58]Adam Smith, *An Inquiry Into the Nature and Causes of the Wealth of Nations* (New York: Modern Library, 1965), p. 324; *Democracy*, vol. I, pp. 52, 98; vol. II, pp. 269, 277.

IV

In the preceding sections, I argued that Tocqueville was indeed "a liberal of a new kind"; that Tocquevillian liberalism was not only a response to the novel political circumstances created by equality, but also a profound critique of the older liberalism which, in the name of liberty, had lent itself as explanation and justification to those tendencies in the democratic soul which threatened centralization and despotism. Toward this end, I found it especially necessary to examine three prominent aspects of liberal doctrine—the purpose of constitutionalism, the character of civil society, and the nature of human liberty—and to situate Tocqueville in relation to these. I also suggested that there was a closer connection between liberal doctrine and the spiritual dynamics of equality than is commonly recognized. It remains for me to show that Tocqueville's praise of municipal institutions and his advocacy of participatory politics as a response to these egalitarian dynamics involves also a fundamental reformulation of the proper relations of reason, sentiment, and interest.

Liberalism has always insisted that political theory take its bearings from civil society. Whatever novelties Tocqueville's "new science" contemplated, it retained the liberal vantage point on the correct relation of theory and practice. "In the end," Tocqueville wrote, "political institutions never fail to become the image and expression of civil society." But Tocqueville's view of the content of civil society dramatically altered the relationship between political "form" and social "substance." From the complex amalgam of opinions, sentiments, and interests that formed civil society, despotism as well as liberty drew nourishment, while the problem of liberty had become the creation and preservation of a certain rarefied taste.

> The whole art of the legislator is correctly to discern beforehand [the] natural inclinations of communities of men, in order to know whether they should be fostered or whether it may not be necessary to check them. For the duties incumbent on the legislator differ at different times.

What are the duties of the legislator in democratic times? What does it mean to "educate" democracy?[59]

The "art" of democratic statecraft includes a knowledge of "propensities" and "causes." The first maxim of this art is that the laws are "infinitely less [efficient]" than the manners and the customs of the people in maintaining democracy. It is especially in regard to manners and customs that the legislator must "foster" as well as "check." Tocqueville's interest in those institutions which are close and palpable (municipal institutions, trial by jury) springs from the efficacy of such structures in shaping the customs and sentiments of democrats. The old liberalism, with its emphasis on the interests, was more familiar (and more comfortable) with the idea of statecraft as limited restraint. Since Locke, liberals have placed great confidence in the power of legislation. Liberty demanded that the actions of both ruler and ruled be restrained and regulated by a "standing rule." In a letter to Mill, Tocqueville sounds this caution: While we must "regulate" and "moderate" the political passions, we must "beware" of "diminishing" them.[60]

In emphasizing the importance of "the moral and intellectual characteristics of men in society," Tocquevillian liberalism pointed to the existence of a more complex relationship between political institutions and civil society than the old liberalism had imagined. The object of the laws should be more than the restraint and regulation of the interests, it should reach to the nurturance of the public affections, for "it depends upon the laws to awaken and direct the vague impulse of patriotism" and consolidate it "into a durable and rational sentiment."[61]

The chief importance of the laws lies in their capacity to mediate between reason and sentiment, and to make more "durable" the natural political affections, for while the political passions are

---

[59]*Democracy*, vol. I, pp. 7, 281; vol. II, pp. 153, 203.

[60]Ibid., vol. I, p. 334; John Locke, *Two Treatises of Government*, ed. Peter Laslett (New York: New American Library, 1963), p. 367; Letter to Mill, Dec. 18, 1840, vol. 1, p. 63. Regarding Tocqueville's opinion of the premier status of customs, his language could not be stronger. Customs are "a central point in the range of observation, and the common termination of all my inquiries" (*Democracy*, vol. 1, p. 334). Concerning the relation of the political order and civil society and the myopias of liberal constitutionalism, see Tocqueville's account of Louis-Philippe, "proud of [his] . . . ingenious mechanism" (*Recollections*, p. 11).

[61]*Democracy*, vol. I, p. 97.

"great," they are also "irregular." Under democratic conditions, the natural ebb and flow of the patriotic "impulse" become pronounced, "all-powerful today, almost imperceptible on the morrow."

> The great utility of popular institutions is, to sustain liberty during those intervals wherein the human mind is otherwise occupied—to give it a kind of vegetative life, which may keep it in existence during those periods of inattention. The forms of a free government allow men to become temporarily weary of their liberty without losing it. When a people are determined to become slaves, it is impossible to hinder their becoming so; but, by free institutions, they may be sustained for some time in independence, even without their own assistance.[62]

It is in light of these reflections that Tocqueville's constitutionalism (and the special status of provincial institutions within that constitutional frame) should be judged. In the past, it often happened that the habits, manners, and traditions of a people were sufficient to sustain the taste for liberty even in the absence of free institutions. But in democratic societies, citizens often "do not resemble their fathers," and sometimes "differ from themselves" as their social condition is "a state of incessant change of place, feelings, and fortunes." Under such circumstances, political "forms" take on greater significance. For Tocqueville, the excellence of democratic institutions is not to be judged by their "regularity" and "methodical order" in the administration of a people's affairs, but as repositories for a "way of life." Institutions such as municipal government and trial by jury are among the most important in this regard because of their "intellectual" and "moral" effects.[63]

The old liberalism deprecated the sentiments and overestimated the capacities of reason when joined to the interests. The Tocquevillian project is an attempt to unite the calculating reason of

---

[62]"France Before the Revolution," in de Beaumot, *Memoir*, pp. 259-60.

[63]*Democracy*, vol. II, pp. 61-62; *Journey to America*, p. 155. See, for example, Tocqueville's discussion of free institutions in the sixteenth and seventeenth centuries in England ("Reflections on English History" in Alexis de Tocqueville, *Journeys to England and Ireland*, trans. George Lawrence and J.-P. Mayer, ed. J.-P. Mayer [London: Faber and Faber, 1958], p. 39).

the democrat to the natural political affections, to create a "common center of the interests and the affections." This effort to turn the political instincts into "intelligent, deliberate and lasting tastes" aims at the rehabilitation of both reason and the affections. As we have seen, calculating reason, "diverted . . . by interest" and loosed from the affections, suffers from certain illusions. Deprived of a knowledge of action, and ignorant of those distinctive pleasures which accompany action, reason is left uncertain as to its proper objects. Unarmed, the political affections become increasingly vulnerable to the claims of interest and subject to great vicissitudes—sometimes "wild," more often "tepid."[64]

For Tocqueville, political action transforms the democratic self. The special virtue of "provincial institutions" is their ability to expand the opportunities for "act[ing] together."

> The Americans have combated by free institutions the tendency of equality to keep men asunder, and they have subdued it. The legislators of America did not suppose that a general representation of the whole nation would suffice to ward off a disorder at once so natural to the frame of democratic society and so fatal; they also thought that it would be well to infuse political life into each portion of the territory in order to multiply to an infinite extent opportunities of acting in concert for all the members of the community and to make them constantly feel their mutual dependence. Their plan was a wise one.

Political action dispels the illusions of independence. It teaches the truth about strength and weakness that the pretense of a calculating reason tries to hide from itself.[65]

By inclination, the democrat prefers neither to "see" nor "feel" his fellow citizens. Thus "a general representation" of political freedom is insufficient. Representative institutions leave democrats in their "natural" social condition: unattached. "Free institutions," on the other hand, "invade the conscience." In Tocqueville's discussion of such institutions, there is a muted language of coercion.

---

64 *Democracy*, vol. I, pp. 83, 99; *Recollections*, p. 74.
65 *Democracy*, vol. II, pp. 61, 110.

The democrat is "snatched . . . from self-observation" and "forced" to "acquaint" and "adapt" himself to his fellows.[66]

Political liberty is a peculiar pedagogy. Action can be learned only in action. Without "experience," the "realities of public life" remain *"terra incognita."* On this, Mill and Tocqueville agree. But for Mill, the "foremost" consequence of the "education" provided by "local popular institutions" is simply "the diffusion of intelligence." While Tocqueville agrees that free institutions give rise to certain "clear practical notions," he is more interested in their capacity to "change [the] character" of both reason and the affections, to create an intelligent, deliberate, and lasting taste for liberty.

> Men attend to the interests of the public, first by necessity, afterwards by choice; what was intentional becomes an instinct, and by dint of working for the good of one's fellow citizens, the habit and the taste for serving them are at length acquired.[67]

Possessed by the joys of concerted action, the democrat finds his "aim[s]" altered and his "exertions" guided by a new purposefulness. Confident of his strength, the aristocrat could stand alone and retain the spirit of liberty, finding the objects of his self-devotion in the remembrance of a past or the contemplation of a future. But in democratic times, strength is to be found only in numbers. Paradoxically, that spirit of "masculine independence" that bespeaks a taste for liberty must now be nurtured by making citizens "constantly feel their mutual dependence" upon their fellow-citizens.[68]

The experience of the Americans, for whom public life was "one half of . . . existence" and their "only pleasure," demonstrated the power of political action to shape the sentiments and make authoritative claims upon "a conscience . . . otherwise based on reflection and calculation." But the American experience also showed the precariousness of the "rational sentiments" of public liberty. Under

---

[66]Ibid., pp. 61, 109, 111.

[67]*Old Regime*, p. 140; Mill, *Works*, vol. 18, pp. 168-70; *Democracy*, vol. I, pp. 70-71; vol. II, p. 112.

[68]*Democracy*, vol. I, pp. 276-77; vol. II, p. 110.

egalitarian conditions, the taste for liberty, too, comes to resemble "the flow of the Rhone," disappearing and reappearing again. As we saw earlier, even the Americans, that most fortunate people, were unable to find a language adequate to give voice to their public pleasures. They hid these joys from their fellows (and perhaps even from themselves) behind the language of a calculating reason. Among democrats, the illusion of independence always threatens to return, and the doctrine of interest sinks its roots deep in their pride. In democratic times, the maintenance of political life "will ever be the product of art." In aristocracies, the taste for liberty benefits from the continuity and endurance of human things. In democracies, where "each new generation is a new people," the knowledge of the joys and devotions of political life is especially hard to preserve.[69]

While it is probably true that the love of action is refined and cultivated only through action, under conditions of equality the pretense of reason and the claims of interest make the taste for liberty increasingly dependent upon experiential knowledge. To those who "have never had the inclination or the time to act together," the power and the pleasure that accompany concerted action "must be shown . . . in order to be understood." Thus "nowhere" are provincial institutions "more necessary" than in a democratic society, not only because their palpable existence more easily attracts the affections of the people, but, perhaps more importantly, because they are well adapted to the pretensions of the democrat's epistemology. Democrats must find things out for themselves. The legislator cannot teach the truth about political liberty. He must, instead, endeavor to put the people in the way of the truth, "multiply[ing] to an infinite extent opportunities for acting in concert."[70]

But this is also the limit of the new science and the origin of Tocqueville's melancholia.

> [For] where will people get their real taste for liberty if they do not know it or if they have lost it? Who will teach

[69]Ibid., vol. I, p. 260; vol. II, pp. 62, 313; *Journey to America*, p. 211; *European Revolution*, p. 152.
[70]*Democracy*, vol. I, p. 99; vol. II, pp. 4, 61, 124.

> them these noble pleasures? Who can make them love liberty if that love has not been originally planted in their hearts? Who will even pretend to make them understand those pleasures of liberty which men can no longer even imagine once they have lost their habitual experience?

The enduring questions of Tocquevillian liberalism—they are no less our own.[71]

---

[71]*European Revolution*, p. 167.

4

Democracy and Pantheism

Peter Augustine Lawler

The theme of this essay is the theme of Part I of Volume II of Alexis de Tocqueville's *Democracy in America,* the effect of democracy on "intellectual movements." The core of democratic thought or theory is the use of reason to destroy allegedly illegitimate or oppressive distinctions. This destruction in thought is both caused by, and is a cause of, democratic political action. Democratic political action and democratic intellectual vision are, for a long time, interdependent. Democratic theory, finally, asserts its primacy over democratic practice. It shows the necessity for the destruction of politics or human assertiveness altogether in the name of reason's consistency.

At first glance, one of Tocqueville's most remarkable suggestions is that the wholly consistent or wholly democratic philosophical system is pantheism. Pantheism is the view that the fundamental distinctions between material and spiritual, visible and invisible, time and eternity, and creator and created are merely apparent. Its system, most fundamentally, synthesizes into one idea: materialism's homogeneity and spiritualism's divinity.

This idea, as the most general of general ideas, satisfies reason's desire for unity without offending human pride and while requiring no intellectual exertion. It is a belief in which the human being "gladly reposes," because it denies the possibility and the desirability of the human struggle to achieve distinctive excellence or greatness. Why should human beings want to be distinctive if the homogeneous whole is already divine? Pantheism, it is easy to see, "naturally attracts" the democratic imagination.

It is impossible to imagine a more democratic idea or system.[1]

Pantheism, in its opposition to any form of distinctiveness, destroys the idea of "human individuality."[2] But Tocqueville himself calls at least democratic individualism an error.[3] Democratic thought's passion for unity or generality perhaps cannot help but be the cause of the eventual recognition of this error.[4] Individualism in any form must not really be wholly democratic. It requires some support from aristocratic pride or passion for distinction.

The democratic individualist, having used his "philosophical method" or skepticism to render human assertions of qualitative distinctions or heterogeneity incredible, seeks his individual distinctiveness in quantitative ones.[5] But, because such distinctions are never definitive and hence are an unreasonable means for establishing one's own humanity, he inevitably fails. His awareness of this failure, perhaps, brings individualism to an end. The democrat at this point abandons the idea of the individual for the idea of the species, and eventually he loses the species in a completely indiscriminate, pantheistic account of the whole.[6]

This destruction of individualism is the basis of pantheism's "charms" for democrats, who eventually find the incoherence of their account of individuality too difficult to sustain. These charms, however, are "secret," because democratic thought begins and is moved a great distance by the vision of the liberation of the individual from intellectual and political bondage. Because pure pantheism negates the idea of human distinctiveness and hence human assertiveness, it cannot consciously motivate democratic political actors. It is too general an idea to be the cause of distinctively human motion. When its truth is wholly affirmed,

---

[1]Alexis de Tocqueville, *Democracy in America*, ed. J.-P. Mayer, trans. George Lawrence (Garden City, N.Y.: Doubleday, Anchor Books, 1969), pp. 451-52. Hereinafter cited as *Democracy*.

[2]Ibid., p. 452.

[3]Ibid., p. 506.

[4]Ibid., pp. 436, 439, 451.

[5]Ibid., pp. 429, 615, 617.

[6]Ibid., p. 451. See p. 688 on the "instinct for centralization" as the "one permanent feature" of democratic motivation.

human striving and hence politics comes to an end. Tocqueville remarks that he discusses pantheism before he discusses the effects of the democratic attraction to general ideas on politics.[7]

Tocqueville notes the progress of pantheism in the German philosophy of his time. Affirmation of pantheism in the writing of the "Young Hegelians" of the 1830s is well known. Engels himself called Hegel's idea of God modern pantheism. It showed humanity and divinity to be identical in essence. Engels discovered this idea in D. F. Strauss's interpretation of Hegel's "speculative theology" in *The Life of Jesus*, and it both attracted him to, and showed him the plausibility of, Hegelianism rightly understood.[8]

For Strauss, "the idea of the unity of the divine and human natures" becomes "a real one in a more lofty sense" when viewed as realized "in the entire human race and not merely in one man." The "fact" of the "individual" is significant only in the context of the "idea" of the "race." "[T]he idea of humanity as one with God" means the negation of "the merely natural and sensual life" of the individual in favor of the "spiritual life" of humanity as a whole, a life which reveals itself in, and is equivalent to, history.[9]

The realization of the species' spiritual goal, or the fulfillment of its historical destiny, is the political goal of the "Young Hegelians." They were, as the phrase is used today, theologians of liberation. They refused to believe that pantheism was already true and hence history had come to an end. As Karl Löwith writes: "The young Hegelians represented the party of youth, not because they themselves were youths, but in order to overcome the consciousness of being epigones."[10] They were and are the "effectual truth" of Hegelianism, because they acted on the opinion that they had reconciled the democratic idea of pantheism with the

---

[7]Ibid., p. 451. See p. 462 on the "secret charm" of "vagueness" in language for democrats.

[8]Karl Marx and Frederick Engels, *Collected Works*, vol. 2 (London: Lawrence and Wisort, 1975), pp. 489-90. This source was called to my attention by Terrell Carver, *Marx and Engels: Their Intellectual Relationship* (Bloomington: Indiana University Press, 1983), pp. 8-10.

[9]D. F. Strauss, *The Life of Jesus, Critically Examined*, trans. George Eliot (Philadelphia: Fortress Press, 1972), pp. 777-81.

[10]Karl Löwith, *From Hegel to Nietzsche: The Revolution in Nineteenth Century Thought*, trans. David Green (New York: Holt, Rinehart, and Winston, 1964), p. 66.

possibility of their own effective political or historical action.

But this Hegelian pantheism, to the extent that it generates political idealism, is not really pure pantheism and not purely democratic. It still distinguishes between human freedom and brute necessity, between history and nature. For the Young Hegelian, pantheism is still to be made true by human beings, both through thought and through practice. Thought eventually reveals the ideal in its rational consistency, but free human action is responsible for making it true.

The democratic movement in thought, Tocqueville shows, does not come to an end with the emergence of the doctrine of the historical development of reason and freedom of Hegelian idealism. It is, moreover, right not to do so, because this doctrine cannot coherently defend itself as a manifestation of human freedom. Tocqueville shows why this is the case through his account of the approach of the wholly democratic historian.[11] This account includes, for Tocqueville, all democratic theorists, those who take their bearings wholly from analysis of the causes of historical change. Those who are able to scorn this success for some higher standard are not wholly democrats.

The aristocratic historian, for Tocqueville, is one who understands historical change in terms of the "will and character" of remarkable individuals. The causes of this change are, then, extraordinary and unpredictable. From a scientific or democratic perspective, they are accidental. Hence, the aristocratic historian denies the possibility of articulating an historical "system." For him, the ideal individual in full command of his soul ought to and can rule the world, but one cannot say with certainty when or how he will.[12]

The democratic historian sees "the whole world moving without anyone moving it." He sees a whole society of human beings moving "simultaneously in the same direction." The cause of such motion must be great, impersonal, and have nothing to do with the free will of particular individuals. The individual must be determined by some comprehensive social force, and society itself

---

[11]*Democracy*, pp. 493-96.
[12]Ibid., pp. 493-95.

seems to "obey some superior dominating force." There is a "general law" that produces "irresistible and inflexible progress" toward "a fixed destiny which no efforts can change." For the consistently democratic historical system: "Generation is firmly bound to generation, and so going back from *age to age,* from *necessity to necessity,* they reach the origin of the world, forging a tight enormous chain which girds and binds the human race." The necessary destiny of the species over time is proof of the nonexistence of individual or even species freedom.[13]

Any historical system, Tocqueville indicates, is a human product. Its existence requires a willful or indolent ignorance of the effects of individual freedom. The only individual it satisfies is the historian or theorist. He believes himself to be rightly proud of his mastery of the whole of humanity through his methodical comprehension of it in a single system.[14] But Tocqueville shows his true or democratic vulgarity. Instead of criticizing history with reference to a transhistorical ideal, he denies the effectiveness of such criticism and hence the existence of the phenomenon of human choice. He shows "events could not have happened differently."[15]

This vulgarity is characteristic of contemporary social science which, when its partisans consistently articulate its premises, is nothing but Tocqueville's democratic theory of history. The social scientist's first principle is simply the denial that politics or humanity really exist at all. He asserts that what seems to be change caused by political choice is really caused by sociological or economic or technological forces. He asserts that the "political" is merely a reflection of the "social" or "economic."

The social scientist claims to be too scientific to accept hypotheses which are based on human partisanship. He knows that all values or human attachments are irrational, that they have no place in science. Those hypotheses that deny that distinctions among human beings and between humanity and nonhumanity really exist are sounder starting points for investigation than those which recognize these distinctions because they are more

---

[13]Ibid., pp. 495-96. Emphasis mine.
[14]Ibid., pp. 496, 544.
[15]Ibid., p. 496.

neutral. They are based on the scientific principle that no particular set of values has any support in reality.[16]

The social scientist tends to see the political system as, in truth, part of the social system which, in turn, is part of some "general system." His fact-value distinction points to a "general systems theory" which affirms the truth of homogeneous materialism. He presupposes, in other words, that the "whole" is, in truth, radically democratic. Consequently, he presupposes that human freedom or distinctiveness do not really exist.

Although democratic history or theory is not completely true, Tocqueville argues it could become at least almost wholly true. The denial of the effectual existence of human freedom may well contribute to that freedom's destruction. The popularization of democratic theory paralyzes democratic action.[17] The reductionistic thrust of the democratic way of thinking, although perhaps largely praiseworthy for a long time for its ability to render incredible aristocratic notions of freedom, culminates in the conclusion that even the most democratic account of freedom—that history is the manifestation of human freedom—is an illusion.

The way this conclusion is reached is easily summarized. Democratic thought begins by locating human progress toward reason and freedom in history. The candid awareness of the effects of human embodiment of democratic materialism opposes the idea of individual completeness. Humanity endures in time and perfects itself as a species or race.[18]

The historical idealist asserts that the progress of history is progress toward the perfection of human freedom. This ideal or ideology of progressivism is the justification, consciously or unconsciously, of individual, social, and political striving in democratic times.[19] The historical idealist requires freedom to be rational freedom, for at least three reasons. First, only reason can destroy

---

[16]See Harvey Mansfield, Jr., *Representation* (Washington, D.C.: The American Political Science Association, 1978), chap. 1. Mansfield wrote this monograph with Robert Scigliano, but chap. 1 was written by him alone.

[17]*Democracy*, p. 496.

[18]Ibid., pp. 453, 459.

[19]Ibid., pp. 452-54.

the illusory or undemocratic obstacles to humanity's unity.[20] Second, reason's technical mastery of nature in the service of human need materialistically conceived is the most concrete (or uncontroversial) evidence of human progress.[21] Third, human freedom must be a freedom in which human beings can reasonably take pride, or really recognize their distinctive superiority.[22] Reflection on the inability to defend rationally any of these assertions on an historical basis reveals the incoherence of the historical idealist's assertion that human freedom is both historical and rational.

To begin with, is not the same democratic or scientific way of thinking which abolishes the distinction between "aristocrat" and "democrat" through its skeptical materialism capable of challenging the distinction between "human" and "nonhuman"?[23] If reason's power of generalization has any limits, do not they suggest limits to the democratic assertion of the reasonableness of complete equality and freedom? Will a democrat be satisfied as long as any such limits exist?[24]

From the perspective of the homogeneous materialism of modern or "democratic" science, is not all distinctively human behavior extraordinary? But to believe in what is extraordinary is undemocratic, and the pure democrat refuses to acknowledge its existence.[25] Is the assertion of any distinctively human behavior, then, "deviant" or even insane from the perspective of democratic "science"? (Consider Marxism, behaviorism, or even just Hobbes here.) Reason compels the democratic thinker to question the real existence of humanity. Does he manifest his humanity by destroying humanity? He shows he is radically free by demonstrating reason's unlimited power. By brutalizing humanity he almost seems to become a god.[26] Is he who proudly abolishes distinctions that seemed to separate beast, man, and God an atheist or a pantheist?

---

[20]Ibid., pp. 437-41, 451.
[21]Ibid., p. 459.
[22]Ibid., pp. 452, 609-10, 632, 672. Also vol. I, pp. 402-03.
[23]See my "Tocqueville on Slavery, Ancient and Modern," *The South Atlantic Quarterly* 80 (Autumn 1981), pp. 466-77. Also *Democracy*, pp. 544, 692-94.
[24]Consider *Democracy*, p. 673.
[25]Ibid., p. 430.
[26]Ibid., p. 544.

The democratic theorist or, more precisely, the modern intellectual opposes God in order to replace Him. His atheism is a means to his own divinization. But, even if he succeeded in using his method to bring the whole of humanity under his control, would he become distinctively divine? Is the uniform control of thoughtless and will-less beings a task worthy of a god or even a human being?[27]

The democratic theorist really has no argument for why he can exempt himself from his homogeneous materialism. He cannot show why his pride in his power is reasonable. His account of power is wholly indiscriminate,[28] and no quantity of power can really overcome his own bodily limitations. Because he cannot sustain his divine or human distinctiveness, he cannot oppose the truth of pantheism. Even atheism, after all, must for him imply an illegitimate distinction. (This conclusion applies also, of course, to the modern tyrant, who is dependent for his "ideas" or goals on the democratic thought of the modern intellectual.[29])

It is also possible to question whether technical progress is human progress, even if the human being can be adequately defined in terms of bodily need. The purpose of technology is to free human beings from this need, from pain, death, and labor. It points to a life of security and freedom from any form of compulsion. It points, in other words, to pure democracy. Consciousness of one's own mortality or of the scarcity of time might be viewed as *the* anti-democratic experience, because it compels one to rank one's possible activities according to some standard.[30] Perhaps only the necessities connected with time and death give human activity weight.[31] Consequently, the pure democrat hates every form of necessity. Those who attempt to call attention to it are the only ones who can disturb his easygoing relativism.[32]

Can technology eliminate the experiences connected with the

---

[27]Consider ibid., p. 694: If the ruled "fall below the level of humanity," there will be no one to recognize the power and wisdom of the single, godlike ruler.
[28]Ibid., pp. 631, 670, 673.
[29]Consider ibid., p. 670. The ideas which "recur in the most fantastic utopia" of democratic thought "strike the imagination of princes even more forcibly."
[30]Consider carefully ibid., pp. 536-58.
[31]Consider ibid., p. 461 on Pascal.
[32]Consider ibid., p. 673.

human consciousness of death? Can it make pure democracy and the pure democrat possible? Technology may eventually eliminate death as a *necessity*. It may find a way of postponing indefinitely bodily decay. It cannot, however, eliminate death as a possibility because it cannot remove all contingency from the infinite universe. If death were no longer a necessity, would not the human being's fear of it increase immeasurably? An accidental death of a human being who did not have to die would be infinitely more terrible than anything human beings now experience. Would anyone be able to choose to accept or even risk death to affirm one's own human nobility or distinctiveness under such circumstances?[33]

Tocqueville is right to emphasize that technological success increases human insecurity and anxiety or unhappiness. The comfort it provides is nothing when compared to the way it increases the individual's sense of his own contingency. When the individual conceives of himself wholly as a time-bound being in an infinite universe, he sees himself as hopelessly weak. He sees that his capabilities have no possibility of fulfilling his longings.[34] Consequently, he cannot affirm the goodness of his individuality or even his humanity, and he continues to work only to avoid self-contemplation by avoiding leisure. He has no use for, or even hates, the "free time" which is allegedly one of technology's most important products.[35] Technological striving, it is easy to see, cannot make the individual human being free. Instead, it makes him feel more and more unfree.

According to Tocqueville, the human being inevitably has a "taste for the infinite and love of what is immortal."[36] He can neither satisfy nor destroy this longing through his own effort, at least, and remain a human being. Consequently, his soul or his consciousness of desires which do not admit of material satisfaction cause him to become "bored, restless, and anxious" when he is enjoying the fruits of technological success.[37] Reason cannot tell him,

---

[33]See Michael Platt, "Would Human Life Be Better Without Death?" *Soundings* 63 (Fall 1980), p. 331.

[34]Consider, for example, *Democracy*, pp. 435, 537, 596, 643, 672.

[35]Ibid., p. 536.

[36]Ibid., pp. 534-35.

[37]Ibid., p. 535.

he believes, how to deal with the "strange melancholy" that haunts him "in the midst of abundance."[38] What keeps him from concluding, quite reasonably, that rational calculation and materialistic enlightenment (the sources that he believes to be his distinctively human qualities) have nothing to do with freedom and happiness? Is his partisanship on behalf of his humanity unreasonable? If he avoids self-destruction, does he do so unreasonably?[39]

The democrat cannot help but come to see that technical and even political or historical progress do not fundamentally transform the human condition of the individual. Although its overcoming of what at one time seemed to be insurmountable limitations may temporarily fill him with self-confidence, in the long run its primary effect is to make him aware of his hopeless weakness. Yet progress must have some significance; it reveals and strengthens the idea of humanity. It is humanity—the species—not the individual which seems to clearly progress over time. Consequently, it is easy for the democratic individual to attempt to lose himself in this idea. If each part of the whole is more or less identical, and petty and puny standing alone, the strength and grandeur of each part must be as a part of a spectacle of collective or mass movement.[40]

But is it reasonable for the skeptical materialist to forget his individuality in this way? He still dies alone and is aware of it, and he knows that reason is a means for self-preservation. His abandonment of his own self-interest in the name of humanity's or the species' future perfection must be unreasonable. Is it a willful abandonment of reason and even a willful abandonment of will? It is based on an "opiate" or "reverie."

Democratic thought, despite its use of reason as its tool, seems to have a propensity to become increasingly unreasonable. Tocqueville shows the process by which democratic thought loses its rational limitations in his account of democratic poetry. For him, "poetry is the search for and the representation of the ideal."[41]

---

[38]Ibid., p. 538.
[39]Ibid., pp. 535, 538.
[40]Ibid., p. 486.
[41]Ibid., p. 483.

All poetry or idealism "ennobles nature"; it is the product of the imagination beautifying reality. It appears, at this point, that Tocqueville believes that reality or "nature" is not inherently beautiful or capable of inspiring idealism. Ideals, as a result, are human creations out of materials which are inherently almost worthless.[42]

Elsewhere, however, Tocqueville contends that there are things which are really good and bad and noble and base independently of human making and that nature gives some guidance to human thought and imagination.[43] He also asserts that the opinion that all "forms" or ideals are simply human creations is self-destructive and untrue.[44] Because human beings are neither totally ignorant nor wise, it appears, imagination must complete what reason discovers in order to give a human being the comprehensive view of himself and the "whole" he needs to order and direct his life. Only God really comprehends the whole; consequently, only God fully comprehends the parts.[45] God has no need of poetry. No human being can be "scientific" enough to do without it.[46]

It is hard for democrats to find subjects for poetry. They refuse to believe in the supernatural or the invisible. They refuse to give the "aristocrat" the distance he needs to seem superior. They claim to know too much about the truth of every human life to idealize any particular individual. Skeptically rejecting any hearsay evidence about the past, and believing dogmatically in the existence of fundamental human progress, they are unable to idealize tradition.

---

[42]Ibid.

[43]Ibid., pp. 481, 698-99.

[44]Consider ibid., pp. 447-49, and Tocqueville's remarks on religion generally. See my "Tocqueville on Religion and Human Excellence," *The Southeastern Political Review* 11 (Fall 1983), pp. 139-60.

For other evidence on "forms," see Harvey C. Mansfield, Jr., "The Forms and Formality of Liberty," *The Public Interest* 70 (Winter 1983), pp. 121-31. Consider also Robert Eden's precise summary of Tocqueville's position: "It is human to be attached to forms. . . ." ("Tocqueville on Political Realignment and Constitutional Forms." Paper presented to the 1984 American Political Science Association Convention, p. 5.) Such attachments are a constituent part of humanity; humanity cannot be conceived without them. The desire to use reason to destroy forms is one which, in truth, opposes and/or denies the real existence of humanity.

[45]*Democracy*, pp. 437, 754.

[46]Ibid., p. 487.

They candidly acknowledge that all of human existence has the same prosaic roots, and they believe, more or less, that everything human reason and imagination can comprehend cannot be disconnected from these roots.

Having reduced the aristocratic sources of poetry to merely human or prosaic proportions, the democrat turns to "inanimate nature" as a source for poetry. But it cannot inspire him. He knows nothing about it, and it means nothing to him. Nature enters his vision only after he has subdued it in the service of human need. It exists for him only as a resource for human productivity. It has no independent existence.[47]

The democratic "soul," the unadorned heart, and "the incomprehensible miseries" of the time-bound being, is a subject of democratic poetry. It is, Tocqueville remarks, this poetry's "fittest subject," perhaps because it is the one which reveals the most truth. But it is surely virtually impossible to idealize. Perhaps the imagination cannot work with too much self-knowledge. Preoccupation with knowledge of the destiny of the individual, at least as it is conceived from the democratic perspective, is the enemy of beauty or nobility. An imagination that can inspire a democrat and a democracy must include more.[48]

The only "magnificent vision" in a democracy is humanity's collective conquest of nature, a constantly moving picture which seems to know no limits. The contribution of the particular individual to this spectacle is growing smaller and more indistinct. The whole called humanity is daily revealing more of the truth of its homogeneity. The world is becoming "one vast democracy" composed of "men on the move." The meaning of this movement for "[t]he destiny of the entire human race" is "a fertile theme for poetry." Its revelation is the still-uncompleted task of *the* democratic poet.[49]

The individual democrat works hard to satisfy his petty, materialistic desires. But he cannot help but see on occasion the futility and even absurdity of his joyless quest for joy. He cannot

---

47Ibid., pp. 484-85.
48Ibid., pp. 486-87.
49Ibid., pp. 485-86.

work hard enough to eradicate completely the longings of his soul. He cannot help but hope that his efforts are also part of a vast movement toward human perfection, and the massive progress he sees around him seems to make this hope reasonable. There seems to be no reason for him not to believe that the future will overcome what appear to be human limitations in the present.

Still, he does not know what human perfection is. All he knows is that he feels the exhilarating possibility of unlimited freedom. He knows that the movement he perceives is in the direction of consistency, universality, and homogeneity. It somehow shows the power of reason. It is a revelation of the thought of God, the democratic evidence that God exists. Humanity's collective progress is evidence that "God guides mankind" by directing the action of each individual toward a goal which transcends the perspective of the particular individual. The "design" of human progress must be divine, because no particular human being chose it. The task of the democratic poet is to reveal God's plan and so the destiny of humanity as a whole.[50]

The democratic poet reveals the "ideal" toward which the growing universality and consistency of humanity's visible and tangible or historical achievements point. Democratic poetry seems to presuppose the possibility of, and considerable knowledge of, the democratic historical "system." For both the democratic poet and the democratic theorist, history is all there is. The poet denies that history has ended; consequently, imagination must provide that for which evidence is not yet available. But the future is not a product of free human creation; it is a revelation of God's plan. Historical "idealism," then, seems to be incoherent if understood as a manifestation of human freedom. The projection of the "end of history" or the total revelation of divinity or pantheism would seem to require only logical deduction and not poetic imagination.[51]

---

[50]Ibid., p. 486.

[51]The use of the phrase "the end of history," which is completely justified in the context of Tocqueville's analysis, calls to mind Alexandre Kojève's remarkable *Introduction to the Reading of Hegel*, ed. Allan Bloom, trans. James H. Nichols (New York: Basic Books, 1969). See especially pp. 160-61, n. 6, where Kojève makes it clear that he believes we have entered the "post-historical" period already. He observes that "post-historical animals of the species *Homo sapiens*" lose their distinctive

It is easy to see, certainly, that the end of history would be the end of poetry. More than that, one could say that once one sees the *necessity* of the end of history, one must dispense with poetry or "idealism."

Still, the poet looks for human significance in historical progress. All it shows to him is his own very insignificant self and the human race as a whole, composed of selves like himself. Because he can see no human distinctions, he seems to be free to imagine anything for the human future. "Find[ing] no stuff for the ideal in what is real and true," he has no choice but to abandon "truth and reality" and "create monsters." He cannot take his bearings from the human beings of the past because humanity has manifested its freedom by progressing beyond them. He cannot take his bearings from democratic history or theory because it denies the real existence of poetry or idealism. He must create "a whole fantastic breed of brainchildren" that have never existed, but perhaps could if human beings become free. For him, freedom means that whatever can be imagined can be brought into being.[52]

Democratic history or theory teaches that the future is beyond human control, but it is intelligibly determined by some superior force. Human beings are enslaved to the force which controls the historical process. The democratic poet traces this force to God, who is capable of doing anything. He ends up reconciling the "idealism" of human freedom with the truth of materialistic determinism by finding freedom at the end of the deterministic process. At this point the content of freedom can be the product of human imagination and human will, because anything will be possible. The distinction between humanity and divinity, or materialism and idealism, will disappear. The democratic poet believes that anyone who criticizes this conclusion with reference to "the real world" is unnecessarily or dogmatically enslaved to human experience.[53] Democratic poetry, then, ends up simply "dreaming about the future," and it knows of nothing to limit or direct its dreams. It is

---

humanity and, as a result, "live amidst abundance and complete security." The disappearance of humanity at the end of history is the real fulfillment of the modern (or democratic) project.

[52]*Democracy*, pp. 488-89.

[53]Ibid.

wholly "beyond measure"; it is beyond reason (or calculation), time, and mortality.[54]

The democratic poet's or idealist's imagination of the future is a judgment concerning the democratic present, where there is too much calculation and too much consciousness of time, and in which every form of immortality seems incredible. The enslavement and misery can be justified only if they can somehow transform themselves into their opposites. One can endure the present only by imagining the future. The present can be "idealized" only as a means to the future.

Consider here that Karl Marx is a good example for Tocqueville of a democratic poet, as would be any "Young Hegelian." For Marx, the meaning of the historical abolition of human distinctions is the liberation of humanity from every form of limitation. His dedication was to the historical actualization of a vision of freedom in which humanity finally comes into its own.

There is, as there is with any democratic poet, a tension between Marx's view of the human significance of the vision and the materialistic-deterministic basis of his historical theory. Whenever this tension seems to be about to change into a debilitating incompatibility, however, Marx and his politically effective followers were, and are, disconcertingly willing to alter the "general" theory to fit what the actualization of the vision seems to require in particular circumstances.

Marx was an idealist. His objection to what he calls idealism was from the perspective of what he believed to be the only realistic idealism. In the decisive cases, his "humanistic" imagination—however distorted and indistinct (or monstrous) the vision of humanity it produces—took precedence over democratic theory's standard of impersonal consistency.

The foundation of the liberating revolution is the great mass of humanity's hatred of its existing condition. Individuals become united through their common perception of individualism's worthlessness. The revolution is total, the commitment to a wholly new future is total, because the present offers nothing but total misery. The experience of extreme or wholly unsupported individualism is

---

[54]Ibid., p. 485.

the precondition of complete human emancipation. It brings into being the opposite of, or the negation of, the isolated individual—the "species being."

For Marx, this being comes into existence with the end of history or the emergence of "communism." Communism is primarily the abolition of the distinction between what belongs to the individual and what belongs to the universal and homogeneous society or the species considered as a whole. Not only the things of the mind but the things of the body can be held in common without doing violence to the needs of each particular human being.

But communism is not only "the *definitive* resolution of the conflict . . . between individual and species." It also resolves "the antagonism between man and nature."[55] It "for the first time consciously treats all natural premises as the creatures of men, strips them of their natural character and subjugates them to the power of individuals united."[56] Humanity becomes master of nature; nature becomes humanity's own. Communism means liberation from any form of enslavement to natural necessity. It is the democratic dream come true.

After communism comes into being, man becomes "the highest being for man," because man cannot imagine a more perfect condition than complete freedom. Because human suffering really disappears, moreover, there will be no need to imagine a world better than the real one. Religion and, it seems, even poetry, at least in Tocqueville's sense, will disappear.

Probably the most attractive feature of Marxism for human beings is its assertion that "bourgeois" misery is not a permanent aspect of the human condition or human nature but was created by, and will be destroyed by, history. But it is impossible to see how history can overcome the experience of democratic individualism in a way which is both materialistic and human. Will not the individual human being still die and feel pleasure and pain alone and be aware of it at the end of history? If so, the overcoming of

---

[55]Karl Marx, "Private Property and Communism" in *The Portable Karl Marx*, ed. E. Kamenka (New York: Penguin Books, 1983), pp. 149-50.

[56]Karl Marx, *The German Ideology*, ibid., p. 189. The remarks on Marx in this essay are indebted to Thomas G. West, "Marx and Lenin," *Interpretation* 11 (1983), pp. 73-85.

economic scarcity cannot create wholly satisfied species beings.

The fundamental scarcity for human beings, of course, is scarcity of time.[57] This scarcity is experienced only by human beings, not by beasts or gods. If human beings were to become truly immortal, really to become free from the fundamental natural limitation of human existence, they would cease to be human and become gods.

Marx never says, and does not mean to imply, that the individual human being will ever really become immortal. If he will die but is not aware of it, he will still be free from consciousness of time. It would seem that at the end of history man becomes a beast. But at the end of history, Marx says, man will be fully conscious of his freedom. He will be, for this reason, fully human.[58] Yet it is impossible for a fully self-conscious mortal being (if such a being is possible) to say he is completely free from necessity.

Marx cannot offer a coherent vision of humanity's future freedom. His vision's credibility depends on the vague, indistinct way in which democrats typically view the future. Surely Marx, in his willingness to abolish the distinction not only between God and man but between man and nature in his vision of radical freedom, is on the verge of pantheism. Only the poetic dimension of his thought causes it to retain an impossibly vague aspect of human distinctiveness.

Marx's revolutionary poetry is intended to be a wholly democratic solution to the problems of modern individualism. The first, and still probably the most profound, partisan of such a solution was Rousseau. He had, I think, a more consistent view of the goal of the democratic movement than did Marx. If Tocqueville could, in effect, anticipate Marx's thought and criticize it in advance, maybe it is because he was a student of Rousseau.

Rousseau saw clearly the incoherence of modern or enlightenment individualistic materialism. On one hand, it is based on the individual's awareness of his distinctiveness and his legitimate desire to protect what is his own. On the other, its view of nature is in terms of a homogeneous materialism which denies the possibility

---

[57]See George Friedman, *The Political Philosophy of the Frankfurt School* (Ithaca, N.Y.: Cornell University Press, 1981), pp. 279-88.
[58]Marx, "Private Property," in *The Portable Karl Marx*, pp. 149-52.

of human distinctiveness. The allegedly enlightened beings who feel compelled to strive incessantly and futilely to overcome this incoherence are chained to a joyless, miserable existence which ends only with death.

If there is no natural support for human striving and if such striving makes human beings miserable, then why do they continue to assert their human distinctiveness? It is because they have acquired over time the human passions of fear and pride, both of which are by-products of the acquisition of reason. Human beings defend their humanity because they believe it is worth preserving. Rousseau, perhaps more consistently than any other thinker, shows why this belief is unreasonable.

If there is really no natural support for humanity, then the awareness of human beings of their individuality or self-consciousness and its by-products—reason, fear, and pride—can be understood as accidental, unfortunate, and inessential acquisitions of some evolutionary or historical process and not part of the human being's genuine being. If humanity is an accident, then human pride is unreasonable. If the human being is true to himself, he can negate the "unnatural" unhappiness produced by his unnecessary desires.

Surely he can say that his enlightened, "bourgeois" pre-occupation with rational calculation, time, and mortality is not healthy or "life-enhancing" and not even conducive to mere bodily self-preservation. He can even say that humanity does not really exist. It can be discovered only if he deviates from a wholly consistent materialism, and the partisan of modern or democratic science knows of no method for accounting for such "deviant behavior."

According to the human standards of truth and happiness, he must conclude that his partisanship on behalf of his human distinctiveness, his pride in his individuality, is unreasonable. If he can but forget his "historical" acquisition of reason or self-consciousness and the insatiable desires it generates, he can find, Rousseau claims to know through personal experience, that his natural state of being is a simple and sweet sentiment of existence. If human beings unconsciously or accidentally made themselves humans, can they consciously recognize their error and consciously undo their work?

If they can, all that will remain is a feeling that, in its way, is godlike in its self-sufficiency. Its "reveries" contain no awareness of the human being's mortality or neediness. They allow him to be idle with guilt. "Scarcity" has been overcome not by unparalleled productivity, but by the destruction of those desires which brought scarcity into being. The ultimate scarcity, to repeat, is scarcity of time, and there is no longer any consciousness of time. The human being has destroyed the distinctions which separated man, beast, and god, and he can affirm the truth of pantheism.[59]

Marx and other democratic poets come close to, but do not reach, pantheism because their inability to purge themselves willfully or imaginatively of their humanity prevents them from thinking with complete consistency. Unlike Rousseau, they cannot help but think they have found human significance in human progress. As Tocqueville says, their vision of the future is full of monsters because their simultaneous partisanship on behalf of both humanity and democracy stands in the way of their thought's or imagination's coherence. They refuse to see the possibility that humanity itself is time-bound, that the democratic movement points to the abolition of humanity. Perhaps they refuse to imagine a future without poetry, a particularly human activity.

Tocqueville follows Rousseau in his ability to see more clearly the effect the democratic movement could have on human possibilities than can the democratic poet. One of his chapters is entitled "How Excessive Love of Prosperity Can Do Harm to It."[60] Its purpose seems to be to show democratic materialists that cultivation of the soul is in their self-interest rightly understood: "Whatever elevates, enlarges, and expands the soul makes it more able to succeed even in those undertakings which are not the soul's concern." Consequently, "[t]here is a closer connection than is

---

[59]These general remarks on Rousseau, which are based on Walk Five of *Reveries of the Solitary Walker* as read in light of the teaching on nature and the emergence of humanity in *Discourse on the Origin and Foundation of Inequality*, might seem to be misleading or incomplete. They are meant to present the democratic "core" of Rousseau's theory. They ignore the aspects of his doctrine which might be called democratic poetry and which might reveal his ultimate partisanship on behalf of humanity or even human excellence.

[60]*Democracy*, pp. 546-57.

supposed between the soul's improvement and the betterment of physical conditions."

From the perspective of material prosperity, human beings are "better than brutes" because they are capable of using the soul (that is, what raises them above "the things of the body" and leads them "even to scorn life itself") to meet bodily needs. "In man," Tocqueville says, "an angel teaches a brute how to satisfy its desires."

Tocqueville's point seems to be that it is necessary to satisfy the angel to satisfy the brute. But, in the final paragraph of the chapter, he implies that the angel is responsible not only for a remarkable expansion of productive capacity but for a corresponding or even greater expansion in human need. Does the angel give and make the brute aware of "angelic" needs, the satisfaction of which will elude every brute? Does not this awareness infuse itself even into the pursuit of "brutish" or bodily pleasure?

The classic document of American democracy, *The Federalist*, No. 51, says, in effect, that the fact that men are not angels but want to be produces unlimited human desires. These desires are so powerful that a particular desire can be controlled effectively only by a different and opposing manifestation of that desire. Limited government is only possible once one candidly acknowledges and deduces the consequences of the fact that the desires of individual human beings, insofar as they have an "angelic" dimension, cannot be satisfied. They cannot even be moderated effectively by morality, religion, or any other form of education which aims at the improvement of the soul, but only through strong institutions which forcefully keep the individual in line.

Consider Tocqueville's final paragraph:

> If men ever came to be content with physical things only, it seems likely that they would gradually lose the art of producing them and would end up enjoying them without discernment and without improvement, like animals.

If human beings could enjoy "physical things only . . . without discernment and without improvement like animals . . . they would gradually lose the art of producing them" because they would no longer need to produce them. They would be satisfied with what is readily available. They would be, it seems, infinitely more content than is the brute with the angel in him.

Perhaps only the restless materialist's incoherent pride in his material achievements makes it possible for him not to want to cast out the angel. His pride is even unreasonable if understood to be in the service of the strictly materialistic perspective which is the foundation of self-interest rightly understood. The angel does not produce material satisfaction, after all, but a restless materialist who can never be satisfied.

The problem with the quest for prosperity, for Tocqueville, is that it may well cause the human being, "in the end," to "lose the use of his sublimest faculties."[61] This loss, from a wholly democratic perspective, is perfectly reasonable and even choiceworthy. A democrat cannot really give an argument for why he should want to retain what is "angelic" or distinctly human about himself.[62]

Consider how Tocqueville introduces the chapter of *Democracy* following his moderate praise of "self-interest rightly understood": "However hard one may try to prove that virtue is useful, it will always be difficult to make a man live well if he will not face death."[63] This chapter and the ones immediately thereafter contain a large number of references to the democrat's inability to confront the significance of his awareness of time and death.[64] There Tocqueville also states that democratic striving cannot satisfy or destroy but only distort the human being's longing for immortality. The partisan of self-interest-rightly-understood's voluntary self-enslavement to the results of materialistic calculation appears at first to be the most sober of human decisions. But Tocqueville eventually makes it clear that his adherence to this doctrine is more a foundation for a willful suppression of, than a rational satisfaction of, human desire.

For the democrat, first reason gives way and then will, which apparently cannot sustain itself indefinitely against reason or, more precisely, against "the *general apathy*" which is the product of

---

[61]Ibid., p. 543.

[62]Ibid. Consider in particular p. 535.

[63]Ibid., p. 528.

[64]Ibid., especially chap. 13: "Why the Americans Are Often So Restless in the Midst of Their Prosperity."

reason's destruction of the supports for individuality.[65] According to Tocqueville, the democrat's self-destruction in the service of rational consistency is the final fruit of his unreasonable faith in the power of human reason. He believes that reason will free him from all bondage. He refuses to acknowledge the possibility of "salutary bondage."[66]

The individual's quest for an absolutely rational independence from every form or limitation he has been given actually reduces his power of choice and leads to "anarchy and impotence." In truth, human progress in thought and action depends upon "fixed ideas" about God and human nature. Human reason, by itself, is too weak to establish for certain the first principles which support human striving even in the minds of philosophers. The pressures of "daily life" deprive most human beings of the time or inclination to think profoundly about "primordial" or "metaphysical" questions.[67]

When all "fixed ideas" are abandoned in the name of reason or real personal freedom, all that remains is doubt and confusion about "the matters of greatest importance." Opinions about human freedom, in particular, can no longer be defended. Given both the inability of human reason to replace questionable first principles with unquestionable wisdom and the democrat's inability to recognize the legitimacy of any standards but human ones, individuals have no choice but to "ignobly give up thinking about" the fundamental human questions.[68] In the democrat's language, or "tool for thought," Tocqueville says, "metaphysics and theology will slowly lose ground."[69]

The democratic individual's decision to give up thinking about the foundation of his individuality or human freedom and distinctiveness is ignoble. If in truth everything is in flux or nothing is fixed, there is no reason for him not to be afraid of thought. It cannot show him why thought or courage or any distinctively human quality is worth possessing and defending. It cannot show

---

[65]Ibid., pp. 735-76n. BB. Also pp. 538, 638.
[66]Ibid., p. 434.
[67]Ibid., p. 443.
[68]Ibid., p. 444.
[69]Ibid., p. 478.

him why his human pride can be reasonable. It cannot show him why he ought to assert his humanity. The specter of "limitless independence" revealed by reason undermines the will.[70] More precisely, it shows the individual why it is reasonable to surrender willingly his free will or individuality, to accept the most radical intellectual and political bondage. It shows him why he ought to abandon his attachment to, and concern for, forms and details or distinctions which cause him to see that pantheism is untrue, to see that humanity in general and human beings in particular really exist.[71]

Tocqueville's conclusion is that "[a]ll those who still appreciate the true nature of man's greatness should struggle against it [pantheism]."[72] But, if a society could universally affirm pantheism's truth, it might well really exist in a "state of happiness" (or, better, contentment) which is "uniform and peaceful."[73] Consequently, Tocqueville must agree with Solzhenitsyn: "If, as claimed by humanism, man were born only to be happy, he would not be born to die."[74]

The great enemy of human distinctiveness is the radical incoherence of the doctrine of radical liberation of modern, democratic humanism. This radical liberation, as has been seen, is finally not a "humanism" at all, because it can be achieved only through the overcoming or negation of the human being's existence as a being which exists "in between" beast and God, as part beast and part angel. Eliminating the incoherence of democratic thought while retaining its goal of radical liberation means affirming the truth of pantheism. Because pantheism cannot be true if the existence of human distinctiveness is true, the democratic movement in thought points to the abolition of humanity in the name of a vulgar or materialistic understanding of happiness.

Tocqueville indicates that partisanship on behalf of man's greatness or freedom as something which is choiceworthy for human

---

[70]Ibid., p. 444.
[71]Ibid., pp. 437, 694.
[72]Ibid., p. 452.
[73]Ibid., p. 632.
[74]Aleksandr Solzhenitsyn, *A World Split Apart* (New York: Harper & Row, 1978), p. 57.

beings in its own right is fundamentally a product of pride.[75] He "confess[es] that this genuine love of freedom," which is "a privilege of noble minds which God has fitted to receive it," in truth "defies analysis." It is "something one must *feel* and logic has no part in it."[76] This "feeling" is not the most powerful cause of animation for most human beings.[77] Consequently, the project of Tocqueville and others who "appreciate the true nature of man's greatness" is an aristocratic one: to oppose as far as possible with "art" the "natural" direction of democratic thought and practice.[78] They use every means at their disposal, not only reason[79] (which cannot be abandoned in view of the inability of the will to sustain or control itself without it) but poetry[80] and even naked indignation,[81] to revitalize the aristocratic opinion that human beings exist for more than the enjoyment of vulgar pleasures.[82]

The successful defense of human freedom in democratic times is perhaps the strongest possible evidence that such freedom really exists. It is surely evidence that one's pride in one's freedom is reasonable. Perhaps even the grandeur of efforts of the partisans of freedom, their wholehearted pursuit of a weighty and difficult goal, makes them "worthy of success," even if, by chance or for

---

[75]*Democracy*, p. 632. See p. 461 on the "ardent, *proud*, disinterested love of truth" (emphasis added). Consider also the account of Pascal's failure on p. 461. Did Pascal self-destruct because he could not appreciate his own worth? Did he lack *proper* pride? Was this error the result of a democratic fundamental presupposition?

See also Delba Winthrop, "Race and Freedom in Tocqueville," paper delivered at the 1982 American Political Science Association Convention, p. 23 and n. 34.

[76]Alexis de Tocqueville, *The Old Regime and the French Revolution*, trans. Stuart Gilbert (New York: Anchor Books, 1955), p. 168. See also *Democracy*, p. 695.

[77]See *Democracy*, p. 689. But this feeling can perhaps find its way in "the heart and mind of every man" in a democracy to *some* extent. The universalization of the love of freedom is democracy's true greatness (p. 668). See p. 702: The democratic love of freedom is strong enough to be an effective tool in the statesman's art.

[78]Ibid., p. 674.

[79]The reconciliation of reason or the love of the truth with pride or human partisanship is perhaps what is to be discovered through "the study of Greek and Latin literature" (ibid., pp. 474-76). See also the praise of "Platonic philosophy" on p. 545.

[80]Tocqueville views religion properly understood as the most salutary form of poetry in a democracy. Ibid., pp. 447-49, 288-89, 483 with 486. Political life, it might be said, is better off remaining largely prosaic.

[81]Note the use of the term "pernicious" in *Democracy*, pp. 543-44. Taking pride in the destruction of humanity "revolts" Tocqueville.

[82]Ibid., p. 632.

some reason, they fail.[83]

But whoever means to support effectively this freedom of "dignity" in democratic times is required to make "equality his first principle." He must appear to be, and to a great extent really be, equality's friend. He must moderate his pride in the light of the truth. He must recognize the limits of what he can reasonably hope to accomplish. He cannot deny that democratic thought is largely true if he is to be politically effective and avoid his own destruction, if he is to keep it from becoming wholly true.[84]

---

[83]Ibid., p. 418.

[84]Ibid., pp. 695, 704-05. See Eden, "Tocqueville on Political Realignment and Constitutional Forms," especially p. 26.

5

Political Sociology Versus Speculative Philosophy

Catherine H. Zuckert

Tocqueville's analysis of politics in terms of two fundamental alternatives, aristocracy and democracy, seems itself to lie between two theoretical alternatives: Aristotle's analysis of politics in terms of regime and Hegel's philosophy of history. All three thinkers share the view that the ruling principle or idea in any society has effects that extend far beyond the "form of government" described institutionally.[1] However, the three authors differ fundamentally both on the character or embodiment of the ruling principle in politics and on the necessary historical progression of such regimes or principles.

Where Aristotle insists that there are at least five different pure types of regime as well as several possible kinds of mixtures, Tocqueville argues that there are only two—aristocracy and democracy—defined in the first instance by number, as the rule of the few or the many, but, more fundamentally, as the rule of the rich or the poor. Even these two do not exist as alternatives at any given place and time, moreover, because, Tocqueville insists, we are witnessing an "irresistible" historical movement from aristocracy, the only existing regime in the past, to democracy, i.e., rule based on the conviction that all human beings are essentially or

---

[1]Aristotle speaks of the ruling group (*politeuma*) rather than the ruling principle, but he also observes that every ruling group justifies its power on the basis of a particular understanding of justice or political right. *Politics*, 1280a, 1301a, 1309a.

by nature equal.[2]

In light of this historical progression, Tocqueville dismisses Aristotle as too "antiquated" to be of much interest to modern readers.[3] He makes the grounds for this dismissal and the fundamental difference between his view and Aristotle's explicit in *Democracy in America*:

> The profoundest and most wide-seeing minds of Greece and Rome never managed to grasp the very general but very simple conception of the likeness of all men and of the equal right of all at birth to liberty. They were at pains to show that slavery was natural and would always exist. . . . Jesus Christ had to come down to earth to make all members of the human race understand that they were naturally similar and equal.[4]

If all men are by nature equal, there is no *just* alternative to democracy. The central political issue is not, then, who should rule. The people should rule. The only question remaining for those who have witnessed the development of Western history is whether popular rule will be free or despotic.

Like Hegel, Tocqueville thus sees modern politics as the product of an historical development which limits the political alternatives by bringing to light a new truth. Like Hegel, Tocqueville sees this truth first enunciated in Christian doctrine; and again like Hegel, Tocqueville also sees the need to secularize this truth in the form of a liberal polity.[5] Unlike Hegel, however, Tocqueville sees that there is still uncertainty with regard to the outcome. Men who

---

[2]Aristotle also describes a certain historical progression from monarchy to aristocracy or oligarchy to democracy based primarily on military technology. *Politics*, 1297b16-20. He also teaches that the government must be suited to the people (i.e., to the actual conditions), not only in order to last but also in order to be just. He does not regard the historical progression as irreversible, certainly in the long run. Nor, of course, does he regard democracy as the best regime.

[3]Letter to M. Corcelle, Paris, 6 juillet 1836, from Alexis de Tocqueville, *Oeuvres Complètes* (Paris: Michel Levy, 1867), VI, p. 61. Hereinafter cited as *O.C.*

[4]Alexis de Tocqueville, *Democracy in America*, ed. J.-P. Mayer, trans. George Lawrence (Garden City, N.Y.: Doubleday, Anchor Books, 1969), p. 439. Hereinafter cited as *Democracy*.

[5]See ibid., "Author's Introduction," p. 12, and vol. II, pt. III, chap. 20, "Why Great Revolutions Will Become Rare," pp. 634-45.

recognize the essential equality of all human beings may live in freedom, but the mere recognition of human equality will not suffice to produce that outcome.[6] Indeed, Tocqueville thinks that Hegel's teaching with regard to the necessary course of history undermines the fundamental condition for the perpetuation of liberal democracy—the human being's belief in his ability to control his own fate.

"You undoubtedly know the role philosophy, especially the Hegelian school, has played in Germany over the last fifty years," Tocqueville writes his friend, Corcelle. "[T]his school has become the protégé of the government, because the political consequences of this doctrine are to establish that everything that happens is acceptable and legitimate, that a government merits obedience for the sole reason that it has come into existence." Hegel's doctrine with regard to the necessary course of human history undermines political freedom, Tocqueville suggests, first, by denying the rationality or grounds of all political opposition. Hegelian philosophy received official support because it seemed to support the status quo. But by teaching in effect that might makes right, Tocqueville goes on to observe, Hegelian philosophy finally produced widespread moral and political confusion. "This doctrine ended up giving birth to all the anti-Christian and anti-spiritual schools of thought which have sought to pervert Germany for the last twenty years, . . . and finally to the socialist school which supported the confusion of 1848."[7]

Hegelian philosophy appears to represent an example par excellence of the most dangerous tendencies Tocqueville identifies in the study of history under democratic conditions. Seeing that no individual has much effect on the fate and future of his people,

---

[6]See G.W.F. Hegel, *Philosophy of History*, of course; but also *Philosophy of Right*, especially Part III. Hegel and Tocqueville agree not only that history is moving inevitably toward democracy and that Christianity represented an essential step in that development, but also that the constitutional monarchy is a desirable form of modern state. See Alexis de Tocqueville, *Recollections*, trans. Alexander Teixeira de Mattos (New York: Meridian Books, 1959). Both thinkers emphasize the importance of pluralism in the modern liberal state. Upon examination, however, the similarities prove to be rather superficial. Where Hegel regards the bureaucracy as the embodiment of rationality, Tocqueville worries that centralization will eventually stifle all liberty along with all initiative. Fundamentally, the two thinkers evaluate the role of reason in politics very, very differently.

[7]Letter to M. Corcelle, Bonn, 22 juillet 1854, *O.C.*, pp. 260-61.

Tocqueville worries, democratic historians are apt to deny the efficacy of statesmen or leadership altogether and conclude that events are the product of essentially uncontrollable forces.

> As it becomes extremely difficult to discern and analyze the reasons which, acting separately on the will of each citizen, concur in the end to produce movement in the whole mass, one is tempted to believe that this movement is not voluntary and that societies unconsciously obey some superior dominating force. . . . A cause so vast that it acts at the same time on millions of men, and so strong that it bends them all together in the same direction, may easily seem irresistible. Seeing that one does yield to it, one is very near believing that one cannot stand up to it.[8]

By convincing human beings that they have no real influence over their own fate, democratic historians will destroy the belief in human freedom and hence freedom itself.

How serious is the danger, however? That is, how much effect does Tocqueville actually think any philosophy or any history can have on politics, especially in democratic times? Tocqueville's objections to Hegelian philosophy raise some rather serious questions about the character and effects of his own endeavor in *Democracy in America.* Does not Tocqueville himself argue that we are witnessing an "irresistible" historical movement toward greater and greater equality, and that "great revolutions will become rare?"[9] How exactly does his doctrine differ from Hegelian philosophy? To what extent does Tocqueville think that the human mind can rise above or beyond its particular historical circumstances? And even if the mind can achieve some independence from the

---

[8]*Democracy*, p. 495.

[9]Tocqueville denies ancient "republics" were actually democratic: "What men called 'the people' in the most democratic republics of antiquity was very unlike what we designate by that term. In Athens all the citizens played a part in public affairs, but there were only 20,000 citizens in a population of over 350,000. All the rest were slaves who performed most of the functions of our lower or even middle classes. Athens, then, with her universal suffrage, was no more than an aristocratic republic. . . . The struggle between patricians and plebeians at Rome must be seen in the same light as an internal quarrel between the elder and younger branches of the same family." Ibid., vol. II, pt. I, chap. 15, pp. 475-76.

particular historical conditions, what effect can it have on those circumstances or the course of history? Is the effect of speculative philosophy always or necessarily negative, destructive of public morality and political liberty, as Tocqueville's criticism of the Hegelian school suggests?

Nature, History, and Political Efficacy

If we look at Tocqueville's analysis of *Democracy in America,* the grounds for his presupposing independence of thought are by no means clear. Surely Tocqueville's argument in his introduction that we are witnessing an inevitable historical development toward increasing equality raises fundamental questions about the extent and effectiveness of intentional political action, because this historical development is clearly greater or broader than the intentions and designs of political leaders in the West over generations. Indeed, Tocqueville's argument with regard to this inevitable historical development makes his analysis resemble Hegel's more philosophical interpretation of history.

Nevertheless, there are fundamental differences. Unlike Hegel, who sees the course of history as the unfolding of one fundamental principle (*Geist*), Tocqueville thinks that several relatively independent developments or factors have conjoined to make human beings more and more equal to one another. Through the course of Western history, as Tocqueville sketches it, we see steadily increasing differentiation of function with an accompanying rise of interdependency and consequent fragmentation, hence equalization of power. The causes of the extension of the division of labor are several, however: the commitment to the equality of all men before God which made the Church a more egalitarian route to power and influence than the landed aristocracy; the complication of social relations which resulted from the economic development facilitated by political stability; the consequent need for civil laws (and lawyers); the political competition between monarchs and nobility, which worked to improve both the economic and the political standing of the middle classes, expanding respect and taste for intellectual achievement as a result of both economic development and the Protestant Reformation;

technological innovations which changed the nature of both military combat and the spread of information; and, finally, the discovery of America. The conjunction of these somewhat independent developments means that all modern Western regimes (and with the extension of trade and technology, we might generalize to the non-West also) will be egalitarian. But Tocqueville never reduces the political, economic, moral, or ideological and technical causes to one. He remains an emphatic pluralist.

Precisely because the movement toward greater and greater equality results from a conjunction of several different factors, rather than from one all-controlling driving force or "spirit," he argues, there is room for intentional action to affect the balance or result. Although lawmakers cannot check the movement toward greater and greater human equality, they can guide the interaction of the forces producing the new democratic social condition, if they acquire the requisite knowledge of its causes and effects.

> A law-giver is like a man steering his route over the sea. He, too, can control the ship that bears him, but he cannot change its structure, create winds, or prevent the ocean stirring beneath him.[10]

Although human beings can neither entirely control nor remake the circumstances in which they find themselves, they can rise above them by learning how laws interact with circumstances to form public opinion. That is, of course, the essence of the "new political science" Tocqueville himself promises to teach.

No political outcome is ever the product of one single factor, Tocqueville insists, even human equality. Thus in the preface to Volume II, he states:

> Noticing how many different effects I hold due to equality, [the reader] might suppose that I consider equality the sole cause of everything that is happening now. That would be a very narrow view to attribute to me. There are nowadays a great number of opinions, feelings, and instincts due to circumstances strange, in some cases even

---

[10]Ibid., p. 163-64.

antipathetic to equality.[11]

Like Aristotle, Tocqueville argues that every regime consists of an ordering or conjunction of different parts. The first and most fundamental is the material.

> It will always be easy theoretically to divide each people up into three classes. The first class is composed of the rich. The second of those who, without being rich, are in all respects comfortably off. The third class includes those with little or no property, who live primarily from the work which the other two classes provide for them.[12]

Since those who control the government use it to further their own interest, there will always be grounds for political opposition.

> No one has yet found a political structure that equally favors the growth and prosperity of all the classes composing society. These classes have formed something like distinct nations within the same nation, and experience has proved it almost as dangerous completely to entrust the fate of all to one of these as it is to make one nation arbiter of the destiny of another. When the rich alone rule, the interests of the poor are always in danger; and when the poor make the law, the interests of the rich run great risks.[13]

A nonoppressive government is therefore likely, under modern as well as ancient circumstances, only where there is a sizeable middle class. And a sizeable middle class is likely to develop, Tocqueville argues, only under "democratic" or egalitarian social conditions.

> [I]f you think it profitable to turn man's intellectual and moral activity toward the necessities of physical life and use them to produce well-being, if you think that reason is more use to men than genius, if your object is not to create heroic virtues but rather tranquil habits . . . if in place of a

---

[11]Ibid., p. 417.
[12]Ibid., p. 209.
[13]Ibid., p. 233.

> brilliant society you are content to live in one that is prosperous . . . then it is good to make conditions equal and to establish a democratic government.[14]

Differences among human beings are not limited to their material interests, however, because there is a fundamental, irreducible division within each single human being between body and soul which is reflected in the mind itself:

> [T]hough one part of the human mind inclines to the banal, the material, and the useful, there is another side which is naturally drawn toward the infinite, the spiritual, and the beautiful. Physical needs hold it to the earth, but when these are relaxed it rises of its own accord.[15]

Men will continue to pursue artistic, scientific, even religious endeavors under democratic conditions, Tocqueville thus teaches, even though these endeavors will take markedly democratic or egalitarian forms.

Just as Tocqueville's differences from Aristotle stem from his view of human nature, so do his differences from Hegel. Where Hegel teaches that human beings come to recognize their freedom only through an historical development which shows them that mind controls nature by actually reshaping nature technologically to accommodate human needs, Tocqueville insists that freedom exists in all ages, aristocratic as well as democratic, because the human soul is always, by nature, potentially free from simply material concerns. The outcome of history is uncertain because human beings are truly, by nature, free. Since material concerns are primary, however, it is possible that human freedom will be stamped out in modern ages. Whether human beings will remain free depends, indeed, on whether individuals learn the organizational techniques to defend themselves, morally and intellectually as well as politically and economically, from pressures to conform to the opinion of the ruling majority. Human beings can rise above their circumstances, but there is no necessity that they do so. Rather than teach

---

[14]Ibid., p. 245.
[15]Ibid., p. 457.

the primacy of mind over nature, Tocqueville emphasizes that narrow concentration on the requirements of self-preservation may reduce human life to the level of physical necessity.

Whether human beings remain free depends on the form of political organization, and the form of political organization is not determined by either nature or recognition of the truth about human nature. Aristocracy is contrary to both the deepest instincts and the truth of human nature:

> An aristocratic body is composed of a certain number of citizens who, without being elevated very far above the mass of the citizen, are nevertheless permanently stationed above them. . . . One can conceive of nothing more contrary to nature and to the secret instincts of the human heart than subjection of this sort.[16]

Yet Tocqueville observes that until modern times, there were none but aristocratic governments to be found.[17]

But the fact that government has been instituted contrary to the natural order does not prove the freedom or power of the mind or human will over physical or historical circumstances. On the contrary, thought itself seems to have been bound by the extant political order.

> All the great writers of antiquity were either members of the aristocracy of masters or, at the least, saw that aristocracy in undisputed possession before their eyes. Their minds roamed free in many directions but were blinded there.[18]

Christianity did not suffice to show men that they were by nature equal, however. Circumstantial developments beyond human control were also necessary to set the stage not only for the emergence and spread of Christianity but also for the emergence of later, more skeptical and egalitarian, philosophic doctrines.

---

[16]Ibid., p. 399.
[17]Cf. Machiavelli, *Prince*, trans. Robert M. Adams (New York: W. W. Norton, 1977), chap. VI, p. 17: ". . . since men don't really believe in anything new till they have had solid experience of it, . . ."
[18]*Democracy*, p. 439.

> At the time when Christianity appeared on earth, Providence, which no doubt was preparing the world for its reception, had united a great part of mankind, like an immense flock, under the scepter of the Caesars. The men composing this multitude were of many different sorts, but they all had this in common, that they obeyed the same laws, and each of them was so small and weak compared to the greatness of the emperor that they all seemed equal in comparison to him. One must recognize that this new and singular condition of humanity disposed men to receive the general truths preached by Christianity, and this serves to explain the quick and easy way in which it then penetrated the human spirit.[19]

When the empire broke up, however, "each nation reverted to its former individuality . . . [and there] soon developed within these nations an infinite hierarchy of ranks."[20] Although Christianity did not lose sight of its central tenets, it adapted these as much as possible to prevailing aristocratic conditions.

Only when the social, economic, and political conditions changed, could a new, more democratic philosophic understanding of man's condition emerge. Indeed, Tocqueville suggests, philosophic questioning of the existing order actually followed the gradual breaking up or transformation of that order.

> The sixteenth-century reformers subjected some of the dogmas of the ancient faith to individual reason, but they still refused to allow all the others to be discussed by it. In the seventeenth century Bacon, in natural science, and Descartes, in philosophy strictly so called, abolished accepted formulas, destroyed the dominion of tradition, and upset the authority of masters. The eighteenth-century philosopher turned this same principle into a general rule. . . . Finally [Descartes'] method came out of the schools, worked its way into society, and became the common coin of thought.[21]

---

[19]Ibid., p. 446.
[20]Ibid.
[21]Ibid., p. 431.

Tocqueville may not agree with Hegel that mind transforms nature, but he does seem to agree that human beings come to learn the truth about human nature only through history, after the fact.

But if the truth is not politically effective, if human perception of the "truth" depends on the historical circumstances, what is the basis of Tocqueville's own new "science"? Is his "science" not as much a reflection of "democratic" social conditions as ancient philosophy was of "aristocratic"?

Upon further examination, we shall see, Tocqueville's recourse to "nature" proves to be problematic, because Tocqueville himself admits that no one actually knows the structure or character of the human "soul." Insofar as Tocqueville's science then comes to rest on "the effective truth" (i.e., what people are willing to believe), his "science" becomes very much tied to prevailing democratic conditions; for, as Tocqueville himself stresses, what most people believe reflects their immediate circumstances. Very few are able to see beyond.[22]

By highlighting the role and indirect means of the formation of public opinion, Tocqueville gives an unparalleled account of the way in which liberal democracies actually work. His analysis of *Democracy in America* thus provides an excellent guide for public policy—within the framework of liberal democracy, for the sake of perpetuating liberal democracy. Because his analysis is so tied to prevailing egalitarian conditions, however, his political science does not reveal the full range of political or intellectual possibilities. Nor does it provide an adequate account of its own philosophic foundation.

Tocqueville's Science of "Mores"

Believing that they are essentially the equals of all others, Tocqueville argues, people in democratic times are unwilling to take many propositions on the basis of authority. Following if not reading Descartes, they will rather attempt to decide all issues on the basis of their own experience. Such popularized "empiricism"

---

[22]Ibid.

and resistance to authority "on principle" will not, however, destroy all dogma or intellectual authority.

No man, not even a great philosopher, can actually examine all the opinions upon which he acts each day, Tocqueville observes.

> Anyone who undertook to go into everything himself could give but little time or attention to each question. He would keep his mental faculties in a state of perpetual excitement, which would prevent his going deeply into any truth or being firmly convinced of anything at all.

Even the greatest philosopher thus limits himself to pursuing the most important or fundamental questions: "[T]he conception men have of God, of His relations with the human race, of the nature of their soul, and of their duties to their fellows."[23] Very few will spend much time or effort on philosophy, however.

> Only minds singularly free from the ordinary preoccupations of life, penetrating, subtle, and trained to think, can at the cost of much time and trouble sound the depths of these truths that are so necessary. . . . Studies of this sort are far above the average capacities of men, and even if most men were capable of such inquiries, they clearly would not have time for them.[24]

Over the centuries, moreover, even the philosophers have proved unable to answer these questions determinatively.

> Indeed we see that philosophers themselves are almost always surrounded by uncertainties, . . . and that for all their efforts they have done no more than discover a small number of contradictory ideas on which the mind of man has been ceaselessly tossed for thousands of years without ever firmly grasping the truth or even finding mistakes that are new.[25]

Tocqueville thus attempts to found his new "science" on a philosophical skepticism. The "truth" is not effective in politics:

---

[23]Ibid., pp. 442-43.
[24]Ibid., p. 443.
[25]Ibid.

Certainly we cannot see its effect because we do not, in truth, possess it. No one knows, indubitably, whether God or the soul exists, what the character of the cosmos or universe is, and hence the *true* foundation of man's duty, if any, to others.

What, then, of the natural equality on the basis of which Tocqueville dismisses the ancients? Like Hobbes, Tocqueville seems finally to be committed to equality less on the basis of similarities in physical power or mental ability than on the basis of the unwillingness of most human beings to admit real or essential inequality.[26] What, then, of the existence of the soul, however, on which Tocqueville ultimately seems to base his hopes for the perpetuation of human liberty?

Whether human beings can ever learn the truth or not, Tocqueville observes, they cannot act without opinions. They do not automatically or instinctively react to external stimuli. Materialism is even less well founded on empirical observation or knowledge than the general principles of the Christian religion.

Since we can only have opinions where we have no knowledge, Tocqueville concludes, we ought to prefer those opinions which leave future possibilities open to those which destroy human liberty, in effect or in fact, by convincing men that they are not free.

If people living under democratic social conditions really try to investigate each question for themselves, Tocqueville observes, they will condemn themselves to indecision and inaction.

> There is hardly any human action, however private it may be, which does not result from some very general conception men have of God, of His relations with the human race, of the nature of their soul, and of their duties to their fellows. . . . It is therefore of immense importance to men to have fixed ideas about [such matters] . . . for doubt about these first principles would leave all their actions to chance and condemn them, more or less, to anarchy and impotence.[27]

---

[26]Cf. *Leviathan*, pt. I, chap. 13 with chap. 15: "If nature therefore have made men equal, that equality is to be acknowledged; *or if nature have made men unequal, yet because men that think themselves equal will not enter into conditions of peace but upon equal terms, such equality must be admitted*" (emphasis added).
[27]*Democracy*, p. 443.

Unlike Rousseau, Tocqueville does not advocate the propagation of a "civil religion," however, because he sees that the anti-authoritarian bias of men living in democratic conditions will make them resist any officially sponsored creed or code.[28]

But if it is impossible for human beings to act without presupposing some general ideas concerning God (or the character of the universe), their souls (or the character of their existence as individuals), and the moral obligations to others, how or where do most skeptical citizens of modern democracies then acquire such ideas, if they cannot generate them for themselves and yet will not accept them on authority from their intellectual betters? They tend to adopt the opinion of the majority, Tocqueville answers; and once this opinion is formed, it will prove extraordinarily difficult to change.

People who regard themselves as, essentially, the equals of all others will not tend to accept the statements of other individuals "on authority," he argues, but that resistance to authority will not prevent them from perceiving their own limits. When they know that they themselves do not know the answer to a question and cannot find it, they will therefore look for assistance. If all are essentially equal, they are apt to reason, won't most people be right most of the time? They will, therefore, be apt to adopt the opinion of the greatest number.

Although "the truth" has no perceptible political effect, primarily because we do not know what "the truth" is, what people think is true, does. Tocqueville's political science could, indeed, be described primarily as the study of the origins and effects of such popular opinions or even less articulate attitudes and sentiments (the "*moeurs*").[29] And this shift from seeking the truth about human affairs to discovering the origins and effects of what most men think is true has some paradoxical results.

---

[28]See Catherine H. Zuckert, "Tocqueville on the Role of Religion in American Democracy," *Review of Politics*, April 1981, vol. 43, pp. 259-80, for a lengthier discussion of this difference.

[29]"The importance of mores is a universal truth to which study and experience continually bring us back. I find it occupies the central position in my thoughts; all my ideas come back to it in the end" (*Democracy*, p. 308).

Why Free Political Institutions Do Not Foster Free Thought in America

Contrary to general impressions about the power of "Madison Avenue," the fact that political order depends ultimately on the opinions or "mores" of most people does not make political order either very manipulatable or very unstable. Once egalitarian conditions are established, Tocqueville argues, basic popular attitudes will be exceedingly difficult to change. After the revolution overthrowing the old landed aristocracy, the institution of a free press and freedom of speech will not have much effect.

The Cartesian skepticism characteristic of people living in democratic conditions would seem to undermine their religious convictions. If they judge everything solely on the basis of their own experience, they are certainly likely to doubt the existence of anything supernatural.

> Seeing that they are successful in resolving unaided all the little difficulties they encounter in practical affairs, they are easily led to the conclusion that everything in the world can be explained and that nothing passes beyond the limits of intelligence. Thus they are ready to deny anything which they cannot understand. Hence they have little faith in anything extraordinary and an almost invincible distaste for the supernatural.[30]

For this reason, Tocqueville argues, people living in democratic conditions will not be receptive to new religious inspiration or dogma. At the very most, under exceptional circumstances like those in America, they will retain the basic elements of their traditional faith.

According to Tocqueville, two somewhat separate circumstances have prevented Americans from taking their Cartesian skepticism to its logical conclusion. One is their Puritan heritage; the other, the fact that they never actually experienced a democratic revolution. The strength of the Puritan heritage is, indeed, dependent on

---

[30]Ibid., p. 430.

the absence of a democratic revolution.

> Every revolution must shake ancient beliefs, sap authority, and cloud shared ideas. So any revolution, to a greater or lesser extent, throws men back on themselves and opens to each man's view an almost limitless empty space.[31]

The Americans never really experienced a truly democratic revolution because the immigrants were basically equal when they arrived in the New World. A landed aristocracy was never really established, even in the South, so there was no truly aristocratic power to revolt against. The "American Revolution" is more accurately described as a "War of Independence," fought against a foreign power.

But only those aspects of the Puritan faith that were compatible with existing egalitarian conditions lasted. In attempting to institute a literalistic biblical theocracy, the Puritans transported "the legislation of a rough, half-civilized people . . . into the midst of an educated society with gentle mores."[32] So unsuited were such laws to the character of the people and the circumstances in which they found themselves, that the Puritans themselves did not live up to the severity of their own codes; "[T]he death penalty has never been more frequently prescribed by the laws," Tocqueville notes, "or more seldom carried out."[33]

The basic tenets of the Christian faith—the existence of one God, ruling all men as His children, as equals—are perfectly compatible with equal social conditions, however. Indeed, the fact that members of virtually all the sects who came seeking freedom in a new land could agree on these basic tenets as well as the fact that they were taught by advocates of liberty of the individual conscience and rule by the people rather than by representatives of a state church gave them additional strength, because they were perceived to be the opinion of the majority, freely adopted. The establishment of freedom of speech and a free press in the colonies did not, therefore, undermine the faith of the general populace.

---

[31]Ibid., p. 432.
[32]Ibid., p. 42.
[33]Ibid.

When first instituted, freedom of speech may shake existing beliefs, Tocqueville admits, but after a while people see that no one can give an indubitable proof or answer to such basic questions as the existence of God. Seeing the "experts" disagree and tiring of the interminable arguments, most will conclude that one opinion is just as good (or as bad) as any other, so they might as well stick to their own. Since their "own" was some form of Christianity to which they saw their neighbors also subscribed, most Americans have continued to adhere to the basic tenets of the Christian faith. And, Tocqueville concludes, this generalized faith is *the* reason for the preservation of liberty in America!

Tocqueville's teaching with regard to the central importance of religion in preserving liberty in America is paradoxical because, as he describes it, religion works to preserve liberty, fundamentally, by curtailing thought.

> If the spirit of the Americans were free of all impediment, one would soon find among them the boldest innovators and the most implacable logicians in the world. But American revolutionaries are obliged ostensibly to profess a certain respect for Christian morality and equity, and that does not allow them easily to break the laws when those are opposed to the executions of their designs. . . . [As a result] till now no one in the United States has dared to profess the maxim that everything is allowed in the interests of society, . . .[34]

The commitment of the American public to limited government thus reflects the confining effects of general religious beliefs on the mind and imagination.

> In the United States it is not only mores that are controlled by religion, but its sway extends even over reason. . . . Christianity reigns without obstacles, by universal consent. . . . So the human spirit never sees an unlimited field before itself. . . . Before innovating, it is forced to accept certain primary assumptions and to submit its boldest

---

[34]Ibid., p. 292.

> conceptions to certain formalities which retard and check it. The imagination of the Americans, therefore, even in its greatest aberrations, is circumspect and hesitant. . . .[35]

Political experimentation in the United States is restrained by almost unquestioning acceptance of the freedom and integrity of the individual conscience, respect for the lives and liberties of all human beings, a sense of the limitations of all human knowledge, and hence the desirability of limiting all human power, even the power of the majority itself.

Such self-limitation is essential for the maintenance of limited government and hence individual freedom in a democracy, Tocqueville argues. Where all power is ultimately derived from the people (as James Madison argues in *The Federalist* No. 39), the majority always has the power to change the laws. Americans have shown how it is possible to avoid the political tyranny of the majority by adopting a constitutional separation of powers.[36] Such institutional checks on the power of the majority, however, will last only so long as the majority itself is convinced that such limitations are desirable.

Tocqueville's insistence on the importance of Puritanic mores in preserving liberty in America represents, in effect, a two-pronged critique of Montesquieu. Montesquieu had argued that eighteenth-century England represented a new form of government in which the liberty of all was secured through the separation and balancing of the powers of government among the three classes or principles of the older, purer regimes—the people (whose "virtues" constituted the basis of republican government), the aristocracy (whose honor provided the ruling principle of the feudal monarchy), and the monarch (or potential despot). Montesquieu also argued that the morals of such a liberal regime will necessarily be somewhat corrupt, because of the freeing of the economic drive from all public moral restraints and the mixing of cultures and ideas as a result of international trade.[37] The American example is so important for

---

[35]Ibid.
[36]Ibid., vol. I, pt. II, p. 253.
[37]Montesquieu, *Spirit of the Laws*, trans. Thomas Nugent (New York: Hafner, 1949), pt. I, chaps. 11, 17.

Tocqueville, in part, because the Constitution of the United States shows that it is possible to preserve freedom through a separation of powers on a wholly democratic base.

> I have always considered what is called a mixed government to be a chimera. There is in truth no such thing as a mixed government . . . since in any society one finds in the end some principle of action that dominates all the others.[38]

Although Tocqueville thinks that there is an enduring division in every society between the rich and the poor, those who would like to extend the power of the state and those who would like to limit it, he also believes that the conflict will come to some sort of resolution. One party will prove that it is more powerful than the other. Eighteenth-century England was, in fact, an aristocracy with some democratic elements. And like all aristocracies in the modern era, England is also gradually becoming more and more democratic. If the possibility of liberty depends upon a mixture of regimes or a balance of classes, the chances of maintaining liberty in the modern world are slight.

The influence of Puritanic mores in American republic shows, moreover, that a free people need not be corrupt. On the contrary, Tocqueville suggests, the interaction of commercial interest with inherited Christian principles can produce a very strict moral code.[39] Those who calculate their self-interest properly will see that community action is to their own long-term benefit; and where such calculations fail (as in justifying military service), minimal religious beliefs will suffice to make human beings wonder at least about the advisability of endangering the chance that they may attain eternal salvation for a more immediate, but obviously much shorter-term, pleasure.[40]

True, Tocqueville admits, citizens of ancient "republics" sacrificed more for their nation than modern democrats are apt to, but the concern these leading citizens displayed for their honor is but one sign that these ancient "republics" were actually aristocracies, not

---

[38]*Democracy*, p. 251.

[39]See especially ibid., vol. II, pt. III, chaps. 9-11.

[40]Cf. ibid., vol. II, pt. II, chap. 9.

truly democracies. Like all aristocracies, the ancient "republics" were based on conquest and forced slavery, not the consent of the people. The virtues of their leaders were largely military, and the great learning of some of these societies was confined to the few.[41] The signal characteristic of modern "democracy" is that it operates through public opinion on the basis of a near-universal consensus on the standard of political right.

Nevertheless, Tocqueville presents the rule of public opinion under democratic conditions as a new form of tyranny, at least potentially, worse than any of the various forms of physical oppression in the past! Indeed, Tocqueville takes the very consensus upon the general Christian principles he argues is the essential condition for the preservation of liberty in America to be a sign of the extreme suppression of freedom of thought there as well.

> I know no country in which, speaking generally, there is less independence of mind and true freedom of discussion than in America. . . . In America the majority has enclosed thought within a formidable fence. . . . In Spain the Inquisition was never able to prevent the circulation of books contrary to the majority religion. The American majority's sway extends further and has rid itself even of the thought of publishing such books.[42]

The power of the majority is greater than the power of any past tyrant, Tocqueville suggests, precisely because it is so soft, involving no forceful oppression at all.

> Under the absolute government of a single man, despotism, to reach the soul, clumsily struck at the body, and the soul, escaping from such blows, rose gloriously above it; but in democratic republics . . . [t]he master no longer says: "Think like me or you die." He does say: "You are free not to think as I do; you can keep your life and property and all; but from this day you are a stranger among us. . . ."[43]

---

[41]Ibid., pt. I, chap. 15, p. 476.
[42]Ibid., pp. 255-56.
[43]Ibid.

Secured by a limited government, the political freedom of the Americans seems, paradoxically, to depend upon a more subtle, but more thorough and insidious, form of intellectual oppression. But as such, the political liberty of the Americans appears to be rather empty, formal rather than actual. What is the political liberty secured by limited government, after all, but freedom from external oppression or interference? If that "freedom" is based on a deeper and more thorough silencing of all dissent or opposition to the ruling part of society (the majority), it would seem to have little actual value or existence.

In fact, Tocqueville seems to overstate the power of majority opinion over the integrity of the individual soul itself. He observes, for example, that "[o]ne finds unbelievers in America."[44] Perhaps they are unable to publish, but they are still able to think. The danger that concerns him seems less to be the absence of actual disagreement, dissent, and freedom of thought, and more that the majority will no longer recognize the evils of oppression because the oppression is not explicit, physical, external, or exercised over the many by the few.

> Absolute monarchies brought despotism into dishonor; we must beware lest democratic republics rehabilitate it, and that while they make it more oppressive toward some, they do not rid it of its detestable and degrading character in the eyes of the greatest number.[45]

The difficulty of convincing a majority that they are exercising tyrannical power over public debate without explicit prohibitions or the use of force is far different from the actual ability of the majority to form or suppress dissent by invading the soul itself. The "tyranny" of majority opinion may be more difficult to resist or overthrow, because it becomes difficult to find allies to resist it. But such tyranny is not different in kind; it is recognizable, at least by its victims, as such. The unprecedented danger posed by the soft tyranny of the majority seems ultimately to be that by cutting off a dissenter from all effective human communication, without

---

[44]Ibid.
[45]Ibid., p. 256.

explicitly repressing him or his opinions in any way, the majority will lead the individual to despair not merely of having an effect but even of his own sanity.

Tocqueville does not give us any examples of such despair, and in Volume II he argues that the circumstances which have curtailed the American mind and imagination do not exist on the European continent. In close communication with Europe, American "dissenters" are not apt to feel themselves utterly alone. If Tocqueville has overstated the danger of the "tyranny of the majority" in his analysis of *Democracy in America* in Volume I, it would seem that he may also have overstated the dangers of materialistic "social science" in Volume II as well. He may have overstated the power of public opinion altogether. If so, the political alternatives may be greater than his "science" of "mores" would allow.

Why Democratic Social Conditions *per se* Do Not Discourage Intellectual Endeavor

Where landed aristocracies have to be overthrown by force, ancient religious beliefs will be thrown into question, especially in nations where the Church has been closely identified with the old political order. When free speech and a free press are introduced into such circumstances, they will have a somewhat different effect than they did in America. Here old beliefs will be even further shaken. So when people tire of the interminable debate on first principles which ensues, they will not have any "beliefs" of their own to which to return or to adhere.

After the revolution, Europeans will therefore be apt to act more exclusively on their materialistic or class interests.

> When opinions are in doubt, men end by clinging only to instincts and material interests, which by nature are more visible, tangible, and permanent than opinions. It is a very difficult question to decide whether aristocracy or democracy governs best. But . . . [t]his is a self-established truth which it is needless to discuss: you are rich and I am poor.[46]

---

[46]Ibid., pp. 187-88.

Such class politics might result in leveling oppression. "It is possible to conceive a people without castes, hierarchy, or classes, in which the law, recognizing no privileges, divides inheritances equally, and which, at the same time, has neither culture nor freedom."[47] But, Tocqueville urges, such an intellectual desert is by no means a necessary consequence of the democratic revolution.

On the contrary, where hereditary privileges are destroyed and each person is allowed to make his own way, individuals will be apt to compete in intellectual endeavors much the way they do in economic enterprise. Indeed, intellectual and economic competition are fundamentally related.

> Where there is no more hereditary wealth, class privilege, or prerogatives of birth, and when every man derives his strength from himself alone, it becomes clear that the chief source of disparity between the fortunes of men lies in the mind.[48]

Having discovered the value of intellectual endeavor, many will enter the fray.

> As soon as the crowd begins to take an interest in the labors of the mind it finds out that to excel in some of them is a powerful aid to the acquisition of fame, power, or wealth. Restless ambition born of equality turns to this as to all other directions. The number of those studying science, literature, and the arts becomes immense. There is vast activity in the realms of the mind; everyone tries to blaze a trail for himself and attract public attention.[49]

The materialistic interests characteristic of men living under democratic conditions will thus encourage intellectual investigations.[50]

---

[47]Ibid., p. 456.
[48]Ibid., p. 458.
[49]Ibid.
[50]"[T]he example of the Americans does not prove that a democratic people can have no aptitude or taste for science, literature, or the arts." Ibid. (vol. II, pt. I, chap. 7, p. 454). Rather: "It may be assumed that the more democratic, enlightened, and free a people is, the greater will be the number of these selfish admirers of scientific genius, and the more profit will be made out of discoveries immediately applicable to industry, bringing renown and even power to their inventors" (chap. 10, p. 463).

Competition for place and profit will, of course, affect the character of intellectual endeavor in a democracy. For example, where everyone is busy trying to earn a living, "the darting speed of a quick, superficial mind is at a premium, while slow, deep thought is excessively undervalued."[51] When science is pursued largely for its practical applications, moreover, the theoretical foundations may be neglected.

Nevertheless, Tocqueville thinks that, given the opportunity, some people will always pursue the most fundamental questions.

> Democracy may not lead men to study science for its own sake, but it does immensely increase the number of those who do study it. Nor is it credible that among so great a multitude a speculative genius should not from time to time arise inspired by the love of truth alone. Such a one will surely penetrate the deepest mysteries of nature, whatever be the spirit of his time and place. His spirit's flight needs no help; it is enough if it is not impeded.[52]

The competition of so great a number to discover something of practical application will itself probably produce theoretical innovation also. "[W]ith new experiments every day, it is almost impossible that very general laws should not frequently be brought to light."[53] At the very least, the new data constantly generated would seem to require continual revision of accepted theory. Democratic social conditions will not, therefore, of themselves destroy freedom of thought.

Scientific investigations are too important in satisfying the materialistic desires of people living under democratic conditions to make it prudent or desirable for any government to attempt to ban them. The problem Tocqueville sees seems, rather, to be that scientific searches for general laws, particularly with regard to human behavior, will undermine the conditions for political freedom by undermining the individual's belief in his own ability to control his fate.

---

[51]Ibid., p. 461.
[52]Ibid., p. 463.
[53]Ibid.

The danger arises first from observation of the apparent facts of human existence under democratic conditions.

> [W]hen all citizens are independent of one another and each is weak, no one can be found exercising very great or, more particularly, very lasting influence over the masses. At first sight individuals appear to have no influence at all over them, and society would seem to progress on its own by the free and spontaneous action of all its members.[54]

The virtues, vices, particular characteristics, and actions of individuals do have an effect on what happens, Tocqueville insists, but these effects are each very small and hence difficult to identify.

Scholars working in democratic conditions are not apt to have either the taste or the leisure for the meticulous, detailed studies necessary to show the influence individuals actually exercise on the course of history. In the first place, such scholars will be apt to work rapidly, anxious to make a name and fortune for themselves as quickly as possible. They will be attracted to general ideas in conducting their historical studies, first, because such general ideas make judgment about particular events much easier, quicker, and hence more efficient. They will also be tempted to generalize about human behavior, because looking at the people around them, they see that they are, in fact, very similar. General causes or explanations seem to fit the facts.

Nevertheless, Tocqueville warns, the promulgation of such general, impersonal laws or causes of the course of human history can have pernicious political results.

> If this doctrine of fatality, so attractive to those who write history in democratic periods, passes from authors to readers, infects the whole mass of the community, and takes possession of the public mind, it will soon paralyze the activities of modern society.[55]

Will freedom of thought thus undermine its own political preconditions? Not necessarily, Tocqueville argues. The potentially

---

[54]Ibid., p. 494.
[55]Ibid., p. 496.

pernicious effects of deterministic theories of history can be checked or counteracted through constitutional legislation establishing a system of "decentralized administration."

Americans are much less attracted than the French to abstract theories of politics or history, Tocqueville observes, because their experience in practical politics shows them the simplification involved in all such generalizations.[56] People living in democratic conditions judge first and foremost by their own experience. And by participating in the policy-making deliberations of a local council, citizens learn that by working with others they can have a concrete effect on their own fate and circumstances. Such an experience gives them not only the confidence to undertake projects, public as well as private, on their own, outside the state apparatus, but also the organizational means with which to resist the tyranny of majority opinion. It is, after all, much easier to stand with a group of like-minded individuals against the majority than it is to stand alone. So Tocqueville concludes, "The morals and intelligence of a democratic people would be in as much danger as its commerce and industry if ever a government wholly usurped the place of private associations."[57]

The problem is not that Hegelians or Marxists will convince people that they have no power to affect the course of history, because that course is predetermined, so much as the fact that people will not actually have any power to determine their own fate unless they learn to organize. Practical popular political education is much more effective than speculative philosophic or historical doctrine. What people believe, after all, largely reflects the reality they see around them.

Free thought and free politics are not, then, necessarily antithetical. The greatest check or limit on government is what people can do for themselves. Religion is helpful insofar as it checks the debilitating effects of skeptical doubt. Nevertheless, in Volume II, Tocqueville suggests that the Puritanic mores of the

---

[56]Ibid., vol. II, pt. I, chap. 4, pp. 441-42.

[57]See Catherine H. Zuckert, "New and Old Federalism," *Review of Politics*, vol. 45 (July 1983), No. 2, pp. 421-32, for a more detailed account of Tocqueville's understanding of the "political effects" of decentralized administration.

Americans with the corresponding informal limitations on thought and imagination may not be necessary to check the growth of government under democratic conditions. In Part IV, he even goes so far as to list the Church as one of the institutions most likely to be centralized under State control (although in Volume I he argued that the influence of religion depends upon the separation of Church and State).[58] In the end, freedom of speech and press, formal procedure, protection of property rights, and decentralized institutions, all appear to be more important in fostering liberal popular political attitudes than the informal propagation of Christian principles (which he neglects even to mention).[59]

Conclusion

If democratic legislators do not establish institutions which give their people practical experience in politics, Tocqueville warns, there may well be serious consequences.

> When social conditions are equal, every man tends to live apart, centered in himself and forgetful of the public. Should democratic legislators not seek to correct this fatal tendency . . . it might happen . . . that . . . the unruly passions of certain men, aided by the foolish selfishness and pusillanimity of the greater number, will in the end subject the fabric of society to strange vicissitudes.[60]

Tocqueville does not even speculate on the nature of these "vicissitudes." Prompted by the "unruly passions" of a few, these future possibilities would seem to include "aristocracy" or the rule of the many by a few on the basis of superior force.[61]

Although Tocqueville concludes that he is "convinced that *in the age now opening before us,* those who try to base authority on privilege and aristocracy will fail,"[62] he cannot finally (or

---

58 *Democracy*, vol. II, pt. IV, chap. 5, p. 681.
59 Ibid., chap. 6, pp. 697-99.
60 Ibid., p. 639.
61 Ibid., Introduction, pp. 12, 446, 704-05.
62 Ibid., p. 695. Emphasis added.

consistently) disallow the possibility of the eventual reemergence of aristocracy on the grounds of historical necessity, because Tocqueville himself sees no historical *necessity*.[63] The progress of Western history toward greater and greater equality is an act of "Providence," Tocqueville repeats; determination of the course of history, he thus suggests, exceeds the powers of the human intellect.[64] In fact, we see, Tocqueville rests his case for the "impossibility" of maintaining feudal aristocracy on his observation of existing conditions in Europe. When human beings are more alike than unlike, they will not willingly tolerate the rule of most by a few others. But, he finally admits, these conditions can change, if not within the immediate or foreseeable future.[65]

If the actual political possibilities are greater than Tocqueville would have his readers believe, so are the questions of political philosophy, for it is by no means clear that democracy is simply superior to aristocracy. Tocqueville himself certainly does not claim as much. On the contrary, he poses two alternatives:

> Do you wish to raise mankind to an elevated and generous view of the things of this world? Do you want to inspire

---

[63]For this reason, Marvin Zetterbaum, in *Tocqueville and the Problem of Democracy* (Stanford: Stanford University Press, 1967), concludes that Tocqueville's insistence on the necessary course of history constitutes a part of a "public" teaching which he, Tocqueville, does not really think is true. I have disputed this thesis elsewhere ("Tocqueville on Religion") on the grounds that "public teaching" is contrary to Tocqueville's own argument concerning the sources of public belief or opinion under democratic conditions. By presenting his understanding of democracy in terms of a description (explicitly modified) of the United States rather than a response to Montesquieu and Rousseau, Tocqueville does attempt to capitalize on the persuasive advantages of "experience" in contrast to theory.

[64]Here, of course, is the source of the fundamental disagreement between Tocqueville and Hegel, because Hegel claims that the course of history is intelligible. Tocqueville's response that Hegel's teaching of "reason in history" has deleterious effects does not in itself constitute an adequate response. If Tocqueville can show that human beings can intentionally change the course of history, as he wishes to do through his practical teaching, such a change would constitute a response.

[65]Hannah Arendt, in *The Origins of Totalitarianism* (New York: Harcourt, Brace & World, 1951), pp. 1-38, suggests that the Nazis arose out of circumstances Tocqueville could explain, the isolation of individuals in the middle class, and a consequent feeling of ineffectiveness, especially on the part of intellectuals. But Tocqueville would not seem to have predicted the emergence of something like Nazi doctrine; i.e., a political ideology emphasizing the *natural inequality* of human beings on the basis of birth (race). Neither, it seems, would Hegel's philosophy; so the actual course of European history, ironically, puts both historical doctrines seriously into question.

> men with a certain scorn of material goods?. . . Do you desire poetry, renown, and glory? Do you set out to organize a nation so that it will have a powerful influence over all others? . . . [D]o not support democratic government. . . .[66]

If, on the other hand, you wish to foster peace and prosperity, he advises, you should become a democrat.

Tocqueville himself finally appears to prefer democracy to aristocracy and so seeks primarily to see how liberty can be maintained under egalitarian conditions on the grounds of the natural equality of all human beings. Yet if, as he himself asserts, no one has actually been able to prove the existence of God or any other sort of enduring order, whether individual human beings have a soul or what that soul is, it becomes rather difficult to appeal to a doctrine of natural right, because no one really knows what is "by nature" or what is the character of the natural order.

In the face of uncertainty about the fundamental questions, Tocqueville seems to appeal to the "effective" or the "practical" truth. But there are difficulties at this level also, because, as he repeatedly admits in different places, force can be effective. It can, for example, stamp out human liberty.

Tocqueville's science of mores thus appears to be very much limited to democratic conditions. Where people are observably more like than unlike in condition, they are not apt *willingly* to accept the rule of a few who claim to be better "by nature" or even by virtue simply of superior wealth. Whether they are able to resist oppression will depend upon their political experience, especially their ability to organize. And where government rests ultimately on popular consent, the opinion of the majority will be the dominant power. Where the majority is not in control, even where minorities despair of ever getting a majority on their side, it is not so clear that their opinion will be decisive.[67] In stressing the power of public

---

[66]*Democracy*, p. 245.

[67]Ibid. In vol. I, pt. II, pp. 193-95, Tocqueville argues that freedom of association is not dangerous in the United States because every group acts in the hope of bringing a majority over to its side. Should a group lose all hope of securing majority backing, he observes, it organizes "not to convince but to fight" (p. 194). And, he admits, such groups exist in Europe.

opinion virtually to the exclusion of physical force, Tocqueville's science seems to reflect the characteristic myopia of the majority he himself points out.

Upon examination, moreover, the potential "tyranny of the majority" does not appear to be so different in kind from older forms of oppressive rule as Tocqueville would have it appear. The majority may, to be sure, have difficulty recognizing its own oppressive power, both because that power is exercised by many rather than by a few and because it is exercised informally, through social convention, rather than explicitly with force. Aristocrats of the ancient regime did not think that their rule rested fundamentally on force either. Ruling groups tend, indeed, to convince themselves that they are right. So long as those under them see no hope of overthrowing the existing regime, they are apt to acquiesce in silence.

Tocqueville's admission that we do not, in fact, know either the course of human history or the enduring characteristics of human nature means, I think, that he finally distinguishes democracy and aristocracy as the rule, respectively, of consent and force. But the difficulty of distinguishing forced (or despairing) acquiescence from passive consent makes this distinction look far too superficial and democratic in bias to hold to on the basis of real philosophical skepticism.

On the basis of such skepticism, we might well conclude that the most pressing practical political necessity is to teach people the organizational means of resisting the dominant element in society—whatever that element is. If some, given the opportunity, will always rise to confront the fundamental issues, the threat posed to intellectual freedom by the "tyranny of the majority" does not appear so great as Tocqueville sometimes makes it seem. But if neither Tocqueville nor anyone else actually knows the psychic structure of the individual human being, neither he nor we can be sure that some will rise to confront the fundamental issues. We can be certain that they will not have any opportunity to do so unless the physical power of the ruling element in society is checked.

Possessing the means will not necessarily give people the will to resist, however. They need to believe not only in their ability but also in their right. It is impossible, therefore, to ignore the substantive question of justice; i.e., the fundamental issues of political philosophy.

And if political order persists only when and where one segment of society has become dominant, the critical power of philosophy becomes extremely important in showing the limited justice of any existing form of rule. Philosophy is sometimes confused with ideology, the subordinate or reflective form of thought rather than the critical; but the distinction is easily drawn, insofar as philosophy brings out the conflicting claims to rule (and hence the partial character of any particular form of rule), where ideology criticizes any existing form of government for only partially realizing *one claim*. And if such criticism is beneficial, the effect of philosophy cannot be described as simply negative.

In denigrating the importance of speculative philosophy, Tocqueville denigrates the fundamental source or manifestation of freedom, as he defines it. It is possible, of course, to define political liberty simply as freedom from external oppression or physical restraint. Such a definition does not appear to satisfy Tocqueville, however.

> What good is it to me, after all, if there is an authority always busy to see to the tranquil enjoyment of my pleasures and going ahead to brush all dangers away from my path without giving me even the trouble to think about it, if that authority, which protects me from the smallest thorns on my journey, is also the absolute master of my liberty and of my life?[68]

If liberty consists merely in the absence of physical restraint, there would be no particular or new danger of the "tyranny of the majority." And if freedom consists primarily in the ability to think for oneself, philosophy is its greatest manifestation. Unfortunately, Tocqueville himself does not provide an example of the ability of the mind to rise above its historical circumstances, even though he proclaims the possibility. At most, he seems to think that this is possible only with regard to the eternal questions, not

---

[68]Ibid., p. 93.

political alternatives.

To say that the mind is free is not to say that philosophy can have an immediate or direct popular effect. There is, to be sure, a necessary difference or distance between philosophic investigation and popular opinion for reasons Tocqueville specifies. Most people cannot engage in philosophic investigations, so they must accept the opinions of others. But to acknowledge that philosophy is not apt to have a direct effect is not necessarily to agree that philosophy has either a negative effect or none at all.

Some have argued that the United States was founded on recognizably Lockean principles.[69] Although he praises the work of the framers of the United States Constitution, Tocqueville suggests that neither their principles nor their institutions were so important as prevailing conditions.[70] To say that institutional reform alone will not suffice to effect a change of regime does not require one to deny the importance of institutions (or ideas) altogether; and peculiarly American political principles and institutions both have identifiably philosophical roots. If the United States does represent an entirely new kind of regime, as Tocqueville himself insists, modern political philosophy is responsible for some of the novelty. Tocqueville himself argues that the institutions Europeans adopt will determine their future. It seems, therefore, that he finally does not take sufficient cognizance of the philosophic foundations, not merely of modern politics as a whole but even of his own particular enterprise.

---

[69]E.g., Carl L. Becker, *The Declaration of Independence* (New York: Alfred A. Knopf, 1922); Louis Hartz, *The Liberal Tradition in America* (New York: Harcourt, Brace & World, 1955). Even the recent commentators who have questioned the specifically Lockean foundations of the American republic have located them in other philosophic sources. Cf. Garry Wills, *Inventing America* (New York: Vintage, 1979), *Establishing America* (Garden City, N.Y.: Doubleday, 1980); Morton White, *The Philosophy of the American Revolution* (New York: Oxford, University Press, 1978).

[70]Tocqueville concludes his account of the work of the framers of the American Constitution by observing: "Sometimes, after a thousand efforts, a lawgiver succeeds in exercising some indirect influence over the destiny of nations, and then his genius is praised, whereas it is often the geographical position of the country, over which he has no influence, a social state which has been created without his aid, mores and ideas whose origin he does not know, and a point of departure of which he is unaware that give to society impetuses of irresistible force against which he struggles in vain and which sweep him, too, along" (*Democracy*, vol. I, pt. I, chap. 8, p. 163).

Politics

"In times of democracy private life is so active and agitated, so full of desires and labor, that each individual has scarcely any leisure or energy left for political life.

"I am certainly not the one to say that such inclinations are invincible, for my chief aim in writing this book is to combat them."

6

Misunderstanding the American Founding

Thomas G. West

Tocqueville's book has so much good sense in it that it seems almost meanspirited to raise a complaint. But since its flaw is important, and happens to be shared by many contemporary writers on America, it needs to be exposed.

Among today's leading scholars and politicians, there is a striking aversion to the political thought on which this country is founded. That aversion, shared by many liberals as well as conservatives, centers on the idea that all men are created equal, and that their Creator endows them with equal natural rights to life, liberty, and property.

Liberals are suspicious of individual natural rights because rights place limits on what government may do in the name of justice. When the law treats rights as belonging to individuals rather than groups, for example, it does not permit discrimination against white or Asian males in order to give jobs to less qualified women or blacks. (Thus the Supreme Court now openly admits that affirmative action, which the Court generally endorses, "trammels the rights" of individuals who do not happen to belong to the "minorities" favored by government.)[1] In short, liberals are wary of equal rights because rights permit individual achievement to flourish in accord with

Thanks to the Earhart Foundation for a grant supporting the revision of this essay for publication.

[1] *Johnson vs. Transportation Agency, Santa Clara County*, 94 L. Ed. 2d 615 (1987), at 627, 634.

individual intelligence, ambition, and hard work. This allows groups composed of some individuals to do better than groups composed of other individuals. Equal opportunity does not lead to equality of conditions.

Liberals therefore sometimes pay mouth-honor to the Founding while disagreeing with it, as Senator Biden did during the confirmation hearings on Judge Bork's nomination to the Supreme Court in 1987. Biden embraced the Founders' language of natural rights while denouncing Bork for refusing to read into the Constitution the partisan agenda of today's activist judiciary. Liberals who are more frank simply dismiss the Founding, and the Constitution, as pro-slavery and anti-women, as Supreme Court Justice Marshall did in a 1987 speech. In Justice Brennan's words, echoed by liberal historian Gordon Wood, the Founders' principles belong to "a world that is dead and gone."[2]

Many conservatives, on the other hand, are also suspicious of individual rights because they fear that the idea of rights provides liberals with an open-ended license to promote extremist policies in the name of social justice. These conservatives therefore prefer to remember the traditionalist aspects of the Founding, rather than the radical principle that all men are created equal.[3]

Tocqueville's account of the Founding has the practical effect of encouraging these current tendencies, although his view is in fact quite different from the views that prevail today.

Tocqueville does explain brilliantly much of what makes American democracy work so well. He does so in a way that cuts against the grain of many fashionable trends in our time. Particularly impressive are his account of the importance of religion in maintaining liberty, his focus on small towns as the heart of everyday democratic life, and his warnings about the despotic threat

---

[2]Thurgood Marshall, Remarks at the Annual Seminar of the San Francisco Patent and Trademark Law Association, Hawaii, May 6, 1987, mimeographed. William J. Brennan, speech to the Text and Teaching Symposium, Georgetown University, Oct. 12, 1985, in *The Great Debate: Interpreting Our Written Constitution* (Washington, D.C.: The Federalist Society, 1986), p. 17. Gordon S. Wood, "The Fundamentalists and the Constitution," *New York Review of Books*, Feb. 18, 1988, p. 39.

[3]Irving Kristol, "The American Revolution as a Successful Revolution," is a typical example of this conservative view of the Founding. In *America's Continuing Revolution* (Garden City: Doubleday, Anchor Books, 1976).

of the cradle-to-grave welfare state.

Yet Tocqueville misunderstands the American Revolution. He never mentions that in our Founding we Americans understood ourselves to be dedicated to the truth that all men are created equal, and that this dedication, and this truth, are what justified the break with Britain and made us a nation. Tocqueville's total silence on the Declaration of Independence—in a 700-page book on America!—is characteristic.

To this extent, at least, Tocqueville did not understand America as Americans understood themselves.

Against Tocqueville stands the view that most American citizens and statesmen held through most of our history—although not today. This view has been shared by such statesmen as Washington, Jefferson, John Quincy Adams, Lincoln, and Coolidge, and such scholars as Andrew McLaughlin and Harry Jaffa, all of whom regarded the principles of the Declaration as the heart of America.

I

If we begin at the surface, we notice that Tocqueville's account of the origins of American democracy gives little weight to the political theory and political actions of the Founders themselves. The decisive movement toward formal independence from 1765 to 1776 is barely mentioned, and he is altogether silent on the Americans' increasing clarity during this period concerning their political principles. The contribution of those principles to the early state constitutions as well as the federal Constitution is not discussed.

For Tocqueville, the decisive moment for American democracy is not the Founding but the point of departure of the first colonists, especially of New England.[4]

Tocqueville argues that three things—liberty, religion, and equality of conditions—formed America. First, the spirit of liberty was nourished from the start by the extraordinary independence of the colonies in determining the rules under which they would live.

---

[4]Alexis de Tocqueville, *Democracy in America*, ed. J.-P. Mayer, trans. George Lawrence (Garden City, N.Y.: Doubleday, Anchor Books, 1969), vol. I, pt. I, chap. 2. Hereinafter cited as *Democracy*.

From the start, they governed themselves for the most part through elected colonial assemblies. Further, within each colony the towns were self-governing in all the ordinary details of public life. So the people quickly became accustomed to act for themselves and not to wait for a central authority to take care of their needs. They developed the habits of free men by performing for themselves the duties of citizenship.

Second, says Tocqueville, the spirit of religion placed necessary limits on liberty, so that the freedom of public life did not become destructive of morals or of the rights of the minority. In agreement with the New England Puritans, Tocqueville insists that a man enslaved to his passions cannot be free.[5]

The third inheritance from the colonies was equality of conditions, for Tocqueville "the creative element from which each particular fact [in American society] derived."[6] Land was easily available, and the price of labor was high. Large fortunes were made, but they were also easily lost. Few families preserved their wealth beyond two or three generations. No hereditary aristocratic or impoverished classes could form under these conditions. Tocqueville argues that this equality in the social order made it impossible for inequality to be established in the political order.

Such is Tocqueville's explanation of America's point of departure, "the germ of all that is to follow and the key to almost the whole work." Tocqueville stresses subpolitical causes, as opposed to the conscious choices made by citizens and statesmen. He believes that a man or a country becomes what it is in its earliest, prerational development, not in its adult, rational deliberation about its form. "Go back, look at the baby in its mother's arms. . . . The whole man is there, if one may put it so, in the cradle."[7]

The premise of this argument, and of Tocqueville's political science as a whole, is that "in the long run political society cannot fail to become the expression and mirror of civil society."[8] This means that what goes on in private life determines the character of

[5]Ibid., pp. 46, 318.
[6]Ibid., p. 9.
[7]Ibid., pp. 31-32
[8]Ibid., p. 586.

the community more decisively than anything government does. The state does not form society; society forms the state. Accordingly, Tocqueville's analysis of democracy places greater weight on the manners and morals of the people than on their formal laws and institutions.

Thus when Tocqueville asks what is most responsible for sustaining American democracy, he answers, "The laws contribute more to the maintenance of the democratic republic in the United States than do the physical circumstances of the country, and mores do more than the laws." (By "mores" Tocqueville means the customs, opinions, habits, and forms of behavior of the people.) "The importance of mores is a universal truth [which] occupies the central position in my thoughts; all my ideas come back to it in the end."[9] In other words, what occurs in the subpolitical realm is more important than—and actually determines—what happens in politics.

In contrast to Tocqueville's approach, the political science of the Founders maintains that government forms society. Although habits and beliefs are crucial to the success of decent republicanism, their ultimate cause is politics and law. Accordingly, the Founders' political studies concentrated on the deliberations of statesmen and the laws and institutions of government.

The Founders' view may be seen in these passages from *The Federalist.* "Why has government been instituted at all? Because the passions of men will not conform to the dictates of reason and justice without constraint." The passions are not merely coerced by the penalty of law. The laws shape the passions, forming the people's habits and character—their mores—for better or worse. Actions of irresponsible state legislatures "have occasioned an almost universal prostration of morals"; but constitutional provisions protecting contracts will "inspire a general prudence and industry, and give a regular course to the business of society."[10]

Similarly, in his *Notes on the State of Virginia,* Jefferson shows how the opinions and character of the people can be formed by the right kinds of laws, including the establishment of state-controlled

---

[9]Ibid., pp. 307-08.

[10]*The Federalist,* ed. Clinton Rossiter (New York: New American Library, Mentor, 1961), No. 15, p. 110; No. 44, p. 283; No. 85, p. 522.

popular education. He proposed a thorough revisal of Virginia's law code because many of the laws inherited from colonial days inculcated "principles inconsistent with republicanism." The laws, that is, do teach principles. Although the people are "the only safe depositories" of government, "to render even them safe their minds must be improved to a certain degree." Government, not society, is entrusted with the task of *rendering* them safe.[11]

From the Founders' point of view, Tocqueville's account is true but partial. Social conditions place limits on, as well as make possible, what can be accomplished politically. The Founders were well aware of this. "[A]ll governments rest on opinion"; "republican government presupposes the existence of [virtue] in a higher degree than any other form."[12] But they thought that however much government is affected by popular mores, those mores are finally formed by government. Indeed, the leading theme of *The Federalist* is how to arrange things so that government by consent of the governed can control the people's passions and not be controlled by them.

The consequence of Tocqueville's mode of analysis is that he feels little need to examine either the publicly pronounced principles or the formal constitutions established by the states and union during the Founding era. Thus there are no quotations or even explanations of the principles of free government as they were articulated during the period 1765-1787. There is a short account of the state constiutions, but this occupies about three pages of his fifty-page chapter on the states. The rest of the chapter is mostly devoted to an account of township government and administrative decentralization. True, Tocqueville does include a long chapter on the federal Constitution, but, much as he admires this document, he concludes that it is not decisive for democracy in America. For the existence of the union is weak and precarious; the people's first allegiance goes to their states and home towns; and almost all the business of government is undertaken locally.

---

[11]*Notes on the State of Virginia,* Query 14, in Thomas Jefferson, *Writings* (New York: Library of America, 1984), pp. 263, 274. Hereinafter cited as Jefferson, *Writings.* Harvey C. Mansfield, Jr., "Introduction," in Thomas Jefferson, *Selected Writings,* ed. Harvey C. Mansfield, Jr. (Arlington Heights, Ill.: AHM Publishing Corp., 1979), p. xxii.

[12]*The Federalist* No. 49, p. 314.

II

The democratic principle, for the Founders, is a precise deduction from a rational insight. That insight is the equality of men, in the sense that no human being is so far superior to another human being that he has the right to rule him without his consent. From this equality follows the inalienable right to liberty; and to life, without which there can be no liberty; and to property, which is the material condition for making liberty practically effective. This equal liberty is not absolute; it is bounded by the moral law, or the law of nature, which prescribes man's duties and limits.

Books have been written and will continue to be written spelling out the implications of these principles, but this simple course of reflection is the basis of the Founders' conception of democracy.

Because Tocqueville does not recognize the Founders' moral conception of liberty, he looks elsewhere for the source of the moral restraint that he correctly observes in American democracy. That is why, in his analysis of America's point of departure, he insists that the spirit of religion and the spirit of liberty are two "perfectly distinct" things. According to Tocqueville, religion establishes right and wrong on an absolute basis: Thanks to religion, "in the moral world everything is classified, coordinated, foreseen, and decided in advance." Religion is not essentially democratic, although it is compatible with democracy. In fact, it is a "precious heritage from aristocratic times." The spirit of liberty, on the other hand, as Tocqueville presents it, has no internal source of direction: "In the world of politics everything is in turmoil, contested, and uncertain." Thus the proper understanding of liberty, including "the divine source of its rights," comes from religion alone. The drift of Tocqueville's presentation is this: For democracies, the only source of moral restraint is the authority of divine revelation; as far as democracy left to itself is concerned, everything is relative and everything is permitted. Without religion, liberty would run wild.[13]

The actual relationship between religion and democracy in America is more complicated. American statesmen from the Founders

---

[13]*Democracy*, pp. 47, 544.

on have been keenly appreciative of the support provided by Christianity, Judaism, and other religions for the moral principles of American politics. But they made a distinction between religious support for those principles and the principles themselves, which they thought were evident in human nature and therefore inseparable from democracy.

For most practical purposes, the foundation of political moral obligation for Americans is the equal rights of all. In Jefferson's words:

> All, too, will bear in mind this sacred principle, that though the will of the majority is in all cases to prevail, that will to be rightful must be reasonable; that the minority possess their equal rights, which equal law must protect, and to violate which would be oppression.[14]

Tocqueville praises the doctrine of individual rights on several occasions. It can help protect weak, isolated individuals from the overwhelming power of society or the state. Yet Tocqueville strangely severs the doctrine of individual rights from democracy. He maintains that the Americans "have taken from the English aristocracy the idea of individual rights. . . ."[15] This odd assertion not only deprives American democracy of its central principle ("that all men are created equal, that they are endowed by their Creator with certain inalienable rights"), but it then treats that principle as an accidental inheritance of an anti-democratic age.

Tocqueville's admirers sometimes forget his praise of individual rights because they are so impressed by his constant reminders of the dangers of equality. Equality tempts democratic citizens to drag down those who excel to the level of the average, which at the extreme could lead them to prefer equality in slavery to inequality in freedom. Equality also fosters what Tocqueville calls "individualism." Democratic citizens are not part of a preexisting social and political hierarchy as they were in aristocratic times. They therefore tend to withdraw from the larger community into their own private world of family, friends, and career. The impression left on

---

[14]First Inaugural Address, in *Writings*, pp. 492-93.
[15]*Democracy*, p. 676.

many readers is that since equality is dangerous and individualism is bad, equal individual rights are part of the problem. Yet at the conclusion of the book Tocqueville affirms that the support of those rights ought to be "the chief aim of any legislator in the age opening before us."[16]

But the rights of man are not the only democratic limit on democracy. The idea of liberty itself contains its own limit. When John Locke spoke of the law of nature as the bound of man's liberty in the state of nature, Americans understood him to mean that human beings "are inherently independent of all but moral law."[17] At least in principle, no one is free to do evil to himself or another. In practice, of course, much evil must be tolerated by the laws, but there is much that the laws can forbid and encourage.

For example, public respect for religion was enforced by Sabbath-breaking laws of the kind quoted with some amazement by Tocqueville.[18] The states also carried detailed legislation governing morals in the ordinary sense. Pornography was forbidden, as were sex outside of marriage, homosexual acts, and in some places even profanity.[19] Naturally, the religious convictions of the citizens provided strong impetus for these laws, but the support of a Jefferson shows that Americans thought these limits were also supported by the teachings of reason. In a word, Americans thought there was a right and a wrong use of the passions, and, in the words of *The Federalist,* a people that cannot guard themselves against "the tyranny of their own passions" will not long remain free.[20]

However, there is a sense in which the Founding principles, both of liberty *and* of self-restraint, may be said to be religious. In the Declaration, the equal right of all men to life, liberty, and the pursuit of happiness derives from the Creator, as do the laws of

---

[16]Ibid., p. 701. One Tocqueville admirer who made this error was Pierre Manent, "*Democracy in America:* The Classic Text on Liberty," *Wall Street Journal,* Jan. 30, 1985, p. 27.

[17]Thomas Jefferson, letter to Spencer Roane, Sept. 6, 1819, in *Writings,* p. 1426.

[18]*Democracy,* pp. 712-14.

[19]I have given striking examples in "The Founders' View of Education," to be published in a book on education edited by Robert L. Utley, Jr. For an easily accessible example, see the morals provisions in Jefferson's proposed revisal of the Virginia laws, *Notes on the State of Virginia,* Query 14, in *Writings,* p. 271.

[20]The quotation is from No. 63, p. 384, but the sentiment is in No. 55, p. 346.

nature and of nature's God. The expression "nature's God" was the Founders' way of speaking of God insofar as He is accessible to all human beings, regardless of their particular religious faith.

The philosopher Thomas Hobbes is famous for the doctrine that liberty by nature has no moral limits. In this respect Tocqueville is surprisingly Hobbesian. During the Revolution, Alexander Hamilton denounced Hobbes for his amoral conception of liberty, appealing against him to the moral obligation in the law of nature as taught by such men as Pufendorf and Locke. Hamilton also spoke there of man's *natural* rights as *sacred* rights, "written, as with a sunbeam, in the whole volume of human nature, by the hand of the Divinity itself."[21] The spirit of liberty properly understood is inseparable from the eternal order of things established by "nature and nature's God." This religious dimension of the Founding is so far from being aristocratic that it is the very foundation of democracy.

One may even speak of the spirit of liberty and the spirit of religion as two sides of the same coin, as long as it is clear that "religion" here means the nonsectarian theology of the Declaration of Independence, not the specific doctrines of Christian revelation. More recently, Solzhenitsyn expressed the Founders' nonsectarian religiosity perfectly when he said: "[I]n American democracy at the time of its birth, all individual rights were granted because man is God's creature. That is, freedom was given to the individual conditionally, on the assumption of his constant religious responsibility." And on the fiftieth anniversary of the Constitution, John Quincy Adams, after summarizing the second paragraph of the Declaration, said: "All this, is by the laws of nature and of nature's God, and of course presupposes the existence of a God, the moral ruler of the universe, and a rule of right and wrong, of just and unjust, binding upon men, preceding all institutions of human society and of government."[22]

In spite of the above criticism of Tocqueville, there is practical truth in his claim that without religion, liberty would know no moral

---

[21]Hamilton, "The Farmer Refuted" (1775), in *Papers of Alexander Hamilton*, ed. Harold C. Syrett (New York: Columbia University Press, 1961), pp. 86-87, 122.

[22]Alexander Solzhenitsyn, "A World Split Apart" (Harvard Commencement Address, 1978), in *National Review*, July 7, 1978, p. 841; John Quincy Adams, *The Jubilee of the Constitution* (New York: Samuel Colman, 1839), pp. 13-14.

limits. Although the Founders' idea of equality includes a moral aspect, that aspect would not be effective were it not supported on religious grounds by the leading Christian, Jewish, and other American sects. That is because religious conviction in this country is always associated with one sect or another, rarely appearing as a generalized endorsement of this nonsectarian democratic theology.

Calvin Coolidge caught well the complex weave of the spirits of religion and liberty in America in this statement:

> Equality, liberty, popular sovereignty, the rights of man—these are not elements which we can see and touch. They are ideals. They have their source and their roots in religious convictions. They belong to the unseen world. Unless the faith of the American people in these religious convictions is to endure, the principles of our Declaration will perish.[23]

Tocqueville rightly sees that a form of government in which the people rule is bound to need restraints on popular excesses. Tocqueville believes that those restraints are either extra-democratic or accidental. Yet the central ground of moral restraint on popular government lies in the very principle that justifies popular rule. There is no need to go outside the democratic ethos for limits on abuses of liberty. Tocqueville's neglect of the moral principles inherent in the Founding weakens his case for democracy and distorts the source of its fundamental decency. It makes American neo-Tocquevillians doubt the worth of democracy, for it makes their country appear to be good only to the extent that it is governed by religion, which it cannot publicly acknowledge as part of the regime, or only to the extent that it curbs the very thing of which it is most proud: democracy. As one conservative admirer of Tocqueville sums up his author: "[T]he problem with America is too much democracy."[24]

---

[23]Calvin Coolidge, "The Inspiration of the Declaration," in *Foundations of the Republic* (New York: Scribner's, 1926), p. 451. For a fuller account of the Founding, see my essay "The Classical Spirit of the Founding," in *The American Founding: Essays on the Formation of the Constitution*, eds. J. Jackson Barlow, Leonard Levy, and Ken Masugi (Westport, Conn.: Greenwood Press, 1988).

[24]Peter Augustine Lawler, "The Problem of Democratic Individualism," *The University Bookman*, 28:3 (1988), p. 9. The *Bookman* is edited by Russell Kirk, a prominent conservative intellectual.

III

Because Tocqueville did not notice that equality was a *political* principle in America, not just a fact of democratic life, he could not anticipate the Civil War, in which the nation split apart over the equality principle, over the rightness or wrongness of slavery, manifested in a dispute over the further expansion of slavery into the territories.

Tocqueville traces the root of the Southern problem, which is really the problem of slavery, to the earliest colonial days. The Southern colonies were at first populated by adventurers without families looking for quick riches, and slavery suited their idle and pleasure-seeking manner of life. The South gradually became more civilized as men married and settled down, and as English mores began to penetrate the region. But the difference always remains and endures, Tocqueville observes, as long as slavery does. The presence of a permanent underclass frozen by strict laws into their inferior station gives the South aristocratic qualities. They include an aspiration to graciousness and even grandeur but also a contempt for work and lack of common sense. Thus Tocqueville's South was an anomaly in an otherwise democratic land. Its most ominous aspect was its tendency to deny the humanity of its slaves, a consequence of the jarring conflict between the modern belief that men are equal and the actual fact of a class of degraded and slavish creatures.[25]

Tocqueville analyzes quite plausibly the effect of slavery on Southern blacks and whites. Yet he does not anticipate the growing Northern resistance to slavery, not only on religious grounds, but also on the grounds of the Founding principles articulated in the Declaration. Considering the accuracy of several of Tocqueville's other predictions, his anticipation of a successful Southern secession and a future race war between Southern blacks and whites is surprising in retrospect.

Tocqueville's lapse can best be explained by his misunderstanding of equality. The equality principle not only justifies majority rule but also imposes a moral obligation to respect the rights of the minority.

---

[25]Tocqueville's contrasts of North and South are in *Democracy*, pp. 34-35, 80-81, 308, 340-95.

This was understood by most leading politicians, North and South, during the Founding era and by most northern politicians thereafter. In the South, however, the Declaration gradually came to be ignored and after 1835 was explicitly repudiated. Southerners understood the importance of the principle and they rejected it with their eyes open. Calhoun, Fitzhugh, and many others wrote theoretical tracts attacking human equality. The tendency culminated in Alexander Stephens' Corner Stone Speech in 1861, which asserted that the theory of black racial inferiority, based upon advances in modern science, was the central principle of the new Confederacy.[26]

Lincoln's political rise after 1854 was grounded upon the continued vitality of the equality principle in the North. Lincoln's appeal to the moral obligation inherent in that principle was the foundation of his policy to keep the territories free of slavery. The Lincoln-Douglas debates show that Lincoln understood the political quarrel of the day as a contest over whether America was going to remain faithful to the Declaration, its ancestral law of moral obligation, or whether it was going to reject that respect for the equal rights of all in the name of self-interest. Lincoln's firm grasp on principle, and the tenacity and skill he displayed in his presidency, enabled him to fight secession and, as the length and bloodiness of the war radicalized northern sentiment, to abolish slavery altogether. Tocqueville knew that the majority might well turn to a superior man in a time of crisis,[27] but he did not anticipate how such a man could establish a policy that would lead to the resolution of the slavery question. That whites would end up fighting whites, and not blacks (as Tocqueville expected), over the future of slavery, is a sign of the moral power of the idea of equality. Of course in fairness to Tocqueville we must acknowledge that few men other than Lincoln himself could have accomplished what he did.

Lincoln epitomizes what is missing in Tocqueville's book. Lincoln renewed and deepened the American understanding of the connection

---

[26]Representative pro-slavery speeches and tracts are conveniently assembled in *Slavery Defended: The Views of the Old South,* ed. Eric L. McKitrick (Englewood Cliffs, N.J.: Prentice Hall, 1963). Stephens' Corner Stone speech is quoted and analyzed by Harry V. Jaffa in *How to Think About the American Revolution* (Durham, N.C.: Carolina Academic Press, 1978), pp. 155-61.
[27]*Democracy,* p. 199.

of equality, moral obligation, and divine justice. Jefferson trembled for his country when he reflected that "God is just: that his justice cannot sleep for ever."[28] Lincoln continued and deepened Jefferson's theme in his Second Inaugural, which makes the case that the Civil War may be a divine punishment of the whole nation for the sin of slavery.[29]

IV

One consequence of Tocqueville's presentation is that it misleads its present-day readers about what happened to America. Because of his minimal attention to our political principles and their importance, Tocqueville did not anticipate the reasons why America would change as it did.

The analysis of Volume II of his book, where he traces the effect of the equality of conditions on the private convictions and habits of the people, is brilliant, but few of his admiring readers heed the proviso of his preface. Tocqueville says there that he deliberately abstracts from everything but equality as a cause, and he frankly admits that he is hardly explaining America in Volume II at all![30] This should not come as a surprise as long as we remember that Tocqueville's main concern was with France, and that he studied democracy here in order to teach his own countrymen how to respond to the new era of equality.

Generally, Volume II shows the effects of equality of conditions on democratic life. Many of these effects are dangerous to liberty. We are warned, for example, that the more conditions become equal, the more insistent will be men's demand for even greater equality. This demand, Tocqueville worries, could become a consuming passion that might eventually welcome a despotism that would establish equal conditions for all but the despot himself. He also predicts a growing hedonism on the part of the people, leading them to self-

---

[28]*Notes on the State of Virginia,* Query 18, in Jefferson, *Writings*, p. 289.

[29]My account of Lincoln is based on Harry V. Jaffa, *Crisis of the House Divided: An Interpretation of the Issues in the Lincoln-Douglas Debates* (Chicago: University of Chicago Press, 1982, repr. Seattle: University of Washington Press, 1973, originally published 1959, Garden City, N.Y., Doubleday Press).

[30]*Democracy*, p. 417.

indulgence at the expense of sound moral habits, and a growing individualism, leading them to withdraw from public concerns. Weakened by petty passions and distracted by private affairs, the people are threatened with a soft despotism that

> provides for their security, foresees and supplies their necessities, facilitates their pleasures, manages their principal concerns, directs their industry . . . [and in the end] relieve[s] them from the trouble of thinking and all the cares of living.[31]

From today's perspective, Tocqueville's argument sounds like a prediction of the welfare state as we have come to know it, where men are not trusted to judge their own safety without a Washington-directed Consumer Products Safety Commission, OSHA, EPA, etc., to protect them, where affirmative-action programs try to make everyone come out equal, and where government abandons its traditional task of setting the moral tone. There is obviously some similarity between Tocqueville's predictions and the character of American life today.

Yet contrary to what Tocqueville seems to predict, these changes have generally come about either without much support from the people or in the face of their opposition. If America today stands on the edge of despotism, it has been brought there not by the people corrupted by equality, but by politicians imbibing the doctrines of intellectuals.

Tocqueville praises the federal Constitution for its several devices designed to check majority tyranny. Still, he expects the people to get their way in the end. Popular sovereignty remains for him the brute fact of American life. "The people reign over the American political world as God rules over the universe."[32]

It is true that the people will prevail concerning anything they set their minds to. But the Constitution really did create a government in which the people's rulers are considerably insulated from public opinion. Besides, the people defer to their leaders to a

---

[31]Ibid., pp. 503-08 (equality and despotism), 530-34 (hedonism), 690-95 (soft despotism).

[32]Ibid., p. 60.

greater extent than Tocqueville seems to think, even when they do not agree with them. If we consider some of the most dramatic changes in our political life over the past twenty-five years, it is striking how few of them were initiated by, let alone supported by, the people, especially in the initial stages. Abortion, busing, the legitimization of obscenity, and the near-abolition of the death penalty were forced onto a protesting people by the Supreme Court. Affirmative action was never voted on by Congress or signed into law by a President until several years after the policy had been invented in the executive branch and consolidated with the active support of the judiciary. Presidential elections over the past twenty years have been won consistently by candidates who ran "against Washington," that is, against the centrally administered state that was erected during the late '60s and early '70s. Congressmen who support the administrative state have found that winning elections is much easier when they conceal their partisan political convictions from the voters.[33]

When we seek out the origin of the opinions of America's post-1965 political elites, we find them in intellectual currents that go back at least a century. During the Progressive Era of the late 1800s, many American intellectuals, following the lead of European writers, turned against the principles of the American Founding. The rights of man and limited constitutional government, many of them believed, stood in the way of the benevolent, efficient regulatory state. Woodrow Wilson provides a classic statement of the Progressive view:

> "State socialism" . . . proposes that all idea of a limitation of public authority by individual rights be put out of view. . . . The thesis of the state socialist is, that no line can be drawn between private and public affairs which the state may not cross at will. . . . [I]n fundamental theory socialism and democracy are almost if not quite one and the same. . . . Men as communities are supreme over men as individuals. . . . [T]he individual rights which the democracy of our own century has actually observed, were suggested to it by a

---

[33]John Marini, "Money in Politics," in *The 1984 Election and the Future of American Politics*, ed. Peter W. Schramm and Dennis J. Mahoney (Durham, N.C.: Carolina Academic Press, 1987).

> political philosophy radically individualistic, but not necessarily democratic.[34]

Like Tocqueville, Wilson severs democracy from individual rights. Unlike Tocqueville, Wilson knows this means repudiating the Founders' constitutionalism and embracing "socialism."

Not only were the Founding principles subjected to attack. The idea of *any* transcendent principles of right was rejected. Progressive-era intellectuals no longer accepted the idea of an eternal human nature and inalienable rights inseparable from moral obligation—not even to speak of a God who establishes and guarantees the moral order of the universe. Eternal natural right was replaced by the ideas of History and Progress. Principles and constitutions have to be kept up with the times, and the times now demand an abandonment of individual rights and an abandonment of limited government. Here is the intellectual germ of the modern bureaucratic state.

Woodrow Wilson personally remained a religious believer, but at the extreme, as Solzhenitsyn explained it in his Harvard address, the Progressive intellectuals' new principle was anthropocentricity, "the proclaimed and enforced autonomy of man from any higher force above him."[35] Consequently, in these same intellectual circles an attack on traditional American religion was mounted. The rejection of God went hand in hand with the rejection of natural right.

The intellectuals of the 1960s, who were so enthusiastic about the Great Society that they thought they were creating, were the same people who were easily persuaded to believe the worst of America when it was attacked from the extreme left as a racist, sexist, capitalist cesspool that deserved to lose the war in Vietnam. These people held political power under Kennedy, Johnson, and Nixon, but they were not typical of the American people. Theodore White, the chronicler of recent presidential elections, calls them a snobbish priesthood that by 1980 "could not recognize where their own

---

[34]"Socialism and Democracy," unpublished 1887 manuscript by Wilson, in *Papers of Woodrow Wilson*, ed. Arthur S. Link (Princeton, N.J.: Princeton University Press, 1968), vol. 5, p. 561.

[35]Alexander Solzhenitsyn, "A World Split Apart," p. 840.

diagnoses and prescriptions had gone wrong."[36] He may be right, but they continue to hold substantial political power. They also exercise great influence from their strongholds in the universities, the legal profession, the media, and the mainstream clergy. Yet it was from lawyers and the churches that Tocqueville expected sensible restraints on *popular* excesses.

When French intellectuals involved themselves in politics during the eighteenth century, the consequences were disastrous for liberty. Tocqueville describes their ideas in *The Old Regime*.[37] American intellectuals, especially over the past hundred years, share with their earlier French counterparts many of the same attitudes and convictions. It is remarkable how familiar these eighteenth-century French ideas sound in today's context. There is the same taste for centralization, for bureaucracy, and for governmental control of the details of social life, and a corresponding hostility toward the independence of local communities and private ownership of property. It is to American intellectuals and their teachers, not to "equality of conditions," that we must look if we are to explain how America got to where it is today.

V

How then are we to evaluate Tocqueville? That is not easy to say, because he conceals his thoughts so well. To some extent, as I argued earlier, Tocqueville's misunderstanding of our Founding proceeded from his "sociological" approach to politics: looking at the political in light of the subpolitical. But there are other considerations that may have led him to "misunderstand" the Founding quite deliberately.

In the first place, we have to remember that Tocqueville's chief concern was France, not America. He studied us in order to teach his fellow citizens "a new political science . . . for a world quite new."[38]

---

[36]Theodore White, *America in Search of Itself* (New York: Harper & Row, 1982), p. 255.

[37]Alexis de Tocqueville, *The Old Regime and the French Revolution*, trans. Stuart Gilbert (Garden City, N.Y.: Doubleday, Anchor Books, 1955), pt. 3, chap. 1.

[38]*Democracy*, pp. 12, 18.

In the French Revolution an attempt had been made to sweep away the old aristocratic-Catholic politics and replace it with an entirely secular, democratic politics. That attempt had proven unsuccessful. Anti-religious "rationalism" had culminated in the terror. In the aftermath of the Revolution, the aristocratic-Catholic party and the democratic-secular party remained bitter enemies, and neither could defeat the other. In Tocqueville's view, neither deserved to defeat the other.

Tocqueville's account of America is accommodated to the French political scene. His strong distinction between an American aristocratic-religious tradition and a democratic-rational tradition in fact fits France better than America. In America, as we have seen, the idea of liberty itself contained moral limits, supported, as Tocqueville says, by all religious sects. But in France the spirit of religion and the spirit of liberty were not only disjoined but at war with one another. By presenting our history as he does, Tocqueville makes it more useful to the French. In his account of our past, America becomes a model for the solution of the French quarrel between aristocracy and democracy, and between Catholicism and secularism. Through the American example, French Catholics learn that religion can thrive in democracy. French aristocrats learn that aristocratic habits and restraints will still be needed in the emerging democratic era. French democrats learn that they are in need of religious and aristocratic mores, adapted to be sure to the democratic age, in order to avoid repeating the failure of the French Revolution.

Nor is this all. I have argued that Tocqueville exaggerates the extent to which American institutions and principles do not stem from democracy. One striking example, mentioned above, is his attribution of individual rights to aristocracy. By this and other means, Tocqueville is able to tell aristocrats that *their* ideas and mores are what make democracy work in America. By flattering them in this way, he perhaps hopes to reconcile them to their real defeat. After all, they are being asked to give up forever the attempt to revive their regime and instead to accept and even promote democracy in France.

There are, however, other reasons why Tocqueville might have avoided speaking about the equality doctrine. One of the major discoveries of Tocqueville's new political science was the democratic tendency toward centralization of administration.[39] And one thing that pushes democracy in that direction, in his opinion, is the "taste for generalizations." This taste, which easily becomes "an ardent and even blind passion of the human spirit to discover common rules for everything," discredits the idea of particular, local communities doing things in different ways. Consequently, "the idea of a single centralizing power directing all the citizens slips naturally into their consciousness without their, so to say, giving the matter a thought."[40] Given the danger that Tocqueville sees in general ideas, he is not likely to be eager to make them the centerpiece of his interpretation of democracy. If America is to be any sort of model for the French, all those American features that check centralization must be stressed, while those that foster it must be criticized or, if it is futile to attack the generalization that "all men are created equal," passed over as silently as possible.

But Tocqueville is not simply concerned with the *danger* of the idea of equality. He also doubts its *truth*. In the only chapter where he affirms "the very general but very simple conception . . . of the equal right of all at birth to liberty," he also says in effect that all general ideas are false. They may be necessary distortions without which imperfect human thought cannot proceed, but "God has no need of general ideas." Wisdom and generalizations are opposites. Thus it should be no surprise when Tocqueville attributes the teaching that all men are "naturally similar and equal" not to philosophers but to Christianity. He implies that human reason, strictly speaking, will not support it.[41]

Tocqueville apparently wished to avoid either an outright assault on the equal natural rights of men or a Lincolnian celebration of those rights as the heart of democracy. He accepted equality as a political principle only in a cautious, provisional way. In the background is Tocqueville's major thesis that ours is ineluctably the age of equality and that opposition to it is fruitless and destructive of liberty. Equality will be the starting point for all politics, free or

---

[39]See John Marini, "Centralized Administration and the 'New Despotism,'" chap. 10 of this book.

[40]*Democracy*, pp. 439, 668.

[41]Ibid., pp. 437, 439.

despotic, for the foreseeable future. There is no "legislator, however wise or powerful, who could maintain free institutions without making equality his first principle and watchword. Therefore all those who now wish to establish or secure the independence and dignity of their fellow men must show themselves friends of equality." As Tocqueville observed earlier in the book, moralists (i.e., writers like himself) should be willing to teach salutary doctrines even if they do not believe them to be true, adapting themselves to the spirit of their age and country.[42] No doubt Tocqueville followed his own advice. The question is, how far?

Tocqueville evidently shared the opinions of the classical political philosophers that all writing has a political character. Writers, especially "moralists," therefore incur a political responsibility. It is not enough to tell the truth. Men must be persuaded not only to see but also to do what is right. In our time, "The unbeliever, no longer thinking religion true, still considers it useful. . . . Therefore he regrets his faith after losing it, and deprived of a blessing whose value he fully appreciates, he fears to take it away from those who still have it." So he will "hide his incredulity" and pretend to believe what he does not.[43]

But Tocqueville goes way beyond this. Do *any* natural standards of right and wrong remain behind the conventional veil of religion and equality? Perhaps not. In a striking passage Tocqueville speaks of justice not as a principle inherent in the natural or divine order of things but as a law "made, or at least adopted, . . . by the majority of all men." In other words, it is authoritative not because it is in accord with eternity but because all men accept it. Tocqueville says he appeals here "from the sovereignty of the people to the sovereignty of the human race."[44] He does not appeal to the sovereignty of God and nature. For Tocqueville, the general will of humanity seems to replace natural or divine right. Justice becomes a product of human agreement or convention.

All ideals, he maintains in his discussion of poetry, are fictitious; nature and reality are prosaic. The ideal is the realm of the

[42]Ibid., pp. 695, 527, 548.
[43]Ibid., pp. 299-300.
[44]Ibid., pp. 250-51.

imagination, not of reason. What links men together in communities are therefore creations and illusions, for civilized men cannot live without faith in ideals. Thus Tocqueville teaches that neither ideals nor general ideas are true. Rather, the truth is that all things are unique and can be understood only with exactitude as absolutely particular. This is God's view of things, he says. It is therefore, he implies, the philosopher's view as well. There are no ideas or classes that bind men together by nature; God's idea of unity is the totality of infinite variety.[45] Tocqueville implies that each human being by nature is a pure self, alone. As soon as a man begins to understand himself as belonging to a group that defines itself by ideals or general ideas, he loses touch with his original nature. At the deepest level, that would be why liberty has no purpose.

But man cannot live alone in the civilized world. He must be part of a community. He can participate in community in two ways: as a free man or a slave. Tocqueville's purpose is to teach men how to retain some fraction of their pure particularity by nature. That is what he means by "liberty." This is to be accomplished above all through "administrative decentralization," that is, people actively taking care of their own everyday affairs and needs in small towns. Only when men are artificially drawn out of their natural selves by the vigorous public life of local democracy can they prevent themselves from succumbing to despotic government, which would prefer to make their choices for them. What liberty finally means for Tocqueville, then, is the self-assertion or self-determination of the individual against external authority. It is the "spirit of resistance."[46]

Tocqueville's theoretical framework is kept well concealed in his book. He is not vain. He feels no need to shock or dazzle his readers or display his sophistication to intellectuals. But behind his seemingly empirical and historical approach lies a radical account of man, nature, and society. It is hard to say where he learned to think this way. We do know that in 1836 Tocqueville wrote to a friend: "There are three men with whom I live a bit every day, Pascal,

---

[45]Ibid., pp. 483, 542-46, 437, 735.
[46]Ibid., p. 312.

Montesquieu, and Rousseau."[47] Could Rousseauan radicalism lie at the foundation of Tocqueville's sobriety?

Whatever Tocqueville's deepest private thoughts may be, it must be emphasized that, with the important reservations noted in this chapter, his book remains one of the very best on American democracy. In our time liberty needs friends wherever she can find them. His book is especially valuable because he foresees the specific tendencies within democracy that open it up to the dangers of socialism and communism. He already discerns the drift toward centralization, apolitical individualism, and the passion that craves equality of conditions even at the expense of freedom. He maintains without hesitation or apology that the greatest threat to liberty in the modern world is a despotism that promised to establish perfect equality if only the people turn over to the central government their control over the details of their lives. In all this he was right. My modest corrections are intended to help citizens and statesmen today who love liberty as deeply as Tocqueville did.

---

[47]Quoted by James T. Schleifer, *The Making of Tocqueville's "Democracy in America"* (Chapel Hill: University of North Carolina Press, 1980), p. 26.

7

Jefferson and Tocqueville

James T. Schleifer

"Jefferson . . . I consider him the most powerful advocate democracy ever had."[1] So wrote Tocqueville in the pages of his famous book on America. Yet even more noteworthy than such praise is Tocqueville's careful reading of Jefferson. The Virginian's writings are cited repeatedly in the text and manuscripts of the 1835 *Democracy*; at least twenty-one specific references appear, disclosing direct links between Jefferson and Tocqueville's effort to define equality, his fascination with inheritance laws,[2] his accounts of the American Revolution, his analysis of the legislative and judicial branches, and his discussions of Indians, blacks, and Anglo-Americans. Perhaps only *The Federalist* is cited in as many places and in relation to so many different topics.[3]

The Jefferson known to Tocqueville came primarily from two printed sources: an edition of *Notes on the State of Virginia*[4]; and a

---

[1]Alexis de Tocqueville, *Democracy in America*, ed. Phillips Bradley, trans. Henry Reeve, rev. Francis G. Bowen, 2 vols. (New York: Alfred J. Knopf, Vintage Books, 1945), vol. I, p. 280. Hereinafter cited as *Democracy*.

[2]In part, Tocqueville's stress on the importance of changes in land inheritance laws during and after the American Revolution came from his reading of Jefferson who is cited specifically on the topic in drafts of *Democracy*. Tocqueville failed to realize that Jefferson himself exaggerated the significance of the abolition in Virginia of the laws of primogeniture and entail.

[3]On Tocqueville's use of *The Federalist*, see especially James T. Schleifer, *The Making of Tocqueville's "Democracy in America"* (Chapel Hill, N.C.: University of North Carolina Press, 1980), chaps. 7 and 8. Hereinafter cited as Schleifer, *Making*. Two other sources frequently cited by Tocqueville were the two *Commentaries* by James Kent and Joseph Story; his use of those works was largely restricted to legal and constitutional issues, however.

[4]Originally printed in 1785. The edition read by Tocqueville is still unidentified.

two-volume selection from Jefferson's letters and memoirs, edited and translated into French by L. P. Conseil.[5] Tocqueville digested these two books in 1833 and 1834 as he composed the first half of his *Democracy.* From Conseil's work, he drew the several quotations from Jefferson's correspondence which would appear in his own book.

The American journey also exposed Tocqueville to Jefferson, though more indirectly. As the visitor talked with Americans, he heard ideas which, once widespread among the revolutionary generation, were by 1831 and 1832 part of accepted opinion in the United States. In part, this *consensus universalis,* as Tocqueville labeled the American ideology,[6] was shaped by Jefferson[7]; in part Jefferson only shared commonly held beliefs. But whenever Tocqueville and his hosts discussed the need for education, the evils of slavery and its pernicious influence on the character of the South, or the future of the races in America, he heard opinions which he would find again in Conseil or in *Notes on the State of Virginia.*

Tocqueville's interest in Jefferson's works also hints at broader affinities between the ideas of the two men as political theorists and moral philosophers. And, indeed, striking parallels do appear when they examine human nature, the requirements for a free society, and the proper functions and role of government. In these cases, similar ideas imply not borrowings by the Frenchman from the American, but a common background. Both writers accepted certain presuppositions of the Enlightenment, whether Scottish, English, French, or American. Concepts, for example, such as an "aristocracy of talent," the "pursuit of happiness," or the need for virtue in a republic, were found in the works of many of the

---

For this chapter I have used the convenient Harper Torchbook paperback edition introduced by Thomas Perkins Abernethy (New York: Harper & Row, 1964). Hereinafter cited as *Notes.*

[5] *Mélanges politiques et philosophiques extraits des mémoires et de la correspondance de Thomas Jefferson,* 2 vols. (Paris: ww 1833). Hereinafter cited as Conseil.

[6] *Democracy,* vol. I, pp. 433-39; also see pp. 408-10, 443-44.

[7] Winthrop Jordan, *White Over Black: American Attitudes Toward the Negro, 1550-1812* (Chapel Hill, N.C.: University of North Carolina, 1968), chap. XII: "Thomas Jefferson: Self and Society." Hereinafter cited as Jordan, *Attitudes.* In this chapter, Jordan remarks about Jefferson's powerful influence in the early 19th century on American opinion about race and slavery (see p. 429).

philosophes.[8] And the men of the eighteenth century in turn drew upon even earlier inheritances from the seventeenth century or the ancient world. Jefferson and Tocqueville shared this heritage, and to their words it sometimes gave similar coloration.

Human Nature and Equality

Tocqueville and Jefferson joined in certain fundamental assumptions about human nature. Men[9] everywhere, they believed, were essentially the same.[10] All possessed what Jefferson called "moral sense":

> [Man] was endowed with a sense of right and wrong. . . . This sense is as much a part of his nature as the sense of hearing, seeing, feeling; it is the true foundation of morality. . . . The moral sense, or conscience, is as much a part of man as his leg or arm.[11]

---

[8]In this chapter I have not attempted to explore in any detail the Enlightenment roots of Jefferson and Tocqueville; such an effort would require an entirely different sort of essay. Instead I have concentrated on exploring some key similarities and differences between the two men and on presenting significant new Tocqueville materials which highlight those parallels and divergences. On their Enlightenment heritage, however, see especially Henry Steele Commager, *Jefferson, Nationalism and the Enlightenment* (New York: George Braziller, 1975), pp. 88, 93-96, 101-03. Hereinafter cited as Commager, *Enlightenment*. Also Garry Wills, *Inventing America: Jefferson's Declaration of Independence* (New York: Random House, 1975), especially chap. 13. Hereinafter cited as Wills, *Inventing*. Consult as well Merrill D. Peterson, *Thomas Jefferson and the New Nation: A Biography* (New York: Oxford University Press, 1970). Hereinafter cited as Peterson, *Jefferson*. And the fine survey by Henry F. May, *The Enlightenment in America* (New York: Oxford University Press, 1976).

[9]The two also shared a blind spot concerning the equality of women. Tocqueville was willing to entertain a "separate but equal" position for women (*Democray*, vol. III, pp. 212-14, 222-25). For Jefferson's attitude, see Edmund S. Morgan, *The Meaning of Independence: John Adams, George Washington and Thomas Jefferson* (Charlottesville: University of Virginia, 1976), pp. 61-62. Hereinafter cited as Morgan, *Meaning of Independence*. Jordan, *Attitudes*, p. 475.

[10]For Jefferson, see *Notes*, p. 115: "Human nature is the same on every side of the Atlantic, and will be alike influenced by the same causes." For Tocqueville, see *Democracy*, vol. I, p. 336.

[11]Jefferson to Peter Carr, Paris, August 10, 1787; *The Papers of Thomas Jefferson*, ed. Julian P. Boyd, 20 vols. to date (Princeton, N.J.: Princeton University Press, 1950), 12:14-19. Hereinafter cited as Boyd, *Papers of Jefferson*. Also see Peterson, *Jefferson*, pp. 55-56.

Of this conscience, Tocqueville wrote in a discarded draft of the *Democracy*:

> If we consider the human species as a whole, we will discover that to live and prosper, the species must obey certain moral laws which are derived *necessarily* from the nature and needs given by God to every man without distinction.[12]

On another sheet he elaborated:

> To survive and prosper the human species taken as a whole needs to submit to certain moral laws which are found wherever men are found and which cannot be modified by time, political constitution, or place. These laws are indicated to each man by individual conscience. They are proclaimed by the common sense (*raison publique*) of all. What we call virtue is exact and willing obedience to these laws which all men instinctively acknowledge. . . .[13]

Human beings also possessed natural liberty.[14] Using language similar to Jefferson's and common to much of the Enlightenment, Tocqueville, in a deleted portion of *Democracy*, reflected:

> In a society founded on the dogma of the sovereignty of the people . . . each individual, born free and perfectly independent of his fellow men, master of his fate, is presumed able to govern himself. When he combines with others for social ends, he voluntarily concedes a part of his independence to the governing majority which he hopes sooner or later to join. But it is evident that such a concession can

---

[12]Yale Tocqueville Manuscripts Collection, CV g, "Rubish" two large boxes of original drafts of the 1840 *Democracy*, tome 4, sheaf A, for the chapter on honor. Hereinafter cited as Yale, "Rubish." CV g; previously unpublished. All translations of new Tocqueville materials are the author's.

[13]Yale, "Rubish," CV g, tome 4, sheaf C for the chapter on honor. Previously unpublished. Compare *Democracy*, vol. II, pp. 242, 254-55.

[14]For Jefferson, see Preamble of the Declaration of Independence, and J. R. Pole, *The Pursuit of Equality in American History* (Berkeley, Cal.: University of California Press, 1978), chap. 2, especially pp. 48, 51-58. Also consult Wills, *Inventing*, especially chaps. 14-16; and from Peterson, *Jefferson*, pertinent discussions of natural law and natural rights, especially pp. 93-96.

> only be made for a social purpose. The man who yielded for that end wanted only to unite his individual strength with that of his fellows and to have some control over the use of their combined force. He certainly did not intend to put himself in tutelage. So in all that concerns him alone, he reserves the inalienable (*imprescriptible*) right of his liberty and is responsible only to God.[15]

Nowhere in the published *Democracy* would Tocqueville so clearly develop his understanding of social contract and of the natural liberty and independence of every human being.[16]

Everywhere the same by nature, formed by Providence with a moral sense or conscience, made free and independent, and endowed with certain inalienable rights, all men were—in these characteristics at least—created equal. But both Jefferson and Tocqueville quickly added that natural inequalities also existed. In a famous letter to John Adams, Jefferson described his concept of "a natural aristocracy among men. The grounds of this are virtue and talents."[17]

In a clear example of Jefferson's influence (or at least of Tocqueville's recognition of a common view), the Frenchman copied the Virginian's name and idea into an early sketch for his chapter on "The Social Condition of the Anglo-Americans." While cataloguing some of the many meanings of equality, he listed the middling level of intellectual attainments which marked American society.[18] An outline of the chapter presented a qualification:

> Intellectual equality (*égalité des intelligences*). In the equality of means that they use. The lower rise; the higher descend. It happens that intellectual abilities

---

[15]Yale Toc. Mss., CVI a, Original Working Manuscript of *Democracy*, tome 1, for the chapter "Necessity of Examining the Condition of States Before That of the Union at Large." Hereinafter cited as Yale, OWM, CVI a. Compare *Democray*, vol. I, p. 67.

[16]Note, however, that Richard Herr, in *Tocqueville and the Old Regime* (Princeton: Princeton University Press, 1962), p. 129, offers a similar excerpt written by Tocqueville in 1836.

[17]Monticello, Oct. 28, 1813, ed. Lester J. Cappon, *The Adams-Jefferson Letters*, 2 vols. (Chapel Hill, N.C.: University of North Carolina Press, 1959), vol. II, p. 388.

[18]See *Democracy*, vol. I, p. 54, where the French word *intelligences* is misleadingly translated simply as "acquirements." The sense is, rather, intellectual attainments or

> (*intelligences*), still unequal as Providence intended, at least find equal means at their disposal. The inequality which comes most directly from God is inequality of intellect (?). Jefferson.[19]

More pointedly, in the text of the 1835 *Democracy,* Tocqueville cited "the natural aristocracy of knowledge and virtue."[20] Once, in his working manuscript, he declared that "[t]here are virtuous and peaceful individuals whose pure morality, quiet habits, opulence, and talents fit them naturally to be the leaders of their fellow men."[21] And in the 1840 portion of his book, he twice again discussed the natural inequality of minds "which [comes] directly from the hand of God."[22]

Equality, Race, and Slavery

Inequalities did not cease with differences of morality or intellect; other distinctions among men also existed. Here we approach the thorny issue of race. How did Native Americans and blacks differ from white Americans? What could be done about slavery? What did the future hold for race relations in America? When Tocqueville wrestled with these questions, he read Conseil's volumes and *Notes on the State of Virginia* with particular care. So here especially, *Democracy* echoes Jefferson.

Both men began with the assumption of differences among races. In *Democracy,* Tocqueville observed:

> Almost insurmountable barriers had been raised between [the three races in America] by education and law, as well as by their origin and outward characteristics; but fortune has brought them together on the same soil, where, although they are mixed, they do not amalgamate, and

---

intellectual accomplishments.

[19]Yale Toc. Mss., *Drafts of Democracy,* CV h, cahier 5, pp. 7-8. Hereinafter cited as Yale, *Drafts.* Previously unpublished. The copylist notes that in this passage one word, which I have marked "(?)" is illegible; it is almost certainly "intellect," however. Compare *Democracy,* vol. I, p. 54.

[20]*Democracy,* vol. I, p. 54.

[21]Yale, OWM, CVI a, tome 1, from Tocqueville's Introduction; compare *Democracy,* vol. I, p. 13, where, in the translation, the word "naturally" is omitted.

[22]*Democracy,* vol. II, pp. 39-40, 146.

> each race fulfills its destiny apart.[23]

And Jefferson, after defending the intellectual powers of the Native Americans, declared: "I do not mean to deny that there are varieties in the race of men, distinguished by their powers of body and mind."[24]

Traits peculiar to Native Americans fostered admiration by Jefferson and Tocqueville.[25] From the *Notes,* Tocqueville learned of Chief Logan's speech which reinforced in his thinking the familiar image of the Noble Savage. In December 1831, along the Mississippi, he witnessed the forced westward removal of the Choctaws. This experience and others in America also taught him about the pride and resignation of the native population of America, their disgraceful treatment, and the grim future which they faced.[26]

Like Jefferson, he had a good opinion of the mental endowment of the Indians. Any deficiencies could be explained by circumstances. In passages deleted from the working manuscript of *Democracy,* Tocqueville declared:

> You have only to see the native population of North America to be convinced that their race cedes nothing to ours. Social conditions have, so to speak, enclosed the Indian mind in a narrow circle, but within this circle, they show themselves the most intelligent of men. . . . Admitted to schools for whites, the young Indians astonish people with the rapidity of their progress; and if you think about the innumerable difficulties which surround the Cherokees you cannot doubt that . . . they have displayed as much and perhaps more natural genius than the people of Europe in their greatest undertakings.[27]

---

[23]Ibid., vol. I, p. 344; also see p. 373.

[24]*Notes,* p. 63.

[25]On Native Americans, for Jefferson, see *Notes,* pp. 55-64, 90; for Tocqueville, *Democracy,* vol. I, pp. 343-69.

[26]The basic message expressed in *Democracy* was that due to pride, fierce independence, and inflexibility, the Indians faced inevitable destruction.

[27]Both passages are included in Yale, OWM, CVI a, tome 2, from the subsection on "The Present and Probable Future Condition of the Indian Tribes." Both previously unpublished. Compare *Democracy,* vol. I, p. 359.

For blacks, Jefferson and Tocqueville showed sympathy,[28] but not admiration. Both commented pointedly that different standards of physical beauty characterized blacks and whites; they left no doubt about their own preferences.[29] And on the critical matter of racial equality, Jefferson equivocated. He insisted that both red and black men possessed a "moral sense," the characteristic which, for him, most defined humanity.[30] In this feature, all men were similar; so Jefferson could still argue for equal creation.[31] But in the *Notes* he also seemed to imply the probable equality with whites of Native Americans[32] and the probable inequality of blacks. After a painful and lengthy discussion, he ultimately skirted the issue by concluding: "I advance it, therefore, as a suspicion only, that the blacks, whether originally a distinct race, or made distinct by time and circumstances, are inferior to the whites in the endowments both of body and mind."[33]

In Tocqueville's case, however, distinctions certainly did not mean inherent racial inferiority; differences were explained in *Democracy* by training, legal status, history, and physical appearance. In several fragments of his working papers he denounced racism explicitly and, in one, announced: "I do not believe that there are races destined to freedom and others to servitude; the ones to happiness and enlightenment, the others to misfortunes and ignorance. These are cowardly doctrines."[34]

If their opinions about racial equality differ, the views of Jefferson and Tocqueville concerning slavery are nonetheless remarkably parallel. Both began with vigorous condemnation;

---

[28]For Tocqueville, see *Democracy*, vol. I, pp. 344-46. And especially note Tocqueville's sympathetic treatment of free blacks in the North, pp. 373-74, 382-83.

[29]For Jefferson, see Jordan, *Attitudes*, pp. 458-59. For Tocqueville, see *Democracy*, vol. I, p. 372.

[30]*Notes*, p. 90 (on Indians), and pp. 133-39, especially p. 137 (on blacks).

[31]See Wills, *Inventing*, chap. 15, pp. 218-28. Also consult Daniel Boorstin, *The Lost World of Thomas Jefferson* (Chicago: University of Chicago Press, 1981, reprint of 1948 ed.), chap. 2. For an interpretation which stresses Jefferson's racism, consult Jordan, *Attitudes*, chap. 12.

[32]*Notes*, p. 59.

[33]Ibid., p. 138.

[34]Schleifer, *Making*, pp. 68-69 and chap. 5. Compare *Democracy*, vol. II, p. 352. Also see Seymour Drescher, ed., *Tocqueville and Beaumont on Social Reform* (New York: Harper & Row, 1968), p. 99. Hereinafter cited as Drescher, *Social Reform*.

they found slavery morally repulsive and destructive.[35] The Europeans who first enslaved Africans, Tocqueville asserted, "violated every right of humanity."[36] And by the 1830s, "The legislation of the Southern states with regard to slaves [presented]... such unparalleled atrocities as suffice to show that the laws of humanity have been totally perverted."[37] In a draft, Tocqueville declared: "Slavery . . . is an evil which is perpetuated from generation to generation, is constantly renewed, and can only end by events more harmful than itself."[38]

Slavery had helped to create the chasm which separated blacks and whites in the United States. Eventual harmony between the two races was unlikely. "Wherever the whites have been the most powerful, they have held the blacks in degradation or in slavery; wherever the Negroes have been strongest, they have destroyed the whites: this has been the only balance that has ever taken place between the two races."[39] "I do not believe that the white and black races will ever live in any country upon an equal footing."[40] To emphasize this observation in *Democracy*, Tocqueville included a quotation from Conseil's edition of Jefferson which made the same point.

For both writers, the great stumbling block to an end of slavery was the presence in the South of large numbers of people of African descent. "If the South abolished slavery," queried Tocqueville, "what would it do about the black population?"[41] And Jefferson asked: "What further is to be done with [the newly freed slaves]?"[42]

Options were limited. Both Jefferson and Tocqueville thought racial amalgamation impossible. In a discarded passage,

---

[35]*Notes*, pp. 85-86, and *Democracy*, vol. I, pp. 395-97.

[36]*Democracy*, vol. I, p. 396.

[37]Ibid., p. 395.

[38]Yale, Drafts, CV h, cahier 2, pp. 92-93. Previously unpublished.

[39]*Democracy*, vol. I, p. 373; also see p. 372.

[40]Ibid., pp. 388-89; the Jefferson quotation (from Conseil, I, p. 214) presented by Tocqueville appears in a footnote on those pages.

[41]Yale, OWM, CV I a, tome 2, for the subsection "Situation of the Black Population in the United States"; previously unpublished. Compare *Democracy*, vol. 1, p. 385.

[42]*Notes*, pp. 138-39. Also consult John Chester Miller, *The Wolf By the Ears: Thomas Jefferson and Slavery* (New York: Macmillan, 1977).

Tocqueville wrote:

> In several European countries we have seen the various branches of the same race gathered together. They were similar in traits and in religion, homogeneous; yet they took centuries to mingle. The Moors, who scarcely differed from the Spanish, were not able to mix with them. If the various branches of the same human family have so much difficulty mingling and blending, how will two radically different races ever succeed? If a slight natural difference has been a nearly insurmountable obstacle, what will happen with a difference so enormous that what appears beautiful to one is extreme ugliness to the other?[43]

In another sentence deleted from the working manuscript, he even admitted: "I regard the mixing of races as the greatest of human misfortunes."[44] According to both Jefferson and Tocqueville, the most likely result of the joint presence of blacks and whites on the same soil was race warfare, "the most horrible of civil wars."[45] In still another passage deleted from his manuscript, Tocqueville explored the future:

> And if they do not intermingle, then what? Examine the various possibilities without dogmatism. No fear for the white race in America. But for the Black raçe. Perhaps they will separate? Perhaps there will be a war of extermination? . . . Finally the reason to maintain *slavery* and all its *hardships* for the good of the two races. If the two cannot mix in the southernmost states of the Union, what then will be their fate? It will be readily understood that we are here left to vague conjectures. In all human affairs an immense part is left to chance and to secondary causes which escape entirely from predictions and calculations.[46]

---

[43]Yale, OWM, CV I a, tome 2, for the subsection "Situation of the Black Population in the United States"; previously unpublished.
[44]Ibid.
[45]*Democracy*, vol. I, p. 394; also see pp. 390, 396-97.
[46]Yale, OWM, CV I a, tome 2, for the subsection "Situation of the Black Population in the United States"; previously unpublished.

Elsewhere in working papers and in his published text, he was more definite and declared racial conflict inevitable.[47]

Given the impossibility of intermingling and the danger of race warfare, only one course of action remained for Southern whites according to the Frenchman: "to keep [the Negroes] in slavery as long as possible."[48] In *Democracy,* Tocqueville's message is so hedged about, even convoluted, that readers often miss it. But his working papers are more emphatic. In one deleted fragment, he set forth the following alternatives for the South: ". . . either to *blend* with the blacks or to be *exterminated* by them." Given this choice, Tocqueville bluntly stated his conclusion: *"To keep slavery."*[49] In two other deleted pieces, he wrote: "I am obliged to confess that all of the ways to accelerate the coming of the struggle between the two races in the South, the abolition of slavery seems to me the most powerful."[50] "I confess that if I had the misfortune to live in a country where slavery had been introduced and if I had the liberty of the Negroes in my hands, I would refrain from opening them."[51] So in *Democracy,* Tocqueville presented no proposal to end slavery. In this, his book differed markedly from Jefferson's *Notes on the State of Virginia*.[52] But within four years he would draft a Report on Abolition which detailed plans for freeing the slaves in the French colonies and served as the basis for subsequent French action.[53] No champion of freedom for blacks in America, he became

---

[47]*Democracy,* vol. I, pp. 391-92; also see vol. II, p. 270.

[48]Ibid., vol. I, p. 394; also see pp. 396-97. Note that in *Democracy,* Tocqueville argued that the earlier Northern answer—gradual abolition—was inappropriate for the South (pp. 386-87) and that the contemporary Southern answer—colonization—was unworkable (pp. 387, 392-94). On the latter point, he disagreed with Jefferson who supported the colonization idea.

[49]Yale, OWM, CV I a, tome 2, for the subsection "Situation of the Black Population in the United States"; previously unpublished.

[50]Ibid.

[51]Ibid. See Tocqueville's qualification in *Democracy,* vol. II, p. 394: "God forbid that I should seek to justify the principle of Negro slavery, as has been done by some American writers! I say only that all the countries which formerly adopted that execrable principle are not equally able to abandon it at the present time."

[52]For Jefferson's early proposal, see *Notes,* p. 132. Of course, Jefferson never acted on his convictions in this matter.

[53]Consult Drescher, *Social Reform,* pp. 98-136. Drescher has pointed out the minor sensation which Tocqueville's Report caused in the United States, especially among American abolitionists, pp. 98-99. Why did Tocqueville's position change? The most

an abolitionist at home.

All along, however, he recognized that even in the United States slavery would end. "Whatever may be the efforts of the Americans of the South to maintain slavery, they will not always succeed. Slavery . . . cannot survive. By the act of the master, or by the will of the slave, it will cease."[54] Jefferson, in similar words, hoped that "under the auspices of heaven," society was moving toward "a total emancipation and that this is disposed, by the order of events, to be with the consent of the masters rather than by their extirpation."[55]

Tocqueville also believed that the tragedy of slavery had a message for humanity. Seeing the blighted present and dim future, "Men are able to say: 'Here at last is the justice of God.'"[56] Jefferson found the same moral. "Indeed I tremble for my country when I reflect that God is just; that His justice cannot sleep forever."[57]

So on the matters of slavery and race, Tocqueville often echoed Jefferson. They both condemned slavery, rejected the likelihood or even the desirability of intermingling, saw the presence of a large black population as an enormous difficulty for the future, predicted race war, and believed that one way or another slavery would end. Important differences are clear as well, however. In his book, Tocqueville offered no plan to end slavery in the United States. But he paid close attention to the deleterious effects of slavery not only on the masters, but also on the slaves. (This Jefferson had failed to do in the *Notes*.) He showed much greater sympathy for American blacks, both slave and free, than Jefferson had. And most important, he explicitly denounced the idea of inherent racial inferiority. Tocqueville would not suffer the shameful fate that some apologists for racism imposed on Jefferson.

Tocqueville's working papers present several other fascinating

---

striking difference between the 1835 *Democracy* and the 1839 Report is the absence in 1839 of predictions about race war. Tocqueville apparently believed that, for the French colonies, harmonious relations between the two races were possible after slavery had ended.

[54]*Democracy*, vol. I, p. 397.

[55]*Notes*, p. 156.

[56]Yale, OWM, CV I a, tome 2, for the subsection "Situation of the Black Population in the United States"; previously unpublished.

[57]*Notes*, p. 156.

unpublished passages on American slavery. The institution stood out as an anomaly in an overwhelmingly democratic society.

> The slavery which reigns in the South of the Union is the only aristocratic institution which the Americans have. Examine (I think) this solitary element of aristocracy after I examine all the consequences of democracy. How American slavery, which exists in the midst of a complete democracy of whites, does not have the same general results that would be expected if it were only an appendage of an aristocratic system. Contradictory effects: It increases the feeling of equality among whites; however, in some ways, it gives whites aristocratic habits, turn of mind, character. When you accuse the American democracy of atrocities against Blacks, you [illegible word] against yourself. Americans have only one aristocratic side and it is there that they are heinous.[58]
>
> The minds of Americans are narrow, . . . backward, rigid, and full of prejudices and limits on the subject of Blacks. . . .
>
> When you see the Americans outrage reason and nature in the way they treat Blacks, you say that these are the effects of an immoderate and unpitying democracy! But wait a moment. Democracy need not blush for the crimes which you impute. The only aristocracy which exists in America is that of whites. The only aristocratic idea is that of color and race. The whites reveal their only aristocratic side vis-à-vis the Blacks and show what legislators, placed by birth in a position superior to and different from the governed, can do. The evil gets worse as the state governments become more aristocratic; that is, as a privileged portion of the nation becomes more absolutely the master of another because of its independence from any foreign sovereign or central government. Always come back to this central idea that no single principle should be allowed to dominate and reach its most extreme consequences.

---

[58]Yale, *Drafts*, CV a, pp. 48-49; previously unpublished.

> As for me, far from considering what happens in America concerning Blacks as an argument against democracy, I would be afraid that an exaggerated and unjust argument against aristocracy might be made, and that what results from particular circumstances which are not inherent, such as the differences of color, might be attributed to aristocracy in a general way.[59]

From this analysis of slavery as an aristocratic institution, Tocqueville shifted to a discussion of America's lessons for the world.

> What I limit myself to saying at this moment is this: of all modern people, the Americans have pushed equality and inequality among men the farthest. They have universal suffrage and servitude. They therefore seem to have wanted to prove the advantages of equality by contrasting arguments. Some claim that by establishing universal suffrage and the dogma of sovereignty [of the people], the Americans have shown the world the advantages of equality. But I think that they have above all proved this by establishing servitude; and I find that they demonstrate the advantages of equality much less by democracy than by slavery.[60]
>
> The entire political doctrine of Americans rests on the principle of equality, but the benefits of this doctrine are still debatable. The Americans prove the need and the goodness of equality better and in a more irrefutable way with *slavery* than with *democracy*.[61]

"If the principle of equality among men needed to be advocated, the most perfect demonstration would be found here."[62] Out of slavery Tocqueville derived an additional proof for the principle of human equality.

---

[59]Ibid., CV h, cahier 1, pp. 23-25; previously unpublished. Compare *Democracy*, vol. I, p. 389. Also consult Schleifer, *Making*, pp. 217-23.

[60]Yale, OWM, CV I a, tome 2, for the subsection "Situation of the Black Population in the United States"; previously unpublished.

[61]Yale, Drafts, CV h, cahier 2, pp. 85, 90; previously unpublished.

[62]Ibid., p. 45; previously unpublished.

Education and the Pursuit of Happiness

Jefferson is widely known for a commitment to education, and his views on the topic are familiar. He urged those around him to "Enlighten the people generally, no other sure foundation can be devised for the preservation of freedom and happiness. . . . Preach a crusade against ignorance; establish and improve the law for educating the common people."[63] "Above all things," he confided to James Madison, "I hope the education of the common people will be attended to; convinced that on their good sense we may rely with the most security for the preservation of a due degree of liberty."[64] Education helped not only to preserve freedom but also to further the pursuit of happiness. Jefferson acted on these convictions, especially by proposing for Virginia a system "to diffuse knowledge more generally through the mass of the people"[65] and, near the end of his life, by bringing the University of Virginia into being.

Tocqueville's concern with education is less obvious, even overlooked by many readers. Yet his diaries of travel in 1831 and 1832 record numerous conversations about the various state systems of support for public education and contain several long reflections about the apparently universal American faith in education as a guarantee of social order, good government, and individual development.[66] In France in 1835, as Tocqueville planned the second half of his book, he projected three possible chapters on American education: "(1) On academic institutions under democracy; (2) On the necessity for learned societies (*corps savants*) in democracies; [and] (3) On education in the United States and in democratic countries in general." "The influence of democracy on the education of men, or rather their instruction," he declared in another note, "is a necessary chapter." He even prepared a chapter jacket with the

---

[63]Letter to George Wythe, August 13, 1786, as quoted in Commager, *Enlightenment*, pp. 113-14.

[64]Letter to James Madison, Paris, Dec. 20, 1787, Boyd, 12, p. 442.

[65]For his proposal, see Yale, *Notes*, pp. 139-43.

[66]See for example, J.-P. Mayer, ed., *Journey to America*, trans. George Lawrence (New Haven, Conn.: Yale University Press, 1960), pp. 31-32, 47-48, 56-57, 77-78, 91, 196, 219-20, 256. Hereinafter cited as Mayer, *Journey*. Concerning the American belief in education, also see *Democracy*, vol. I, pp. 409-10.

title "Influence of Equality on Education."[67]

But instead of a comprehensive analysis, gathered into a single major chapter, the topic became one of the great submerged themes of *Democracy*, poking out in various places in Tocqueville's drafts and working manuscript and appearing on scattered pages throughout both parts of his book.[68] "The great, the capital interest of the century," he exhorted his countrymen in one unused fragment, "is the organization and the education of the democracy."[69] After stating in *Democracy* that the people must be enlightened at all costs, Tocqueville wrote: "The time is fast approaching when freedom, public peace, and social order itself will not be able to exist without education."[70]

The access to ideas and to education which Americans enjoyed fascinated Tocqueville.[71] Drawing upon what he had seen in the New World, he suggested that, with liberty and education equally available to all, the extreme dangers of a mass society could be avoided.[72] Elsewhere in *Democracy* he observed:

> Give democratic nations education and freedom and leave them alone. They will soon learn to draw from this world all the benefits that it can afford; they will improve each of the useful arts and will day by day render life more comfortable, more convenient, and more easy.[73]

Here once again was Jefferson's concept of the pursuit of happiness facilitated by learning.[74]

Jefferson and Tocqueville valued education because it offered benefits which they both desired for democracies. For society,

---

[67]For these brief fragments on education, consult Schleifer, *Making*, p. 21.

[68]See especially *Democracy*, vol. I, pp. 7, 54-55, 326-30, 408-10; and vol. II, pp. 39, 65-67, 132, 153, 209-11, 316-17, 323.

[69]For this piece, see Schleifer, *Making*, pp. 266-67.

[70]*Democracy*, vol. II, p. 132; also see vol. I, 7, pp. 335-37, 341-42.

[71]See especially ibid., vol. I, pp. 326-30. Also Mayer, *Journey*, pages cited in n. 66.

[72]*Democracy*, vol. II, p. 39.

[73]Ibid., p. 153.

[74]What kind of learning did Tocqueville have in mind? See ibid., p. 66, where he argues that, for most people in a democracy, education should be "scientific, commercial, and industrial." Also note his comment that book-learning is sometimes overemphasized as the path to knowledge; practical experience, he suggests, is often more effective instruction, especially in politics and public life (ibid., vol. I, p. 329).

learning helped to mold the mores and the virtue necessary for freedom.[75] It made popular participation in government more responsible and created an enlightened citizenry. Tocqueville even argued that knowledge was a protection against the seductions of centralized administration.[76] For the individual, education opened new possibilities for self-development and broadened opportunity. It smoothed the road to independence, achievement, and happiness.

But perhaps a shared enthusiasm for the life of the mind most fundamentally explains their parallel attitudes toward education. Both theorists were fiercely committed to intellectual liberty. Tocqueville spoke of "freedom of thought as a holy thing."[77] And Jefferson declared: "I have sworn upon the altar of God, eternal hostility against every form of tyranny over the mind of man."[78] The two men, both devoted to culture, recognized that the emergence of new ideas and the continuing development of science and the arts demanded freedom of inquiry and education.

The Nature and Functions of Government

Still another example of the broad similarity of views which resulted from a shared heritage is their understanding of the object of government. Jefferson followed Francis Hutcheson and other figures of the Enlightenment in the belief that the end of government was the greatest happiness of the greatest number.[79] For his part, Tocqueville declared: "[T]o my mind, the end of a good

---

[75]The two men also shared the common 18th-century conviction that particular mores were necessary for a free society; they agreed that a republic demanded morality and virtue. Jefferson wrote, for example: "It is the manners and spirit of a people which preserve a republic in vigor. A degeneracy in these is a canker which soon eats at the heart of its laws and constitution" (*Notes*, p. 158). This idea of the central importance of *moeurs* is a fundamental argument throughout Tocqueville's *Democracy*; see especially *Democracy*, vol. I, pp. 326-42.

[76]*Democracy*, vol. II, pp. 316-17; also vol. I, p. 93.

[77]Ibid., vol. II, p. 13. Also see Schleifer, *Making*, chap. 14.

[78]Letter to Benjamin Rush (1800) as quoted in Commager, *Enlightenment*, p. 6. Also see Merrill D. Peterson, *Adams and Jefferson: A Revolutionary Dialogue* (Athens, Ga.: University of Georgia Press, 1976), pp. 77-78. Hereinafter cited as Peterson, *Adams and Jefferson*.

[79]See Wills, *Investing in America*, chaps. 10, 17, 18.

government is to ensure the welfare of a people."[80] In his book he argued that a key advantage of democracy was its contribution to "the well-being of the greatest number."[81]

On the relative powers and dangers of the legislative, executive, and judicial branches, however, what the American statesman had to say interested Tocqueville much more specifically. For these topics, citations of Jefferson's writings appear repeatedly in his manuscripts and text. In 1835 Tocqueville theorized that in a democracy the legislature most directly represented the sovereign people and would therefore most likely become the instrument of popular tyranny. One of his primary fears for America was legislative despotism. So in the pages of *Democracy,* the similar views of Jefferson are carefully presented: "The executive power in our government is not the only, perhaps not even the principal object of my solicitude. The tyranny of the legislature is really the danger most to be feared, and will continue to be so for many years to come."[82]

Tocqueville's drafts contain still another reference to Jefferson. In *The Federalist* No. 48, cited by Tocqueville, James Madison quotes his mentor to demonstrate the inherent danger of legislative usurpation. "All the powers of government, legislative, executive, and judiciary, result to the legislative body. The concentrating of these in the same hands is precisely the definition of despotic government. It will be no alleviation that these powers will be exercised by a plurality of hands, and not by a single one. One hundred and seventy-three despots would surely be as oppressive as one."[83]

In *Democracy,* Tocqueville summarized:

> To concentrate the whole social force in the hands of the

---

[80]*Democracy,* vol. I, p. 95n. 10.

[81]Ibid., pp. 246-50, especially p. 249; and pp. 262-63.

[82]Ibid., p. 280.

[83]For the original quote, see *Notes,* p. 113; also consult Schleifer, *Making,* pp. 147-48. Tocqueville cited and summarized *The Federalist* No. 48 in a draft; see Yale, *Drafts,* CV b, p. 25. So striking were Jefferson's words that in 1840 Tocqueville would perhaps unconsciously echo them: "For myself, when I feel the hand of power lie heavy on my brow, I care but little to know who oppresses me; and I am not the more disposed to pass beneath the yoke because it is held out to me by the arms of a million men" (*Democracy,* vol. II, p. 13). Note, however, that by then Tocqueville was concerned not with the despotic behavior of many legislators but with the tyrannical pressure

legislative body is the natural tendency of democracies; for as this is the power that emanates the most directly from the people, it has the greater share of the people's overwhelming power, and it is naturally led to monopolize every species of influence. . . . The existence of democracies is threatened by two principal dangers: namely, the complete subjection of the legislature to the will of the electoral body, and the concentration of all the other powers of the government in the legislative branch.[84]

Agreement between Jefferson and Tocqueville did not last once thoughts turned to the judiciary, however. The former President's concerns were noted in Tocqueville's manuscripts: "Opinion of Jefferson on the dangers of the extreme independence of the judiciary in the United States. See Conseil, Volume I, page 232."[85] But in *Democracy,* Tocqueville chose to reproduce the contrary analysis of the judiciary which he found in *The Federalist* and elsewhere.[86] He argued that the judiciary was by nature the weakest of the three branches and that liberty had little to fear from courts and judges. Instead, the judicial power served as one of the few effective barriers to democratic excesses; it checked, or at least slowed, the potentially despotic actions of both the people and the legislature. The independence of the judiciary must therefore be protected in democracies. Tocqueville simply could not credit Jefferson's concern that judges not responsible to the people might somehow threaten freedom.

Tocqueville also disagreed with Jefferson's mature interpretation of the federal relationship. The Frenchman presumably read Jefferson's contention, expressed in several letters contained in Conseil's volumes, that the states were losing power to the central government and that the Union was sliding toward consolidation. The Virginian cited many examples and pointed to the elastic clauses of the Constitution and the interpretations of the federal

---

of the mass.

[84]*Democracy,* vol. I, pp. 160-61.

[85]Yale, *Drafts,* CV h, cahier 5, pp. 29-30.

[86]For evidence of Tocqueville's reliance on *The Federalist,* see especially Yale, *Drafts,* CV h, cahier 3, pp. 10-11; and cahier 5, pp. 16-25, 39-41.

courts to support his opinion.[87] But once again Tocqueville followed *The Federalist* and other authorities and, in his book, argued for the constant weakening of the federal bonds and for the inevitable dissolution of the Union.[88] In his working papers he even blamed a particular American leader—Thomas Jefferson—for setting the American republic on the road to debility. This critical interpretation of Jefferson's policies was deleted in later stages of revision, however.[89]

In his use of Jefferson as an analyst of potential tyranny, Tocqueville made a common mistake. He never adequately recognized the shifts in Jefferson's views as time passed and circumstances changed. In 1785, in the *Notes*, for example, the Virginian focused most clearly on the threat of legislative despotism. By 1787, in letters commenting on the proposed Constitution, he was raising concerns about an executive who might become a king for life.[90] Later, his attention shifted to the active role the federal courts had assumed as interpreters of the Constitution and as champions of the prerogatives of the central government, and he began to warn about an overly independent judiciary.

In 1835, Tocqueville, then also troubled by the dangers of legislative tyranny, turned with approval to Jefferson's words. By 1840, however, his worry went not to the judiciary or to federal aggrandizement, but to a new sort of despotism: administrative or bureaucratic tyranny. So, although he noticed Jefferson's fears of the courts and of increasing federal power, he never read or cited them with appreciation. The two theorists started at the same place, but their paths of analysis rapidly diverged. On matters of government, Tocqueville learned only from the earlier Jefferson.[91]

---

[87]Consult Schleifer, *Making*, pp. 108-11, 278, 282.

[88]Ibid., chaps. 7 and 8.

[89]Ibid., p. 109.

[90]See especially letter to John Adams, Paris, Nov. 13, 1787, and letter to James Madison, Paris, Dec. 20, 1787; Boyd, 12, pp. 351 and 439-42, respectively.

[91]Tocqueville also quoted Jefferson (from Conseil) to support his view that legislative instability was one of the weaknesses of American democratic government; see *Democracy*, vol. I, pp. 213-14, 267-68.

Concerning the President, Tocqueville and Jefferson agreed that he should not be reeligible. Reelection opened the door to office for life, to political desperation, and to foreign intrigue. But they differed over the issue of Presidential power. Jefferson

Jefferson and Tocqueville are most commonly associated with limited government, with that government which governs least. Both certainly were suspicious of governmental power if it attempted too much.[92] Especially remembered are Tocqueville's warnings against administrative centralization and his chilling portrait of the new soft despotism of the bureaucratic state which meddles in all public and private affairs and inexorably loosens the springs of individual will, purpose, and action.[93]

This interpretation of the two statesmen can be overdone, however. Jefferson, we are reminded by his biographers and other commentators, strove for the vigorous application of his own power and authority as President. Throughout his life he looked to government-instituted reform measures, including land distribution to landless, adult, white males, and public educational systems. Most of all, he consistently advocated government support for various cultural and scientific activities, from the Lewis and Clark expedition to the creation of the University of Virginia.[94]

Tocqueville, too, urged the French government to inaugurate reforms, including a new prison system and the abolition of slavery in the French colonies. All the familiar planks in his political program for France (including decentralization, wider suffrage, liberty of the press, and freedom of association) assumed significant governmental initiative. At least twice in his book on America he reminded leaders of their obligation to conduct personal lives and to set public policies which would exemplify the moral standards required in a democratic society.[95] During the late 1830s, as he penned his warnings against bureaucratic tyranny, he was also

---

worried that the Chief Executive might be an elective king. Tocqueville, on the other hand, was convinced that weak executives were a major flaw of democratic government and that the executive should be as strong as possible. *Democracy* described the President, despite the enormous potential power which Tocqueville recognized, as pathetically subservient to the legislature. For Jefferson, see especially letter to John Adams, Paris, Nov. 13, 1787; letter to William Stephens Smith, Paris, Nov. 13, 1787; and letter to James Madison, Paris, Dec. 20, 1787; Boyd, 12, pp. 351, 356-57 and 439-42, respectively. For Tocqueville, see especially *Democracy*, vol. I, pp. 125-43.

[92]See *Democracy*, vol. II, p. 117.

[93]Ibid., pp. 336-37.

[94]See Peterson, *Adams and Jefferson*, pp. 735-39, 762-67, 802, 855-60.

[95]*Democracy*, vol. II, pp. 156, 160.

advocating subsidized hospitals and other institutional safeguards for the poor. And by 1847, Tocqueville was proposing tax relief and free education and legal aid for the poor; support for mutual insurance companies which would provide various kinds of social security; and new public institutions to aid the widowed and orphaned, the disabled, and others in difficult or impoverished circumstances.[96]

A fascinating example of this stance toward government action appears in sketches of the proposed chapter mentioned earlier on "Academic Institutions Under Democracy." Tocqueville wrote:

> An Academy whose object is to keep minds on a certain path and to impose a method is contrary to the genius of democracy; such an Academy is an aristocratic institution.
>
> But an Academy whose end is to honor men engaged in the arts and sciences and to grant them at state expense the modest comfort and leisure which is withheld by democratic social conditions is an eminently democratic institution. Such an Academy, though perhaps not to the tastes of a democratic nation, is nonetheless always compatible with, and sometimes necessary to, the existence of a democracy.
>
> The necessity for learned societies which are supported monetarily in democracies. This necessity grows as the people turn increasingly to democracy. This truth is hard for the democracy to understand. Natural tendency is in the opposite direction which must be resisted. The Americans give in to it. The result: science abandoned to the ordinary encouragement which democracy can provide; that is, only application, no theories are produced by the men who are doing work.[97]

What Tocqueville proposed here was government subsidy for activities he believed essential for intellectual creativity, but

---

[96]Consult Seymour Drescher, *Tocqueville and England* (Cambridge, Mass.: Harvard University Press, 1964), chap. 7, especially pp. 138-40, 142-43, 145. Also André Jardin, *Alexis de Tocqueville: 1805-1859* (Paris: Hachette, 1984), pp. 382-83.

[97]Drafts, CV a, pp. 2-3; previously unpublished. Compare *Democracy*, vol. II, p. 48.

which he did not think democratic societies would adequately support either through the marketplace or by voluntary contribution. His passion for the life of the mind once again shows through.

So—particularly for Tocqueville—let us consider a modest revision. For Jefferson and Tocqueville, public power was an instrument to be used, but only for particular purposes, which especially included the pursuit of science, education, culture, and certain kinds of equal opportunity. They championed the judicious use of government. And the ends thought worthy of public action were precisely what Jefferson and Tocqueville considered most vital for a free society and for individual independence. In some cases, at least, they were willing to put the government where their hearts were.

Individual Independence

Central to the thinking of both Jefferson and Tocqueville is respect for the dignity of each human being and the idea of individual independence.[98] This concept explains both their interest in education and their attitude toward the proper functions of government. Education (and a basic level of material comfort and security) were preconditions for knowledgeable, self-confident, and responsible individuals. And such individuals, willing to play a role in public affairs, made an intrusive government unnecessary; willing to work together for common purposes, they had little need to call for governmental action. So individual independence had two quite different dimensions: self-fulfillment or the pursuit of happiness, and effective participation in public life. For neither Jefferson nor Tocqueville did the idea have a selfish connotation. In one of the most famous parts of *Democracy*, Tocqueville specifically denounced the narrow, materialistic pursuit of purely personal goals

---

[98]For Jefferson, see especially Morgan, *Meaning of Independence*, pp. 62, 67-72. Morgan also notes Jefferson's blind spots: women, blacks, and the "mechanics in America's cities." See as well Joyce Appleby, "What is Still American in the Political Philosophy of Thomas Jefferson?" in *William and Mary Quarterly*, 39:2 (April 1982), pp. 287-309, especially pp. 293-97. Hereinafter cited as Appleby, "What is Still American?" For Tocqueville, see Schleifer, *Making*, chaps. 17 and 18.

as *individualisme,* one of the great plagues of democracy. For both theorists, individual independence had an essential social dimension. The individual was to be self-sufficient and wise enough to work toward public as well as private ends. This sensitivity to the proper blend of individual and social ends is still another distinguishing mark of the thinking of both men.

Other Parallels of Mind and Personality

Apart from similarities of ideas, Jefferson and Tocqueville also shared certain affinities of mind and personality. Both valued privacy and frequently showed an aristocratic aloofness or detachment which some observers thought cold. Both had a passion for ideas and enjoyed the constant reconsideration of familiar concepts; they exhibited what Merrill Peterson has called "intellectual spaciousness."[99] Jefferson and Tocqueville also shared the mental habit of thinking in contraries or pairs in tension.[100] And neither was a system-maker. Time, a tendency always to look at things in new ways, the dangers of thinking in dichotomies, and a belief that social and political principles had to fit the circumstances of particular societies kept both from devising any closed formulas for the guidance of others. One result of this open-ended nature of their thinking has been the rich and varied images of Jefferson and Tocqueville cast by readers over the years. Their writings can be read in a multitude of ways and have been used to demonstrate a broad range of not-always-compatible viewpoints.[101]

Some significant differences also existed between Jefferson and Tocqueville, however. Four are especially striking. Although they thought human beings everywhere were fundamentally the same, the first was more optimistic about human nature; the second, more pessimistic. Jefferson, for example, believed that, given the

---

[99]Peterson, *Adams and Jefferson,* p. 104.

[100]For Jefferson, see Jordan, *Attitudes,* pp. 475-77. For Tocqueville, see Schleifer, *Making,* p. 279.

[101]Consult Merrill D. Peterson, *The Jefferson Image in the American Mind* (New York: Oxford University Press, 1960); and Robert Nisbet, "Many Tocquevilles," *The American Scholar,* 46 (Winter 1976-77), pp. 59-75.

opportunity, people would choose natural aristocrats as leaders.[102] In contrast, Tocqueville worried constantly about the poor choices democratic peoples seemed to make; for him, the quality of leadership was one of the weakest points of democracies. Sometimes Tocqueville was more inclined to think in terms of original sin than of natural goodness. Once in his working manuscript, for instance, he lamented that "men have at their command so large a reservoir of baseness that they always turn out to be more or less the same in the service of all despots, whether people or king."[103] In Joyce Appleby's wonderful phrase, "Science and education pulled [Jefferson's] carriage of hopes."[104] For Tocqueville, however, nothing could entirely erase the foreboding which he often felt as he surveyed the probable future of modern societies.[105]

The American was also more of an activist than the Frenchman. Jefferson was, after all, a revolutionary. And throughout his life he often made efforts to put his favorite schemes into effect, sometimes with considerable success. Tocqueville was better at exhorting than acting. His political career was less successful, and Seymour Drescher and others have noted his tendency to write or speak for a proposal and then to stand aside. If his ideas were to be translated into reality, others had to respond to his words.

In addition, Jefferson's interests ranged over a wider field; his genius was broader. What excited him and what he observed, studied, and wrote about was much more varied than was true for Tocqueville. And he often approached his many interests in a detailed and scientific manner; Tocqueville's usual approach, by contrast, was theoretical and deductive. What the two men collected when abroad is telling. Tocqueville returned to France with a head full of ideas and trunks stuffed with books and papers. Jefferson, too, came home with ideas and books, but tucked away as well were seedlings and other specimens of a new way of life that he imagined for America.

---

[102]For example, see Jefferson's letter to John Adams, Monticello, Oct. 28, 1813, Cappon, II, pp. 388-89.

[103]OWM, CV I a, tome 1, for the chapter "The Principle of the Sovereignty of the People of America"; previously unpublished.

[104]Appleby, "What Is Still American?" p. 294.

[105]See Schleifer, *Making*, pp. 186-87, 333nn. 47, 48.

But if Jefferson was more universal and empirical, I believe we may sustain the argument that Tocqueville was more original than the Virginian. Jefferson exquisitely mirrored the presuppositions of his age and excelled at putting them in beautiful and memorable prose. Tocqueville was also a superb stylist known for his lucid and concise phrasing. But he went beyond the accepted to achieve significant new insights about modern society. As J.-P. Mayer demonstrated over forty years ago, his careful analysis of the consequences and especially of the dangers of mass society broke new ground.[106] And we have just noted still another example of Tocqueville's talent for putting a new twist on a familiar idea: Out of the horrors of American slavery he drew an additional proof for the advantages of equality.

Conclusion

The purpose of Tocqueville's usual textual citation of Jefferson was to present an authoritative witness to seal an argument. Where Jefferson disagreed markedly from Tocqueville's other major sources, especially *The Federalist*, the Frenchman's habit was simply to acknowledge the difference in his sketches or drafts and then to ignore the Virginian's dissent. Perhaps the major exception to this method is the topic of race and slavery; there, if anywhere, Tocqueville learned from Jefferson or from the American mind-set which Jefferson had helped so much to create. On these matters, the chain of ideas presented in *Democracy* is remarkably like that found in *Notes on the State of Virginia* and other Jefferson writings. But overall, Tocqueville did not so much as learn from Jefferson (even from the Jefferson of 1785) as share a heritage with him, agree with many of his opinions, and resonate to a certain fellowship of spirit and intellect.

---

[106]J.-P. Mayer, *Prophet of the Mass Age: A Study of Alexis de Tocqueville* (London: J. M. Dent, 1939).

8

Modern Commerce

John Adams Wettergreen

Freedom, and freedom alone
can extirpate these vices.[1]

Tocqueville, 1854

One hundred and fifty years after *Democracy in America,* the United States enjoys a degree of material prosperity which might have surprised even Tocqueville. Yet the causes of this economic progress and its worth have never been more in dispute. In the presidential elections of 1980 and 1984, for example, the nature of American economic enterprise has been the central issue, and the nation was divided between those who hope for economic progress and those who fear it.

Fear of industrial progress can be found on the Left and the Right. The list of dangers and evils is old and long: Industrialization despoils Nature; fosters greed over social responsibility; widens economic, social, and political inequality; and breeds an irrational faith in technological solutions to human problems. Such disgust at American commerce is most common among socialists or liberals, but it is easily discovered among conservative intellectuals, who often seem to differ from their brothers on the Left only by regarding American commercialism as a necessary, not an unnecessary, evil.[2]

---

[1]Alexis de Tocqueville, *The Old Regime and the French Revolution,* trans. Stuart Gilbert (Garden City, N.Y.: Doubleday, Anchor Books, 1955), p. xii. Hereinafter cited as *Old Regime.*

[2]See, on the right, e.g., George Will, *Statecraft as Soulcraft: What Government Does* (New York: Simon & Schuster, 1983), and Irving Kristol, *Two Cheers for Capitalism*

The contemporary American Center, in contradistinction to the criticism of the Left and Right, has attempted an intellectual defense of the morality—indeed, the piety—of American free enterprise. In large part, Middle America has reacted to the economic failure and political success of the highly bureaucratized or "mixed" economy that was created in the United States between 1964 and 1974. In particular, George Gilder and Michael Novak argue that the American economy produces not only wealth, but also what they regard as best in human nature: faith, hope, and charity.[3] That is, ultimately these critics look upon the American commercial system as positively good because it advances the cause of Christianity.

Given today's uncertainty about political economy, it is useful to turn to the writings of Alexis de Tocqueville. Tocqueville's historical vantage point was superior to that of contemporary American intellectuals; it comprehended the American democracy, but included also premodern, pre-American, and predemocratic societies. Moreover, unlike the writings of the American Left, Right, and Center, Tocqueville's account of American commercialism is intentionally scientific. That is, it could be simply true, insofar as it is based upon a comprehensive understanding of human nature.

Tocqueville's Relevance

Most contemporary scholars doubt the claim that Tocqueville is our contemporary and blame his understanding of political economy, claiming that he was "blind to capitalism."[4] The overt complaint is not that Tocqueville was not a socialist or Marxist, which would, of course, be perfectly sound so far as it goes, but that he did not comprehend or could not have foreseen the leading features of the

---

(New York: Basic Books, 1978); on the left, e.g., John Kenneth Galbraith, *Economics and the Public Purpose* (New York: Houghton Mifflin, 1973), and Robert N. Bellah, *The Broken Covenant: American Civil Religion in a Time of Trial* (New York: Seabury Press, 1975).

[3]George Gilder, *Wealth and Poverty* (New York: Basic Books, 1981), and Michael Novak, *The Spirit of Democratic Capitalism* (New York: Simon & Schuster, 1982).

[4]The common scholarly view is well expressed by Irving M. Zeitlin, *Liberty, Equality, and Revolution in Alexis de Tocqueville* (Boston: Little, Brown & Co., 1971), pp. 48-64. No one, so far as I know, accuses him of being blind to socialism. Hereinafter cited as Zeitlin, *Liberty*.

contemporary political economy, especially industrialization and urbanization. This interpretation is founded, in part, on the assumptions that he was "under the influence of his predominantly agrarian model of America," and that, consequently, he "systemmatically obscured" the growth of manufacturing, as distinguished from agriculture and trade.[5] However, as shall now appear, this interpretation and its foundations are incorrect.

In a single chapter of *Democracy in America,* "What Gives Almost All Americans a Preference for Industrial Callings," Tocqueville both noticed the continuing decline of agriculture as a mode of living and explained why this trend would continue in the United States and elsewhere: "[A]lmost all the tastes and habits born of equality naturally lead men in the direction of trade and industry," while giving them "a distaste for agriculture."[6] Of course, he did not suppose that agriculture would cease to be a way of life. By becoming commercialized, agriculture would become just one more means of earning a living among many. Already, Tocqueville noted, "[a]lmost all farmers combine some trade with agriculture; most of them have made agriculture itself a trade."[7] All that would have remained to bring about the present, fully commercialized condition of agriculture (sc., "agri-business"), then, would be its industrialization. That too, as shall appear presently, was easy for Tocqueville to foresee.

In common with every great social scientist after John Locke, Tocqueville understood the technicalization of production, which we call industrialization. The following passage states the principles of industrialization with perfect clarity and simplicity:

---

[5]Ibid., pp. 49 and 56, which follows Jack Lively, *The Social and Political Thought of Alexis de Tocqueville* (Oxford: Clarendon Press, 1962), p. 217. Hereinafter cited as Lively, *Thought.*

[6]Alexis de Tocqueville, *Democracy in America,* ed. J.-P. Mayer, trans. George Lawrence (Garden City, N.Y.: Doubleday, Anchor Books, 1969), pp. 551-52. Hereinafter cited as *Democracy.*

[7]Ibid., p. 554; see also p. 53: "Now, as soon as landowners are deprived of their strong sentimental attachment to the land, based on memories and pride, it is certain that sooner or later they will sell it, for they have a powerful pecuniary interest in so doing, since other forms of investment earn a higher rate of interest, and liquid assets are more easily used to satisfy the passions of the moment." Cf. Xenophon, *Oeconomicus,* XX, p. 29.

> It is acknowledged that when a workman spends every day on the same detail, the finished article is produced more easily, quickly, and economically.
>
> It is likewise acknowledged that the larger the scale on which an industrial undertaking is conducted with great capital assets and extensive credit, the cheaper will its products be.
>
> People had formed some inkling of these truths long ago, but it is in our day that they have been demonstrated. They have already been applied to several very important industries, and in due turn even the smallest will take advantage of them.[8]

Industrialization, then, is not just mechanization, but the application of science to the problems of production altogether. Its power was obvious in pre-Revolutionary France, and in England as well as in the United States. Thus Tocqueville expected the number of those engaged in industry to multiply "without limit."[9] In other words, everyone, including farmers, would come to be engaged in industry.

Tocqueville saw, as clearly as a contemporary social scientist, that there could be no industrialization without urbanization. Again, this was obvious from observations in England, France, and the United States. For example, the "influx of workers into Paris from all parts of France and the development of districts of the city inhabited almost exclusively by the [industrial] working class" began well before the Revolution there, and was a cause of it.[10] The same movement, Tocqueville argued, would be inevitable in the United States.

For this reason, Tocqueville declared that the development of an urban, industrial working class in America is "serious and claims the particular attention of legislators," even at a time when "[t]here is not yet any great capital in America." Such a class of citizens, Tocqueville feared, could become a rabble—so

---

[8]*Old Regime*, p. 555.
[9]*Democracy*, p. 555. See also pp. 539, 552, 554, 637, 684. On English industrialization, see, above all, p. 730. On French industrialization, see *Old Regime*, pp. 133, 179.
[10]*Old Regime*, p. 76n. 24.

economically dependent, miserable, and politically ignorant that it could be ruled only by force.[11] Moreover, far from being blind to the possibility of a labor movement, which was to develop in the United States after his journey here, Tocqueville recommended the formation of associations of industrial workers as one means to counter the demoralizing effects of industrialization and urbanization. More: He urged a free-labor movement and cautioned against governmentally organized labor unions; i.e., one of the hallmarks of the twentieth-century's socialistic tyrannies.[12]

It was easy for Tocqueville to see what both the Marxists and half-Marxists call the class-structure of capitalist society and what they call its contradictions. Industrial societies, he argued, tend to develop an urban proletariat dependent upon a grand bourgeoisie. The members of neither of these classes, he feared, would recognize moral obligations to the other. Tocqueville believed that this absence of bonds of mutual obligation would pose a special problem for modern democracies because such societies, when fully commercialized, "are subject to very unexpected and formidable industrial crises."[13] Indeed, "the recurrence of these industrial crises is an endemic disease." The reason for these great depressions is obvious because almost everyone is engaged in industrial activities, all prosper or fall at once. Given these developments, it was not difficult for Tocqueville to foresee the welfare state: "[T]he industrial aristocracy of our day, when it has impoverished and brutalized the men it uses, abandons them in time of crisis to public charity to feed them."[14]

He also foresaw the possibility, declared to be a fact by the American Left today,[15] that government could be dominated by the industrial capitalists: "From being a class exceptional in society, there is a danger that it will become the chief and, one might almost say, the only one. . . ."[16] That had already happened

---

[11]*Democracy*, pp. 584, 278n.
[12]Ibid., p. 686. Cf. Zeitlin, *Liberty*, pp. 53-54.
[13]*Democraacy*, p. 554.
[14]Ibid., pp. 557-58.
[15]See e.g., Michael Walzer, *Spheres of Justice: A Defense of Pluralism and Equality* (New York: Basic Books, 1983), p. 310.
[16]*Democracy*, p. 685.

forty years before the French Revolution.

> The number of persons having monetary dealings with [the central government], subscribing to its loans, living on wages paid by it, and speculating in government-sponsored enterprises had enormously increased. Never before had the interests and fortunes of private individuals been so closely bound up with the State.[17]

In sum, all the features of what today's social scientists call "capitalism," "late capitalism," or "post-industrial society" were adequately understood by Tocqueville.

Socialism, too, was obvious to Tocqueville.

> It is commonly thought that the subversive theories of what today is known as socialism are of recent origin. This is not so. . . . In Morley's *Code of Nature* [1755] may be found not only the ideas . . . regarding the unlimited rights of the State but also several of the alarming political theories which we were inclined to think had made their first appearance in our own generation; for example, community of property, the right to be provided with work, absolute equality, State control of all activities of individuals, despotic legislation, and the total submerging of each citizen's personality in the group mind.[18]

Just as the intellectuals of Tocqueville's day supposed that socialism was a century younger than it was, so today's intellectuals suppose that Tocqueville could not have foreseen even the obvious features of modern society. Not only did he see them, he tried to penetrate to their roots.

Today's scholars believe they will be on safe ground by asserting that, great as he was, Tocqueville had to be mistaken about America and about democracy because he could not have foreseen our future; such a dogmatic belief freed Henry Steele Commager, for example, from making a careful investigation of

---

[17] *Old Regime*, p. 179.

[18] Ibid., p. 164. Cf. Alexis de Tocqueville, *Recollections*, trans. George Lawrence, eds. J-P. Mayer and A. P. Kerr (Garden City, N.Y.: Doubleday & Co., Inc., 1971), pp. 94-95.

what Tocqueville actually did think about big government.[19] Of course, it is true that no one can foresee the future in detail, but it is equally true that the future is easily foreseen insofar as it is like the present: All one needs to know is what is permanent and what is transitory in one's present condition. The aspects of social and political life which contemporary intellectuals single out as characteristic of our time—free enterprise and socialism, democracy and bureaucracy, industrialization and urbanization, and so on—were also present in nineteenth-century Western societies. Therefore, it was easy, especially for a great mind like Tocqueville's, to grasp what contemporary intellectuals believe to be the major features of the political economies of the contemporary Western democracies.

The Moral and Political Causes of Modern Commerce

Tocqueville had a clear and certain idea of three causes, or rather three sets of moral principles, which distinguish the contemporary economic system: democracy, modernity, and Christianity.

Democracy

As Marvin Zetterbaum has remarked, he saw that "the rise of the commercial spirit" was characteristic of modern democracies because the commercial mode of living—as distinguished from nomadry, hunting, war, fishing, and agriculture—best satisfies the desire for material comforts. Or, in Tocqueville's words:

> It is not trade and industry that give men the taste for physical pleasures, but rather the taste for them which induces men to go into trade and industry, so as to satisfy this taste more completely and quickly.[20]

19"Tocqueville's Mistake," *Harper's Magazine* (Aug. 1984), CCLXIX, no. 1611, p. 70.
20*Democracy*, p. 552n. See also pp. 539, 550n. 10.

Tocqueville reasoned that the modern democrats' belief in equality teaches that each human is the best judge of his own good, since bodily pleasures are the most obvious of goods, most democrats "strive eagerly to gratify their immediately felt and immediately intelligible desires to improve their conditions in life."[21]

Tocqueville supposed that the affinity between the spirit of commerce and democracy is natural or universal. Accordingly, he insisted that the ancient democracies, like the modern, were commercial societies:

> We are told of small democracies in antiquity whose citizens gathered in public places garlanded with roses and spent the best part of their time dancing or at the theater. I do not believe in the existence of such republics any more than in that of Plato. . . .

Rather, in democracies, whether ancient or modern, all "those who are not ambitious to control the commonwealth devote all their energies to increasing their private fortunes."[22]

Conversely Tocqueville maintained that a commercialized aristocracy is freakish, "an exception to the rule":

> [A]ristocracy is not at all favorable to the progress of industry or trade. . . . When wealth has become the only indication of aristocracy, it is very difficult for the rich to keep power for themselves alone and to exclude all the rest.
>
> An aristocracy of birth and a pure democracy are the two extremes of the social and political state of nations. Aristocracy of wealth [sc., England] comes in between.[23]

In France, Tocqueville saw that when commercialism, the devotion of a people to wealth-getting as a way of life, is fostered

---

[21]Marvin Zetterbaum, "Alexis de Tocqueville," in *History of Political Philosophy*, eds. Leo Strauss and Joseph Cropsey (Chicago: Rand McNally & Co., 1972), p. 727.
[22]*Democracy*, p. 610. Cf. Montesquieu, *Spirit of the Laws*, trans. Thomas Nugent (New York: Hafner Press, 1949), bk. XXI, chap. 6, pp. 334-39.
[23]*Democracy*, p. 730. Cf. Montesquieu, *Spirit of the Laws*, bk. XX, chap. 7, pp. 320-21.

in an aristocracy, a democratizing revolution must soon follow.[24] In America, he saw that the commercial interests were powerfully favorable to the perpetuation of democracy.[25]

Modernity

Although Tocqueville was aware of the contribution of modern natural science, via technology, to economic prosperity, he traced technological and scientific progress to the same cause as commercialism, to the moral principle of democracy.[26] Yet, however commercial the ancient democracies may have been, their commerce was not industrialized or technologized. Modern commerce, that is, is modern as well as democratic.

In his *Correspondence with Gobineau*,[27] more clearly than in his major work, Tocqueville explored the precise difference between modernity and democracy:

> [A] new kind of social and political morality is being established, a kind which antique peoples hardly knew but which is, in reality, a combination of some of their political ideas with the moral principles of Christianity.[28]

Christianity alone, not modernity, had effected a genuine moral revolution by standing antique morality on its head.

> [Christianity] did not establish entirely new virtues; but it changed their relative position. Certain rude and half-savage virtues had been at the top of the list; Christianity put them on the bottom. The milder virtues, such as neighborly love, pity, leniency, the forgetfulness even of injuries had been on the bottom of the antique list;

---

[24]The argument is developed throughout *Old Regime*, but see especially pp. xii, 118, 123, 133, 135-36, 171, 175, 179, 237n. 17, p. 238.

[25]*Democracy*, p. 634-45 ("Why Great Revolutions Will Become More Rare").

[26]Ibid., pp. 459-65.

[27]Alexis de Tocqueville, *"The European Revolution" and Correspondence with Gobineau*, ed., trans. John Lukacs (Gloucester, Mass.: Peter Smith, 1968). Hereinafter cited as *European Revolution*. That Tocqueville believed the thoughts of these letters were worthy of preservation appears from p. 195.

[28]Ibid., p. 193.

Christianity placed them above all others.

However, modernity did politicize Christianity.

In particular, modernity is an attempt to remedy "the only weak facet" of Christian morality—"the public virtues seem . . . to have been inadequately defined and considerably neglected"—with "the only strong facet of the moral system of the antique nations." Ancient morality is characterized by public-spiritedness or the passionate love of political liberty.[29] Indeed, "almost all that we call modern principles should be considered as new consequences drawn from the old Christian principles because of our present political and social conditions."[30]

Nevertheless, modernity is not only this-worldly or politicized Christianity, because modernity's this-worldliness, unlike antique this-worldliness, lacks a foundation. The antique morality, like Christianity, looked upward.

> [T]he ancient religions found it easy to dignify morality by establishing it under the aegis of divinity. Now it has been brought down to earth, and it has not yet been possible to discover its sources.[31]

Modern society is "much more alienated from the theology than from the philosophy of Christianity, [and so] morality has become more concerned with the legitimacy of material needs and pleasures."[32] To put it somewhat bluntly, modernity is agnostic, not to say atheistic and materialistic, Christianity.

Tocqueville's life was devoted to understanding and improving the practical effects of the modern morality. Or, as he put it, "[M]y main purpose [is] above all to find and show what is really new and divorced from Christianity in these modern moral systems."[33] Modern commerce is one of those really new things.

---

[29]Ibid., p. 167-68.

[30]Ibid., p. 211.

[31]Ibid., p. 203.

[32]Ibid., p. 192.

[33]Ibid., p. 208. "Kant seems to me beyond, rather than within, Christianity." Kant's categorical imperative could provide a basis in human nature and reason for the characteristic of Christian morality that Tocqueville prized most highly: "Christianity put in grand evidence the equality, the unity, the fraternity of all

"Every cause which makes love of things of this world predominate in the human heart," Tocqueville reasoned, "also favors trade and industry."[34] Thus modernity augments to the utmost democracy's natural proclivity for commerce, for modernity's this-worldliness, being baseless, includes no limit to material progress. Indeed, not even self-interested calculation can curb the modern egalitarians' improvements upon their material conditions. Tocqueville tried to capture the almost-blind pursuit of wealth that results from modernity's baselessness in two chapters of *Democracy in America*: "Why Americans Are Often So Restless in the Midst of Their Prosperity" and "How the Aspect of Society in the United States is at Once Agitated and Monotonous."[35] In these chapters, we see that no amount of wealth could ever cause the Americans to turn away from their relentless commercialism, not because they are unusually greedy or profligate, but because they know no ambitions beyond wealth and because they see how easily fortunes could be lost in their commercial ventures, as well as for specifically "American" reasons (see "American Commerce," pages 217-20).

Although Tocqueville was dismayed, and even frightened, by modern democracy's commercial spirit, he did not condemn it absolutely, nor could he hold it in aristocratic contempt. He did not condemn, because he hoped to cure the worst maladies of modern commerce, and he could not despise commerce, because he knew that modern material prosperity is an improvement of the human condition.

Christianity

According to Tocqueville, in modern times the practice of the Christian religion has encouraged economic progress. In the chapter of *Democracy in America* devoted to the practical limits of

---

men" (p. 191). However, Tocqueville was not at all convinced of the practicality of Kantian morality. On the contrary, he was almost as disgusted by Kantian universalism as he was by materialism: "I am convinced that the interests of the human race are better served by giving every man a particular fatherland than by trying to inflame his passions for the whole of humanity" (p. 170).

[34] *Democracy*, p. 552n.

[35] Ibid., vol. II, pt. II, chap. 13, pp. 535-38ff., and vol. II, pt. III, chap. 17, pp. 614-16.

materialism, "How the Excessive Love of Prosperity Does Harm to It," the desire for material comforts and conveniences, a desire which is elsewhere called "this mother of all desires,"[36] is shown to be so inadequate a motive for material progress that it can actually destroy material progress. The greatness of the human imagination and the mind, not the greatness of the human body's desires, moves humans to produce prosperity. Otherwise, Tocqueville reasoned with infallible accuracy, cows would enjoy a more thriving commerce than human beings. Thus, Tocqueville concluded, "Whatever elevates, enlarges, and expands the soul makes it more able to succeed [in commercial undertakings, among other things]."[37]

Nevertheless, specifically modern commerce, i.e., industrial enterprise, is soulless, and even soul-destroying: An extreme division of labor, more than anything else whatsoever, tends to turn men into machines and to deprive the things made of any trace of soul.[38] So all religions are contradistinguished from industrial enterprise, because they place "the object of man's desires outside and beyond worldly goods and naturally lift the soul into regions far above the realm of the senses."[39] Tocqueville did not expect that modern democrats would be capable of traditional, i.e., feudal, Christianity's severe restraints on the passions, and he knew that modern morality indulged the passions, hoping to rationalize them.[40] Indeed, he expected that for most of the busy members of a democratic society, religion would be the only soulful activity. This proved to him that religious belief was crucial for the health, including the economic health, of modern democracies. By strengthening the soul, religion would be the only well-established curb upon the excesses of the spirit of commerce. At the same time, religion would be the chief inspiration for economic progress. No wonder Tocqueville found the American laws compelling the observance of the Sabbath to be wonderful! Only on

---

[36]Ibid., p. 448.
[37]Ibid., vol. II, pt. II, chap. 16, pp. 546-47.
[38]Ibid., p. 403.
[39]Ibid., p. 444.
[40]*European Revolution*, p. 202.

the Sabbath did Americans find any respite from the incessant demands of commercial life, and only the enforced rest of the Sabbath refreshed them enough to continue the breakneck pace of their commercial enterprises on Monday.[41]

With these things in mind, Tocqueville remarked: "I should be even more inclined to believe in the coming of some new religion than the continuation of the prosperity and the greatness of modern societies without religion. . . ."[42] Of course, Tocqueville did not suppose that a new religion would be necessary for the prosperity of modern democracy. On the contrary, Christianity is well suited to modern democracy's commercialism or materialism because, as has already been argued, Christian morality has so much in common with modern morality. In particular, "the idea that all men have a right to certain goods, to certain pleasures, and that our primary moral duty is to procure these for them," is the secularization of the Christian moral idea of "the equality, the unity, the fraternity of all men."[43]

Tocqueville supposed that the combination of modern commercial enterprise with the Christian religion in a modern democracy would be extraordinarily powerful. For example, he disagreed with Gobineau's expectation that the West would decline to the level of oriental depotism in the coming centuries.

> A few million men who, a few centuries ago, lived nearly shelterless in the forests and in the marshes of Europe will, within a hundred years, have transformed the globe and dominated the other races.[44]

However, to repeat, this superior material power of the West depends upon the tempering of modernity's materialism by religion. Is modern democracy really capable of such temperance? It was, above all, the American example which gave Tocqueville confidence in the future of the West.

---

[41]*Democracy*, pp. 712-14.
[42]*European Revolution*, p. 212.
[43]Ibid., pp. 191, 193; cf. p. 293.
[44]Ibid., p. 267.

American Commerce

In general, the world would be dominated by the West and, in particular, the United States would dominate the commerce of the world. Tocqueville expected this American dominance because it was the most democratic and the most religious of the modern Western nations of his day. More importantly—because other nations could become as modern, as democratic, and even as religious as the United States—other nations lacked the unique American spirit of commercial enterprise. When the American dominates in commerce, he "is not just working by calculation but is rather obeying an impulse of his nature."[45] Thus, "American trade," Tocqueville declared, "can not only face competition on its own ground, but can even compete to advantage with foreigners on their own."[46]

Tocqueville saw something about the American economy that contemporary social scientists usually miss. American prosperity "depends upon purely intellectual and moral qualities."[47] Material advantages, like superior fertility of soil, abundance of natural resources, or moderation of climate, have not made the United States economically superior. Nor are Americans any more greedy or materialistic than other modern democrats. Of course, the Americans love the material gains which trade and manufacturing bring them, but even more "they love the emotions it provides."[48]

The daring, intelligence, and versatility of American commercial enterprise amazed Tocqueville. Americans would brave the savagery of the Indians and of the ocean's storms for the sake of a profit, to be sure, but even more for the thrill of commercial competition. "For an American, the whole of life is treated like a game of chance, a time of revolution, or the day of battle,"[49] from all of which the American expects to prosper. Indeed, for Americans, commerce is the moral equivalent of war.

---

[45]*Democracy*, p. 403.
[46]Ibid., p. 401.
[47]Ibid., p. 402.
[48]Ibid., p. 553.
[49]Ibid., p. 404.

> [In war, the French] did everything at the double and had no hesitation in risking men's lives to attain the end in view. . . . The Americans have introduced a similar system in commerce. What the French did for the sake of victory, they are doing for the sake of economy.[50]

Yet commerce cannot be the practical equivalent of war, because economic power is not the same as military power. Accordingly, Tocqueville remarked, "Reason suggests and experience proves that there is no lasting commercial greatness unless it can, at need, combine with military power."

The extraordinary, warlike, commercial venturesomeness of the Americans is a moral quality, whose intellectual equivalent is belief in the perfectibility of man or in the idea of progress. Since, to the Americans, all motion seems to be an advance, they are constantly attempting new ventures; some are great and many are small, but almost everyone is engaged in an enterprise. Although the idea of progress is not peculiarly American, nor even peculiarly modern or democratic,[51] that idea inspires the Americans more than any other people. Consequently—because they are so versatile, i.e., so capable of changing and adapting to each new commercial circumstance—they are more commercially intelligent than any other people. This versatility keeps American enterprise genuinely free, i.e., ever more thriving and diverse. It is free, that is, not just because governmental influence is minimal, but above all because commerce is not highly differentiated. When Tocqueville was here (and, relatively speaking, even in the late twentieth century), economic specialization, professionalization, and the division of labor were not very far advanced. That is, there were (and are) not many legally and/or hereditarily defined vocations, nor were there many governmentally defined and certified professions. To the extent that commerce is not differentiated, Americans can pride themselves on being "Jacks-of-All-Trades," an attitude, I believe, which still prevails among American workers.

Tocqueville saw that this lack of—indeed, distaste for—

---

[50]Ibid., p. 402.
[51]Ibid., pp. 452-53.

economic specialization was the economic strength of the Americans. Of course, lack of specialization often makes for poor workmanship. It also permits far more to be attempted in a much more intelligent manner. So, if there are more commercial failures, and there are, there are also far more successes.

It is not simply economic underdevelopment that made Americans versatile, intelligent, and daring in trade and manufacturing. Their versatility is born of their "natural" spirit, i.e., of their love of independence.[52] The Americans that Tocqueville saw could not even conceive of servility, for "the servant may at any time become the master, and he wants to do so."[53] Characteristically, Tocqueville traced this spirit of independence to the American's religion, that is, to their Protestant Christianity. Christianity in general, and Roman Catholicism in particular, he thought to be "most favorable to equality of conditions" and so to democracy. "However," Tocqueville declared with some emphasis, "I say that Protestantism in general orients men much less toward equality than toward independence," for that religion teaches its adherents to "acknowledge no religious supremacy," a teaching that is the point of departure for everything, like versatility, that is specifically American.[54] Of course, Protestantism's spirit of independence is not necessarily contrary to the spirit of equality, but it is different from that spirit. As such, it can serve to moderate democracy's worst excesses, including its materialism, without being at all anti-democratic.

Tocqueville admired American commercial prosperity for the usual reason; he did not despise or fear the ever-higher standard of living it provided for all. However, he admired American commercialism even more for the goodness of the way of life it encouraged than for that way's comfort and convenience. It is a way characterized by regularity or good order, both in politics and

---

[52]For example, the popularity of "Do-It-Yourself" in America is certainly not due to considerations of comfort, convenience, or economy! On the other hand, in France today virtually all artisans are the children of artisans (because of tax laws), and most professional waitresses and waiters are state-trained and certified. This seems almost feudal.

[53]*Democracy*, p. 576.

[54]Ibid., p. 288.

in society, for commercial men usually favor nothing more than stability. It is, above all, a moral way of life, one free from the worst excesses of the passions. Commercialism, then, is an integral part of the *mores*, which, Tocqueville said, "allow a democratic people to remain free."[55]

Commercialism is only a prop, not the foundation, for democratic liberty.

> [D]emocratic societies which are not free may well be prosperous, cultured, pleasing to the eye, and even magnificent, such is the sense of power implicit in their massive uniformity; in them may flourish many private virtues, good fathers, honest merchants, exemplary landowners, and good Christians, too—since the patrimony of the Christian is not of this world and one of the glories of the Christian faith is that it has produced such men under the worst governments and in eras of the utmost depravity. . . . But, I make bold to say, never shall we find under such conditions a great citizen, still less a great nation. . . .[56]

In America, Tocqueville saw real citizenship, in company with a thorough-going, if somewhat wild, commercial spirit. He found this combination to be rare, perhaps even inimitable and, therefore, very valuable. America, therefore, must have been Tocqueville's practical demonstration that modern morality has some foundation.

In sum, Tocqueville saw that American greatness—commercial and otherwise—is born of the Americans' spirit of individual independence, which makes us demand of each other that we rule ourselves. This spirit must be distinguished from what Tocqueville called "individualism," which is an anti-social and anti-political moral attitude. Protestant theology is the principal carrier of this spirit of individual independence, which he thought could both inspire and temper modern commerce.

---

[55]Ibid., p. 315. Strangely, commercialism is not among the "habits of the heart" of which Professor Bellah and his school have written; see Robert N. Bellah, et al., *Habits of the Heart: Individualism and Commitment in American Life* (Berkeley: University of California Press, 1985).

[56]*Old Regime*, p. xiv.

Tocqueville's Critique of Modern Commerce

For all his admiration of free enterprise, Tocqueville concluded that it could cause the most profound difficulties for modern democracy. Indeed, his criticism of modern commerce was in many respects as harshly and bitterly contemptuous as contemporary socialism's criticism of capitalism. Yet, as shall now be shown, he differed from the socialists in the diagnosis of the ills of modern commerce, in his etiology, and even more in his prescription for them.

Tocqueville held that modern industrialization could be soul-destroying ("alienating" in the vocabulary of contemporary social science). His fear is most obvious in a famous chapter, "How an Aristocracy of Manufacturers Might be Created by Industry." There Tocqueville claimed that modern mass production—of precisely the kind which Adam Smith advocated and Marx condemned—would alienate workers from the products of their labor and from society. When they focus the attention of their labors upon some one small part, not the whole, of their product, the minds of the workers are narrowed to the point that they no longer can see the place of their labors in society as a whole. Beyond this, Tocqueville believed that production-line labor so narrowed and constrained the life of the worker that "he no longer belongs to himself, but to his chosen calling."[57] Thus, the moral and material conditions of factories appeared to him to be little different from prisons.[58] The final result of the habits of industrial labor, Tocqueville thought, would be the sapping of the industrial worker's capacity for self-rule, and thus an alienation of that worker from his fellow citizens. So, as Tocqueville saw it, this system of production brutalizes and stupefies the worker by killing his spirit of independence.

The effects of industrial commerce upon the owners or bosses are no less pernicious. In the first place, it degrades government and

---

[57]*Democracy*, p. 555; cf. Karl Marx and Friedrich Engels, *Basic Writings on Politics and Philosophy*, ed. Lewis Feuer (Garden City, N.Y.: Doubleday & Co., 1959), pp. 135, 147-60, 489-97.

[58]Gustave de Beaumont and Alexis de Tocqueville, *On the Penitentiary System in the United States and Its Application in France*, trans. Francis Lieber (Carbondale, Ill: Southern Illinois University Press, 1964), p. 165.

politics. "In democracies nothing has brighter lustre than commerce,"[59] and industrial enterprises are among the greatest and most challenging. As such, they attract the attention and stir the imagination of the most talented and ambitious citizens. Consequently, the bosses have no more time for civic life than the industrial workers:

> Such things are all right for idlers to play at [says the typical businessman], but they do not become men of weight occupied with the serious business of life. Such folk think they are following the doctrine of self-interest, but they have a very crude idea thereof, and the better to guard their interests, they neglect the chief among them, that is, to remain their own masters.[60]

The results can be catastrophic. Public offices are despised by, and so not really authoritative for, the most talented citizens. Moreover, democracy's politicians, being less talented and less ambitious than its commercial leaders, are easy prey for businessmen; one thinks, for example, of how easily Commodore Vanderbilt ruined the whole New York State legislature when it attempted to deprive him of his railroad franchise.[61]

Modern commerce atomizes society. Bosses or owners become removed from general social life and, especially, from daily personal contact with employees. So isolated, employers become "administrators" (a term of contempt for Tocqueville); that is, managers. Because administrators as such have no personal relations with those they administer, they lack that sense of moral obligation to their employees which characterized even the relation of a feudal lord to his retainers or serfs. Consequently, "there is no true link between rich and poor . . . no true association." Accordingly, Tocqueville judged that a business aristocracy would be "one of the hardest that has appeared on earth," but that politically it would be "one of the most restrained and least

---

[59]*Democracy*, p. 553.
[60]*Recollections*, p. 540.
[61]See Forrest McDonald, *The Phaeton Ride: The Crisis of American Success* (Garden City, N.Y.: Doubleday & Co., 1974), pp. 52-53.

dangerous," for the business aristocracy, as he saw it, would not want to rule its workers. That would be too troublesome. Rather, it would just make use of them.

These trends could be dangerous to liberty, both in America and elsewhere. On the one hand, the stupefied industrial worker, sapped of political intelligence and social responsibility and periodically thrown upon governmental welfare programs by economic contractions, comes to look upon the central political power as the only one capable of protecting him.[62] Likewise, the administrators of industrial enterprises, "the aristocracy of manufacturers," increasingly turn to the central power for their own aggrandizement:

> In proportion as a nation becomes more industrialized, it feels a greater need for roads, canals, ports, and other semipublic works which aid the growth of wealth. The more democratic a society becomes, the harder it is for private people and parochial communities to undertake such matters on their own.[63]

By such means, the central power daily increases the population's dependence upon it. Although both industrial orders at first become dependent upon the central power only for what is called today "the infrastructure of the economy" and "the safety net for the truly needy," public finance and its regulation soon expand dependency to every aspect of economic life. Indeed, dependency is preferred over economy. For example, Tocqueville observed that where the central power might impose some new tax, it instead has "recourse to a loan": "So little by little the state comes to owe money to most of the men of wealth and thus centralizes the bulk of capital in its hands."

Likewise, the central regulation of "the poor man's savings bank" sucks "the smallest capital into [the central power's] keeping." The consequence is that the whole wealth of the nation is "perpetually circulating around the government and

---

[62]On the egalitarian and Christian origins of the welfare state, see *European Revolution*, p. 209.
[63]*Democracy*, p. 686.

falling into its hands."[64]

While the central power becomes crucial for the use of public and private wealth, that easily provides the pretext for the regulation of almost every other aspect of social life. Tocqueville had already seen in Europe that centralization of administration (i.e., bureaucratization) could extend into all the details of individual citizens' choices: their vocations and professions, their education, their entertainment; the disposal of their estates; and the organization of all professional, civic, and commercial associations. Indeed, there was already a more alarming development: "[R]eligion is in danger of falling under government control."

> It is not that the rulers are overzealous to fix dogma themselves, but they are getting more and more of a hold over the wills of those who interpret it . . . and with their help they reach right down into the depths of each man's soul.[65]

So long is the reach of bureaucracy!

It is a mistake to suppose that modern industrial commerce and central administration of the economy are antithetical. Tocqueville observed, what is easily observed today: Industrial administrators do not naturally favor *laissez-faire* capitalism any more than industrial workers do. Of course, industry and trade do produce ever more wealth, and the influence of the industrial orders does grow ever greater as a result. Yet, "industrial wealth does not extend to rights in proportion to its importance":

> [M]anufacturing classes do not become less dependent as they become more numerous. On the contrary, it would seem that they bring despotism along with them and that it naturally extends in proportion to their growth.[66]

Every aspect of industrial society—its large size, its novel and complex social relations, its economic instability, the danger of its work to health and life—are occasions for further

---

[64]Ibid., p. 682.
[65]Ibid., p. 681.
[66]Ibid., p. 685.

centralization of administration.[67] Therefore, for Tocqueville, industrialization itself is an exercise in materialism and, as such, it is the cultivation of servility.

Tocqueville considered the possibility that the industrial owners would rule society through the state, but, unlike Marx and other socialists, he expected exactly the opposite consequence:

> Governments [will] appropriate to themselves and put in their own use the greater part of the new force which industry has created in the world of our time. Industry leads us along, and they lead industry.[68]

In other words, the organization of means of production is determinative of social life, but social life is not simply determinative of political life. Tocqueville was a political sociologist. As such, he could see that the political form, bureaucracy, is possible either with or without industrialization.

Centralization of administration, as distinguished from centralization of government,[69] is a more fundamental threat to liberty than industrialization. This is obvious in a chapter of *Democracy in America* entitled "What Sort of Despotism Democratic Nations Have to Fear," but, in fact, the "chief aim" of the whole book—if not the central purpose of Tocqueville's whole life—was to combat centralized administration, "bureaucracy," in America and anywhere else it might appear.[70] The characteristic of this kind of despotism is not the harsh subjection of a people to the will of some tyrant, but the gentle strangulation of the spirit of individual independence in a people by the progressively meddlesome regulations of a central bureaucracy.

In the long run, bureaucratization is economically crippling, but that is not why Tocqueville hated it.

> You will see tranquil and prosperous peoples amidst free institutions. They grow, they become rich, they shine.

---

[67]Ibid., p. 684.
[68]Ibid., p. 687.
[69]On this all-important distinction, between kinds of political authority, see ibid., p. 87.
[70]Ibid., p. 671; see also p. 95, and *European Revolution*, p. 252.

> Do not then believe that their independence will endure if it is only these material goods which attach them to liberty. For they may be deprived of these goods in a moment; on the other hand, despotism may procure these goods at least for a time. . . . Material interest will never be sufficiently permanent and tangible to maintain the love of liberty in the hearts of men unless their taste for it exists. . . .[71] [Ellipses in the original.]

Nor did he object to bureaucratization only because it corrupted private morality:

> [T]hat craving for material well-being which leads the way to [bureaucracy] . . . which, while morally debilitating, can be singularly tenacious and insidious . . . often operates in close association with such private virtues as family love, a sense of decorum, respect for religion, and even a lukewarm but punctilious observance of the rites of the established Church. While promoting moral rectitude, it rules out heroism and excels in making people well-behaved but mean-spirited citizens.[72]

He hated centralization because it is contrary to what he regarded as the best instinct in human nature.

Tocqueville believed that, by nature, all humans have some taste for liberty, in the form of "an instinctive tendency, irresistible and hardly conscious, born out of the mysterious sources of all great human passions."[73] Although present in all humans, this "common source not only of political liberty but of all of the high and manly virtues" dominates in the souls of only a very few men. Above all, bureaucracy violates this "instinct." From this, it does not necessarily follow that aristocracy, being the rule of a few, is more favorable to liberty than democracy. After all, aristocracy is based upon the principle of inequality, not liberty, and there is no guarantee that those who are by nature superior in the passion for

---

[71]*European Revolution*, p. 167.
[72]*Old Regime*, p. 118.
[73]Cf. Rousseau, *The First and Second Discourses*, ed. Roger Masters, trans. Roger Masters and Judith Masters (New York: St. Martin's Press, 1964), p. 117.

liberty will be the rulers in an aristocracy. On the other hand, just because aristocracy is the rule of a few, the prospect of a society ruled by nature's liberty-lovers in their own right exists only in an aristocracy. Conversely, democracy, in Tocqueville's view, practically guarantees the rule of those in whom the love of liberty does not predominate. So he declared emphatically that in democracies liberty is the product of art and that "[c]entralized government will be the natural thing" to them.[74] Perhaps it is true that, on the ground of justice, Tocqueville preferred democracy to aristocracy, i.e., socio-political equality to socio-political inequality.[75] Did he prefer justice to liberty? "To me," Tocqueville wrote to Gobineau, "human societies, like persons, become something worthwhile only through their use of liberty."[76] There is nothing in modern industrial commerce which cultivates, but there is much that undermines that natural taste for liberty.

Because he thought the love of liberty is natural to all humans, Tocqueville—unlike Marx and the rest of the socialists, who trace everything to historical socio-economic conditions—did not despair of industrial democracy. Indeed, *Democracy in America* was written to combat its worst propensities. Yet Tocqueville had no doubt that, in the absence of sound democratic statesmanship and citizenship, bureaucratic despotism would only be strengthened by industrialization.

Tocqueville's Prescription for Modern Commerce

In matters of political economy, the great danger to liberty does not come from the socialists' stupid equalitarianism or the *laissez-faire* capitalists' narrowly calculated selfishness. Rather, Tocqueville pointed out, we should fear the intellectuals. Disgusted with

---

[74]*Democracy*, p. 674. Cf. *European Revolution*, p. 309: "I have always said that it is more difficult to stabilize and to maintain liberty in our new democratic societies than in certain aristocratic societies in the past."

[75]Zetterbaum, "Alexis de Tocqueville," p. 734.

[76]*European Revolution*, p. 309. Consider also: "[I]t is the nature of every government to wish continually to increase its sphere of action" (*Democracy*, p. 672n). Equality can inspire a love of liberty (p. 667), but so can inequality: "Thus any notion that the old regime was an era of servility and subservience is very wide of the mark" (*Old Regime*, p. 119).

democracy's propensity to reward commercial—not intellectual or artistic—talents, intellectuals of the right and the left prefer the following proposal:

> [C]oncentrate all wealth in the hands of a central power whose function it should be to parcel it out to individuals according to their merits. That would . . . [be] a way of escaping from the complete and eternal equality which seems to threaten democratic societies.[77]

We may call this proposal bureaucratic redistributionism. In practice, redistributionism has proven to be both socialistic, e.g., when aiming to raise the least-advantaged classes to the socio-economic status they are thought to deserve, and capitalistic, e.g., when seeking to encourage those who produce what is to be redistributed to produce more so that more can be redistributed. Indeed, bureaucratic redistributionism can be capitalistic and socialistic simultaneously. It is essential only that every redistribution of wealth be administered centrally.

Against bureaucratic redistributionism, Tocqueville proposed the following policy:

> [G]ive privileges to none, but equal enlightenment and independence to all, and leave it to each man to make a place for himself. Natural inequality will soon make itself felt, and wealth will pass spontaneously into the hands of the most capable.[78]

This policy runs contrary to the natural preferences of intellectuals, of course. However, as we have already seen, it could also run contrary to the interests of the industrial orders, which at various times might well favor the intellectuals' plan. What then can be done to control the march of industrial democracy toward bureaucracy?

We mention, in the first place, Tocqueville's general admonition that "princes and other leaders of democracies should remember that it is only the passion for freedom, habitually

---

[77]*Democracy*, p. 457. The proposal is characteristic of positivism.
[78]Ibid., p. 457. Cf. Aristotle's critique of Phaleas, *Politics*, 1267a ff.

enjoyed, which can do more than hold its own against a habitual absorption in well-being."[79] In other words, politicians must be careful to point out the pleasures of freedom, however small they might seem, especially when they are connected to the pleasures of material well-being. We must break the present habit of pointing out and even of imagining every abuse of commercial liberty. Conversely, what regulations do exist should be painful—not only costly, but also humiliating—reminders of a citizen's failure to rule himself; nothing is more ill-advised than the current regulatory policy—common throughout the West, but especially in the United States—of negotiated compliance out of court.

In the second place, the actual administration of the economy must be kept or made as decentralized as is possible. For example, a national "industrial policy," which is the current form of bureaucratic redistribution, should be resisted, because central administration can only exacerbate the ills of modern commerce. Instead, autonomous centers of economic life in the private sector and of regulatory authority in the public sectors ought to be tolerated.

In this regard, the major institutions of modern commerce in the United States today are relatively healthy. Labor unions and business corporations are still, in the main, free associations. Small business is still possible. In commerce as in every other aspect of democratic social life, such free associations are the institutional bulwark against bureaucratization. By their very nature, free associations teach their members to recognize for themselves what they have in common with their fellows, train them in the skills of compromise and leadership which are essential to self-government, and strengthen them against the central power. Of course, unions, corporations, and other commercial associations are sanctified by various agencies of state or federal governments, but this sanctification amounts to a certification that each association has been freely organized; i.e., that no one was constrained to associate by force or by ignorance. Indeed, one of the glories of the New Deal is that, in establishing the Securities and Exchange Commission and the National Labor Relations Board to regulate

---

[79]*Democracy*, p. 663.

national industries, it managed to preserve freedom of commercial association.

The major difficulty with unions and corporations is not the freedom of their organization but the involvement of their interests with the central administration. Increasingly, labor unions have become involved with bureaucracy: first, by the preference of unions for central administrative agencies, like the Occupational Safety and Health Administration and a score of others, to perform functions of unions; then, by the organization of governmental employees in the same unions as industrial workers. Similarly, the interests of corporations have become heavily involved with central administration: Many federal regulatory agencies perform functions for an industry, which each could do for itself, but which no single corporation in that industry is willing to do. For example, no automobile manufacturer is willing to set its own standard for noxious emissions, out of fear that it would put itself at a competitive disadvantage, but all are happy to live up to an industry-wide standard set by the Environmental Protection Agency. As this matter turns out, the companies do not cease competing over emissions control, but now they compete for the favor of bureaucrats, not the favor of automobile buyers. Thus do corporations acquire a competitive interest in the regulatory process. Moreover, the interests of unions and corporations are profoundly influenced by the fact that government is the largest single employer and the largest single consumer; government can quite often make the market for goods and services.

The consequences of the heavy involvement of commercial interests with central administration are not at all what the politicians who encouraged it might expect. Tocqueville's careful study of the French Revolution proves this:

> [I]t was the *rentiers*, merchants, manufacturers, businessmen, and financiers—the section of the community usually most adverse to violent political changes, warm supporters of the existing government, whatever it may be, and essentially law-abiding even when they despise or dislike the laws—that now proved to be the most strenuous and determined

advocates of reform.[80]

Political support for decentralization of administration, including deregulation, is most likely to come from those economic interests which are most heavily involved with the bureaucracy because they can see and feel the oppression of bureaucracy immediately. Of course, those interests would be selfish, not political. Bureaucracy is objectionable to them, not because it is oppressive of the citizens' liberties, but because it squanders taxpayers' money:

> On the one hand was a nation in which the love of wealth and luxury was daily spreading; on the other a government that while constantly fomenting this new passion, at the same time frustrated it.[81]

The recent attempts of the Carter and Reagan administrations to deregulate commerce illustrate the difficulty to which Tocqueville points. Deregulation has not decentralized the regulation of commerce: The authority of the central regulatory agencies remains intact, but they tend to exercise it more gently or less arbitrarily. As long as central authority is not applied against their interests, unions and corporations prefer to keep central authority intact, apparently hoping that it can be used against their competitors.

Thirdly, democratic statesmen ought to foster the prosperity of religion, especially Protestant Christianity, for the health of commerce—the productivity that comes only with self-restraint—depends upon the spirit of independence. Of course, the encouragement of religious observance cannot be accomplished directly; e.g., by the establishment of Protestant Christianity or any other faith. Perhaps even Sunday-closing laws are no longer possible in many places.

Tocqueville suggested a number of indirect means. Politicians ought, for example, "daily to act as if they believed [in the doctrine of the immortality of the soul] themselves."[82] Also, they

---

[80]*Old Regime*, p. 179.
[81]Ibid.
[82]*Democracy*, p. 546.

ought to "give daily practical examples" proving to men that worldly successes come only with long, hard, troublesome work.[83] However, the chief vehicles of these religious and moral lessons are not really politicians, but women—that is, mothers and wives:

> [Religion] is often powerless to restrain men in the midst of innumerable temptations . . . [and] cannot moderate their eagerness to enrich themselves, which everything contributes to arouse, but it reigns supreme in the souls of women, and it is women who shape moral behavior.[84]

Tocqueville went further than this: "[T]he chief cause of the extraordinary prosperity and growing power of this nation . . . is due to the superiority of [American] women."[85]

Marriage laws permitting divorce on demand and an equal division of the family's assets and liabilities (including the children) between the husband and wife would appall Tocqueville. These are the chief cause of the inferiority of our women, they are a cause of much unhappiness, and they are also the cause of the great bulk of economic dependency.[86] Even if the material condition of women and children without husbands and fathers could be improved by such bureaucratic programs as Affirmative Action/ Comparable Worth and publicly financed child-care centers, the moral and religious education, which is essential for the continued happiness and prosperity of the nation, cannot be accomplished by the bureaucratization of women and children.

The health of a democratic society, including the health of its economy, requires the strength of families as autonomous associations, for it is from these associations, above all, that citizens learn the fundamentals of decentralized administration. Good families can cultivate that spirit of independence, which is the basis of both political liberty and prosperity. Yet such families are materially and morally impossible for almost all without the

---

[83]Ibid., p. 549.
[84]Ibid., p. 291.
[85]Ibid., p. 603.
[86]Of late, even feminists have begun to recognize this. See Lenore Weitzman, *The Divorce Revolution* (New York: The Free Press, 1985).

constant, cooperative presence of a mother and a father. From Tocqueville's point of view, no finer regulation of commerce would be possible than reform of the divorce laws, and of the foolish notion of the equality of the sexes upon which the present laws are based.

The Limit of Tocqueville's Relevance

There is so much good sense and perspicacity in Tocqueville's analysis of commerce in modern democracy that we are reluctant to consider its merely theoretical defects. Accordingly, we notice the difficulty in Tocqueville's political philosophy only insofar as it explains a defect in his practical judgment. Simply stated, Tocqueville seems to have overestimated the capacity of industrial commerce to produce a servile, stupefied, atomized, and depoliticized civic body and underestimated the capacity for violence of modern centralized administration.

We have seen in this century—above all, in the Soviet Union—a fully centralized administration more violent than any regime in history. And such regimes would have to be called modern democracies by Tocqueville's standard because their public principle is "equality."

Nor is it clear that the industrial system *as such* has been destructive of civic virtue. For example, not only are industrial workers in the United States among the most patriotic, they are also among the most martial of habit, which is the best measure of willingness to sacrifice for the well-being of the community. Indeed, one's impression is that servility and incivility are more common in universities or in the federal bureaucracy than on an assembly line or a construction site. Furthermore, if it is true that the economic independence of the American people has decreased while industrialization has progressed, it is not clear that it has decreased as a necessary consequence of industrialization. That is, more enlightened social, economic, taxation, and regulatory policies could encourage economic independence and reduce dependence. For example, Individual Retirement Accounts (IRAs) could replace or supplement Social Security. Furthermore, it is at least plausible that the current stage of industrial development favors decentralization of production, and so of regulation, as much as the development of mass production favored centralization. Certainly, the electronics industries offer many new opportunities and have already resulted in the development of many new centers of wealth (and many newly wealthy citizens). What is necessary to sustain and increase individual independence and to turn it toward civic virtue, as Tocqueville demonstrated with unrivaled excellence, is that independence be publicly prized. Let us hope, then, that today's social reformers turn away from the victimology of Affirmative Action/Comparable Worth, and other forms of bureaucratic redistributionism, and toward policies which foster political as well as economic independence.

Tocqueville's two misevaluations of industrial democracy are connected. If the industrial orders are capable of more civic virtue than Tocqueville supposed, then bureaucratic rule of industrial society would have to be more violent than he supposed. The theoretic root of both errors is Tocqueville's understanding of man's natural political capacity. If most humans really are so lacking in capacity for self-government (i.e., for participation in political rule) that they can be reduced to the level of a well-managed dairy herd, then Tocqueville's mild bureaucratic despotism would seem to be almost inevitable. On the other hand, if all men are created equal in capacity for self-government, then the prospects of industrial democracy are brighter than Tocqueville supposed, and the specter of bureaucracy is darker.

To understand Tocqueville's estimate of the natural human capacity for politics, we turn now to the two distinguishing features of his political philosophy: its libertarianism and what may be called its religiosity. We have already treated the libertarianism, i.e., Tocqueville's preference for liberty over justice.

Tocqueville's religiosity is best seen in his contempt for modern philosophy's anti-religious prejudices:

> Eighteenth-century philosophers had a very simple explanation for the gradual weakening of religious faith. Religious zeal, they said, was bound to die down as enlightenment and freedom spread. It is tiresome [to note]

> that the facts do not fit this theory at all.[87]

Again, respecting the nineteenth century:

> [O]ur pedants find . . . that all is fine in America except just that religious spirit. . . . I am informed that on the other side of the ocean freedom and human happiness lack nothing but Spinoza's belief in the eternity of the world and Cabanis' contention that thought is a secretion of the brain.[88]

As we have observed in detail, America proves that almost the opposite is the case: Enlightenment and freedom depend upon religious conviction. So Tocqueville insisted—for the sake of liberty but against today's left-liberalism—that free government and decent social life in modern democracies presupposes a religious citizenry. Religion, that is, is not merely a private matter between the abstract individual and his God.

Scholars like to suppose that Tocqueville's religiosity was merely utilitarian, as though he did not concern himself with the truth of religion.[89] However, much of the evidence cited to support this contention proves just the opposite. For example, the fact that Tocqueville was certain that "the doctrine of metempsychosis is not more reasonable [but is more useful] than that of materialism,"[90] clearly does not prove that Tocqueville was a materialist, but does show that he entertained religious truths.

The theoretical connection between Tocqueville's libertarianism and his religiosity appears most clearly in a remarkable passage on evangelical Christianity. To explain why he thought being "born again" is the characteristic American reaction against the headlong pursuit of physical gratifications, he remarked:

---

[87]*Democracy*, p. 295. He sketches the development of this modern idea on pp. 430-31.
[88]Ibid., p. 294.
[89]See Zetterbaum, "Alexis de Tocqueville," p. 733; Zeitlin, *Liberty*, pp. 45-46; Lively, *Thought*. J.-P. Mayer does not quite agree; see his *Alexis de Tocqueville: A Biographical Essay in Political Science* (New York: The Viking Press, 1940), pp. 163-71, for a view closer to that of this essay.
[90]*Democracy*, p. 544.

> It was not man who implanted in himself the taste for the infinite and the love of what is immortal. These sublime instincts are not the offspring of some caprice of the human will; their foundations are embedded in nature; they exist despite man's efforts. Man may hinder and distort them, but he cannot destroy them.[91]

A natural human instinct for eternity could be the basis for both freedom and religion, if it is that instinct which liberates humans from the constantly changing desires of their bodies and from the fickle prejudices of their society.

Tocqueville made it as clear as needs be that the passion for eternity can be expressed, if not satisfied, by national inquiry or philosophy. Yet, in his opinion, religion is a worthy expression of that concern, even for the greatest minds, and it is the only such expression for which the great bulk of the members of any society can have time.[92] Accordingly, the highest or distinguishing principle of human reality—of the natural *"ordre du coeur,"* as distinguished from the *"ordre logique"*—would be just this passion or taste for eternity (and liberty), which finds expression as religion. The various aristocratic or democratic articulations of this reality in political, economic, or social life are secondary and cannot ever rightly command a man's deepest passions. Every human knows that "societies do not have eternal lives."[93] In other words, not political excellence, but the free flowering of the individual soul is the central and highest concern of Tocqueville's social science. Not public reason, but private passion, and not political justice, but individual liberty are definitive of humanity. Tocqueville admitted, however, and even demonstrated, that the passion for justice (e.g., for equality) is stronger than the passion for liberty.[94] Given Tocqueville's categories then, the preservation of democratic liberty would be fortuitous indeed.

---

[91]Ibid., pp. 534-35.

[92]On the need of all humans for answers which they do not have time to discover, see ibid., pp. 459-65. See the reference to Pascal, ibid., p. 461, and the other two references, pp. 198, 629-30; see also J.-P. Mayer, *Alexis de Tocqueville: A Biographical Essay* (Salem, N.H.: Ayer, 1979), pp. 24, 147.

[93]*European Revolution*, p. 292.

[94]*Democracy*, p. 503-06.

Reason could not suggest to Tocqueville the harmony of equality with liberty. For him, the passion for equality is the principle of democracy, not its reason, just as the passion for liberty is the principle of humanity. Yet, in the American political tradition, that harmony is reasonable: Equality means, above all, the equality of natural rights among all individual members of the human race, and those include the right of liberty. That is, the American tradition affirms the equal capacity of all humans for self-government. However, to Tocqueville, America's doctrine of individual rights is not something reasonable and democratic. Tocqueville called it our precious inheritance from "the English aristocracy."[95]

This is historically erroneous. Historically, the American doctrine of individual rights is not the doctrine of the rights of Englishmen, including English noblemen. Indeed, the doctrine was used in the Declaration of Independence to explain why Americans were not, and ought not be, Englishmen! Furthermore, even if it is historically true that Americans were prepared to accept the doctrine of natural individual rights by their English heritage, it is also historically true that the perpetuation of that doctrine has been accomplished by the repudiation of nonuniversalistic or non-rational conceptions of individual rights. Because of this historical error, Tocqueville could not guess that, politically, the enemies of liberty are invariably the enemies of equality. That is, today as in the past, the enemies of liberty—on the Right and on the Left—deny the natural (i.e., universal or nonhistorical) basis of individual rights and affirm some doctrine of right founded in American law, relative social condition, history, traditional norms or formalities, subjective feelings, race, or socio-economic class; not nature and not reason. They, like Tocqueville, cannot learn the lesson of Abraham Lincoln:

> "All men are created equal" remains the decisive *political* truth, because . . . those who do deny it [the hypothesis of our nation], can only do so because of an unjust motive.[96]

---

[95]Ibid., p. 676.

[96]Harry V. Jaffa, *Crisis of the House Divided: An Interpretation of the Issues in the*

They, like Tocqueville, prefer to believe in the providential march of history, rather than affirm the simple truth of equality.

Tocqueville's affirmation of the natural habits of the heart, against bureaucracy's relentless "rationalization" of human life, amounts to a denial that the natural order is a rational order. So, as much as we admire the nobility of Tocqueville's struggle against centralization of administration, we should recognize that it is not rational, but fundamentally sentimental. After all, the rationalization of society promised by bureaucratization, whether in the regulation of commerce or in the regulation of the relation between the sexes, is empty or merely formal: Bureaucracy promises that all will be subject to the same rule, without bothering to specify in relation to what all are the same. In contradistinction, the rational society promised by the American democracy's doctrine of natural equality would treat all the same in relation to those things in which they are the same: their natural rights.

In the past two decades, something very much like Tocqueville's bureaucratic despotism has begun to grow up in the United States. Just as Tocqueville argued, the failure (or unwillingness) of the commercial orders to govern themselves has been a principal condition for, and the proposals of leading intellectuals have been the cause of, American bureaucratization. Appeals to the passion for individual independence have been to little avail against the bureaucratization of free enterprise, because they appear to be merely selfish or irrational. Furthermore, for the reasons already given, American businesses have already found many ways to make bureaucracy profitable. So the danger to free government which Tocqueville foresaw with such acuity (and worse dangers which he did not foresee) cannot be forestalled by appeals to interest, any more than by appeals to passions. The friends of freedom, including commercial freedom, must prepare themselves to give moral and economic reasons for the decentralization of administration. We have more reason to hope for success than Tocqueville had, because all humans are possessed of the capacity to rule themselves. We also have more reason to fear failure.

Lincoln-Douglas Debates (Garden City, N.Y.: Doubleday & Co., Inc., 1959), p. 222; (reprinted Chicago: University of Chicago Press, 1982).

9

The Illiberal Tocqueville

Edward C. Banfield

Democracy in America has been called the greatest book ever written about one country by a citizen of another. It is certainly the greatest book ever written by anyone about America. After 150 years there is hardly a page that does not open the reader's eyes to the larger implications of some familiar fact. It may appear perverse of me, then, to use this occasion to discuss not Tocqueville's illuminating view of America but rather his—as I think—unilluminating one of the nature and future of democracy. My excuse for doing so is not that this essay celebrates the Bicentennial of the Constitution (which is based on principles quite contrary to Tocqueville's). Rather, it is that Tocqueville considered the nature and future of democracy to be his real subject. "America," he wrote to J. S. Mill, "was only the frame, my picture was Democracy."[1]

In the memoir he wrote after Tocqueville's death, Beaumont listed the questions he said had filled Tocqueville's thoughts before they began their journey together—questions which brought Tocqueville to the New World and which were to be the business of his life.[2] There were four:

This essay was the second annual Constitutional Statesmanship Lecture in The Claremont Institute's *Novus Ordo Seclorum* Bicentennial Project, delivered Sept. 26, 1985.

[1]*Memoir, Letters and Remains of Alexis de Tocqueville* (Boston: Ticknor and Fields, 1862), vol. II, p. 38. Hereinafter cited as *Memoir*. Tocqueville says essentially the same in his introductory chapter. Alexis de Tocqueville, *Democracy in America* (New York: Alfred A. Knopf, 1945), vol. I, p. 14. Hereinafter cited as *Democracy*.

[2]*Memoir*, vol. I, pp. 19-20.

> How to reconcile equality, which separates and isolates men, with liberty? How to prevent a power, the offspring of democracy, from becoming absolute and tyrannical? Where to find a force able to contend against this power among a set of men, all equal, it is true, but all equally weak and impotent? Was the fate of modern society to be both democracy and despotism?

I shall discuss Tocqueville's reflections on these four questions, drawing mainly upon *Democracy in America* but also upon his other published writings, including letters.

I

Tocqueville writes as a French patriot, a member of the lesser nobility, who aspires to a career as a statesman and literary figure; who sees France in the turmoil of a social and political revolution likely to end in either anarchy or despotism; and who wants passionately to show the leaders of both right and left how they may guide events to an outcome which, although far from ideal, will nevertheless combine liberty with order and justice—a regime decent men will find tolerable. His purpose is frankly hortatory. He will paint a picture of democracy that will reassure extreme conservatives in France while at the same time dampening the enthusiasm of radical egalitarians.[3]

He finds it almost as difficult for a man to be inconsistent in his language as to be consistent in his conduct, but he himself uses his key concepts in at least two—usually vague—senses.[4] Thus "democracy" has two quite unrelated meanings: "general equality of social conditions" and "the absolute sovereignty of the majority."[5] In America, general equality of social conditions has developed farther than anywhere else: Indeed, it has approached its "natural

---

[3]Ibid., pp. 376-78. This letter is reprinted in Roger Boesche, ed., *Alexis de Tocqueville: Selected Letters on Politics and Society* (Berkeley: University of California Press, 1985), pp. 98-99. Hereinafter cited as Boesche, *Selected Letters*.
[4]*Democracy*, vol. I, p. 16; see also vol. II, p. 69.
[5]Ibid., vol. I, pp. 3, 254.

limits."[6] Equality of social conditions does not necessarily imply popular government; thus Tocqueville can speak of a "democratic people ruled by a despot."[7] Although in both meanings "democracy" was more advanced in the United States than elsewhere, it was not likely that the nations of Europe could learn much from it. Tocqueville was well aware of this. He saw the United States as the unique product of its origins. The Puritan colonists of the seventeenth century, he writes, brought into an admirable combination two distinctive elements that hitherto had often been at war: the *"spirit of religion"* and the *"spirit of freedom"* (emphasis in the original).[8] The first Puritan carried with him the whole of the political future.[9] "There is not an opinion, not a custom, not a law, not even an event, that the origins of the Americans will not explain."[10] What is most important in the development of national character is not climate, law, or even institutions; rather, it is habits, opinions, usages, and beliefs.[11] New England, he points out, is very different from the West and the South.[12] Mexico, which has the same laws as the United States, is unable to govern itself democratically.[13]

If American democracy is unique, one wonders, what can be learned from it that will have any application elsewhere? What can France, for example, which never had a Puritan, learn from a country whose political tradition was decisively influenced by Puritanism? Tocqueville acknowledged the problem: A careful distinction must, he says, be made between the institutions of the United States and democratic institutions in general, adding that if human nature or social conditions are very different in America and Europe there is no possibility of making predictions about democracy in general on the basis of American experience.[14] Finally, he

---

[6]Ibid., p. 13.
[7]Ibid., vol. II, p. 26.
[8]Ibid., vol. I, p. 43.
[9]Ibid., p. 290.
[10]Ibid., p. 28.
[11]Ibid., p. 322.
[12]Ibid.
[13]Ibid., p. 321.
[14]Ibid., pp. 323-24.

recognizes that what may be learned about democracy from American experience may not bear transplanting: A democracy, he says, can obtain truth only as a result of experience, meaning, presumably, *its own* experience.[15] Having acknowledged these methodological limitations, he proceeds as if they do not exist.

II

> How to reconcile equality, which
> separates and isolates men, with liberty?

All men at all times, Tocqueville says, have a passion for equality—one that is "ardent, insatiable, incessant, invincible."[16] Where conditions permit of rising in the world, there is universal competition to do so.[17] In Europe, over many centuries there has been a gradual but accelerating tendency to break down all forms of social hierarchy. The further advance of equality, that is, of democracy, constitutes a social revolution which cannot be stopped, although it may be guided and controlled.[18] Equality of social conditions, he writes in the first paragraph of *Democracy*, is "the fundamental fact from which all others seem to be derived. . . ."

By separating and isolating men, equality of social conditions gives rise to individualism, a state in which every man's feelings are turned toward himself alone. The individualist, with his family and friends, draws apart from others: He turns his back upon society, leaving it to take care of itself.

> As social conditions become more equal, the number of persons increases who, although they are neither rich nor powerful enough to exercise any great influence over their fellows, have nevertheless acquired or retained sufficient education and fortune to satisfy their own wants. They owe nothing to any man, they expect nothing from any man; they acquire the habit of always considering themselves

---

[15]Ibid., p. 231.
[16]Ibid., vol. II, p. 97.
[17]Ibid., vol. I, p. 201; vol. II, p. 138.
[18]Ibid., vol. I, p. 7.

as standing alone, and they are apt to imagine that their whole destiny is in their own hands.

Thus not only does democracy make every man forget his ancestors, but it hides his descendants and separates his contemporaries from him; it throws him back forever upon himself alone and threatens in the end to confine him entirely within the solitude of his own heart.[19]

At first individualism attacks only the virtues of public life, but eventually it destroys all others as well. Equality is bound to spread and, with it, individualism. This being the case, how can liberty be maintained?

Clearly much depends upon how one conceives of liberty. Tocqueville has mutually antagonistic concepts of it.[20]

In an article written for a review edited by J. S. Mill, he defines it very much as Mill was to define it himself twenty years later:

According to the modern, and democratic and, we venture to say, the only just notion of liberty, every man, being presumed to have received from nature the intelligence necessary for his own general guidance, is inherently entitled to be uncontrolled by his fellows in all that only concerns

---

[19]Ibid., vol. II, p. 99.

[20]In his account of the origins of the Americans, Tocqueville quotes the "fine definition" of liberty made by the Puritan leader John Winthrop in the seventeenth century (ibid., vol. I, p. 39). Civil or moral (as opposed to natural) liberty, Winthrop said, "is a liberty to do only that which is good, just, and honest"; such liberty, he added, "is exercised in subjection to authority." What Tocqueville finds admirable in this definition is the combination of the *spirit of religion* with the *spirit of liberty* (vol. I, p. 43). That the Puritans freely voted laws that were "fantastic and oppressive" he acknowledges, calling it an error "discreditable to human reason" (vol. I, pp. 39, 42; also vol. II, Appendix E). But of course it is precisely because men who are separated and isolated, acknowledging no principle of authority, are prone to error that the question of how to maintain liberty among them arises. Winthrop's notion of liberty is irrelevant to the kind of society with which Tocqueville is concerned.

When addressing English readers, Tocqueville seems to use the word "liberty" differently than when addressing French ones. In a letter to J. S. Mill, he says he loves liberty "by taste" whereas he loves equality by "instinct and reason" (Boesche, *Selected Letters*, p. 100). Writing to his publisher, Henry Reeve, he says he has only one passion: "love of liberty and human dignity" (ibid., p. 115). To Madame Swetchine and to Beaumont, he takes a different tone. To the former he writes that liberty is "one of the most fertile sources of manly virtues and great actions" (ibid., p. 326), and to the latter it is "the necessary condition without which there has never been a truly great or virile nation" (ibid., p. 366).

himself, and to regulate at his own will his own destiny.[21]

What Tocqueville here calls the "only just notion of liberty" sounds very much like what in the first volume of *Democracy* he describes as the "grand maxim" of American society; namely, that Providence has given to every human being the degree of reason necessary to direct himself in the affairs that interest him exclusively.[22] This, however, is the principle of individualism, which he detests. A nation devoted to it, he says, must eventually slide into despotism.[23]

What Tocqueville meant by liberty was no more than the absence of despotism.[24] He was much mistaken when, writing Mill to thank him—before reading it—for a copy of *On Liberty*, he said that liberty "is a field in which we cannot but walk hand in hand."[25] But even by this weakest of definitions he contradicts himself. In *The Old Regime and the French Revolution*, he condemns as despotic the ideas of the Physiocrats, who, he says, believed the function of the state was not only to rule but also to shape the mentality of the population by instilling the ideas and sentiments they thought desirable.[26] But instilling ideas and sentiments was exactly what his own program for turning individuals into citizens entailed. In *Democracy* he proposes laying down "certain extreme limits which the state should never be allowed to overstep."[27] How, one must wonder, are "those who direct our [French] affairs" to keep within any limits while carrying out the duties Tocqueville says are imposed upon them:

> . . . to educate democracy, to reawaken, if possible, its religious beliefs: to purify its morals: to mold its actions: to

---

[21]*Memoir*, vol. I, p. 247.
[22]*Democracy*, vol. I, p. 418.
[23]Ibid., p. 420.
[24]See Joseph Hamburger, "Mill and Tocqueville on Liberty," eds. John M. Robson and Michael Laine, *James and John Stuart Mill: Papers of the Centenary Conference* (Toronto and Buffalo: University of Toronto Press, 1976), p. 124.
[25]*Memoir*, vol. II, p. 428.
[26]Alexis de Tocqueville, *The Old Regime and the French Revolution*, trans. Stuart Gilbert (Garden City, N.Y.: Doubleday, Anchor Books, 1955), pp. 158-64. Hereinafter cited as *Old Regime*.
[27]*Democracy*, vol. II, p. 248.

> substitute a knowledge of statecraft for its inexperience, and an awareness of its true interest for its blind instincts. . . .[28]

This list of reforms is lengthened in the second volume. The "leaders of modern society" should expose the community to difficulties and dangers "in order to raise ambition. . . ."[29] Government should do what it can to restore men to a love of the future.[30] A policy of giving democratic nations education and freedom and then leaving them alone will not suffice in the end, and it is likely to cause man "to lose the use of his sublimest faculties."[31]

III

> How to prevent a power, the offspring of democracy, from becoming absolute and tyrannical?

Tocqueville could answer this question in principle, but, alas, *only* in principle.

The self-interested individual must be taught the ways of citizenship: He must learn to accept his share of responsibility for the welfare of the community. What is needed is a decentralization of government that will put the conduct of local affairs in local hands: The individual will then of necessity acquire the skills and habits of a citizen. American experience suggests a number of other "democratic expedients" having this tendency: among them the spread of associations for political and social ends, the jury system, a free press, and an independent judiciary.

Unfortunately, these "democratic expedients" would not be expedient in Europe, and the most important of them, local self-government, was rapidly ceasing to be so in the United States. Townships, Tocqueville remarks, must be "self-produced," and municipal freedom is "rarely created by others."[32] Developed societies, he says, are apt to be impatient with the blunders that

---

28Ibid., vol. I, p. 7.
29Ibid., vol. II, p. 248.
30Ibid., p. 151.
31Ibid., p. 144.
32Ibid., vol. I, p. 60.

result from local independence.[33] Moreover, both the interests of the politicians in power and the tastes of individuals are forces pressing for centralization.[34] It is far easier for a central government to destroy local independence than to create it.[35]

A somewhat more promising possibility lies in the American principle of self-interest rightly understood. Recognizing the futility of urging lofty ideas of man's duty upon self-interested individualists, American moralists content themselves with holding that it is to the individual's self-interest to serve others. This principle, Tocqueville points out, produces no great acts of self-sacrifice: It cannot make a man virtuous, but it does discipline men in habits of regularity, temperance, moderation, foresight, and self-command, and so it draws them in the direction of virtue.[36] If they could be drawn far enough, they would be good—no, fair—citizens.

Unfortunately they cannot be drawn far enough. "No power on earth," he says,

> can prevent the increasing equality of conditions from inclining the human mind to seek out what is useful or from leading every member of the community to be wrapped up in himself. It must therefore be expected that personal interest will become more than ever the principal if not the sole spring of men's actions. . . .[37]

If self-interest narrowly conceived comes to dominate, "freedom, public peace, and social order itself will not be able to exist. . . ."[38] Except as men take account of the public interest, "it is difficult to foresee to what pitch of stupid excesses their selfishness may lead them. . . ."[39]

The defining principle of democracy is the sovereignty of the majority, but the majority, it appears, cannot be educated to

---

[33]Ibid.
[34]Ibid., vol. II, pp. 367-68.
[35]Ibid., vol. I, p. 60.
[36]Ibid., vol. II, p. 123.
[37]Ibid., p. 124.
[38]Ibid.
[39]Ibid.

citizenship. Moreover, that the people have a right to do anything they wish is an "impious and detestable maxim."[40] In America, Tocqueville finds, the principle of the sovereignty of the people has acquired "all the practical development that the imagination can conceive"[41]: "The people reign in the American political world as the Deity does in the universe. They are the cause and aim of all things: Everything comes from them, and everything is absorbed in them."[42] The American Founders, he mistakenly thinks, carried the principle of popular sovereignty to its extreme by providing that the legislature be elected by the people *directly* and for *a very brief term* (the emphasis is his) in order to make it responsive not only to the convictions but "even to the daily passions" of the people.[43] (He was under the misapprehension that the national government was of little importance as compared to state governments.) The power of the majority in the United States, he concludes, "is harmful in itself and dangerous for the future."[44] The states, he thinks, must move toward indirect democracy or "risk perishing miserably among the shoals of democracy."[45]

The best government, Tocqueville wrote from America to a friend, "is not that in which all have a share, but that which is directed by the class of the highest moral principle and intellectual cultivation."[46] Democracy cannot be the best government since its very essence "consists in the absolute sovereignty of the majority. . . ."[47] But he wonders if in some country—France?—the people would consent to be ruled by their betters. Unmindful of American constitutional arrangements, Tocqueville speculates:

> Might not a democratic society be imagined in which the forces of the nation would be more centralized than they are in the United States; where the people would exercise a less direct influence upon public affairs, and yet every citizen,

---

[40]Ibid., vol. I, p. 259.
[41]Ibid., p. 57.
[42]Ibid., p. 58.
[43]Ibid., p. 254.
[44]Ibid., p. 256.
[45]Ibid., p. 205.
[46]*Memoir*, vol. I, p. 297.
[47]*Democracy*, vol. I, p. 254.

> invested with certain rights, would participate, within his sphere, in the conduct of the government?"[48]

Democratic institutions of this kind might be introduced elsewhere than in America, he thinks, if it were done gradually and without greatly disturbing the habits and opinions of the people.[49]

IV

> Where to find a force able to contend against
> this power among a set of men all equal,
> it is true, but all equally weak and impotent?

The "power" to which the question refers is that of an unenlightened majority. Tocqueville believes that two forces are able to contend against it: religion and patriotism. These, he says, are the only motives that can long urge all the people toward the same end.[50] Both are natural instincts, and both have been weakened by the effects of equality, especially excessive desire for physical gratifications and for the acquisition of wealth.

The compelling need is to direct men's attention away from the petty pleasures of the present and from theories of materialism and to point it toward distant objects. Legislators and all virtuous and enlightened men should endeavor to raise the souls of their fellow citizens and to keep them lifted up toward heaven.[51]

Religious belief should be awakened "if possible."[52] The purpose being a political one (Tocqueville says he is discussing religion "from a purely human point of view"),[53] it is not necessary that the awakening be to a true religion; any one will do, even one that is "false and dangerous"; indeed, even one that does not promise a personal immortality.[54]

---

[48]Ibid.
[49]Ibid.
[50]Ibid., p. 93.
[51]Ibid., vol. II, p. 145.
[52]Ibid., vol. I, p. 7.
[53]Ibid., vol. II, p. 22.
[54]Ibid.

Although he believes that man instinctively turns to religion, Tocqueville recognizes that the forces that have turned him from it—especially materialism—are not easily overcome. The only way by which rulers can get the doctrine of the immortality of the soul respected is to act *as if* they believe it themselves.[55] Will the rulers of an atheistic democracy act *as if* they believe? Tocqueville has his doubts. The American clergy, he notes, not wanting to be conspicuously out of step with public opinion, are far from vigorous in their efforts to turn attention from this world to the next.[56] How could it be otherwise? "The taste for well being," Tocqueville says, "is the prominent and indelible feature of democratic times."[57]

The other instinct able to unite men is patriotism. In a letter written late in his life, Tocqueville conjectures that nations were formed by God in order to show more clearly the ties by which individuals ought to be mutually attached.[58] (He adds that God's purpose was probably better served by giving men particular fatherlands than it would have been by trying to inflame their passion for all humanity!)[59] National pride is often puerile and absurd, he writes in another letter, but "with all its absurdities and weaknesses [it] is still the greatest sentiment that we [the French] have. . . ."[60] In the first of these two letters, Tocqueville goes on to say that he wishes the clergy would emphasize that a Christian belongs to his nation:

> I wish the clergy to instill into their very souls that everyone belongs much more to this collective Being [the nation] than he does to himself; that towards this Being no one ought to be indifferent, much less, by treating such indifference as a sort of languid virtue, to enervate many of our noblest instincts; that everyone is responsible for the fortunes of this collective Being; that everyone is bound

---

[55]Ibid., p. 147.
[56]Ibid., p. 27.
[57]Ibid., p. 26.
[58]*Memoir*, vol. II, p. 333.
[59]Ibid.
[60]Boesche, *Selected Letters*, p. 144.

> to work out its prosperity, and to watch that it be not governed except by respectable, beneficent, and legitimate authorities.[61]

This, Tocqueville recalls, was the teaching of his grandmother, a very saintly woman who, after urging her young son to perform the duties of private life, never failed to add: "And then, my child, never forget that a man above all owes himself to his homeland; that there is no sacrifice that he must not make for it. . . ."[62]

Tocqueville distinguishes categorically between public and private virtue and exalts the former over the latter. Commerce he finds repellent because the "paltry desires" and "vulgar pleasures" it engenders distract men from "manly virtues and great actions," "lofty enterprises," "heroic deeds," and "altruistic sacrifices." He says that in a society consisting of good fathers, honest merchants, exemplary landlords, and even good Christians, there cannot be a great citizen, still less a great nation.[63] Why is it, he wonders, that in proportion as private virtue increases, "the great family of the nation seems more corrupt, more base, and more tottering."[64]

It is manly virtues that make a nation glorious. War is, of course, the activity in which these virtues are most conspicuously displayed. War "almost always enlarges the mind of a people and raises their character."[65] Although he yields to no man in his hatred of the revolutionary spirit, Tocqueville writes to a friend in 1836 that he finds the French revolutionaries' belief in man's innate virtue "admirable," the basis of a new religion that freed them of "self-regarding emotions": Indifferent to the petty amenities of life, unchecked by any scruples, able to act with unprecedented

---

[61]*Memoir*, vol. II, p. 333.

[62]Ibid., p. 329. This letter is included in Boesche, *Selected Letters*, p. 338.

[63]*Old Regime*, p. xiv.

[64]*Memoir*, vol. II, p. 317. In his famous address to the Chamber of Deputies of Jan. 27, 1848, Tocqueville condemns the idea that there are two moralities, a public and a private, a view which he later pressed upon Madame Swetchine (*Memoir*, vol. II, p. 328; see also Boesche, *Selected Letters*, p. 338). In his address he says that private mores affect public life, a matter "to cause disquiet and alarm to good citizens." His address to the Chamber is Appendix III of the George Lawrence translation of *Democracy in America*, ed. J.-P. Mayer (New York: Doubleday, 1969), pp. 750-51.

[65]*Democracy*, vol. II, pp. 261-62.

ruthlessness, they were "the first of a new race of men."[66] He has unstinting praise for the British record in India: "Nothing under the sun is so wonderful as the conquest, and still more the government, of India by the English."[67]

In the absence of the manly virtues that inspire lofty enterprises and heroic deeds, Tocqueville concludes, "a nation can but relapse into a servile state."[68]

All this is reminiscent of Robespierre, whose vision of political life, Stephen Holmes has written, was dominated by a dichotomy between base self-interest and noble virtue, for whom citizenship presupposed a preference for the public interest over all private interests, and for whom the first duty of a politician was to form and preserve public morality.[69]

V

Was the fate of modern society to be
both democracy and despotism?

The answer to the question must be "yes" if one follows the logic of Tocqueville's argument. Here is that logic in summary:

1. All men at all times have an insatiable passion for equality; the movement toward equality of social conditions in all Christian countries is "a providential fact."[70]

2. Individualism, which spreads with equality, saps the virtues of both public and private life.[71]

3. Equality produces an excessive taste for small comforts[72] and, worse, for money-making, and—worse yet—materialism. These distract men from their public duties.[73]

---

[66]*Memoir*, vol. I, p. 383.
[67]Ibid., vol. II, p. 387.
[68]Ibid., *Old Regime.*
[69]Stephen Holmes, *Benjamin Constant and the Making of Modern Liberalism* (New Haven, Conn.: Yale University Press, 1984), pp. 48-49.
[70]*Democracy*, vol. I, p. 6.
[71]Ibid., vol. II, p. 98.
[72]Ibid., p. 128.
[73]Ibid., pp. 133, 141.

4. Democratic tastes and habits lead to commerce and manufacturing, the tendency of which is to degrade the worker ("What can be expected of a man who has spent twenty years of his life making heads for pins?")[74] and to make the master an "aristocrat" who feels no responsibility for his workers.

5. The growth of commerce and manufacturing necessitates large governmental undertakings (roads, canals, etc.), and the principle of equality itself imparts a taste for strong, centralized government.[75]

6. Centralization of government eventuates in a new kind of tyranny. In former times it was impossible for a tyrant to administer strict and uniform regulations; now he can reach into every detail of everyone's life.[76]

Some of Tocqueville's most eloquent language describes the coming "democratic despotism":

> After having thus successively taken each member of the community in its powerful grasp and then fashioned him at will, the supreme power then extends its arm over the whole community. It covers the surface of society with a network of small complicated rules, minute and uniform, through which the most original minds and the most energetic characters cannot penetrate, to rise above the crowd. The will of man is not shattered, but softened, bent, and guided; men are seldom forced by it to act, but they are constantly restrained from acting. Such a power does not destroy, but it prevents existence: it does not tyrannize, but it compresses, enervates, extinguishes, and stupifies a people, till each nation is reduced to nothing better than a flock of timid and industrious animals, of which the government is the shepherd.[77]

---

[74]Ibid., p. 158.
[75]Ibid., pp. 296, 284; also app. Z.
[76]Ibid., p. 318.
[77]Ibid., p. 319; also vol. I, p. 329.

VI

Perhaps because his purpose was hortatory, Tocqueville chose not to follow where his logic led.[78] In the final paragraphs of *Democracy,* he says again that nations cannot prevent the conditions of men from becoming equal. But then, ignoring all that this "fundamental fact" entails, he asserts that for democratic nations to be virtuous and prosperous, they "require but to will it." His argument has been that they will *not* will it. But he passed over this in silence.

Brilliant as are his insights into so many aspects of life, Tocqueville's analysis fails utterly to explain the most massive facts of recent and current history. He foresees tyrannies that have not occurred, while failing to see the ones that have. Centered as it is on the condition of equality, on individualism, the commercial mentality, and the displacement of national glory by petty pleasures and comforts, his analysis points in exactly the wrong directions. It is the values of his saintly grandmother, not those of the despised moneymaker, that supported the Nazi regime, that are exploited by the Soviet one, and that fire the fanaticism that is endemic in much of the Third World. In the commercial societies which Tocqueville considers doomed—and only in them—has freedom constantly been extended and combined with order and justice. It is to these societies that the world owes the relative material welfare of its many billions of people.

There are many reasons to fear for the future of modern society, but they are not Tocqueville's. By now we know enough about individualism and materialism to understand that they need not

---

[78]That Tocqueville saw the full implications of his argument is evident from recently published notes and chapter drafts. See James T. Schleifer, *The Making of Tocqueville's "Democracy in America"* (Chapel Hill: University of North Carolina Press, 1980), especially chap. 16, "Would Democracy Usher in a New Dark Ages?"

Richard Herr, after pointing out Tocqueville's failure to acknowledge the pessimism of his *Old Regime* suggests that he was temperamentally incapable of stating a pessimistic conclusion explicitly. See his *Tocqueville and the Old Regime* (Princeton, N.J.: Princeton University Press, 1962), p. 91.

Tocqueville himself argued that to see events as determined is a "false and cowardly" doctrine of historians who live in democratic ages—one that, once it gets possession of the public mind, "will soon paralyze the activity of modern society and reduce Christians to the level of the Turks." *Democracy,* vol. II, p. 88.

destroy private and public virtue. We know also that the pursuit of happiness, even when it leads to paltry pleasures, is compatible with the maintenance of freedom and justice. We know that the seamy side of a commercial society is only one of its many sides.

A principal defect of Tocqueville's analysis, I think, is his assumption that only insofar as men are good can they produce a good society and that they will be good—or good enough—only if some central authority educates and guides them. The teaching of Mandeville and Adam Smith, that favorable outcomes often occur without anyone's intending them, was alien to his way of thinking.

Like the American Founders, Tocqueville believed that man is more a creature of passion than of reason and that his leading passion is self-interest—"the only immutable point in the human heart."[79] The Founders accepted the necessity of taking man as he was and endeavored to arrange institutions so that in the pursuit of happiness (paltry pleasures, most often), men would be distracted from socially more dangerous activities ("lofty enterprises," perhaps). Tocqueville thought—perhaps I should say wanted to believe—it possible for some authority to educate and guide men, if not to real public virtue, then at least to a more enlightened self-interest, at any rate, to something better than they were by nature. He could not bring himself to believe that if they were left alone the social outcome might be tolerable, let alone in some respects admirable.

It seems to me that the Founders had a much better understanding of things than did Tocqueville. If government can change the nature of man for the better, one would want it to do so right away. But it cannot. And therefore the best course—a perilous one, certainly—is to protect him from others in his pursuit of happiness, and to hope for the best.

---

[79]*Democracy*, vol. I, p. 246.

10

Centralized Administration and the "New Despotism"

John Marini

Alexis de Tocqueville is well known for his elaboration of the principle of equality as the animating force of modern democratic politics. Less well known, and often less well understood, is his analysis of the concept of centralization. Centralization was a primary concern of Tocqueville throughout much of his life. From the time he attended Francois Guizot's lectures on the *History of Civilization in France*, at age twenty-four in Paris, to his own classic account of centralization in *The Old Regime and the Revolution*, he became increasingly and ever more profoundly concerned with this issue. After reading Guizot's *History of Civilization in Europe*, in the summer of 1829, Tocqueville was so impressed with the historical analysis of the development of modern society that he wrote Beaumont: "We must re-read this together this winter my dear friend, it is prodigious in analysis of ideas. . . ."[1] In that work, Guizot "developed the theme that European civilization was shaped by the theory and practice of monarchy, aristocracy and democracy, and that the victory of the democratic force was the essential thread of Europe's history."[2] However, Guizot observed, the development of free political institutions was constantly challenged by the irresistible centralizing

---

[1]Edward T. Gargan, *De Tocqueville* (London: Bowes & Bowes, 1965), p. 28. Hereinafter cited as Gargan, *De Tocqueville.*
[2]Ibid., p. 27.

tendencies of modern government. Guizot was among the first to consider the modern state as a form of administration. In his lectures, he noted:

> [U]nder the most general point of view, administration consists in an aggregate of means destined to propel, as promptly and certainly as possible, the will of the central power through all parts of society and to make the face of society, whether consisting of men or money, return again, under the same conditions, to the central power.[3]

Modern society really begins in the sixteenth century, Guizot maintained, by virtue of the "silent and hidden process of centralization, both in social relations and in the opinions of men—a process accomplished without premeditation or design."[4] Centralization, in Guizot's view, is the inevitable concomitant of democracy. Tocqueville, although impressed with Guizot's method and his analysis, never appeared to believe that the process of centralization was a providential fact. But, for reasons of his own, he devoted much of his scholarly life to the elucidation and elaboration of this idea. In Tocqueville's hands, centralization received its most profound treatment.

In Tocqueville's view, it is the principle of equality which is the irresistible force of modern times. All democratic regimes are characterized by a commitment to equality, and all modern regimes will be democratic. In post-democratic times, therefore, it is no longer principled issues which are of decisive importance in practical life, but the growth and development of the administrative state shapes the essential character of social life. Centralization, though not fated, is the silent, continuous, almost natural tendency, which threatens to undermine that legitimate passion for equality which is compatible with liberty. Alongside the "manly and legitimate passion for equality," Tocqueville asserts, "the human heart also nourishes a debased taste for equality, which leads the weak to want to drag the strong down to their level, and which

---

[3]Francois Guizot, *Historical Essays and Lectures*, eds. Stanley Mellon and Leonard Krieger (Chicago: University of Chicago Press, 1972), p. 257.
[4]Gargan, *De Tocqueville*, p. 29.

induces men to prefer equality in servitude to inequality in freedom."[5] The modern bureaucratic state becomes the vehicle which reduces the individual to servitude. It does so by supplying all the needs of the body; in the process it enslaves the soul. The centralized administrative state becomes the "protective power which is alone responsible for securing [man's] enjoyment and watching over [his] fate." This power, Tocqueville noted:

> . . . is absolute, thoughtful of detail, orderly, provident, and gentle. It would resemble parental authority if, fatherlike, it tried to prepare its charges for a man's life, but on the contrary, it only tries to keep them in perpetual childhood. . . . It gladly works for their happiness but wants to be sole agent and judge of it. It provides for their security, foresees and supplies their necessities, facilitates their pleasures, manages their principal concerns, directs their inheritances. Why should it not entirely relieve them from the trouble of thinking and all the cares of living.[6]

The "slow process of bureaucratic government," Seymour Drescher has observed, "is the Frankenstein of the egalitarian process . . . it silently subverts the integrity of individuals and associations."[7] Tocqueville hoped to call attention to this process, almost before it began, by elaborating the theoretical and practical aspects of centralization.

In *The Old Regime and the Revolution,* Tocqueville documented the growth and development of the centralized administrative state. He traced its origin to the theory and practice of modern democratic egalitarianism. The French intellectuals and philosophers, as well as the monarchy, contributed to the administrative centralization which would become the hallmark of the modern nation-state. Moreover, the French Revolution succeeded in accelerating those centralizing tendencies, while destroying the elements

---

[5]Alexis de Tocqueville, *Democracy in America,* ed. J.-P. Mayer, trans. George Lawrence (Garden City, N.Y.: Doubleday, Anchor Books, 1969)), p. 57. Hereinafter cited as *Democracy.*

[6]Ibid., p. 668.

[7]Seymour Drescher, "Tocqueville's Two Democracies," *Journal of the History of Ideas* 25 (April-June 1964), p. 249.

in French society which could resist them. However, it was "towards the middle of the eighteenth century," he observed, "that a group of writers known as the 'Physiocrats' or 'Economists' who made the problem of public administration their special study, came on the scene."[8] The form of tyranny "sometimes described as 'democratic despotism' . . . was championed by the Economists well before the Revolution." In fact, he suggested, "the germinal ideas of practically all the permanent changes effected by the Revolution can be found in their works."[9] Their chief targets of attack "were those institutions which the Revolution was destined to sweep away forever." More importantly, he noted, "their writings had the democratic-revolutionary tenor characteristic of so much modern thought. For they attacked not only specific forms of privilege but any kind of diversity whatsoever; to their thinking all men should be equal even if equality spelled servitude."[10] Tocqueville analyzed their political program:

> They were for abolishing all hierarchies, all class distinctions, all differences of rank, and the nation was to be composed of individuals almost exactly alike and unconditionally equal. In this undiscriminated mass was to reside, theoretically, the sovereign power, yet it was to be carefully deprived of any means of controlling or even supervising the activities of its own government. For above it was a single authority, its mandatory, which was entitled to do anything and everything in its name without consulting it. This authority could not be controlled by public opinion since public opinion had no means of making itself heard, the State was a law unto itself and nothing short of a revolution could break its tyranny.[11]

In Tocqueville's opinion, the Economists or Physiocrats were forerunners of those socialist thinkers who called for "the unlimited

---

[8]Alexis de Tocqueville, *The Old Regime and the French Revolution*, trans. Stuart Gilbert (Garden City, N.Y.: Doubleday, Anchor Books, 1955), p. 158. Hereinafter cited as *Old Regime*.
[9]Ibid.
[10]Ibid., p. 159.
[11]Ibid., p. 163.

rights of the State." He believed that "socialism and centralization thrive on the same soil; they stand to each other as the cultivated to the wild species of a fruit."[12] Tocqueville's theoretical analysis of the concept of centralization required bringing to light the development of the modern bureaucratic state. At the same time, he hoped to shed new light on the character of modern despotism. In the process, he hoped to preserve the civic spiritedness necessary to allow men to be free.

Tocqueville was impressed with the absence of a centralized administration in the America of the 1830s. He noted in the first volume of *Democracy in America*: "We have seen that in the United States there was no administrative centralization. . . . But there is a high degree of governmental centralization in the United States."[13] What Tocqueville most admired was "not the administrative but the political effects of decentralization."[14] The most important political effect of decentralization—or provincial institutions—was the creation of a kind of civic spiritedness and love of liberty necessary to keep individuals from becoming completely preoccupied with their own private interests and pleasures. He observed:

> What good is it to me . . . if there is an authority always busy to see to the tranquil enjoyment of my pleasures and going ahead to brush all dangers away from my path without giving me even the trouble to think about it, if that authority, which protects me from the smallest thorns on my journey, is also the absolute master of my liberty and of my life? If it monopolizes all activity and life to such an extent that all around it must languish when it languishes, sleep when it sleeps, and perish if it dies?[15]

Tocqueville was convinced that the democratic tendency was toward centralizing administrative and governmental authority in the same hands: the central power. In the past several decades,

---

[12]Ibid., p. 164.
[13]*Democracy*, p. 89.
[14]Ibid., p. 95.
[15]Ibid., p. 93.

American government has become centrally administered at the national level. Tocqueville's predictions of the political effects of such centralization have been largely borne out. However, his warning concerning the despotic character of centralization has been widely ignored, especially by that most sophisticated and informed segment of society: the intellectuals. Intellectual, or elite, opinion—which often shapes the most influential public opinion on these matters—sharply diverges from the common-sense understanding of what is now called bureaucratization. The intellectual elite's acceptance of a certain "taste" for equality, which necessitates those "general ideas" and the kind of uniformity from which administrative centralization inevitably springs, has undermined Tocqueville's treatment of the despotic character of such centralization. Tocqueville's "philosophic analysis" of centralization was aimed at a similar intellectual elite, whose views began to dominate public discourse on this issue in the nineteenth century. It was not the first time that decent political practice required such a defense.

Recently, Henry Steele Commager criticized Tocqueville for what he described as "Tocqueville's Mistake."[16] Commager insisted that "centralization and a strong national government have extended not curtailed our liberties." He implies that the contemporary conservative criticism of centralization is only part of an attack on the social programs of liberal governments. He suggests, therefore, that "those who declaim against Big Government as the enemy of liberty are ignorant of American history."[17] He contends that the central government abolished slavery and extended the civil rights of various minority groups. Consequently, he is unable to comprehend the contemporary popular animus against centralization. He states: "Perhaps the most astonishing feature of the current attack on centralization, an attack that President Reagan has turned into a crusade, is the argument that the United States today has not a strong national government but a Big Government."[18] Commager insists that the national government is

---

[16]Henry Steele Commager, "Tocqueville's Mistake," *Harper's* (August 1984), p. 71.
[17]Ibid., p. 72.
[18]Ibid.

not "Big Government," when compared with most governments of the world. Moreover, he implies that Tocqueville's analysis is no longer relevant. "What Tocqueville failed to see," he asserts, "was that in a federal system like the American, the problem of the role of local and central governments has taken on a new character."[19]

Unlike Commager, most Americans believe that the national government is a "big government," and for that reason not as strong as it ought to be. Popularly understood, big government is bureaucratic government, government concerned not with the general or public principles of the regime but, increasingly, the minute regulations of the private and particular details of social existence. This view is closely akin to the distinction Tocqueville makes between government and administration. Commager appears not to have considered the importance of this crucial distinction in Tocqueville's analysis of centralization. Tocqueville observed: "For my part, I cannot conceive that a nation can live, much less prosper, without a high degree of centralization of government." He noted, however: "I think that administrative centralization only serves to enervate the peoples that submit to it, because it constantly tends to diminish their civic spirit."[20] Free men must take an active part in the conduct of their affairs. Elite opinion appears to have championed a conception of equality which denigrates liberty and leads to ever-greater uniformity. The contemporary intellectual understanding of centralization is so alien to the spirit of Tocqueville's views that his analysis must be recovered by considering its origins.

Centralization — A "Philosophic Analysis"

"Centralization," John Stuart Mill observed in 1862, is "one among the political questions of the age which bears the strongest marks of being destined to remain a question for generations to come."[21] The importance of this question, Mill asserted, "is

---

[19]Ibid.

[20]*Democracy*, p. 88.

[21]John Stuart Mill, "Centralisation," *Collected Works*, ed. John M. Robson (Toronto: University of Toronto Press, 1977), vol. 19, p. 581. Hereinafter cited as Mill, "Centralisation."

constantly tending to increase, by the perpetual growth of collective action among mankind and the progress made in the settlement of other questions which stand before it in the natural order of discussion." The more "exciting subject of Forms of Government," which had for so long dominated political debate, he suggests, "is likely to be much sooner, at least theoretically settled." This is so because "it is simpler in itself," and "it admits . . . of a more definite answer."[22] The question of the legitimacy of popular government, not to mention its form, appears to admit of almost no further debate. "Centralization; or in other words, the limits which separate the province of government from that of individual and spontaneous agency, and of central from local government." This is the issue, Mill asserts, "which is destined to dominate political discourse for the foreseeable future."[23]

There is little doubt that Mill's understanding of this question was decisively shaped by Tocqueville. Mill recorded his debt in his *Autobiography*. He noted there that a

> subject on which I derived great benefit from the study of Tocqueville was the fundamental question of Centralization. The powerful philosophic analysis which he applied to American and to French experience, led him to attach the utmost importance to the performance of as much of the collective business of society, as can safely be so performed by the people themselves.[24]

The value of Tocqueville's contribution, quite apart from his practical conclusions, derived from his "philosophic analysis," which elevated the issue of centralization to a new theoretical level.

Mill suggested that it was as a result of Tocqueville's powerful analysis of this issue, that he himself was alerted to the danger of centralization. European attitudes toward central and local government and administration, derived largely from experience and habit. Mill noted that in England, unlike the Continent,

---

[22]Ibid.
[23]Ibid.
[24]John Stuart Mill, *Autobiography* (New York: Liberal Arts Press, 1957), p. 124.

"centralization was . . . the subject not only of rational disapprobation, but of unreasoning prejudice; where jealousy of Government interference was a blind feeling preventing or resisting even the most beneficial exertion of legislative authority."[25] If popular opinion depended upon habit and circumstance, and perhaps chance, Tocqueville was responsible for informing "philosophic" opinion. As Mill observed: "[T]he more certain the public were to go wrong on the side opposed to Centralization, the greater danger was there lest philosophic reformers should fall into the contrary error." Mill, himself, was "actively engaged in defending important measures" that would have led to increased administrative centralization, and "had it not been for the lessons of Tocqueville,"[26] he would have failed to see that the prejudice of his countrymen was more enlightened than the opinions of the philosophic reformers. "The reaction . . . against governmentalism and centralization, and in favor of individual and local agency is at present intense," Mill noted, and "the renewed and more serious movement in this beneficent direction is usually dated from the publication of the great work of M. de Tocqueville."[27]

Mill insisted that Tocqueville's thought was indispensable in the creation of the "serious movement" in the direction "against governmentalism and centralization and in favor of individual and local agency." There were few issues which Tocqueville considered with greater care or seriousness than the problem of centralization. Indeed, he commented in a letter concerning this subject: "I sense that I am treating there the most important idea of our time."[28] In his *Journeys to England and Ireland*, Tocqueville recorded in his notes the following observation: "Centralization . . . Preparation for despotism."[29] Tocqueville always believed that "despotism would be the inevitable but (almost) silent companion to

---

[25]Ibid., pp. 124-25.

[26]Ibid., p. 125.

[27]Mill, "Centralisation," p. 582.

[28]James T. Schleifer, *The Making of Tocqueville's "Democracy in America"* (Chapel Hill, N.C.: University of North Carolina Press, 1980), p. 165. Hereinafter cited as Schleifer, *Making of Democracy*.

[29]Alexis de Tocqueville, *Journeys to England and Ireland*, ed. J.-P. Mayer (Garden City, N.Y.: Doubleday, Anchor Books, 1968), p. 63. Hereinafter cited as *Journeys*.

the centralized state."[30] In focusing on centralization, Tocqueville hoped to expose the sinister aspect of the passion for equality. Toward the end of the second volume of *Democracy in America,* Tocqueville observed:

> Every central power which follows its natural instincts loves equality and favors it. For equality singularly facilitates, extends, and secures its influence.
>
> One can also assert that every central government worships uniformity; uniformity saves it the trouble of inquiring into infinite details, which would be necessary if the rules were made to suit men instead of subjecting all men indiscriminately to the same rule. Hence the government loves what the citizens love, and it naturally hates what they hate. This community of feeling which in democracies continually unites each individual and the sovereign in common thought establishes a secret, and permanent bond of sympathy between them. The government's faults are forgiven for the sake of its tastes. . . .[31]

Consequently, Tocqueville suggests, "the chief and, in a sense, the only condition necessary in order to succeed in centralizing the supreme power in a democratic society is to love equality or to make believe that you do so. Thus the art of despotism, once so complicated, has been simplified; one may almost say that it has been reduced to a single principle."[32] For this reason, Tocqueville believed that "it is easier to establish an absolute and despotic government among a people whose social conditions are equal than among any other."[33] Although "democratic peoples are instinctively drawn toward centralization of power," he noted, "this attraction is uneven. It depends on particular circumstances which may promote or restrain the natural effects of the state of society."[34] In America, those circumstances were extremely propitious.

---

[30]Schleifer, *Making of Democracy*, p. 177.
[31]*Democracy*, p. 673.
[32]Ibid., pp. 678-79.
[33]Ibid., p. 695.
[34]Ibid., p. 674.

Tocqueville's practical task was to clarify the meaning of centralization. His philosophic analysis required a clarification of the idea which lay at the heart of modern political practice.

The Practical Problem

If centralization were to be recognized as an issue of the first magnitude, it was imperative that Tocqueville clarify its meaning and establish the ground upon which the issue would be debated. "When we speak of centralization," he noted, "we are always fighting in the shadows because of a failure to make the distinction between governmental and administrative centralization."[35] In his famous definition, he seeks to make this distinction with precision:

> Certain interests, such as the enactment of general laws and the nation's relations with foreigners, are common to all parts of the nation.
>
> There are other interests of special concern to certain parts of the nation, such, for instance, as local enterprises.
>
> To concentrate all the former in the same place or under the same directing power is to establish what I call governmental centralization.
>
> To concentrate control of the latter in the same way is to establish what I call administrative centralization.[36]

However, it is almost impossible, theoretically, to maintain this celebrated distinction; it is full of ambiguity in practice. Tocqueville was aware of the difficulty. He noted, almost in the same breath, "[T]here are some points where these two sorts of centralization become confused."[37]

The difficulty is a practical one; how does one distinguish national from local interests? There cannot be a principle to regulate this distinction which would not succumb to necessity—particularly war. Far from defending decentralization, Tocqueville

---

[35]Quoted in Schleifer, *Making of "Democracy,"* p. 135. Schleifer is quoting manuscript drafts of *Democracy*. Yale, CV b, Paquet 13, pp. 57-58.
[36]Ibid., p. 87.
[37]Ibid.

makes it clear that in America, administrative decentralization has been carried too far in ordinary times. "We have seen that the Americans have almost entirely isolated the administration from the government," he observed. "In doing this they seem to have overstepped the limits of sane reason, for order, even in secondary matters, is still a national interest."[38] Is it possible that Tocqueville was unaware of this difficulty? It seems unlikely. Marvin Zetterbaum has noted in this regard:

> Tocqueville not only does not provide a simple formula to distinguish matters concerning the general interest, from matters that may safely be left to local authorities; he recognizes that if a nation is subject to significant external pressures, local autonomy in anything other than trivial matters is impossible. In such a case, the distinction between national and local becomes arbitrary and meaningless.[39]

But Tocqueville was not concerned to resolve the issue as a practical matter, it is practically insoluble. In bringing the distinction to light, he hoped to expose the practical consequences of modern philosophic or ideological politics. Hence Tocqueville served a theoretical rather than a practical need. In his elaboration of the distinction between administration and government, Tocqueville brought to light the inherent tension between the general and particular, the common and self-interest, and the public and private spheres.

Mill's comments on centralization are helpful in clarifying Tocqueville's purpose. Mill, in his definition of centralization, distinguishes the governmental and private, as well as the central and local. This juxtaposition is not without significance, for he recognized two separate kinds of authority: the private, individual, and self-interested, he associates with local government, or what Tocqueville called administration; the general, uniform, and the public interest form the heart of central authority, or

---

[38]Ibid., p. 90.

[39]Marvin Zetterbaum, *Tocqueville and the Problem of Democracy* (Stanford, Cal.: Stanford University Press, 1967), p. 99. Hereinafter cited as Zetterbaum, *Problem*.

what Tocqueville characterizes as government. This analysis is instructive, for it offers a corrective to the interpretation commonly held in our time. The contemporary understanding falls prey to the very tendency Tocqueville sought to expose in his analysis. Tocqueville, like Mill, was of the opinion that the different kinds of authority, implicit in the distinction "of central contrasted with local authority, as of government contrasted with the individual," ought to be preserved with the view to tempering in practice the principle of popular sovereignty.

The contemporary understanding admits to a single legitimate center of authority: the public, the general, or the governmental. If the locus of that authority had shifted from the states to the national legislature, since Tocqueville's time, the principle is clear; there is nothing that government—primarily the legislature—cannot do. The democratic instinct that tends toward the nation-state also moves in the direction of uniform government and legislative supremacy. In Tocqueville's time, it was the state legislatures that he looked to as the "locus of the tendency towards democratic centralism."[40] He noted:

> The duties and rights of the federal government were simple and easy to define because the Union has been formed with the object of providing for certain great general needs. But the rights and duties of the government of the states were many and complicated, for such a government was involved in all the details of social life.[41]

It is now the national government which has become involved in all the "details of social life," but the principle remains the same. Tocqueville observed that the legislative power is the "authority which springs most directly from the people, it is also that which shares its all-embracing power most."[42] A recent observer, John Koritansky, has stated: "The legislature tends to be supreme

---

[40]John C. Koritansky, "Decentralization and Civic Virtue in Tocqueville's 'New Science of Politics,'" *Publius*, vol. 5 (Summer 1975), p. 68. Hereinafter cited as Koritansky, "Decentralization."

[41]*Democracy*, p. 114.

[42]Ibid., p. 154.

because, strictly speaking, legislative supremacy is a necessary implication of democracy . . . not only is the legislature most directly responsible to the people . . . it is the legislative function that corresponds to the kind of political activity the people themselves would perform if they actually assembled."[43] Legislative supremacy appears to be the closest thing to direct popular rule, but it tends also "in the direction of a simple rule of law unimpeded by any perception of the need for administrative discretion or provincial autonomy."[44] The tendency is toward greater centralization as a consequence of the necessity to treat everything in a uniform manner. As Koritansky notes:

> Any argument that limits the ability of the law to govern every last detail of human life always involves some allegation of complex circumstances that need special, particular accommodation. But democracy is always impatient with such claims. The image that corresponds most closely to the democracy's vision of society is a social atomism; the atoms themselves being simple and perfectly interchangeable are suitably governed by a few majestic generalities. Democratic citizens always suspect the allegation of special circumstances to be a cover for inequality, and they reject inequality in turn because it is the source of these complexities that impede the simple rule of law.[45]

This leads necessarily to the creation of an "administrative class" formed to handle in a uniform and general way the details of everyday life.

This tendency in the direction of legislative supremacy and administrative unity, not to say uniformity, is so compelling—the notion of popular sovereignty so pervasive—that Tocqueville's analysis of centralization has been undermined. Administrative centralization becomes necessary in democratic times to ensure greater efficiency and rationality, not to mention equity. Furthermore, the distinction between government and administration,

---

[43]Koritansky, "Decentralization," p. 68n. 39.
[44]Ibid., p. 68.
[45]Ibid., pp. 68-69.

in Tocqueville's sense, has been replaced by the distinction between policy-making and execution. As Martin Diamond observed:

> [T]he most common understanding of Tocqueville's distinction is the following: Government centralization means that policy should be made centrally, the power of legislation belongs to the central government, administrative decentralization requires that central policies be locally administered; the power of execution belongs to the localities.[46]

However, in Tocqueville's view, both government and administration form an autonomous whole. Both are concerned with law-making and execution. The difference lies in the kind of authority characterized by each; administrative authority concerns the details of social life, it is private and self-interested, not to say particular. Governmental authority is principled and uniform, not to say general.

In Tocqueville's view, the proper reconciliation of these two kinds of authority can occur only on the level of the community or township. It is there that both public and private interests can be properly considered. Such a resolution involves the necessity of abstracting from one's private interest in the conduct of the ordinary details of life. Such an abstraction leads to the realization that every citizen must consider the whole or the common good first, or at least at the same time that he considers his own good. As a result, every citizen's private interest is inseparable from his public duty. Private interest moderates public policy, by attempting to preserve individual autonomy or freedom, and public spiritedness is engendered in the act of self-legislation. "There will be no stable order," Tocqueville noted in *Le Commerce,* "as long as the law does not give to each citizen a political existence which bestows on each person both rights and duties; and thereby, a civic conscience, a respect for authority . . . a reasoned respect for the law."[47]

---

[46] "The Ends of Federalism," *The Federal Polity*, ed. Daniel J. Elazar (New Brunswick, N.J.: Transaction Books, 1974), p. 139.

[47] Roger Boesche, "Tocqueville and *Le Commerce*: A Newspaper Expressing His Unusual Liberalism," *Journal of the History of Ideas* 44 (April-June 1983).

The Theoretical Problem

Tocqueville's analysis is, in the fundamental respect, primarily theoretical. It involves nothing less than the attempted reconciliation—on the level of political history—of the inherent tension which exists between the public and private; the general and particular. In the process he hoped to forestall the worst aspect of democratic life, the tendency to administrative despotism. "To what degree," he asked, "can these two principles of private and public welfare be blended? To what point can a conscience born of reflection and calculation overcome political passions not yet visible, but which cannot help arising?"[48]

Tocqueville's distinction provided the conceptual means of isolating the tendency of modern government toward unity or centralization. He hoped to buttress those elements—provincial institutions—which could serve to mitigate its growth. He was aware that provincial institutions and local liberty "are not the natural government" of the modern world. They grew "almost in secret, amid a semibarbarous society." Left to themselves, "the institutions of a local community can hardly defend themselves against a strong and enterprising government."[49] Their existence depends upon the civic virtue of a people. Thus Tocqueville insisted that "decentralization, like liberty, is a thing which leaders promise their people, but which they never give them. To get and keep it, the people must count on their own sole efforts; if they do not care to do so the evil is beyond remedy."[50] In teaching democratic man the necessity of civic virtue, he would show them how to remain free.

Nonetheless, it is hard "to make the people take a share in government." And, "it is even harder to provide them with the experience and to inspire them with the feelings they need to

---

[48]Zetterbaum, *Problem*, p. 118.
[49]*Democracy*, p. 62.
[50]Quoted in J.-P. Mayer, *Alexis de Tocqueville: A Biographical Essay in Political Science* (New York: Viking Press, 1940), p. 26. Hereinafter cited as Mayer, *Biographical Essay*.

govern well."[51] Such a task requires the service of a legislator. The difficulty of Tocqueville's project was nowhere better stated than in Rousseau's *Social Contract*:

> Sages who wish to use their own language in addressing the vulgar instead of vulgar language cannot possibly make themselves understood. For . . . there are a multitude of ideas which it is impossible to express in the language of the people. Views that are too general . . . objects . . . too remote, are equally beyond their comprehension; and every individual, relishing no scheme of government but that which promotes his own private interest, cannot easily be made sensible of the benefits to be derived from continual privations imposed upon him by wholesome laws. For a newborn people to relish wise maxims of policy and to pursue the fundamental rules of statecraft, it would be necessary that the effect should become the cause; that the social mind, which should be the product of such an institution, would prevail even at the institution of society; and that men should be, before the formation of laws, what those laws alone can make them. The legislator being, from these reasons, unable to employ either force or argument, he must have recourse to an authority of another order, which can bear men away without violence, and persuade without convincing them.[52]

To what authority did Tocqueville have recourse to assist in the legislator's task? He seems to have turned to "historical philosophy" to accomplish his purpose.

In his review of *Democracy in America* in 1840, John Stuart Mill stated: "It is perhaps the greatest defect of M. de Tocqueville's book, that . . . his propositions even when derived from observation, have the air of mere abstract speculation."[53] This criticism is rarely noted. Subsequently, Tocqueville's own work was praised for

---

[51]*Democracy*, p. 315.

[52]Rousseau, *The Social Contract* (New York: Hafner, 1947), p. 38.

[53]John Stuart Mill, *Essays on Politics and Culture*, ed. Gertrude Himmelfarb (Garden City, N.Y.: Doubleday, Anchor Books, 1963), p. 238.

the soundness of his practical observations. It was not "abstract speculation" which characterized his work, but incisive analysis of sociological and political phenomena. His work is often thought to be a series of brilliant observations without theoretical coherence. One commentator, Marvin Zetterbaum, has remarked, "like other nineteenth-century theorists, Tocqueville was in revolt against those of his predecessors who had looked on political things in an abstract way."[54] Paradoxically, both Mill and Zetterbaum are right. Tocqueville was concerned with placing politics within a proper historical framework, but he was aware that every society is animated by certain ideas. Tocqueville believed that the science of politics gave

> birth or at least form to those general concepts whence emerge the facts with which politicians have to deal, and the laws of which they believe themselves the inventors. They form a kind of atmosphere surrounding each society in which both rulers and governed have to draw intellectual breath, and whence—often without realizing it—both groups derive the principles of action. Only among barbarians does the practical side of politics exist alone.[55]

It is for this reason that Tocqueville desired a new political science for a new age.

America appeared to offer Tocqueville the historical material from which he could undertake an analysis of democracy. In his first letter written from American soil, Tocqueville seemed to have grasped the meaning of the opportunity presented to him. He wrote:

> Picture to yourself . . . a society which comprises all nations of the world . . . people differing from one another in language, in beliefs, in opinions; in a word, a society possessing no roots, no memories, no prejudices, no routine, no common ideas, no national character. . . . The whole world over here seems to consist of malleable matter which forms and fashions to his liking.[56]

---

[54]Zetterbaum, *Problem*, p. 86.
[55]Mayer, *Biographical Essay*, p. 149.
[56]Ibid., pp. 37-38.

America offered Tocqueville the opportunity to "form those general concepts" of democratic society, in the process of describing "the general facts with which politicians have to deal."

He noted his purpose in another way in another context: "I must find somewhere a solid, lasting basis of fact for my ideas. I can find this only as I write history."[57] If his study of the French Revolution provided an opportunity in this regard, he pointed to the greatest difficulty he encountered in pursuing his method. "The one that troubles me most," he wrote, "arises from the mingling of history proper with historical philosophy. I do not yet see how I can mix the two things (and it is most important that this should be done, for one can put it that the former is the canvas, the latter the color—and both these are necessary to make a picture)."[58]

In blending history and historical philosophy, Tocqueville's task is at once practical and theoretical. It was only by proceeding in this way that he could hope to moderate a politics that was in the process of becoming ideological. He noted:

> It was political science, and often that science at its most abstract, which put into our father's heads the germs of those new ideas which have since suddenly blossomed into political institutions and civil laws unknown to their forebears. . . . Among all civilized peoples the political sciences create, or at least give shape to, general ideas, and from these general ideas are found the problems in the midst of which politicians must struggle, and also the laws which they imagine they create. The political sciences form a sort of intellectual atmosphere breathed by both governors and governed in society, and both unwittingly derive from it the principles of their action.[59]

As a consequence of the unification of politics and a certain kind of modern philosophy, which occurred as a result of the French Revolution, the "natural link" between "opinions" and "tastes,"

---

[57]Ibid., p. 110.

[58]Ibid., p. 111.

[59]Alexis de Tocqueville, "The Art and Science of Politics," trans. J.-P. Mayer, *Encounter* 36 (Jan. 1971), pp. 29-30. Hereinafter cited as "Politics."

"acts" and "beliefs," "feelings" and "ideas" had been severed. It "was the French," Tocqueville observed in the chapter in which he described the "Philosophical Approach of the Americans," who "turned the world upside down." The reason "is not simply that they changed their ancient beliefs and modified their ancient morality. The reason is that they were the first to generalize and call attention to a philosophic method by which all ancient things could be attacked and the way opened for everything new."[60] Tocqueville had observed the result in his "Introduction" to *Democracy in America*:

> I search my memory in vain, and find nothing sadder or more pitiable than that which happens before our eyes; it would seem that we have nowadays broken the natural link between opinions and tastes, acts and beliefs; that harmony which has been observed throughout history between the feelings and ideas of men seems to have been destroyed, and one might suppose that all the laws of moral analogy had been abolished.[61]

Tocqueville's purpose is to inspirit democratic man by forging artificial links to replace the broken natural link. In the process he will have established new laws of moral analogy. "Whereas only observations and facts are necessary to demonstrate mathematical truths," Tocqueville noted, "to understand and believe moral truths, mores are needed."[62]

Centralization and Despotism

At its most fundamental level, centralization is derivative of the desire for perfectibility, and the taste for general ideas, or the quest for rationality and uniformity. It is the practical culmination of the transformation of modern political life and institutions, brought about by modern political philosophy and science. "It is hard to realize," Tocqueville observed, "how much follows

---

[60]*Democracy*, p. 431.
[61]Ibid., p. 16.
[62]"Politics," p. 32.

naturally from this philosophic theory of the indefinite perfectibility of man and what a prodigious influence it has even on those who, concentrating solely on action to the exclusion of thought, act according to this theory of which they know nothing."[63] What is the idea to which theory and practice are made to conform? Tocqueville wrote:

> Equality puts many ideas into the human mind which would not have come there without it, and it changes almost all the ideas that were there before. I take the concept of human perfectibility as an example, for that is one of the chief ideas which the mind can conceive and which by itself constitutes a great philosophical theory, a theory whose effects can be seen at every moment in the conduct of affairs.[64]

Like Rousseau, Tocqueville regards perfectibility as the distinguishing characteristic of man. "Though man resembles the animals in many respects," Tocqueville noted, "one characteristic is peculiar to him alone: he improves himself, and they do not."[65]

"[P]erfectibility," Tocqueville asserted, "is as old as the world," but equality "has given it a new character." When citizens were classified by rank, profession, birth, men believed they could see the "ultimate limits of human endeavor quite close in front of [them], and no one attempted to fight against an inevitable fate." In his view, aristocratic societies thought in terms of "amelioration, not change." They imagined that "the conditions of the societies of the future will be better but not really different."[66]

When "castes disappear and classes are brought together," when "men are jumbled together and habits, customs and laws are changing . . . when old conceptions vanish and new ones take their place," Tocqueville remarked, "then the human mind imagines the possibility of an ideal but always fugitive perfection." Under these circumstances, individuals see "changes continuously take place,"

---

[63]*Democracy*, p. 453.
[64]Ibid., p. 452.
[65]Ibid.
[66]Ibid., pp. 452-53.

they observe "that many men improve their lot," and they conclude "that man in general is endowed with indefinite capacity for improvement."[67] When change occurs and conditions become more equal, Tocqueville observed that "each individual becomes more like his fellows, weaker, and smaller, and the habit grows of ceasing to think about citizens and considering only the people." Individuals are forgotten and "the species alone counts." At such times, he noted, "the human mind seeks to embrace a multitude of different objects at once, and it constantly strives to link up a variety of consequences with a single cause." The "concept of unity" then "becomes an obsession."[68] Throughout much of the second volume of *Democracy in America*, Tocqueville attempted to show the manner in which the "predominating taste of democratic people for very general ideas" manifested itself in politics, philosophy, and religion.

Centralization appeared to be the almost inevitable concomitant of the desire for uniformity and the taste for general ideas. In a conversation with John Stuart Mill in England in 1833, Mill made it clear to Tocqueville that it was the English abhorrence of general ideas which was largely responsible for the administrative decentralization in that country. In his notes, published as *Journeys to England and Ireland*, Tocqueville recorded his conversations with Mill on this subject. In questioning Mill on the danger of centralization, he asked if he feared "the present tendency of his country toward centralization." Mill replied that he did not, because "up to now centralization has been the thing most foreign to the English temperament." He noted further:

> Our habits or the nature of our temperament do not in the least draw us towards general ideas; but centralization is based on general ideas; that is the desire for power to attend in a uniform and general way, to the present and future needs of society. We have never considered government from such a lofty point of view. So we have divided administrative functions up infinitely and have

---

[67]Ibid., p. 453.
[68]Ibid., p. 451.

> made them independent of one another. We have not done this deliberately, but from our sheer inability to comprehend general ideas on the subject of government or anything else. The tendency of English politics up to now has been to remain as free as possible to do what was convenient. The taste for making others submit to a way of life which one thinks more useful for them than they do themselves, is not a common taste in England.[69]

But "could it not be," Tocqueville asked, "that what you call the English temperament, is the aristocratic temperament?" Mill admitted he had not considered the possibility. Is it not the "aristocratic temperament," Tocqueville inquired, which is likely "to isolate oneself . . . to be more afraid of being disturbed in one's own domain, than wishful to extend it over others?" Is not "the instinct of democracy exactly opposite," Tocqueville asked, "and may it not be that the present tendency which you consider as an accident, is an almost necessary consequence of the basic cause?"[70] The demise of the aristocracy, Tocqueville implied, leads almost inevitably to centralization. Why is this so?

Tocqueville's analysis of the problem was developed in his study, *The Old Regime and the Revolution.* This work only strengthened his belief that the destruction of the aristocracy accelerated the tendency toward centralization. But, in one of the novel findings of his research, Tocqueville discovered that centralizing tendencies were already apparent in the old regime. However, there was no principle involved in centralization prior to the French Revolution. It was the greed of the aristocracy, and the desire for money and power on the part of the monarchy, which resulted in increased centralization prior to the Revolution. In the decades preceding the Revolution, "feudal institutions had broken down to such an extent that the nobility had retained many of the privileges, but virtually none of its political authority."[71] In *The Old Regime,* Tocqueville demonstrated the means by which

---

[69]*Journeys,* pp. 66-67.
[70]Ibid., p. 67.
[71]Delba Winthrop, "Tocqueville's *Old Regime*: Political History," *The Review of Politics,* vol. 43 (Jan. 1981), p. 98.

"the monarchy centralized all administrative power under its own authority." The central power "controlled either directly, or indirectly, virtually every aspect of provincial and local life including public order."[72] Local autonomy nearly disappeared, and the nobility ceased to play an administrative role in the community—it was virtually powerless. Moreover, it ceased to concern itself with public affairs and was wholly preoccupied with its private pleasures. The aristocracy in France relinquished its power in exchange for its privilege—primarily the exemption from taxes. Tocqueville asserted that the old regime succumbed on the day that the French people "permitted the king to impose a tax without their consent and the nobles showed so little public spirit as to connive at this, provided their own immunity was guaranteed—it was on that fateful day that the seeds were sown of almost all the vices and abuses which led to the violent downfall of the old regime."[73]

The lack of public spiritedness on the part of the French aristocracy stood in sharp contrast to the British nobility. "The English aristocracy," Tocqueville noted, "took upon itself the heaviest public charges in order that it would be allowed to govern; in France the nobility retained to the very end its exemption from taxes to console itself for having lost control of the government."[74] If the French nobility lost its political virtue and ceased to be an aristocracy, becoming instead what Tocqueville called a caste—composed of individuals concerned with private economic advantage—with its destruction, every barrier to centralization was removed.

However, when "that ancient institution, the French monarchy, after being swept away by the tidal wave of the Revolution, was restored in 1800," Tocqueville asked, "how was it possible for this part of the old regime to be . . . integrated into the constitution of modern France?" The centralization of power "did not perish in the Revolution," he noted, because "whenever a nation destroys its

---

[72]Irving M. Zeitlin, *Liberty, Equality, and Revolution in Alexis de Tocqueville* (Boston: Little, Brown, 1971), p. 126.
[73]*Old Regime*, pp. 98-99.
[74]Ibid., p. 160.

aristocracy, it almost automatically tends toward a centralization of power."[75] The revolutionaries, despite their hatred of central power, could not prevent even greater centralization of authority. Nonetheless, prior to the Revolution, "it (was) due to habits and not to ideas that . . . centralization remained strongly established." In spite of the fact that "the future revolutionaries themselves"—in their pamphlets—were "opposed to centralization and in favor of local rule."[76] Tocqueville demonstrated that "the democratic revolution, though it did away with so many institutions of the past, was led inevitably to consolidate this one; centralization fitted in so well with the program of the new social order that the common error of believing it to have been a creation of the Revolution is easily accounted for."[77]

In his *Correspondence with Gobineau,* Tocqueville took Gobineau to task for asserting that *The Old Regime* was a book about "administrative institutions." As Tocqueville recorded in his "Notes" on what was to have been the second volume of *The Old Regime*: "The influence of administrative practices on the destiny of a people should not be exaggerated. The principal source of these (political) vices and virtues are always to be found in the original ideas."[78] He outlined the principle "ideas at the base of the new social and governmental system" in his *Notes*:

> Natural equality must be represented in all institutions. . . . The sovereign power resides in the nation. It is one and omnipotent. It is not from traditions, not from examples, not from precedents, not from the particular rights of certain bodies or classes, not from the rights achieved, not from established religions that these principles derive, but from *general* reason, from the natural and primordial laws regulating the human species.[79]

---

[75]Ibid., p. 60.
[76]Alexis de Tocqueville, *"The European Revolution" and Correspondence with Gobineau,* trans. John Lukacs (Gloucester, Mass.: Peter Smith, 1968), p. 103. Hereinafter cited as *European Revolution.*
[77]*Old Regime,* p. 60.
[78]*European Revolution,* p. 101.
[79]Ibid., pp. 101-02.

The triumph of general ideas goes hand in hand with the destruction of all intermediate powers. Thus Tocqueville noted: "[C]entralization does not spread in a democracy simply in step with the progress toward equality, but also depends on the way in which that equality was established."[80] It is true, he observed, that "among democratic nations, the only form of government which comes naturally to mind is a sole and central power and that they are not familiar with the notion of intermediate powers." This is particularly true in regard to "those democratic nations which have seen the principle of equality triumph with the help of a violent revolution." In such a circumstance, "the classes that managed local affairs were suddenly swept away in that storm, and as the confused mass which remains has as yet neither the organization nor the habits which would allow it to take the administration of these affairs in hand, the state alone seems capable of taking upon itself all the details of government." Centralization "becomes a fact, and in a sense, a necessity."[81]

For this reason, Tocqueville insisted that "One must not praise or blame Napoleon for concentrating almost all administrative power in his own hands, for which nobility and the upper ranks of the middle classes abruptly brushed aside, these powers fell automatically into his hands; it would have been almost as difficult for him to reject as to assume them." However, this was not the case in the United States, because the Americans derived from the aristocracy of England "the idea of individual rights and a taste for local freedom, and they have been able to keep both these things because they have had no aristocracy to fight."[82]

In Tocqueville's view, aristocratic institutions form a bulwark against those tendencies in democratic society toward centralization. He commented in detail on the differences in the old societies. Unity and uniformity "were nowhere to be found." Nor had there developed a taste for general ideas in aristocratic societies. Tocqueville more than once points to the fact that the English had an aversion to generalization. But, he noted, "a more or less highly

---

[80]*Democracy*, p. 675.
[81]Ibid.
[82]Ibid., p. 676.

developed culture is not by itself enough to account for a taste for or aversion from generalization." Rather, it is in aristocratic societies that he discerns a distaste for generalization:

> When standards are very far from equal and the inequalities are permanent, individuals gradually become so dissimilar that one can almost talk of as many types of humanity as there are classes. Attention is never fixed on more than one of these at the same time, and losing sight of the connecting thread which links them all within the vast bosom of mankind, it is invariably not man but certain men who are observed. Members, therefore, of aristocratic societies never make grand generalizations about themselves, and that is enough to give them a habitual distrust and unconscious distaste for all generalizations.[83]

Tocqueville traced the origin of the taste for generalization to Christianity. Societies of antiquity were aristocratic. To illustrate his point, Tocqueville argued that "the profoundest and most wide-seeing minds of Greece and Rome never managed to grasp the very general but very simple conception of the likeness of all men and of the equal right of all at birth to liberty." They were at pains to show that slavery was natural and would always exist: "All the great writers of antiquity," Tocqueville insisted, "were either members of the aristocracy of masters or . . . saw that aristocracy in undisputed possession before their eyes. Their minds roamed free in many directions . . . Jesus Christ had to come down to earth to make all members of the human race understand that they were naturally similar and equal."[84] Christianity made egalitarian societies possible, and unity and uniformity in politics and society likely.

Unlike man in aristocratic society, democratic man "sees nothing but people more or less like himself around him, so he cannot think about one branch of mankind without widening his view until it includes the whole." Truths which apply to himself seem equally to apply to all men. "Having acquired a taste for generalizations in the matters which most closely take up his attention, and touch his

---

[83]Ibid., pp. 438-39.
[84]Ibid., p. 439.

interests, he carries it with him when dealing with everything else." Thus, says Tocqueville, "It becomes an ardent and often blind passion of the human spirit to discover common rules for everything, to include a great number of objects under the same formula, and to explain a group of facts by one sole cause." The equality of conditions and standards "induce[s] each man to look for truth for himself." It is "easy to see that such a method insensibly directs the human spirit toward generalizations." When traditions of class, of profession, and of family are repudiated and "the dominion of precedent is left behind for the search by one's unaided reason for the way to follow," Tocqueville observes, "one has a natural inclination to deduce the motives for one's views from the very nature of man, and that leads of necessity and almost in spite of oneself to a great number of very broad generalizations."[85]

However, Tocqueville insisted that "[g]eneral ideas do not bear witness to the power of human intelligence but rather to its inadequacy, for there are no beings exactly alike in nature, no identical facts, no laws which can be applied indiscriminately in the same way to several objects at once."[86] Nature is hostile to uniformity. Nonetheless, a central power attempts to oversee all the details of the life of a nation. But, such a power, Tocqueville asserted, "however enlightened and wise one imagines it to be, can never alone see to all the details of the life of a great nation." It cannot do so "because such a task exceeds human strength."[87] Tocqueville noted the sterile character of such an attempt in the following observation:

> Men think that the greatness of the idea of unity lies in means. God sees it in the end. It is for that reason that the idea of greatness leads to a thousand mean actions. To force all men to march in step toward the same goal—that is a human idea. To encourage endless variety of actions but to bring them about so that in a thousand different ways all tend toward the fulfillment of one great design—that is a

---

[85]Ibid., pp. 439-40.
[86]Ibid., p. 437.
[87]Ibid., p. 91.

> God-given idea. The human idea of unity is almost always sterile, but that of God is immensely fruitful. Men think they prove their greatness by simplifying the means. God's object is simple but His means infinitely various.[88]

Democratic peoples "naturally favor the concentration of political power." The idea of secondary powers, "between the sovereign and his subjects, was natural to the imagination of aristocratic peoples, because such powers were proper to individuals or families distinguished by birth, education, and riches, who seemed destined to command."[89] However, Tocqueville suggested, "Opposite reasons naturally banish such an idea from the minds of men in ages of equality; it can then only be introduced artificially and retained with difficulty; but the idea of a single central power directing all citizens slips naturally into their consciousness without their, so to say, giving the matter a thought."[90]

Consequently, Tocqueville noted, "in politics, as in philosophy and religion, democratic peoples give a ready welcome to simple general ideas. They are put off by complicated systems and like to picture a great nation in which every citizen resembles one set type and is controlled by one single power." Once the idea of a single central power is grasped,

> next . . . that of uniform legislation equally spontaneously takes its place in the thoughts of men. . . . As each sees himself little different from his neighbors, he cannot understand why a rule applicable to one man should not be applied to all the rest. . . . The faintest differences in the political institutions of a single people give him pain, and legislative uniformity strikes him as the first condition of good government.[91]

Democratic man as a result of the breakup of intermediate powers, the uniformity of ideas and feelings, comes at this moment to place all powers into the hands of the only authority which stands above

---

[88]Ibid., pp. 734-35.
[89]Ibid., p. 668.
[90]Ibid.
[91]Ibid.

all equally: the central power.

It is at the time when all things have conspired to deprive the individual of any support in the society, when he is most isolated and alone, that the central power assumes the greatest authority over the individual. Moreover, it is in these circumstances that the individual is least concerned with the conduct of public affairs. Tocqueville noted: "It is just at the moment when a democratic society is establishing itself on the ruins of an aristocracy that this isolation of each man from the rest and the egoism resulting therefrom stand out clearest."[92] Because every person finds his beliefs within himself, "all his feelings are turned in on himself." Thus Tocqueville alerts us to the new and dangerous element of democratic society, what he calls individualism. "Individualism is a calm and considered feeling which disposes each citizen to isolate himself from the mass of his fellows and withdraw into the circle of family and friends; with this little society formed to his taste, he gladly leaves the greater society to look after itself."[93] The individual becomes isolated and alienated and is concerned primarily with his pleasure and physical comfort. At such time, Tocqueville remarked, "men are carried away and lose control of themselves at sight of the new good things they are ready to snatch. [A]nd the better to guard their interests, they neglect the chief of them, that is, to remain their own masters."[94] Men are following two separate roads to servitude. He observed that "the taste for their own well-being withholds them from taking a part in government, and their love of that well-being forces them to closer and closer dependence upon those who govern."

Despotism, Tocqueville wrote, "sees the isolation of men as the best guarantee of its own permanence. So it usually does all it can to isolate them." The problem is that "[e]quality puts men side by side without a common link to hold them firm. Despotism raises barriers to keep them apart. It disposes them not to think of their fellows and turns indifference into a sort of public virtue."[95] How is it

---

[92]Ibid., p. 508.
[93]Ibid., p. 506.
[94]Ibid., p. 540.
[95]Ibid., pp. 509-10.

possible, Tocqueville asked, "that a society should escape destruction if the moral tie be not strengthened in proportion as the political tie is relaxed?"[96]

Recently, Roger Boesche has suggested that "previous theorists assumed that despotism required an extremely hierarchical society. Tocqueville agrees that despotism hinges on isolation, but he recognizes a new and modern historical development encouraging a despotism that need not rely on force (but instead can make servitude delightful)."[97] This new despotism is particularly to be feared because it may be unrecognizable. Tocqueville attempted to teach democratic man the "feeling" and "attitudes" of oppression, for modern despotism will be accompanied by ever-greater physical comforts. It endangers not the body but the soul. As Tocqueville noted:

> Fetters and headsman were the coarse instruments that tyranny formerly employed; but the civilization of our age has perfected despotism itself, though it seemed to have nothing to learn. . . . Under the absolute sway of one man the body was attacked in order to subdue the soul; but the soul escaped the blows which were directed against it and rose proudly superior. Such is not the course adopted in democratic republics; there the body is left free, and the soul is enslaved.[98]

In Tocqueville's view, only freedom could forestall the worst aspects of the new despotism. In his Foreword to *The Old Regime,* he articulated his mature reflection on the issue:

> Freedom and freedom alone can extirpate these vices, which indeed are innate in communities of this order; it alone can call a halt to their pernicious influence. For only freedom can deliver the member of a community from that isolation which is the lot of the individual left to his own

---

[96]Quoted in Harry D. Gideonse, "De Tocqueville, Liberal of a New Type," *American Journal of Economics*" 19 (July 1960), p. 412.

[97]Roger Boesche, "The Prison: Tocqueville's Model for Despotism," *Western Political Quarterly*, 33 (Dec. 1980), p. 553.

[98]Ibid., p. 556.

> devices and, compelling them to get in touch with each other, promote an active sense of fellowship. In a community of free citizens every man is daily reminded of the need of meeting his fellow men . . . of exchanging ideas, and coming to an agreement as to the conduct of their common interests. Freedom alone is capable of lifting men's minds above mere mammon worship. . . . It alone replaces at certain critical moments their natural love of material welfare by a loftier, more virile ideal.[99]

Tocqueville insisted that "in the dawning centuries of democracy, individual independence and local liberties will always be the products of art. Centralized government will be the natural thing."[100] In his "most enlightened speculation" on the issue of administrative centralization, Tocqueville offered the legislator's art in the service of genuine liberty.

In an important respect, Tocqueville has been remarkably influential in shaping the "attitudes" and "feelings" of the individual in modern society, particularly with regard to the problem of what is now called bureaucracy. His success can be seen in the remark of a contemporary observer:

> The contempt in which bureaucracy is held in modern thinking and prejudice, the insensitivity to honour that is also present in this function of government—this contempt was for all time given respectability by Tocqueville's history.[101]

---

[99] *Old Regime*, p. xiv.
[100] *Democracy*, p. 674.
[101] Gargan, *De Tocqueville*, p. 65.

11

Political Science, Political Culture, and the Role of the Intellectual

James W. Ceaser

Alexis de Tocqueville left America in 1832 with the intention not merely of describing its political and social institutions, but of creating a "new political science for a world itself quite new."[1] The object of the new political science was to clarify the forces shaping the modern world and to provide "those who now direct society" with the knowledge to meet its greatest challenge: reconciling liberty and democracy (the social state characterized by an "equality of conditions").[2] As Tocqueville told John Stuart Mill in 1836, "America was only the frame, my picture was Democracy."[3] Mill recognized the scope and novelty of Tocqueville's project when he described *Democracy in America* as "the first philosophical book ever written on Democracy as it manifests itself in modern society."[4]

Tocqueville addressed *Democracy in America* to the entire

Originally published as "Alexis de Tocqueville on Political Science, Politics and the Role of the Intellectual," *American Political Science Review*, vol. 79, Sept. 1985, p. 656.

[1]Alexis de Tocqueville, *Democracy in America*, ed. J.-P. Mayer, trans. George Lawrence (Garden City, N.Y.: Doubleday, Anchor Books, 1969), vol. I, p. 17. Hereinafter cited as *Democracy*.

[2]Ibid., pp. 9, 12.

[3]Alexis de Tocqueville, *Memoirs, Letters, and Remains of Alexis de Tocqueville*, 2 vols. (Boston: Ticknor & Fields, 1862), vol. 2, p. 38.

[4]John Stuart Mill, "M. de Tocqueville on *Democracy in America*," in *The Philosophy of John Stuart Mill*, ed. Morris Cohen (New York: Modern Library, 1961), p. 122.

generation of modern readers, but his immediate audience was clearly European, not American. No narrow chauvinism was at work here, but instead a frank assessment of the status of philosophy in different nations of the world. Nineteenth-century America hardly needed and could scarcely digest a work like *Democracy in America*: "The spirit of the Americans is averse to general ideas. . . . They pay very little attention to the rival European schools [of philosophy]. Indeed, they hardly know their names."[5] America at the time lay at the intellectual periphery, but, for the moment at least, ignorance was bliss. Without either a taste for abstract political thinking or a large class of intellectuals, America alone had succeeded in reconciling democracy and liberty. Nor was this a mere coincidence: America, Tocqueville contended, had met the challenge of the modern age not in spite of, but in large measure because of, the lack of influence of recent doctrines in political philosophy and the absence of a class of intellectuals to spread them.

According to Tocqueville, the role of political philosophy in Europe could hardly have been more different. Contemporary thought, purveyed by a powerful intellectual elite, had a tremendous influence on European societies. Political philosophy in Tocqueville's time was divided between two basic schools that were openly competing for dominance over the public mind—philosophe rationalism (the more influential school) and traditionalism. In Tocqueville's view, the tenets of both of these schools tended ultimately to undermine liberty. Political thought had lost a constructive role as a guide to political action and was promoting the march toward despotism. This intellectual crisis demanded a theoretical response—a new political science—the rudiments of which Tocqueville discovered in his study of America's ostensibly unsophisticated political culture. Seldom has an anthropological expedition yielded so much for a philosophic debate.

Although not the first to study what political scientists today call political culture, Tocqueville applied that concept to the analysis of democratic states with greater rigor than any previous

---

[5]*Democracy*, pp. 301, 429.

thinker. The character of a regime, in Tocqueville's view, is determined more than anything else by its *moeurs*, defined as "the sum of the moral and intellectual dispositions of men in society . . . the habits of heart . . . [and] the sum of ideas that shape mental habits."[6] The importance Tocqueville ascribed to *moeurs* (or political culture) accounts both for the scope of his political science, which extends to what we today would consider to be sociological and cultural elements of society, and for its distinctive method of studying a political system, under which institutions are analyzed as much in terms of their impact on the mental habits of the citizens as by their internal efficiency. Of all the aspects of the American regime, it was the *moeurs* of the people that Tocqueville believed best accounted for America's success. The United States was characterized by less brilliance and possessed less efficient political institutions than some nations in Europe, but it had developed the mental habits that could sustain liberty.[7]

In searching for the factors that form a political culture, Tocqueville, following Montesquieu, discussed the influence of such fundamental causes as geography, history, and laws.[8] Because these factors are in some degree particular to the experience of each nation, it is more correct in discussing Tocqueville's thought to speak in the plural of political cultures than of a single political culture. Yet what struck Tocqueville about the modern age was the emergence of certain factors that might influence all developed nations along the same lines: "Democratic peoples . . . in the end come to be alike in almost all matters. . . . [T]he same ways of behaving, thinking and feeling are found in every corner of the world."[9] The two most important forces Tocqueville identified as causes of this common development were the spreading social condition of equality

---

[6]Ibid., pp. 287, 305.

[7]Ibid., pp. 307-08.

[8]As Tocqueville wrote in a letter to Kergorlay in 1836, "There are three men with whom I commune a little every day; they are Pascal, Montesquieu, and Rousseau." Of these, Montesquieu seems to have been the most influential, and 15 years later Tocqueville wrote the same friend that he was modeling his next work, *The Old Regime*, on Montesquieu's *Considerations on the Causes of the Grandeur and Decadence of the Romans* (Richard Herr, *Tocqueville and The Old Regime* [Princeton, N.J.: Princeton University Press, 1962], pp. 48-49).

[9]*Democracy*, pp. 660, 615.

and the emergence of modern political thought as an active force capable of influencing the political cultures of all societies.

To understand the possibilities implicit in this path of development, Tocqueville abstracted from the particular nations and political cultures of his day (e.g., the United States, France, and England) in an effort to discover the picture of a common regime or political culture.[10] This abstract regime, which Tocqueville originally referred to as "Democracy," consisted of a set of properties and tendencies that, if left to their normal course of development, would more likely eventuate in despotisms, whether of the usual or new tutelary variant, than republics. Although these tendencies operated in some degree on all modern societies, they were refracted by the special characteristics of each nation's political culture, with the result that different nations were more or less likely to control the despotic tendencies of democracy and establish liberty. Tocqueville chose the United States as the obvious place to study the properties of democracy, but it turned out that the United States was in many respects atypical of his general model of democracy, mainly because of the special intellectual foundation of its political culture.[11]

This article proposes to demonstrate that Tocqueville intended his new political science as an alternative to rationalism and traditionalism that could help shape the political culture of modern states to avert despotism. In light of the threat to liberty posed by these rival schools, Tocqueville held that political science could not remain aloof or detached, but had to become an active force in history. Yet in no sense did he conceive of the new political science as an ideology that could convince public opinion by the force of its popular appeal. Rather, it represented a complex teaching that synthesized certain epistemological elements of rationalism and

---

[10]Ibid., pp. 417-29.

[11]Tocqueville had trouble with his use of the term "democracy" to describe a regime that was not free, and by the end of his life ceased using the term in the earlier sense. See his notes for vol. II of *The Old Regime and the French Revolution*, trans. Stuart Gilbert (Garden City, N.Y.: Doubleday, Anchor Books, 1955, originally published in 1856). Hereinafter cited as *Old Regime*. The key passage is translated in Raymond Aron, *Main Currents in Sociological Thought*, trans. Richard Howard and Helen Weaver (Garden City, N.Y.: Doubleday, Anchor Books, 1968), vol. I, pp. 240-41.

traditionalism into a truer picture of reality that was intended to help his contemporaries make responsible choices about their future. The factors shaping the development of democracy, although increasingly common to all nations, were not entirely beyond human control, either within each nation or within the developed world as a whole. The decisive choice between freedom and despotism would be largely determined by the doctrines and ideas that guided people's thought.[12]

In developing this thesis, it will be helpful at the outset to indicate the different parts of the argument. I begin by tracing Tocqueville's account of the development of rationalism and traditionalism, turn next to a sketch of the purpose and general character of his new political science, then outline his stratagem for inserting the teachings of the new political science into society, and finally indicate the manner in which he mixed rationalism and traditionalism to create his distinctive synthesis.

Rationalism and Traditionalism

Tocqueville's point of departure in both of his major works was the reaction of his contemporaries to democracy and to the shattering event that brought democracy to the center stage of European consciousness, the French Revolution. On one side, according to Tocqueville, stood the proponents of a radical version of rationalism, who saw themselves as the heirs of the French philosophes. For these thinkers, the French Revolution marked the dawn of a new era in which philosophy for the first time became an active force in transforming society. Philosophy stripped away the cloak of tradition that had supported superstition, injustice, and parochialism, providing in its place universally valid principles, derived from reason, that could instruct the enlightened on how to remake society and construct new political orders.[13]

On the other side were the proponents of traditionalism or "organicism," who turned for their inspiration chiefly to the writings of Edmund Burke. This school, which emerged as a conscious

---

[12]*Democracy*, p. 705.

[13]Ibid., pp. 429-33; *Old Regime*, pp. 13-169.

reaction to philosophe ideas, attacked the abstract, "speculatist" character of rationalist thought, seeing in its universalism and contempt for tradition a dangerous doctrine that threatened political stability, diversity, and the noblest elements of civilization. Only by a renunciation of this doctrine and a return to respect for tradition—meaning an appreciation for hierarchy, diversity, and transcendence—could the world be saved from the ambition of the philosophes, who, according to Burke, had ushered in "a barbarous philosophy" that had "rudely torn off . . . all the decent drapery of life."[14] About all both schools could agree on was that philosophe ideas had prepared the way for, if indeed they had not been the chief cause of, the French Revolution.[15]

Tocqueville analyzed the development of rationalist thought up to his time by distinguishing four different stages. The first stage, which occurred in the sixteenth century, focused on the relationship of man to God; religious reformers "subjected the dogmas of ancient faith to reason," while still maintaining a belief in the Deity.[16] The second stage, a development of the seventeenth century, saw the application of this way of thinking by Bacon and Descartes to the realms of natural science and philosophy (metaphysics); these philosophers consciously defined the mode of thought known as "method" and launched a philosophic project that "destroyed the dominion of tradition and upset the authority of masters."[17] The essence of method was a reliance on individual reason, in the light of experience, as the standard for evaluating truth, rather than prejudice, revelation, or tradition.[18]

It remained, however, for a third stage to extend the principles

---

[14]Edmund Burke, *Reflections on the Revolution in France* (Indianapolis: Liberal Arts Press, 1955, originally published in 1790), p. 87.

[15]The idea of studying Tocqueville's thought as a response to these two schools was suggested by J.-P. Mayer in *Alexis de Tocqueville* (New York: Harper, 1960), pp. 111-12, who also noted that the influence of Burke on Tocqueville has never been sufficiently explored in the scholarly literature. For my treatment of rationalism, I also rely heavily on the ideas of Peter Augustine Lawler and Edward Gargan, *De Tocqueville* (New York: Hillary House, 1965); and Pierre Manent, *Tocqueville et la nature de la democratie* (Paris: Julliard, 1982).

[16]*Democracy*, pp. 430-31.

[17]Ibid., p. 431.

[18]Ibid., pp. 429, 431.

of method to the social and political spheres, turning the world upside down and spreading in the public mind a mode of thinking "by which all ancient things could be attacked and the way opened for everything new."[19] This approach was popularized by the eighteenth-century thinkers, and in particular by the French philosophes and economists.[20] The key to the philosophe position was the idea that "what was wanted was to replace the complex of traditional customs governing the social order of the day by simple, elementary rules deriving from the exercise of human reason and natural law"[21] Tocqueville was aware, of course, of other strands of contemporary rationalist political thought that were not as radical or abstract as the French school, and he was personally very appreciative of certain English rationalists like Hume.[22] Yet his purpose here was not to survey the thought of different writers, but to sketch the core principles of the ideas that had helped to shape the political cultures of his day. In Tocqueville's view, the philosophe school had clearly exercised the greatest impact upon the public mind, becoming "the common coin of thought" throughout much of Europe.[23]

Under the influence of the philosophes, French writers of the next generation extended their mode of thinking to "an unrestrained passion for generalizations."[24] This marked yet a fourth stage in the evolution of rationalism contemporaneous with Tocqueville. "No writer . . . is satisfied with an essay revealing truths applicable to one great kingdom, and he remains dissatisfied with himself if his theme does not embrace the whole of mankind."[25] French thought, which in contrast to English thought brought almost no practical

---

[19]Ibid., p. 431.
[20]Ibid.; *Old Regime*, pp. 158-69.
[21]*Old Regime*, p. 139.
[22]Ibid., pp. 152-54.
[23]*Democracy*, p. 431. The account of rationalism here is presented from Tocqueville's point of view. An account from the outside would also be helpful, and one reader of this article suggested distinguishing between an analytic rationalist tradition, which went from Bacon and Descartes through Hume, Smith, Montesquieu, and Tocqueville, and a rationalist tradition, in which the thinker adopts the perspective of an omniscient observer, which would include Saint Simon and Hegel.
[24]Ibid., p. 438.
[25]Ibid.

experience to bear in writing on politics, was characterized by a "literary spirit" largely devoid of any contact with reality.[26] It built abstract, utopian models, ignoring the real world and real constraints. In France at least, this "literary spirit" came to shape the public's intellectual dispositions: "It was this vision of the perfect state that fired the imagination of the masses. . . . Turning away from the real world around them, they indulged in dreams of a far better one and ended up by living, spiritually, in the ideal world thought up by the writers."[27]

By the end of the eighteenth century, what passed for rationalist thought was something very different from the original rationalist method identified by Bacon and Descartes and later pursued by Hume and Montesquieu. Whereas rationalism had begun as an inductive or empirical mode of thought characterized by the careful movement from the particulars of experience to generalizations, it evolved by the end of the eighteenth century into an abstract and deductive mode of thought in which authors fabricated their own internal systems and then sought to impose them on reality. Tocqueville regarded this shift from an empirical mode of thought to "a passion for generalization" as a clear perversion of the original spirit of rationalism. All that remained was a suspicion of tradition, and even this had been transformed into an irrational prejudice against the old. Although Tocqueville did not object to the spread of all general ideas, and in particular endorsed the idea of the rights of man, he was convinced that the mental habits inculcated by modern rationalist writers were destructive of the cause of liberty. It was only in America that rationalism in its original, empirical form was practiced in daily politics: "America is the one country in which the precepts of Descartes are least studied and best followed."[28]

Traditionalism received a less systematic treatment from Tocqueville, probably because of its more recent origin. Although

---

[26]Alexis de Tocqueville, *Recollections*, trans. George Lawrence (Garden City, N.Y.: Doubleday, Anchor Books, 1971), p. 84. Hereinafter cited as *Recollections*. *Old Regime*, p. 148.
[27]*Old Regime*, p. 146; cf. p. 670; *Recollections*, pp. 78-79.
[28]*Democracy*, p. 429.

Tocqueville was thoroughly familiar with the precepts of this school from the thought of French writers like Joseph de Maistre, he apparently did not trace these ideas to their source until making an in-depth study of Burke's thought during his visit to England in 1833.[29] Tocqueville ultimately disagreed with the traditionalist outlook, but he shared many of its points of criticism of philosophe rationalist thought, and among his contemporaries he clearly directed his works to moderates of the traditionalist persuasion, hoping to change their minds.[30]

Although the traditionalists of Tocqueville's time ranged across a broad spectrum of opinion, their diagnosis of the evils of philosophe rationalism contained a common theoretical position. Traditionalists rejected abstract, metaphysical thought in politics and dismissed *a priori* reasoning. Burke,[31] for example, regarded political science as a "practical science" and emphasized the need to view political phenomena in terms of concrete circumstances and particulars. Traditionalism thus presented itself partly as a defense of the realm of prudence for the statesman against the misinformed intrusion of speculative philosophers. In this respect, traditionalism was consistent with the pragmatic character of original rationalist thought, which counseled making judgments on the basis of experience. But traditionalism went far beyond a reliance on this form of reason in its assault on rationalism.

First, traditionalists attacked metaphysical speculation, and sometimes reason itself, in the name of a veneration for the old and familiar. They upheld the "prejudices" of the community and glorified an "instinctive patriotism."[32] For the traditionalist, Tocqueville explained, "the idea of evil is indissolubly linked with

---

[29]For the influence of Burke on French thought, see Robert Nisbet, *Tradition and Revolt* (New York: Vintage Books, 1970), p. 48; and B. Reardon, *Liberalism and Tradition* (Cambridge: Cambridge University Press, 1975), p. 22. Hereinafter cited as Reardon, *Liberalism.* Burke was also highly influential in German conservative thought, which Tocqueville studied directly and learned about through Gobineau (George Chapman, *Edmund Burke, The Practical Imagination* [Cambridge, Mass.: Harvard University Press, 1967], pp. 4-12; hereinafter cited as Chapman, *Imagination*).

[30]*Democracy*, pp. 16-17.

[31]*Old Regime*, p. 69.

[32]*Democracy*, p. 235.

that of novelty."[33]

Second, and following from this depreciation of reason, traditionalists celebrated the heritage of each nation as it emerged as the product of the particular and accidental forces that shaped its development. According to traditionalists, historical bonds of union formed the only sound basis for community, not individual reason or the individual's calculation of interest.[34] Each nation's constitution was the product of—and ought to be bounded by—its particular historical development. Beginning from this "organic" perspective on society, traditionalists viewed the homogenizing effects of universalistic ideas with profound suspicion. Universal ideas eroded the basis of community at the same time that they destroyed the charm of diversity in the world.

Finally, traditionalists strongly supported religious faith, especially as it manifested itself in the particular religious institutions of each society. Traditionalists identified speculatist philosophy with irreligiosity and sought to make common cause with the faithful by contending that religion was one part of an integral world view being attacked by rationalist ideas.[35]

All of these properties of traditionalism can be found in Burke's writings, but they received a simpler, and more extreme, expression by Joseph de Maistre:

> [Man's] cradle should be surrounded by dogmas; and when his reason awakes all his opinions should be given him. . . . Nothing is more vital to him than prejudices. . . . Religion and political dogmas, mingled and merged with each other, should together form a general or national mind sufficiently strong to repress the aberrations of the individual reason.[36]

After sketching the development of these two schools of thought up to his day, Tocqueville turned to their likely evolution and to their consequences on political culture. Although each school claimed in its own way to support liberty, Tocqueville contended

---

[33]Ibid., p. 17.
[34]Ibid., p. 236.
[35]*Old Regime*, p. 154.
[36]Reardon, *Liberalism*, p. 24.

that both ultimately denied that individuals could control their own destiny and therefore eroded a fundamental belief that supported liberty. To maintain liberty, Tocqueville argued, requires more than the acceptance of an idea of rights and certain favorable institutional arrangements, however important each of these may be. Liberty requires a metaphysical foundation in certain views respecting historical causality and free will. It depends on the fact that people can choose and that their choices can make a difference, and on the fact that people *believe* that they can choose and that their choices can make a difference.[37] Without this belief, people lose their "will" to choose and can see no reason to support the idea of rights or legal institutions designed to protect liberty.[38] It was precisely this belief in man's free will, according to Tocqueville, that rationalism and traditionalism called into question.

Philosophe rationalism began with the seeming assertion of boundless human choice: "It has been said that the character of the philosophy of the eighteenth century was a sort of adoration of human intellect, an unlimited confidence in its power to transform at will laws, institutions, customs."[39] Man can make the world according to the dictates of reason, overthrowing the tyranny of tradition and accident. Yet in its ever-expanding quest for universal principles of explanation, philosophe rationalism led paradoxically to the negation of the conditions for choice. The search for general and universal causes ended by positing the source of human activity not in the decisions of particular individuals, but in mankind as a whole or, beyond, in some immanent force in nature or history. Tocqueville labeled this mode of thinking "philosophic pantheism." By tracing the springs of human activity to abstractions like mankind or history, this doctrine rendered human choice meaningless. Choices for mankind or societies, Tocqueville argued, can only be made by

---

[37]In his correspondence with Gobineau, who contended history was the product of racial characteristics, Tocqueville told his friend, "I believe that [your doctrines] are probably quite false; I know that they are certainly very pernicious." Tocqueville judged an idea by the dual criteria of its "philosophic merits" and "its moral and political effects." *"The European Revolution" and Correspondence with Gobineau*, ed. John Lukacs (Gloucester, Mass.: Peter Smith, 1968), pp. 227, 232.

[38]*Democracy*, p. 705.

[39]*Old Regime*, p. 281.

individuals on behalf of the species; the species itself cannot choose. Once one posits the power over human affairs in the species, that power lies with no one in particular and hence with an invisible system that operates on all: "Individuals are forgotten, and the species alone counts."[40] With vast, general causes thought to be controlling their destiny, people lose all will to assert themselves, and they become weak and phlegmatic.

If philosophe rationalism carried to the extreme leads to one form of denial of human choice, traditionalism carried to the extreme leads to another. The result is equally paradoxical in light of the traditionalists' expressed goal of preserving a realm of discretion for the statesman. Yet by depreciating reason and making the heritage of each society both the cause and standard for its regime, traditionalists implied that there were no fundamental choices; all was as it had to be, or nearly so. The protection traditionalists sought to gain for the statesman in the realm of prudential decision-making was thus bought at the cost of denying human choice on fundamental questions. "Each nation," in the traditionalist view, "is inexorably bound by its position, origin, antecedents, and nature to a fixed destiny which no effort can change . . . [it is] the product of preexisting facts, of race, or soil, or climate."[41] Following Tocqueville, John Stuart Mill gave his classic formulation of the traditionalist position: "[Governments] are a sort of organic growth from the nature and life of that people: a product of their habits, instincts, and unconscious wants and desires, scarcely at all of their deliberate purposes."[42]

Traditionalism, then, leads to a doctrine of historical inevitability, although not of the sort with which we are most familiar today. Ever since Hegel, and especially Marx, doctrines of historical inevitability have tended to assume the form of universalistic theories in which the forces at work in history are said to include all of mankind. This post-Hegelian form of historicism folds the universalistic ideas inaugurated by the philosophes into an

---

[40]*Democracy*, p. 451.
[41]Ibid., pp. 705, 496.
[42]Alexis de Tocqueville, *Journey to England and Ireland*, trans. George Lawrence and J.-P. Mayer (New Haven, Conn.: Yale University Press, 1958), p. 4.

inevitable movement of *world* history in which all are swept along in accord with some plan that flows either from the movement of Mind or material forces. But doctrines of historical inevitability were originally an outgrowth of traditionalism, and their source can be traced to Burke. This earlier form of historicism sought to demonstrate that the cause of human societies lay with the particular and accidental forces that operate on each nation (or *Volk*).[43] Although Tocqueville glimpsed the possibility of a universalistic historicism and advanced one such mild variant of his own, he identified the historicism of his day mainly with those who sought to explain the fate of *particular* nations or peoples.

Notwithstanding their attempt to defend rank and hierarchy, traditionalist doctrines of historical inevitability represented a democratic mode of thought in the sense that peoples, races, or climates, but not individuals, control historical development. While Tocqueville thought that traditionalist historicism might preserve a certain diversity in the world among nations or races, he believed that it was no less hostile than philosophic pantheism to the idea of human choice. It left man with the view that his actions could make no difference and that "societies unconsciously obey some superior dominating force," which was precisely the belief that prepared the way for despotism.[44] By extending Tocqueville's analysis, one can glimpse in this organic variant of historicism, as transformed by the atheism of Nietzsche, the seeds of the radical "democratic" Right (fascism), just as it is possible to see in rationalism, as modified by Marx, the grounds of the radical

---

[43]For historicist accounts that see a movement or plan for the whole world, see Hegel's *Philosophy of History* and Marx's and Engels's *Communist Manifesto*. For the origin of historicist thought in Burke, see Leo Strauss, *Natural Right and History* (Chicago: University of Chicago Press, 1953), pp. 294-321; and Thomas Pangle, *Montesquieu's Philosophy of Liberalism* (Chicago: University of Chicago Press, 1973), pp. 192-93. Hereinafter cited as Pangle, *Philosophy*. Although Burke shied away from anything like a pure doctrine of historical inevitability, the latter tendency became much more pronounced in those who drew their inspiration from his thought. It is also possible to trace the seeds of Burke's emphasis on history and circumstance in Montesquieu, whom Burke considered "the greatest genius which has enlightened this age" (Chapman, *Imagination*, 1967), p. 23. But the emergence of history as possibly the most important standard is far more evident with Burke and with those who drew directly on his thought.

[44]*Democracy*, p. 495.

"democratic" Left (communism).

Thus rationalism, by leading to philosophic pantheism, and traditionalism, by leading to historicism, deny free will. To promote the beliefs that sustain liberty, Tocqueville sought to free man from the sway of these ideologies. His alternative, the new political science, presupposed a significant, although not unlimited, degree of choice: "One may say that it depends on us whether in the end republics will be established everywhere, or everywhere abolished."[45] Political science was designed to help man choose well, which demanded knowledge of the true historical situation and the capacity to face reality, avoiding the mistakes of the rival schools of alternatively exaggerating and underestimating the possibilities that were available.

Against the philosophe's excessive pride that all societies could be remade according to the simple principles of reason, Tocqueville countered with the claim that regimes were still bound by the particular experiences of each nation. Despite the homogenizing forces set in motion by growing equality and the spread of modern thought, the political culture of each nation retained certain distinct characteristics, and Tocqueville certainly had no desire to impose uniformity for its own sake. Insofar as political science might assist those who directed society, it was not by prescribing precise models that should be adopted in the same fashion in every nation, but by illustrating general principles that should be applied in their own way as far as circumstances within each nation would permit: "The laws of the French republic can be, and in many cases should be, different from those prevailing in the United States. . . . [L]et us adopt the principles rather than the details of her laws."[46]

Against the traditionalists, Tocqueville countered with a twofold argument to meet their two very different (and conflicting) assumptions. On the one hand, traditionalists virtually denied that there could be a general science of politics that could assist legislators. As the world, in the traditionalists' view, is governed by contingencies and accident, and as constitutions are the product of

---

[45]Ibid., p. x.
[46]Ibid., p. xiv.

particular cultures, the best the legislator can do is modify a constitution according to standards that emerge from understanding a nation's particular genius. According to Tocqueville, this view underestimates the degree of choice and the role that a general science of politics might play in informing the tasks of legislating and constitution-making.

On the other hand, traditionalists assumed that the movement toward equality of conditions and away from a respect for hierarchy and forms could be thwarted by the development of a counter-ideology. For Tocqueville, this option was closed: "Burke did not see . . . that there could be no question of putting the clock back."[47] Although traditionalists purported to look at facts, they refused to acknowledge that the movement toward the social state of democracy and the penetration of society by some form of rationalism were historical facts in their own right that could be neither denied nor reversed. In his Introduction to *Democracy in America,* Tocqueville advanced a mild variant of universalistic historicism that challenged traditionalists to see that the real choice lay not between the old order and democracy, but between democratic despotisms and democratic republics.[48] Given the traditionalists' expressed concern for liberty, they might, when faced with this choice, be persuaded to become adherents of the new political science.

The New Political Science

Tocqueville's new political science combines generals and particulars to form a body of knowledge designed to promote the cause of liberty in modern times. It can thus be characterized not only by its normative goal, which makes it quite different from modern political science, but by its distinctive epistemological foundation. Tocqueville's political science falls into a middle ground between rationalism, which extended general ideas to the point of eliminating any prudential consideration of specific

---

[47]*Old Regime*, p. 21.

[48]See Marvin Zetterbaum, *Tocqueville and the Problem of Democracy* (Stanford, Cal.: Stanford University Press, 1967).

circumstances, and traditionalism, which virtually denied the existence of any general ideas that could inform or instruct prudential judgment. But it is much easier, Tocqueville tells us, to imagine the existence and utility of such a middle ground than to put it into practice.

The central problem for a science of politics concerns the epistemological status of "general ideas." All general ideas, Tocqueville maintains, distort reality in some degree by comprehending the distinctness of different objects under the same concept. Human thought creates a world of partially fictitious wholes that assigns greater similarity to things than actually exists in the real world: "General ideas do not bear witness to the power of human intelligence but rather to its inadequacy, for there are no beings exactly alike in nature."[49] It was this difficulty, among other concerns, that led Burke and other traditionalists to doubt the worth of a theoretical political science. For Tocqueville, however, the proper response was not to deny the value of general ideas, but rather to recognize their limitations and avoid using them in an extreme or abstract fashion. Without recourse to general ideas, no science, indeed no advancement in human understanding, would be possible, for man "would soon be lost in a wilderness of detail and not be able to see anything at all."[50]

Political science is the careful construction of knowledge in which general ideas are founded not on abstract principles that flow elegantly from self-contained intellectual systems, but on the painstaking study of particular cases and the "slow, detailed, and conscientious labor of the mind."[51] "One man . . . notices a fact and another conceives an idea; one man finds a means and another discovers a formula."[52] Yet even this knowledge, because it relies on general ideas, is imperfect and does some violence to the understanding of particular circumstances. This difficulty creates an inevitable—although not unbridgeable—gap between the statesman and the political scientist, "For while it is sometimes necessary

---

[49]*Democracy*, p. 437.
[50]Ibid., and Gargan, *De Tocqueville*, pp. 42-44.
[51]*Democracy*, p. 440.
[52]Ibid., p. 268; cf. p. 438.

to brush rules of logic aside in action, one cannot do so in the same way in treatises, and man finds it almost as difficult to be inconsistent in his words as he generally finds it to be consistent in his actions."[53] Tocqueville prepares his readers for this problem by warning them that he must sometimes bring his own ideas "to the verge of the false and impracticable" although he never consciously "fitted the facts to opinions instead of subjecting opinions to the facts."[54]

A perfectly accurate understanding of reality, Tocqueville tells us, cannot be attained, for it would require a humanly impossible method that could somehow reap all the benefits of generalizing while avoiding all of its defects. Only God can employ such a method, for He alone "can survey distinctly and simultaneously, all mankind and each single man."[55] Science does the best it can using the limited tools of human intelligence to emulate this godlike standard.

The thought of philosophe intellectuals, by contrast, ignores completely this godlike standard by attempting to subsume more and more of "reality" into abstract general ideas without regard to the existence of particulars. Instead of minimizing the defect inherent in the structure of human thought, the philosophe intellectual exacerbates it. If all that were involved in this process was the activity of some isolated individual interpreting the world, the danger would be slight. But, in fact, philosophe thought was designed expressly to create a popular political program, the aim of which was to eliminate complex customs and traditions and reshape reality in accord with the "rules of logic and a preconceived system."[56] In line with this program, the rationalists of Tocqueville's day tended to support the powers of the largest unit of authority, the central government, no matter whether it was a strong, "enlightened monarchy or a centralized republic."[57] Philosophe intellectuals saw the central government with its centrally

---

[53]Ibid., p. 20. I have changed Lawrence's translation in this passage.
[54]Ibid., pp. 19-20.
[55]Ibid., p. 704; cf. p. 437.
[56]*Old Regime*, p. 147.
[57]*Democracy*, pp. 97, 723-24.

directed administrative apparatus as one of the chief instruments for "recasting [a nation] in a given mold, of shaping the mentality of the population as a whole and instilling the ideas and sentiments [of the intellectuals] into the minds of all."[58]

Even more important for Tocqueville than the philosophe's program for change was the consequence of its framework of thought on the mental habits of society. By its inattentiveness to particulars, philosophe thought promoted a disregard for diversity and a partiality for uniformity. By contrast, the new political science, in its concern for facts and practice, implicitly encouraged a respect for diversity. Thus, apart even from a consideration of the content of their programs, the new political science embraced a mode of thought more favorable than philosophe rationalism to a political culture that supported liberty. In his most general and revealing statement on the consequences of rationalist general ideas, Tocqueville wrote:

> To force all men to march in step toward the same goal—that is a human idea. To encourage endless variety of actions but to bring them about so that in a thousand different ways all tend toward the fulfillment of one great design—that is a God-given idea. The human idea of unity is almost always sterile, but that of God is immensely fruitful. Men think they prove their greatness by simplifying the means, God's object is simple but His means infinitely various.[59]

Rationalist intellectuals were either ignorant of the distortion of reality in their thought or else chose from ambition to disregard it. Yet far from reducing their influence on society, this defect tended to increase it, for "what is merit in the writer may well be a vice in the statesman, and the same things that often make beautiful books can lead to great revolutions."[60] Here Tocqueville suggested the central problem of the intellectual in politics; theoretical constructs that are a false reflection of reality are apt to

---

[58]*Old Regime*, p. 162.
[59]*Democracy*, pp. 734-35.
[60]*Old Regime*, p. 147; cf. *Recollections*, pp. 84-85.

have a much greater impact on the public mind than those that present a true picture of reality. The products of a "literary spirit" result in "beautiful" works, whereas the products of a scientific spirit must sacrifice beauty for accuracy.

Traditionalists had correctly identified this homogenizing tendency of modern philosophe thought as its most characteristic and dangerous trait. But while sharing their concern, Tocqueville rejected their standards and doubted the efficacy of their methods for combating philosophe ideas. Unlike the traditionalists, Tocqueville upheld reason at the same time that he attacked the reason of his contemporaries and defended the intellect at the same time that he attacked the modern intellectual.

The underpinnings of Tocqueville's new political science were not entirely original. Concern about the consequences of philosophe thought and about the need to blend the universal and the particular can be found in the works of the writers whom Tocqueville studied most closely (Rousseau, Montesquieu, and Pascal). Yet the fact that Tocqueville owed a debt to other thinkers, and especially to Montesquieu, does not reduce the significance of his call for a new political science, for on Montesquieu's own grounds political philosophy must be "presented not only in the form of a philosophic treatise but simultaneously in the form of a tract for the times."[61] Just as the principles of political science must be adapted to each country, so the principles of political philosophy must be adapted to each new age.[62] In the brief period between Montesquieu's death and Tocqueville's publication of *Democracy in America*, modernity had undergone one of its greatest transformations. Tocqueville's claim to originality (if his words can be read in those terms) was not for a new political science per se, but for a "new political science . . . for a world itself quite new." Tocqueville's achievement lay, as Mill had said, in writing "the first philosophic book . . . on Democracy."

---

[61]Pangle, *Philosophy*, p. 305.
[62]*Democracy*, p. 543.

Political Science as an Active Force in the World

Given the complicated character of his new political science, one immediately wonders how Tocqueville hoped to make it into an active force in modern society. Although the goal of political science—reconciling liberty and democracy—was not hostile to the general spirit of modern times, its complexity left it without widespread appeal. It could, of course, be taught directly to the few who studied his works, but Tocqueville was under no illusions that it could become a popular ideology that could, like philosophe thought, "fire the imagination of the masses." "Generally speaking, simple conceptions take hold of people's minds. A false but clear and precise idea always has more power in the world than one which is true but complex."[63]

Since political science could not win a public war of ideas against philosophe ideology, Tocqueville employed a more indirect strategy based on encouraging certain mental habits in society that would be compatible with, if not necessarily exactly the same as, the lessons taught by political science.[64] These mental habits were characterized less by any particular content (in the sense of a set of ideas outlining a program or agenda) than by a way of thinking that people would employ. Tocqueville did not seek to fight ideology with ideology, not only because such a battle would have been futile, but also because a society directed by ideology (and intellectuals) could not, in his view, remain a free regime.

To be more specific, Tocqueville's strategy involved showing those who direct society what kinds of social and political institutions could limit the intellectuals' influence over public opinion and help citizens to learn to reason from particulars to generals rather than from generals to particulars. Under Tocqueville's strategy, public opinion would form more along the lines of the American than the French model. The influence of ideas produced by intellectuals at the "top" would diminish, whereas that of other sources of authority (e.g., political leaders and lawyers) and of opinion generated from the "bottom" would increase.

---

[63]Ibid., p. 164.
[64]Ibid., p. 287.

Opinion generated from the bottom was a reflection of democratic sentiments and concrete interests as these were modified by the knowledge and experience gained by citizens involved in the task of self-government.

In this section, I shall examine Tocqueville's application of the practical aspects of the new political science to the press, the legal system, and local government, noting how he employs his distinctive standard of judging institutions by their effect on mental habits. In each case, Tocqueville illustrates how American institutions, especially when compared with those in France, serve to reduce the influence of general ideas and to promote reasoning from particulars to generals. Tocqueville's method of analysis here is slightly unexpected given his starting point of studying America in order to see the picture of democracy. Yet American political culture, as noted, does not follow democracy's natural path of development. In the instances discussed below, France becomes the picture for certain democratic tendencies in their pure (and dangerous) form, whereas America becomes the (partial) model for how these tendencies can be corrected in a framework that is consistent with democracy.

The Press[65]

Tocqueville's discussion of the press is the most striking case of his effort to limit the influence of modern intellectuals. In line with the position of most *philosophe* thinkers, Tocqueville was a staunch advocate of a free press, arguing that citizens in free regimes need a free flow of information to govern themselves and that the possession by government of the power to regulate the press could lead by stages to despotism. Yet unlike the philosophe thinkers, who saw the press as a perfect vehicle for spreading their version of enlightenment to the public, Tocqueville preferred an arrangement of the press that would limit the intellectual's influence.

As an independent source of power over public opinion, the

---

[65]In this section, I borrow freely from the excellent discussion of Tocqueville's thought by Francis Bourricaud, *Le Bricolage Ideologique: Essai sur les intellectuals et les passions democratiques* (Paris: Presses universitaires de France, 1980), pp. 37-69.

French press had no equal. The "vital part" of its newspapers was devoted to political discussion, and the "spirit" of French journalism demanded a "lofty and eloquent way of arguing about the great interests of state."[66] French journalists were highly esteemed, as the relatively small number of newspapers was concentrated in Paris and attracted talented and cosmopolitan writers. It was with the aid of the press that intellectuals were able to spread their thought from the center to the peripheries and to enlighten the provinces with the latest and most advanced ideas.

The American press could hardly have been more different. Newspapers were filled with advertisements, and the presentation of the news lacked the kind of "burning argument" and lofty commentary that was commonplace in France.[67] There was an extraordinarily large number of newspapers in America, which were widely dispersed throughout the nation. The effect of this arrangement was to divide and limit the influence of the American press in comparison with that of the French press. In addition, American journalists were generally of low educational status and possessed only modest talents. When they expressed political viewpoints, they did so not by adopting an intellectual perspective and hiding their appeals to passions in philosophic language, but instead by making crude appeals to lower passions, often "attacking people [and] revealing their private lives and vices."[68] Although American journalists won a wide audience by these techniques, the public, and certainly its more enlightened elements, sensed the narrow spirit of their inquiry and had little respect for journalists as a group.

Even though the press in America was less powerful than in France, its influence was still very great: "After the people, the press is nonetheless the first of powers."[69] Yet it was not journalists as opinion-makers who held most of this power; rather, it derived from the newspapers' role in communicating ideas among groups in society, such as political parties and associations. The American

---

[66]*Democracy*, pp. 183, 185.
[67]Ibid., p. 184.
[68]Ibid., p. 185.
[69]Ibid., p. 186.

press therefore contributed to the formation of public opinion by political associations rather than by intellectuals, allowing opinion to build from the bottom to the top, rather than from the top to the bottom.[70]

By any criterion of literary or journalistic excellence, the American press was inferior to that in France, and Tocqueville never doubted that the "deplorable abuse of thought" that took place in the American press would adversely affect "the taste and morality" of the American people.[71] But the harm done to American mental habits in this respect was more than offset by the benefit derived from blocking a portal of access for the intellectuals' general ideas. Tocqueville was quite willing to sacrifice sophistication and even to admit a degree of coarseness into society as the price for protecting citizens from the thinkers who sought to run their lives.

The Legal Profession

Tocqueville's discussion of the legal profession provides a second example of his effort to limit the power of intellectuals and general ideas.[72] Tocqueville sought to promote the legal spirit in society to serve as a counterweight to the literary spirit, and lawyers as a counterweight to intellectuals.[73] The legal way of thinking, with its roots in the judicial process, has something in common with the empirical strain of early rationalist thought: "[I]t pronounces on particular cases and not on general principles."[74] Judges and lawyers are trained to reason from particulars to generals and therefore develop an affinity for order and forms that leads them as a rule to shun momentary popular passions. To the extent that the legal profession influences the thinking of society as a whole, it imbues the citizenry with some of its mental habits. Tocqueville, for

---

[70]Ibid., p. 520.
[71]Ibid., p. 185.
[72]Ibid., p. 267; cf. p. 185.
[73]Tocqueville provides a rough definition of spirit (*l'esprit*) as, in any particular case, "certain ways to which all must conform . . . the sum of these common ways is called a spirit; there is the spirit of the bar, the spirit of the court" (p. 185). We are obviously also meant to think of Montesquieu's usage of the term.
[74]*Democracy*, p. 160.

example, considered the importance of the institution of the jury as much in terms of its impact on mental habits as on its efficiency as an instrument of justice.

After sketching the general spirit of the legal profession, Tocqueville turned to the particular spirit of French and Anglo-Saxon lawyers. Although lawyers in both nations reason from particulars to generals, French lawyers, following continental theories of jurisprudence, analyze particulars in the light of general principles, whereas Anglo-Saxon lawyers, working in the common-law tradition, consult "the law of precedents" and consider particulars in light of "the legal judgments of their fathers." "The first thing an English or American lawyer looks for is what has been done, whereas a French one inquires what one should wish to do." The spirit of French law is more abstract, as it is based on a "whole system of ideas," whereas that of English and American law is more historical.[75]

The spirit on which Anglo-Saxon law rested antedated not only philosophe thought, but the emergence of rationalism. It incorporated many characteristics of traditionalism, and Tocqueville's discussion of English and American law virtually reads as a commentary on traditionalist thought. English and American lawyers proceed with "a superstitious respect for all that is old"[76] and value laws "not because they are good but because they are old."[77] With their expertise resting on an "obscure" tradition, they relate to the public "somewhat like the Egyptian priests, being, as they were, the only interpreter of an occult science."[78] English lawyers will introduce change, but only by hiding the fact and going to "absurd lengths" to avoid admitting to the "crime" of being an "innovator."[79] The character of English law is decidedly organic—a point Tocqueville emphasizes by employing the metaphor of a "trunk of an old tree" on which lawyers continually graft "the strangest shoots."[80]

Although Tocqueville appreciated much in the traditionalist

---

[75]Ibid., p. 267.
[76]Ibid., p. 269.
[77]Ibid., p. 268.
[78]Ibid.
[79]Ibid.
[80]Ibid.

character of Anglo-Saxon law, his ironic tone and admission that this system of legal thought was filled with "defects" leave no doubt that he considered traditionalism to be unsuitable as the first principle for the entire government.[81] In any case, its merits aside, the Anglo-Saxon legal spirit could not serve openly as the foundation for a modern society, as its premises were out of step with rationalist standards of legitimacy. Anglo-Saxon lawyers could "raise no banner of their own" and won a measure of influence not by openly defending their principles, but by insinuating their spirit into society, "penetrating each component class and constantly working in secret upon its unconscious patient."[82] In spite of these reservations, however, Tocqueville thought that the Anglo-Saxon legal spirit provided a salutary corrective to the excesses of certain democratic tendencies, moderating the citizenry's fascination with novelty and limiting its susceptibility to the appeal of the intellectual's general ideas. The legal spirit in the United States served in its context to promote the ends of the new political science, even though it was not grounded strictly on the mental habits of early rationalist thought.[83]

Communal Government[84]

Tocqueville's discussion of communal liberty and citizen participation in local governments is the best-known example of his application of the principles of the new political science to practical affairs. It is important, however, to avoid confusing his ideas on citizen participation with an endorsement of populism in national politics.[85] Tocqueville was a staunch opponent of direct democracy in national politics and a strong defender of the American Founders' goal of establishing representative institutions that

---

[81] Ibid.

[82] Ibid., p. 270.

[83] Ibid., p. 268.

[84] Lawrence sometimes translates "commune" as "township," where Tocqueville was suggesting a connection between the American local community and local communities found everywhere. When referring specifically to the American local unit of government, Tocqueville often included the English word "township" in parentheses. I have substituted "commune" for "township" in some of the translations in this section.

[85] *Democracy*, p. 253.

preserved broad discretion for deliberation and statesmanship. His idea of participation emphasized activities in matters falling within the sphere of the citizens' own experience, not in affairs of state such as foreign policymaking. The importance of participation was based as much on the mental habits promoted by the activity of deciding as on the content of what people decided.[86]

By taking part in political affairs, citizens learn the mental habits of the pragmatic strain of rationalism. These habits serve to reduce the influence of general ideas and increase the weight of experience in the formation of public opinion: "If, then, there is a subject concerning which a democracy is particularly liable to commit itself blindly and extravagantly to general ideas, the best possible corrective is to make citizens pay daily practical attention to it."[87] For citizens to become enlightened in more than a cosmetic sense depends, in fact, on their being able to complete their literary education by participating in the practical task of governing: "True enlightenment is in the main born of experience, and if the Americans had not gradually grown accustomed to rule themselves, their literary attainments would not help them much toward success."[88]

Local government also functions for Tocqueville as a major "secondary power" that stands between the individual and the central state.[89] Tocqueville seldom discussed liberty without also discussing the practical means by which it could be secured, and these included the possession by citizens of a sense of their *power* to defend their rights. Secondary powers in Tocqueville's thought serve as rallying points for citizens to resist the overwhelming weight of central authority. Yet secondary powers are threatened in democratic times by the many forces tending toward concentration of authority in central governments, and it is only by great effort and intelligence that they can be maintained: "In the dawning centuries of democracy individual liberty and local liberties will always be products of art; centralized government will be the natural thing."[90]

---

[86]Ibid., pp. 511, 694.
[87]Ibid., p. 442.
[88]Ibid., p. 304.
[89]Ibid., p. 676.
[90]Ibid., p. 674.

Of the secondary powers Tocqueville identified—civic associations, political associations, and business enterprises—he considered the commune to be the most durable, for it alone rested on a "natural" foundation (although it, too, could be maintained only by "art"). The commune is "natural" in the sense of being a form of social organization that grows organically rather than being consciously constructed: "[It] is the only association so well rooted in nature that wherever men assemble it forms itself. . . . [M]an creates kingdoms and republics, but communes seem to spring directly from the hand of God."[91] Tocqueville introduces here a key distinction between the "natural" (in the sense of the organic) and the conventional (that which man makes by the application of his own intelligence). Tocqueville's final standard, it should be observed, is not the natural in the organic sense, but rather "nature" or "natural right" as discovered conventionally by human reflection on the world and its possibilities.[92] In contrast, however, to the fabricated "human ideas" propagated by philosophe intellectuals, Tocqueville's understanding of natural right never departs entirely from the natural in the organic sense, in part because the failure to recognize organic needs leads to social dysfunctions. A satisfactory modern regime must combine a man-made principle of rule with respect for the natural foundations of community that are found in the communes.

The conflict Tocqueville identified between the standards of philosophe rationalists and the standard of the natural (organic) is played out on the plane of practical politics in the conflict over the role of local governments in the modern state. The commune develops outside the sphere of human contrivance and derives much of its operating spirit not from abstract theory or ideology, but from custom and practical experience. Philosophe intellectuals, who rely for their power on units of central opinion formation and their alliance with central authority and centralized administration, regard communal liberty as an enemy of their designs. They want to impose their standards on the commune and thus run roughshod over communal custom and local experience: "A very civilized society

---

[91]Ibid., p. 62.
[92]Ibid., p. 237.

finds it hard to tolerate attempts at freedom in a local community; it is disgusted by its numerous blunders and is apt to despair of success before the experiment is finished."[93] Here Tocqueville depicts the characteristic vice of modern intellect, which is an absence of forbearance and an impatient impulse to do things for people rather than to let them act for themselves. Philosophe rationalists prefer to impose the right opinion in every case rather than inculcate the mental habits that would allow people to decide for themselves (and therefore inevitably to make mistakes).

The question of where to draw the line between central and communal authority was for Tocqueville a complicated matter that depended on such considerations as security needs, the stage of economic development, and the degree of enlightenment in the communes. Although not a dogmatic opponent of all "intrusions" of the central authority in local affairs, Tocqueville nonetheless expressed a strong preference, all other things being equal, for decentralization.[94] In the northern states of the United States, Tocqueville found his practical ideal of the modern commune. Free of feudal customs, these localities had developed a new tradition based on equality and the exercise of pragmatic rationalism in politics. These communes were enlightened, but they were still far from being the centers of sophistication adored by philosophe intellectuals. Tocqueville had no hesitation, however, in defending them, as his goal was not a society directed by the most advanced discoveries of modern thinkers, but one that allowed free and enlightened citizens to practice the art of self-government.

Tocqueville's comparison of opinion formation in France and America risks slipping at times into an ideal-type analysis in

---

[93]Ibid., p. 62.

[94]Ibid. Tocqueville acknowledged the need for greater centralization in Europe than the United States because of the necessity of reforming its feudal mores (p. 90). In the U.S., he suggested that the federal government would have a similar role to play with respect to eliminating prejudice against Indians and Blacks (p. 337). In future times, economic conditions would call for a very active role for the federal government as protector and regulator (p. 684). Finally, although Tocqueville clearly preferred as a general rule to strengthen decentralizing trends against the tendencies of democracy toward constant centralization, in the U.S. he felt that the drift toward decentralization was too strong and threatened the nation's unity and security (pp. 390-93).

which the United States, in order to be contrasted with a nation influenced by philosophe rationalist thought, is presented as a society devoid of intellectual reflection and successful only because of the unconscious operation of certain geographical and historical advantages. In fact, while Tocqueville pointed to many of the fortunate circumstances that contributed to America's success, his analysis makes clear that the establishment of the Constitution in the 1780s was a remarkable achievement of political sagacity. America was adverse to "general ideas," if by general ideas one means the sort of ideas generated by the philosophes and their opponents. But the American Founders were certainly not adverse to the study of the first principles of politics, and important elements of the American public grasped the principles of science on which they had based their work.[95]

Although Tocqueville had nothing but praise for the intelligence of America's Founders, it is nevertheless significant that he did not consider any American to have been a "great writer" on politics.[96] The understanding of what made America work was only partly contained in the thought of *The Federalist*, which, because it concentrated on the principles for establishing a *national* government, provided an incomplete account of state and local governments and the fundamentals of American political culture.[97] Tocqueville's analysis in effect combined the concerns of *The Federalist* and the small republic or anti-Federalist traditions in American political thought by blending certain attributes of the small republic—or at any rate worthy facsimiles thereof—with the qualities needed to sustain a great, modern commercial republic.[98] The result, he evidently thought, was a more complete political science than that of any American thinker.

---

[95]Ibid., pp. 113-14, 152, 164.
[96]Ibid., p. 301.
[97]Ibid., p. 61.
[98]Ibid., p. 287.

The Synthesis of Rationalism and Traditionalism

To promote liberty in modern times, Tocqueville sought to reduce the influence of intellectuals and general ideas and to instill in citizens the mental habits of the early rationalist method of reasoning from experience and particulars. Although Tocqueville was as critical as Burke of the modern philosophe strand of rationalism, he nevertheless made rationalism, not traditionalism, his principal standard for modern society. He rejected traditionalist notions of prejudice, superstition, and emotion as the foundation for government on the grounds that they were inconsistent with the spirit of modern times and incapable of supporting a regime of equality in liberty.

Tocqueville's project can therefore be described as an effort to rescue the original core of rationalism from its later distortion. Yet this statement needs to be qualified, for Tocqueville thought that rationalist standards, even those derived from the early inductive approach, were not entirely adequate as a foundation for a free and healthy society. Moreover, the distortion of early rationalist thought that took place in the eighteenth and early nineteenth centuries was not, in Tocqueville's estimation, a mere accident, but a logical result of certain flaws and limitations implicit in the original rationalist position. Thus, even to save the original core of rationalism, Tocqueville argued that it had to be supplemented and modified. These changes were based on insights Tocqueville drew from traditionalist principles, although he sought to apply these insights in ways that were compatible with the spirit of rationalism.

The originality of Tocqueville's new political science inhered largely in its synthesis of these two schools. Although predominantly a rationalist and a liberal, Tocqueville sought to integrate certain traditionalist values such as religiosity, community, and spiritedness into the democratic liberal state. These values Tocqueville considered worthy in themselves, but he also stressed their utility. The failure of liberal rationalist regimes to incorporate these values would lead to severe dysfunctions that in the end would threaten their prosperity and freedom. The dual nature of Tocqueville's analysis, at once friendly to liberalism but mindful of its problems, helps to explain his powerful influence on both liberal thinkers and those of the European sociological tradition who have stressed the major difficulties of liberal society.[99]

Tocqueville discussed the central problem posed by the entire rationalist project in his extensive treatment of the nature of intellectual authority in modern times.[100] The original rationalist position as it filtered into society held that each person could make up his own mind, using his personal assessment of reality as the standard of truth. But this position, Tocqueville argued, was untenable, for most human beings lack the time, inclination, and capacity to decide on a great many matters of fundamental importance: "Man has to accept as certain a whole heap of facts and opinions which he has neither leisure nor power to examine and verify for himself . . . [s]omewhere and somehow authority is always bound to play a part in intellectual and moral life."[101]

Aristocratic societies were arranged implicitly in acknowledgment of this fact, and people experienced no great problem in receiving opinions from tradition or from those considered wiser. In democratic societies, however, individuals are imbued with the rationalist idea that they can make up their own minds, and, considering themselves fully equal with everyone else, refuse to accept the intellectual authority of any other individual. Nevertheless, sensing their own weakness and needing to resolve matters, they turn to public opinion as the source for their ideas.[102] By bowing to no one in particular, they flatter themselves that they have not sacrificed their own judgment. With their minds thus at ease, they accept a source of intellectual authority that is potentially even more powerful than those found in aristocratic societies. Rationalism, which begins from the supposition that each person can make up his own mind, may paradoxically end with a state of affairs in which few think for themselves and in which "public opinion becomes more and more mistress of the world."[103]

---

[99]Included on this list would be Emile Durkheim and, in the U.S. today, Robert Nisbet and Peter Berger.
[100]*Democracy*, pp. 429-500.
[101]Ibid., p. 434.
[102]Ibid., p. 435.
[103]Ibid.

The central question in Tocqueville's analysis of democratic society thus becomes who or what forms public opinion. Tocqueville provides two basic answers: first, public opinion may emerge from the interests and sentiments of the people; second, public opinion may be formed by intellectuals. There are differences in the character of opinion as it derives from these two sources, though not as great as one might suppose. The opinion that emerges from the people is coarser and reflects, among other things, untutored desires for material gratification and for some kind of equality[104]; the opinion formed by intellectuals fans the passions for equality and uniformity, dressing them in highbrow philosophic language and endowing them with utopian expectations.[105] Accordingly, both sources produce opinions that are democratic in content; but the opinion that derives from intellectuals is rigid and dogmatic, whereas that which derives from sentiment is more amenable to modification by political experience and to direction by political leaders.[106]

To explain why the opinions fostered by intellectuals are democratic, Tocqueville presents a three-part sociology of ideas and intellectuals. First, he argues that only those ideas that are broadly consistent with prevailing social conditions can attract public support.[107] Social conditions do not determine the exact content of thought or the ideas of every thinker. But social conditions do suggest certain ways of thinking about reality, which most thinkers then ascribe—often erroneously—to all times and places. For example, given the weakness of individuals in democratic times, most thinkers are led to posit that history is moved by general causes rather than individual efforts.[108] More important, social conditions set boundaries to the kinds of ideas that are potentially acceptable. Thinkers who stand outside these boundaries—like traditionalists—are unable in the end to exercise much influence. Thus, although intellectuals may shape the public mind,

---

[104]Ibid., pp. 552, 504.
[105]*Old Regime*, pp. 158-59.
[106]Ibid., p. 142.
[107]*Democracy*, p. 431.
[108]Ibid., pp. 439, 494-96.

they can do so only so far.

Second, intellectuals in the modern era are perhaps especially prone to reflecting the common views of their times. Those who become intellectuals are not members of a distinct class having a set of values fundamentally different from the rest of society, but rather emerge from society after having been initially formed by democratic tastes and passions. They employ their thought to give expression to these sentiments and are often little more than the most articulate conveyors of democratic prejudices.[109]

Finally, Tocqueville suggests a narrower and more self-interested reason for the intellectual's adherence to democratic ideas. Like all others in democratic times, intellectuals must earn a living and make their way in the world by practicing a career; they engage in their trade as a vocation, not an avocation.[110] As a result, their success depends on how well they can sell their ideas to their contemporaries. The intellectual *qua* intellectual is not accorded deference, but rather can gain influence only by his ability to appeal to a portion of the public and supply it with the kinds of ideas it can grasp. The intellectual is therefore led by ambition and the desire to secure a livelihood to produce ideas that can meet with widespread approval. In content, this means purveying ideas that are consistent with the democratic passions, chiefly equality and uniformity; in style, it means writing in broad generalities, because democratic citizens, needing "sound" opinion on many matters but unwilling or unable to spend time on difficult inquiries, crave general ideas.[111]

Although the opinion generated by intellectuals tends to be democratic, it differs, as noted, from the opinion that emerges directly from popular democratic sentiments. Intellectuals create opinions that appeal to the imagination and that move people beyond a common-sense calculation of their interest to imagine utopian visions; and even though intellectuals must sell their ideas, they are not (with the exception of the masters of popular entertainment and culture) bound by the immediate views of the mass

---

[109]Ibid., pp. 457, 460.
[110]Ibid., p. 458.
[111]Ibid., p. 442.

public. They produce for a more limited high-brow or literary-minded public that is more likely to get excited by their new thoughts.[112] The intellectual's influence over the public mind is exercised by a two-step process in which potentially quite radical ideas are first digested by a literary-minded sector and then by degrees disseminated to the public at large.

If this analysis helps explain the intellectuals' ability to manage opinion in modern society, the problem for Tocqueville was how their influence could be limited by mental habits reflecting the empirical strand of original rationalist thought. For this, Tocqueville thought it better to work with opinion as it emerged naturally from democratic passions and sentiments, educating and moderating it by means of the solutions noted in the last section. Yet for these solutions to work, Tocqueville made it clear that steps would also have to be taken to deal with certain fundamental moral and intellectual problems that rationalism, even in its empirical form, left unresolved. It was here that Tocqueville turned to traditionalist insights.

Tocqueville's most important qualification of a rationalist foundation for society was his assertion of the need for religious belief. Tocqueville stands out as one of the staunchest supporters of religion among the great liberal thinkers, and it is on this point that his break with rationalist intellectuals of his time was most explicit.[113] In matters of belief about religion, as on the question of the rights of man, Tocqueville made an exception to his position against general ideas, or rather took the occasion to clarify his position about the domains of opinion in which general ideas were needed: "General ideas respecting God and human nature are . . . the ideas above all others which ought to be withdrawn from the habitual action of human judgment."[114] If the scope of critical inquiry in these areas was not limited, people would be thrust into an intellectual vacuum leading to despair, paralysis, and eventually susceptibility to false and dangerous pseudo-religions.

By contrast, the philosophes held that people could live

---

[112]Ibid., pp. 461, 473.
[113]Ibid., p. 295; *Old Regime*, pp. 148-57.
[114]*Democracy*, p. 443.

without a religious dimension in their lives. But this view, according to Tocqueville, was both false and detrimental to society. People possess a "taste for the infinite," which, if repressed in one form, must surface in another.[115] Two results follow from the attempt to destroy religious beliefs. In one case, most people abandon religious faith and immerse themselves in a consuming pursuit of material gratification. But within this secularized society, people experience a gnawing feeling of emptiness, causing some to turn to fanatical religious sects or to mysticism.[116] In the other case, people displace their religious sentiments onto politics, thus creating a religion of revolution. This had already occurred in France, where the French Revolution "though ostensibly political in origin . . . assumed many of the aspects of a religious revolution."[117] Tocqueville here identified the mindset of the modern intellectual revolutionary—a revolutionary of a "hitherto unknown breed"—who saw no meaning to life outside the political realm, but who, because of this denial, infused politics with all of his repressed spiritual feelings.[118]

In contrast to rationalism, Tocqueville's new political science recognized the spiritual needs of man as a fact of human existence which a healthy social order must take into account and channel in a constructive way. Tocqueville based his view in part on the traditionalist view regarding man's incapacity to support intellectual doubt, but he did not extend this principle to a reliance on "prejudice" in political affairs. His model for the intellectual foundation for modern society was taken from the United States, where citizens managed to join a belief in God with a pragmatic rationalist approach to truth in other spheres. Although resting on different foundations, religion and rationalism were joined together in America into an intellectual whole, with religion not only coexisting with rationalism, but actually enhancing its role in practical affairs. The limitation of rationalist inquiry on a few metaphysical questions provided spiritual comfort and solace,

---

[115]Ibid., p. 535.
[116]Ibid.
[117]*Old Regime*, p. 11.
[118]Ibid., p. 157.

enabling people to exercise rationalism more effectively in the domain of politics.[119] Hence Tocqueville's famous claim: "I am led to think that if [man] has no faith he must obey, and if he is free he must believe."[120]

In addition to neglecting man's spiritual needs, rationalism in Tocqueville's view promoted the vice of a radical and asocial individualism. According to rationalist tenets, each individual separately judges truth on the basis of his own reason and experience: "[E]ach man is narrowly shut up in himself, and from this basis makes the pretension to judge the world."[121] This leads to a malady that Tocqueville called "individualism," but which, given the modern connotation of that term, might better be called privatism. Privatism has the effect of making individuals ignore all political and social concerns and withdraw into a life preoccupied with the well-being of self and family. It helps pave the way for despotism, which "sees the isolation of man as the best guarantee of its own permanence."[122]

Although Tocqueville argued that people possessed a natural yearning for community, he did not think it was sufficient to withstand the disintegrating impact of rationalist intellectual doctrines and modern social conditions. To integrate man into the community required a mixture of rationalist and traditionalist principles. Unlike traditionalists, Tocqueville thought that the fundamental bond between the individual and community in modern times had to rely on a calculation of interest, not on feelings of patriotism.[123] To a certain extent, rationalism contained the remedy of its own defect, for citizens could learn from participating in politics that their private interest would be promoted in the long run by furthering the public interest. As a result of the mental habits formed by this principle of "self-interest rightly understood," citizens would develop a concern for the community as such.[124]

Yet the integration of the individual into the community, which

---

[119]Ibid., p. 153; *Democracy*, p. 444.
[120]*Democracy*, p. 444.
[121]Ibid., p. 430.
[122]Ibid., p. 509.
[123]Ibid., p. 236.
[124]Ibid., pp. 510-11.

is essential to fulfilling man's yearning for a social existence, could not be accomplished without also relying on the effective attachment of individuals to their communities as a supplementary bond: "Every citizen of the United States may be said to transfer the concern inspired in him by his little republic to love of the common motherland."[125] Tocqueville's view of the political community thus reflected a synthesis of rationalism and traditionalism. A modern state is not, as certain traditionalists would have it, a mere enlargement of an organic unit. Neither, however, is social organization entirely a human convention created by asocial individuals who contract to form a community, as so many rationalists posited. The two conceptions need to be combined into a view of the state that recognizes individual rights but that also accords a great deal of independence to local governments.

The final difficulty with rationalism, in Tocqueville's view, lay in its inability to account for the deepest source of man's attachment to liberty. Rationalism can help people see their interest in liberty and, through the principle of self-interest rightly understood, lead them to appreciate its utility for producing such goods as wealth and power. Ultimately, however, this utilitarian standard is inadequate. Liberty can be maintained in the final analysis only if people value it as an end worthwhile in itself. This kind of commitment to liberty inheres in the "will" rather than any calculation of self-interest.[126] As human "will" falls into the category of a moral sentiment of the heart, it must be evoked by a rhetoric that goes beyond interest and that appeals to traditionalist notions of pride and spiritedness. Tocqueville accordingly urges those who direct democratic society to exhort citizens to have a "higher idea of themselves and of humanity"[127]:

> What has made so many men, since untold ages, stake their all on liberty is its intrinsic glamour, a fascination it has in itself, apart from all "practical" considerations. . . . The man who asks of freedom anything other than itself is born to be a slave. [The love of liberty] is something one must *feel* and logic has no part in it. It is a privilege of noble minds

---

[125]Ibid., p. 162; cf. p. 94.
[126]Ibid., p. 705.
[127]Ibid., p. 632.

> which God has fitted to receive it, and it inspires them with a generous fervor. But to meaner souls, untouched by the sacred flame, it may well seem incomprehensible.[128]

Conclusion

In analyzing the thought of any major political theorist, it is necessary to begin by making an effort to understand the world in the same terms as that theorist. Yet in Tocqueville's case, to stop at that point would fail to fulfill the spirit of his enterprise. Tocqueville's political science calls on others to continue the project of attempting to reconcile liberty and democracy by engaging in concrete analysis of the specific social conditions and institutions in each era and each regime: "Different times make different demands; the goal alone is fixed . . . the means of getting there ever change."[129]

Here, of course, is not the place to pursue such inquiries, but it is clear that America has experienced fundamental changes since Tocqueville's time in some of the elements shaping its political culture. America's intellectual elite, once shut off from the latest ideas and fashions, now often sets the trend for Western intellectual development. Although American political culture probably continues to remain more resistant to the immediate influence of deductive intellectual thought and "general ideas" than the political cultures of certain European nations, recent studies of American society—especially the literature on the emergence of the so-called "new class"—point to a growing influence of America's intelligentsia in shaping the way people think.[130]

This increased influence of the intellectual stratum in America has been accompanied by a weakening of the specific counterweights to the rapid transference of "general ideas" throughout society. In comparison to Tocqueville's time, the dominant jurisprudential theories are less tradition-bound and more open to influence by contemporary intellectual ideas. The news media have become more

---

[128]*Old Regime,* p. 169.
[129]Ibid., p. 543.
[130]Daniel Bell, *The Coming of Post-Industrial Society* (New York Basic Books, 1973); Barry Bruce-Briggs, ed., *The New Class?* (New York: Basic Books, 1979).

centralized, and major journalists, who now enjoy an extraordinarily high status, have developed close ties to intellectual centers. Finally, the political system, at least until quite recently, has become more centralized, with many matters previously considered local now decided at the level of the federal government. America can no longer rely, as it could in Tocqueville's time, on its insularity or the peculiar character of its institutions to escape the consequences of the propagation of intellectual ideas in society. Like the European nations he addressed in the nineteenth century, contemporary America requires, by Tocqueville's standards, a science of politics to combat the potential hazards of the easy ideas produced by literary writers about politics.

Over the past two decades, students of American politics have rediscovered the concept of political culture, using it to investigate areas of society that for a time had been considered outside the normal boundaries of political science. Despite many recent advances in the techniques for studying social phenomena, modern researchers may still find that Tocqueville's approach offers some important insights. Whether or not one accepts his view about the relationship between basic "mental habits" and political values, it at least provides criteria for determining what is worthwhile and thus suggests a way of avoiding the sort of inquiries that catalogue every societal factor imagined to have a bearing on political beliefs. Moreover, far from merely making ritualistic claims about the centrality of political culture, Tocqueville shows how one can keep the concept continually in mind to analyze and evaluate institutions and public policies. Finally, Tocqueville's analysis of the connection between political thought and political culture—and between changes in the one and transformations in the other— points to the need to transcend the artificial modern division between political theory and empirical political science. If one follows Tocqueville's approach, political culture must be understood ultimately by reference to the philosophic ideas that form the mental structures which govern how people see the world and formulate their opinions. The task of maintaining a political culture of liberty leads to a consideration of the philosophic ideas capable of being embodied in the mental habits of citizens which can provide people with the means and the will to maintain their freedom.

Mores

"The social state is commonly the result of circumstances, sometimes of laws, but most often of a combination of the two. But once it has come into being, it may itself be considered as the prime cause of most of the laws, customs, and ideas which control the nation's behavior; it modifies even those things which it does not cause."

12

The Quest for the Self: Individualism, Morality, Politics

Robert N. Bellah

It was the belief of the authors of *Habits of the Heart*[1] that the discussion of individualism in Tocqueville's *Democracy in America* illuminates contemporary American social life. Our research was in many ways a continuing conversation with Tocqueville as well as with our fellow citizens. In this essay I would like to bring Emerson into the conversation and suggest how close attention to these nineteenth-century texts is helpful in illuminating current social reality.

Tocqueville and Emerson on Individualism

In a famous chapter entitled "Of Individualism in Democracies," Tocqueville points out that "'Individualism' is a word recently coined to express a new idea. Our fathers only knew about egoism." Individualism is more moderate and orderly than egoism, but in the end its results are much the same: "Individualism is a calm and considered feeling which disposes each citizen to isolate himself from the mass of his fellows and withdraw into the circle of family and friends; with this little society formed to his taste, he

---

[1]Robert N. Bellah, Richard Madsen, William M. Sullivan, Ann Swidler, and Steven M. Tipton, *Habits of the Heart: Individualism and Commitment in American Life* (Berkeley: University of California Press, 1985). Much of this chapter derives from our joint authorship.

gladly leaves the greater society to look out after itself."[2] As this tendency grows, he wrote, "there are more and more people who, though neither rich nor powerful enough to have much hold over others, have gained or kept enough wealth and enough understanding to look after their own needs. Such folk owe no man anything and hardly expect anything from anybody. They form the habit of thinking of themselves in isolation and imagine that their whole destiny is in their hands." Finally such persons come to "forget their ancestors," but also their contemporaries. "Each man is forever thrown back on himself alone, and there is danger that he may be shut up in the solitude of his own heart."[3]

Tocqueville saw the isolation to which Americans are prone as ominous for the future of our freedom. It is just such isolation which is always encouraged by despotism. And so Tocqueville is particularly interested in all those countervailing tendencies which pulled people back from their isolation into social communion. Immersion in private economic pursuits undermines the person as citizen. On the other hand, involvement in public affairs is the best antidote for the pernicious effects of individualistic isolation: "Citizens who are bound to take part in public affairs must turn from their private interests and occasionally take a look at something other than themselves."[4] It is precisely in these respects that the mores become important. The habits and practices of religion and democratic participation educate the citizen to a larger view than his purely private world would allow. These habits and practices rely to some extent on self-interest in their educational work, but it is only when self-interest has been to some degree transcended that they will have succeeded. Tocqueville even saw the family as playing an important role in tempering individualism, particularly through the role of women who, under the influence of religion, counter the economic self-interest of their husbands and communicate to children a morality transcending the interests of the self.[5]

---

[2]Alexis de Tocqueville, *Democracy in America*, ed. J.-P. Mayer, trans. George Lawrence (Garden City, N.Y.: Doubleday, Anchor Books, 1969), p. 506. Hereinafter cited as *Democracy*.

[3]Ibid., p. 508.

[4]Ibid., p. 510.

[5]Ibid., p. 291.

Tocqueville is at his most brilliant in his analysis of the social consequences of American individualism. He is, however, not without interest in his observations about its personal consequences. He comments on the competitiveness of Americans and their "restlessness in the midst of prosperity." "In America," he says, "I have seen the freest and best educated of men in circumstances the happiest to be found in the world; yet it seemed to me that a cloud habitually hung on their brow, and they seemed serious and almost sad even in their pleasures," because they "never stop thinking of the good things they have not got." This restlessness and sadness in pursuit of the good life make it difficult to form "strong attachments between man and man." The efforts and enjoyments of Americans are livelier than in traditional societies, but the disappointments of their hopes and desires are keener, and their "minds are more anxious and on edge." Of such restless, competitive, and anxious people, Tocqueville says, "they clutch everything and hold nothing fast."[6]

Ralph Waldo Emerson, writing at much the same time, gives a remarkably similar picture of American individualism except for his more positive, even celebratory tone. But that more positive tone is perhaps related to an effort to give individualism a moral meaning that for Tocqueville it did not have. Toward the end of his Phi Beta Kappa address of 1837, "The American Scholar," Emerson also describes something that he sees as new in his time:

> Another sign of our times, also marked by an analogous political movement, is the new importance given to the single person. Everything that tends to insulate the individual,—to surround him with barriers of natural respect, so that each man shall feel the world is his, and man shall treat with man as a sovereign state with a sovereign state;—tends to true union as well as greatness. "I learned," said the melancholy Pestalozzi, "that no man in God's wide earth is either willing or able to help any other man." Help must come from the bosom alone.[7]

---

[6]Ibid., pp. 535-38, 565.

[7]Ralph Waldo Emerson, *Essays and Lectures* (New York: The Library of America,

At moments Emerson tends to inflate the self until it is identical with Universal Being, with unfortunate consequences for any mere earthly attachments:

> Crossing a bare common, in snow puddles, at twilight, under a clouded sky, without having in my thoughts any occurrence of special good fortune, I have enjoyed a perfect exhilaration. I am glad to the brink of fear. . . . I become a transparent eye-ball; I am nothing; I see all; the currents of Universal Being circulate through me; I am part or particle of God. The name of the nearest friend sounds then foreign and accidental: to be brothers, to be acquaintances,—master or servant, is then a trifle and a disturbance.[8]

Emerson's devotion to what he calls "the capital virtue of self-trust" makes him leery of the dependence of the self on others but also of others on the self: "A sympathetic person is placed in the dilemma of a swimmer among drowning men, who all catch at him, and if he gives so much as a leg or a finger, they will drown him."[9] The conclusion of these views for social ethics is clear enough, confirming Tocqueville's analysis. In the famous essay on "Self-Reliance" Emerson wrote:

> Then, again, do not tell me, as a good man did to-day, of my obligation to put all poor men in good situations. Are they *my* poor? I tell thee, thou foolish philanthropist, that I grudge the dollar, the dime, the cent, I give to such men as do not belong to me and to whom I do not belong.[10]

Here we see tangible evidence of Emerson's rejection of the normative authority of the New Testament and his intention to deliver a comparable revelation for his own day.

Finally Emerson confirms Tocqueville's observation that individualism cuts us off from the past. He advises us to "desert the tradition" because "[t]he perpetual admonition of nature to us, is, 'The world is new, untried. Do not believe the past. I give you

---

1983), p. 70. Hereinafter cited as Emerson, *Essays and Lectures*.

[8]Ibid., Introduction to *Nature*, p. 10.

[9]Ibid., "Experience," p. 490.

[10]Ibid., p. 262.

the universe a virgin to-day.'"[11]

What is surprising about this quick look at the teachings of Tocqueville and Emerson on individualism is how accurately they describe our condition today, whether we like it or not. The contemporaneity of Emerson as well as the sharply conflicting views about his significance are evidenced in two recent essays, one by John Updike and the other by Harold Bloom.[12] Updike, in a long appreciative essay, finds Emerson finally too optimistic about the self and too coldly absorbed in it to be much help to Americans today. Bloom, in an essay that is clearly a rejoinder to Updike, significantly entitled "Mr. America," glories in just those aspects of Emerson's teachings that Updike deplores. Brushing aside Updike's objections as "churchwardenly mewings," Bloom praises Emerson for proclaiming the only God in which Americans can any longer believe, "the god in the self."[13]

Ordinary Americans may be less conscious of their link to an earlier America than the literary intellectuals, but in the interviews we gathered for *Habits of the Heart*[14] we found that the individualism Tocqueville described and Emerson exemplified is more vigorous than ever among middle-class Americans. We will consider briefly toward the end of this paper whether the mores Tocqueville found holding that individualism in check are still vigorous today.

The Quest for the Self

Middle-class Americans share Emerson's emphasis on self-reliance and his belief that help comes only from our own bosom. As one of the therapists we interviewed put it, "In the end you're really alone and you really have to answer to yourself." They also tend to share Emerson's view that society is inimical to the individual and that the quest for the self involves freeing ourselves

---

[11]Ibid., "Literary Ethics," p. 100-01.
[12]John Updike, "Emersonianism," *The New Yorker*, June 4, 1984, pp. 112-32; Harold Bloom, "Mr. America," *The New York Review of Books*, Nov. 22, 1984, pp. 19-24.
[13]Ibid., p. 24.
[14]"Habits of the heart" is a phrase Tocqueville uses to describe the mores. *Democracy*, p. 287.

from society. As Emerson put it, "Society is everywhere in conspiracy against the manhood of every one of its members."[15] Thus the quest for the self is a quest for autonomy, for leaving the past and the social structures that have previously enveloped us, for stripping off the obligations and constraints imposed by others, until at last we find our true self which is unique and individual.

One of the strongest imperatives of our culture is that we must leave home. Unlike many peasant societies where it is common to live with parents until their death and where one worships parents and ancestors all one's life, for us leaving home is the normal expectation, and childhood is in many ways a preparation for it. For some the process is quite smooth; for others there is considerable conflict. The presence of conflict does not mean that the cultural pattern of leaving home is in doubt. Indeed a degree of conflict over this issue is to some extent expected. However painful the process of leaving home, for parents or for children, the really frightening thing would be the prospect of the child never leaving home.

For the middle-class child, the process of leaving home, though associated with becoming gainfully employed and starting a family of one's own, often occurs earlier, when one goes away to college. Leaving home involves not only leaving the family but often leaving one's local community, going to a "good college," where one's chances of getting a really good job and perhaps attaining higher status than one's parents will be enhanced. Part of the "self-reliance" implicit in leaving home involves taking care of oneself without immediate dependence on parents, perhaps working to contribute toward paying for one's education. But an equally important aspect of self-reliance is taking responsibility for one's own views. Very often this means not only leaving home but leaving church as well.

One may not literally have to leave one's church. One may continue to belong to the church of one's parents. But the expectation is that at some point one will decide on one's own that that is the church to belong to. One cannot defend one's views by saying that they are simply those of one's parents or of the church in which one

---

[15]From "Self-Reliance," in Emerson, *Essays and Lectures*, p. 261.

was raised. On the contrary, they must be particularly and peculiarly one's own. Traditionally, Protestant piety demanded that a young person experience a unique conversion experience of his own, even while specifying more or less clearly the content of that experience. More recently we expect even greater autonomy. On the basis of our interviews, we were not surprised to learn that a 1978 Gallup poll found that eighty percent of Americans agreed with the statement: "An individual should arrive at his or her own religious beliefs independent of any churches or synagogues."[16]

Finding the right occupation is certainly an important part of the quest for the true self. But for middle-class Americans today, work is less of a calling and more of a career; less something one deeply identifies with and more a means toward self-fulfillment. Getting locked into a particular slot or organization is often seen as constricting to the autonomy of the self, and mid-life job changes or even career changes are widely advocated.

Where work is frustrating and confining and contains few intrinsic satisfactions, as it is for many Americans at all status levels, the quest for the true self may be pursued most urgently in the sphere of leisure and private life. In urban middle-class America, the choice of private "lifestyle" is probably freer than ever before in our history. Most of the constraints of traditional marriage have been called into question. (The expectation that it is normal to get married at all has dropped sharply over the past thirty years.[17]) One young mother of two whom we interviewed decided that it was immoral to go on living with her husband when sex had lost its excitement, so the couple separated, each had therapy, and only after a year and the resolution of the problem did they resume living together. Many of those to whom we talked, involved in long and apparently satisfying marriages, indicated that their commitment to the marriage was contingent on the continued satisfactions that it offered. We may not believe they will actually act on their ideology to notice how powerfully the

---

[16]Reported in Dean R. Hoge, *Converts, Dropouts, Returnees: Religious Change Among Catholics*, Washington, D.C.: United States Catholic Conference (New York: Pilgrim Press, 1981), p. 167.

[17]Joseph Veroff, Elizabeth Douvan, and Richard A. Kulka, *The Inner American: A Self-Portrait from 1957 to 1976* (New York: Basic Books, 1981), p. 147.

ideology of self-fulfillment undercuts all sustained commitments in our society.

The quest for the self then, pursued under the predominant ideology of individualism, involves separating out from family, religion, and calling as sources of authority, duty, and moral example. It means autonomously pursuing happiness and satisfying one's own wants. But what are the wants the self satisfies, and by what measure does it identify its happiness? In the face of such insistent questions, the predominant ethos of American individualism seems determined more than ever to press ahead with the task of letting go of all criteria other than a radically private validation. And it is very frequently to psychology that Americans turn. As Robert Coles says, "Psychology, in this instance, means a concentration, persistent, if not feverish, upon one's thoughts, feelings, wishes, worries—bordering on, if not embracing, solipsism: the self as the only or main form of (existential) reality."[18]

Frequently when we sought to discover the criteria that Americans use to measure the success of their quest for the true self we found them using the term "values." "Values" turn out to be the incomprehensible, rationally indefensible thing that the individual chooses when he or she has thrown off the last vestige of external influence and reached pure contentless freedom. The ideal self in its absolute freedom is completely "unencumbered," to borrow a term from Michael Sandel.[19] The improvisational self chooses values to express itself, but it is not constituted by them as from a preexisting source. The language of "values" as commonly used is self-contradictory precisely because it is not a language of value, of moral choice. It presumes the existence of an absolutely empty, unencumbered, and provisional self.

I want to make it clear that we do not believe that the people to whom we talked have empty selves. Most of them are serious, engaged people, deeply involved in the world. But insofar as they are limited to a language of radical individual autonomy, as many of them are, they cannot think about themselves or others except as

---

[18]Robert Coles, "Civility and Psychology," *Daedalus* (Summer 1980), pp. 136-37.

[19]Michael Sandel, *Liberalism and the Limits of Justice* (New York: Cambridge University Press, 1982).

arbitrary centers of volition. They cannot express the fullness of being that is actually theirs.

Reaching Out

However much Americans extol the autonomy and self-reliance of the individual, they do not imagine that a good life can be lived alone. Those we interviewed would almost all agree that connectedness to others in work, love, and community is essential to happiness, self-esteem, and moral worth. We must now consider how they, as autonomous individuals, reach out to others and how they conceive of the community that results.

Radical American individualism seems to contain two conceptions of human relatedness that at first glance may appear incompatible, but which were firmly asserted by Emerson and many Americans today. Looking at individuals as "sovereign states," one might imagine the only relations possible between them to be by treaty, that is, by contract. The contractarian model has long been popular in America and takes new, psychologically nuanced, forms today. But Emerson also noted that "sovereign" individuals, when they have freed themselves from convention and tradition, are identical to "nature," which is the same for all. The idea that deep within our unique and individual selves there is an expressive identity with all other selves is an idea that we found widespread among the Americans with whom we talked. But these two notions of relatedness apply to radically different spheres. Expressive identity applies most of all to situations of love and intimacy, usually intense but of short duration. Contractual bargaining is the norm of everyday relationships, even the everyday aspects of marriage and friendship. What links the two seemingly disparate types together is the fact that both depend on the absolutely autonomous wills of the individuals involved. What both types avoid is the notion that there is any objective normative order governing the relationship, any transcendent loyalty above the wishes of the individuals involved, any community that is really there independent of the wills of the individuals who compose it. Naturally, relationships that are dependent entirely on spontaneous feeling or contractual bargaining alone are fragile, frustrating, and difficult to sustain.

Since "conventional roles" no longer have authority for many middle-class Americans and spontaneous feeling (though highly valued) is often untrustworthy and transient, the contractual model, long familiar in our economic life, has more and more entered the sphere of private relationships, often under the aegis of popular psychology. It is, however, not always an easy model to live with and exacts a high price in terms of the stability of relationships. "Commitments take work, and we're tired of working," sighs Alec, a young therapist, "and we come home from work, the last thing I want to do, you know, is for people to sit down and say, 'Well, let's sit and work on our relationship. Let's talk about it.' Yes, but I worked eight and a half hours today, you know. Let's just sit down and watch the boob tube." His protest ends in a confession: "It's like you periodically ask yourself, like, 'Is this worth my effort? Is this worth that?'" Faced with ongoing demands to work on their relationships as well as their jobs, separate and equal selves are led to question the contractual terms of their commitments to each other: Are they getting what they want? Are they getting as much as they are giving? As much as they could get elsewhere? If not, they are tempted to withdraw and look elsewhere for fulfillment. Therapeutic experts may counsel them that lasting commitments are necessary for self-fulfillment. But within this "giving-getting" model, each person must test such claims against his experience, case by case, and judge them in the light of his own "values." Because each person's feelings and values are subjective, the difficulties in figuring out the bottom line and interacting appropriately with others are daunting enough to make "long-term relationships" almost as unstable in their actual prospects as they are formidable in their therapeutic demands.

Yet many of those with whom we talked who seem to be committed to a radically individualistic ideology, do not really seem to live in accordance with their belief, or better, they find their usual individualistic language inadequate to explain how they actually live. A successful California lawyer who has sustained a long marriage and who is accustomed to explain all his actions in cost/benefit terms, was finally pressed in our interview to see that no interest-maximizing calculus could really account for what was in those terms an irrational commitment. At last he affirms that his happiness with his wife comes from "proceeding through all these stages together. It makes life meaningful and gives me the opportunity to share with somebody, have an anchor, if you will, and understand where I am. That, for me, is a real relationship." Here he is groping for words that would express his marriage as a community of memory and hope, a context that actually defines who he is, not a forum in which an empty self maximizes satisfactions.

In another case, a woman who had renewed her commitment to Judaism at first explained her action in individualistic terms. Judaism provides "structure" in a chaotic world. In the religious community she has found help with day-care as well as a place where the joys and sufferings of everyday life can be shared. In her highly educated mentality it was as though communal ties and religious commitments can be recommended only for the benefits they yield to the individual, for the social, emotional, and cultural functions they perform. But there was a moment in our conversation with her when she transcended these presuppositions. She told us, "The woman who took care of my daughter when she was little was a Greek Jew. She was very young—nine, ten, eleven—when the war broke out, and was lying at the crematorium door when the American troops came through. So she has a number tattooed on her arm. And it was always like being hit in the stomach with a brick when she would take my baby and sit and circle her with her arm, and there was the number." In that moment she was no longer in the "giving-getting" mode. She knew herself as a member of a people, which includes the living and the dead, parents and children, inheritors of a history and a culture that tells her who she is and that she must nurture through memory and hope.

Many of those to whom we talked seemed caught in the tensions created by radical American individualism. We strongly assert the value of our self-reliance and autonomy. We deeply feel the emptiness of a life without sustaining social commitments. Yet we are afraid to articulate our sense that we need each other as much as we need to stand alone, for fear that if we did we would lose our independence altogether. The tensions of our lives would be even greater if we did not, in fact, engage in practices that constantly limit the efforts of an isolating individualism, even though we cannot articulate these practices nearly as well as we can the quest for autonomy.

Politics and the Public Sphere

If the ideology of American individualism creates problems in sustaining intimate relationships, it causes even greater difficulty for involvement in the public sphere. Just as, in spite of our individualism, Americans do sustain long-term relationships, so do they also frequently become publicly involved. But our individualism skews and limits the kinds of public undertaking we are likely to engage in as well as our understanding of them.

Middle-class Americans view success in the occupational sphere as an essential prerequisite for a fulfilled life. But many of them do not think that personal success is enough. Only if one makes a personal, voluntary effort to "get involved" in helping others will one's life be complete. And Americans in larger numbers than in many societies do join voluntary associations, service clubs, and church societies whose main purpose is to help the unfortunate or better the community. Such activities bring great personal satisfaction. The happiness and joy of giving are earned by making a free individual decision to join such an organization, to accept its discipline, and to participate in its charitable work. For these Americans, the self-interest demanded by the individualistic pursuit of success needs to be balanced by the sympathy of the voluntary act of concern for others. Without the joyful experience of support from such a community, an individual would find it difficult to make the effort to be a success, and success achieved would likely turn to ashes in his mouth. Without some individually deserved success, an individual would have little voluntarily to contribute to his chosen community.

It is, of course, no easy task to strike a balance between the kind of self-interest implicit in the individualistic search for success and the kind of concern required to gain the joys of community and public involvement. A fundamental problem is that the ideas which Americans have traditionally used to give shape and direction to their most generous impulses no longer suffice to give guidance in controlling the destructive consequences caused by the pursuit of economic success. It is not, as many recent social critics have claimed, that Americans have today become less generous than in the past. Practically all of those we talked with are convinced, at least in theory, that a selfish seeker after purely individual success could not live a good, happy, joyful life. But when they think of the kind of generosity which could redeem the individualistic pursuit of economic success, they often imagine voluntary involvements in local, small-scale activities resembling a family, club, or idealized community in which individuals' initiatives interrelate to improve the life of all. They have difficulty relating this ideal image to the large-scale forces and institutions shaping their lives. This is what provides the pathos underlying many of our conversations about work, family, community, and politics. Many of those with whom we talked convey the feeling that sometimes their very best efforts to pursue their finest ideals seem senseless.

It is rarely "getting involved" as a moral act that is thought senseless. Instead, the difficulty has to do with the realm of politics. For a good number of those with whom we talked, the very notion of politics connotes something morally unsavory, as though voluntary involvement is commendable and even fulfilling up to the point at which it enters the realm of office-holding, campaigning, and organized negotiating. Thus their judgments about the goodness of citizenship in the wide sense of public involvement and responsibility turn negative in peculiar ways when they extend beyond the bounds of their local concerns and into the activities and institutions Americans term "politics."

In one sense, politics is making operative the moral consensus of the community, where that consensus is thought to flow from agreement among individuals reached through free face-to-face discussion. The process of reaching such a consensus is one of the central meanings of the word "democratic" in America. It idealizes an individualism without rancor. For this understanding, citizenship is virtually co-extensive with "getting involved" with one's neighbors for the good of the community. Many times Americans do not think of this process as "politics" at all. But where this understanding is seen as a form of politics, it is the New England township of legend, the self-governing small town singled out by

Tocqueville, that remains as the ideal exemplar.

In sharp contrast to the image of consensual community stands another understanding, for which politics means the pursuit of differing interests according to agreed-upon, neutral rules. This is the realm of coalitions among groups with similar interests, of conflicts between groups with opposing interests, and of mediators and brokers of interests, the professional politicians. The "politics of interest," which is what we call this second type, is what Americans frequently mean by the term "politics." It is sometimes celebrated by political scientists as "pluralism," but for ordinary Americans the connotation is often negative. The politics of interest is frequently seen as a kind of necessary evil in a large diverse society, as a reluctantly-agreed-to second best to consensual democracy.

Instead of a realm of spontaneous involvement with others to whom one feels akin, one enters the politics of interest for reasons of utility, to get what one or one's group needs or wants. To the extent that many of those we interviewed see "politics" as meaning the politics of interest, they regard it as not entirely legitimate morally. Hence the generally low opinion of "the politician" as a figure in American life. Politics suffers in comparison with the market. The legitimacy of the market rests in large part on the belief that it rewards individuals impartially on the basis of fair competition, a legitimacy helped by the fact that economic transactions are widely dispersed and often invisible. By contrast, the politics of negotiation at local, state, and federal levels, though it shares the utilitarian attitudes of the market, often exposes a competition among groups in which inequalities of power, influence, and moral probity become highly visible as determinants of the outcome. At the same time, the politics of interest provides no framework for the discussion of issues other than the conflict and compromises of interests themselves. Thus the routine activities of interest politics, visibly conducted by professionals and apparently rewarding all kinds of inside connections while favoring the strong at the expense of the weak, must appear as an affront to true individualism and fairness alike.

Citizenship in this second understanding of politics is more difficult and discordant for the individual than in the ideal of community consensus. It means entering the complicated, professional, yet highly personal business of adversarial struggles, alliance building, and interest bargaining. It requires dealing with others from quite different consensual communities. For most people it lacks the immediacy of everyday involvement unless urgent interests are at stake. Thus supporting candidates by voting is the typical expression of this understanding of politics for most people, keeping politics at arm's length.

Thus the culture of individualism does not prevent Americans from entering the public sphere, but it does limit and distort their understanding of it. If human action is always either the spontaneous expression of sympathy or the rational calculation of self-interest, then when the former fails only the latter is left. The public realm is not considered exclusively as a realm of Hobbesian conflict because most Americans see the national community, at moments at least, as a local community writ large. Thus millions of Americans could identify with the individual American athletes competing in the Los Angeles Olympic Games and root for "U.S.A.! U.S.A.!" as they would for the local high school football team. But where it is a question not of our similarities but of our differences, then most Americans see only conflict and power. Objective political norms that speak not only of individual rights and fair procedures, but of substantive justice, are hard to comprehend within an individualist vocabulary. Thus national politics, when the veneer of local rhetoric, of "family, neighborhood, and work," is removed, makes little sense to most Americans. It is not narcissism or hedonism that prevents Americans, who continue in many ways to be a generous and compassionate people, from understanding those different from themselves. It is the limitations of their cultural resources.

Individualism and American Mores

We have described American individualism from Emerson to the present and have considered some of its consequences for private and public life, for morality and politics. It is time to return to Tocqueville to consider whether the restraints he saw the American mores of his day placing on individualism are still operative or whether the destructive consequences he feared an unchecked individualism would have are beginning to materialize.

By way of summary of what has been said so far, we may reformulate Tocqueville's argument in a way somewhat more explicit than he ever does himself. We have characterized individualism, following Tocqueville and with the help of Emerson, as a way of thinking about human action which can conceive of human relatedness only as the result of spontaneous feeling or calculated interest. Tocqueville is fully aware of both of these aspects of an individualistic culture. He stresses repeatedly the "natural compassion" or "sympathy" which citizens in a democracy feel for one another:

> It often happens in the most civilized countries of the world that a man in misfortune is almost as isolated in the crowd as a savage in the woods. That is hardly ever seen in the United States. The Americans, always cold in manner and often coarse, are hardly ever insensitive, and though they may be in no hurry to volunteer services, yet they do not refuse them.[20]

Tocqueville, who is fully aware of the importance of self-interest in the motivation of Americans, often sees sympathy and interest working together to promote public-spirited actions. At times Tocqueville even seems to feel that a combination of sympathy and an educated self-interest, a "self-interest properly understood," would be enough to sustain free institutions in America.

There is an ambiguity in the way Tocqueville uses the term "mores." On the one hand, it is a purely descriptive term. American mores are simply the way Americans do things, the pattern of American life, close to what we would mean when we speak of "American culture." On the other hand, "mores" has a normative meaning. It includes the notion of duty, obligation, or moral rightness, and refers particularly to social obligations. Here "mores" is close to the German *Sittlichkeit*, the institutionalized pattern of social obligations. From this understanding of mores, individualism is ambiguous. It is certainly part of a cultural pattern. It even has a normative component, one we can understand better perhaps with

---

[20] *Democracy*, p. 571.

the help of Emerson than Tocqueville: the obligation to remain true to the self regardless of all other considerations. Yet from individualism a *social* ethic does not flow. Social relatedness depends entirely on the spontaneous feeling or rational calculation of individual wills. The social order has no normative validity in itself. It is merely the instrument or the expression of individual selves. From this point of view individualism cannot be part of the mores but is antithetical to them.

I think it is clear that however subtly Tocqueville analyzes the possibility that individualism in America can be turned to the service of the common good and the preservation of free institutions, in the end he does believe that only an objective moral order, with obligations that transcend individual feelings and interests, will be equal to that task. In the narrower sense, therefore, the term "mores" refers to that objective moral order. As we have said, there are two spheres where Tocqueville finds mores in this second sense significant: political participation and religion.

In both of these spheres in America an objective moral order is problematic because both of them are so heavily invaded by self-interest. In the important chapter "How the Americans Combat the Effects of Individualism by Free Institutions," Tocqueville points out how it is self-interest, including quite petty self-interest, that often motivates Americans to participate in the public sphere. But in the end, he says:

> The free institutions of the United States and the political rights enjoyed there provide a thousand continual reminders to every citizen that he lives in society. At every moment they bring his mind back to this idea, that it is the duty as well as the interest of men to be useful to their fellow.[21]

It is precisely the element of duty that cannot be derived from the interests and feelings of individuals alone.

In the chapter "How the Americans Apply the Doctrine of Self-Interest Properly Understood to Religion," Tocqueville comments on

---

[21]Ibid., p. 512.

the American tendency to propagate religion on the basis of its earthly or at least heavenly rewards. "Nevertheless," he says, "I refuse to believe that all who practice virtue from religious motives do so only in hope of reward."[22] And a few pages later on, in one of the most earnestly admonitory chapters in the whole book, Tocqueville says, "By their practice Americans show that they feel the urgent necessity to instill morality into democracy by means of religion. What they think of themselves in this respect enshrines a truth which should penetrate deep into the consciousness of every democratic nation."[23] Tocqueville had already pointed out in Volume I that religion provided for Americans a morality that was objective, certain, and stable, which the unimpeded pursuit of interest in the economic and political spheres could never do.[24]

And so we may ask whether today there exists in America, in the midst of our triumphant individualism, mores in the sense of *Sittlichkeit*, that would resist our proclivity to become a collection of atomized individuals who would be easy prey to administrative despotism.

We have already indicated that the ideology of individualism does not describe adequately the lives even of those who espouse it. A completely empty self that operates out of purely arbitrary choice is theoretically imaginable but performatively impossible. The family, the church, the local community, which the middle-class person seeks to shuffle off in the effort to rise in the social hierarchy free of encumbrances, cannot be wholly denied, for we are indelibly constituted by them. On the other hand, for those many Americans for whom objective moral communities still exist, most frequently in the form of churches or other religious associations but often also in political associations, the insistent language of individualism constantly threatens to make commitment contingent on psychological or material reward.

This is not the place to review our findings on the present state of American mores. At best what we found are signs of the times, which are far from allowing a prediction of future trends. We did

---

[22]Ibid., p. 528.
[23]Ibid., p. 542.
[24]Ibid., p. 292.

find many Americans for whom an objective moral order embodied in living communities clearly does exist. Indeed in *Habits of the Heart* we describe a number of people that one could call genuine heroes and heroines of everyday life, dedicated to the common good and joyful in their dedication. We also found a great deal of nostalgia for a more coherent America, for "traditional values" and stable communities. The image of the small town we found to be deeply attractive to Americans regardless of their political or ethical views. Yet it would be hard to deny that the individualism that Tocqueville described and Emerson embodied is stronger than ever today. For many Americans, the world is indeed divided into the two realms of rational calculation and spontaneous feeling, even though the emptiness of a life that alternates between those realms alone is increasingly recognized.

Perhaps not surprisingly, the alternatives to radical individualism that we discovered among present-day Americans are not different from those pointed out by Tocqueville: republican politics and biblical religion. Reappropriating those traditions and reviving the communities that carry them seem to be our best hope. Only they can overcome the chasm between person and society that individualism creates. Only they show us that we can be true to ourselves, individualists in the best sense, only when we are true to our ethical commitments and collective loyalties in private and public life. Indeed it is only such commitments and loyalties that constitute a real self, that tell us who we are. Biblical religion and republican politics involve us in communities of memory and hope within which we can sustain the moral ecology that makes a good life possible. The fact that in the research for *Habits of the Heart* we found so many serious, dedicated citizens for whom these communities are still alive and effective gives grounds, if not for optimism, at least for hope.

13

The Uses and Hazards of Christianity in Tocqueville's Attempt to Save Democratic Souls

Ralph C. Hancock

"The Spirit is so contrasted with flesh that no intermediate thing is left." — John Calvin

On the face of it, Tocqueville's political endorsement of Christianity in *Democracy in America* could hardly be more straightforward: The religious beliefs of Americans, he argues, provide them with a stable, common morality that moderates or contains the otherwise destructive passion of a democratic people for innovation.[1] Thus religious authority supplies the defect of political authority in a democracy:

> How could society escape destruction if, when political ties are relaxed, moral ties are not tightened? And what can be done with a people master of itself if it is not subject to God?[2]
>
> . . . I doubt whether man can support complete religious independence and entire political liberty at the same time.

The author gratefully acknowledges the support of a 1985 Summer Stipend from the National Endowment for the Humanities in preparing this essay.

[1]Alexis de Tocqueville, *Democracy in America*, ed. J.-P. Mayer, trans. George Lawrence (Garden City, N.Y.: Doubleday, Anchor Books, 1969), vol. I, pt. II, chap. 9. Hereinafter cited as *Democracy*.

[2]Ibid., p. 294.

> I am led to think that if he has no faith he must obey, and if he is free he must believe.[3]

Tocqueville's argument appears quite simple: The people will not accept the right to rule of any man or class of men; the people cannot be trusted to rule themselves absolutely; therefore, the people must be ruled by God or by their beliefs about God.

In these passages Tocqueville clearly subordinates the question of the truth of Christianity to that of its political utility. Similarly, in other contexts, he admits to "considering religions from a purely human point of view"[4] and indicates that, from the standpoint of "legislators for democracies," any firmly established religion that includes "belief in an immaterial and immortal principle" will serve. Tocqueville is even willing to include among potentially useful religions those that teach the doctrine of metempsychosis, though he considers that doctrine "not more reasonable than that of materialism."[5] Thus, if Tocqueville is "firmly persuaded that at all costs Christianity must be maintained among the new democracies," this political judgment does not seem to rest upon a religious conviction.

Tocqueville's analysis of the human condition in his chapter "Concerning the Principal Source of Beliefs Among Democratic Peoples,"[6] in fact, suggests that religious beliefs rest inevitably on human or political foundations. Both social bodies and individual human beings, he argues, have daily need of more "truths" than they can discover or verify for themselves. As an individual, every man must accept on trust the "foundation" on which he "builds the house of his own thought"; as a citizen each man must accept the "leading ideas" by which "all the minds of the citizens [are] rallied and held together." In a later chapter,[7] Tocqueville identifies these leading or fundamental ideas, which are "indispensable to men for the conduct of daily life"[8] as those concerning

---

[3]Ibid., vol. I, pt. I, chap. 5, p. 444.
[4]Ibid., pt. II, chap. 9, p. 297.
[5]Ibid., vol. II, pt. II, chap. 15, pp. 543-44.
[6]Ibid., pt. I, chap. 2.
[7]Ibid., chap. 5.
[8]Ibid., p. 443.

"God and human nature":

> There is hardly any human action, however private it may be, which does not result from some very general conception men have of God, of His relations with the human race, of the nature of their soul, and of their duties to their fellows. Nothing can prevent such ideas from being the common spring from which all else originates.[9]

Thus the "inflexible laws of his existence" render man subject to "dogmatic beliefs"; that is, to beliefs the only verifiable source or ground of which is not God or nature but other men. It is thus inevitable that human beings—or at least the great majority of human beings—depend on other human beings for their opinions about the most important matters. Tocqueville does not recoil before the harsh implication of his analysis: "It is true that any man accepting an opinion on trust from another puts his mind in bondage."[10] The bondage of the mind thus appears to be the natural and inevitable condition of humanity.

This bondage is inherently political in the sense that the "fixed ideas" that individuals must accept on trust are precisely the "leading ideas" by which citizens are "rallied and held together." Consequently, the character of this bondage varies with the character of the political order; it varies, in particular, according as the regime is fundamentally aristocratic or democratic:

> When standards are unequal and men unalike, there are some very enlightened and learned individuals whose intelligence gives them great power, while the multitude is very ignorant and blinkered. As a result men living under an aristocracy are naturally inclined to be guided in their views by a more thoughtful man or class, and they have little inclination to suppose the masses infallible.

---

[9]Ibid., pp. 442-43.

[10]Compare Doris S. Goldstein, who, in order to defend Tocqueville against charges of "conservatism" or "flawed liberalism," must distinguish radically between "manipulation and coercion" and "belief and persuasion." *Trial of Faith: Religion and Politics in Tocqueville's Thought* (New York: Oxford University Press, 1975), pp. 126-27. Hereinafter cited as Goldstein, *Trial of Faith.*

> In times of equality the opposite happens. The nearer men are to a common level of uniformity, the less are they inclined to believe blindly in any man or any class. But they are readier to trust the mass, and public opinion becomes more and more mistress of the world.[11]

In both aristocracies and democracies, men are bound intellectually to other men. In democracies, however, this bondage is more self-conscious and more confining than in aristocracies. When men are equal they "look into themselves or into their fellows for the sources of truth," whereas, under conditions of inequality, the people accept the authority of a "more thoughtful man or class" whom they regard as a medium of access to a truth assumed to reside "beyond and outside humanity." Whether or not this assumption is correct, an aristocratic people, while necessarily accepting on trust the ideas of certain human beings on the most important questions, thus implicitly assumes that there exists a ground of truth higher than humanity. This is perhaps what Tocqueville means when he observes, in the first volume of *Democracy in America*,[12] that the principle of the sovereignty of the people lies at the bottom of almost all human institutions, although it has been brought fully to light and made effective only in American democracy.

Thus, although the bondage of the mind is the inflexible law of human existence, there are, according to Tocqueville, better and worse forms of bondage. The political use of religion in *Democracy in America* may therefore aim at securing a better form and avoiding a worse, and not simply at keeping the people in check—that is, at maintaining order in the bare sense of material security or prosperity. In other words, the apparently straightforward idea that Tocqueville is interested in the political utility of religion rather than in its truth reveals itself as problematic once one sees that utility cannot be interpreted in a utilitarian or materialistic sense and, indeed, that the question of what is useful to human beings and the question of religious or metaphysical truth may not

[11] *Democracy*, vol. II, pt. I, chap. 3, p. 435.
[12] Ibid., vol. I, pt. I, chap. 4.

be entirely separate.[13] Thus Tocqueville, though he has no hope of delivering mankind from the "inflexible laws" of intellectual bondage, believes that this bondage can be "a salutary bondage, which allows him to make a good use of [his] freedom."[14] On the other hand, democracy, which seems precisely to hold out the promise of liberation from intellectual bondage to other men, actually threatens to "confine the activity of private judgment within limits too narrow for the dignity and happiness of mankind."[15]

That Tocqueville is able to judge between a stifling or degrading intellectual confinement and a "salutary bondage" that serves as a basis for the "good use of freedom" and is consistent with "the dignity and happiness of mankind" implies that he does not believe himself to be enslaved to groundless human opinions; he thus seems implicitly to claim access to some standard "beyond and outside humanity." And it is true that in the chapter "How Religion in the United States Makes Use of Democratic Instincts,"[16] Tocqueville suggests that certain men of rare natural ability can, under favorable material circumstances, lay hold on truths about "God, their souls, and their duties toward their Creator and their fellows":

---

[13]Thus Goldstein, *Trial of Faith* (p. 124) is right to take Jack Lively, *The Social and Political Thought of Alexis de Tocqueville* (Oxford: Oxford University Press, 1962), p. 197, and Marvin Zetterbaum, *Tocqueville and the Problem of Democracy* (Stanford: Stanford University Press, 1967), p. 122, to task for jumping from the observation that Tocqueville takes a "functional" approach to religion to the conclusion that "he considered religion 'solely from the point of view of these [political] effects,' or that he advocated 'the propagation of spiritualistic myths.'" But Goldstein's alternative, the view that "Tocqueville's religious outlook is the inextricable meshing in his mind of 'faith,' 'truth,' and 'utility,'" merely raises the question that I hope to begin to address—that is, the question of the character and interrelationship of faith, truth, and utility. See also p. x, where Goldstein states her methodological principle: "I assume that Tocqueville's thought consists of a network of interconnected themes, with no fixed order of primacy among them." Hereinafter cited as Zetterbaum, *Problem*.

A notable attempt to integrate Tocqueville's views of notions such as faith, truth, and utility by showing their common subordination to, or emanation from, a certain idea of freedom is *Ute Uhde, Politik und Religion: zum Verhältnis von Demokratie und Christentum bei Alexis de Tocqueville* (Berlin: Dunker & Humblot, 1978).

[14]*Democracy*, p. 434.

[15]Ibid., p. 436.

[16]Ibid., vol. II, pt. I, chap. 5.

> Only minds singularly free from the preoccupations of life, penetrating, subtle, and trained to think, can at the cost of much time and trouble sound the depths of these truths that are so necessary.[17]

It is not clear whether Tocqueville intends to include himself in the class of these rare minds. In any case, he makes no attempt to reveal the content of the "depths of these truths," but seems rather to maintain a distinction between these depths and any "fixed ideas" that can be revealed to the public. Those who sound the depths can see the truth in religious dogmas that are "clear, precise, intelligible to the crowd, and very durable," but the truth they see in the depths is not precisely identical to what is visible or can be made visible to all.[18] Thus the ground of Tocqueville's judgment concerning "salutary bondage" or "the dignity and happiness of mankind," remains unclear, and the precise manner in which religion serves these ends is not treated thematically. In particular, it is not clear how American religion can contribute to widening the people's intellectual horizons and thus to their happiness and dignity if, as Tocqueville observes in the very midst of his discussion of the degrading intellectual bondage of democracy, "religion is strong less as a revealed doctrine than as part of common opinion." But it appears that Tocqueville's intention is to define the visible limits of freedom in order to approximate the deep or hidden truths about God, the soul, and duty. To understand Tocqueville's use of religion, we must therefore see how it is that religion may help to create a space of the right dimensions for human activity and thus for human happiness and dignity, or for the good use of freedom.

In other words, to understand the political utility of religion it is necessary first to understand the purpose of politics. In discussing "How Religious Beliefs at Times Turn the Thoughts of Americans Toward Spiritual Things,"[19] Tocqueville observes that

---

[17]Ibid., p. 443.

[18]Compare Catherine Zuckert: Tocqueville "endorses those opinions which *reflect* fundamental truths." See her chapter entitled "Not by Preaching: Tocqueville on the Role of Religion in American Democracy" in *The Review of Politics,* vol. 3 (April 1981), pp. 277.

[19]*Democracy,* vol. II, pt. II, chap. 15.

the legislative art has a fixed goal, but he does not spell out just what that goal is. It is thus necessary to discern this end in the means to it that Tocqueville recommends. These means are ever-changing, since they must be fitted to the particular circumstances of the societies in question. But societies come in two main types, Tocqueville observes, and he recurs to the basic dichotomy which shapes his entire consideration of democracy in America; that is, the contrast between aristocracy and democracy. Tocqueville does not attempt to describe the lawgiver's art abstractly or dogmatically, but exhibits it in its application to each of these general conditions of society.

In aristocracies, when men are held "in a state of torpor" because their attention is "fixed on the contemplation of another world," the business of the lawgiver is to turn men's attention to this world, to their physical needs. Under such conditions, Tocqueville writes, "I should try to send them hunting for prosperity."

On the other hand, "legislators for democracies have other cares." Democratic men are all too ready to hunt after prosperity; they thus risk degrading themselves or losing the use of their sublimest faculties.

> In a democracy therefore it is ever the duty of lawgivers and of all upright educated men to raise up the souls of their fellow citizens and turn their attention toward heaven. There is a need for all who are interested in the future of democratic societies to get together and with one accord to make continual efforts to propagate throughout society a taste for the infinite, an appreciation of greatness, and a love of spiritual pleasures.[20]

The utility of religion for Tocqueville's project thus seems clear: Democracy tends to degrade men, and religion helps statesmen and "upright educated men" to raise them up. But this does not fully explain Tocqueville's intention, since the religious elevation of man is not presented as the fixed goal of the lawgiver's art but only as a means appropriate to a democratic age. And Tocqueville has

[20]Ibid., p. 543.

already implied that it is possible for men to be too religious or elevated for them to attend too much to the other world. Just as men risk losing their sublimest faculties in an age of equality, so, in an age of excessive inequality, they risk falling into "a state of torpor," a condition unlikely to elicit "the best efforts of the best brains." The common goal of democratic and aristocratic lawgivers thus seems to be the fullest activity of the best human faculties. Thus Tocqueville endorses "belief in an immaterial and immortal principle" less for its own sake than because it is "indispensable to man's greatness," and he subordinates an "appreciation of greatness" in the abstract, that is, as bound up with "a taste for the infinite . . . and a love of spiritual pleasures," to a concern for a specifically human greatness. Furthermore, if he is convinced that "at all costs Christianity must be maintained among the new democracies," this seems to be because Christianity is at present the only viable form of "belief in an immaterial and immortal principle."

> Thus, then, when *any* religion has taken deep root in a democracy, be very careful not to shake it, but rather guard it as the most precious heritage from aristocratic times. Do not try to detach men from their old religious opinions in order to establish new ones . . . .[21] [Emphasis added.]

In sum, Christianity comprises belief in an immaterial and immortal principle, and such a belief in a greatness beyond human control is indispensable to human greatness and particularly in need of support in a democratic age. Tocqueville's governing intention is thus to make human greatness possible in a democratic age. The goal is neither precisely a religious one nor an aristocratic one, but a fixed political end that now requires the support of religion understood as an aristocratic heritage.

Materialism as Idealism

To understand more fully Tocqueville's political use of Christianity in *Democracy in America,* it is necessary to examine

[21]Ibid.

further the democratic disease for which he proposes Christianity as a cure or part of a cure. The disease of democracy, we have seen, consists in an excessive concern for bodily needs and a failure to exercise the higher human faculties; this appears to be an adequate definition of the condition that Tocqueville often deplores under the name of "materialism." However, on closer inspection we will see that "materialism" can refer not only to the inactivity of the intellect, but also to a certain form of intellectual activity.

In a chapter on the life of the mind in American democracy,[22] Tocqueville alludes to one of the most ancient metaphors of political philosophy to express his horror of a society in which the light of the mind would be extinguished altogether:

> It is possible to conceive a people without castes, hierarchy, or classes, . . . which . . . has neither culture nor freedom. . . .
>
> . . . The poor, without either culture or freedom, would not so much as conceive the idea of raising themselves, and the rich would let themselves be dragged down into poverty without knowing how to defend themselves. They would soon both be reduced to complete and permanent equality. Then no one would have time or taste for the labors and pleasures of the mind. They would all stay benumbed in a like ignorance and equal slavery.
>
> When I conceive a democratic society of this kind, I fancy myself in some low, close, and gloomy abode where the light which breaks in from without soon faints and fades away. A sudden heaviness overpowers me, and I grope through the surrounding darkness to find an opening that will restore me to the air and to the light of day.[23]

But before Tocqueville or his reader is overwhelmed by the suffocating confinement of the cave, he informs us that this dreadful condition does not seem to apply to a modern, enlightened democracy:

---

[22]Ibid., vol. II, pt. I, chap. 9.
[23]Ibid., p. 456.

> But none of that would apply to men already enlightened who retain their freedom after abolishing those peculiar and hereditary rights which perpetuated the tenure of property by certain individuals or certain classes.

It is true that certain "special causes," including "their strictly Puritan origin," have "concurred to fix the mind of the American on purely practical objects," or "to draw the American's mind earthward." But the nature of democracy itself, in fact, favors the extension of intellectual interests to a greater number of citizens[24] than under conditions of inequality. Thus "the circle of readers continually increases and finally includes all the citizens." It seems, then, that, far from confining mankind to the darkness of the cave of ignorance, the long-term tendency of democracy is, in fact, to bring enlightenment within the reach of every man.

On closer inspection, however, Tocqueville clearly has certain reservations about the quality of light in a democracy. In the next chapter, he will explain "Why the Americans are More Concerned with the Applications than with the Theory of Science,"[25] but it is clear from the present chapter that this tendency is not peculiar to Americans:

> Even the crowd can now plainly see the utility of knowledge, and those who have no taste for its charms set store by its results and make some effort to acquire it. . . .
>
> As soon as the crowd begins to take an interest in the labors of the mind it finds out that to excel in some of them is a powerful aid to the acquisition of fame, power, or wealth. . . . The number of those studying science, literature, and the arts becomes immense . . . ; and though each individual achievement is generally very small, the total effect is always very great.[26]

Thus, Tocqueville concludes, the natural tendency of democrats is not to neglect intellectual pursuits but rather to "cultivate them in their

---

[24]Ibid., p. 458.
[25]Ibid., vol. II, pt. I, chap. 10.
[26]Ibid., p. 458.

own fashion"—that is, in a fashion that conceives of intellectual activity only as a means to material ends, or which subordinates theory to practice.

In opposing "materialism," the author of *Democracy in America* may thus fear the form of intellectual activity in a democracy as much as the prospect that intellectual activity will cease. Indeed, this is clear from the moment we see that Tocqueville's energies are directed not only against the natural human tendency to care excessively for the body, but against a doctrine propounded by certain intellectuals, that is, by the "materialists."

> Democracy favors the taste for physical pleasures. This taste, if it becomes excessive, soon disposes men to believe that nothing but matter exists. Materialism, in its turn, spurs them on to such delights with mad impetuosity. Such is the vicious circle into which democratic nations are driven.[27]

The specific malady of modern, enlightened democracy consists in the vicious circle that is formed when men engaged in the life of the mind publicly propound the teaching that mind is subject to body, or when philosophers outdo men of affairs in asserting the priority of practice, when they give the name "light" to the darkness of the cave.

"There are many things that offend me about the materialists," Tocqueville writes in this same context; and to understand his political use of religion, we must understand his repugnance. In explaining what he finds offensive in the materialists, Tocqueville emphasizes less the doctrine of materialism itself than the disjunction or disproportion that he sees between this theory and the attitude or practical disposition of those who teach it. He seems ready to allow, in fact, that under certain conditions a doctrine unflattering to humanity might serve the purpose of "giving man a modest conception of himself." But there is nothing useful in the doctrine of the champions of modern civilization, Tocqueville observes, and he rebukes the materialists with this epigram:

---

[27]Ibid., vol. II, pt. II, chap. 15, p. 544.

> When they think they have sufficiently established that they are no better than brutes, they seem as proud as if they had proved that they were gods.[28]

In this sentence one can find encapsulated Tocqueville's critique of the intellectual framework of modern democracy. The materialists assert themselves proudly on the basis of theories that cannot account for the possibility of self-assertion; as they debase humanity as a whole in theory, they implicitly arrogate to themselves the prerogatives of gods. And it appears that it is only implicitly and surreptitiously that their claim to divinity can be effective, since its only theoretical representation is the inarticulate standpoint of power from which mankind is seen to be powerless. The materialists make themselves gods by making men brutes; indeed, the more their theories establish the brutishness of humanity, the more they in practice assert their own divinity. Thus the subordination of theory to practice results in a grotesque divorce of theory and practice: The theory of the materialists cannot account for the practice of theorizing; that is, for the choice of the life of the mind over a life devoted to the body. Because the materialists cannot give an account of themselves or will not stand up for themselves as theoretical men, they, in practice, assert themselves as gods.

This dislocation of theory and practice can be seen to lie at the heart of the "alarming spectacle" presented by "the Christian nations of our day" which Tocqueville describes in his introduction to the first volume of *Democracy in America*:

> In the heat of the struggle [surrounding the French Revolution] each partisan is driven beyond the natural limits of his own views by the views and the excesses of his adversaries, loses sight of the very aim he was pursuing, and uses language which ill corresponds to his real feelings and to his secret instincts. . . .
>
> . . . [I]t would seem that we have nowadays broken the natural link between opinions and tastes, acts, and beliefs; that harmony which has been observed throughout history

---

[28]Ibid.

> between the feelings and the ideas of men seems to have been destroyed, and one might suppose that all the laws of moral analogy had been abolished.[29]

Tocqueville then offers a number of examples of this alarming rupture between ideas and actions:

> Men of religion fight against freedom, and lovers of liberty attack religions; noble and generous spirits praise slavery, while low, servile minds preach independence; honest and enlightened citizens are the enemies of all progress, while men without patriotism or morals make themselves the apostles of civilization and enlightenment![30]

When the "laws of moral analogy" are abolished, or all likeness between God and man is denied, then man can only imitate God by debasing mankind. This state of "intellectual squalor" where "nothing is connected" ultimately portends complete theoretical and practical chaos, "[w]here nothing any longer seems either forbidden or permitted, honest or dishonorable, true or false."[31]

The leading representatives of this intellectual squalor, and thus Tocqueville's principal enemies, are the self-styled champions of modern civilization, who seek to "find out what is useful without concern for justice, to have science quite without belief and prosperity without virtue." If Tocqueville is to redirect the course of modern civilization, he must challenge the leadership of these champions; that is, of those men "whose object is to make men materialists." *Democracy in America* may therefore be understood as a sustained attack on the doctrine of materialism, or, more precisely, on those materialists who claim political leadership with the pride of gods while reducing mankind to the level of brutes. Thus, in the concluding exhortation of the whole work,[32] Tocqueville finds the occasion for a final denunciation of his chief rivals:

---

[29]Ibid., Introduction, p. 16.
[30]Ibid., p. 17.
[31]Ibid., p. 18.
[32]Ibid., vol. II, pt. IV, chap. 8, p. 705.

> I am aware that many of my contemporaries think that nations on earth are never their own masters and that they are bound to obey some insuperable and unthinking power, . . .
>
> These are false and cowardly doctrines which can only produce feeble men and pusillanimous nations.

The Poetry of Democracy

It is necessary to return to Part I of Volume II of *Democracy in America* in order to see the roots of the "intellectual squalor" that Tocqueville deplores. The rupture between theory and practice or the destruction of "the laws of moral analogy" effected by democratic intellectuals is perhaps most clearly exhibited in Tocqueville's chapter 20, "Some Characteristics Peculiar to Historians in Democratic Centuries." Whereas classical historians tend to exaggerate the influence of individuals, Tocqueville here observes, democratic historians exhibit the opposite and more dangerous tendency; they deny individuals and whole peoples "the faculty of modifying their own lot and make them depend either on an inflexible providence or on a kind of blind fatality." And somehow these historians' low view of the powers of mankind generally does not lead them to despair of their own faculties; indeed, "they pride themselves" on proving that men are not free. Tocqueville hints briefly at the political implications of this anomalous standpoint.

> Classical historians taught how to command; those of our own time teach next to nothing but how to obey. In their writings the author often figures large, but humanity is always tiny.[33]

What disturbs Tocqueville most about materialists and democratic historians is not their implicit claim to superiority over ordinary men and women but, on the contrary, the fact that their point of view pervades the democratic mind. Indeed, he is offended less by the pride of democratic authors than by the fact that they elevate themselves, not by explicitly claiming exemption from the

---

[33]Ibid., p. 496.

weaknesses of the rest of humanity but, rather, in the very act of reducing themselves to the common level. The disproportion between authors and subjects that Tocqueville describes is one that exhibits itself within each author as he projects a low view of himself as subject and within each subject as he adopts the viewpoint of the democratic author on his own humanity. As Tocqueville writes in another, closely related, context, "writer and public join in corrupting each other."[34] The democratic historian thus exhibits the divorce between theory and practice that, more than the natural tendency to care excessively for the body, threatens the soul of democratic man.

The content of the groundless pride of democratic historians and the way in which this pride and this groundlessness threaten democratic man in general are presented somewhat obliquely by Tocqueville in his chapter "Some Sources of Poetic Inspiration in Democracies."[35] "For me," Tocqueville writes, "poetry is the search for and representation of the ideal . . . it is . . . not the poet's function to portray reality but to beautify it and offer the mind some loftier image." In the realm of the poetic, we may thus discover the hidden ideal that makes it possible for the historian to take pride in his low view of human reality and thus of his own humanity.

At first Tocqueville's view of poetry and democracy seems to be that the two tend to be mutually exclusive: "It must first of all be acknowledged that the taste for ideal beauty and the pleasure derived from seeing it expressed are never as lively or as widespread in democracies as in aristocracies." Poetry requires leisure, or considerable freedom from the care of the body, and such freedom is in short supply in democracies, where "the love of physical pleasures, the hope to better one's lot, competition, and the lure of success" dominate the soul. Whereas, under aristocracies, men are inclined to believe in "intermediate powers" between man and God, and "the universe is peopled with supernatural beings," democracy "brings the poet's imagination back to earth and shuts it up in the actual, visible world." Poetry requires a reference beyond the real

[34]Ibid., p. 488.
[35]Ibid., vol. II, pt. I, chap. 17.

or actual to the ideal, and democracy tends to deprive men of such reference.

Thus one might expect poetry to wither away in a democratic society. But this is not Tocqueville's argument; instead, he writes that "the spread of equality over the earth dries up the old springs of poetry. We must try to show how other springs are revealed." Contrary to our original impression, Tocqueville does not believe that the poetic imagination is necessarily stifled when it is brought back to earth and shut up in the actual, visible world. The "other springs" that democracy reveals are somehow consistent with being "shut up" in the actual. From the viewpoint of the old poetry, the ideal has to be added to the real; the new poetry, on the other hand, finds the ideal "shut up" within the real or actual.

The new poets of democracy, as they renounced the ideals of the past, at first found their attention fixed on inanimate nature: "Gods and heroes gone, they began by painting rivers and mountains." But this descriptive poetry is only "a transitional phenomenon":

> In the long run I am sure that democracy turns man's imagination away from externals to concentrate it on himself alone.
>
> Democratic peoples may amuse themselves momentarily by looking at nature, but it is about themselves that they are really excited.

A question immediately arises: What are democratic peoples so excited about? Tocqueville has just observed that "[i]n democratic societies . . . all are insignificant and very much alike. . . ." How can this monotonous insignificance stir the imaginations of democratic men? An answer seems to be implied in the next sentence, where Tocqueville notes that "poets in democracies can never take a particular man as the subject of their poetry." Thus, it is not any particular man or woman that exalts the poetic imagination of Americans, but "themselves" taken collectively. But this hardly diminishes our puzzlement; for how can a mass of insignificant and essentially similar individuals, any more than a single such person, strike us as significant, even exciting?

Tocqueville introduces his answer to this question by referring us back to his chapter on "How Equality Suggests to the Americans the

Idea of the Indefinite Perfectibility of Man."[36] It is "the ideas of progress and the indefinite perfectibility of the human race" that make confinement to "the actual visible world" consistent with poetic excitement. More precisely, it is not the actual, visible world itself that stirs democratic souls, but the idea of this world's movement toward an indefinite perfection. And since the perfection envisaged is indefinite—that is, since it cannot be represented among a democratic people in any particular, concrete, embodied form—the democratic imagination focuses on the movement itself. Thus, "[t]he American people see themselves marching through wildernesses, drying up marshes, diverting rivers, peopling the wilds, and subduing nature." It is the very indeterminacy of the character of a democratic people that allows the people's attention to concentrate on themselves as a movement or activity; undiverted by any qualitative differences among men or among the ends that men pursue, or by any "intermediate powers" between God and man, a democratic people can be fully present to itself:

> The very likeness of ends . . . helps the poet to group them in imagination and make a coherent picture of the nation as a whole. Democracies see themselves more vividly than do other nations. . . .

The indefinite end projected as the future of a democratic people at once makes this people visible to itself by reducing individuals to indistinguishable parts of a homogeneous whole and infuses this vision with a poetic excitement that has no basis—indeed, must have no basis—in the nature of any of the parts taken individually.

The spread of equality thus reveals new springs of poetry only by drying up the old springs; indeed, the excitement of an indefinite perfectibility represents itself concretely only in the active and perpetual leveling of any individual assertion that claims to represent a definite idea of perfection. The universalization of the democratic vision requires the leveling of any particular causes that might attempt to stand independent of the universal democratic movement or to "dispute the supremacy of the earth." The effectual

---

[36]Ibid., chap. 8.

truth of a progress purified of every reference to intermediate powers is thus perpetual destruction: The Americans, "one may almost say . . . do not see the marvelous forests surrounding them until they begin to fall beneath the ax."[37] "A taste for the infinite," it appears, may not lead naturally to "an appreciation of greatness."

Tocqueville's chapter on democratic poetry thus explains the fundamental paradox of democratic theory; it shows how it is possible for the insignificance of human beings to redound to the pride of humanity: When men assume the perspective of an omnipotent god whose only purpose is the conquest of nature for humanity, then the powerlessness of men appears as equivalent to the limitless power of mankind. This means that the theory of democracy is explained and governed by its poetry: The characteristic pride of the champions of modernity is rooted in a poetic inspiration they cannot account for; modern materialism does not comprehend its own idealism. And one could say equally that modern idealism does not comprehend its own materialism; the poetry of progress cannot articulate the indefinite perfectibility it posits as the direction of the material conquest of nature; it must accept without question a material interpretation of its inspiring ideal.[38] Thus the champions of modernity are not really leaders but followers of a democratic inspiration they do not understand. In this they resemble the average American, whose "petty, insipid . . . anti-poetic" daily life is supported by the "hidden sinews" of the poetry of progress. The champion of modernity merely continues and radicalizes the tendency of democratic man to employ and devote his noblest faculties to the leveling of all that is noble. Thus the point of view that poses as most theoretical (that is, most detached from the needs and wants of ordinary men) turns out to be the most practical; i.e., the most subservient to those very needs and wants. Similarly, by focusing his devotion on one supreme God to the exclusion of all "intermediate powers," human or divine, the

---

[37]Ibid., p. 485.

[38]Compare Friedrich Nietzsche, *Beyond Good and Evil*, trans. Walter Kaufmann (New York: Random House, 1966), pt. I, no. 13, on the residual teleology of modern thought.

democratic citizen harnesses his God to the enterprise of material progress. The attempt to adopt a standpoint altogether above humanity thus tends to reduce one's standpoint to that of the most common humanity.

Democracy, Aristocracy, Christianity

It is not, therefore, the natural tendency to care excessively for material things but a certain poetic or idealistic materialism that Tocqueville must defeat in order to save the democratic soul from degradation. This understanding of the disease of democracy, however, makes it much more difficult to see how Christianity can be a cure. For in the course of describing the poetry of modern materialism, Tocqueville clearly suggests that this democratic idealism is, to say the least, compatible with Christian spiritualism:

> Even when equality does not bring religions crashing down, it simplifies them and turns attention away from secondary beings to concentrate chiefly on the Supreme Being.[39]

It may therefore be not only in the form of "skepticism" but in the form of Christianity that equality "depopulated heaven."[40] Thus Tocqueville by no means presents idealistic materialism as the enemy of Christianity but, in fact, offers a Christian, or at least theistic, version of the poetry of worldly progress:

> Just when every man, raising his eyes above his country, begins to see mankind at large, God shows himself more clearly to human perception in full and entire majesty.
>
> Seeing the human race as one great whole, [democratic men] easily conceive that its destinies are regulated by the same design and are led to recognize in the actions of each individual a trace of the universal and consistent plan by which God guides mankind.[41]

---

[39]*Democracy*, vol. I, pt. II, chap. 17, p. 483.
[40]Ibid., p. 484.
[41]Ibid., p. 486.

That the intellectual paradigm of democracy is compatible with Christianity as well as with skepticism is confirmed in the chapter "How Religion in the United States Makes Use of Democratic Instincts."[42]

This chapter, in fact, has a lot to say about how democracy makes use of religious instincts:

> The . . . observation . . . that equality leads men to very general and very vast ideas . . . is especially applicable to religion. Men who are alike and on the same level in this world easily conceive the idea of a single God who imposes the same laws on each man and grants him future happiness at the same price. The conception of the unity of mankind ever brings them back to the idea of the unity of the Creator. . . .[43]

One might argue, of course, that, although Christianity can be made to conform to the intellectual paradigm of democracy, it need not do so, or that the essence of Christianity is really distinct from democracy. And it is true that Tocqueville observes here: "Christianity itself has in some degree been affected by the influence of social and political conditions on religious beliefs." Perhaps, one might think, Tocqueville intends to treat the disease of democracy with a form of Christianity purged of democratic influences.

This does not seem to be Tocqueville's intention, however, for he does not, in fact, recommend that American Christianity resist the democratic attack on intermediate powers:

> In democratic ages, therefore, it is particularly important not to confuse the honor due to secondary agents with the worship belonging to the Creator alone.[44]

Furthermore, the primary example Tocqueville offers of the social and political conditions of Christianity concerns, not the modification of the Christian faith, but its very origins. Thus he

---

[42]Ibid., pt. I, chap. 5.
[43]Ibid., p. 445.
[44]Ibid., p. 447.

clearly suggests that, if Christianity has an essential character, this character is much more in tune with democracy than with aristocracy. Referring to the unification of "a great part of mankind" under the Roman emperors, Tocqueville argues that "this new and singular condition of humanity disposed men to receive the general truths preached by Christianity. . . ."[45] The subsequent, more aristocratic interpretation of Christianity which, "unable to subdivide the Deity . . . could at least multiply and aggrandize His agents beyond measure" was thus an aberration, a departure from the essence or origins of the Christian faith. Tocqueville thus refers to the medieval worship of angels and saints as "almost idolatrous." Christianity, by its very nature, thus has something fundamental in common with democracy: both incline powerfully toward "very general and very vast ideas."[46]

The problem of general ideas is treated thematically by Tocqueville in the third chapter of Volume II, Part I: "Why the Americans Show More Aptitude and Taste for General Ideas Than Their English Forefathers." This chapter is of the first importance because it invites us to compare the characteristic points of view of aristocracy and democracy with the one true perspective, that is, God's perspective.

"God has no need of general ideas," Tocqueville explains, because "he sees every human being separately and sees in each the resemblances that make him like his fellows and the differences which isolate him from them." God knows each and every individual thing fully and precisely, and has no need to use one identical concept or "label" to cover many individual things that are not the same but only similar. Human beings, on the other hand, "would soon be lost in a wilderness of detail" if they tried to know each individual thing fully as it is in itself. Thus "general ideas do not bear witness to the power of human intelligence but rather to its inadequacy." Furthermore, paradoxically, this crutch of the human mind is not cast aside as humanity progresses in knowledge and civilization, but is actually relied upon more and more: "So the use of general ideas and the taste for them will always increase the

---

[45]Ibid., p. 446.
[46]Ibid.

older a people's culture and the wider their knowledge." The more a people knows, one might say, the more it must ignore.

It is true that there are better and worse uses of this crutch of general ideas. The better forms minimize the distortion that accompanies every generalization; this kind of general idea "results from the slow, detailed, and conscientious labor of the mind, and . . . widens the sphere of human knowledge." The inferior kind of general idea, on the other hand, "springs up at once from the first quick exercise of the wits and begets only very superficial and uncertain notions." Now aristocratic peoples tend to fix their attention on differences among things just as they take for granted the social inequalities that exist among men; they thus show "an ill-considered scorn" of even the better or more truthful kind of generalization. A democratic people, on the contrary, is likely to develop an "injudicious warmth" for the inferior kind of generalization:

> When traditions of class, of profession, and of family are repudiated and the dominion of precedent is left behind for the search by one's own unaided reason for the way to follow, one has a natural inclination to deduce the motives for one's views from the very nature of man, and that leads of necessity and almost in spite of itself to a great number of very broad generalizations.[47]

The democrat repudiates artificial inequalities but has little time or aptitude for the "slow, detailed, and conscientious labor" necessary to distinguish judiciously between natural and unnatural inequality. He thus understands the universal "nature of man" as opposed to inequality simply; he assumes that "truths applicable to himself [are] equally applicable, *mutatis mutandis*, to his fellow citizens and to all men."[48] Thus the tendency to generalize and, in particular, to reduce mankind as a whole to one's own level "becomes an ardent and often blind passion of the human spirit."

Tocqueville chooses a remarkable example, or contrasting pair of cases, to support his theory that aristocratic peoples tend to

---

[47]Ibid., pp. 435-40.
[48]Ibid., p. 439.

distrust and democratic peoples to embrace general ideas. Immediately after describing "the ardent and blind passion" of democrats for general ideas, he asserts that "the views of the ancient world about slaves clearly demonstrate the truth of this proposition." In its present context, one might expect "this proposition" to refer to the blind passion of democrats for general ideas, but the first example chosen leads us to believe that Tocqueville intends rather to illustrate his general argument comparing aristocrats with democrats:

> The profoundest and most wide-seeing minds of Greece and Rome never managed to grasp the very general but very simple conception of the likeness of all men and the equal right of all at birth to liberty. They were at pains to show that slavery was natural and would always exist.

The "great writers of antiquity," Tocqueville argues, were unable to see through the conventional inequalities of their own societies to the truth about human nature. But what, then, is the truth about human nature? And how were men empowered to see this truth?

> Jesus Christ had to come down to earth to make all members of the human race understand that they were naturally similar and equal.[49]

God had to become his own mediator, to descend to the level of our common humanity, in order to destroy the claim of certain men to the right to mediate between men and God, to lord it over other men. Tocqueville thus introduces the most general of general ideas, the idea of the natural equality of all mankind, as a dogmatic truth grounded in Christianity.[50] He allows his Christian and

---

[49]Ibid.

[50]Zetterbaum, apparently agreeing with this "natural" truth but not with its dogmatic foundation, simply chooses to ignore the "theological" character of Tocqueville's "most prominent justification for democracy." Zetterbaum, *Problem*, p. 22n. 49.

Compare Manent's brilliant and much more balanced discussion (chap. vii) of "*La Démocratie et la Nature de l'Homme.*" For example, p. 113: "*La démocratie, c'est la nature qui met en danger la nature.*" Pierre Manent, *Tocqueville et la Nature de la Démocratie* (Paris: Julliard, 1982). Hereinafter cited as Manent, *Tocqueville et la Nature*.

egalitarian reader to focus on the errors or alleged errors of pagan writers and to forget for the moment that the central thrust of the whole chapter in which this passage appears is to expose the weakness of general ideas and particularly the reductionist tendency of general theories of humanity. However, if careful attention is paid to the context of Tocqueville's comparison of pagan antiquity to Christianity, it appears that the political interpretation of the Christian idea of equality, and the Christian prejudice against the philosophic defense of inequality, may indeed constitute the supreme example of an "ardent and blind passion" for general ideas. Perhaps it is not so much "the views of the ancient world about slaves" as the Christian and modern reading of those views that "clearly demonstrates the truth of this proposition."

In any case, Tocqueville's chapter on general ideas clearly indicates that the Christian religion is not to be understood fundamentally as an aristocratic phenomenon; indeed, it seems that it was the religious doctrine of the incarnation that gave decisive power to the political idea of "the likeness of all men and the equal right of all at birth to liberty."

One might quite plausibly argue, however, that the democratic idea of political equality does not stem from Christianity but is, in fact, a perversion or "secularization" of a fundamentally spiritual doctrine. Indeed, by Tocqueville's own account, God himself does not even need general ideas, and so the Christian idea of the equality of mankind can only be an approximation of the divine point of view, an approximation little suited to political application. But Tocqueville does not believe that the mutual influence of political and religious beliefs can be prevented: "Nothing can prevent such ideas from being the common spring from which all else originates." Man is by nature in bondage to general ideas, whether in the more restricted form of aristocratic ideas that see the whole world, both human and divine, from the point of view of a largely artificial inequality or, in the more radical, democratic form which finally rejects inequality altogether, excepting, perhaps, the inequality that divides man and God. Thus, however much a Christian might resist the political use of the doctrine of spiritual equality (that is, of an equality that is only visible from the standpoint of God), such a doctrine, in destroying intermediate or secondary powers between

God and man, necessarily erodes the intellectual foundations of any nondemocratic order. And since neither individual action nor political order is possible except with reference, explicit or implicit, to dogmatic beliefs about ultimate reality, Christians must choose between an "almost idolatrous" introduction of beliefs in intermediate powers, or proceed to the politicization or secularization of Christianity itself. As long as Christianity is addressed to human beings, it cannot escape involvement in politics, whether aristocratic or democratic.[51]

Against the background of Tocqueville's analysis, in Volume II, of the deep affinity between Christianity and democracy, it is possible to see that an awareness of this affinity subtly shapes Tocqueville's account of the rise of democracy within the Christian West in the very first pages of *Democracy in America.* In the introduction to the first volume, the first moment of the "great democratic revolution [which] is taking place in our midst" is traced to the emergence of "the political power of the clergy." The authority of Christianity was the first to oppose the power of the nobility:

> Through the church, equality began to insinuate itself into the heart of government, and a man who would have vegetated as a serf in eternal servitude could, as a priest, take his place among the nobles and often take precedence over kings.

It is not obvious, however, how the political power of priests could constitute the germ of the modern idea of equality; and, after mentioning the clergy in introducing his account of the seven-hundred-year march of equality, Tocqueville surveys various apparently discrete developments which seem to have little to do intrinsically with Christianity: the rise of lawyers and of

---

[51]Leo Strauss, whom one would expect to understand this at least as well as anyone, seems to ignore it in his discussion of Max Weber's attempt to associate Calvinism with the rise of capitalism. There Strauss maintains a rather rigid distinction between true Puritanism and "the Puritanism that had already made its peace with 'the world.'" Leo Strauss, *Natural Right and History* (Chicago: University of Chicago Press, 1953), p. 61n.)

Compare Manent: *"La religion elle-même . . . ne peut se donner aux hommes que dans un site conventionnel, qu'en en étante autorisée—au double sense du terme—par certains hommes ou certains institutions."* Manent, *Tocqueville et la Nature,* p. 144.

tradesmen, the emergence of the intellect as "a social force," and the leveling influence of the monarchy and of inventions and improvements in trade and industry. This survey of the causes of the democratic revolution might leave the impression that Christianity was at most one factor among many in the rise of democracy, but Tocqueville prevents us from drawing this conclusion. He invites the reader to reflect on the problem of the overarching cause which integrated the effects of the particular factors he has enumerated:

> Everywhere the diverse happenings in the lives of peoples have turned to democracy's profit; all men's efforts have aided it, both those who intended this and those who had no such intention, those who fought for democracy and those who were the declared enemies thereof; all have been driven pell-mell along the same road, and all have worked together, some against their will and some unconsciously, blind instruments in the hand of God.[52]

The mysterious principle that integrates these various discrete causes of democracy is thus referred to God. But in declaring the power of the democratic revolution to be irresistible, Tocqueville bows before the "sacred character" bestowed on this revolution, not directly by God, but by the "patient observation and sincere meditation" of "men of the present day," men who can find no bearings for themselves except in the "gradual and measured advance of equality." If such patient and sincere men can see no alternative to equality, then "to halt democracy *appears* as a fight against God himself" (emphasis added).[53]

The force of the inability of patient and sincere men to know themselves except in and through the idea of equality[54] is, for Tocqueville, like God in its irresistibility; furthermore, it seems to derive from God or from a certain idea of God, since it is a phenomenon encompassing, not mankind in general, but "Christian

---

[52]*Democracy*, Introduction, pp. 11-12.

[53]Ibid., p. 12.

[54]See Manent, *Tocqueville et la Nature*, p. 95: "*. . . l'égalité* [devient] *l'horizon même de l'existence social, le principe au nom duquel tour est éprouvé et jugé . . .*"

lands," "the Christian nations of our day,"[55] or "the Christian world."[56]

Thus Tocqueville's discussion of the democratic revolution of the last seven hundred years returns to the problem of Christianity with which it began, and the impression that modern democracy is somehow rooted in Christianity is inescapable, although it is far from clear just how this is so. Indeed, Tocqueville appears willing to confine himself to the perspective of patient and sincere men of Christian lands and thus to consider the march of democracy as much beyond human understanding as it is beyond human control. Still, in distinguishing the Christian world from the world simply, and in referring to the power of the opinion of his patient and sincere contemporaries, Tocqueville invites the careful reader to look beyond the providential power of equality to the human cause of this power, to search for the intellectual cause of the subordination of all other causes to the progress of equality.

I will quote in its entirety the paragraph in which Tocqueville comes nearest to explaining this overarching cause:

> Once the work of the mind had become a source of power and wealth, every addition to knowledge, every fresh discovery, and every new idea became a germ of power within reach of the people. Poetry, eloquence, memory, the graces of the mind, the fires of the imagination and profundity of thought, all things scattered broadcast by heaven, were a profit to democracy, and even when it was the adversaries of democracy who possessed these things, they still served its cause by throwing into relief the natural greatness of man. Thus its conquests spread along with those of civilization and enlightenment, and literature was an arsenal from which all, including the weak and poor, daily chose their weapons.[57]

The emergence of the intellect as a source of power seems to be associated very closely with the equalization of society. Tocque-

---

[55]*Democracy*, p. 12.
[56]Ibid., p. 11.
[57]Ibid.

ville has already drawn our attention to the centrality of the fact that "the mind became an element of success; knowledge became a tool of government and intellect a social force. . . ."[58] But it is far from obvious why the rising status of the intellect should ineluctably serve the cause of democracy, for clearly, as the paragraph quoted above indicates, all intellects are not created equal, and many superior intellects are likely to be possessed by the adversaries of democracy. What, then, is this force which turns all causes, and in particular intellectual inequality itself, toward the progress of equality?

Tocqueville's only answer seems to be that inequality served equality essentially by "throwing into relief the natural greatness of man"—that is, not the greatness of any man in particular or of a certain unequal kind of man, but the greatness of mankind in general, of the species man. But on what ground, precisely, is every assertion of human excellence or inequality interpreted as supporting "the natural greatness of mankind" understood as a homogeneous species? Tocqueville does not undertake to explain this in detail, but he points to this ground in the words he chooses to describe human inequality: All forms of intellectual excellence are presented as gifts "scattered broadcast by heaven" (*dons que le ciel répartit au hazard).* When the unequal is interpreted as random or arbitrary, as having no basis accessible to human understanding, then the natural can be understood only as the equal; when intellectual virtues are interpreted as *"graces de l'esprit,"* then nature can assert itself only in the form of equality. When supernatural "graces of the mind" were pressed into the service of humanity, the only natural ends accessible to that mind were "power and wealth," that is, the needs of mankind understood as "weak and poor." In sum, the Enlightenment, in opposing the worldly power of priestly claims to transcend nature, in effect took up the cause of nature implicitly understood as the correlate of a radically transcendent God; it was fundamentally derivative of Christianity even when it took the form of an attack on Christianity. It is as created that the creation asserted itself against the Creator. Thus the "natural greatness of

---

[58]Ibid., p. 10.

man" joined itself to the cause of equality on the basis of a fundamentally Christian orientation toward the world.[59]

The Separation and Union of Religion and Politics

The deeper one penetrates into Tocqueville's understanding of the nature and origins of democracy, the harder it is to see what use he intends to make of Christianity in addressing the ills of democracy. Indeed, Tocqueville gives every indication that the Christian devaluation of nature is, to say the least, part of the problem:

> Thus, far from thinking that we should council [*sic*] humility to our contemporaries, I wish men would try to give them a higher idea of themselves and of humanity; humility is far from healthy for them; what they most lack, in my view, is pride. I would gladly surrender several of our petty virtues for that one vice.[60]

To put the problem bluntly: How can Christianity cure democracy, if it is its cause?

To address this question, it is necessary to examine Tocqueville's account of the particular situation of religion in American democracy. Whereas, in Europe, the great democratic revolution has produced the anomaly of a struggle between the proponents of equality and the defenders of the very religion from which the doctrine of human equality is derived,[61] the Americans have somehow been spared this "intellectual squalor." The pilgrims "in some way" transplanted the principle of democracy in the New World, where it could "grow in freedom and, progressing in conformity with mores, develop peacefully within the law."[62] The precise nature of this transplantation and the key to the development of American

---

[59]Compare Karl Lowith, "Conclusion" in *Meaning in History* (Chicago: University of Chicago Press, 1949), and Hans Blumenberg, *The Legitimacy of the Modern Age* (Cambridge, Mass.: Harvard University Press, 1983), pt. I, chap. 4, p. 47: "There was no 'worldliness' before there was the opposite of 'unworldliness.'"

[60]*Democracy*, p. 632.

[61]Ibid., p. 16.

[62]Ibid., p. 18.

democracy and to Tocqueville's strategy for saving it are revealed in the chapter, "Concerning Their Point of Departure and Its Importance for the Future of Anglo-Americans."[63]

"The whole man is there . . . in the cradle." The truth about Americans can be found in its beginnings. This is the methodological principle with which Tocqueville introduces his account of the settlement of North America. The point of departure of the American people, he argues, gives us the rare opportunity to examine the origins and thus the nature of a society "in broad daylight,"[64] under conditions, as it were, of experimental control. He presents this scientific opportunity as a gift of God: "Providence has given us a light denied to our fathers and allowed us to see the first causes in the fate of nations, causes formerly concealed in the darkness of the past." Thus Tocqueville offers this chapter on the point of departure as "the germ of all that is to follow and the key to almost the whole work."

Tocqueville locates the key to American civilization in Puritan New England, "whose influence now extends . . . over the whole American world."[65] "The foundation of New England was something new in the world," he argues, in that its basis was not greed or necessity but "a purely intellectual craving." He thus identifies the religious zeal of the Puritans with an intellectual passion; if we can now see the infancy of America in broad daylight, this is because the first Americans aspired to making a radically new beginning under God.

This new beginning was to be a rebirth, not only of man but of society: "Puritanism was not just a religious doctrine; in many respects it shared the most absolute democratic and republican theories."[66]

> It must not be imagined that the piety of Puritans was merely speculative, taking no notice of the course of worldly affairs. Puritanism . . . was almost as much a

---

[63]Ibid., vol. I, pt. I, chap. 2, p. 32.
[64]Ibid.
[65]Ibid., p. 35.
[66]Ibid., p. 36.

political theory as a religious doctrine.[67]

Just as the intellectual squalor of Europe can be represented by the unnatural separation and conflict between piety and liberty, so the genius of American democracy and of its Puritan point of departure consists in their union:

> Anglo-American civilization . . . is the product (and one should continually bear in mind this point of departure) of two perfectly distinct elements which elsewhere have often been at war with one another but which in America it was somehow possible to incorporate into each other, forming a marvelous combination. I mean the spirit of religion and the spirit of freedom.[68]

The union of Christianity and freedom which Tocqueville seemed to present in his introduction as the natural harmony of elevation of soul and love of liberty, now appears as a "marvelous combination . . . of two perfectly distinct elements" which was not natural but "somehow possible." Indeed, it appears that it was precisely the radical theoretical distinction the Puritans made between these two elements that made their practical combination possible. At the deepest level, Puritanism was a political theory as well as a religion because it attempted, on religious grounds, radically to separate the political from the religious, or the worldly from the otherworldly. If the Puritans could "with almost equal eagerness . . . seek either material wealth or moral delights, either heaven in the next world or prosperity and freedom in this,"[69] it was because they drew a clear boundary between the material and the spiritual. Such an inviolable boundary implies the radicalization of what lies on either side: "The founders of New England were both ardent sectarians and fanatical innovators. While held within the narrowest bounds by fixed religious beliefs, they were free from all political prejudices."[70]

It seems, then, that Puritanism was a political theory mainly in

---

[67]Ibid., p. 38.
[68]Ibid., pp. 46-47.
[69]Ibid., p. 47.
[70]Ibid.

the sense that it implied the liberation of the political from theological constraints:

> Under [the Puritans'] manipulation political principles, laws, and human institutions seem malleable things which can at will be adapted and combined. The barriers which hemmed in the society in which they were brought up fall before them; old views which have ruled the world for centuries vanish; almost limitless opportunities lie open in a world without horizon, the spirit of man rushes forward to explore in every direction. . . .[71]

The political significance of Puritanism was not, however, limited to the removal of theological constraints from political action. It also contributed positively to the spirit of democratic politics:

> Religion regards civil liberty as a noble exercise of men's faculties, the world of politics being a sphere intended by the Creator for the free play of intelligence.

God withdraws His authority from the political world, but He does not withdraw His care; in asserting their freedom from God to manipulate the formless matter of politics, men are fulfilling God's purpose.

In practice, of course, the Puritans did not understand this freedom as absolute, since the limits of politics were not defined politically but were accepted on religious authority or simply taken for granted:

> [T]he spirit of man rushes forward to explore in every direction; but when that spirit reaches the limits of the world of politics, it stops of its own accord; in trepidation it renounces the use of its most formidable faculties; it forswears doubt and renounces innovation; it will not even lift the veil of the sanctuary; and it bows respectfully before truths which it accepts without discussion.

The Puritans understood the spiritual world to have a definite

---

[71]Ibid.

moral content that was not, after all, politically irrelevant. In some cases this moral content was taken directly and literally from Scripture, as when Connecticut lawgivers laid down "ten or twelve provisions . . . taken word for word from Deuteronomy, Exodus, or Leviticus."[72] Tocqueville does not show much respect for the spiritual authority of these provisions, but describes them as "the legislation of a rough, half-civilized people. . . ."[73] Indeed, although he certainly approves the combination of religion and freedom in America, on close inspection he shows no great liking for either of the two elements of the combination as Americans understand them; that is, for either rigid moralism or boundless freedom:

> In the one case obedience is passive, though voluntary; in the other there is independence, contempt of experience, and jealousy of all authority.[74]

What Tocqueville means by freedom or liberty or by "salutary bondage" corresponds no more to absolute contempt for experience and authority than to absolute and passive submission. He shows us, in fact, in this very chapter that what was most valuable in the Puritan founding of American civilization did not issue from Puritan theory in either its specifically religious or its political dimension. If the Puritans "had more acquaintance with the notions of rights and principles of true liberty than most of the European nations at that time," this was not directly owing to their Puritanism but because, "born in a country shaken for centuries by the struggle of parties, a country in which each faction in turn had been forced to put itself under the protection of the laws, they had learned their political lessons in the rough school. . . ."[75] Similarly, Tocqueville seems to take a less favorable view of the religious and theoretical freedom according to which "political principles, laws, and human institutions seem malleable things which can at will be adapted

---

[72]Ibid., p. 41.
[73]Ibid., p. 42.
[74]Ibid., p. 47.
[75]Ibid., p. 33.

and combined"[76] than he does of "the dogma of the sovereignty of the people" understood as present in the free institutions of local government that "had already taken deep root in English ways"[77] under the Tudor monarchy.

If the Puritan point of departure is the key to the whole of *Democracy in America,* it cannot therefore be in the way the author first suggests. The religious and intellectual aspiration to a new birth of man and society in broad daylight proves to be a delusion.[78] The civilization of the pilgrims was not, as it implicitly claimed, like an infant competent to preside over its own birth; on the contrary, fortunately, "democracy more perfect than any of which antiquity had dared to dream sprang full-grown and fully armed from the midst of the old feudal society."[79] Still, the belief in a new beginning or creation in broad daylight, though largely false, may illuminate the whole of American democracy, as Tocqueville suggests. For it appears that it was because this fundamentally religious belief emerged first under the explicit auspices of a positive religion that religion was able to ally itself with this belief and to moderate it: "In America it is religion which leads to enlightenment and the observance of divine laws which leads men to liberty."[80]

We have seen that the situation in Europe was less favorable to the harmony of religion and freedom or enlightenment. There, under the influence of an aristocratic or "almost idolatrous" Christianity, the claims of the other world had intruded far into this world, provoking an emphatically worldly and revolutionary reaction. In the ensuing conflict, defenders of both worlds were blinded to their deep agreement on the separation of God and man, or on the equality of men.[81] In the New World, where Christianity was truer to its fundamental separation between God and the world, religion was able to exercise a more enduring influence on politics than in the Old

---

[76] Ibid., p. 47.
[77] Ibid., p. 33.
[78] Thus Tocqueville does not simply accept "the legend of the [Puritans] founding fathers," as Goldstein believes (*Trial of Faith,* p. 21).
[79] *Democracy,* p. 39.
[80] Ibid., p. 45.
[81] Ibid., pp. 300-01.

World, which priests tried to rule, anomalously, in the name of an otherwordly God. Similarly, the theological and geographical separation of the New World from the Old World secured the survival of certain vestiges of the Old World within the New; the New World was thus less radically separated in practice from the Old World and from the other world where it was more clearly separated from them theologically and geographically. The New World that was to rise up within the Old World would not enjoy this advantage.

It is clear, then, that Tocqueville favors the results of the radical, Calvinist separation between God and man more than he does the separation itself. In particular, he admires the traditional English liberties and experience in local self-government that the Puritans brought to America and that the veil of sectarianism helped to protect from the broad daylight of radical democracy. Tocqueville loves the practical harmony of religion and politics, of elevation of soul and political liberty, rather than the theological and theoretical guardian of this harmony; that is, the combination of absolute submission and absolute freedom.

Tocqueville affirms his preference for the practical effects of American religion over its theoretical basis in his discussion of religion in a chapter on "The Main Causes Tending to Maintain a Democratic Republic in the United States." He prefaces this discussion with a theoretical statement:[82]

> Every religion has some political opinion linked to it by affinity.
>
> The spirit of man, left to follow its bent, will regulate political society and the City of God in uniform fashion; it will, if I dare put it so, seek to harmonize earth with heaven.[83]

The harmony of religion and politics, which Tocqueville is taking such pains to secure, thus seems to be the natural inclination of humanity. Tocqueville's objective, however, to be more precise, is to secure the harmony of religion with a certain political liberty,

---

[82]Ibid., vol;. I, pt. II, chap. 9.
[83]Ibid., p. 287.

and this may be a more difficult matter. It is clear in any case that a certain harmony of the more general kind has existed in America from its point of departure: "From the start politics and religion agreed, and they have not since ceased to do so."[84] But it appears that the nature of this harmony has undergone a profound evolution since the days of the Puritans. At that time the religious sectarianism of Americans seemed to dominate their political liberalism or radicalism; at present, the religious consensus of Americans is defined largely in terms of political beliefs. In describing the Puritan point of departure, Tocqueville thus quoted at length from an account of the early settlement of New England and called the reader's attention to "the solemn religious feeling thereof; one seems to breathe the atmosphere of antiquity and to inhale a sort of biblical fragrance."[85] He then went on to explain the politics of the Puritans against the background of their remarkable piety. But in discussing his contemporaries, the order is reversed. It is true, he observes, that there is "only one mental current in America," and this current is democratic Christianity: "For the Americans the ideas of Christianity and Liberty are so completely mingled that it is almost impossible to get them to conceive of the one without the other."[86] But the relationship between Christianity and democracy seems to have been reversed. Thus this consensus is no longer fundamentally sectarian but includes Catholics who have accepted the Protestant strategy for making the two worlds agree by radically separating them:

> American Catholic priests have divided the world of the mind into two parts; in one are revealed dogmas to which they submit without discussion; political truth finds its place in the other half, which they think God has left to man's free investigation.[87]

Likewise in this chapter, as in his discussion of the severe piety of the Puritans, Tocqueville quotes a religious source at length. But

---

[84]Ibid., p. 288.
[85]Ibid., p. 37.
[86]Ibid., p. 293.
[87]Ibid., p. 289.

this quotation is the prayer of a priest whose piety seems to consist almost entirely in devotion to the cause of world democracy:

> Lord, who has created all men in the same image, do not allow despotism to deform thy work and maintain inequality upon the earth . . . arouse at last the French nation, that, forgetting the apathy in which its leaders lull, it may fight once more for the freedom of the world.[88]

One is left with the impression that this priest and the democratic Christianity he represents identify "the freedom of the world" with "the salvation of all men" for which Christ died. Thus Americans have preserved the agreement between religion and politics secured by a radical separation between religion and politics, but the terms have changed; the radical separation of worlds, asserted against the otherworldly interpretation of this world, seems to have provided the intellectual framework for a worldly interpretation of transcendence or for the spiritual pursuit of material ends.

No wonder, then, that Tocqueville expects less help from this "direct action of religion on politics" than from its "indirect action." That Tocqueville does not espouse the agreement of religion and politics as understood by the Puritans or their successors is unmistakable: "[I]t is just when [religion] is not speaking of freedom at all that it best teaches the Americans the art of being free."[89] It is not the freedom that comes from regarding "political principles, laws, and institutions as malleable things" subject to human manipulation that he supports, but the "certain and fixed" moral beliefs or "formalities" which serve as "insurmountable barriers" to this freedom.[90] In particular he praises the moral regularity of American women as essential to the perpetuation of an orderly society. Nevertheless, Tocqueville's final objective is no more to support the moral rigor of Americans than to encourage the formless freedom contained by that morality. Nor does he aim at a complete agreement of religion and democracy on the basis of their radical

---

[88]Ibid., pp. 289-90.
[89]Ibid., p. 290.
[90]Ibid., p. 292.

separation, for such an agreement could only take the form of a fuller identification of the salvation of the soul with the worldly liberation of mankind. If, therefore, Tocqueville favors the "joint reign" of religion and freedom under the banner of their separation as "the natural state of man with regard to religion at the present day,"[91] this is not because he believes religion and politics can really be separated. For he has shown that, where the political world is not understood as ordered by religious truth, then political ends are stripped of all concrete religious content but pursued all the more fervently as ultimate or religious ideals. Rather, Tocqueville endorses the democratic absorption of religion in America because he believes the union of religion and politics takes a less radical form there than among the "ardent adversaries"[92] of religion who, in Europe, attack belief with the zeal of true believers—"ardent adversaries" who may, in fact, be identified with those materialists who exhibit the pride of gods in reducing humanity to the level of brutes.

It is thus precisely because the agreement of religion and politics understood as the spiritual pursuit of material ends is incomplete in America that Tocqueville endorses it. The residue of positive Christianity presents an obstacle to the synthesis of idealism and materialism and thus preserves a space in which an older form of liberty or self-government, rooted in a long aristocratic experience, can survive:

> Religion, which never intervenes directly in the government of American society, should therefore be considered as the first of their political institutions, for, although it did not give them the taste for liberty, it singularly facilitates the use thereof.[93]

---

[91]Ibid., p. 299.
[92]Ibid., p. 300.
[93]Ibid., p. 292.

Pantheism and Mediation

That positive religion may serve as an obstacle to the synthesis of religion and politics, that is, to the spiritualization of the politics of worldly freedom, is confirmed by a further examination of Tocqueville's account of the intellectual paradigm of democracy in Volume Two, Part I, of *Democracy in America.* It is in a brief and at first rather puzzling chapter on the subject of Pantheism[94] that Tocqueville reveals the vanishing point of the democratic synthesis of religion and politics. The full title of the chapter is "What Causes Democratic Nations to Incline Toward Pantheism." "Pantheism," Tocqueville argues, is a form of thought that has begun to appear in German philosophy and French fiction, not for accidental reasons, but because it is the theoretical outlook toward which democracy drifts of its own accord; it is the final form of the democratic passion for universalization or "general ideas," and is thus "most fitted to seduce the mind in democratic ages."[95]

> The concept of unity becomes an obsession. Man looks for it everywhere, and when he thinks he has found it, gladly reposes in that belief. Not content with the discovery that there is nothing in the world but one creation and one Creator, he is still embarrassed by this primary division of things and seeks to expand and simplify his conception by including God and the universe in one great whole. If one finds a philosophical system which teaches that all things material and immaterial, visible and invisible, which the world contains are only to be considered as the several parts of an immense Being who alone remains eternal in the midst of the continual flux and transformation of all that composes Him, one may be sure that such a system, although it destroys human individuality, or rather just because it destroys it, will have secret charms for men living under democracies.[96]

---

[94]Ibid., vol. II, pt. I, chap. 7.
[95]Ibid., p. 452. See "On Democracy and Pantheism," chap. 4 of this book.
[96]*Democracy*, pp. 451-52.

The final achievement of the democratic passion for likeness or unity would thus consist in the obliteration of the only remaining representative of qualitative differentiation, and thus the last ground of human individuality: God. Tocqueville makes plain his attitude toward this deep temptation of the democratic intellect: "All those who still appreciate the true nature of man's greatness should combine in the struggle against it." The struggle against the consummation of the idealistic materialism of democracy in the pantheistic synthesis is thus one of Tocqueville's central purposes in *Democracy in America.*

Returning to the chapter on "Poetic Inspiration," it is clear that Tocqueville here describes the drift of democracy toward Pantheism, but without naming the final outcome. Indeed, he seems in one passage to describe the democratic mind as perched precariously on the edge of the cliff of radical monotheism that overlooks the abyss of pantheism:

> Just when every man, raising his eyes above his country, begins at last to see mankind at large, God shows himself more clearly to human perception in full and entire majesty.

Here the vision of the unity of God is practically but not explicitly identified with that of the unity of mankind. In the following paragraphs Tocqueville retreats slightly from this near-pantheistic version of the democratic imagination to a somewhat less radical statement, referring to "God's intervention in human affairs" and to "the universal and consistent plan by which God guides mankind."[97] Tocqueville thus seems to hope to employ the universalizing movement of democracy against itself by fixing the imagination of the democrat on that final stage of monotheistic progressivism in which, although the ends of God are almost wholly identified with the worldly progress of mankind, some distinction between God and the world persists.[98] As long as such a distinction exists, the claim of the democrat to see all mankind "in

---

[97]Ibid., p. 486.

[98]Cf. Manent: ". . . *pour appréhender sans vertige sa liberté illimitée . . . [le citoyen démocratique] doit se dédoubler et se réfléchir dans l'image de l'homme naturellement soumis à Dieu.*" Manent, *Tocqueville et la Nature*, p. 135.

broad daylight" is qualified and limited by reference to the point of view of a God who is not yet wholly transparent to him; as long as the distinction between God and the world exists, there is a point at which the restless democratic spirit "stops of its own accord."[99] Beyond this point, the poet has the opportunity "to connect the general designs of God for the universe and, without showing the hand of the Supreme Governor, reveal His thought." The name of God thus offers the poet of democracy a standpoint outside and potentially above democracy; it might therefore allow the poet to employ the idea of the indefinite perfectibility of man in the service of the idea of "the true nature of man's greatness."

To prevent the identification of the extreme of powerlessness with the extreme of power, and thus to teach democratic man how to stand up for himself, Tocqueville, as guide to democratic poets, must somehow locate "man's true greatness," a moderate kind of greatness that, because it is moderate, does not pass over into its opposite.

What is man's true greatness? And how can it be made visible to democratic man? Tocqueville offers no dogmatic teaching on these fundamental problems.[100] He offers only his example of deferring to the direct influence of Christian democracy in order to be able to preserve certain of its indirect consequences. He thus seems to have little hope of reversing the progress of general ideas, however "superficial and uncertain" they may be. Clearly there can be no question of reviving the "almost idolatrous" worship of angels and saints[101] or the poetry of gods and heroes[102] by which aristocratic man represented to himself the "intermediate powers between God and man." Perhaps because of this theoretical and rhetorical difficulty, Tocqueville generally indicates the gravity of the democratic problem of the missing middle only indirectly or in quite restricted contexts. Thus he provides a sort of image of the

---

[99]*Democracy*, p. 47.

[100]It is only because Zetterbaum assumes that Tocqueville's main purpose is dogmatic (that is, that Tocqueville aspires to produce a theory of politics in the modern sense) that he can then conclude that Tocqueville failed at this and thus finally had to fall back on Rousseauian myth-making. *Problem*, pp. 147, 158-60. But for Tocqueville, not all that is natural is within the compass of such theory.

[101]*Democracy*, vol. II, pt. I, chap. 5.

[102]Ibid., pt. II, chap. 17.

fundamental dilemma of the democratic mind in a chapter on the apparently peripheral subject of monuments:

> Thus democracy not only encourages the making of a lot of trivial things but also inspires the erection of a few very large monuments. However, there is nothing at all between these extremes.

Similarly, in chapter 18, Tocqueville takes up the apparently secondary subject of American oratory and finds the occasion to explain that American speakers and the writers who imitate them swing from the vulgar and banal to the bombastic, whereas "the space between is empty." Thus "they achieve gigantism, missing real grandeur." It is thus only after seeming to conclude his apparently sympathetic discussion of the poetic inspiration of democrats that Tocqueville discloses the key to interpreting that discussion:

> We have noted before that in democracies the springs of poetry are fine but few. . . . Finding no stuff for the ideal in what is real and true, poets, abandoning truth and reality, create monsters.

What was just presented as "the full and entire majesty of God" is thus identified with an ugly "gigantism," and the illumination "by exaggeration" of "certain dark corners of the human heart" appears as the creation of "monsters."

The concluding part (IV) of Volume II likewise shows the problem of the empty "space between" the democratic extremes to have a central importance, both intellectually and politically, that one might easily have failed to appreciate in earlier chapters. In undertaking a summary of the intellectual framework of democracy, Tocqueville begins by noting that "the idea of secondary powers, between sovereign and subject [which] was natural to the imagination of aristocratic peoples . . . can only be introduced artificially and retained with difficulty in a democracy."[103] The immediate context is political, but Tocqueville points here to a basic intellectual paradigm governing politics, philosophy, and religion.

---

[103]Ibid., p. 668.

In each of these manifestations of the democratic mind, "the idea of intermediate powers is obscured and obliterated."[104] This is the fundamental, intellectual cause of the primary political fact that so alarms Tocqueville: "The idea of rights inherent in certain individuals is rapidly disappearing from men's minds."

In reviewing the causes of this disappearance, Tocqueville clearly echoes earlier and apparently more favorable accounts of the democratic mind: Equality, he explains, seems to make men independent but soon brings them to accept equal and absolute dependence on a "huge entity which alone stands out above the universal level of abasement." Modern democratic man, like his intellectual champion, is thus described as "both proud and servile." The lack of an intellectual framework that would allow human beings to locate "the true greatness of man" somewhere in the space between absolute power and complete subjection thus threatens modern civilization with theoretical and practical squalor. The prospect of this squalor inspires in Tocqueville, as he notes in the general introduction, "a kind of religious dread."[105]

By now it should be clear that it is no accident that Tocqueville here describes his dread of the universal progress of democracy as religious.[106] Similarly, in discussing the ills of democratic revolutions in the next to last chapter of *Democracy in America,* he remarks that "there is always a danger of their becoming permanent or eternal."[107] If it were an easy matter to refute and replace the intellectual framework of democracy, if it were possible to give a dogmatic or scientific account of a distinctively human or intermediate form of greatness, then the danger and the dread would not be nearly so great. But man, in attempting to achieve the standpoint of God, either religiously or philosophically, destroys the secondary powers of aristocratic worlds until he is left with only

---

[104]Ibid., p. 669.

[105]Ibid., p. 12.

[106]Goldstein, in cautiously endorsing the view of Tocqueville as a "Christian moralist," completely overlooks this ambivalence toward the Christian idea of absolute transcendence (*Trial of Faith*, p. 125). That is, she simply identifies a "*Christian* philosophy of history" with a "belief in the superior desirability and effectiveness of *moral* forces" (emphasis added). Ibid., p. 123.

[107]*Democracy*, p. 700.

the pantheistic god of "continual flux," a god who can manifest himself only as destroyer of all that is unequal or distinct, all that stands up for itself.[108]

Tocqueville does not, however, succumb to the awesome power of this very religious and very rational dread. His critical examination of man's essential moral and political predicament, while it makes clear the impossibility of a complete theoretical or dogmatic articulation of what is highest in man, at the same time brings what is highest into view as the very standpoint from which inferior ways of life and thought are understood. In the last part of *Democracy in America,* therefore, Tocqueville concedes that his own elevated tastes cannot be grounded with any precision in the standpoint of God, but finds the courage to assert a human standpoint from which the democratic distribution of goods may not compensate for its debasement of the quality of those goods. Whatever one may say about a divine standpoint that must remain hypothetical, "no man on earth can affirm, absolutely and generally, that the new state of societies is better than the old."[109] And if Tocqueville attempts to enter into the perspective of the democratic poetry of Providence, it is not only to cultivate a moderate appreciation for the benefits it promises to provide, but especially to carve out a space within it in which to affirm the

---

[108]Cf. Manent's eloquent conclusion: *"[L'ami immodéré de la démocratie} sidere [l'humanité démocratique] par l'assurance vertigineuse de somnambule avec laquelle, dans chaque société, dans chaque institution, dans chaque homme, il met le pied, pour se soutenir en l'écrasant, sur tout ce qui est libre, sur tout ce qui est heureux, sur tout ce qui a forme humaine."* Manent, *Tocqueville et la Nature,* p. 181.

[109]*Democracy,* p. 704. Cf. Manent: *"Et ce qu'il sent dans son ame (la liberté humaine), il ne l'évacuera pas pour complaire au jugement supposé de Dieu"* (ibid., p. 175.

This would seem to supersede Manent's earlier judgment that Tocqueville failed to find an anchor for his defense of liberty independent of social conventions, aristocratic or democratic (p. 144). Manent may have arrived at this judgment by taking too seriously Tocqueville's conventional statements that such an anchor can only be religious or other-worldly (pp. 137-38). If liberty can be more than *simply* political, it perhaps can be less than simply other-worldly. Manent does not seem to see that the reason Tocqueville is content that Christianity and democracy should modify and compromise each other is that this compromise between twins (who must not learn that they are twins) is the condition of the compromise of both with, and the modification of both by, a third element—human liberty in the highest sense—that otherwise is threatened with extinction. Manent, in effect, finishes by exaggerating the practical identity in America of Christianity and democracy because he begins by exaggerating their theoretical separateness.

worth of goods it does not:

> Providence has, in truth, drawn a predestined circle around each man beyond which he cannot pass; but within those vast limits, man is strong and free, and so are peoples.[110]

In his study of human opinions about the meaning of human life, Tocqueville has discovered the impossibility of defending the honor of humanity from the standpoint of a radically transcendent God as well as from that of an abstract universal reason,[111] but he has also found reason to affirm that "the hierarchy of words" derives "from the very nature of things."[112] His confidence in the ground of his own true nobility, and the standard by which he strives to judge and mold his contemporaries, thus emerges along with a recognition of the impossibility of giving a full theoretical account of the noble. From his study of human things, Tocqueville, by some miracle, derives the insight and the courage needed to mediate between a God who does not speak directly to the political and moral life of man and a mankind that cannot bespeak its own humanity. Having learned that a humanity that takes itself too seriously may issue into the most insidious and extreme form of pride, he knows that he can only hope to save the souls of democrats and Christians by affirming, however indirectly, the natural grace of his own soul. Thus he remarks, in his preface to the second volume of *Democracy in America*, that success in the task he has set for himself is less important than "pursuing the undertaking in a spirit which could make me worthy of success."[113]

The essence of Tocqueville's politics and of his political use of religion is well summed up in an observation by Harold Laski:

> There is a fascinating sense in which the whole effort of his thought was to discover the secret of a social order in which there was scope for the manner of man he himself was.[114]

---

[110]*Democracy*, chap. II, pt. IV, chap. 8, p. 705.
[111]Ibid., pt. III, chap. 18.
[112]Ibid., vol. I, pt. I, chap. 16, p. 481.
[113]Ibid., p. 418.
[114]"Alexis de Tocqueville and Democracy," in *The Social and Political Ideas of Some*

Representative Thinkers of the Victorian Age, ed. F.J.C. Hearnshaw (Westport, Conn.: Greenwood Press, 1983), p. 114.

This remark seems to me to hold the key to integrating Tocqueville's concern for utility with his concern for truth, or for bringing together his "deeply personal" interest in religion with the concerns of "the man of knowledge" (Goldstein, *Trial of Faith*). See Ude, *Politik und Religion*, pp. 19-26, on the unity of theory and practice in Tocqueville's work.

Zetterbaum also quotes Laski's remark with approval (*Problem of Democracy*, p. 84). But this is hard to reconcile with his argument that the foundation of Tocqueville's view is a belief in natural rights as asserted by Hobbes and Locke (pp. 21-40) or that Tocqueville's ultimate objective is identical to Rousseau's (p. 92; see also pp. 159-60). Nor is it easy to reconcile these two arguments with Zetterbaum's belief that, for Tocqueville, there exists an "intelligible" common good that is "superior to private interests" (p. 98).

14

Rights: A Point of Honor

Delba Winthrop

Anglo-American moral philosophy has recently been spared the fate of degeneration into utilitarianism or death by positivism with an infusion of "rights." Contemporary rights theorists have attempted to recover or improve upon the theory and practice of liberal democracy by returning it to its proper beginning in rights. True, there has been disagreement about what these rights are, whether they are claims upon government or against government, and thus whether they justify a welfare state or a minimal state. Yet on both sides there is substantial agreement—and misunderstanding—about the nature of the rights that make liberal democracy worth reinvigorating. As I shall argue with the assistance of Tocqueville, prevailing theories of rights will ultimately only enervate liberal democracy.

For a variety of political and intellectual reasons, it is now fashionable to view politics from the perspective of rights.[1] Tocqueville, too, took rights seriously. He went so far as to insist that respect for individual rights is essential to democracy's

[1]Rights, of course, came into their own in academia with the publication of John Rawls's *A Theory of Justice*. The notion of rights was embraced by moral philosophers who saw it as a new value-neutral way of talking about values after other ways had been foreclosed by the authority of positivism. Since then, rights theories have been embraced by social scientists, economists, and law professors, each of whom could employ their peculiar intellectual tools in treating the subject. The political appeal of rights to lawyers and others initially was their obvious utility in promoting the welfare state. Robert Nozick then showed conservatives what advantages rights theories offered them.

preservation of liberty and human dignity.[2] Yet his understanding of rights differs considerably from ours. Most obviously, he asserts that the idea of rights is not democratic at all but, rather, aristocratic.[3] While urging the necessity of imbuing democracy with an idea of rights,[4] he contends that democracy is naturally hostile to individual rights.[5] At the same time, Tocqueville acknowledges that aristocracy ensured not rights, but privileges,[6] and he concedes the superiority of democracy to aristocracy with respect to justice.[7] Surely he knew that the theoretical justifications of rights, if not their historical origins, are to be found in the seventeenth and eighteenth-century political thought underlying the French and American Revolutions.[8] What, then, are we to make of Tocqueville's apparent—not to say, glaring—error concerning the origin of the very idea of rights? To make sense of it is to appreciate Tocqueville's critique of modern politics and of the opinions with which we attempt to sustain it.

Current notions of rights have two principal sources in the history of political philosophy, even though they depart from both of these sources. According to natural rights theories, propounded

---

[2]Alexis de Tocqueville, *De la démocratie en Amérique*, ed. J.-P. Mayer (Paris: 1961), vol. II, pt. IV, chap. 7, pp. 699-701. All quotations and page references are from *Democracy in America*, ed. J.-P. Mayer, trans. George Lawrence (Garden City, N.Y.: Doubleday, Anchor Books, 1969). Hereinafter cited as *Democracy*. The translation has been corrected where necessary.

[3]Ibid., vol. I, pt. I, chap. 2, p. 28; pt. II, chap. 4, pp. 192, 197; chap. 7, p. 258; vol. II, pt. IV, chap. 4, pp. 674-76.

[4]Ibid., vol. I, pt. II, chap. 6, pp. 236, 238, 239.

[5]Ibid., vol. II, pt. IV, chap. 2, p. 669; chap. 3, p. 673; chap. 7, p. 699.

[6]Ibid., vol. I, pt. II, chap. 6, p. 234. See also "*État social et politique de la France avant et depuis* 1789" in *L'Ancien régime et la révolution* (Paris: 1953), p. 62. Hereinafter cited as *L'Ancien régime*.

[7]*Democracy*, vol. II, pt. IV, chap. 8, p. 704; "*État social et politique de la France avant et depuis* 1789," p. 62.

[8]At the beginning of vol. II of *Democracy* (pt. I, chap. 1, pp. 429-33), Tocqueville traces the politics of revolutionary and post-revolutionary France to the philosophy of Descartes and his followers. He seems to deny that American politics has a basis in philosophy—the Americans are Cartesians without ever having read Descartes—but he ultimately contends only that pre-modern politics had first causes of its own: the eighteenth-century French employed "a philosophic method by which all ancient things could be attacked and the way opened for everything new" (p. 431). His denial that America ever had a democratic revolution, the obverse of his insistence that rights are our aristocratic heritage, may well explain his remarkable silence about America's Declaration of Independence.

most notably by Thomas Hobbes and John Locke and presupposed in the American Declaration of Independence, every human being has an equal natural right to his preservation and to a determination of the means of his preservation. All have this right because it is in the nature of a human being to be moved most powerfully by an aversion to his destruction, and no one can prove him wrong in this. Each human being always retains the right to his preservation, but all may transfer to one sovereign authority the right to determine the means thereunto. Politics, conducted by whomever and however many, is the means to the end of preservation or, effectively, of security and material prosperity. According to the moral philosophy of Immanuel Kant, however, the right of every human being is to the respect befitting a moral being possessed of a good will. The duty to grant this right universally follows from an understanding of what it means to think of a human being as the rational being each of us necessarily flatters himself to be. Politics secures the external freedom moral action presupposes; its end is nothing more nor less than provision of an equal opportunity to all who are supposed to be capable of morality, and therefore worthy of respect, to show themselves as moral.

Thus rights belong either to each and every natural human being or to each and every rational, moral being. In either case, the necessary beginning is the autonomous individual, equal to all other individuals in freedom. If human beings are by nature or by rational presumption free and equal, then every legitimate political order must originate in their mutual consent, actual or assumed. Every legitimate political order need not grant a right to equal political participation once a government has been consented to, however.

Today's rights theorists share these fundamental postulates of their predecessors. But they attempt to bridge the differences between them, combining Hobbes's essential concern for happiness with Kant's exclusive concern for dignity. The apparent disadvantages of Hobbes and Kant—the vulgarity of Hobbesian preservation and the austerity of Kantian moralism—are overcome by expanding our rights to the "primary goods" individuals might need to design and achieve "life plans." It is in designing and achieving life plans that human beings attain their proper dignity and happiness together. The goods acquired by, or distributed to, these choosers-of-life plans are theirs by right, and politics either protects or provides these economic and psychic goods, according as sympathies lie with the minimal state or the welfare state.

Tocqueville, no less than today's rights theorists, seems to accept the primacy of rights, and he too seeks to reconcile happiness ("interest") with dignity through the idea of rights. But his way is very different. What Tocqueville clearly saw and what he shows us in *Democracy in America* is that all theories meant to ground a politics defined by rights on a contract among autonomous and equal individuals are at least practically, if not theoretically, unsound. When these theories are adapted to political practice, they engender sentiments and ideas that almost inevitably vitiate individual liberty. The idea of rights can foster neither our true interests nor our dignity if interest and dignity are not linked through rights to self-government. Yet, for Tocqueville, even in modern liberal politics self-government ultimately requires an appeal not just to rights, but to a sense of honor. Honor, paradoxically, is the animus of pre-liberal, aristocratic politics. Thus for Tocqueville, protection of the rights that distinguish liberal democracies depends on a recollection of, and respect for, an understanding of politics that does not fit the mold of any current moral or political theory.

Tocqueville's endeavor to connect democratic rights to a sense of honor will succeed only if democrats can be made to feel the passions and appreciate the interests of aristocrats. But his endeavor ought to succeed only if he can adequately address two difficulties. First, honor, which is essentially conventional, must nonetheless not be altogether arbitrary. Second, honor, which is necessarily inegalitarian, must nonetheless be compatible with some plausible notion of democratic equality. I shall first explain how Tocqueville shows that liberal contract theories vitiate in practice the rights they assume in theory. I shall then show how Tocqueville suggests another, more adequate way of using the idea of rights to promote the well-being and dignity of human beings.

I

In his only thematic discussion of rights, Tocqueville links or equates them with virtues: "Next to virtue as a general idea, nothing, I think, is so beautiful as that of rights, and indeed the two ideas are mingled. The idea of rights is nothing but the conception of virtue applied to the world of politics."[9] Informed by it, every citizen can be "independent without arrogance and obedient without servility."[10] The idea of rights, we might say, makes possible the two political virtues of assertiveness or courage and moderation, virtues essential to self-government. Indeed, that idea is recommended as engendering "the spirit of the city"[11] and as animating political activity,[12] respect for law,[13] and enlightened patriotism.[14] Thus, for Tocqueville, rights are primarily political rights. They serve to conjoin human beings to one another in a civilized manner compatible with both liberty and dignity.[15]

Tocqueville also links rights to self-interest. More fundamentally, in a famous phrase he urges democratic moralists to propound the doctrine of self-interest well understood (*l'interet bien entendu*) as democracy's moral doctrine.

> I am not afraid to say that the doctrine of self-interest well understood appears to me the best suited of philosophical theories to the needs of men in our time. . . . Contemporary moralists therefore should give their attention principally to it. Though they may well judge it imperfect, they must nonetheless adopt it as necessary.[16]

Self-interest well understood is always preferable to self-interest grossly or wrongly understood, for individuals and perhaps for societies. What is peculiar to the modern era, however, is

---

[9]*Democracy*, vol. I, pt. II, chap. 6, pp. 237-38.
[10]Ibid., p. 238.
[11]Ibid., p. 236.
[12]Ibid., pp. 242-44.
[13]Ibid., pp. 240-41.
[14]Ibid., pp. 237-38.
[15]Ibid., p. 238; vol. II, pt. IV, chap. 7, p. 699.
[16]Ibid., vol. II, pt. II, chap. 8, p. 527.

the need not merely for self-interest well understood, but for a *doctrine* of self-interest, a "philosophical theory." How this theory links rights or political virtue to self-interest and what its effects on democratic politics are constitute a major theme of Volume II of *Democracy*.

As Tocqueville's democratic moralists formulate the doctrine of self-interest well understood, it engenders habits of regularity, temperance, moderation, foresight, and self-mastery—habits without which morality, political stability, and even social intercourse are impossible.[17] Although not self-evident in all respects,[18] the doctrine is effective because it is "clear and definite" and "wonderfully suited to human weaknesses."[19]

The doctrine of self-interest is intended to turn self-interest against itself. Tocqueville anticipates that calculations of self-interest are ever more likely to become the basis of all actions, so a morality based on self-interest must somehow replace "the sublime conception of the duties of man" that sustained "instinctive virtues" by recommending "the beauties of virtue" and the glory of self-forgetting.[20] Looking to put something more suitable in its stead, democratic moralists seek an example in which acting for a common interest is also to one's personal advantage, present their discovery as a general rule, and persuade their fellows to sacrifice some of their private interests to the public for the sake of preserving the rest. They do not argue that virtue is beautiful and sacrifice grand, but that these are useful.[21] They insist not that what is good is also useful, but that "what is useful is never wrong."[22] So instructed, Americans deny that they are ever moved to act "by the disinterested, spontaneous impulses natural to man," preferring "to honor their philosophy rather than themselves."[23]

Democratic moralists begin with self-interest because they know they must. Because they are too cowardly, they do not go

---

[17]Ibid., pp. 527-28; cf. vol. I, pt. II, chap. 6, pp. 237-39.
[18]Ibid., vol. II, pt. II, chap. 8, p. 528.
[19]Ibid., pp. 526-27.
[20]Ibid., pp. 525, 528.
[21]Ibid., p. 525.
[22]Ibid., p. 527.
[23]Ibid., p. 526.

beyond self-interest.[24] Americans are individualists.[25] By individualism, Tocqueville does not mean mere egoism, or excessive self-love. Self-love is a natural, universal passion. Individualism is a new, democratic opinion, a greatly exaggerated opinion of self-sufficiency. When conditions are roughly equal, as they are in a democracy, everyone has some wealth and some education, while no one has much. Each man is tempted to think he has enough to get along by himself, without the help of others. He is not tempted to think he has enough to assert authority over others, or to allow that anyone else is so privileged as to assert authority or even influence over him. Men set their ambitions and extend their concern no further than their powers, and their powers rarely exceed provision for their own needs and those of their families. Because they wish to think of themselves as self-sufficient wholes, neither do their thoughts soar above their powers.

This "erroneous judgment" of individualism[26] is, however, not merely a consequence of democracy, but its premise.

> Providence has given each individual the amount of reason necessary for him to look after himself in matters of his own exclusive concern. That is the great maxim on which civil and political society in the United States rests. . . . Extended to the nation as a whole, it becomes the dogma of the sovereignty of the people.
>
> Thus in the United States the creative principle underlying the republic is the same as that which controls the greater part of human actions.[27]

Nowhere does Tocqueville name the source of the judgment of individualism. He does point out that the Americans are exemplary Cartesians without ever having read Descartes.[28] Similarly, they seem to have made the principles of the state of nature, as described by natural rights theorists, the basis of their society. Or

---

[24]Ibid., p. 525.
[25]Ibid., chap. 2, pp. 506-08.
[26]Ibid., p. 506.
[27]Ibid., vol. I, pt. II, chap 10, p. 397.
[28]Ibid., vol. II, pt. I, chap. 1, p. 429.

rather, they try to make them the essence of their society.[29] The Americans described by Tocqueville would live as self-sufficient individuals even in society; that is, they would live in society as men live in the pre-social, pre-political state of nature of Hobbes and Locke. In contrast to the individuals of contract theory, these of modern (democratic) practice[30] do not leave the state of nature once and for all. Their departure is reenacted on each and every occasion of social activity. Indeed, they must be shown that *each* departure is necessary or that it is in the self-interest of *each* would-be individual to act collectively *now*. This is the task of the American doctrine of self-interest well understood, designed to "combat individualism" and used to facilitate the "associations" without which civilization is imperiled.[31]

To repeat, American, or modern democratic, moral doctrine is meant to overcome individualism and encourage association. That it is a doctrine of self-interest well understood is as much the statement of a problem as a solution to it. Not merely the practice, but the theory underlying modern democracy lends credence to a misguided presumption of individual autonomy. Tocqueville's appreciation of this problem leads him to elevate the right of association among rights[32] and to place exaggerated emphasis on "artificially" created associations for democracy's social and political well-being, not to mention civilization's survival. Only after creating and re-creating associations of all sorts can democratic individuals go about the usual business of people who have not been taught to take seriously the political theorists' state of nature. "Associating" is what politics and civilized life are all about. In presenting his analysis of associations, Tocqueville forces us to ask whether the modern moral doctrine of self-interest well understood is up to its self-defined task.

Theories notwithstanding, Tocqueville's Americans seem to

---

[29]See Pierre Manent, *Tocqueville et la nature de la démocratie* (Paris: 1982), pp. 46-48.

[30]Tocqueville identifies all of modern politics with the democratic politics of which he speaks (*Democracy*, vol. II, pt. III, chap. 26, p. 663; cf. vol. II, pt. IV, chap. 8, pp. 704-05).

[31]Ibid., vol. II, pt. II, chap. 8, p. 525; chap. 5, p. 514.

[32]Ibid., vol. I, pt. II, chap. 4, p. 193.

excel at creating associations.

> Americans of all ages, all stations of life, and all types of disposition are forever forming associations. There are not only commercial and industrial associations in which all take part, but others of a thousand different types—religious, moral, serious, futile, very general and very limited, immensely large and very minute. Americans combine to give fetes, found seminaries, build churches, distribute books, and send missionaries to the antipodes. Hospitals, prisons, and schools take shape in that way. Finally, if they want to proclaim a truth or propagate some feeling by the encouragement of a great example, they form an association. In every case, at the head of any new undertaking, where in France you would find the government or in England some territorial magnate, in the United States you are sure to find an association.[33]

They associate for economic, social, political, and even moral and intellectual ends. In doing so, they should acquire an "art" and a "science" of associating.[34] Economic and social (or quasi-economic) associations are generated easily enough by a kind of sympathy compatible with democratic self-preoccupation. "Equality which makes men feel their freedom also shows them their weakness. They are free, but liable to a thousand accidents, and experience is not slow to teach them that although they may not usually need the help of others, a moment will always arrive when they cannot do without it."[35] Anticipating their own necessity, they can put themselves in the place of others who are in the tough situations in which they fear to find themselves someday. So they sympathize and come to one another's aid.

Economic and social associations enable democratic individuals to meet daily needs that they could not meet individually. But these associations occur by chance and are of short duration.[36] Even

---

[33]Ibid., vol. II, pt. II, chap. 5, p. 513; cf. vol. I, pt. II, chap. 4, p. 189; vol. I, pt. II, chap. 6, p. 242.

[34]Ibid., vol. II, pt. II, chap. 5, pp. 514, 517, 522.

[35]Ibid., pt. III, chap. 4, p. 571.

[36]Ibid., pt. II, chap. 7, p. 520; pt. III, chap. 7, p. 582.

though often successful, they involve risks and promise limited benefits.[37] They neither enlarge self-interest nor set sights beyond provision for common immediate needs. These associations for little objects enable participants to perfect the technique of associating.[38] But they do not provide a strong incentive for making the effort, especially if citizens believe their needs could be met in some other way.[39]

It is in politics, not economics, Tocqueville contends, that individualism becomes truly incredible.[40] Here the necessity of associating, the vast numbers and therefore the power of associates, and the importance of the ends at stake should be obvious. So it is above all in political association that the art of associating will be acquired.

A political association like the New England township of which Tocqueville speaks at length, is "a true association permanently established by law."[41] It is, at the same time, "coeval with humanity," "the only association . . . well rooted in nature."[42] It is sustained by a "spirit of liberty" independent not only of transient passions, interests, and circumstances, but also of rational calculations of how interests are most efficiently served.[43] The township's free political institutions "are to liberty what primary schools are to science."[44] Participating in them, citizens acquire a taste for freedom and learn its habits. In Tocqueville's New England township, citizens meet frequently to discuss public business and serve for short tenures in numerous elective offices. The link between self-interest and a stable general good is made visible, as when all citizens vote to impose a tax on themselves to pay for a new school that benefits the children of each and all. Here, too, one can see that choices have an effect on the world: the school they chose to build stands. "Americans," Tocqueville says, "love their towns for

---

[37]Ibid., vol. II, pt. II, chap. 7, p. 521.
[38]Ibid.
[39]Ibid., chap. 5, p. 515.
[40]Ibid., chap. 7, p. 521.
[41]Ibid., chap. 6, p. 518; vol. I, pt. II, chap. 4, p. 189.
[42]Ibid., vol. I, pt. I, chap. 5, p. 62.
[43]Ibid., pp. 62-63.
[44]Ibid., pp. 63.

much the same reason that highlanders love their mountains. In both cases the native land has emphatic and peculiar features; it has a more pronounced physiognomy than is found elsewhere."[45] The township is individual self-government writ large.[46]

The township's self-governing institutions are supported by a "spirit of liberty." They arouse or accommodate political passions. At the least, self-assertiveness in making claims on others is shown to be useful and respectable, hence desirable. At best, will is rationalized as it is asserted, for the township limits ambition, even as it encourages it. In the assembly attended by all voting adults, self-interest is linked through deliberation to a common good. In the numerous offices designed to fulfill specific duties, personal ambition is attached to the performance of these duties, and public opinion demands respect for this performance. "In [this] restricted sphere . . . [the townsman] learns to rule society; he . . . develops a taste for order, understands the harmony of powers, and in the end accumulates clear, practical ideas about the nature of his duties and the extent of his rights."[47] One clear, practical idea accumulated is that rights are coextensive with civic duties.

While the township is the primary school of liberty, political associations like parties are "great free schools to which all citizens come to be taught the general theory of association."[48] Political parties do not require a sacrifice of self-interest nor do they suppose an identification of it with the interests of all. Hence they are "free schools"; they make demands neither onerous nor unreasonable. Rather, parties unite similarly interested selves to advance their common interest. The self-interested ambition of individuals is enlarged to partisanship. At the same time, it is recognized as partisan, as merely partial. In the township it was still possible to identify the interest of an overwhelming majority with the common good simply.[49] In party politics it becomes clear for all to see that human beings have different sentiments and

---

[45]Ibid., p. 69.
[46]Cf. ibid., p. 61.
[47]Ibid., p. 70.
[48]Ibid., vol. II, pt. II, chap. 7, p. 522.
[49]Ibid., vol. I, pt. I, chap. 5, p. 70. In the township "injustices which affect only isolated individuals are forgotten in the general contentment."

ideas, all of which must be given a hearing before we can determine what the common good is, or even whether there is a good that is truly common. We learn, among other things, about the partisanship of democracy itself—the regime that first insists that all citizens are equal and similar, even if they are not, and then serves the interests of the majority, not of all.[50]

The core of an association, according to Tocqueville, is a newspaper.[51] A newspaper articulates the sentiments and ideas of its readers; an association is comprised of readers who share sentiments and ideas and for whom communication with one another would otherwise be difficult. There is, Tocqueville insists, not only a necessary correlation between associations and newspapers, but between newspapers and local self-government. The number of newspapers will be proportionate to the extent of political decentralization; and in America the number of newspapers is "enormous."[52] The ostensible reason for the connection between newspapers and political liberty is that people who are required to conduct public affairs must be informed about them. But why need there be an enormous number of newspapers through which to share particular sentiments and ideas? An enormous number is needed only if the necessity of acting politically brings to light a truth otherwise obscured in democracy's economic associations; namely, that the sentiments and thoughts of human beings can vary greatly.

Tocqueville calls to his reader's special attention associations less obvious than economic and political associations: America's moral and intellectual associations. Through these, "feelings and ideas are renewed, the heart enlarged, and the understanding developed . . . by the reciprocal action of men one upon another."[53] The repeated example of a moral and intellectual association is the temperance society.[54] At first Tocqueville thought a society of 100,000 members publicly pledged to abstinence from alcoholic beverages was a joke. Why not just sit at home, self-righteously

---

[50]Ibid., vol. I, pt. II, chap. 6, p. 241.
[51]Ibid., vol. II, pt. II, chap. 6, p. 518.
[52]Ibid., p. 518-19.
[53]Ibid., chap. 5, p. 515.
[54]Ibid., p. 516; vol. I, pt. II, chap. 6, p. 242.

sipping Perrier? We, in turn, might be surprised at Tocqueville's suggestion that a temperance society is an intellectual association. But inebriation is the characteristic problem of American democracy, manifest above all in the erroneous judgment of individualism. Democrats, like drunks, may feel independence but display only dependence. Their failing is intellectual as well as moral when they do not see the need for associations.[55] Each democratic association is a human artifice that is not formed either by immediate perception of necessity or by mere habit. An act of will is required to establish and maintain it, as is a choice of an end for which to associate. To the extent that it is chosen, each association is both moral and intellectual.

For the same reason, democratic associations are also "political." When Tocqueville marvels at the amount of political activity in America, he mentions diverse, seemingly nonpolitical activities: building churches, planning roads and schools, forming temperance societies.[56] In each case the real activity taking place, for whatever end, is speaking or deliberating in common. The art of association perfected and practiced in political association by Tocqueville's Americans is the knowing and willing pursuit in common of shared, though partial, interests. But association is said to be completed by a science as well as an art. The science of association might emerge only when the full range of human sentiments and ideas is brought to light by associations. Then sober reflection on the variety of sentiments and ideas and a determination of which might be worthy of pursuit can begin. For Tocqueville, associations are necessary above all to reveal what human nature is and what is possible for it, so as to enable us to ponder mankind's true interests.

American moralists intend their "imperfect" doctrine of self-interest well understood to encourage association by combating individualism. In combating individualism, however, they inadvertently undermine individuality in such a way as to discourage association. Even without a doctrine, democratic citizens would realize soon enough that they are not self-sufficient and that they

---

[55]Ibid., vol. II, pt. II, chap. 5, p. 516.
[56]Ibid., vol. I, pt. II, chap. 6, p. 242.

must either associate with one another to pursue interests effectively or rely on an external power to meet their everyday needs. Indeed, the economic and quasi-economic associations that tend to proliferate are "almost unintentional."[57] But what of associations to meet other needs, less keenly or less universally felt, but no less essential?

Democracy's would-be individuals become accustomed to pursuing their interests in a certain way, and they are constrained to associate with one another according to democratic forms. With its fixed customs and forms, democracy makes it difficult for individuals properly to understand a "self" and to become aware of the full range of the self's possible interests. Democratic moralists who suit their teachings to human weaknesses share responsibility for democracy's deficient self-understanding. The effectual truth of their doctrine of self-interest well understood is an exacerbation of democracy's self-destructive tendency to turn inflated self-esteem into self-depreciation.

Each democratic individual "pretends . . . to judge the world" for himself,[58] wishing to defer to the opinions of no one else, present or past. But even under the best conditions, no man arrives by himself at knowledge of everything he needs to know in order to live his life, much less to judge the lives of others. Almost insensibly, democratic individuals come to put their trust not in themselves, but in a public opinion that seems to have been formed by no one in particular, or by no one easily identified. Not the choices of individuals, but an unreflective, unassailable mass opinion reigns over democracy. Few individuals feel qualified to challenge it, fewer are courageous enough to attempt the challenge, and virtually none can expect to succeed.[59] Democrats can act as if they understood their interest well only if democratic public opinion embodies that sound understanding.

Democratic public opinion holds to three dogmas: individualism, egalitarianism, and materialism. Equality, that is, an equal ability to judge one's own interests, is the necessary presupposition

[57]Ibid., vol. II, pt. III, chap. 4, p. 572.
[58]Ibid., pt. I, chap. 1, p. 430.
[59]Ibid., chap. 2, pp. 433-36; pt. III, chap. 21, pp. 640-45.

of both individualism and democratic politics. But democratic peoples also make "equality of condition" (what we today call "equality of result") an end. After all, if individuals are equal in the most important respect, why should they not have equal results to show for equal exertions? In truth, equality endears itself especially to those who do not care to exert themselves much at all. Democracy's would-be individuals, Tocqueville contends, love equality because they can take it for granted, because it does bring to all daily small pleasures, and because the pleasures of equality are bought with little expenditure of effort.[60]

Just as individualism and egalitarianism have the same root, so they nourish and are nourished by materialism. The equality of intellect democracy posits is, in fact, contrary to nature.[61] If it can be assumed, it can never be achieved. Intellectual accomplishments could be fully equalized only by being hindered, not by being pursued. People might—and once did—take a more or less equal interest in the well-being of their immortal souls, finding their satisfaction in piety.[62] But this supposed great good is too doubtful or too far off or too hard-earned to inspire democrats. Not even America's clergy, much less her moral philosophers, insist that this good be pursued as an end in itself.[63] But the well-being or comfort of their bodies does recommend itself as an end for democrats. Enjoyment of physical pleasures is individual, and all are equally capable of it.

All human beings necessarily take some interest in their physical survival and comfort. But democratic individuals, who are, by definition, equally able to attend to their own affairs, must also take an interest in the preservation of their capacities for independent judgment and action. They can never pursue one interest so that it endangers the others. To do so, however, is precisely what the democrat is inclined to believe is in his interest.[64]

The Americans Tocqueville observed were "preoccupied caring

---

[60]Ibid., vol. II, pt. II, chap. 1, pp. 503-06.

[61]Ibid., vol. I, pt. I, chap. 3, p. 56; vol. II, pt. II, chap. 13, p. 538.

[62]Ibid., vol. II, pt. II, chap. 10, p. 531.

[63]Ibid., pt. I, ch. 5, pp. 448-49; pt. II, chap. 9, p. 530.

[64]Ibid., pt. II, chap. 15, p. 543.

for the slightest needs of the body and the trivial conveniences of life."[65] To their credit, American moralists do urge everybody to forgo a thousand passing pleasures for the sake of enduring happiness in this world.[66] But someone might ask, in response, what the enduring happiness of a mortal body is. Proselytizing nonsmokers notwithstanding, it is not all that clear that human beings act reasonably in seeking the preservation of the body at the expense of its passing pleasures, for it is not clear that the body can experience any sensation that is not passing.

Tocqueville's Americans are not happy. They are "grave and almost sad" in their ardent, yet soft materialism.[67] Because they think happiness can be nothing but the experience of the mortal body's pleasures, they fret under the awareness that they have a limited time within which to experience happiness. So while they methodically pursue desire after desire, they are saddened at the thought of not tasting all pleasures. The Americans find no happiness in their pleasures because they know their desires for pleasure cannot be satiated.

To the extent that the Americans regulate their petty desires, they tend to seek life's rewards by means of commercial and industrial careers.[68] In democracy, everyone seeks wealth, and no one can afford to take it for granted. So men chose risky, lucrative occupations that promise to bring them great wealth quickly. In particular, industrial enterprise seems to present an opportunity for those with ambition and genius. Since the efficient maximization of material goods in any society is subject to two laws of economics, division of labor and concentration of capital, workers concern themselves with putting heads on pins while owners find themselves conducting vast enterprises. In utilizing as much daring and intelligence as their tasks require, captains of industry perfect their faculties. Workers lose theirs through disuse. In this way a permanent inequality—of ability as well as condition—between "masters" and workers is created, and democracy issues in a new

---

[65]Ibid., chap. 10, p. 530.
[66]Ibid., chap. 9, p. 528.
[67]Ibid., chap. 13, p. 536.
[68]Ibid., chap. 19, pp. 551-52.

industrial aristocracy.[69] To restate this point, if men posit their end as material well-being and act most effectively in pursuit of it, democratic equality will be undermined. Thus democratic desires for material well-being and equality are not only insatiable, but contradictory.

Tocqueville remarks that whereas in France the suicide rate is increasing alarmingly, in America madness is common, and that these are symptoms of the same malady.[70] The Americans cannot wish to deny that man is a rational animal, a being who reasons about how to satisfy desires, if not about which desires he ought to satisfy. If Americans choose to act almost like brutes, satisfying only the needs instinct might dictate, as they do when thoughtlessly pursuing material well-being, they risk the loss of the capacities that distinguish men from brutes.[71] If the Americans reasoned about their situation, they would conclude that their inadequate understanding of their interests endangers their very selves. Instead, the strength of their desires or the absence of an explicit and forceful correction of them causes the Americans to abandon reason—to go mad. Tocqueville likens madness to suicide because it, too, means the destruction of man as a rational animal.

If democratic public opinion recommends interests that are self-destructive, it also requires men to associate in ways that make it almost impossible for them to acquire the self-understanding that might alert them to the destruction that threatens them. Democracy gives people similar habits and opinions, puts them in more or less equal social and economic conditions, and makes them believe they are equal.[72] So merely by casting "a rapid glance" at themselves and imagining themselves in the place of another, they can appreciate his sufferings.[73] Sensing their own needs, they attribute them to another who, as an equal, must also feel them. Their sympathy accords with their perception of their self-interest because they perceive themselves as weak individuals. "There is a

---

[69]Ibid., chap. 20, pp. 555-58.
[70]Ibid., chap. 13, p. 538.
[71]Ibid., chap. 16, pp. 546-47.
[72]Ibid., vol. II, pt. III, chap. 5, pp. 576-77.
[73]Ibid., chap. 1, p. 564.

sort of tacit and almost unintentional agreement between them which provides that each owes to the other a temporary assistance which he in turn can claim at need."[74]

Democracy's most common associations are thus made possible by a dogmatic belief in human equality and a preoccupation with need rather than ability. As Tocqueville makes clear, the American neither knows nor cares to know much about his fellow citizens.[75] He judges others poorly because he has never experienced or reflected on the need for knowledge of the variety of human natures. Lacking this knowledge, he relies on democratic dogma to define his relations to others. He simply assumes that the most obvious needs are universal and that these make people equal. Nor does the American know much about himself. His self-knowledge consists in an awareness that he, too, is subject to these universal human necessities.

Precisely the cognizance that urges the utility of democratic associations undermines their very possibility. Because democrats are preoccupied with their material well-being, the associations they most frequently seek are economic. Individuals need to associate because they are weak, and they will associate when they can anticipate that it will be in their self-interest to have assisted another. But how can this calculation be relied upon? Mutual assistance is not a matter of duty and right.[76] Nor can a collection of weak individuals be supposed to be all that strong. Were any one individual strong enough to be of real help, he would only be suspected as privileged, envied, and hated.[77] Consequently,

> . . . the citizen of a democracy develops extremely contradictory instincts. He is full of confidence and pride in his independence among his equals, but from time to time his weakness makes him feel the need for some outside help which he cannot expect from any of his fellows, for they are both impotent and cold. In this extremity, he naturally turns his eyes toward that huge entity which alone stands

---

[74]Ibid., chap. 4, pp. 572.
[75]Ibid., chap. 3, pp. 567-71.
[76]Ibid., pt. IV, chap. 3, p. 672.
[77]Ibid., pp. 672-73.

> out above the universal level of abasement [that is, the government]. His needs, and even more his longings, continually put him in mind of that entity, and he ends by regarding it as the sole and necessary support of his individual weakness.[78]

He, himself, finds little time away from business to spare for the conduct or oversight of the affairs of this huge and powerful entity. He loses interest in both economic and political associations. Eventually, the very idea of an association as a "secondary power" standing between individual and central power becomes, so to speak, inconceivable.[79]

Tocqueville's worst fear for democracy is that it will degenerate into little more than the benevolent despotism we now call big government. While the government meets the perceived needs of citizens, it ultimately deprives them of "several of the chief attributes of humanity,"[80] namely, the will and reason sustained and developed in associations. Democratic political equality comes to mean equal political apathy and consequent impotence and servitude.[81] The democratic despotism Tocqueville foresees differs from the modern welfare state not in the range and scope of the services it seeks to perform for citizens, but in the absence of economic and social demands as claims of right. Tocqueville's democrats willingly surrender individual rights in return for satisfaction of their wants. The impetus to democratic despotism is the desire of democratic individuals to secure their interests as they understand them. Good intentions notwithstanding, democratic moralists who espouse the doctrine of self-interest well understood effectively recommend rather than oppose this despotism when they concede that whatever is useful must be good.

Tocqueville observed that with their doctrine of self-interest well understood, American moralists persuade people to sacrifice some of their interests to save the rest. The part of their interest democrats are inclined and encouraged to sacrifice is their interest in

---

[78]Ibid., p. 672.
[79]Ibid., chap. 2, p. 668.
[80]Ibid., chap. 7, p. 695.
[81]Ibid., chap. 2, p. 668; chap. 7, p. 702.

whatever does not immediately strike them as useful; namely, the honorable and beautiful.[82] They surrender their rights to these in exchange for provision for their most obvious needs. They cultivate only the virtues without which no society can be preserved, not the ones that bring dignity to human beings.[83] Given this assessment of our situation and prospects, we could well join contemporary moral philosophers in faulting utilitarianism, as they do. But we could endorse their reintroduction of an interest in rights only if they appreciated the necessity and possibility of preserving democratic selves by ennobling as well as interesting them.

II

The doctrine of self-interest well understood that Tocqueville describes is essentially that of natural rights theorists. Its ignobility had already been recognized by Kant, who sought to imbue rights with moral dignity by making them independent of self-interest. Although Kantian idealism had barely begun to be taken up by America's popular moralists, Tocqueville's analysis allows us to see the deficiencies of these theories as well. Kantian (and today's so-called Kantian) rights theories, like the natural rights theories, posit a contract made by autonomous and equal individuals in a pre-political condition. In these theories, too, respect for the rights of each is a requirement of justice, though now dictated by an *a priori,* disinterested reason. One's dignity depends essentially on fulfillment of this requirement. Tocqueville might well have asked whether this understanding allows for motives strong enough to sustain the exercise of rights. For him, rights have less to do with justice than with honor, and in the first instance they are not deduced from reason, but express an instinct or taste.

Tocqueville pleads that the idea of rights be linked in the modern world to personal interest. He means that interest, not piety or a sense of duty, must become the principal motive for claiming, exercising, and conceding rights. But he also means that human beings do not understand their interest well if they do not take an

---

[82]Ibid., pt. I, chap. 11, p. 465; pt. II, chap. 8, p. 525.

[83]Ibid., vol. II, pt. II, chap. 11, pp. 533-34; pt. III, chap 19, p. 632; chap. 21, p. 645.

interest in rights. Democrats, he notes, will ill preserve their liberty, not to mention their dignity, if not given "the rights and a political spirit that suggests to each citizen some of the interests that influence the behavior of nobles in aristocracies."[84] If the aristocratic noble cannot strictly be said to have had an "interest" in political rights, he surely had a taste for them.[85] That taste prompted him to claim and preserve his rights with far more passion than do most democrats. In order to see how Tocqueville could have said that rights are of aristocratic origin and to grasp somewhat more clearly the kind of interest to which rights must be linked, we must consider some aspects of the political demeanor of Tocqueville's aristocrats.

In aristocratic ages, obedience without servility and independence without arrogance were sustained by the serf's religious beliefs and the noble's judgment of what duty and honor required of him.[86] The official moral doctrine of aristocracy held it to be "a glorious thing to forget oneself and . . . to do good without self-interest, as does God himself."[87] In fact, however, Tocqueville's aristocrats are not as selfless as gods. Nor is their virtue, as distinguished from the serfs', grounded in piety. Aristocratic demeanor is formed by a regard for honor, not merely duty, and graced by a love of beauty.[88] While the Americans believe that both justice and honor are deduced from self-interest,[89] aristocrats deny that they are ever moved by any consideration but honor.[90] And though they may study in silence the utility of virtue, they speak incessantly of its beauty.[91] Unlike the Americans, they do not reduce the beautiful to the useful.[92] As we have seen, self-interest as understood by democrats and as partially obscured by the democratic fancy of

---

[84]Ibid., vol. II, pt. III, chap. 26, p. 663.

[85]In *Democracy*, Tocqueville does not use the word "interest" in any precise or technical sense. Only later, in *The Old Regime*, does he deliberately contrast it to instinct or taste.

[86]Ibid., vol. II, pt. III, chap. 1, p. 562.

[87]Ibid., pt. II, chap. 8, p. 525.

[88]Ibid., pt. I, chap. 10, p. 462; chap. 17, p. 483; pt. III, chap. 14, p. 608.

[89]Ibid., vol. I, pt. II, chap. 10, p. 374.

[90]Ibid., chap. 18, p. 550.

[91]Ibid., vol. II, pt. II, chap. 8, p. 525.

[92]Ibid., pt. I, chap. 11, p. 465.

equality[93] leads naturally to despotism.[94] Self-interest as understood or denied by aristocrats and as veiled by aristocracy's ennobling and beautifying forms leads to an exaggerated respect for particular rights.[95]

In the modern world, opinions that rights are either "divine" or "moral" are not credible, so the idea of rights must be linked to interest.[96] We link rights to interest through the notion of contract. By means of contracts, individuals freely consent to provide for their mutual needs in relations of temporary inequality while still retaining an illusion of equal self-sufficiency.[97] It is Tocqueville who best teaches us to appreciate how the notion of contract and an opinion of its justice spare us from degrading, demoralizing confrontations with necessity.[98] Yet he rejects the premises of theories that posit contracts as the origin of morality.

Tocqueville speaks of natural rights,[99] but he emphatically, if tacitly, denies that there was a state of nature (or an original position or any other pre-political condition) in which rights

---

[93]Ibid., pt. III, chap. 5, p. 577.

[94]Ibid., pt. IV, chap. 2, p. 669; chap. 3, p. 673; chap. 7, p. 699.

[95]Ibid., chap. 7, p. 701.

[96]Ibid., vol. I, pt. II, chap. 6, p. 239. Tocqueville attributes to the American Puritans the opinion that their rights were divine in origin (vol. I, pt. I, chap. 2, p. 47). He elaborates no further on moral notions of rights than he does in the passage in vol. II, pt. III, chap. 1, p. 602, in which rights are identified as political, not natural, and their support said to lie either in piety or in duty and honor.

[97]Ibid., vol. II, pt. III, chap. 5, p. 576.

[98]Ibid., p. 579.

[99]The natural rights of which Tocqueville speaks are the rights of parents to direct and educate their children (ibid., vol. I, pt. I, chap. 3, p. 45; vol. II, pt. III, chap. 8, p. 586), of a magistrate to choose among legal provisions that which binds him most tightly (vol. I, pt. I, chap. 6, p. 102), of a judicial tribunal to punish agents of the executive power when they violate the law (p. 104). The most natural and perhaps inalienable rights are of individual liberty and then of association (vol. I, pt. II, chap. 4, p. 193). Nature's own rights are expressed as indomitable sexual passion (vol. I, pt. II, chap. 10, pp. 343-44). Familial rights are also said to be sacred, as are property rights (Preface, p. xiv), and the right of society to choose the law that binds it is said to be more sacred than the magistrate's natural right to choose (vol. I, pt. I, chap. 6, p. 102). The Puritans saw religion as the divine source of their rights (vol. I, pt. I, chap. 2, p. 47), and rights must now be linked to interest because divine and moral notions of rights have been undermined (vol. I, pt. II, chap. 6, p. 239). Thus it is not as clear as Zetterbaum suggests that Tocqueville's adoption of the idea of rights is an adoption of natural rights. Marvin Zetterbaum, *Tocqueville and the Problem of Democracy*, (Stanford, Cal.: Stanford University Press, 1967), p. 39.

originated.[100] For it is the conception of an original, pre-political existence that makes possible the erroneous judgment of individualism and can easily be interpreted to recommend egalitarianism and materialism. Thus for Tocqueville, rights can be neither the natural rights of Hobbes and Locke nor the rational constructs of Kantians and contemporary rights theorists. He says rights are our aristocratic inheritance. Yet he observes that aristocrats think of what are, in truth, their inherited privileges or "political rights"[101] as "parts of themselves, or at least as natural rights and inherent in their persons."[102] While consciously portraying mankind's natural condition as a political condition, he concedes the power of the opinion that rights have a ground in nature and do not merely subsist by aristocratic or democratic convention.

Just as Tocqueville gives no clear account of the origin of rights, he gives no precise definition of the virtue of which rights are the political manifestation. In the first volume of *Democracy,* he remarks that the idea of rights makes possible "independen[ce] without arrogance and obedien[ce] without servility." In the second volume, he comes close to identifying political virtue with courage.[103] (The doctrine of self-interest well-understood, he acknowledges, is conducive to moderation [*supra,* page 392].) But courage is sustained only by honor. Both courage and honor, he stresses, assume different forms in different times and places. Yet if honor is conventional, it is never simply arbitrary. If rights are identified with political virtue and thereby made to depend on honor, their natural ground is in whatever need or needs generate a code of honor. Tocqueville cannot give a clear account of the origin of

---

[100]Not only did the Anglo-Americans arrive with a fully developed civilization, but even the noble savages they encountered on arrival are said to be descended from a once-superior civilization (*Democracy,* vol. I, pt. I, chap. 1, pp. 29-30). Neither Tocqueville's query about what ought to be the natural state of religion now (vol. I, pt. II, chap. 9, p. 299) nor his reference to others' expectations that the South American nations will return to their *natural* (nonrevolutionary) *state* (vol. I, pt. II, chap. 5, p. 226) can be taken as evidence of his acceptance of the notion of a prepolitical state of nature. Indeed, "a republic seems to me the natural state for the Americans" (vol. I, pt. II, chap. 10, p. 395).

[101]Ibid., vol. II, pt. III, chap. 1, p. 562.

[102]Ibid., chap. 16, p. 613.

[103]Ibid., chap. 18, p. 620.

rights if he believes a sense of honor to be a surer basis for them than is interest because the origins of honor may not be honorable in themselves.[104] He cannot give a comprehensive and precise definition of political virtue if codes of honor and the needs that generate them admit of variation. The only universal and permanent need he mentions is that "men should not kill each other,"[105] as if the principle to which it pointed were the mere preservation of the human race.[106] Honor, in contrast, tends to equate the whole of virtue with the specific virtue of courage[107] because it is meant to sustain the dominion of the human race—over one another if need be—but, more fundamentally, over natural necessity. As befits their situation in the New World (as well as their desiderata), the Americans have reshaped the look of courage from military valor to commercial daring.[108] They have not obviated or denied the need for courage. Indeed, Tocqueville speaks more confidently of America's changed conception of honor than of her justice. His Americans rarely, if ever, allow their actions to be bounded by considerations of justice.[109]

Prescriptions of honor, we are told, are conventional. These conventions are not universally rational. The best-known form of honor, feudal honor, is only one species of it. American democrats have a conception of honor that leads them to praise as virtues what aristocrats deem vices.[110] "The Americans make an equally arbitrary classification of [virtues and] vices." The conventions are not altogether arbitrary, however. They derive from the peculiar needs of those who govern, and from what is needed to maintain

---

[104] Ibid., p. 617. Tocqueville explicitly refuses to discuss the origins of medieval aristocracy itself.

[105] Ibid.

[106] This is the modern principle of justice taken to its root. Tocqueville places trust in God's justice above trust in his own understanding (ibid., Introduction, p. 18). He submits his judgment to the divine and natural view that democracy is good because it is egalitarian and therefore just (vol. II, pt. IV, chap. 8, p. 704). But cf. vol. I, pt. II, chap. 8, pp. 270-76: Tocqueville subordinates the concern for justice to his concern for politics, which he presents as a mode of education.

[107] Ibid., vol. II, pt. III, chap. 18, p. 620.

[108] Ibid., p. 621; cf. vol. I, pt. II, chap. 10, p. 402.

[109] Ibid., vol. I, pt. II, chap. 7, pp. 251-53, 252n; chap. 10, p. 339, 339n. At most, the Americans pay lip service to justice.

[110] Ibid., vol. II, pt. III, chap. 18, p. 621; cf. vol. I, pt. ii, chap. 9, p. 284.

their authority.[111] The apparent peculiarity of the prescriptions, the comprehensiveness and detail with which they are formulated, and the degree to which they are respected in society are functions of the peculiarity and strength of the needs that dominate a given nation. If aristocratic honor seems arbitrary to democrats, it is because it judges men and actions from the perspective of rare and impermanent, albeit strong, needs rather than universal and permanent needs. In truth, however, the arbitrariness of aristocratic honor arises not from its peculiarity but its generality, for the honorable man obeys the code, not his felt need, in each instance.

More importantly, honor is never wholly arbitrary because the conditions that allow a ruling class or a nation to maintain its authority are not wholly arbitrary or subjective, no matter how accidental or arbitrary the origins of that authority may have been. Democratic honor should judge men by the standard of the virtues that enable them all equally to govern themselves, or by what is needed to sustain the idea of rights. What makes self-government possible must always be kept in view. (Only because there is a connection between the political liberty of citizens and the nation's commercial hegemony, are the Americans correct in honoring the virtues that secure this hegemony.)[112] While Tocqueville distinguishes in this context between the kind of virtue that depends on public recognition, or honor, and "simple virtue [which] feeds upon itself contented with its own witness,"[113] "virtue applied to the world of politics," that is, rights, obviously does depend on public recognition. For Tocqueville, democracy's commitment to rights is a point of honor—a point of honor necessary to it.[114]

Honor becomes weak in democracy, however. Its precepts are imprecisely perceived, indecisively applied, or simply forgotten. As inequalities diminish, honor becomes more like the morality of

---

[111]Ibid., vol. II, pt. III, chap. 18, pp. 617-18.

[112]Ibid., pt. II, chap. 14, pp. 539-41; vol. I, pt. II, chap. 10, pp. 404, 413.

[113]Ibid., vol. II, pt. III, chap. 18, p. 626.

[114]Tocqueville's rather rosy picture of American republicanism in the fourth section of the last chapter of the first volume of *Democracy* (vol. I, pt. II, chap. 10, pp. 395-96) must be considered in the context of his indictment of American democracy throughout the second part of that volume. This is America's boast, a boast necessary to justify popular sovereignty.

right and wrong common to all humanity. Should it ever come about that "all had the same interests and needs, and there was no characteristic trait distinguishing one from another, the practice of attributing a conventional value to men's actions would then cease altogether. Everyone would see them in the same light. The general needs of humanity . . . would form the common standard."[115]

In losing sight of honor, democrats are in danger of losing the virtue that evokes it, for if people "all had the same interests and needs, and there was no characteristic trait distinguishing one from another," they would have no virtue, or virtue would have no moral value. The only morally relevant considerations would be equality or inequality of need and similarity or dissimilarity of equally weighted interests. This, we might suggest, is why today rights are almost invariably associated not with virtue, but with basic human needs or with interests to which one can apply an essentially economic calculus.

Yet the virtue of assertiveness or courage, and therewith honor, remains necessary insofar as the boast of self-rule is essential to humanity. Even democracy's justice stands or falls with the dogma of popular sovereignty; that is, the sovereignty of the human race.[116] Tocqueville's contention that rights are aristocratic in origin serves to remind us that, from a broader perspective, self-governing human beings constitute nature's aristocracy. As his analysis of democratic associations shows, it is possible for human beings to be preserved without their exercising the peculiar human faculties of will and reason that enable them to live with liberty and dignity. But such beings are not quite fully human.[117] Thus even if honor is not usually thought of as a universal and permanent need of mankind, it is one nonetheless. Yet the fact that a sense of honor is not universal and permanent in the same way hunger is, the fact that it must be sustained, if not prompted, by reasonings about its specifications and significance permit us to distinguish this unique

---

[115]Ibid., vol. II, pt. III, chap. 18, p. 627.
[116]Ibid., vol. I, pt. II, chap. 7, p. 250; chap. 10, p. 395.
[117]Ibid., chap. 10, pp. 317-18; vol. II, pt. IV, chap. 7, p. 695.

need as something that bestows dignity on mankind.[118]

If honor, however conventional, has this much of a natural and nonarbitrary basis, other difficulties remain in attempting to identify rights more closely with honor than with what usually passes for self-interest well understood. Honor, Tocqueville readily acknowledges, is essentially inegalitarian, while democratic rights are egalitarian.[119] And honor is usually thought of as something to be earned by individuals, while rights are held to be ours by virtue of some common attribute of our humanity. Tocqueville can be said to have addressed both of these difficulties in his insistence that individuals will have rights only as long as they are willing to exercise them and that rights are most fully exercised in democracy's political associations. Associations are democracy's "aristocratic bodies."[120]

In Tocqueville's *The Old Regime and the French Revolution,* we learn about the English aristocrats, from whom American democrats are said to have inherited our idea of rights. They willingly abandoned their haughty pride and economic privileges to retain the right to govern.[121] In this regard, Tocqueville compares the French aristocracy unfavorably with the English. Yet from his lengthy description of pre-revolutionary France, we nonetheless learn something important about not only aristocratic liberty, but liberty as such.[122] In aristocratic France, liberty was a matter of privilege, not of right.[123] This privilege engendered in those who were given it, and in others by their example,[124] a spirit of independence, and a proud resistance to tyranny, if not to all government. Independence could be asserted against government because dependence could not be bought.[125]

---

[118]Ibid. At vol. II, pt. II, chap. 18, p. 551, Tocqueville at least attributes to the Americans an assumption that there can be "honorable necessities."

[119]Ibid., vol. II, pt. III, chap. 18, p. 627.

[120]Ibid., vol. I, Introduction, p. 14; vol. II, pt. IV, chap. 7, p. 697.

[121]*L'Ancien régime.* All quotations and page references are from *The Old Regime and the French Revolution,* trans. Stuart Gilbert (Garden City, N.Y.: Doubleday, Anchor Books, 1955), corrected as necessary, vol. I, pt. II, chap. 10, p. 98.

[122]Ibid., chap. 11, p. 108.

[123]Ibid., p. 119.

[124]Ibid., p. 111; cf. *Democracy,* vol. II, pt. III, chap. 5, pp. 573-75.

[125]Cf. *Democracy,* vol. II, pt. III, chap. 20, p. 638.

Eighteenth-century man had little of that craving for material well-being which leads the way to servitude. A craving which, while morally debilitating, can be singularly tenacious and insidious, it often operates in close association with such private virtues as family love, a sense of decorum, respect for religion, and even a lukewarm but punctilious observance of the rites of the established Church. While promoting moral rectitude, it rules out heroism and excels in making people well-behaved but mean-spirited as citizens. The eighteenth-century Frenchman was, in short, both better and worse than ourselves.

The French in these days were pleasure seekers, all for the joy of life. They were perhaps more irregular in their behavior, more extravagant in their passions and ideas than our contemporaries, but on the other hand, they had none of that decent, well-regulated sensualism which prevails today. The upper classes were far more interested in living beautifully than in comfort; in making a name for themselves than in making money. Even the middle classes did not devote themselves exclusively to the pursuit of material comforts; they often aspired to loftier, more refined satisfactions and were far from regarding money as the supreme good. As a contemporary writer put it . . . "I know my nation well; versed though it is in making and squandering precious metals, it is not so constituted as to bestow perpetual adoration on them, but at any moment may return to its ancient idols: valor, glory, and, I make bold to say, magnanimity."[126]

This aristocratic liberty of privilege did not give to all citizens "the most natural and necessary guarantees,"[127] nor did it prepare the way for the orderly, lawful liberty that American democracy at its best achieves.[128] It did grace France with individuals who exhibited virile virtues, who had pride in themselves and a taste

---

[126]*L'Ancien régime*, vol. I, pt. II, chap. 11, pp. 118-19.
[127]Ibid., p. 119.
[128]Ibid., p. 120.

for glory. It formed the vigorous souls, the proud and audacious geniuses who made the Revolution.[129] These are the men Tocqueville himself took so much pleasure in contemplating.[130]

It is the aristocrat, not the democrat, who has a natural taste for liberty and therefore a passion for politics. Yet if aristocrats are correct in sensing that this taste is distributed unequally among human beings, they err in believing that the taste can be inherited like property and justly manifested in the privileges aristocratic conventions establish. But democrats err no less in thinking that a passion for liberty for its own sake is either unnecessary or found naturally and equally in all human beings.

> Interest will never be permanent enough and visible enough to sustain the love of liberty in the hearts of men, if taste does not fix it there. . . .
>
> There is a reasoned and interested taste for liberty that has its source in a view to the benefits it procures. Then there is an instinctive penchant for it, irresistible and almost involuntary, that gives birth to the invisible source of all great passions. Never forget that when you reason. A taste that is found, it is true, among all men, but which holds first rank in the hearts of only a very small number. . . . It is the common source not only of political liberty, but of all the virile and high virtues. . . . It is less a view of the advantages liberty brings than the pleasure of being free that attaches [men] so strongly to their rights and makes them so jealous of them.[131]

This "sublime taste" that "enters by itself in the great hearts God has prepared to receive it" must be experienced and cannot be analyzed.[132] How wrong the Americans are in "honor[ing] their philosophy rather than themselves"!

Democrats would also err if they failed to see how free

---

[129]Ibid.

[130]Cf. *Democracy*, vol. II, pt. IV, chap. 8, p. 704.

[131]*L'Ancien régime*, vol. II, p. 345.

[132]Ibid., vol. I, pt. III, chap. 3, p. 169.

institutions and the political right to form associations[133] might spark the taste for liberty that moves men to exercise and defend their rights. Where the institutions of political freedom flourish "at first it is of necessity that men attend to the public interest, afterward by choice. What had been calculation becomes instinct. By dint of working for the good of his fellow citizens, he in the end acquires a habit and a taste for serving them."[134] Democracy will still be graced by natural aristocrats, who have a passion for political liberty.[135] They will be required to dissemble—not sacrifice—their pride.[136] Having done this, their task is to put themselves or to cause others to put them at the head of democratic associations. What Tocqueville claims to have learned in America is that democracy can combat its natural envy with the idea of rights[137] and its enervating egalitarian individualism with the right of association.

Tocqueville could not have warned more clearly than he did against attempting to impose aristocratic forms on democracy, or even to judge it by aristocracy's standards.[138] Yet he could not have suggested more forcefully throughout *Democracy* that a proper evaluation of liberal democracy presupposes an awareness of the alternative to it, aristocratic or pre-modern politics. His paradoxical contentions that rights are aristocratic in origin and that democracy is naturally hostile to them should make the necessity of a comparison clear. *Pace* Socrates, aristocracy, not democracy, is the natural home not only of love of liberty, but of political philosophy, for in it alone is found the full complement of human natures displayed for contemplation,[139] the leisure for contemplation, and the appreciation of beauty and subtlety that sustain it.[140] The democratic associations that best fulfill this function are already the product of an art that respects the tastes, if not the forms,

---

[133]*Democracy*, vol. I, pt. II, chap. 4, p. 193; vol. II, pt. II, chap. 7, pp. 522-24.
[134]Ibid., vol. II, pt. II, chap. 4, pp. 512-13.
[135]Ibid., chap. 1, p. 505; pt. III, chap. 14, p. 608.
[136]Ibid., pt. II, chap. 4, pp. 510, 512.
[137]Ibid., vol. I, pt. II, chap. 9, p. 311.
[138]Ibid., vol. II, pt. IV, chap. 8, pp. 704-05.
[139]Ibid., pt. III, chap. 17, pp. 614-15.
[140]Ibid., pt. I, chap. 10, pp. 460, 462.

of aristocracy.[141]

There is no reason to doubt that Tocqueville means what he says when he urges democratic moralists to pay principal attention to the doctrine of self-interest well understood and to link rights to interest. They must accept the doctrine as necessary, though imperfect. But a moral philosophy that seeks no further than to reflect on democracy's considered convictions can hardly be adequate to its task. It is even less adequate to that task if it neglects reflection on what rights are *for* in favor of a preoccupation with current conceptions or misconceptions of what rights are *to.* For Tocqueville, rights are *to* self-government and *for* the political liberty whose exercise calls forth the virtues that bring honor to human beings. Tocqueville is not a flatterer of democracy because he is not an enemy of it.[142] His adoption of the idea of rights reminds us of his account of how America's Federalist party benefited democracy by introducing the principles of aristocracy under the slogans of its democratic adversaries.[143]

---

[141]Ibid., vol. II, pt. II, chap. 5, p. 517; pt. IV, chap. 3, p. 674.
[142]Ibid.; Preface, p. 418.
[143]Ibid., vol. I, pt. II, chap. 2, p. 177.

15

On the Central Doctrine of *Democracy in America*

George Anastaplo

Aude, hospes, contemnere opes et
te quoque dignum finge deo . . . .
— Virgil, *Aeneid*, VIII, 364

I

Alexis de Tocqueville's *Democracy in America* is a huge book with a great reputation. Whether it is ultimately, or primarily, about the United States can be doubted. But that the American regime of the 1830s is used, and in a most instructive way, to examine perennial questions has long been evident. The meanings and effects of both equality and liberty, and the proper relation of one to the other, are examined at length. The decisiveness of equality for this study, and in the modern world, is recognized from the outset. Thus, it is reported in the author's introduction: "So the more I studied American society, the more clearly I saw equality of conditions as the creative element from which each particular fact derived, and all my observations constantly returned to this nodal point." Among the consequences, at least in America, of triumphant equality had been the development of a vigorous individualism—and this, too, the author must (in a statesmanlike way) put in its place.

I propose on this occasion, in an effort to suggest how one might begin to think about this massive book, to look at one chapter in some detail. This seems to me consistent with the understanding of things proposed by the author himself. Thus, he argues for the importance in the continental American nation of local township government (and of the family as well). These are the vital materials of which the great American edifice is constructed. A part, he seems to suggest, can reveal much about the whole. But which part should we settle upon? Why not that which is at the heart of the work, the central chapter of the ninety-three chapters of the entire book? For this purpose, the sizes of the chapters do not matter, just as the sizes of localities and families (so long as they do remain localities and families) do not matter for some purposes.

The central chapter of *Democracy in America* is found in the second volume of the book. This means the author had the entire work before him when he placed this chapter where he did. This short chapter, which is Chapter 8 of Part II of Volume Two, is entitled "How the Americans Combat Individualism by the Doctrine of Interest Well Understood." (That which is here translated as "interest" is often translated as "self-interest.") I found, on settling upon this chapter as central to the book, that it has been designated as vital by other students of the book as well, albeit on other grounds.

A careful (however awkward) translation is needed for the detailed commentary I offer here. As I go along, I will try to speak to questions (including old questions about the relations of moderns to ancients) which are raised not only by each paragraph in succession but also by the entire chapter and by the book as a whole. Those who know this book better than I do should be able to tell us what major differences there may be between the first and second halves of the book (when divided according to chapters). I have found it convenient to divide the central chapter into the following sections:

Section I:	Paragraphs 1 and 2
Section II:	Paragraphs 3, 4, 5, 6, and 7
Section III:	Paragraphs 8, 9, and 10
Section IV:	Paragraphs 11 and 12
Section V:	Paragraphs 13, 14, and 15
Section VI:	Paragraphs 16, 17, 18, 19, and 20
Section VII:	Paragraphs 21 and 22.

The entire chapter is set forth, paragraph by paragraph, in the course of this commentary.

II

The opening section of this chapter (made up of paragraphs 1 and 2) is devoted to "history," a recapitulation of the doctrine that had once prevailed, and to an introduction to another doctrine, which is now about to prevail.

First, then, the recapitulation, as found in the opening paragraph of this central chapter:

> [1] When the world was conducted by a small number of powerful and rich individuals, these liked to form for themselves a sublime idea of the duties of man; it pleased them to profess that it is glorious to forget oneself and that it is fitting to do good without [regard to] interest, as God himself [does]. That was the official doctrine of the times in matters of morality.

A pervasive opinion is reported here, one that is presented as having once been generally accepted, at least in the West ("the world"). Was it a time in which a few stood out—and in which truly political judgments were not relied upon? Is this suggested by the use of "conducted" in place of a word such as "governed"? That is, were human affairs in those times *managed* rather than being subjected to political ordering? The managers were a few, who were "powerful and rich individuals." The usual translations here accommodate themselves to the English idiom, making the passage read, "rich and powerful individuals." But this reversal of "powerful" and "rich" conceals questions left by the French original. Were these few managers rich because they were powerful? Did they seek power in order to secure wealth?

These few are designated "individuals." They stood out from all the others; perhaps they even considered everything around them *theirs*. Were they the only ones who "counted"? Certainly, they, as the visible ones, were the only ones who had access to glory; for them, sublimity meant something and was perhaps available. It is difficult for more than a few to share in glory, since its effect is heightened (if not even made possible) by its rarity. The "duties of man" are spoken of—but, it seems, these were duties that only a few could be expected to perform. Only a few could, under this dispensation, be truly human. To be truly human meant, for them, to be godlike: An imitation of God, by conduct that was concerned for the good alone without regard to personal advantage, was their aspiration. A great distance is opened between these few and all the others. One is pleased to forget oneself; but one does derive considerable satisfaction from the recognition that one is thereby a benefactor and otherwise virtuous. Still, whatever the implications of the text here, that one does enjoy doing the right thing should not be held against one. Indeed, is it not the mark of a virtuous man that he takes pleasure in doing the right thing, knowing that it *is* the right thing? Or are we to assume that all superiority *is* spurious or otherwise undeserved?

Whether it is indeed virtuous to forget oneself (however glorious it can be in some circumstances) remains a question. That is, one may at times have a duty to preserve oneself. Besides, habitual disregard for oneself can encourage one to be unaware of, if not even callous toward, the prosaic needs of others. One must be careful about the tendency of the noble to "do right" without sufficient regard for the consequences, especially in circumstances where deprivations and pains are shared by all while the glory and other pleasures are monopolized by a few. What is truly moral remains a question here.

All this is referred to as "the official doctrine of the times." *When* these times were is not made clear. They precede the present era, of course, but how far back do they go? They seem to run back through the Christian era—there are indications of that in what is said about sacrifice and great abnegations—but not so far back as the classical period. A certain line of development—perhaps even a virtually inevitable line of development—may be assumed. Little, if anything, is said in this chapter about what prompted this development. One has the impression, here as elsewhere, that all this is viewed from the French, or at least from the European, perspective: For *them*, there are all around them (in buildings, in names and language, and in history) many reminders of the claims upon them of the nobility.

To say that the doctrine was "official" may be to suggest that it was not necessarily adhered to generally. Still, an official doctrine, even when tainted by the hypocrisy that any long-established profession of faith is liable to, can set the tone of a time. For lack of something better—a general unease, if not resentment, is *not* something better—the official doctrine of a time shapes by and large the general opinions of a time. In this case, the official doctrine could even be understood to provide meaning to much of what might otherwise seem a bleak and exploited life. To refer to it as a *doctrine* may recognize that it is a *teaching* or an *instruction,* a set of opinions which, whatever their truth, it is considered salutary to transmit and support. In this way, both the few and the many were once taught and reassured about how all that went on around them, as well as within them, could be understood.

We can now turn, in the next paragraph, to the doctrine which (according to the author) was coming to prevail in his time:

> [2] I doubt that men were more virtuous in aristocratic ages than in others, but it is certain that the beauties of virtue were talked about incessantly; they studied only in secret the side of it which is useful. But, to the extent that the imagination takes a less lofty flight and that each concentrates on himself, moralists are frightened at this idea of sacrifice and they no longer dare offer it to the human spirit; they are then reduced to inquiring whether the individual advantage of citizens would not work to the happiness of all, and, when they have discovered one of those points where particular interest does meet with the general interest, and conforms to it, they hasten to place it in the light; little by little like observations are multiplied. What was an isolated remark becomes a general doctrine, and one comes finally to perceive that man in serving his like serves himself, and that his particular interest is to do well.

The "official doctrine" of a former age had been set forth in the first paragraph of this chapter. When the author turns to more recent times, he walks in the path marked out, two centuries earlier, by an even greater French questioner of official doctrine, René Descartes. Thus, our author, like his predecessor, begins here with the expression of personal doubt. Other traces of the Cartesian approach may be seen elsewhere in this book and even, further on, in this very chapter. The author seems to call into question, if only to give full force to the contemporary alternative, the received opinion of the preceding age.

What is meant by the suggestion that men were not "more virtuous in aristocratic ages than in others"? Does this judgment depend on an assessment not of a few men then and now but rather of the bulk of men in both kinds of times? Certainly, there is an indication later in this chapter (in paragraph 15) that a time could come when the best men would not be as remarkable as the best men once were. Does the author draw the comparison he does here, at the outset of this discussion, to make as plausible a case as possible for the contemporary doctrine and its consequences?

It is a case which is to rely much upon utility. To prepare the way, the author seems to disparage those who talked "incessantly" about "the beauties of virtue." No doubt, such talk can be little more than the expression of vanity and ostentation; it is consistent with a way of life that made much of glory and the sublime. Yet, to take pleasure in doing what is right—which I have already spoken of as the mark of the truly virtuous man—is to be drawn to the attractions of virtue, as something worthy for its own sake, not just for its consequences. Is not this included in any insistence upon "the beauties of virtue"? Does not such an insistence somehow ratify human existence as something desirable in itself, as a thing of beauty, especially when well-conducted, however transitory it may be?

Why were aristocrats inclined to study "only in secret" the usefulness of virtue? Is there something shameful about an emphasis upon utility here? Is there something ugly in making much of an effort to show that virtue pays—or, at least, is there something ugly about those who are taught to expect this to be shown to them? Not only is it thereby tacitly recognized that virtue is inherently painful—why else endeavor to make so much of its supposed utility?—but also it is virtually conceded that one need not act virtuously in those instances when the personal utility of a virtuous act cannot be shown. To proceed pursuant to the expectation that honesty in such circumstances is the best policy may encourage one to resort to dishonesty when honesty obviously does not "pay." At the least, an unseemly calculating spirit can be promoted.

Be all this as it may, the author seems to say, these times are less high-minded, and moralists and statesmen must adapt themselves to a lowering of sights if they are to be effective in what they teach and do. We are not told here how it was that the flight of the imagination became "less lofty" when each "concentrate[d] on himself." The new general doctrine, which leads one "to perceive that man in serving his like serves himself," is designed to serve men in their more self-centered condition; it does not seem to have brought men to this condition; something else, it seems, is responsible for that.

In any event, the "idea of sacrifice" is no longer resorted to. Why are "moralists" so "frightened" by it? Only because it is no longer persuasive? Or because it is too dangerous in its persuasiveness, in that it has been invoked all too often with disastrous consequences? Does this latter consideration suggest that man has an innate tendency toward self-sacrifice, and its awful beauties, so much so that a reliance upon the useful is apt to be temporary or at least vulnerable?

Much is now made of the correspondence between "the individual advantage of citizens" and "the happiness of all." We notice it is here that the citizen emerges in this chapter. Citizens had been made much of in antiquity, we recall; but there may not have been much room for citizens in the post-classical aristocratic ages evidently referred to in the first paragraph. Only a few were full citizens then—and those few were as much individuals as they were citizens: Their own glory meant more to them, perhaps, than "the happiness of all."

Must not modern citizens be distinguished from their predecessors? Is not the tendency of modern citizens (particularly in democratic times) to make much of "all," of their "like," of "the general interest," rather than of local allegiances? Do we not hear echoes here of the Rights of Man and of the brotherhood of man (or at least of European man)? Does this come, at least in part, from the legitimation of the "particular interest" of each citizen, teaching him that he is entitled to identify himself with all others like himself as human beings, especially if much should be made of his economic interest with its dependence upon repeated transactions with peoples of other lands? Thus, modern man moves *en masse* first into the citizen body and then into the bourgeoisie.

Is it here suggested by the author that the isolated instances of correspondences between particular interests and the general interest do not really add up to the "general doctrine" they are gathered together to make? Still, it is this general doctrine which has replaced the earlier "official doctrine." Why is it not *designated* the new official doctrine? Perhaps because there is not yet an authoritative body, in the new age, to provide such ratification? May the authoritativeness of any body be in principle improper in a truly egalitarian age?

So much, then, for the history of two doctrines, the official doctrine of aristocratic ages, which is fading away, and the general doctrine of modern times, which is emerging to take its place to some extent. The reference in paragraph 2 to "light" may anticipate the call for enlightenment with which this chapter concludes and upon which the modern project is believed to depend.

III

The second section of this chapter (made up of paragraphs 3, 4, 5, 6, and 7) testifies to the application of the newly emerging general doctrine among a particular people, and the consequences of that application.

The author informs the reader,

> [3] I have already shown, in several places in this work, how the inhabitants of the United States almost always know how to combine their own well-being with that of their fellow-citizens. That which I want to point out now is the general theory which helps them get there.

The Americans first come to view in this chapter as "the inhabitants of the United States." This designation seems more geographical, and even scientific, than political or racial. But is not the geography such that the emphasis on "all" and "his like" in paragraph 2 can easily be shifted to "fellow-citizens" here? That is, Americans do live where virtually all the white men they come in contact with happen to be fellow-citizens. They need not trouble themselves, at least not to the extent that Europeans must, to mediate between the demands of humanity and those of citizenship.

Even so, the emphasis is on the welfare of human beings in their several capacities (whether as individuals or as all of one's fellow-citizens). The welfare of the country, or the community, is not made anything of. Does not this mean, among other things, that the emphasis is apt to be upon the present generation, not upon any identification with the past or upon any concern with the future?

The author's work as a whole is intended to show, among other things, how well the American system works. The question remains, of course, how and why it works as well as it does. The author intends to notice "the general theory which helps" Americans "almost always . . . to combine their own well-being with that of their fellow-citizens." Is that "general theory" itself but a tool, not something which provides ultimate guidance? It is said to *help* Americans do what they do. It, by itself, may not be enough. Perhaps it is not even the principal factor in determining how Americans act. In any event, this "almost always" reminds us that the application of any "general theory" must be tested by a higher standard, if we are to be able to judge whether that which is aimed at by the use of such a theory is indeed achieved. That higher standard, it would once have been said, is looked to by statesmanship. Whether statesmanship can be built into a democratic system, or whether a self-governing people can be statesmanlike, remains a problem.

The next paragraph tells us something about the application by Americans (in a statesmanlike way?) of the general theory they employ:

> [4] In the United States, it is hardly ever said that virtue is beautiful. It is maintained that it [virtue] is useful, and it is proved every day. American moralists do not pretend that one must sacrifice oneself for one's like because it is great to do so; but they boldly say that such sacrifices are as necessary to him who imposes them upon himself as to those whom they profit.

Why do not Americans say that virtue is beautiful? Because it is not so? Or if it is so, do they not say so either because they do not recognize it to be so or because they do not believe it prudent to say it is so? Are Americans fully modern in preferring to rely upon (or at least to voice) "realistic" reasons for what men do?

If it should not be believed that virtue is beautiful, what then is the status of the beautiful? If beauty should be kept separate from morality, which *is* by and large a community concern, then beauty tends to be a private matter, perhaps even something left (more than virtue is) to each man's taste. Again we notice that beauty may be tacitly left to the noble-minded, with their illusions (or pretensions?) and their exotic individuality.

American moralists, unlike European moralists, are "bold," not "frightened," in confronting the idea of sacrifice. Why is this? The answer may depend on why European moralists were frightened. In any event, American moralists make much of sacrifices as mutually beneficial. Do they advocate this because they believe it or because it is useful?

May not the greatness of sacrifice be sacrificed to this new way of seeing things? Perhaps greatness at large is also sacrificed. Is an emphasis upon utility, and upon mutual benefit, much more likely in a commercial republic? Do bodies matter more than spirit in such republics, or at least more so than in aristocracies? Does this shift in emphasis have something to do with the political elements in the talk and lives of Americans? A somewhat self-conscious republic may be more inclined to speak in terms of interest than is a monarchy or an aristocracy (which is more likely to be moved by considerations of pride). Does it not make more sense for a republic to be concerned with utility than with honor? After all, a community is obviously in large part bodily. Utility, then, may have more to do with the broadest base of sovereignty; pride, and hence beauty, may have more to do with the few.

Whatever the soundness of the American position, it does reflect an accommodation to the times. Thus, it is noticed in the next paragraph:

> [5] They have seen that, in their country and in their time, man is brought back to himself by an irresistible force and, losing hope of arresting it, they have dreamed of no more than to conduct him.

The American moralists, it seems, are aware of the limitations both of the arguments for the position they espouse and of any efforts to arrest the development which makes such a position useful. What the ultimate cause is of this "irresistible force" remains unstated here. Again we see that a standard is resorted to in the light of which the public position is taken by the moralists. How much they understand, beyond an awareness of what is immediately needed, is not clear.

The use here of "conduct" can again remind one of Descartes. Conducting takes the form of the proposition reported in the next paragraph:

> [6] They therefore do not deny that each man may pursue his interest, but they do their utmost to prove that the interest of each is to be honest.

Selfishness, it would seem, is not to be condemned; rather, it is to be redirected. One is to be shown what is truly in one's interest, what an informed selfishness leads one to. And so we return to the notion of the utility of virtue, with special emphasis placed here on the virtue of honesty. This word (*honnete*), which has as well the connotations of honorable, upright and just, may be particularly appropriate for a commercial republic, one in which men have to rely on each other's fidelity in the transactions they undertake.

It should be noticed that man (not citizen?) is thus being addressed in this appeal to interest. It should also be noticed that it seems to be suggested that the argument made in the appeal is difficult to prove: It has always been far easier to see that one's honesty helps another than to see that it advances one's own interest as well.

The second section of this chapter, which testifies to the application of the newly emerging general doctrine about interest among the Americans, concludes with a recognition of what American moralists have and have not accomplished by their arguments:

> [7] I do not want to enter here into the details of their reasons, as that would divert me from my subject; it suffices for me to say that they [their reasons] have convinced their fellow-citizens.

One might wonder, of course, whether Americans are better or worse for having been thus convinced of what may be a dubious argument. That is, does not such convincing speak well of their moral concerns, but less well of their intellectual powers? But then, the author himself is less concerned with the validity of the argument here than he is with its consequences and usefulness. In this respect, he may be (at least for the moment) very much an "American," concerned more with utility than with beauty.

IV

The third section of this chapter (made up of paragraphs 8, 9, and 10) looks to antecedents of the doctrine of interest well understood and considers the varied responses to that doctrine in America and in Europe.

Thus, the first paragraph in the third section reports:

> [8] A long time ago Montaigne said: 'If I did not follow the straight road for its straightness, I should follow it from having found, by experience, that in the final reckoning it is commonly the happiest and the most useful.'

This could serve as the culmination of the second section of this chapter (rather than, as I have put it, as the beginning of the third section), suggesting further that utility is to be preferred (at least in practical affairs) to beauty (which is to be seen, presumably, in "straightness"—in virtue for its own sake). But the author also hints at the roots, at least in recent centuries, for the doctrine of interest well understood. He does not go directly (or by the straight road) to Montaigne in his reliance upon him here. Montaigne does speak, in a passage to which we will return when we get to paragraph 18, on the relation of utility to honesty—and perhaps we are intended to be reminded of that discussion by Montaigne. But the Montaigne passage drawn upon here (if the editors of *Democracy in America* are to be trusted in their suggestion as to what *is* drawn upon) is not concerned with the problem of utility; indeed, it is far from saying what Tocqueville here restates it as having said. Consider the supposed source, the opening sentence of Montaigne's essay, "Of Sleep": "Reason orders us always to go on the same path, but not always at the same pace; and whereas the sage should not allow human passions to make him deviate from the right course, he may well, without prejudice to his duty, let them hasten or retard his steps, and not plant himself like a Colossus, immobile and impassable." It is useful to Tocqueville to paraphrase loosely what Montaigne says here, and especially to add a reliance upon the notion of utility in determining what path one is to follow with a view to happiness.

Perhaps a kind of analogy is intended. That is, Tocqueville suggests that there are better and worse reasons for doing what one does; the important thing is to persist in doing what one should, to keep in mind one's objective. Thus, where Montaigne varies the pace of one's movement along the path, Tocqueville varies the reasons for following the path. In both instances, the path is followed and, presumably, the goal is reached.

Would not even more be indicated by the explicit reliance upon this particular passage from Montaigne if it should be evident that another passage (directly on point) could have been used? Perhaps we are meant, in any event, to reflect upon the chapter which *is* used here, the chapter on sleep. There Montaigne shows how certain men were able to sleep soundly despite their circumstances (that is, despite an impending battle or despite an impending suicide). What are we to make of such men, that they were able to forget themselves completely? Or was it rather that they always had an ability to sense what they could and could not do for themselves, regardless of their circumstances (which others around them took so much more seriously)? Were they being highly individualistic? To sleep is to retreat from the everyday world, the world of affairs and of "reality." Is all this to be seen, somehow, as a commentary on the nature and prospects of "interest well understood"? To sleep is to be most private, to be most on one's own. Thus, for example, everyone can be an invincible sovereign while asleep. Does this suggest the limits of any concern for the public? Certainly, the Montaigne chapter alluded to in paragraph 8 does raise questions about the body, about life itself, and hence about the importance of self-interest (however understood)—that is, about the things with which most men are very much concerned.

Whatever Montaigne and Tocqueville are, it would seem, they are not simply straightforward (and the talk about a straight road points this up?). Is not their subtlety an aristocratic, rather than a democratic, trait? Does not subtlety, especially in the form of irony, reflect an awareness of inequalities? One must wonder what really moves each of them, what each is driving at.

In any event, Montaigne has been used (in a preliminary fashion), and we can proceed to the next paragraph:

> [9] The doctrine of interest well understood is then not new; but, among the Americans of our day, it has been universally admitted; it has become popular there: one finds it at the root of all actions; it runs through all discourse. One does not encounter it less in the mouth of the poor than in that of the rich.

To speak of this doctrine as "then not new" may suggest that Montaigne (or perhaps Montesquieu?) is *a* distant source of what the Americans generally believe. It is here spoken of, for the first time (since the title to this chapter), as the "doctrine of interest well understood." Is it among the Americans, perhaps first—or at least more than anywhere else—that it is regarded as a *doctrine,* as a received teaching for all, or almost all, to accept?

It is a popular doctrine, we are told, so popular that both rich and poor mouth it. (Does this say something about the expectations of the poor in the United States? That is, they do not expect to remain poor indefinitely? They believe this way of life serves their interest at least as much as it serves the interest of the rich? And since fortunes are so changeable, the rich are more vulnerable in America than in Europe?)

We must wonder, however, whether a popular doctrine can be correct, whatever its usefulness may be. And, if it is not correct, may not a day of reckoning come? Perhaps not, it can be responded, if the use of the doctrine is conducted by those (those few?) who know what they are doing. Certainly, the statesman knows that few things are useful in all circumstances.

American experience with this doctrine is to be compared with that of peoples elsewhere. This may be seen in the next paragraph:

> [10] In Europe, the doctrine of interest is much more coarse than in America, but at the same time it is less widespread and especially less exhibited, and every day great abnegations are feigned, which are no more.

Curiously, the American version of this doctrine is more refined than the European, whereas one expects the Europeans generally to go in for more refinements than the Americans. But, then, the Americans have taken this doctrine more seriously and have had to live with it—and that can promote a certain refinement.

This doctrine is still suspect in Europe: One does not parade it as in the United States. This seems to be, at least in part, because greatness is still aspired to in Europe, in the form at least of great self-sacrifice, a monumental forgetting of oneself for the sake of others (or is this primarily for the sake of the glory referred to in paragraph 1?).

The truly great is not apt to be widespread; certainly it cannot find popular expression, however widely it may be acclaimed in time. But, we are told, these expressions of greatness are feigned; they are not to be taken seriously; they are illusions of grandeur, resorted to by those who do not recognize that times have changed and that the sublime has been made obsolete.

America, we are given to understand, is the way of the future; Europe looks too much to the past. We are obliged, if we are to be sensible, to reconcile ourselves to arguments from utility, to a doctrine which counsels men that it is truly in their interest to act morally toward their fellows. This, we are further given to understand, is to be sensible—and life will generally be better if the hopeless aspirations of the past for genuine virtue (that is, for virtue for its own sake—or was it for the glory of virtue?) should be surrendered up as ineffectual.

V

But, then, we do have in the fourth section of this chapter (made up of paragraphs 11 and 12) a curious interlude, if not even a digression. For we see indicated here, in the central paragraphs of the chapter, perhaps decisive reservations about the doctrine which is being advocated for general acceptance.

The first of this pair of revealing paragraphs reads:

> [11] The Americans, on the contrary, are pleased to explain, by the aid of interest well understood, almost all the acts of

> their life; they exhibit complacently how an illuminated love of themselves constantly brings them to assist one another and disposes them willingly to sacrifice to the good of the State a part of their time and their wealth. I think that in this they often do not do themselves justice; for one sometimes sees in the United States, as elsewhere, citizens abandoning themselves to the disinterested and unconsidered impulses which are natural to man; but the Americans hardly ever avow that they concede anything to movements of this kind; they like better to honor their philosophy rather than themselves.

That Americans are "pleased" to explain things as they do might mean that they are somewhat superficial in how they regard themselves. This conclusion is reinforced by the use here of "complacently." On the other hand, the author speaks of the Americans' resorting not to the "doctrine of interest well understood" but rather simply to "interest well understood." Does this hint that it is in their interest thus to explain themselves?

We are told that "almost all the acts of their life" are explained in this fashion. That is, virtually nothing is done except as it might contribute to their own well-being? Perhaps the most interesting question here is why, if it should *not* be so, Americans prefer to speak of themselves in this fashion. Is this because of the more "realistic" taste of modernity? Has it become unfashionable to display, or at least to admit to, high-mindedness? Is hard-headedness as much "feigned" as the "great abnegations" spoken of earlier? Is this in part due to the excesses of democratic rhetoric, which had (by the time this book was written) exploited noble sentiments for several generations? Did the resistance to such rhetoric take two forms: the "realism" of the intelligent citizen and the stunning simplicity of literary craftsmen such as Mark Twain and Abraham Lincoln?

Even so, one must wonder whether Americans in the author's time *did* explain themselves almost exclusively by recourse to the doctrine of interest well understood. *Did* the people whom the author talked with express themselves thus? Or did he merely hear them thus, partly because of *his* own interests or predispositions? Somewhat revealing here may be his suggestion that Americans make sacrifices "to the good of the State." Is not this use of "State" highly suspect? Would not Americans have spoken of "community" or of "neighbors" or of "country"? Does not the use of "State" here remind us that the author has a tendency, elsewhere as well as here, to put things in terms that he, as a European, happens to understand?

Perhaps it is the author's own inclinations, both as the social scientist (or sociologist) that he is and as a European, which leads him to make as much as he does in this book of *The Federalist.* Virtually nothing is said by him about the Declaration of Independence. But it is in the Declaration that much more is made of nobility: It is there that one hears echoes of classical antiquity. The more interest-oriented *Federalist*—with its immediate appeals for votes in a local contest—is much more instrumental, presumably serving thereby the grander purposes set forth in the Declaration.

The author leaves us here in paragraph 11 with two criticisms of the Americans. First, there *are* natural impulses which no doubt account for some of American philanthropy. In addition, to say that a people prefer "to honor their philosophy rather than themselves" is to suggest that they can hardly be said to philosophize.

But, then, we must wonder what philosophy means for the author himself. He virtually equates it, here and elsewhere, with something like ideology or august opinion. A related question is whether he recognized *nature* as the source of more than impulses (or desires). Cannot nature, in its most refined and reflective form, lead to calm judgment and mature understanding? Perhaps the author's use here of "justice" is significant. Does this use point to a judgment which is to be made somewhat independent of consequences? Does it remind us of the attractions of virtue as something worthy for its own sake, not just for its utility?

Does the author, then, point to something more than the doctrine of interest well understood not only as the basis of his thought and judgment but as the basis as well of what the Americans do? Are not Americans somewhere between the two tendencies toward which the author's French readers may be inclined, the reckless pursuit of *gloire* by the thoughtless nobility and the determined pursuit of personal gain by the calculating bourgeoisie?

That the author himself prefers to be regarded as looking, at least in conducting *his* affairs, past the doctrine of interest well understood is suggested by the next paragraph:

> [12] I might stop here and not attempt to judge that which I have described. The extreme difficulty of the subject would be my excuse. But I do not want to profit from it, and I prefer that my readers, seeing clearly my goal, should refuse to follow me than that I should leave them in suspense.

The author, it seems, does not make the mistake the Americans do: He does not speak only of interest moving *him* to act as *he* does. His interest (say, in maintaining his reputation or in making his book easy for readers) might seem to be served by stopping here rather than run the risk of so exposing his goal or so complicating his argument as to lose his would-be followers.

Of course, he seeks an effect by his book; he may even be considered to have had an overall social-political purpose. The intended utility of his book in this respect is evident on its surface. But perhaps, also, he wants to be understood, at least by some: The truth about these matters and the beauty of that truth are there to be discerned by those who read carefully. Does he indicate as well that true virtue, including the virtue of wisdom, would be better than utility, especially for the great of soul? But can such virtue be counted on, especially if one has large-scale or long-term political purposes in view? Does not the author, in the way he conducts himself here, attempt to reserve the best for himself?

Thus, paragraph 11 of this chapter shows the Americans being more altruistic (less concerned for their personal profit) than they admit; and paragraph 12 shows the author being more altruistic (less concerned for his own profit) than other authors might be. Thus, both the author and the Americans look out for others, whatever the prevailing "philosophy" might be. Does the author thereby suggest that whatever the utility of virtue—whatever the usefulness of the doctrine of interest well understood—virtue for its own sake (without regard to personal advantage in the ordinary sense) must be at the heart of a healthy and enduring community?

This book, we should remember, is not written for Americans.

Rather, the United States is used as part of the author's efforts to transform and guide Europeans, and especially his fellow-citizens in France. Does he, as teacher-statesman, use the doctrine of utility in order to move his own community to habits and opinions which can make it as virtuous politically as the Americans are or are said to be?

VI

We have seen, in the first half of this chapter (paragraphs 1 through 10), the development of the doctrine of interest well understood, particularly as it is put to work by Americans. We have been reminded, at the center of this chapter (in paragraphs 11 and 12), of the underlying virtue (a disinterested virtue for its own sake) which can make this doctrine work properly, whatever may be said about it by its practitioners. We now go on, in the second half of this chapter (paragraphs 13 through 22), to develop the "goal" the author refers to in paragraph 12. That is, the doctrine of interest well understood is examined in statesmanlike applications, especially to European conditions.

Three sections remain to be touched upon in this commentary, sections in which there is far less said about the United States itself than in the first half of this chapter. The first remaining section is devoted to the consequences, good and bad, of the doctrine of interest well understood; the second remaining section, to the conditions which make acceptance of the doctrine necessary; the third remaining section, to the safeguards which must be resorted to once the doctrine is indeed relied upon.

First, then, in the fifth section of this chapter (made up of paragraphs 13, 14, and 15) there are these observations:

> [13] Interest well understood is not a lofty doctrine, but it is clear and sure. It does not seek to attain great objects; but it attains without too much effort all those it aims at. As it is within the reach of all intelligences, each can grasp it easily and can retain it without trouble. Accommodating itself marvelously to the weaknesses of men, it easily obtains a great empire, and it has no difficulty preserving

> it, because it turns personal interest against itself and uses, to direct the passions, the [same] goad that excites them.

The references to "clear and sure" and to "the reach of all intelligences" once again remind us of Descartes. We are reminded as well of the Cartesian insistence upon modest but certain steps along a way which can eventually lead to great accomplishments, especially if one is not shackled by the past. Sights are to be lowered—perhaps that is to be regretted, but then the targets come within reach, and something is to be said for that. Machiavelli, for one, said much of what could be said here.

This doctrine of interest well understood, since it is "within the reach of all intelligences," is easily grasped and retained. We are reminded of our observations about the popularity of doctrines which may not be correct—which, indeed, are suspect for their very popularity. The author himself had noticed earlier that "an idea [which is] false but clear and precise, will always be more powerful in the world than an idea [which is] true but complex." And we have noticed, in our discussion of paragraphs 11 and 12 (at the heart of this chapter), the extent to which the doctrine of interest well understood may depend on a radically different approach to virtue from that of former times.

Loftiness is discounted—both in paragraphs 1 and 2 of this chapter and now here in paragraph 13 (a second beginning?). But something of the lofty manages to slip back in, for is there not also here something for the great-souled statesman? Consider the invocations of the "marvelous" and of "a great empire." Something of Machiavelli may again be seen perhaps—and not least in the empire that the author of *Democracy in America* will himself achieve if he succeeds in transforming the moral and political sentiments of Europeans.

The author counsels, like Machiavelli and Hobbes before him, that moralists face up to the passions and hence limitations of men, making use of them rather than fighting them. This may perhaps best be seen, for its remarkable effects, in the economic life of a people when acquisitiveness is legitimated (as the free market does). (Whether the same approach can work in foreign policy and war, where honor and great personal sacrifice seem to mean much more is glanced at in the following chapter in this book.)

The way spelled out in our chapter can indeed secure "all [the objects] it aims at." But cannot it lose sight of what it is truly after, of what (for instance) the pursuit of gain serves? We can see in paragraphs 14 and 15 what the doctrine of interest well understood does and does not secure. It is recognized:

> [14] The doctrine of interest well understood does not produce great abnegations; but it suggests each day small sacrifices; by itself alone, it cannot make a man virtuous; but it forms a multitude of orderly, temperate, moderate, foresightful citizens, masters of themselves; and if it does not conduct directly to virtue by the will, it insensibly brings it near by habituation.

Once again we are reminded that we are to turn away from the greatness that the aristocrats sought. What must be looked for now are not virtuous men but, rather, useful citizens. This approach, which both legitimates and redirects the lower passions, can transform most, if not all, of the inhabitants of a land into citizens—that is, into human beings working more or less together, in a reliable fashion, for the good of all, something that the aristocrats could never do or, at any rate, can no longer do.

Who knows what can follow from these habits in regularity? These citizens might "insensibly" become virtuous, almost in spite of themselves. Whether one is truly virtuous in such circumstances remains a question.

The prospect of success for the program implied in this chapter (if not in the work as a whole) leads to further suggestions about what is lost and gained:

> [15] If the doctrine of interest well understood comes to dominate entirely the moral world, extraordinary virtues would no doubt become more rare. But I also think that then the coarser depravities would be less common. The doctrine of interest well understood perhaps prevents some men from mounting far above the ordinary level of humanity; but a great number of others who would fall below encounter it and catch hold of it. Consider some individuals, it debases

them. Survey the species, it elevates it.

We now see it conceded that men of extraordinary virtues have existed, perhaps still exist—and that they are vulnerable to the new way advocated by the author. Once the advantages of the new way have been shown (as in paragraph 14 and earlier), then this concession can be made, whereas it had been doubted at the outset of this chapter that "men were more virtuous in aristocratic ages than in others."

Since it might be questioned whether the loss of men of extraordinary virtues should be accepted with equanimity, a further advantage of the new way is at once suggested: "The coarser depravities would be less common." True, some men would be prevented from "mounting far above the ordinary level of humanity," but "a great number of others who would [otherwise] fall below" are propped up. Thus, a trade-off is indicated: Individuals might be debased, but the species would be elevated.

Is not, however, the use of "species" here curious? This seems to be a scientific term, playing up the supposed malleability of the human race. Perhaps we are meant to appreciate that the author senses that the new way does, in certain aspects, turn away from the fully (or truly) human. Perhaps, also, this fits in with the notion that the useful (or one's interest) sounds more objective and verifiable and hence scientific (especially if it is seen primarily in terms of economic interest) than virtue or goodness (which can seem more "subjective" or a matter of taste). Of course, many of us in this country today *can* appreciate what the elevation of the species that the author speaks of means, when we compare our own personal circumstances with those of our immigrant parents, grandparents, or great-grandparents "in the old country."

Has the species been elevated? Certainly, there are more human beings supported now by the available resources, human beings who tend to be healthier and to live longer than men of a couple of centuries ago. But how have nobility and the quality of thought been affected? Does mankind depend, somehow, on some great ones, if it is to realize its full humanity? Does the elevation of the species invoked here by the author make too much of peace and of comfort?

One must also wonder, of course, whether "the coarser depravities" have indeed been made "less common." Perhaps this is true, in the sense that certain long-accepted depravities (in the form of callousness toward large-scale economic exploitation) have come under general attack. But, on the other hand, we must ask what the unprecedented barbarities of the twentieth century (beginning less than a hundred years after this book was written) can be attributed to. Did the great aspirations and pretenses of earlier centuries make the worst less likely in those times?

Does the author, in what he says about the elimination of the coarser depravities by the new way he advocates, underestimate the effects of technology and secrecy? (This means, among other things, that certain depravities can be carried out with fiendish thoroughness and yet can be concealed from public view and hence from any residual natural resistance to depravity.) Such considerations are critical to any assessment of a book which makes so much of utility. That is, the practical effect of the new way is vital, since this is a way which is recommended not for its own sake but rather primarily for its consequences. Are, then, the "coarser depravities" indeed made "less common," something which had been put forth as compensation for the loss of the highest human types?

Has the eclipse of the highest human types, the men of extraordinary virtues, liberated the very worst to assert itself, and not only because the now-concealed best were (among other things) best equipped to anticipate and to head off (perhaps even by great self-sacrifice) the worst? To what extent have the worst depravities come precisely because men remain open to greatness, because they have an innate taste for greatness, if not in themselves, at least in a few and in the community defined and inspired by those few? We are often reminded of the willingness, if not the eagerness, of some to pull down the high and mighty—and an egalitarian age does all too often cater to envy. But perhaps we need to be reminded as well that there may be in mankind an innate openness to the sublime. Have not the most awful atrocities of the twentieth century been grounded partly in efforts to supply mankind substitutes for the obvious and enduring greatness that our new way of life has virtually eliminated? Has elimination of the appearance of such greatness also depreciated the standards in the light of which certain things were considered great and others considered despicable?

Aside from the question of depravities (to which we will return), there is the question of what happens to genius, both philosophic and artistic, when the new leveling prevails? Is not the fullest expression of genius compromised, and made less likely, when "some individuals" (that is, men of extraordinary virtues) are "debased"? Certainly there is a vast difference between the works of, say, Sophocles and Phideas and Shakespeare, on the one hand, and the most widely acclaimed modern art, on the other. We are reminded of the question touched upon in paragraph 11, which comes up again in paragraph 16, of what philosophy does mean to this author.

We are obliged, then, to return to the question: In what does mankind truly live: in raising the general level of the community at large, or in contemplating the peaks which only a few can reasonably hope to attain? Does the general recognition of distant peaks affect the moral tone of the community and affect also a people's sense of dignity and the meaning for them of life itself? Or can people be satisfied by the placid times to which a rough equality, in effect, aspires? Still, are not extraordinary virtues, including the intellectual virtues, the things that even the generality of mankind somehow lives for? Whatever the social and political consequences of such virtues, the human being comes to fulfillment thus—and mankind can, when properly instructed, take pride in the manifestation of extraordinary virtues just as a healthy family or community can take pride in the offspring or neighbor who rises far above his fellows.

One mark of the man of extraordinary virtues should be his ability to explain men such as himself in such a way as to make them acceptable. Is it not a sign of a people's limitations that it does not sense how critical a man of extraordinary virtues can be for the vitality of the soul of mankind? Is not the author, even though not perhaps of the highest rank as a thinker himself, also somewhat vulnerable to the way of life he advocates? Certainly, one must question any way of life that seems to rule out, almost on principle, the very best.

Paragraph 15, like paragraph 8, can be considered a transition. The limitations of the doctrine of interest well understood have been touched upon here; its compensations, which are developed in the next section of this chapter, are anticipated.

VII

The sixth section of this chapter (made up of paragraphs 16, 17, 18, 19, and 20) considers further what can be said on behalf of the doctrine of interest well understood. Perhaps no section of the chapter makes so much of the first person. Thus, its first paragraph reads,

> [16] I shall not fear to say that the doctrine of interest well understood seems to me, of all the philosophical theories, the one most appropriate to the needs of men of our time, and that I see in it the most powerful guarantee that remains to them against themselves. It is principally toward it then that the spirit of moralists of our time ought to be turned. Even though they may judge it to be imperfect, it still must be adopted as necessary.

The author describes himself at the very outset of this paragraph as not fearful. In this he is like the bold American moralists referred to in paragraph 4, not like the frightened European moralists of paragraph 2. He is, that is, in tune with the times and its inclinations.

We here see again the problem of what philosophy means to the author (a problem that may be seen as well in paragraphs 11 and 15). Philosophy, it seems, is something to be used—and this may be consistent with a greater interest by the author in practice than in speculation. Is not this related to the down-to-earth approach displayed in paragraph 13, with its (Cartesian?) invocation of the "clear and sure"?

Men "of our time," we are told, have certain "needs." It may not matter how they got these needs; it is enough that they have them or, what may be the same in practice, that they believe they have them. Nothing is said about what should be done about these needs, such as changing them, except that they can usefully be turned against themselves. And for this the doctrine of interest well understood is eminently useful.

This doctrine, it is recognized, is imperfect. Yet it should be "adopted as necessary." Thus, the truth is respected here, at least to the extent of acknowledging that the doctrine, however useful, is defective. The truth is thus somehow preserved, at least for a while—but one must wonder how any doctrine can continue to be recognized as imperfect by anyone once it is generally accepted and turns out to be useful. Evidently, in order for this doctrine to be popular, it must not be *presented* as imperfect. The author's immediate readers, then, are not those who are likely to accept the doctrine without reservation. Are his privileged readers to consider all this from a perspective that is somehow superior to those who believe in the doctrine of interest well understood? Upon what does such a statesmanlike perspective depend? Nothing is said about that here. Rather, the author goes on to say something more about how Americans and Europeans differ in one critical respect, presumably because of the effect in the United States of the general acceptance of the doctrine of interest well understood:

> [17] I do not believe, on the whole, that there is more egoism among us than in America; the sole difference is that there it is illuminated and here it is not. Each American knows how to sacrifice a part of his particular interests to save the rest. We want to retain everything and often everything escapes us.

Europeans, it seems, are particularly in need of the moderating effects of the doctrine of interest well understood. That is because of the kind of egoism Europeans have. Egoism, the author had explained six chapters before, "is a passionate and exaggerated love of self which leads a man to think of all things in terms of himself and to prefer himself to all." It "springs from a blind instinct." Individualism, on the other hand, "is based on misguided judgment rather than on depraved feeling"; it is "a calm and considered feeling which disposes each citizen to isolate himself from the mass of his fellows and to withdraw into the circle of family and friends. . . ." Egoism, it seems, is associated more with man (is it almost natural?); individualism, more with the citizen—and it is the individualism of Americans, as citizens, from which this chapter takes its departure. Egoism, it also seems, is more of a problem with Europeans than it is with Americans, perhaps because Europeans remain, by and large, more private and more instinctive in their pursuits. (The concern here with egoism may help account for the considerable use of the first person in this section of our chapter.)

Europeans are, with respect to their personal desires, less "illuminated" (or informed) than Americans. About what matters are Americans better informed? As to how egoistic all are? Or as to how to be effectively egoistic, especially by looking out somewhat for others? One way or another, Americans are sensible: They know how to give up part to save the whole, whatever reasons they give. Has the legitimation of acquisitiveness in America made them less acquisitive? Are they thus on the way to that virtue, by gradual habituation, anticipated in paragraph 14?

We Europeans, on the other hand, the author suggests, are stupidly greedy. How bad *we* are, how much *we* are in need of correction, is evident in the next paragraph:

> [18] I only see around me people who seem to want to teach each day to their contemporaries, by their word and their example, that the useful is never dishonest. Shall I not discover finally some who undertake to make them comprehend how the honest can be useful?

People around him seem to want to teach the wrong thing: An act is moral, they seem to say, if it serves one's interest. That is, European moralists of his day try to rationalize, in terms of the honorable, the selfishness that men are prone to. Does such rationalization only create resentment among the exploited? On what basis were these arguments being made in the author's time? Was it being said that it is not wrong for a man to do what benefits him? Rather, it is only "natural" to do so? Besides, it was perhaps added, only he can look out for himself. In this way, whatever natural regard one might have for the welfare of others was disparaged, if not even suppressed.

The author prefers to see the current teaching reversed: It should be insisted that it pays to be moral. No doubt, moral conduct *can* be useful. Is it always? Are there not instances when it is difficult to believe that one is benefiting personally, in the ordinary sense of "benefit," from one's morality? Or should morality be vitally dependent upon prudence, a prudence which makes much more of consequences than do everyday moral maxims? That is, the right thing to do may often vary with the circumstances. Prudence does look to utility—but whose utility? Is not prudence consistent, at least on rare occasions, with self-sacrifice?

Perhaps this is too sophisticated for the author's immediate purpose. After all, it is a popular doctrine that is needed, one that is, or at least appears to be, "clear and sure." The author seems to identify himself as one of those who "undertake to make [people] comprehend how the honest can be useful." Or is it really that he wants to persuade people to believe that the honest *is* useful, not *how* it happens that it is? For, we notice, it is not precisely spelled out here what the Americans believe they gain by giving up "a part of [their] particular interests," or how they gain by acting morally toward others. What might happen would require a case-by-case analysis to figure out—and that is not the author's concern here. Rather, it is a general attitude that he wants to change: He wants people to begin to believe that it helps *them* to help their fellow citizens, for whatever reason they do it. Perhaps he (as a responsible statesman) would change his emphasis, and the rationale of his position, once Europeans become so convinced by what he advocates that they act more like public-spirited Americans. To begin to change Europeans, they must first believe that one does the right thing toward others primarily for one's own good, even though in fact it may be for the good of the other. Of course, a better community, and better fellow-citizens, are thereby promoted—and so one does benefit, usually, by one's sacrifices.

French readers of these comments by Tocqueville on the relation of the honest and the useful could well have been reminded of Montaigne's essay, almost three centuries earlier, "On the Useful and the Honest." Tocqueville had referred to Montaigne by name, for the only time in the entire book, in paragraph 8 of this chapter; he now implicitly draws upon him, here in paragraph 18. An endorsement of Montaigne's approach may be seen in Tocqueville's resistance to the emphasis in the teaching of his own time upon the proposition that "the useful is never dishonest." After all, Montaigne had virtually concluded his essay on this subject with the sentence, "We poorly argue the honesty and beauty of an action from its utility, and we commit a fallacy in thinking that everyone is obliged to perform—and that it is honest to perform—an action merely because it is useful. . . ." Again and again in his essay, Montaigne argues for the honest in lieu of the useful, even though he recognizes that princes must sometimes violate their consciences in order to do what the common good (or general utility) clearly requires. But private interest, he seems to insist, should not be permitted to sway one from proper conduct; that would hardly be worthy of, or becoming for, the true statesman.

It would take us too far afield on this occasion, however, to consider further what Montaigne says, and how he questions the distinction in common usage between the useful and the honest. A full study of *Democracy in America* should take seriously this subtle essay by Montaigne; it is against this background that Tocqueville speaks. Consider, for instance, the roles of shame (which is related to beauty?) and of conscience in Montaigne, and what happens to these things in Tocqueville.

Perhaps Tocqueville meant to suggest that his entire book should be read in the light of Montaigne, another great "sociological" writer of the French school. And so, special reference may, in effect, be made by Tocqueville to the Montaigne essay on the useful and the honest. Montaigne does seem more elevated with respect to virtue than Tocqueville sometimes allows himself to appear in *Democracy in America.* But, one can suspect upon noticing correspondences between these two French authors' works, Tocqueville knew that Montaigne's public position on virtue was closer than was Tocqueville's to classical models (even though Montaigne, too, did depart from them). (Also, was not philosophy a more serious enterprise for Montaigne?) Tocqueville's public position and emphasis with respect to virtue and politics, he can be understood to have suggested, must appear (and hence be?) different from Montaigne's because times and circumstances have changed so much. We are thus reminded of how this subject might more fully be regarded.

The author goes on, in the following paragraph in this chapter, to remind us also of what has led to the changes in times and circumstances that a statesman must reckon with:

> [19] There is no power on earth able to prevent the increasing equality of conditions from carrying the human spirit to seek out the useful, or from disposing each citizen to shrink into himself.

No "power *on* earth" can prevent what is happening. Is it recognized that God may still do so, but He is not expected to do so? He, in any event, cannot be counted upon to intervene here. The author reconciles himself to the inevitable. Great historical forces are suggested. But could the excesses or debacle of triumphant equality lead to its subversion?

Should the worldwide inclination to equality be catered to (and used) or should it be resisted? Elsewhere in the book, there are indications that a rough justice is available from a dedication to equality which was not evident when liberty reigned, that very liberty which does permit nobility and men of extraordinary virtues to manifest themselves. This opening to justice might make the author himself more inclined than others of his class to go along with, and to guide in a statesmanlike manner, the egalitarian revolution, rather than to resist it. He is not heard to pray to God that this massive historical movement be reversed.

The key to this movement, we are told, is "the increasing equality of conditions." It seems that material conditions, not ideas, are considered by the author to be fundamental to this development, whatever he may say elsewhere about the primacy of the soul. But why have conditions changed? That is not explored here. Perhaps it cannot be, without sacrificing the notion that conditions are critical. That is, really to know why conditions have changed would be to challenge the (sociological?) opinion that conditions are dominant; reason would thereby be considered somehow higher, if not even sovereign, something which the author generally seems to doubt.

What does a dedication to equality mean in practice? We have noticed its opening to justice, especially when contrasted to regimes which find people locked into depressed stations generation after generation. Does equality tend to look to the useful, especially if traditional models and standards are repudiated? The useful in such circumstances is apt to be linked to the pleasant: One is encouraged to look out for oneself; or perhaps that turns out to be the only thing one is left with. It is not surprising then that each citizen becomes disposed "to shrink into himself," even while much is made of judging each man and woman on the basis of merit.

Each can see his merits equal to those of others, if only because (in the absence of authoritative standards) one naturally tends to consider one's own desires to be as worthy as those of others. (And as more and more material goods become generally available, appetites are excited further.) It becomes fashionable to insist, "I'm as good as anyone else"—with the only sure and clear basis of one's claims to equal treatment being the fact of one's existence. Thus, one can insist that one is as good as the next man, without having had to learn anything special or to act in any special way.

Besides, a usefulness keyed to pleasure is easier to "understand." The many can more easily believe that they comprehend what is going on, or at least where their interests lie, when utility is the key to choice. Nature, in any event, becomes suspect as a source of standards, even while it seems to legitimate the desires one happens to have. For one thing, if there should be standards of right and wrong recognized as evident from a study of nature, then it is likely that significant inequalities among men may also have to be recognized. Therefore, if one makes much of equality, one may tend (unless one is thoughtful) to rule out nature as a guide, insofar as nature works from differences among men. Invocations of nature are distrusted, for they have all too often been used to rationalize unjust allocations among men. Or, if nature is to be permitted to have a say, it should be only in the form of serving, as well as legitimating, whatever desires we happen to have. Thus, again, the pleasant is sovereign, which means a determined recourse to the useful.

The author sees two responses by men to prevailing egalitarian conditions. Either they will go out to seek the useful or they will shrink into themselves. Either way, they will try to serve themselves, or at least they will not submit to authority or to authoritative principles. So, he counsels, thoughtful men (that is, statesmen?) should make the moral seem useful. Thus, he closes this section of our chapter with this observation:

> [20] It must then be expected that individual interest will become more than ever the principal, if not the unique, motive for the actions of man; but it remains to be learned how each man seeks his individual interest.

Individual interest will be decisive. The critical question is what each man sees interest to be—that is, how he can be led to see his own interest. The author advocates in this chapter that each man should be led to see that his interest includes a considerable benevolence toward his fellow citizens.

The author does not say more about rightness for its own sake. Perhaps he is too much a modern, and not only in being "realistic," in shying away as he does from that recourse to nature which may be seen in invocations of natural right and in relying upon the natural sociability of men.

VIII

The final section of this chapter (made up of paragraphs 21 and 22) suggests the safeguards that must be resorted to, now that equality is becoming triumphant and should the doctrine of interest be established.

First, the dangers that lie before mankind are dramatized:

> [21] If citizens, in becoming equal, were to remain ignorant and coarse, it is difficult to foresee to what stupid excess their egoism will carry them, and it cannot be said in advance into what shameful miseries they would plunge themselves from fear of sacrificing something of their well-being to the prosperity of their kind.

The author warns against stupid excesses and shameful miseries, especially if citizens remain "ignorant and coarse." Ignorance takes the form, it seems, of a selfishness which is *not* tempered by the doctrine of interest well understood. Here as elsewhere in this chapter, fear is a corrosive element in society; this time it is "fear of sacrificing something of their well-being to the prosperity of their kind." We are reminded of the expectation voiced in paragraph 15 that "the coarser depravities would be less common" if the doctrine of interest well understood should come "to dominate entirely the moral world."

Ignorance and coarseness are seen as dangerous. And yet we now know that perhaps the greatest systematic atrocities in recorded history did come (in our own time) in a highly cultivated country and under the leadership of someone who challenged his people to make great sacrifices for the fatherland. Are not men apt to "plunge" most deeply when asked to sacrifice for the most noble causes, especially if elevated glimpses of the truly great have been systematically denied them? That is, "debasing" extends beyond the few great ones who are dragged down. Of course, those who commit atrocities do not consider their victims to be their equals. They may not even regard their victims as of the same species (or as "their kind"). And so a thoroughgoing dedication to equality *can* promote justice within a community. But, as I have suggested, equality can also be taken by all too many to relieve men of any duty to submit to restraints imposed either by nature or by any who are by nature superior.

Still, the author concludes this chapter by counseling what should be done to make the equality-bound men of our day somewhat respectful of the requirements of the community and of their fellow-citizens:

> [22] I do not believe that the doctrine of interest, as it is preached in America, is evident in all its parts; but it does contain a great number of truths so evident that it suffices to illuminate men for them to be seen. Illuminate them, then, at any cost, for the age of blind abnegations and of instinctive virtues already flees far from us, and I see approaching the time when liberty, the public peace and social order itself will not be able to exist without enlightenment.

It is conceded here that the doctrine of interest is not "evident [or, obvious] in all its parts." One is reminded, by way of contrast, of the Declaration of Independence, with its grounding in self-evident truths. But, the author goes on to assure us, the doctrine "does contain a great number of truths so evident" that one need only point them out in order for men at large to be persuaded.

This pointing out—this lighting up what is there to be seen—is advocated. Such enlightenment does not seem to be genuine education; rather it is to be, as it has been in America, a kind of preaching.

Can the enlightenment called for head off demagoguery and atrocities, to say nothing of a long-term decline? Demagogues, I have suggested, can appeal to the natural taste for sacrifice, for country and for greatness—all of which tend to be neglected by the doctrine of interest well understood, which may rest ultimately upon the opinion that one does not really sacrifice anything when one acts morally, that what one does is for one's personal benefit as ordinarily understood, and that greatness is obsolete and otherwise unrealistic. We suspect that only citizens of democracies are apt to be able to apply systematically the doctrine of interest the author advocates, if only because only they have extensive choices to make in how they conduct themselves in social relations. Are democracies then most vulnerable to the permanent debasing effects of any doctrine which, however highminded in its ultimate goals and in many of its consequences, places the emphasis in its method upon looking out for oneself?

What is the alternative to the doctrine of interest well understood? An old-fashioned answer looks to prudence (preferably a prudence instructed by political philosophy)—prudence in statesmen who minister to a people properly trained with respect to "the duties of man," not just with respect to man's interests and rights. But "blind abnegations" and "instinctive virtues" seem to be ruled out by the author, whereas one might have hoped that one's leaders had been imbued with a spirit of appropriate sacrifice for the common good and that one's people had been so shaped that its virtues were deeply engrained. Does the author, with the sense of sophisticated "realism" he promotes, make a thoughtful prudence (such as was evident among the Founding Fathers) more difficult to develop in leaders and to respond to by peoples, thereby making statesmanship less likely?

Be that as it may, our chapter closes with a reminder of various goods which are threatened: "liberty, the public peace and social order." Liberty, it can be argued, makes nobility (or excellence) possible. It, perhaps more than the others—and more than equality as well—can be, as it were, an end in itself. Liberty is to be found as against the community, perhaps, but still *within* the community—at least if one regards man as a social animal. The natural sociability of man may be reflected in the reaffirmation here of public peace and social order. Do not these point to the community, and not to one's own interest (however well understood), as primary in certain respects? And is not a truly political approach required here, not an effort which seems to assure people that they are entitled to look out first for themselves in their dealings with their fellow citizens? Certainly, political philosophy, not political sociology of the kind seen in this book, is needed to clarify what it is that mankind needs and aspires to and what the place is, in a genuine political community, of men of extraordinary virtues. Perhaps this is also needed if we are to understand what is truly at the heart of the American regime and hence what it is that makes it work as well as it, in fact, does.

IX

We have seen, through an extended examination of one of its shorter chapters, that *Democracy in America* is a book that can be expected to repay detailed examination. Care in composition is evident throughout. Some of the things we have seen in examining the text of this chapter are evident as well in its title, "How the Americans Combat Individualism by the Doctrine of Interest Well Understood."

The author speaks here of *combat* (as in a related discussion four chapters before). This suggests that there is a battle going on—that the Americans have a mission, even a victory, in mind, perhaps even some notion of the common good which they want to see prevail. Without such an objective, the American effort would be but another purposeless skirmish, not part of a meaningful campaign. Thus, the author seems to imply, Americans sense something higher for the sake of which a useful individuality should be curbed. What role do extraordinary men, "by their word and their example," play in reminding Americans of great goals? Our greatest "word," the Declaration of Independence, does make much of the place of prudence, and hence of statesmanship, in human affairs.

Certainly it is difficult, if the doctrine of interest well understood is to be taken both as men ordinarily take it and as decisive in guiding American actions, to make sense of the great civil war in which magnificent passions were enlisted and to which incalculable sacrifices were made—that great war which, coming a generation after this book, could be called the last great war among gentlemen. Perhaps, it can be added, the existence of slavery in the United States meant that early Americans should have emphasized as they did the principle of equality, if only to remind themselves continually that they could do no more than tolerate the unjust institution they were saddled with—tolerate it until the opportunity came (albeit with great disregard for personal interest, as ordinarily understood) to rid themselves and their posterity of this affliction.

Whether equality should continue to be made as much of as formerly among us, now that circumstances have changed, depends on prudential political judgments of the highest order. We are again reminded of the standards to which Americans must have looked in "combating" individualism or in determining what to emphasize and what to play down, both in their efforts to serve the common good and in their personal pursuits of happiness. The doctrine of interest well understood, I have suggested, may help, when properly used, to guide both public opinion and private action. That is, it must rest, if it is to be used well, on a lively sense of right and wrong rooted either in nature or in a sacred tradition so firmly established as to seem natural. The author does not seem to appreciate the significance of the fact, reported by him elsewhere in the book, of the presence of treasured copies of Shakespeare and of the Bible in humble dwellings all over the America he visited. Did not those works teach Americans *not* to insist only upon the utility of virtue but rather to practice it for its own sake as well?

What, finally, does Tocqueville do for that political philosophy upon which an enduring polity rests? He certainly draws upon political philosophy and yet (depending on how he is read) he can be seen to undermine it—or, at least, he can make sound understanding more difficult for his successors. How many of the difficulties implicit in his argument which I have suggested on this occasion did he himself recognize? Or was he, like a gifted artist, inspired to reveal more than he was conscious of? Did he, for example, counsel his more privileged readers not only as to how "insensibly" to lead the many to virtue but also as to how to attain for themselves and others like themselves a noble grandeur by which still others might be enlightened, inspired, and perhaps even educated? To this end, should not much more be made of ideas and reasoning, and far less of mindless conditions and inevitable movements, as the fundamental causes of the soundest opinions and of the most celebrated actions of mankind? It is with such causes and such ends that the dedicated statesman must be preeminently concerned.

I have suggested certain problems with Tocqueville's understanding of moral and political things and their sources. Need I add that this should not be taken as an attempt to deny the extraordinary merits of a majestic oratorio on democracy which, in its inspired appeal, defies all critics?

16

Racial Equality in America

William D. Richardson

The enduring popularity of *Democracy in America* attests both to the tremendous ambitiousness of its subject matter and, even more remarkably, to the uncommon insightfulness of some of Tocqueville's observations. Tocqueville presented a survey of America which examined the unique combination of its natural resources, inhabitants, and political arrangements, with the intent of explaining that nation's singular limitations and prospects. One of the less-remarked-upon subjects of this survey concerned the three distinct American races which were experiencing vastly different degrees of freedom and prosperity. The explanations Tocqueville advanced for these inequalities, and their long-term consequences for the regime, would seem to merit some reexamination, not in the least because some of their more significant aspects have survived to this day.

The Three Races in America

A thorough discussion of Tocqueville's views on race relations in America requires some prefatory remarks about his (indirect) quarrel with Count de Buffon, a renowned French naturalist.[1] In

---

[1]There is a distinct parallel between Tocqueville's views on the perniciousness of Buffon's theories and his familiarity with, and frequent references to, the works of Thomas Jefferson, who also assailed Buffon. For Tocqueville's view of Jefferson, see *Democracy in America*, ed. J.-P. Mayer, trans. George Lawrence (Garden City, N.Y.: Doubleday, Anchor Books, 1969), pp. 29nn. 15 and 16, 334, 356n. 46, 368, 382, 391. Hereinafter cited as *Democracy*. For a discussion of Jefferson's treatment of Buffon, see William D. Richardson, "Thomas Jefferson and Race: The Declaration and *Notes on the State of Virginia*," *Polity*, 16, No. 3 (Spring 1984), pp. 447-66.

brief, Buffon contended that all living things of the New World, be they animal or vegetable, were inferior to their counterparts in the Old World. Since a large part of Buffon's argument revolved around allegations about the New World's unsuitable climate and soil, his thesis also had as a lesser target those animals (including, obviously, men) or vegetables transported to the New World from the Old. Some of the clearest statements of Tocqueville's views on this subject (as well as of a theme undergirding most of *Democracy*) are found in correspondence written many years after his visit to America. In one of his letters to his young friend and protégé Gobineau, Tocqueville remarks:

> Buffon and, after him, Flourens believe in the diversity of *races* but in the unity of the human *species*. The only reason they seem to give is the continuous procreation of the races among themselves, which, for natural scientists, should be complete and incontrovertible proof, since it is difficult to believe that God would have amused Himself by creating two physically almost similar species but then permitting their confusion through the effacement of His original line of demarcation. . . .
>
> Mankind thus belongs to a singular species and, according to Buffon and Flourens, human variations are products of three secondary and external causes: of climate, of food, and of the manner of life.[2]

In another letter, Tocqueville bluntly castigates Gobineau's acceptance of Buffon's theories.

> I never concealed from you that I am greatly prejudiced against what seems to be your principal idea . . . it applies *fatalism* not merely to individuals but to those perennial conglomerations of individuals called races.[3]

Still later, Tocqueville more fully elaborated his opposition to

---

[2]Tocqueville to Gobineau, May 15, 1852. See Tocqueville, *"The European Revolution" and Correspondence with Gobineau*, ed. John Lukacs (Gloucester, Mass.: Peter Smith, 1968), pp. 221-22. Hereinafter cited as *European Revolution*,.

[3]Tocqueville to Gobineau, Oct. 11, 1853. See *European Revolution*, p. 224.

Gobineau's combining of the doctrines of predestination and "matter." Tocqueville's main concern was not with their truth or falsity (though he is convinced they are in error); rather, he is worried about "the practical consequences of these philosophical doctrines."

> You continually speak about races regenerating or degenerating, losing or acquiring through an infusion of new blood social capacities which they have not previously had. . . .
>
> And be assured that should the masses, whose reasoning always follows the most beaten tracks, accept your doctrines, it would lead them straight from races to individuals and from social capacities to all sorts of potentialities. . . .
>
> The consequence of both theories is that of a vast limitation, if not a complete abolition of human liberty.[4]

Tocqueville is concerned that Gobineau could believe that his Buffonian theories presented a truer version of history than the previous practice of seeking the "cause of human events in the influence of certain men, of certain emotions, of certain thoughts, and of certain beliefs."[5] Far from better serving mankind, Tocqueville believes Gobineau's newly adopted doctrines do the opposite.

> What purpose does it serve to persuade lesser peoples living in abject conditions of barbarism or slavery that, such being their racial nature, they can do nothing to better themselves, to change their habits, or to ameliorate their status? Don't you see how inherent in your doctrine are all the evils produced by permanent inequality: pride, violence, the scorn of one's fellow men, tyranny and abjection in every one of their forms?[6]

Tocqueville stresses the view that the "destinies of men, whether of individuals or nations, depends on *what they want to*

---

[4]Tocqueville to Gobineau, Nov. 17, 1853. See *European Revolution*, p. 227, and the antepenultimate paragraph of *Democracy*, p. 705.
[5]*European Revolution*, p. 228.
[6]Ibid., p. 229.

be"[7] (emphasis added). Understanding of this contention may greatly assist one in comprehending Tocqueville's treatment of the subject of race relations in particular, and of the question of democracy's potential for "progress" in general.

Tocqueville was not so naive as to believe that men actually controlled or could control their whole destiny. He recognized that chance plays an impressive part in the affairs of men.[8] What he did seem to believe, though, was that men could control more of their destinies than heretofore had been thought possible. However, in order to convince men of this possibility, Tocqueville had to continue Machiavelli's enterprise of persuading men to concentrate on bettering their earthly existence. In order to accomplish this, he had to overcome the attraction of contrary opinions; consequently, he propagated what have been termed "salutary myths."[9] One such myth held that the triumph of democracy over rival forms of government—particularly aristocracy—is inevitable. Its purpose was to get men to accept democracy and, instead of fighting against it, devote themselves to perfecting it. Through the use of this and lesser salutary myths, Tocqueville hoped to see the bold claim that men can be what they want to be at least partially fulfilled.

Tocqueville does not openly discuss theories of racial inequality. Instead, he is intent on identifying the practical consequences for America contained in the presence of distinct racial groups on her soil (a presence in which he sees slaves representing the "order of nature overthrown").[10] However, before entering into the substance of Tocqueville's examination of American race relations, it is worthwhile to note the structure within which that treatment is presented.

---

[7]Ibid.
[8]*Democracy*, p. 357.
[9]Marvin Zetterbaum, *Tocqueville and the Problem of Democracy* (Stanford, Cal.: Stanford University Press, 1967), p. 19.
[10]*Democracy*, pp. 355, 363.

The Structure of *Democracy in America*

The discussion of race occurs in the tenth and final chapter of the first volume of *Democracy.* It is striking that, up until this chapter, Tocqueville had been almost silent on the subjects of the black race and slavery in America. (He had previously mentioned the subject of blacks in a long footnote which, in illustrating the majority's capacity for despotism, presented the predicament of free blacks who feared to exercise their "rights as citizens.")[11] In other words, it is not until the very last chapter of the first volume (which preceded the second volume by five years and was intended to treat the subject of the American "democratic social order['s] . . . laws and conceptions of public morality")[12] that there is a treatment of the most serious and controversial moral-legal problem confronting the regime founded on Jefferson's principles of rights and equality. As we will see, it is the very seriousness of the problem that may account for its being treated as the "final" issue of the volume.

That this last chapter of Volume I concerns race relations is easily ascertained from its title, "Some Considerations Concerning the Present State and Probable Future of the Three Races that Inhabit the Territory of the United States." What is not so obvious, however, is Tocqueville's reason for placing this particular chapter where he does. To discover this, it is first necessary to examine the order or structure of Volume I, which is divided into two parts. The first is generally concerned with the "social state" of equality in America and with the forms and powers of its various governments. The second part is most concerned with an inquiry into the problems of majority rule in America. Thus, immediately preceding the chapter on the three races is one entitled "The Main Causes Tending to Maintain a Democratic Republic in the United States." Essentially, this chapter is a discussion of the importance of laws, mores, and religious beliefs for maintaining democratic institutions.[13] Their

---

[11]Ibid., pp. 252-53. For a brief discussion of the origins of American slavery and its debilitating effects on the South, see p. 35.

[12]Ibid., p. 417.

[13]Paradoxically, these democratic laws and mores prove to be severe impediments to the removal of slavery and to the acceptance of blacks into white society. In turn, it is slavery which represents the greatest threat to the American democracy. See

influence is of great importance in creating and sustaining a homogeneous society. However, chapter 10 is not so much concerned with a homogeneous society as with a heterogeneous one. In fact, here Tocqueville states that the races in America represent foreign peoples facing each other on the same soil.[14] One way in which Tocqueville seems to indicate his awareness of the grave dangers inherent in such an arrangement is by entitling the central subsection of chapter 10, "What Are the Chances that the American Union Will Last?" A further interesting and suggestive feature of the chapter's structure is that the titles of the subsections following this central one do not indicate a concern with race at all. However, this seeming lack of concern is deceptive. An explanation of it requires a brief consideration of what, in fact, Tocqueville *does* discuss in chapter 10.

In examining the disadvantages attending white enslavement of blacks, Tocqueville concentrates not on the injustice of this slavery but, rather, on the material costs to the masters.[15] The purpose in appealing to American democrats—particularly Southern American democrats—in this manner seems to be a reflection of his concern with turning "self interest" into "self interest properly understood."[16] In a sense, he provides an illustration of how the self-centeredness or individualism of democratic men can be manipulated so as to produce a result that is (or appears to be) good both for the individual and, more importantly, for the regime as a whole. The way in which Tocqueville accomplishes this task is to appeal to the democrat's lowest and most cherished object: his material well-being. By persuading him that this well-being is adversely affected by a reliance on black slavery, Tocqueville achieves more than one objective. First, if he is successful, the democrat, in seeking the furtherance of his own selfish desires, should be convinced of

---

Democracy, pp. 340-41, 343, 355-56.

[14]Ibid., p. 355.

[15]Ibid., p. 345ff (see especially p. 348). Compare this with Thomas Jefferson's treatment of related disadvantages—material and spiritual or intellectual—afflicting the master. See *Notes on the State of Virginia*, ed. William Peden (New York: Norton, 1972), Query 18.

[16]*Democracy*, vol. II, pt. II, chap. 8. (It is possible to see Tocqueville acknowledging this approach when he states that most men "think that knowledge of [their] own interest properly understood is enough to lead a man to what is just and honest." Ibid., p. 374.)

the need to end his involvement with black slavery.[17] (Thus, a base appeal advances a noble end.) Second, the commercial greatness of the United States should be enhanced by former masters being forced to turn to the marketplace in order to make a comfortable livelihood for themselves.

One reason he devotes more than half of this last chapter—a chapter that is, according to its title, supposedly concerned with race relations—to questions of commercial development is that this approach touches the dearest concern of American democrats. While such men would listen very attentively to proposals that promised to increase their wealth, they would probably do no more than pause to hear an indictment of slavery that only attacked that institution's natural injustice.[18] Similarly, the underlying concern of the chapter—and, in particular, of those subdivisions devoted to commerce—with the survival of the United States can be seen as a reflection of the author's concern about what should be done with the blacks once the masters are persuaded that it is in their own best interest to free them.

Finally, before he separately treats the red and black races in America,[19] Tocqueville presents a short introduction to his subject which he concludes by recounting his observation of three females of different races in the forest. He describes the "free, proud, and almost fierce" demeanor of the "young savage," the servility of the Negress, and the white child's "sense of superiority."[20] Part of his emphasis in this section of *Democracy* is certainly on the different types of individuals produced by different conditions, laws, and mores.[21] However, while it is true that Tocqueville makes

---

[17]Admittedly, the question of the injustice of black slavery was understood as a separate issue from the question of what should be done with the blacks once they were freed.

[18]Appropriately, the last subsection of this chapter is entitled: "Some Considerations Concerning the Causes of the Commercial Greatness of the United States."

[19]In an interesting and ironic comment, Tocqueville states, in chapter 10, that he will discuss "topics [which] are like tangents to my subject, being American, but not democratic. . . ." One of these undemocratic topics concerns the "tyranny" of the white race over the other races. In the whole of volume I, this appears to be the only instance in which Tocqueville explicitly undertakes to examine something which is both peculiarly American *and* peculiarly undemocratic.

[20]*Democracy*, p. 320.

[21]John Koritansky argues that Tocqueville's depiction of the three races was intended

comparisons between members of different races and certain regimes,[22] the majority of the comparisons involve members of the white race—specifically, Northerners and Southerners. For instance, he refers to the Southern slavemasters as members of an "aristocracy founded on visible and indelible signs."[23] He then devotes a fair amount of space to a description of the material differences between an aristocracy (represented by Kentucky) and a democracy (represented by Ohio).[24] In one memorable passage, Tocqueville criticizes all aristocracies in a manner which implicitly reserves the severest censure for the American aristocracy based on natural differences. An aristocracy cannot last unless it is founded on "an accepted principle of inequality, legalized in advance, and introduced into the rest of society—all things so violently repugnant to *natural equity* that only constraint will make men submit to them"[25] (emphasis added).

Indian and White Men in America

The separate treatments Tocqueville accords Indian-white and black-white relations may be a reflection of his view that each race "follows a separate destiny."[26] Also, Tocqueville thinks that the Indians are governed by "opinions and mores alone." However, these opinions and mores have a tenacious hold over them. Far from being willing to sacrifice them in favor of the whites' civilization, the Indian "delights in his barbarous independence and would rather die" than give up any part of it.[27] In fact, relations between these barbarous Indians and the supposedly civilized white men produced some startling effects: As a result of being in contact with one another, both Indian and white men frequently became more

---

to symbolize the "three fundamental human conditions: aristocratic but barbaric freedom, abject servitude, and democratic equality." See his "Democracy and Nobility: A Comment on Tocqueville's *Democracy in America*," *The Intercollegiate Review* (Fall 1976), p. 14.

[22] *Democracy*, pp. 328, 357.

[23] Ibid., p. 342.

[24] Ibid., p. 347ff.

[25] Ibid., p. 399.

[26] Ibid., p. 317.

[27] Ibid., p. 319.

barbarous.[28] Accordingly, a proper examination of Tocqueville's views on Indian-white relations has to occur within the larger context of his views on the consequences of this clash between civilization and barbarism.

One may begin, then, with Tocqueville's definition of the conditions or states of civilization and barbarism. He defines the former as "the result of prolonged social endeavor taking place on the same spot, an endeavor which each generation bequeaths to the next."[29]

Later, he elaborates on this definition:

> I would never admit that men form a society simply by recognizing the same leader and obeying the same laws; only when certain men consider a great many questions from the same point of view and have the same opinions on a great many subjects and when the same events give rise to like thoughts and impressions is there a society.[30]

In a more general manner, Tocqueville undertakes to define barbarism or savagery. Aside from the previously mentioned view that Indians or "savage" men are "governed" only by opinions and mores, he emphasizes that a "childish carelessness of the morrow [is] characteristic of savage nature."[31] Furthermore, Tocqueville believes that the Indians are particularly difficult to civilize because they are nomadic hunters and exceedingly prideful.

> Far from wishing to adapt his mores to ours, [the red man] regards barbarism as the distinctive emblem of his race, and in repulsing civilization he is perhaps less moved by hatred against it than by fear of resembling the Europeans.[32]

The Indians' reticence to be civilized is not diminished by the actions of the white race, for the whites consistently exploit those

---

[28]Ibid., pp. 318, 329-30n. 17.
[29]Ibid., p. 327.
[30]Ibid., p. 373.
[31]Ibid., p. 326. This characterization is certainly reminiscent of Rousseau. Cf. Jean-Jacques Rousseau, *The First and Second Discourses*, ed. Roger D. Masters, trans. Roger and Judith Masters (New York: St. Martin's Press, 1964), pp. 117, 137.
[32]*Democracy*, p. 319.

Indians who are forced into attempting some sort of accommodation with them. Consequently, the only impetus Indians have to adopt white ways is necessity—a situation which is usually forced upon them by the whites' destruction of their means of subsistence.[33] In Tocqueville's view, this way of embracing civilization is very deficient, for while "misery drove these unfortunate Indians toward civilization . . . oppression repulses them [back] toward barbarism."[34]

In reflecting on the manner in which various peoples have risen from barbarism to civilization, Tocqueville contends history generally shows that "barbarous people have raised themselves gradually by their own efforts until they reach civilization."[35] However, depending on the circumstances under which they meet, the barbarians' rise to civilization can be either substantially assisted or greatly hindered by a civilized people.

> When the conquered people are enlightened and the conquerors half savage . . . the power which the barbarian has won by his victory enables him to keep on a level with the civilized man and to go forward as his equal, until he becomes his rival; one has force to support him and the other intelligence. . . . But when the side that has the physical force has intellectual superiority too, it is rare for the conquered to become civilized; they either withdraw or are destroyed.[36]

This view of the conflict between civilization and barbarism has relevance not just for the Indian-white confrontation but for the black-white one as well. Both the Indians and blacks shared two important attributes in facing the whites: They were conquered, and they remained (or were kept) "intellectually" inferior to the whites.

The unevenness of the odds in the conflict between the whites and the Indians seemed to have influenced Tocqueville's view when

---

[33]Ibid., pp. 328-29.
[34]Ibid., p. 335.
[35]Ibid., p. 330.
[36]Ibid., p. 330-31.

he considered the options open to the latter.

> There were only two roads to safety open to the North American Indians: war or civilization; in other words, they had either to destroy the Europeans or to become their equals.[37]

Unfortunately (for them), the Indians waited too long to choose the option of waging a war of annihilation against the whites; at the time of Tocqueville's writing, they were already too few in number to pose a formidable threat to the constantly increasing ranks of the whites. On the other hand, the Indians refused to accept the only remaining course of action that could have saved them; if and when they decided to seek civilization's embrace, it would be too late.

Black and White Men in America

Tocqueville's discussion of the black race is forthrightly and perhaps alarmingly heralded by the title "Situation of the Black Race in the United States; Dangers Entailed for the Whites by Its Presence." The attentive reader is thus given notice that the author will be discussing the matter from the perspective of the whites and with special attention to the whites' "self-interest properly understood."

Since one of the most important questions about black-white relations in Tocqueville's time concerned what to do with the blacks if and when they gained their freedom, it is appropriate to begin with it. One aspect of this question involves the matter of making citizens—good citizens—out of former slaves. Tocqueville speaks to this difficulty at several points in chapter 10. It is his view that the black habitually has acquired the "thoughts and ambitions of a slave."[38]

> If he becomes free, he often feels independence as a heavier burden than slavery itself, for his life has taught him to

---

[37]Ibid., p. 326. Note how similar Tocqueville's prescription for the Indians is to his for the blacks: "The Negroes and whites must either mingle completely or they must part." Ibid., p. 355.

[38]Ibid., p. 317.

> submit to everything, except to the dictates of reason; and when reason becomes his only guide, he cannot hear its voice. A thousand new wants assail him, and he lacks the knowledge and the energy needed to resist them. Desires are masters against whom one must fight, and he has learned nothing but to submit and obey. So he has reached this climax of affliction in which slavery brutalizes him and freedom leads him to destruction.[39]

One of the means that Tocqueville mentions for overcoming this problem is the gradual emancipation practiced by the Northern states. By keeping the current generation of blacks enslaved while slowly emancipating their offspring, the freemen, in learning to be masters of themselves, also learn "the art of being free."[40] Tocqueville concedes, however, that this approach produces many problems among the blacks who must remain enslaved, particularly when, as in the South, they represent a large proportion of the total population. These men would understandably be resentful that such a cherished thing as freedom should be given to others while being denied to themselves.[41]

Aside from the problems in educating former slaves to become good citizens, there is the obstacle presented by whites who would resist accepting the blacks as fellow-citizens. Tocqueville cites instances in the North where blacks were blessed with all the rights of American citizenship but exercised some of those rights only at risk of their lives.[42] In his opinion, "race prejudice seems stronger in those states that have abolished slavery than in those where it still exists, and nowhere is it more intolerant than in those states where slavery was never known."[43]

While it is Tocqueville's view that the equality between the blacks and the whites is the result of a "purely legal inferiority,"[44] the effects of this conventional inequality cannot be

---

[39]Ibid., p. 318.
[40]Ibid., p. 354.
[41]Ibid.
[42]Ibid., p. 343.
[43]Ibid.
[44]Ibid., p. 342.

eradicated merely by eliminating the legal difference in status. The resultant racial prejudice is so pervasive that Tocqueville despairs that anyone but God could obliterate its traces.

> A natural prejudice leads a man to scorn anybody who has been his inferior, long after he has become his equal; the real inequality, due to fortune or the law, is always followed by an imagined inequality rooted in mores; . . .
>
> [I]n the modern world the hard thing is to alter mores, . . . This is because in the modern world the insubstantial and ephemeral fact of servitude is most fatally combined with the physical and permanent fact of difference in race.[45]

Tocqueville sees this "intangible and tenacious prejudice" as having three elements: the prejudice of the master, that of race, and that of the white.[46] By means of numerous examples drawn from antiquity, he demonstrates that while it once may have been possible for freed slaves to escape the opprobrium attached to their former condition, such an escape is not possible in America. The reason is that these three elements of prejudice are inseparable; the inequality which motivates the racial prejudice in America "seems to have immovable foundations in nature herself."[47] Thus, while slavery itself may be in decline, prejudice remains fixed (and may even grow stronger). As a result, Tocqueville harbors no delusions that the two races may eventually mingle. He does not see this state of affairs as being peculiar to America, though he contends that, in this country, "the matter will be still harder . . . than anywhere else." In glancing over the whole of the earth, he does not see "that the white and black races *will ever* be brought *anywhere* to live on a footing of equality"[48] (emphasis added).

One must, therefore, view with a judicious eye Tocqueville's speculation that a change in America's government might prove beneficial to race relations.

---

[45]Ibid., p. 341.
[46]Ibid., p. 342.
[47]Ibid.
[48]Ibid., p. 356.

> Some despot subjecting the Americans and their former slaves beneath the same yoke might perhaps force the races to mingle; while American democracy remains at the head of affairs, no one would dare attempt any such thing, and it is possible to foresee that the freer the whites in America are, the more they will seek to isolate themselves.[49]

This statement should be read in light of the discussions which follow it. Tocqueville's subsequent concern with the viability of the Union and its republican government strongly suggests that he believes a despot—at least one who would be so "above the prejudices of religion, country and race" as to actively promote intermingling of the races—is not likely to come into power.

A reason for the seemingly perpetual inequality between the black and white races is grounded in something closely related to, but even more pervasively influential than, "prejudice"; namely, what Tocqueville refers to as "mores." To understand the influence of mores, it is necessary to recognize what the author thought their role was in the formation of men's "characters."

Blacks and Whites: The Influence of Mores

> I have said . . . that I considered mores to be one of the great general causes responsible for the maintenance of a democratic republic in the United States.
>
> I here mean the term "mores" (*moeurs*) to have its original Latin meaning; I mean it to apply not only to "*moeurs*" in the strict sense, which might be called the habits of the heart, but also to the different notions possessed by men, the various opinions current among them, and the sum of ideas that shape mental habits.
>
> So I use the word to cover the whole moral and intellectual state of a people. It is not my aim to describe American mores; just now I am only looking for the elements in them which help to support political institutions.[50]

49Ibid.

50Ibid., p. 287.

Tocqueville later discusses how slavery caused Northerners and Southerners to have different "mores" which, in turn, created men with different "characters" in the two regions.[51] He denies, however, that the two areas consequently have significantly different "interests." "Slavery . . . does not attack the American confederation directly, through interests, but indirectly, through mores."[52]

Since slaves free Southerners from being "preoccupied with the material cares of life,"[53] the latter are able to concentrate their attention on a wide scope of lesser objectives, ranging from the admirable ("greatness") to the useless ("idleness").[54] In contrast, the Northerners must contend directly with the need to satisfy their own requirements, which causes them to "recognize for [themselves] the natural limits of [their] power."[55] Tocqueville later details the differing characteristics produced in Northerners and Southerners by their different mores: The latter are afflicted by both the greatest and the worst qualities of an aristocracy, while the former, as befits the "middle classes," are beset by a much more moderate range of virtues and vices.[56]

As a consequence of the intractability of mores and prejudice in the matter of race relations, Tocqueville does not see much prospect for the blacks becoming the equals or rivals of the whites. Therefore, it is appropriate that his views on the alternatives to racial equality receive some attention.

Blacks and Whites: Alternatives to Racial Equality

One of the more simplistic and attractive solutions to the race problem of the era was that advocated by Jefferson in the eighteenth century and Lincoln in the nineteenth: emancipation by expatriation. Its seeming simplicity was deceptive, however.

---

[51]Ibid., p. 375.
[52]Ibid., p. 376.
[53]Ibid., p. 375.
[54]Ibid.
[55]Ibid.
[56]Ibid., p. 376.

Tocqueville, speaking to and about a materially oriented democracy, approaches this possible solution from a democrat's perspective. He concludes that merely to "counterbalance the natural increase of the black population" would require more than the annual wealth of the whole country.[57] In other words, in order to remove most of the existing American blacks by natural means—allowing them to die of old age—while transporting their progeny to (presumably) an African "America," the commercial republic would have to commit all of its profits, as well as assume an onerous debt, for a period of fifty to seventy years. At the end of this period—assuming that the material sacrifice was worthwhile and the blacks were gone—the republic would be faced with the fact that its progress had been at a standstill for several generations; it would be fifty to seventy years behind its commercial and political rivals. Obviously, such a price was unlikely to be paid by the vast majority of democratic men who would never live to enjoy the benefits of their noble sacrifice. As a consequence, Tocqueville concludes that:

> The Negro race will never again leave the American continent, to which the passions and vices of Europe brought it; it will not disappear from the New World except by ceasing to exist.[58]

Another alternative would have been to maintain the existing institution of slavery. Tocqueville is understandably equivocal about this option. On the one hand, to contend openly that there is no solution other than the status quo to the greatest injustice existing within a regime which claims to be the embodiment of justice (and one must never lose sight of the fact that one of his chief objectives was to reconcile this conception of justice-as-equality with the dictates of human excellence) amounts to a confession of failure on Tocqueville's part. On the other hand, there is a barely imaginable solution which would remove the injustice, but only at the cost of an even greater injustice which quite possibly might destroy the regime altogether: The blacks and whites could engage in a war

---

[57]Ibid., pp. 359-60.
[58]Ibid., p. 360.

whose object would be the complete annihilation of one or the other of the races.

In his treatment of mores, Tocqueville indicated his concern with the problem of reconciling justice, excellence, and the regime's survival. In attempting to persuade democrats of the wrongfulness of slavery, Tocqueville, as I have previously mentioned, adapted his speech to his intended audience. While characterizing the slave-holding South as being more "tolerant and gentle" toward the black than is the North, he does not overlook the fact that America is a commercial republic and that its future lies in its energetic pursuit of wealth. This seems to be the reason he consistently and approvingly emphasized the necessity of engaging in work or "labors."[59] The presence of slavery in the South impedes the willingness of the whites in that section to work; in a sense, slavery permits the whites the luxury of "glorifying idleness." However, Tocqueville does not deny that some of these "aristocratic" Southerners put their idleness to good use. He admits that "the [S]outherner is more spontaneous, witty, open, generous, intellectual, and brilliant" than the Northerner.[60] But these are not the qualities that are esteemed and useful in a commercial republic. The admirable qualities are to be found in the commonsensical, "active," and "skillful" Northerner.

Tocqueville's equivocation on the subject of slavery extends even to an assessment of the advantages and disadvantages accruing to the slaves. He admits that the Southerners have bettered the physical condition of their blacks. At the same time, however, they have instituted a "spiritualized despotism and violence" that seeks to prevent the slave from even "wishing" to be free.[61] This is a clear departure from the practices of the ancient masters. More significantly, it is inconsistent in the sense that it precludes the possibility of the whites ever emancipating their charges. With the slaves lacking an education that would equip them for freedom, the blacks and whites are doomed to be intertwined in a master-slave or provider-dependent relationship for the foreseeable future.

---

[59]Ibid., pp. 343, 346, 349, 351-53, 355.
[60]Ibid., p. 376.
[61]Ibid., p. 361.

Additionally, by employing this form of tyranny, the whites have removed from their arsenal a crucial means of controlling their slaves: Without the hope of ever gaining liberty, the blacks could become, to say the least, much less tractable. The Southerner's actions, which are a consequence of his refusal to free the blacks and mingle with them, only leave him the option of remaining "isolated from them and keep[ing] them as long as possible in slavery."[62]

> From the moment when the Europeans took their slaves from a race different from their own, which many of them considered inferior to the other human races, and assimilation with whom they all regarded with horror, they assumed that slavery would be eternal, for there is no intermediate state that can be durable between the excessive inequality created by slavery and the complete equality which is the natural result of independence.[63]

The problem that so vexed Tocqueville was that not only was there no intermediate state, but there was also little likelihood that either of the extremes would long suffice. Having already indicated the severe impediments to the blacks' ever attaining equality with the whites, Tocqueville believed that slavery, "limited to one point on the globe and attacked by Christianity as unjust and by political economy as fatal," could not last in the American democracy. As a consequence, he saw no long-lasting and peaceable solution to the problem of race relations in America.

---

[62]Ibid., p. 360.

[63]Ibid., p. 362. The seeming insolubility of race relations in America causes Tocqueville to vent his "hatred" of these long-departed Europeans who reintroduced slavery into the Western world.

17

Women's Liberation: The Relevance of Tocqueville

William Kristol

I

Supposing women were liberated—what then? Is there no danger the leaders of the women's revolution will, like other revolutionaries according to Tocqueville, go beyond what is reasonable and fail to secure happiness and virtue?[1] Is it not possible that American women, like young women in an aristocracy who have just escaped from parental authority, will make ill use of their newly acquired but uneducated capacity of free choice?[2] And will it not be tempting for American men, like vanquished aristocrats, to adopt a stance of public submission and flattery which covers over private distaste and resentment?[3] If "the Americans have this great advantage, that they attained democracy without the sufferings of a democratic revolution and that they were born equal instead of becoming so,"[4] what of contemporary Americans, who have enjoyed, or suffered, a democratic revolution on behalf of equality between the sexes?

Perhaps no greater task faces contemporary men and women

---

[1]Alexis de Tocqueville, *Democracy in America*, ed. J.-P. Mayer, trans. George Lawrence (Garden City, N.Y.: Doubleday, Anchor Books, 1969), vol. II, pt. III, chap. 11, p. 597. I have tried to correct the translation where necessary. Hereinafter cited as *Democracy*.

[2]Ibid.

[3]Ibid., vol. I, pt. II, chap. 2, p. 179.

[4]Ibid., vol. II, pt. II, chap. 3, p. 509.

than coming to grips with the consequences of the women's revolution. And who better to look to for guidance than Tocqueville? His guidance can only be suggestive, for with regard to women more perhaps than with regard to any other subject, Tocqueville's America seems not to be ours. But in fundamental ways, Tocqueville still seems to see not differently but further than any contemporary party.[5] By climbing onto his shoulders, we may be able to begin to arrive at an understanding of women's place in post-revolutionary America—an understanding that accords with their true interests and with the interests of men and of society. Such an understanding requires an education of the sort Tocqueville provides throughout *Democracy in America*—but especially, perhaps, in his discussion of the subject of American women.[6]

II

But isn't the very notion of a "woman's place" in contemporary, liberated America fundamentally misleading, not to say pernicious and reactionary? This is a free country—now for women too, and individual women should be able to do what they want. If some wish to devote themselves to careers, and others to families, and others to various combinations of the two—if some women are content to enter traditionally female occupations and others are not—then let the laws be sex-blind, and let each be free to choose her own place. There may be disagreements over whether we need a transitional program of affirmative action, or over how much the government should be involved in the campaign against sex-stereotyping, but surely there is no serious dispute over the fact that we have left notions like "a woman's place" far behind.

This objection is not without force; and it is clear that women will, in fact, find themselves in a greater variety of places, reflecting a greater latitude for individual preference, after liberation than was the case before. But however completely this liberal,

---

[5]Ibid., Introduction, p. 20.

[6]The theme of education is prominent throughout (e.g., Intro., pp. 18-19; vol. II, pt. II, chap. 8, p. 528; chap. 17, pp. 548-49), but the only chapter title in *Democracy* that mentions education is vol. II, pt. III, chap. 9: "The Education of Girls in the United States."

individualist perspective prevails with regard to the formal, legal situation of women, it does not make it unnecessary to reflect on a woman's proper place. For this perspective fails to acknowledge the importance of mores in the broad sense—not just the habits of the heart, "but also the different notions possessed by men, the various opinions current among them, and the sum of ideas that shape mental habits."[7] Our laws can be neutral or sex-blind; but if, as Tocqueville suggests, mores are more fundamental than laws,[8] the decisive question becomes: What should American mores be with regard to the roles and relation of the sexes—even if the laws are silent? (And can the laws ever be truly silent?) Since laws affect mores, different views on desirable mores will lead to disputes over legislation, even within a context of broad agreement on basic legal equality: Do we insist on *every* sex-based distinction falling (e.g., the combat exclusion for women)? Do we want to provide incentives to improve the "maldistribution" of women in certain occupations?

Why can't we, though, try to remain agnostic on the woman question by pushing the refusal to decide up one notch? Why can't we simply say, let whatever mores emerge from individuals exercising their own judgment prevail? After all, as Tocqueville points out, Americans relied on the individual judgment of young women one hundred and fifty years ago; how much the more appropriate today. The whole point of Tocqueville's discussion of "The Education of Girls in the United States" seems to be the capacity of American girls to exercise their own judgment.[9] The education of American girls exposes them to the world and teaches them to see clearly, to judge without illusions, and to control their passions through their own free will. The education of a girl in the United States thus involves "increasing her confidence in her own powers" and "giving her a precocious knowledge of all things." In sum, Americans "have sought to arm her reason" so that she can defend her virtue. Why should we not arm each woman's reason so she can choose her place? The net result of these individual choices

---

[7]Ibid., vol. I, pt. II, chap. 9, p. 287.
[8]Ibid., p. 308.
[9]Ibid., vol. II, pt. III, chap. 9, pp. 590-92. The rest of this paragraph is based on this chapter.

would presumably be a desirable set of mores.

Or would it be? Tocqueville admires the young American woman who results from the "education" he describes, but this education is not quite what it seems. As Tocqueville points out, in trying to arm woman's reason and give her confidence in her powers, Americans are using "the same method as in other circumstances."[10] But this rationalist and individualist educational (or philosophical) "method" of the Americans fails to appreciate the inevitability of dogmatic beliefs: Human beings—men and women— are not capable of acquiring knowledge of all things by themselves.[11] The pretense that they are, means, in a democratic social state, that what, in fact, results is the overwhelming if invisible reign of public opinion.[12]

It is thus no surprise to find in the second chapter on women that the account of the first chapter is modified. Americans may think they are freeing the judgment and arming the reason of their girls so they can govern themselves, but American women are, in fact, guided by "inexorable public opinion" and "firmly established notions."[13] American women do not make up their own minds; the minds of women, like those of men, are, in fact, "rallied and held together by some leading ideas."[14] In this case, one of the leading ideas—probably *the* leading idea, at the heart of "inexorable public opinion"—is the American understanding of "the kind of democratic equality that can be established between man and woman." This understanding rests on the assumption that "because nature has established so great a difference between the physical and moral constitution of the sexes, she clearly meant to give their different faculties diverse employment"—men's in the world, women's at home, with husbands as the "natural head" of the family.[15] Tocqueville's own view of nature's intention may be more problematic—he refers to "the great inequality of man and woman,

---

[10]Ibid., p. 591.

[11]Ibid., pt. I, chaps. 1-2, pp. 429-34.

[12]See especially ibid., also vol. I, pt. II, chap. 7, pp. 254-56, and vol. II, pt. III, chap. 21, pp. 640-45.

[13]Ibid., vol. II, pt. III, chap. 10, pp. 592-93.

[14]Ibid., pt. I, chap. 2, p. 434.

[15]Ibid., pt. III, chap. 12, p. 601.

which has *seemed* until our day, to have its eternal foundations in nature"[16]—but he accepts and defends the American view for the benefit of his readers. It was from this "firmly established notion" that American mores followed, rather than from free individual choice. But in our day the seeming eternal foundations in nature seem to have crumbled. What understanding is now likely to dominate the public opinion that will inexorably guide the individual choices that men and women make? Is that understanding healthy? Might it be modified or educated?

III

The understanding that seems to be emerging as dominant in the wake of women's liberation is a version of the view that Tocqueville saw propounded by some in Europe:

> In Europe there are people who, confusing the divergent attributes of the sexes, claim to make of man and woman creatures who are, not equal only, but actually similar. They would attribute the same functions to both, impose the same duties, and grant the same rights; they would have them share everything—work, pleasure, public affairs.[17]

The version of this view that now seems likely to prevail is not an extreme claim of androgyny but rather a milder form of "second-stage" or "third-stage" feminism.[18] This feminism is committed to full equality without any fixed or discriminatory sex roles. But it urges women to shed their dependence, not by trying to become "male," but rather by affirming certain female qualities of caring and nurturing even as women fully enter the previously male worlds of commerce and politics. On the other side, men are able to share the burdens of the home, and its pleasures, in a way that allows them to be nonoppressively, but still recognizably, male. The

---

[16]Ibid., p. 600 (emphasis added).
[17]Ibid., pp. 600-01.
[18]See Betty Friedan, *The Second Stage* (New York: Summit Books, 1981) and Benjamin R. Barber, "Beyond the Feminist Mystique," *The New Republic*, July 11, 1983, pp. 26-32.

male/female distinction cannot be, and should not be, obliterated; but certainly the worlds of work and home, and the character of men and women, will and should become less distinct, and men and women will each become more whole. The emerging public opinion does not, therefore, embrace simple androgyny; but this new world is still far removed from Tocqueville's world of driven men and restricted women—and of course, we think, far superior to it. The new public opinion seems to be converging on a happy medium beyond sexism but before androgyny, where people are people but some nonoffensive, somewhat distinctive male and female traits remain. But these traits are secondary; fundamentally, we are all yuppies now.

Would Tocqueville judge this mild version of similarity between the sexes—we might call it convergence—much less harshly than the more extreme version? Would he say of this version, too, that "one can easily conceive that this sort of equality forced on both sexes degrades them both, and that so coarse a jumble of nature's works could produce nothing but feeble men and dishonorable women"?[19] I believe he would, even if he might be impressed how smoothly rather than coarsely we seem to be managing to jumble nature's works. Let me elaborate this assertion only briefly, since to defend it thoroughly would require both a full exposition of Tocqueville's political philosophy and a full, neo-Tocquevillian analysis of the new public opinion and its accompanying mores.

Why do "caring" men deserve the epithet "feeble"—at least from a political point of view? Because caring men are not intractable, and it is male intractability that underlies the love of independence. That love blocks the road that equality opens up toward the terrible new form of servitude Tocqueville sees on the horizon.[20] Male intractability, even irrational male aggressiveness, seems to be useful, therefore, in preventing the form of despotism that democratic nations need fear, the schoolmaster state.[21] The new public opinion and its accompanying mores run the risk either of succeeding in enfeebling men, which will be dangerous to liberty, or

---

[19]*Democracy*, vol. II, pt. II, chap. 12, p. 601.
[20]Ibid., pt. IV, chap. 1, pp. 667-68.
[21]Ibid., chap. 6, pp. 690-91.

of failing to do so—in which case men will remain intractable but uneducated in their intractability, a situation also dangerous to liberty and indeed to civilization.[22]

As for women, everything that has a bearing on their status, their habits, and their opinions is of great political importance according to Tocqueville, because women shape mores.[23] Or rather, religion shapes mores through women—because while religion is often powerless to restrain men directly, "it reigns supreme in the souls of women, and it is women who shape mores."[24] And the political importance of religion is very great; it plays a major part in teaching Americans "the art of being free."[25] The liberated woman tends not to be governed by religion; as such, though a great devotee of freedom, she is not in a very good position to guide its use. It seems to me, in sum, that Tocqueville would judge the old association of a spirited man and a religious woman more conducive to liberty and well-being than the new association of more similar and in some ways more attractive types.

Having offered this judgment on Tocqueville's behalf, I should immediately emphasize two points: Tocqueville is by no means Pollyannish about the character of the old association, and he would probably not be surprised that it did not last. Let me develop each of these points in turn.

IV

That the passing of the way men and women lived together in preliberated America should not simply be a matter for nostalgic regret is suggested by Tocqueville's rather chilling picture of the American family in his discussion on "The Young Woman as Wife."[26] Here Tocqueville praises the strength of will of American girls, who give up the amusements of girlhood in order to follow "the only path that can lead to domestic felicity," submitting "without

---

[22]Ibid., vol. II, pt. II, chap. 5, p. 517; chaps. 10-16, pp. 530-47.
[23]Ibid., pt. III, chap. 9, p. 590.
[24]Ibid. vol. I, pt. II, chap. 9, p. 291.
[25]Ibid., p. 290.
[26]Ibid., vol. II, pt. III, chap. 10, pp. 592-94; all quotations in this paragraph are from this chapter.

complaint to the austere duties of their new state." This strength of will manifests itself in the other trials of women's lives—and most of these trials, it turns out, are due to their husbands. Although living comfortably back East, many of them set off for the West in search of more wealth, taking their wives with them and inflicting upon them the dangers and miseries that accompany such expeditions. Tocqueville comments:

> In the utmost confines of the wilderness I have often met young wives, brought up in all the refinement of life in the towns of New England, who have passed almost without transition from their parents' prosperous houses to leaky cabins in the depths of the forest. Fever, solitude, and boredom had not broken the resilience of their courage. Their features were changed and faded, but their looks were firm. They seemed both sad and resolute.

Tocqueville develops this sad picture in the footnote to this chapter.[27] He describes an example of family life in the wilderness, saying that "there is nothing that recommends this picture to the reader except its great truth." In other words, there is nothing to recommend this state of affairs, of a man dragging his family along on a quest in which he uses his reason to do that which can be accounted for only by passion, enduring the life of a savage in order to conquer and civilize the wilderness. For American men (at least American men *in extremis*), civilizing is understood to mean conquering, conquering nature; the danger is that devotion to such conquest can, in fact, reduce men to little more than savages. And the women have no choice but to submit: Tocqueville describes the pioneer woman whose "appearance seemed superior to her condition" but whose "delicate limbs were wasted, her features worn, and her eyes gentle and serious; her whole physiognomy bore marks of religious resignation, a deep peace free from passions, and some sort of natural quiet determination which would face all the ills of life without fear and without defiance."

This picture should put in a new light Tocqueville's famous judgment, at the end of his discussion of American women, that if

---

[27]Ibid., pp. 731-33n. U; all quotations in this paragraph are from this chapter.

anyone were to ask him what he thought was the chief cause of the extraordinary prosperity and growing power of the nation, "I should answer that it is due to the superiority of their women."[28] Superior to whom? Perhaps not only to European women but also to American men, for while the men are driven by their passions (especially the passion for wealth), and they thus put themselves at the mercy of fortune both in a narrow and in a broader sense, the women's desires "seem to contract with their fortune as easily as they expand."[29] Women have the virtue of moderation that men sadly lack—and that lack of moderation, the succumbing by men to the passion for material well-being, is dangerous not just to Americans' liberty but to their humanity.[30]

Yet the women submit. Is there any justification for this submission beyond force or irrational public opinion? At the end of his footnote to chapter 10, after describing the wife's "religious resignation" and "natural, quiet determination," Tocqueville mentions her children, "full of health, high spirits, and energy." They are "true children of the wilderness." Their mother looks at them—not at her husband—with "mingled melancholy and joy; seeing their strength and her weariness, one might think that the life she has given them exhausted her own, and yet she does not regret what they have cost her."[31] Woman submits for the sake of the children, it seems; she preserves civilization in the wilderness; the cabin in which they live has a Bible, some Milton, and some Shakespeare. Tocqueville calls their home—or rather her home—an "ark of civilization lost in an ocean of leaves. A hundred paces away the eternal forest spreads its shade, and solitude begins again."[32] The project of conquering "the eternal forest" seems irrational and runs the risk of making men savage. Women seem to mitigate this danger; perhaps they will be able to bring up the children of the wilderness to become civilized, more civilized than their fathers. Women cannot, it seems, directly confront the love of material well-

---

[28]Ibid., vol. II, pt. III, chap. 12, p. 603.
[29]Ibid., chap. 10, p. 594.
[30]Ibid., pt. II, chaps. 10-16, pp. 530-47 (p. 533n. U).
[31]Ibid., pp. 732-33n. U.
[32]Ibid., p. 733n. U.

being that is the dominant national taste[33]; but perhaps by submitting they can modify it or educate it. And Tocqueville helps in this education by holding up American women as an example not of moderation, which is presumably not a quality that American men much admire, but as an example of courage, independence, and strength of will.[34] Insofar as women's liberation simply liberates women's passion for material well-being side by side with men's, women will no longer shape the mores that can save Americans from the dangers to which the passion for well-being exposes them. Still, the price the unliberated woman pays is high.

V

Tocqueville could not have believed that American women were forever likely to continue paying that price. For one thing, the picture Tocqueville draws is so harsh and unattractive that one would suppose the natural course of mores in democracy toward gentleness and ease[35] should erode this state of affairs. More important, the state of affairs, and its acceptance by women, rests on two pillars: the belief in nature's intention regarding men and women, and religious belief. Yet both of these are endangered by the "natural" course or tendency of democracy. The belief in a fixed natural intention, especially one that mandates difference and inequality, is at odds with the notion that flourishes in a democratic social state of the indefinite perfectibility of man—and, presumably woman—and their "liberation" from traditional limitations.[36] Indeed, in the midst of his portrait of female submission, Tocqueville lets slip in passing that, in fact, the Americans realize that in a democracy "a husband's power [will be] contested."[37] As for the religious belief that counsels resignation and even sacrifice, how strong a support is that in this age when "blind

---

[33]Ibid., vol. II, pt. II, chap. 10, p. 532; and see vol. I, pt. II, chap. 9, p. 291.
[34]Ibid., vol. II, pt. III, chaps. 9-10, pp. 590-94.
[35]Ibid., chaps. 1-2, pp. 561-67.
[36]Ibid., pt. I, chap. 8, pp. 452-54. See on this issue F. L. Morton, "Sexual Equality and the Family in Tocqueville's *Democracy in America*," *Canadian Journal of Political Science*, XVII:2 (June 1984), pp. 322-24.
[37]*Democracy*, vol. II, pt. III, chap. 9, p. 591.

sacrifice and instinctive virtues" are things of the past, and interest reigns supreme?[38]

Tocqueville indicates the tenuousness of the American understanding of the equality of the sexes, and of the mores that follow from this understanding, most clearly, perhaps, in the following way: At the beginning of the first chapter on women, on the education of girls in the United States, Tocqueville says, "There have never been free societies without mores, and as I observed in the first part of this book, it is woman who shapes these mores."[39] He concludes the chapter by saying that "a democratic education is necessary to protect women against the dangers with which the institutions and mores of democracy surround them."[40] The institutions and mores of democracy are in tension with the well-being of women—who allegedly shape these mores. It seems, in fact, that women do not sufficiently shape mores to prevent their own corruption by democratic mores. Now that democratic mores have liberated women, what is to protect us from the dangers with which modern democracy surrounds us?

VI

The answer is education—the education Tocqueville calls for throughout *Democracy in America,* and part of which he presents through his discussion of American women. We have seen that the claim that Americans have successfully educated their women, or women their Americans, is questionable: Women seem more fundamentally shaped by religion and unreflective public opinion, and American men are not much shaped at all. The Americans, typically, have flattered themselves: They believe that they have armed woman's reason and provided that her freedom be able to control itself, "and it is only when they have reached the utmost limits of human strength that they call in the aid of religion."[41]

---

[38]Ibid., pt. II, chap. 8, p. 528.
[39]Ibid., pt. III, chap. 9, p. 590.
[40]Ibid., p. 592.
[41]Ibid., pp. 591-92.

But, in fact, these limits come far earlier than Americans imagine,[42] for it is religion that "reigns supreme in the souls of women."

But now that religion no longer does reign, it would seem necessary to come closer to making that American boast a reality. Now individual freedom really must control itself, and reason govern woman's choice. Tocqueville's description must be taken—as Tocqueville intended it to be taken—as a prescription; American women—and men—need to live up to Tocqueville's flattering portrait. They can do this by moving beyond women's liberation to grasp the following three points: the necessity of marriage, the importance of good morals, and the necessity of inequality within marriage. I shall sketch these points very briefly and inadequately.

The charms of a free-spirited girlhood notwithstanding, the institution of marriage is clearly in the interest of women, who are weaker than men and vulnerable to men, and who can benefit from male assistance in bringing up the children. Stable marriages and strong families are also clearly good for society. But women's liberation, insofar as it is committed to liberation altogether, makes it difficult for women to acknowledge that they have a peculiar interest in the marriage bond—that men unconstrained by marriage are liberated men, and liberated men are likely to enjoy their liberation at the expense of women. Tocqueville hopes that equality of conditions will foster marriage by making irregular morals before marriage more difficult. For in a state of equality, where each can marry whom he or she chooses, "however credulous passion may make us, there is hardly a way of persuading a girl that you love her when you are perfectly free to marry her but will not do so."[43] But this presumes that the girl will require persuading of the man's love, or that she will not be deluded by modern doctrines of equality into believing that she is as able to take advantage of him as he is of her. A competitive liberation of men's and women's passions will work to the disadvantage of women (though in the long run to the disadvantage of men, too) because men's passions are so powerful, as Tocqueville shows, not to say

[42]Ibid., vol. I, pt. II, chap. 9, p. 291.
[43]Ibid., vol. II, pt. III, chap. 11, p. 595.

tyrannical. Could a "democratic education" teach women to support marriage as they once did from tradition and religion, by educating women to their true interest, well-understood?

Once the case for marriage is restored or bolstered, Tocqueville suggests how a democratic education could strengthen those marriages that were made. The freedom to choose should make us more willing to live with our choice, but educating our understanding beforehand should allow us to make choices that we are happy to live with. Americans need to be impressed with the responsibilities of choosing freely. Because we cannot choose time and again, we need to choose well; and we need to be educated in order to be able to choose well. Men, as we have seen, tend to be driven by their desires; women can choose reasonably with an eye to the future, and then uphold that choice by insisting on strict adherence to that choice—on strict morals—once the choice has been made. In a democratic and skeptical age, men tend to "give way to casual and ephemeral desires" and, shunning protracted effort, never achieve anything great or calm or lasting. In the turmoil of democracy, social instability "favors the natural instability of desires," and men think in terms of "chance in every shape and form"; the present looms large and hides the future, and "men do not want to think beyond tomorrow."[44] Women, by choosing with an eye to the future and by insisting on regular morals, combat the present-orientedness of men. They provide what Tocqueville says are necessary: "practical examples to the citizens" of farsightedness and willingness to endure trouble for the sake of distant happiness.[45] Thus, by taking seriously the responsibility and privilege of free choice, women can perhaps accustom American men "to think of the future in this world" and to overcome their passing whims and desires. Thus free choice replaces religion as the ground of good morals; but good morals, and the habit of acting responsibly with an eye to the future, could, Tocqueville suggests, gradually lead citizens without their noticing it back toward religious belief. The democratic education that is made necessary by the decline of religion may be "the only means we still possess for bringing mankind back,

---

[44]Ibid., pt. II, chap. 17, pp. 547-48.
[45]Ibid., pp. 548-49.

by a long detour, to a state of faith."[46]

Is the price women must pay for marriage and morality submission to the husband within the family? The answer appears to be yes. Every association must have a head, and it seems natural, at least in the sense of necessary, that the man be the head. The Americans think that "in the little society composed of man and wife, just as in the great society of politics, the aim of democracy is to regulate and legitimize necessary powers and not to destroy all power."[47] This bow to necessity need not be degrading to women, for American women can find "a sort of glory in the free relinquishment of their will, and it is their grandeur to bear the yoke themselves rather than to escape from it."[48] Because this arrangement was freely chosen by women, they are not degraded by it. And in return for this submission, Americans respect women's honor and their moral and intellectual freedom; for example, American men watch their language out of respect for women.[49] Thus, by submitting to men, American women educate them. For in respecting the honor and freedom of women, American men are forced to respect themselves, whom they assume superior to women; they come to judge themselves, to a degree, by "womanly" standards of morality rather than simply by male standards of conquest and material well-being. In this way, the voluntary submission of women, now based on choice rather than on nature's supposed intention, can reopen the question of nature as providing a standard for human beings to choose to live up to, as opposed to obstacles to be conquered or limitations from which to be liberated.

VII

The title of the first chapter on women, "The Education of Girls in the United States," turns out, therefore, to be ambiguous: for girls, or at least women, educate as much as they are educated. But they educate by submitting. In this respect, women seem to be an example

---

[46]Ibid., p. 549.
[47]Ibid., pt. III, chap. 12, p. 601.
[48]Ibid., p. 602.
[49]Ibid., pp. 602-03.

for political philosophers. Tocqueville comments that American girls steer their thoughts and language through the traps of a sprightly conversation more easily than a philosopher could.[50] One thinks of the political philosopher Tocqueville who also navigates the narrow path along which it is possible to educate democracy. This path requires Tocqueville to accept democracy, as women accept their lot; and the picture of the sad but resolute woman in the cabin in the forest reminds us of Tocqueville, as he describes himself at the end of *Democracy in America*: "When I survey this countless multitude of beings, shaped in each other's likeness, among whom nothing stands out or falls unduly low, the sight of such universal uniformity saddens and chills me. . . ." But rather than regret what cannot be, he resigns himself religiously to necessity or Providence: "What seems to me decay is thus in His Eyes progress; what pains me is acceptable to Him."[51]

Tocqueville says, near the end of his discussion of women, that while the Americans have allowed the social inferiority of women to continue, they have raised her with all their power morally and intellectually to the level of man.[52] But the thrust of these chapters is that American women are, in fact, morally and intellectually superior to men. That superiority must be hidden for the sake of elevating men. Like the woman who submits to her husband, Tocqueville submits to democracy for the sake of educating it and shaping its mores. This would suggest that the cause of American democracy requires not only successful marriages of men and women but a successful marriage of American democrats to the author of *Democracy in America*, who achieved a sort of glory in submitting to American democracy in order to educate it.

---

[50]Ibid., chap. 9, p. 591.
[51]Ibid., pt. IV, chap. 8, p. 704.
[52]Ibid., pt. III, chap. 12, p. 603.

18

An Asian Perspective

Sombat Chantornvong

> Now in the United States it has been the established Custom from the time of His celebrated Presidency President George Washington down for the entire population of the land with one accord to elect persons who are proper to fill the highest grades of office and establish them as President and Vice President to administer the Government as Chief rulers of the Country for a definite limited term of four years or Eight years, that this Custom should continue for so long a period and no disturbance arise or strife to obtain possession of the supreme power as is constantly occurring in other countries, is very remarkable indeed and the custom is one worthy of all praise.
>
> *Letter from King Mongkut of Siam (Thailand) to the President of the United States, February 14, 1861.*

Is Tocqueville's *Democracy in America* in any way relevant to the problems facing non-Western nations of today? Can an Asian possibly learn something from the book that might help him better understand the course of his own and neighboring societies, most of which are classified as "underdeveloped" or "developing" or "less developed," depending on how one wants to euphemize? What parts of Tocqueville's analysis and prescriptions are still valid and applicable in the context of Asian societies? To try to answer such a question requires rereading *Democracy in America*. Reading the

---

The author would like to express his sincere gratitude to Professor Saneh Chammarik, William Klausner, and especially Professor Montri Chenvidyakarn for their valuable comments. This essay was completed in January 1985, but changes to take account of recent political events are unnecessary.

work anew in such a context, an Asian reader would now approach it with an entirely different set of questions in mind. This paper grows out of an attempt to picture how an Asian reader, ever conscious of his own background, would react to Tocqueville. However, just as Tocqueville's references to the Old World are mostly limited to his French homeland, the Asian perspective and experience related in this paper will be limited basically to Thailand and some of her Southeast Asian neighbors.

I

Tocqueville begins the introduction to his book by saying, "No novelty in the United States struck me more vividly during my stay there than the equality of conditions."[1] He later adds that "the more I studied American society, the more clearly I saw equality of conditions as the creative element from which each particular fact derived."[2] Equality of conditions, as used by Tocqueville, seems to mean simply the conditions in a state of society in which the concept of equality has been actualized. It is the state of society in which all men have equal opportunities; for example, to receive education, to take part in the general leveling of wealth, or in the uniform assurance of political rights. The United States is this place where the principle of popular sovereignty happily coincides with the equality of conditions. Thus, it is easy for democracy to take root and develop. According to Tocqueville,

> Anglo-Americans brought equality of conditions with them to the New World. There were neither commoners nor nobles there, and professional prejudices were always as unknown as prejudices of birth. So with this democratic social state it was not hard for democracy to establish its sway.[3]

But if Tocqueville had ever journeyed to Asia, he would most

---

[1]Alexis de Tocqueville, *Democracy in America*, ed. J.-P. Mayer, trans. George Lawrence (Garden City, N.Y.: Doubleday, Anchor Books, 1969), vol. I, p. 9. Hereinafter cited as *Democracy*.

[2]Ibid.

[3]Ibid., p.305.

likely have said that the most pervasive and the most influential principle in Asian states, past and present, is that of inequality. Prior to the middle of the nineteenth century, the social and political inequality which existed and served as a moving principle of Asian agrarian states was basically that associated with birth. People were simply born to different social classes, each with its own duties and functions.[4] But with the coming of Western imperialism and colonialism, new dimensions were added to this inequality. To begin with, Western imperialism significantly distorted the internal cohesiveness of the self-sufficient village economies, forcing economic activities to shift from subsistence agriculture to plantation production of raw materials and foodstuffs for world markets.[5] The colonized Asians now acquired a taste for new consumer goods. This was the beginning of their being dependent on external forces beyond their control. The inroad of capitalism by way of colonization also led to the formation of new social classes—the small entrepreneurial middle class and the new, educated bureaucratic elite. In the West, the expansion of the economic base of the entrepreneurial class has led to the liberalization of the absolutist, mercantilist monarchies. Tocqueville himself observes that "[t]rade makes men independent of one another and gives them a high idea of their personal importance; it leads them to want to manage their own affairs and teaches them how to succeed therein. Hence it makes them inclined to liberty. . . ."[6] The emergence of the entrepreneurial "middle class" in colonial Asia did not, however, produce a similar effect. Part of the reason was that the newly formed and very small middle-class businessmen consisted mostly of alien Asian immigrant population—notably Indians and Chinese.[7] The colonial government administration had also created a new, educated elite which proved to be more significant for the

---

[4]See, for example, H. G. Quaritch Wales, *Ancient Siamese Government and Administration* (New York: Paragon Book Reprint Corp., 1965).
[5]Morris Watnick, "The Appeal of Communism to Underdeveloped Peoples," *Economic Development and Cultural Change*, vol. I, no. 1 (March 1952), p. 28.
[6]*Democracy*, vol. II, p. 637.
[7]John Bastin and Harry J. Benda, *A History of Modern Southeast Asia: Colonialism, Nationalism, and Decolonization* (Englewood Cliffs, N.J.: Prentice Hall, Inc., 1968), pp. 72-74.

immediate future of Asia. This small group of men was most receptive to key ideas of Western democracy: freedom and equality.[8] It was the exposure to the idea of Western democracy by Western-educated elites that sparked the revolutionary nationalism in Asia. These native elites advocated a democratic form of government, espoused the cause of nationalism, and led the uneducated masses in the struggle against colonialism. The single mass party, also a new creation, was often organized by nationalist leaders as the chief instrument to achieve their goal of independence. Naturally, the issue of nationalism dominated all other issues. Internal differences and divisions were subsequently played down. On the surface, it appeared as though the end of colonization and the newly found independence would bring an Asian-style utopia.

But whereas "the Revolution in the United States was caused by a mature and thoughtful taste for freedom, not by some vague, undefined instinct for independence,"[9] the so-called "national revolution" of Asia, which naturally involved violent efforts and disruptions of existing structures of authority, was aristocratic in nature. The masses did not originate the revolution. It was always the elitist few who called for the national revolution. In most cases, mass participation in the nationalist movement was basically associated with the role of loyal followers. Instead of challenging all traditions, all moral rules, established rights, and social values, and substituting for them new ones based on democratic standards, most nationalist movements seemed to focus first and foremost on taking over the state apparatus. In many cases, the indigenous elites, many of whom had previously served as colonial intermediaries, simply took over the political and bureaucratic machinery left behind by their colonial masters.[10]

Thus, national revolutions in Asia tended to strengthen the power of the state but did not go very far in transforming the spirit of the society. At first most former colonies adopted the political

---

[8]Walter F. Vella, *The Impact of the West on Government in Thailand* (Berkeley: University of California Press, 1955), p. 362.
[9]*Democracy*, vol. I, p. 72.
[10]Ferdinand E. Marcos, *Today's Revolution: Democracy* (N. P., 1971), p. 69. Hereinafter cited as Marcos, *Today's Revolution.*

forms of the imperial powers. The case of the Philippines, the only country in Asia whose constitution was patterned after that of the United States, serves as a good example. But unlike the Anglo-Americans who were already cultivated in political affairs as the result of having acquired the taste for freedom from birth, the masses of Asia had neither the desire nor the skills necessary for modern-day political participation. As such, a small number of the new elites who were entrusted with the responsibility of governing an independent country must have felt that they should be allowed a great deal of maneuverability required for a paternal authoritarian rule. It is difficult for the nationalist leaders with different social backgrounds, educational achievements, administrative and political experiences distinguished from the rest of the people, to accept the masses as their equals.[11] It is true that they might have been genuinely concerned about the miseries of the masses, but it certainly was not the kind of concern which one had for one's equals. In short, despite their dedicated role in the uprooting of foreign and exploitative rule, the Western-educated elites often turned out to be a new kind of aristocracy (oligarchy) in their own land.

The end of Western imperialism, therefore, did not necessarily mean the beginning of freedom or the birth of democracy. Instead, it brought about more inequality as the desire of the Western-educated leaders to transform their country into something like the powerful West called for specialized administrative and technical skills. The result was the emergence of the modern bureaucracy. According to Tocqueville, the predominance of social equality, adequate education of the average citizen, the prosperity of trade and industry, and the abundance of land in the United States made the people more inclined to seek the channel of private enterprise rather than official bureaucratic appointment as the means to improve their lot. Thus,

> In the United States, when a citizen has some education and some resources he tries to enrich himself either by trade and industry or by buying a field covered in forest and

---

[11]William J. Foltz, "Building the Newest Nations: Short-Run Strategies and Long-Run Problems," eds. Karl W. Deutsch and William Folly, *Nation Building* (London: Atherton Press, 1963), p. 119.

> turning into a pioneer. All he asks from the state is not to get in his way while he is working and to see that he can enjoy the fruit of his labor.[12]

In contrast, administrative work in the new states has become the main road open to the ambitions of men. Contrary to Tocqueville's United States, in which official appointments are few, ill paid, and insecure,[13] in Asia bureaucracy can be the main source of employment for the educated class. In Thailand, for example, the bureaucracy, until lately, has been the primary outlet for its most ambitious and educated citizens.[14] The bureaucracy, which is by definition a centralizing force with a tendency to boost its own political and material privileges, has thus become even more powerful. As a privileged group, having in a sense their own class interest to promote, the bureaucrats in Asian countries had enlarged their power, influence, and interest to the point where there were no external forces capable of controlling them. In Thailand, the domination of the bureaucracy—the armed forces, police and civil administrators—was so conspicuous that the kingdom was sometimes called a bureaucratic polity.[15] The average American, Tocqueville observed, would, due to the "daily breeding new and impatient desires" occasioned by the equality of conditions, shy away from seeking official appointment and avoid political positions as well.

> In the United States it is men of moderate pretensions who engage in the twists and turns of politics. Men of parts and vaulting ambition generally avoid power to pursue wealth; the frequent result is that men undertake to direct the fortunes of the state only when they doubt their capacity to manage their private affairs.[16]

---

[12]*Democracy*, vol. II, pp. 632-33.
[13]Ibid.
[14]William J. Siffin, *The Thai Bureaucracy: Institutional Change and Development* (Honolulu: East-West Center Press, 1966), p. 131.
[15]See, for example, Fred W. Riggs, *Thailand: The Modernization of a Bureaucratic Polity* (Honolulu: East-West Center Press, 1966). Hereinafter cited as Riggs, *Thailand*.
[16]*Democracy*, vol. I, p. 205.

The opposite was true in Asia. In the new states of Asia, politics, like bureaucracy, was the monopoly of the ambitious few. After all, political independence had turned these new elites into becoming a new element of the ruling class, charged with the main responsibility of nation building and modernization. Besides, political independence often meant the immediate task of its leadership to win over to the nationalist government the loyalty of quarreling factions, constantly threatening to break up the new nation as soon as the common enemy was out of sight. Unlike Tocqueville's America where people speak the same language, believe in the same religion, share the common beliefs, and live under the same material conditions and the same laws,[17] citizens of many new Asian states, such as Burma and Malaysia, still face the problem of divisive cultural pluralism.[18] In sharp contrast to Tocqueville's observation that even religion in the United States is republican,[19] church and state in several Asian countries were either at odds with each other or were too closely linked to each other. In either case—whether a state religion was officially established or there existed serious antagonism between the secular state and the church—prejudice, resentment, and conflicts were bound to grow. Faced with unyielding opposition movements and irridentism—both real and imagined—most leaders often argued for the greater centralization of administrative and political power. They maintained that new nations of Asia needed the kind of regime that would be strong enough to run the affairs of state efficiently.[20]

Even in a relatively more homogeneous society like Thailand, the new elites still faced unsurmountable obstacles and insoluble problems of great magnitude rooted in the feudal and colonial characteristics of their own countries. Unlike the United States, as Tocqueville argues, where equality was the accepted principle of social relations,[21] in Asia the idea of class hierarchy, which included respect for age, status, rank, education, wealth, deference

---

[17]Ibid., p. 56.
[18]Bastin and Bends, *Modern Southeast Asia*, pp. 102-06.
[19]*Democracy*, vol. I, p. 397.
[20]See, for example, the excerpt from Aung San's *Blueprint for Burma* quoted by Muang Muang, *Burma and General Newin* (New York: Asia Publishing House, 1969), p. 300.
[21]*Democracy*, vol. I, p. 9.

and obedience to authority, was still very much alive. In fact, it might be said that, for the most part, the inhabitants of the former colonies regarded themselves more as "subjects" of the traditional regime rather than as "citizens" of the new democratic nations.

Without an adequate basis in social structure—without equality of conditions—the political institutions and the rituals of democracy which were imposed from above merely served to legitimize the power of the ruling class: traditional landowners, hereditary rulers, religious hierarchy, and the military-civilian bureaucracy. Even a free and popular election, though seen as an indispensable aspect of democratic rule, in practice meant manipulation of the political process with attendant corruption. Most political parties, which have proliferated, had personal rather than ideological bases. They functioned mainly as the instruments of mass control and perpetuation of personal rule. Typically, wealth is the assured way of gaining power through the electoral process. Unlike Tocqueville's America where every village was a sort of republic accustomed to self-rule,[22] the villagers of Asia were no more than festival spectators or participants of electoral rituals. At best they tend to view election time as the time to make some small private gain in the vote-buying business. The electorate ended up exercising no real choice. Free elections thus did not lead to substantial social or political change but served merely to legitimize the rule of old oligarchs or new elites to perpetuate their dominance. After all, the supply of qualified candidates was limited, and their characters and attitudes seemed to have changed only little. Despite the right to vote, the masses of Asia remained unfree.

Without a democratic social state, all other conditions which are active factors for the maintenance of independence in the eyes of Tocqueville could exist only in forms. Newspapers, which, according to Tocqueville, were essential for the development and maintenance of any concerted action of democratic citizens,[23] were the tools or under control of a special class or group. Likewise, civil associations, which Tocqueville regards as very important in the

---

[22]Ibid., p. 386.
[23]Ibid., vol. II, pp. 517-20.

formation of independent spirit,[24] often came under the state's control and regulations. In Thailand, for example, all kinds of associations, academic included, can be formed only after the government agencies concerned have examined and authorized their statutes. Even today no associations are allowed to take part in political activities.[25]

As if the inequality of conditions and other unfavorable factors mentioned above were not enough, the conditions of Asian nations were far less conducive to the growth of democracy in other significant ways as well. Unlike the United States which was located in relative geographical isolation and therefore had no neighbors or enemies to fear,[26] most new nations were often hard-pressed by both internal divisions and external threats. The military elites, which were the first to receive Western training in the technological field and also the first to lead the masses in the nationalist struggle for independence, were therefore in a very good position to assume political leadership.[27] How unfortunate this situation can be with regard to the development of democracy may be judged from the following applicable remarks of Tocqueville:

> The Americans have no neighbors and consequently no great wars, financial crises, invasions, or conquests to fear; they need neither heavy taxes nor a numerous army nor great generals; they have also hardly anything to fear from something else which is a greater scourge for democratic republics than all these others put together, namely, military glory.[28]

Furthermore, under military rule, the suppression of opposition groups or leaders and the application of other strong-arm tactics are not uncommon. General respect for the rule of law and peaceful resolution of conflicts which, according to Tocqueville, constitutes

---

[24]Ibid., pp. 520-24.

[25]See Montri Chenvidyakarn, "Political Control and Economic Influence: A Study of Trade Associations in Thailand" (Ph.D. dissertation, University of Chicago, 1979).

[26]*Democracy*, vol. I, p. 278.

[27]David E. Novack and Robert Lekachman, *Development and Society: The Dynamics of Economic Change* (New York: St. Martin Press, 1964), p. 244.

[28]*Democracy*, vol. I, p. 278.

one of the major roots of American habits or customs favorable to the maintenance of freedom, is conspicuously absent.

By Tocqueville's standard, most post-independence Asian states would be classified as aristocracy or oligarchy. Yet the new aristocrats, or rather the new oligarchs of Asia, must not be too readily identified with the kind of aristocracy Tocqueville has generally described. True aristocracy, according to Tocqueville, is a social system based on the inequality of men. But it is not simply the rule by the rich and the powerful man. It is also the system which evokes man's highest spiritual qualities since an aristocrat is someone who is attached to causes beyond himself.[29] The privilege of an aristocrat is not separated from his social responsibility. Even the relationship between a master and his servants in aristocracies is not simply that of an employer and employees.

> In aristocracies the master comes to think of his servants as an inferior and secondary part of himself, and he often takes an interest in their fate by the extended scope of his selfishness.
>
> The servants, for their part, see themselves in almost the same way, and they sometimes identify themselves so much with the master personally that they become an appendage to him in their own eyes as well as in his.[30]

On a larger scale, the relation between the rich and the poor is also one that is psychologically free from oppression or struggle.

> In nations where an aristocracy dominates society, the people finally get used to their poverty just as the rich do to their opulence. The latter are not preoccupied with physical comfort, enjoying it without trouble; the former do not think about it at all because they despair of getting it and because they do not know enough about it to want it.[31]

The new oligarchs of Asia, on the contrary, could never feel free of

---

[29]Marvin Zetterbaum, *Tocqueville and the Problem of Democracy* (Stanford, Cal.: Stanford University Press, 1967), p. 22. Hereinafter cited as Zetterbaum, *Problem*.

[30]*Democracy*, vol. II, p. 575.

[31]Ibid., p. 531.

all wants nor could they be content with their lot. Seeking not just power or glory but also wealth, they necessarily could not look beyond their own class interest.[32]

An aristocracy, observes Tocqueville, also contributes indirectly to the defense against any tyranny over the people by defending its own privilege or "aristocratic liberty."

> Only an aristocracy can preserve the people from the oppression of royal tyranny and from the miseries of revolution, that the privileges which seem established in the sole interest of those who possess them do also form the best guarantee for the tranquility and prosperity even of those who do not have them.[33]

Again it is evident that the new oligarchs of Asia could not perform this function—their interests not coinciding with those of the masses. In this sense, the masses of Asian new states could be worse off than those living under a European aristocracy of the ancient regime. Contrary to the average American who, thanks to the equality of conditions, is never satisfied with his present fortune and is "constantly trying a thousand ways to improve it,"[34] the Asian masses would look up to the government for guidance and accept their fate as inevitable, taking refuge in the hope for a better status in the next world. According to Tocqueville, "when inequality is the general rule in society, the greatest inequalities attract no attention."[35] In an Asian society where conditions were generally unequal and where the hierarchy of command appeared to be firmly established, it naturally would not matter to the majority of the people if the new military or bureaucratic elites should acquire more "liberties" or "privileges" than others. Indeed, it would not matter at all if the so-called democracy would be given up altogether. In such a society, Tocqueville's fear of the vice of

---

[32]See David A. Wilson, "Thailand," *Government and Politics of Southeast Asia*, ed. George M. Kahin (Ithaca, N.Y.: Cornell University Press, 1964), p. 60; and Riggs, *Thailand*, p. 251.

[33]Alexis de Tocqueville, *"The European Revolution" and Correspondence with Gobineau*, ed. and trans. John Lukacs (Garden City, N.Y.: Anchor Books, 1959), p. 73.

[34]*Democracy*, vol. II, p. 637.

[35]Ibid., p. 538.

democracy unchecked—the tyranny of the majority acting through an uncontrolled political assembly—is not applicable. After all, for a tyranny by the majority to take place, the people must first be free. The society in which they live must also be truly democratic so they can exercise their political rights to the fullest.

But while political democracy may be readily given up in some countries on the ground that it is a peculiar product of Western civilization and historical experience (and probably not many people lament its demise), the much-desired modernization and industrialization are never easily forsaken. As a matter of fact, it has often been argued that the failure of democracy to function effectively in these countries was largely due to the leadership's political and economic inability to provide a solid base for the very process of modernization and industrialization to take off. However, modernization and industrialization, believed to be essential to the nation's existence, led to greater centralization and increased inequality of conditions. In order to industrialize, for instance, a nation, as Tocqueville has observed, would have a greater need for such infrastructure as roads, canals, and ports, which only the state can provide. Becoming increasingly involved in such activities, the power of the state grows and its needs necessarily expand. The growth of industry also brings with it a new and complicated system of human relations which requires, in turn, uniform regulation and control. The end result, according to Tocqueville, is further administrative centralization.[36] Obviously, this is especially true as modernization and industrialization has compounded the situation in which the problems of urbanization, overpopulation, the high cost of technological transfers and development, the emergence of technocracy, and the expansion of bureaucracy, seem ungovernable.

In addition, the rise of large-scale industry, observes Tocqueville, may result further in the emergence, on the other hand, of "a new industrial aristocracy"—a much more aristocratic class—and on the other, an increasingly debased and impoverished class of workers. As he says:

> When a workman is constantly and exclusively engaged in

---

[36]Ibid., pp. 684-87.

> making one object, he ends by performing this work with singular dexterity. But at the same time, he loses the general faculty of applying his mind to the way he is working. Every day he becomes more adroit and less industrious, and one may say that in his case the man is degraded as the workman improves. . . .
>
> While the workman confines his intelligence more and more to studying one single detail, the master daily embraces a vast field in his vision, and his mind expands as fast as the other's contracts. Soon the latter will need no more than bodily strength without intelligence, while to succeed the former needs science and almost genius. The former becomes more and more like the administrator of a huge empire, and the latter more like a brute.[37]

To Tocqueville, this "state of dependence and poverty affecting part of the industrial population in our day is an *exceptional fact* running counter to conditions around it."[38] He is not overly concerned with the possibility that unrestrained pursuit of material well-being will become characteristic of any particular group of people.

> Should it happen that some people got too keen on the pursuit of riches and were altogether too enamored of physical delights, I should not be worried at all. Such particular characteristics would be soon lost in the general picture.[39]

But in Asia, where inequality of conditions prevails, the way is open for the industrial aristocrats' passion for wealth to rule over the whole society. In fact, the emerging industrial aristocrats do not merely find it to their advantage to join hands among themselves but also with the rulers to exploit the masses. Even a small middle class, which may have developed as a result of the modernization process, may also go along with the bureaucratic-capitalist partnership as long as they, themselves, can maintain their

---

[37]Ibid., pp. 555-56.
[38]Ibid., p. 584.
[39]Ibid., p. 543.

interests. To understand the position taken by the new upper classes of an Asian society, one probably needs only to remind oneself of Tocqueville's remark that what "most vividly stirs the human heart is certainly not the quiet possession of something precious but rather the imperfectly satisfied desire to have it and the continual fear of losing it again."[40] Meanwhile, the poor masses, being helplessly thrown under the yoke of the capitalist economy, eventually come to depend entirely on the state authority for the improvement of their lot.

Again, the Asian context of industrialization points interestingly to the importance of equality of conditions and other fortunate circumstances surrounding the birth of the United States as a nation which has later developed into a great commercial republic. Yet, at first glance, it would seem that it is America's almost unlimited natural resources and general prosperity alone which makes it all possible. According to Tocqueville:

> The territory of the Union offers unlimited scope to human activity; it provides inexhaustible supplies for industry and for labor. Love of wealth therefore takes the place of ambition, and prosperity quenches the fires of faction.[41]

In fact, it sounds as if Tocqueville is praising the passion for profit-making of the Americans in developing their virgin continent.

> In Europe we habitually regard a restless spirit, immoderate desire for wealth, and an extreme love of independence as great social dangers. But precisely those things assure a long and peaceful future for the American republics. Without such restless passions the population would be concentrated around a few places and would soon experience, as we do, needs which are hard to satisfy. What a happy land the New World is, where man's vices are almost as useful to society as his virtues![42]

---

[40]Ibid., p. 530

[41]Ibid., vol. I, p. 306.

[42]Ibid., p. 284.

The crux of the matter is, as one scholar pointed out, that the desire for well-being inevitably accompanies equality of conditions, quite independently of climatic or geographic factors.[43] In other words, it is the equality of conditions which gives birth to the love of wealth, the spirit of commerce which, in turn, not only makes the country great but also promotes social stability. Or, as the same scholar puts it, "Tocqueville believed that the spirit of commerce would produce a social state in which most men owned some property, thus ending the contrast between the few rich and the many poor that he considered the main source of social instability."[44] In Asia, on the other hand, the limited resources available and inequality of conditions seem to bring out instead the negative side of the self-interest of man.[45] The problems of hunger, poverty, disease, violence, and wretchedness have become more visible. In a sense, the society has become a predatory one. The results of modernization and industrialization seem to carry a threat against the regime itself. Not only economic inequality weakens social cohesion, but it also breeds injustice and inevitably breaks the political bond that binds the social fabric. More than ever, it is now very possible to imagine that the masses, feeling that poverty is indeed a social product, not something predestined, may ask for a radical political, social, and economic change. Here, Tocqueville's remark concerning the relationship between the rich and the poor states of the Union is quite appropriate:

> It is difficult to conceive of a lasting relation between two peoples, one of whom is poor and weak, the other rich and strong, even if it is proved that the strength and wealth of the one are in no way the cause of the weakness and poverty of the other.[46]

---

[43]Zetterbaum, *Problem*, pp. 128-29n. 29.
[44]Ibid., p. 131.
[45]President Ferdinand Marcos of the Philippines had this to say regarding his country: "There seems to be individual but no national progress. Everyone had his own strategy for personal survival but there was no strategy for national survival." See Marcos, *Today's Revolution*, p. 56.
[46]*Democracy*, vol. I, p. 381.

II

Today just about every new nation's response to the basic problem of economic inequality is planned development. But, if economic prosperity is a necessary condition for political stability, can the reverse be argued? If it can, does the quest for economic development, defined as economic growth, plus equal income distribution, necessarily imply the exclusion of the democratic process?[47] For Asian countries which have not yet adopted the central planning system of industrialization, it seems that persisting internal and external threats leave them no choice. The only way they can progress is to establish effective administrative machinery for economic development. In claiming that the government now has the moral obligation to improve the conditions of the poor, the regime leaders often declare that they are working against economic oppression. They call upon the people to sacrifice political freedom in order that the state may break up the concentration of economic powers and promote the economic growth for all.

Interestingly enough, it is on this theme of the relationship between economic development and freedom that Tocqueville's teaching proves to be highly relevant to Asia. As mentioned earlier, Tocqueville's observations of social and historical nature have shed light on the reason why a democratic tree has found fertile soil in America but could not survive and grow in Asia. Yet, at the same time, one cannot simply dismiss Tocqueville's fear of the coming of a new kind of despotism—the one characterized by its drive toward depoliticization and the emergence of the administrative state. Actually in Asia today such a danger can sometimes creep in almost unnoticed. Consider the cases of the Philippines and Singapore. In the Philippines, President Marcos had vowed to eliminate economic inequality, charging that "the wealth of the few, like the power of the few, is a violence on the poor."[48] He then

---

[47]John L.S. Gerling, *The Bureaucratic Polity in Modernizing Societies: Similarities, Differences, and Prospects in the ASEAN Region* (Singapore: Institute of Southeast Asian Studies, 1981), pp. 54-55.
[48]Marcos, *Today's Revolution*, p. 119.

demanded "a democratic revolution"—the building of a New Society in which property will be regulated for collective human ends.[49] It is the job of a democratic government to serve as a faithful instrument of the people's revolutionary aspiration, he argued. From now on, it is the poor who will shape the future of the Philippines.[50] President Marcos is, however, far from being a Marxist. His so-called democratic revolution, he maintained, was actually aimed at preventing the Communist revolution that was destructive of human freedom. While he did not try to please just one particular class, he nevertheless tried to make his New Society everything to everybody. Thus, in explaining that his democratization of wealth simply meant the sharing of private wealth with the society, and not a total abolition of private ownership, he promised the rich security against the Communist threat. He offered peace and order to the middle class, and pledged to the poor that his definition of "equality" meant giving each citizen "three square meals, a roof over his head, efficient public transport, schooling for his children, and medical care for his family."[51] But in order to arrive at such a society in which economic activities, both private and public, would join together in promoting the interest of the individual and the welfare of the whole, the authority of the government must be exerted whenever these ends are not being served.[52] Obviously, the state alone is supposed to be neutral and thus free from any political ideology.[53] Only the political authority can establish the priorities and provide the mechanism of equalization. What is further needed is the modification of the political culture of the Filipinos from that of the populist, personalistic, and individualistic into that of citizens who are equally conscious of the collective or social interest.[54]

---

[49]Ibid.

[50]Ferdinand E. Marcos, *Notes on the New Society of the Philippines* (Manila: Marcos Foundation, Inc., 1976), p. 56. Hereinafter cited as Marcos, *Notes.*

[51]Ibid., p. 116.

[52]Ibid., p. 124.

[53]Alexander R. Magno, *Developmentalism and the "New Society": The Repressive Ideology of Underdevelopment* (Third World Studies Center: The Philippines in the Third World Papers series No. 35, 1983), p. 10.

[54]Marcos, *Notes,* p. 59.

Apparently implicit in this idea is not just his attempt to raise the status of the state to something paternal in nature—something beyond any particular class interest—but it seems to reflect also Mr. Marcos's belief in the necessary links between social conditions and the citizen's habits of mind. The new social conditions, President Marcos seems to say, can be freshly created. Understandably, he is evasive when talking about the legitimacy of his assumed power to bring about the changes he idealized.

Until now not many people have taken the words of Mr. Marcos seriously. They were often dismissed as mere political rhetoric—a crude attempt to justify his rule by martial law. He has often been judged by what has actually been going on in the Philippines, not by what he had proposed to do. The picture of a society deeply troubled by worsening economic crisis, widespread corruption in high places, political assassinations, daily protests and demonstrations, internal divisions and local insurgency, however, seems to draw us away from a more fundamental question: What would happen if he succeeded in delivering the goods? Were Mr. Marcos able to make good his promises of a better society, with or without having to rely so heavily on the support of the military and the civil bureaucrats and technocrats, would his rule be more acceptable? After all, his socio-economic programs which were aimed at reducing mass poverty and at mobilizing mass support for his crumbling regime, have already created demands on it. What would it mean if the Marcos regime were able to handle all these demands? For a student of Tocqueville, an answer to this line of questioning should come before our concern over the final fate of the regime. In other words, one should take seriously the warning of Tocqueville that the threat to liberty may lay no less in citizens refusing the responsibilities of freedom than in their being refused it.[55]

Actually, a New Society à la Marcos has been realized in Singapore, now considered the most "successful" new nation of Southeast Asia, if not the whole of Asia. Separating from the Federation of Malaysia and becoming a fully independent state in 1965, Singapore has since been a showcase of economic progress and

---

[55]*Democracy*, vol. II, p. 540.

political stability.[56] Two and a half million Singaporeans enjoyed the highest per-capita GNP ($5,900) in Asia except for Japan, and had only a 3.3 percent unemployment rate in 1984. They must have been quite happy with the government which has brought them economic prosperity. Indeed, the majority of the Singaporeans may very well be content with the life they are enjoying. The People's Action Party (PAP), which has ruled the island republic since its birth, has accepted from the very start the policy of maximizing the welfare of the people. A subsidized public housing program, aimed at alleviating the acute housing shortage among the poor and lower-income groups, was the first among several other welfare services provided by the social democratic government. In retrospect, the housing development program has served not only as a means to get the economy going but has also brought solid political support for the Lee Kuan Yew regime. By encouraging the poorer sections of the society to accumulate property through purchasing government apartments on an easy installment plan, the PAP government has succeeded in giving them a vested interest in the status quo.[57] In order to ensure the success of its industrialization policy and the expansion of welfare services, the government of Singapore, through its efficient bureaucrats and state enterprises, has become actively involved in other economic projects: commercial, industrial, and financial. Today by all counts, the government of Singapore is the most important entrepreneur in the island economy, and Singapore has become one of the most successful, prosperous capitalist states in the world.[58]

Development and welfare, however, have been used by the regime as a conscious and deliberate effort to discipline the Singaporean people and to subject them to total obedience. Of course, one of the reasons behind this effort may be that Singapore is one of the most racially heterogeneous societies in the world. Another major reason may be purely economic. To ensure the dynamism of its economy, the regime has to take necessary measures to

---

[56]Editorial, *Asia Week*, Sept. 7, 1984, p. 34. Hereinafter cited as *Asia Week*.
[57]T.J.S. George, *Lee Kuan Yew's Singapore* (Worcester and London: The Trinity Press, 1974), p. 205. Hereinafter cited as George, *Yew's Singapore*.
[58]*Asia Week*, p. 34.

organize the social life of the people including family planning.[59] Yet, implicit in this drive for popular discipline is a conscious desire on the part of the government to produce "New Men" among its citizens. Those who admire the system often regard this socialization of a new political culture through strict schooling and community control as a process of nation-building. They are quick to point at the desirable manners, respect for the law, communal harmony, work ethic among labor, popular support for the armed forces, and the spirit of patriotism as among the moral virtues and social precepts successfully developed by the government over the years.[60] But if one were to take a critical look at the whole process of this socialization, what has been created in Singapore is nothing but a culture designed to discourage conflict, disruptive confrontation and free bargaining, and to encourage instead stability, low-risk and orderly petition.[61] The education system, for example, has been completely "officialized." Not only does the regime emphasize the importance of technical and vocational training over humanities and liberal arts, but apparently in order to control the mind of the youth, it also goes as far as to appoint cabinet ministers to join the university staff.[62] In the meantime, the government also employed various tactics to make sure that only young Singaporeans with the right kind of attitude and background get enrolled in college. It has succeeded in instilling in the students, many of whom were born and lived most of their lives under PAP's rule, a conviction they share with their rulers that liberal democracy is a

---

[59]It is only lately that Prime Minister Lee Kuan Yew, sensing the adverse effects of a low fertility rate among the more educated women, began to urge the female professionals who stay single to marry and raise a family.

[60]*Asia Week*, p. 34.

[61]Chan Heng Chee, "Politics in an Administrative State: Where Has the Politics Gone?" in Seah Chee Meow, *Trends in Singapore: Proceedings and Background Papers* (Singapore: Singapore University Press, 1975), p. 43. Hereinafter cited as Chee, "Politics."

[62]The following are some excerpts from the Code of Conduct for the Vigilante Corps Members which may be considered as guidelines for Singapore's ideal citizen: "The concept: Human beings have basic needs. Human beings have basic obligations. Basic security. The state provides our basic needs. The Republic of Singapore is our society. We elected our government and the Government is responsible for the organization of our society. It is through the efforts made by the Government, on our behalf, that we are able to obtain our basic needs." See George, *Yew's Singapore*, p. 134.

dispensable virtue in a society which "must put survival above everything else."[63] Newspapers may have grown in terms of circulation, but they are under strict government control. Claiming that the task of the newspaper consists mainly in disseminating facts and information, citing the economic need to prevent waste of resources and duplication of services, the regime has recently forced the merger of small newspapers under the control of one single corporation. The rationale given by the minister involved is quite characteristic of the regime itself. "[C]ompetition alone does not make quality newspaper. Quality people working in a company that is financially sound make quality paper."[64] Radio and television are also under tight control of the government.

Since rising economic growth and improvement of the people's living conditions seem to prove the PAP's points, the ruling elites have become increasingly authoritarian in their exercise of political power. The regime tolerates no political dissidents, public or private. It has carried out a systematic policy of rigorous internal repression of all opposition groups. The last strike recorded in Singapore was in 1977. Given the small size of the island (226 square miles), it is not difficult to understand why the PAP's drive for the monopolization of power has succeeded so well. In 1967, the PAP successfully turned Singapore into a single-party regime when it won all the parliamentary seats in the general election. Since 1968 it has swept all the general elections, each time with an increasing number of the votes. Rapid economic and social development in Singapore, the regime now argues, necessitates the shift of emphasis from politics to economics. According to the PAP leaders, they succeeded in promoting the welfare of the people only when they gave up their excessive concern with "politics" and turned Singapore into a one-party parliament.[65] At any rate, the regime's achievements in major social welfare programs—public housing, transportation, health, education, and community organization—have already convinced most of the satisfied populace that there is simply no alternative to the nation's economic survival

---

[63]George, *Yew's Singapore*, p. 132.
[64]*Asia Week*, p. 40.
[65]Chee, "Politics," p. 53.

other than the one offered by the PAP. A popular election now turns out to be mere popular mobilization which serves only to maintain the system or to reinforce the power of the ruling party. It seems, as one perceptive observer put it, that "politics" has disappeared from Singapore. There is just no politics any more. Instead, there is only "an administrative state."[66] Apparently, the regime has succeeded too well in producing materially satisfied citizens who are willing to forgo all that the government denies them and absolutely obey the government.

The disappearance of politics and the emergence of the "administration of things," predicts Tocqueville, will result in the tremendous growth of government activities.[67] This has been the case in Singapore as the regime assumes responsibility for the expansion of the economy. It enlarges and extends the role of bureaucracy to cover many new areas of responsibility. Civil servants are now appointed chairmen of public enterprises and private companies. Meanwhile, the regime seeks to retain its socialist-style grass-roots organizations, but at the same time increasingly draws its parliamentary candidates from the highly educated technocratic class as well as from the teaching staff of its university. Senior officers of public enterprises resign from their posts to run for political office. The result is that the distinction between politics and administration has become blurred. Increasingly, politics which concerns the decisions about conflicting ends has been replaced by pure administration, a technical assessment of the correct means to given ends. Centralization is another main feature of the regime. The regime long ago merged the city council with the central government apparently in a move to ensure national unity, and the degree of centralization has now reached the point where "[you] need a license for everything in Singapore. You can't do any business without one—banking, newspapers, right down to taxis and hawkers. Most of them have to be renewed every year."[68] The following words of Tocqueville could have summarized the same situation:

---

[66]Ibid., p. 48.
[67]*Democracy*, vol. II, p. 515.
[68]*Asia Week*, p. 37.

> The central power not only fills the whole sphere of former authorities, extends, and goes beyond it, but also acts with greater speed, power, and independence than it had ever done. . . . All the initiative taken away from private people is constantly going to enrich that of the government. . . . As a result, public administration not only depends on one sole power but also is more and more controlled from one spot and concentrated in ever fewer hands. The government centralizes its activity at the same time that it increases its prerogatives; hence a twofold growth of power.[69]

Yet it is only natural for other Asian leaders to aspire to see their countries become another Singapore. Compared with others, Singapore must appear to be an ideal state. But a student of Tocqueville might ask: What is the point of being one of the best-fed, best-administered, best-educated nations, if the major outlet for grievances and frustration available to ordinary citizens is the letters column in the newspaper or the political rumor mill?[70] Is this not, in fact, symptomatic of a suppressed society where there is no real political participation and no free press? Worse still, does this "capitalist totalitarianism" not remind us of Tocqueville's unnamed new despotism in which the government manages just about every important aspect of life for its people, who, welcoming all of this, think of nothing or cannot think at all?[71] What good is

---

[69] *Democracy*, vol. II, p. 683.

[70] Chee,"Politics," pp. 56-58.

[71] The following telephone conversation was between a visiting Asian editor and his friend, a minister in the PAP government:
Minister: , "Well now, how do you find Singapore?"
Editor (casually): "Great."
Minister: "What do you mean?"
Editor: "Just great."
Minister: "I don't think I like the tone of your voice."
Editor: "I have just come from Djarkarta and Manila. Nothing worked there. . . . Here my telephone works, my flush flushes, everything is clean and antiseptic. Singapore is simply great."
Minister: "All right, old chap, what's bothering you?"
Editor: "Look, what does it all mean? What about people? Don't they have minds? I see no evidence of people here having minds of their own, feelings of their own."
Minister: "They are happy. See those modern high-rise buildings? We gave them decent places to live in."

it to have people whose only concern in life seems to be that of material interest—the people who know "the price of everything and the value of nothing"?[72] Or as Tocqueville put it:

> What good is it to me, after all, if there is an authority always busy to see to the tranquil enjoyment of my pleasures and going ahead to brush all dangers away from my path without giving me even the trouble to think about it, if that authority, which protects me from the smallest thorns on my journey, is also the absolute master of my liberty and of my life?[73]

With this awareness, one may suggest that countries like Singapore and the Philippines, though seemingly worlds apart, in reality belong to the same category. The only difference is that one happens to be economically successful while the other is a disaster. Meanwhile, in between there belongs a host of other nations which contains a mixture of successes and failures. From a comparative perspective, the present situation in the Philippines, bad as it is, is not bad in *all* respects, especially in its political life. At least politics in the sense of conflicts and choices of ends which presupposes the will to liberty on the part of the populace, still exists there. The failure of Mr. Marcos's economic development plan should be viewed as a blessing in disguise because it may make it easier for the people to shun his authoritarian rule. Interestingly enough, in the Philippines more and more businessmen and professionals of the middle class who, according to Tocqueville would be a "natural enemy of any violent commotion,"[74] are joining hands with other political dissidents in their protest against his regime. All of this resistance would not be possible if the Philippines (once a showcase for a working democracy in Southeast Asia) had no

---

Editor: "What have you done to their minds?"
Minister: "Well, we are thinking about it. Having given them a clean city, modern amenities and a strong economy, we are now thinking of what culture we should give them."
Editor (after pause): "Is the culture factory also going to be in the Jurong industrial estate?"
End of conversation. See George, "Yew's Singapore," p. 109.

[72]Ibid., p. 202.

[73]*Democracy*, vol. I, p. 93.

[74]Ibid., vol. II, p. 636.

experience with democratic rule before. Despite its past abuses, the tradition of political democracy in the Philippines has evidently provided the opposition groups with precedents and recognized means to rebel against one man's rule. Moreover, as Tocqueville argues, just as in defending its own "liberty" or "privilege," the aristocracy will end up defending the general liberty,[75] so the emergence of the new opposition groups, apart from the traditional ones in the Philippines, should be regarded as something conducive to the resuscitation of liberal democracy.

III

The relevance of *Democracy in America* to Asia having been argued, it now remains to be seen if a would-be Asian "democratic leader" can draw any guidance from Tocqueville. At first glance, it may appear that such a possibility does not exist. In reading *Democracy in America,* an Asian may find that Tocqueville has indeed brought our attention to a much more fundamental problem facing any would-be democratic nation of today. Foremost in the mind of an average Asian reader of Tocqueville is probably the problem of his own society—that of existing inequality of conditions. He most likely would argue that it is basically the pre-existence of democracy, actualized in the form of the equality of conditions, which makes popular rule in the United States a successful one. It is this peculiar social state which prevents the dogma of popular sovereignty from being just "an isolated doctrine, bearing no relation to the people's habits and prevailing ideas."[76] Tocqueville himself remarks:

> The social state of America is a very strange phenomenon. Men there are near equality in wealth and mental endowments, or, in other words, more nearly equally powerful, than in any other country of the world or in any other age of recorded history.[77]

---

[75]Ibid., vol. I, pp. 72, 88.
[76]Ibid., p. 397.
[77]Ibid., p. 56.

To an Asian reader, Tocqueville could not have exaggerated the significance of this "strange phenomenon"—of equality of conditions. Consider, for example, the case of the United States in which the prevailing equality of conditions leads to the emergence of the democratic mores of individualism, meaning first, the exaltation of individual reason—something not necessarily bad; and second, the concentration on self-interested and largely materialistic ends.[78] In the new aristocracy of Asia, the introduction of the democratic process resulted in the emergence of individualism of the second kind only. This self-centered, self-interested concentration on personal ends was at the very beginning limited to the upper classes and the newly emerging middle classes only, as they were the ones who took full advantage of the new political structure. Then, thanks to modernization efforts, the poor masses now demand that the government must provide them with a better standard of living. The "individualism" as developed by the middle and upper classes in Asia and the rising expectations on the part of the masses both do not seem to lead to aggressive individualistic self-assertion. In most cases, Asian individualism and the Asian mode of modernization made most classes shy away from social obligations, leaving public affairs to the government which consequently extended its power. In a country where the taste for physical pleasures has been more rapidly absorbed by the people than either education or the experience of free institutions, a few men can easily seize control of the state and maintain themselves in power as long as they can satisfy the material needs of the people. In short, the introduction of formal democratic institutions and processes into a society in which the inequality of conditions is the rule may turn that society into something very close to "capitalist totalitarianism," as shown in the case of Singapore.

A question may, then, be raised: Is it possible to modify the existing social state or to construct out of the old one the kinds of societies that are favorable to the emergence of democracy? Before any answer can be given, let us first find out what the social state is. As used by Tocqueville,

---

[78]Jack Lively, *The Social and Political Thought of Tocqueville* (Oxford: Clarendon Press, 1962), p. 85. Hereinafter cited as Lively, *Thought*.

> The social state is commonly the result of circumstances, sometimes of laws, but most often of a combination of the two. But once it has come into being, it may itself be considered as the prime cause of most of the laws, customs, and ideas which control the nation's behavior; it modifies even those things which it does not cause.
>
> Therefore one must first study their social state if one wants to understand a people's laws and mores.

The striking feature in the social condition of the Anglo-Americans is that it is essentially democratic.[79] The combination of "circumstances" and "laws" then constitutes the "social state," which, in turn, characterizes the whole regime. Circumstances and laws also make up two of the three major categories of factors which contribute to the maintenance of democratic rule in the United States—the other being social mores or "habits of mind." As Tocqueville put it:

> I have come to the conclusion that all the causes tending to maintain a democratic republic in the United States fall into three categories: The first is the peculiar and accidental situation in which Providence has placed the Americans. Their laws are the second. Their habits and mores are the third.[80]

Of these, the most vital one is the third factor: the spirit of the people, the feelings, the beliefs, the ideas, the habits of heart and mind of men.[81] A people may differ with regard to an assortment of things. Some may be rich and some may be poor, but they can live together if they share the same mores. In the words of one scholar:

> Differences between social and economic functions would naturally persist, differences between rich and poor might persist, what would go would be the division of society into groups with distinctive mores. And this would result from the egalitarian insistence on the basic comparability of all

[79]*Democracy*, vol. I, p. 50.
[80]Ibid., p. 277.
[81]Ibid., p. 308.

individuals and their subjection to common rules.[82]

To Tocqueville, the ultimate social and political reality is the totality of ideas which form the habits of men's minds. To truly understand what any society means, one must understand these generally held ideas and standards, not just formal institutions.[83] Tocqueville stresses the importance of mores in the following way:

> Europeans exaggerate the influence of geography on the lasting powers of democratic institutions. Too much importance is attached to laws and too little to mores. Unquestionably those are the three great influences which regulate and direct American democracy, but if they are to be classed in order, I should say that the contribution of physical causes is less than that of the laws, and that of laws less than mores.
>
> I am convinced that the luckiest of geographical circumstances and the best of laws cannot maintain a constitution in despite of mores, whereas the latter can turn even the most unfavorable circumstances and the worst laws to advantage.[84]

To an Asian reader of Tocqueville, factors conducive to the actualization of democracy and the ones which maintain it are, therefore, overlapped. Thanks to the social state (i.e., circumstances and laws combined), the idea of popular sovereignty can actualize. The development of "democratic mores" then makes the democratic rule last. Yet it is clear that social state and mores, significant though they may be, are not beyond the reach of human influence. Both of them can always be altered by laws. "A law can modify that social state which seems most fixed and assured, and everything changes with it."[85] In other words, just as every law and political institution to be effective and lasting must be based on or reflect social mores, so it is possible that once put into action, laws and political institutions themselves may be able to modify

---

[82]Lively, *Thought*, p. 244.
[83]Ibid., p. 236.
[84]*Democracy*, vol. I, p. 308.
[85]Ibid., p. 297.

social mores. There are, of course, cases in which factors affecting social mores themselves, as well as the inclinations those factors encourage, may be rather difficult to alter, such as those habits formed by the climate, past history, economic abundance or scarcity.[86] But there are also cases which show that the creation of certain laws or political institutions may have resulted in the emergence of some other passions not intended in the first place. At any rate, to find democratic devices which will fit in with one's particular social state and to construct "democratic mores" through legislation is not impossible. Indeed, Tocqueville seems to have plenty of encouragement for such an attempt.

> American laws and mores are not the only ones that would suit the democratic peoples, but the Americans have shown that we need not despair of regulating democracy by means of laws and mores. If other peoples, borrowing this general and creative idea from the Americans, but without wishing to imitate the particular way in which they have applied it, should try to adapt it to the social state which Providence has imposed on the men of our time and should seek by this means to escape the despotism of anarchy threatening them, what reasons have we to believe that they are bound to fail in their endeavor?[87]

It is not the intention of this paper nor is it possible here to specify how one can go about "adapting" democratic ways to fit in with his particular society or constructing "democratic mores" through legislation. Suffice it to say that each "operational plan," in Tocqueville's opinion, must be based on the principle of self-interest. An American, Tocqueville observes, "obeys the society, not because he is inferior to those who direct it nor because he is incapable of ruling himself—but because union with his fellows seems useful to him and he knows that the union is impossible without a regulating authority."[88] Or, as he later sums it up, "The individual is the best and only judge of his own interest and

---

[86]Lively, *Thought*, p. 237.
[87]*Democracy*, vol. I, p. 311.
[88]Ibid., p. 66.

that society has no right to direct his behavior unless it feels harmed by him or unless it needs his concurrence."[89] Translated into a strategy for future development, it simply means that the problem of balanced development is basically the problem of self-development, of freedom and self-interest, and, as such, it should be treated as a political problem. To think otherwise is to mistake something else rather than social mores as the social glue which can effectively hold the society together. In fact, Tocqueville would have argued, under a nondemocratic regime, any socio-economic program sponsored by the government cannot be truly good, since it has the tendency to limit or separate the ties that bind a citizen's individual freedom with his sense of social responsibility. How can we expect any kind of "development" to grow out of a relation in which the government, taking a paternalistic position, treats the people not as its constituency to whom it is accountable, but rather as something to be patronized and thus controlled? The idea of freedom—beginning with the freedom to choose—must be regarded as an essential part of any development plan. Democratic mores must be cultivated, and this can be done only through meaningful citizen participation. In fact, development itself must be viewed not merely as a goal but positively as a process.[90] Efforts and ways must be devised to make the citizens equal partners in development. Says Tocqueville: "I do say that the most powerful way, and perhaps the only remaining way, in which to interest men in their country's fate is to make them take a share in its government."[91] Of course, there is a danger that the people may lack political maturity. Tocqueville himself was aware of this possibility and warns repeatedly that nothing is harder than freedom's apprenticeship.

> It cannot be repeated too often: nothing is more fertile in marvels than the art of being free, but nothing is harder than freedom's apprenticeship.[92]

---

[89]Ibid.
[90]See Randolf S. David, "Dictatorship and Development: The End of an Illusion," lecture prepared for the "Global Community Lecture Series," sponsored by Sophia University, the United Nations, and the International University of Japan, March 30-31, 1984, Tokyo, Japan.
[91]*Democracy*, vol. I, p. 236.
[92]Ibid., p. 240.

> It is hard to make the people take the share in government; it is even harder to provide them with the experience and to inspire them with the feelings they need to govern well.[93]

But then the only way the people can learn to know the law is by taking part in the framing of the legislation, just as the only remedy for the weakness of association in any society is through experience in associating. Tocqueville never tired of making this observation:

> It is by taking a share in legislation that the American learns to know the law; it is by governing that he becomes educated about the formalities of government. The great work of society is daily performed before his eyes, and so to say, under his hands.[94]

The task of an Asian leader, then, is to see to it that all the ideas of democracy and freedom must guide all socio-economic programs, or the goals of development must be to achieve the kind of society in which these ideas are cherished. Application, of course, may vary according to different circumstances, but the principle must remain the same.

Granting the existence of a myriad of problems facing Asian nations today, we can definitely say that such a development task, to be a success, would have to be carried out by the greatest and the most intelligent statesmen. Yet, in a somewhat similar situation, what Tocqueville offers as food for thought is still that self-interest must be combined with political freedom.

> But sometimes there comes a time in the life of nations when old customs are changed, mores destroyed, beliefs shaken, and the prestige of memories has vanished, but when nonetheless enlightenment has remained incomplete and political rights are ill-assured or restricted. . . . What can be done in such a condition? . . . it is essential to march forward and hasten to make the people see that individual

[93]Ibid., p. 315.
[94]Ibid., p. 304.

> interest is linked to that of the country, for disinterested patriotism has fled beyond recall.
>
> Certainly I am far from claiming that in order to reach this result the exercise of political rights must immediately be granted to every man; but I do say that the most powerful way, and perhaps the only remaining way, in which to interest men in their country's fate is to make them take a share in its government.[95]

To Tocqueville, so it seems, to be fully developed, a country as well as an individual must first be free. To question whether development without democracy is desirable is misleading.[96] Without democracy—that is, without freedom—we cannot have development in the true sense. To trade democracy for economic development under a despotic rule would be a poor bargain, for in the words of Tocqueville:

> If it is true that there will soon be nothing intermediate between the sway of democracy and the yoke of a single man, should we not rather steer toward the former than voluntarily submit to the latter? And if we must finally reach a state of complete equality, is it not better to let ourselves be leveled down by freedom rather than by a despot?[97]

---

[95] Ibid., p. 236.

[96] See Samuel P. Huntington, "Will More Countries Become Democratic?" *Political Science Quarterly*, Vol. 99, No. 2, 1984, pp. 193-218.

[97] *Democracy*, vol. I, p. 315.